eMarketing

eMarketing, 9th edition, equips students with the solid foundation in digital marketing required to excel in practice and "think like a marketer."

The book connects digital marketing topics with the traditional marketing framework, making it easier for students to grasp the concepts and strategies involved in developing a digital marketing plan. With a strategic approach that focuses on performance metrics and monitoring, it is a highly practical book. The 9th edition has been fully updated to include the most cutting-edge trends and topics, including SEO, customer experience, digital media consumption, analytics, big data and AI, and diversity and ethics. Case studies and examples have been updated across the book to demonstrate marketing practice in real organizations globally. Pedagogical features support the theoretical foundation throughout, incorporating "success stories" and "Let's Get Technical" boxes, as well as activities at the end of each chapter, to aid students in their understanding of and ability to execute successful digital marketing strategies.

Highly regarded and comprehensive, this textbook is core reading for undergraduate students studying digital marketing and digital business. Online resources include PowerPoint slides and a test bank.

Raymond D. Frost is Professor of Analytics and Information Systems at Ohio University, USA. He has published scholarly papers in the fields of information systems and marketing.

Alexa K. Fox is Associate Professor of Marketing at The University of Akron, USA. Her research interests include digital marketing, user-generated content, consumer behavior, online privacy, sharenting, and physiological measurement of cognition and emotion, Alexa's work has appeared in various journals, books, and national conferences.

Terry M. Daugherty is the Dean of the Scott College of Business and Professor of Marketing at Indiana State University, USA. His research examines areas of consumer psychology and persuasion, and he is the former Editor-in-Chief of the *Journal of Interactive Advertising*. Terry has authored numerous scholarly publications within the domains of digital marketing and advertising while presenting his work at leading academic conferences worldwide.

eMarketing

Digital Marketing Strategy

International Student Edition

Ninth edition

Raymond D. Frost, Alexa K. Fox,
and Terry M. Daugherty

Routledge
Taylor & Francis Group

NEW YORK AND LONDON

Cover image: © Getty Images

Ninth edition published 2024
by Routledge
605 Third Avenue, New York, NY 10158

and by Routledge
4 Park Square, Milton Park, Abingdon, Oxon, OX14 4RN

*Routledge is an imprint of the Taylor & Francis Group, an informa
business*

Eighth edition published by Routledge 2018

ISBN: 978-1-032-35801-7 (ISE)

DOI: 10.4324/9781003247319

Typeset in Bembo
by Apex CoVantage, LLC

Printed in the UK by Severn, Gloucester on responsibly sourced paper

Access the Support Material: https://www.routledge.com/9781032161587

Contents

Part I

Digital Marketing in Context

Chapter 1

Past, Present, and Future

The key objective of this chapter is to develop an understanding of the background, current state, and future potential of digital marketing. You will learn about digital marketing's important role in a company's overall integrated marketing strategy.

After reading this chapter, you will be able to:

- Explain how the advances in internet and information technology offer benefits and challenges to consumers, businesses, marketers, and society.
- Distinguish between digital business and digital marketing.
- Explain how increasing buyer control is changing the marketing landscape.
- Understand the distinction between information or entertainment as data and the information-receiving appliance used to view or hear it.
- Identify several trends that may shape the future of digital marketing, including the semantic Web.

THE PIANO GUYS STORY

The Piano Guys, an American musical group that has swept the nation with their original blends of classical and modern sounds, has successfully used digital marketing as a key part of the huge success the group has become today. Paul Anderson, a local piano store owner in Utah, was searching for new ways to market his pianos, so he started a YouTube channel and a Facebook page for his store. He created unique music videos to showcase his pianos, which caught on quickly, going viral and generating traffic to his store.

One day, Jon Schmidt, a solo piano performer, came into Paul's store and asked if he could practice for an upcoming concert he was performing in the area. Paul asked Jon if he would be willing to be in a video that could both promote Paul's store and Jon's music. The duo hit it off, and Jon invited his friend and cellist, Steve Sharp Nelson, to join the team. Finally, Al van der Beek approached Steve, who was moving into Al's neighborhood, to show him his elaborate at-home music studio. Al's studio engineering skills would prove to be an invaluable piece that makes The Piano Guys the remarkable musical group they are today.

The Piano Guys started creating music videos that blended classical and modern songs and enhanced the videography with unique special effects such as lightsaber cello bows during a special version of the infamous "The Imperial March" from *The Empire Strikes Back* of the *Star Wars* saga. This video can be found on The Piano Guys' YouTube channel and has garnered over 47 million views, making it a great example of a viral marketing success.

Today, The Piano Guys are known just as much for their remarkable classically influenced instrumental music as they are their highly professional music videos that incorporate unique

DOI: 10.4324/9781003247319-2

special effects and are shot in breathtaking locations. The musicians have 6.92 million subscribers to their YouTube channel, where they have dozens of fascinating videos uploaded. Many people learn about and become fans of The Piano Guys on YouTube first, before purchasing their music and concert tickets to enjoy them offline.

Why do we begin this book with this story? Because a musical group is a product, promoting its benefits to consumers in hopes that they'll purchase songs, albums, or concert tickets, or even engage in another type of "purchasing," by subscribing to The Piano Guys' YouTube channel or liking its Facebook page. The Piano Guys have even blended these two types of purchasing by showcasing the details of their nearest concert and offering the opportunity to purchase tickets as a viewer watches the videos posted to their YouTube channel. The Piano Guys' use of digital marketing is a stellar example for businesses and demonstrates the power of the internet. The Piano Guys created a product (unique and inspiring music and video content), reached people via the media they prefer (online and social media), created a dialog with people, often initiated by the group, and leveraged user-generated content by sharing internet users' posts and comments about their music and videos. Their story successfully generated interest through its viral videos and created a loyal following that has made this group a full-time job for the musicians, completing with a full tour schedule around the United States. What a remarkable way to respect the beauty of classical music and infuse it with the sounds of today that people just can't get enough of. Sources: www.thepianoguys.com and The Piano Guys social media pages.

Digital Marketing Landscape

The Piano Guys example demonstrates that some marketing principles never change. Companies must meet the needs of their customers. Further, markets always welcome good products and demand good company/customer communication. Customers trust well-respected brands and talk to others about them. What is new is that these classic concepts are enhanced and often more challenging when applied to social media, huge databases, mobile devices, the internet of things (IoT), and other internet technologies.

What Works?

The rapid growth of the World Wide Web (basis for "www.") in the 1990s, the subsequent bursting of the dot-com bubble, and mainstreaming of the internet and related technologies created today's climate: the comprehensive integration of digital marketing and traditional marketing to create seamless strategies and tactics. This provides plenty of profitable opportunities, as discussed below. This chapter is just a sampling of what you'll find throughout the text.

- *The customer is CEO.* After all those years of marketers talking about the customer being their focus, finally, this has become a reality. The internet has put the consumer in charge. This power shift means that companies must be transparent, authentic, monitor online discussion about brands, and engage customers to help improve products (a strategy called crowdsourcing).
- *Digital commerce.* US consumers are projected to spend $933 billion online in 2021. While this is a massive amount of money, it still represents less than one-fifth of what is spent in the brick-and-mortar world. But absolute numbers are deceiving. What is more significant is the rate of growth. So while brick-and-mortar sales will grow at about 6 percent, digital commerce sales are growing at three times that rate, or about 18 percent. Investors care about growth potential and thus money continues to flow into digital commerce.

- *Advertising online.* Online advertising the largest portion of media budgets compared to every other medium. Marketers spent more than $189 billion on online advertising in the United States in 2021, with more than $135 billion spent on mobile advertising ("IAB Internet . . .", 2021).
- *Search engine marketing.* This marketing tactic is hugely important. Digital search advertising spending (i.e., purchasing keywords that present advertisements on search engine results pages) yielded more than $78 billion in 2021 ("IAB Internet . . .", 2017). Google controls the lion's share of the user search market, and most digital marketers use search engine optimization to make sure their sites appear near the top of the first page of organic search results (more on search engine optimization in Chapter 12).
- *Owned, paid, and earned media.* Marketing communication planning now involves owned (e.g., website), paid (e.g., banner ads), and earned (e.g., blog and Facebook posts) media. The traditional marketing communication tools of advertising, sales promotion, personal selling, direct marketing, and public relations are used within this new context to generate earned media.
- *Mobile marketing.* Eighty-five percent of American adults now have smartphones, providing plenty of profitable opportunities for smartphone applications and advertising (Pew Research, 2021). When added to mobile computing (iPads and netbooks), the wireless internet offers users anytime, anywhere access for consumers—and where consumers go, marketers follow. Increased mobile device use and faster WiFi connectivity has also led to more long-form content being available and consumed via mobile devices, which yields new opportunities for online advertising.
- *User-generated content.* Now a huge part of online content, this includes everything from consumer-created commercials and product improvement suggestions to YouTube videos, Facebook photos, and Pinterest posts, as well as electronic word of mouth on blogs, social networks, and user review sites (such as the Amazon.com book reviews).
- *Social media communities.* These communities gather users with like-minded interests for conversation and networking. This includes social networking sites such as LinkedIn, Twitter, Facebook, Instagram, and TikTok. Marketers use these virtual communities to build brands and engage customers.
- *Content marketing.* Marketers are becoming publishers, creating content on websites and in social media to attract and engage prospects and customers. Companies publish videos, press releases, blog posts, white papers, infographics, digital books, and more. Content and customer engagement go hand in hand.
- *Local and location-based marketing.* These efforts work well online, thanks to Google local search, eBay classifieds, and the hugely popular Craigslist. Smartphone users can easily find a local business with a global positioning system (GPS) and the Google application or check into local businesses on Facebook.
- *Brand transparency.* This means that marketers are rewarded for being honest, open, and transparent in their communication with internet users. Those who are not get called out under the bright lights of the blogosphere, on product review sites, and on social media.
- *Inbound marketing.* The days of "interrupt" marketing (e.g., television commercials) are waning. Consumers are not waiting for marketing messages but rather are receiving custom messages in real time, often in response to search queries and other behavior. Inbound marketing strategies are about enticing consumers to find companies online (more in this chapter).
- *Analytics.* Web analytics and many other techniques allow marketers to keep track of every mouse click, page visit, cookie, and geotag to improve strategy efficiency and

effectiveness. There are millions of metrics with marketers selecting the most appropriate for their objectives and tactics while following them daily.

- *Privacy.* Profiling of individual consumers has become very sophisticated on the web. That in turn has led to a backlash by consumers concerned about their privacy. Apple has become the corporate icon of the privacy movement. They now have extensive privacy protections built into their platforms that allow easy one-click protection. By contrast, Facebook and Google sell ads and oppose Apple's privacy enhancements to their platforms. Their real objection is that Apple has made it too easy to opt out of tracking without providing the context of the marketing benefit that consumers lose by opting out.

Internet 101

Technically speaking, the **internet** is a global network of interconnected networks. This includes millions of corporate, government, organizational, and private networks. Many of the servers (hard drives and software) in these networks hold files, such as webpages and videos, that can be accessed by all networked computers. Every computer, cell phone, or other networked device can send and receive data in the form of e-mail or other digital files over the internet. These data move over phone lines, cables, and satellites from sender to receiver. One way to understand this process is to consider the internet as having three technical roles: (1) content providers who create information, entertainment, and so forth that reside on Web servers or computers with network access, (2) users (also known as *client* computers) who access content and send e-mail and other content over the network (such as a Facebook comment), and (3) a technology infrastructure to move, create, and view or listen to the content (the software and hardware). Note that individuals can be both users and content providers at various times, so the line between items 1 and 2 is slowly disappearing. In *eMarketing*, we stopped capitalizing the word *internet*. Following *Wired Magazine*'s suggestion, we agree that the internet is not a place (requiring a proper noun's capitalization) but a medium, similar to radio and television.

There are three types of access to the internet:

1. *Public internet*—The global network that is accessible by anyone, anywhere, anytime.
2. *Intranet*—A network that runs internally in a corporation but uses internet standards such as HTML and browsers. Thus, an intranet is like a mini-internet, but with password protection for internal corporate consumption.
3. *Extranet*—Two or more proprietary networks that are joined for the purpose of sharing information. If two companies, or a company and its suppliers or customers, link their intranets, they would have an extranet. The access is limited to extranet members.

Digital business, digital marketing, and digital commerce are internet applications. **Digital business** is the optimization of a company's business activities using digital technology. Digital technologies are things, such as computers and the internet, that allow the storage and transmission of data in digital formats (1s and 0s). In this book, we use the terms *digital technology* and *information technology* interchangeably. Digital business involves attracting and retaining the right customers and business partners. It permeates business processes, such as product buying and selling. It includes digital communication, digital commerce, and online research, and it is used in every business discipline. **Digital commerce** is the subset of digital business focused on transactions that includes buying/selling online, digital value creation, virtual marketplaces and storefronts, and new distribution channel intermediaries. Mobile commerce (M-commerce) and social commerce are subsets of digital commerce (discussed in Chapter 11).

Digital marketing is only one part of an organization's digital business activities. **Digital marketing** is the *use of information technology* for the marketing activity and the processes for creating, communicating, delivering, and exchanging offerings that have value for customers, clients, partners, and society at large. More simply defined, digital marketing is the result of information technology applied to traditional marketing. Digital marketing affects traditional marketing in two ways. First, it increases efficiency and effectiveness in traditional marketing functions. Second, the technology of digital marketing transforms many marketing strategies from a mass approach to more of a one-to-one relationship between a business and customer, as shown in The Piano Guys example. This transformation also results in new business models that add customer value and/or increase company profitability, such as the highly successful Facebook, Twitter, and Google AdSense advertising models.

However, digital marketing involves much more than these basic technologies and applications.

Digital Marketing Is Bigger than the Web

The Web is the portion of the internet that supports a graphical user interface for hypertext navigation, with browsers such as Microsoft Internet Explorer, Mozilla Firefox, and Google Chrome. The Web is what most people think about when they think of the internet. Electronic marketing reaches far beyond the Web. First, many digital marketing technologies exist without the Web, which include mobile apps, software and hardware used in customer relationship management, supply chain management, and electronic data interchange arrangements pre-dating the Web. Second, non-Web internet communications such as e-mail, internet telephony (e.g., Skype), and text messaging are effective avenues for marketing. Some of these services can also use the Web, such as Web-based e-mail. Third, the internet delivers text, video, audio, and graphics to many more information-receiving appliances than simply personal computers (PCs). As shown in Exhibit 1.1, these forms of digital content also go over the internet infrastructure to the television, personal digital assistants, cell phones, and even the refrigerator or automobile (see more about the internet of Things in Chapter 7). Finally, offline electronic data-collection devices, such as barcode scanners and databases, receive and send data about customers and products over an intranet.

It is helpful to think of it this way: Content providers create digital text, video, audio, and graphics to send over the internet infrastructure to users who receive it as information, entertainment, or communication on many types of appliances. As marketers think outside of the

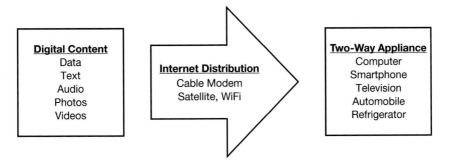

Exhibit 1.1 The Web Is Only One Aspect of Digital Marketing

Web and realize that most users are also now content providers, they find many new possibilities for creating products that provide value and communicate in ways that build relationships with customers.

Digital Marketing Is Bigger than Technology

The internet is like a watering hole for humans. We come for easy, inexpensive, and quick access to digital information, connections, and entertainment, and in turn, it transforms individuals, businesses, economies, and societies. This book focuses on the union of technology and marketing; however, a brief overview of the big picture is useful for understanding digital marketing's impact.

INDIVIDUALS

The internet provides individual users with convenient and continuous access to information, entertainment, networking, and communication. If "information is power," individuals have more power than ever before, as many companies experience. Yet the quality of the information available online is being questioned more than ever before, and companies, including big tech companies, are taking an active role in corporate social responsibility in an effort to connect with consumers in ways never done before. Consumers compare product features and prices using search engines and read product reviews from other consumers at www.Amazon.com, Facebook, and other sites. Further, consumers use the internet to bring music, movies, and other types of entertainment directly to their PCs, iPads and televisions—on their schedule and on their preferred receiving device, not those of the medium distributor. Finally, the internet enables multimedia one-to-one communication through e-mail, social media, and more. The internet continues to affect the way many individuals work, communicate, and consume, and marketers scramble to provide value and earn a piece of the profits.

COMMUNITIES

Strangers in countries worldwide form online communities supporting many-to-many communication to discuss a variety of topics facilitated by the internet. Communities form around shared videos (YouTube) and individual or company profiles (Facebook). See Exhibit 1.2 for an idea of the huge number of internet users belonging to online communities. Companies and consultants gain exposure to customers on Web logs (blogs). **Blogs** are online journals frequently updated on webpages. Micro sites and microblogs, such as twitter.com, allow individuals to follow each other's short posts. Business communities also abound online, especially around shared industries or professions. Another example of online communities is auctions in both business and consumer markets. Finally, independent, private communities have formed around peer-to-peer file sharing. Individual users upload, share, and collaborate on documents and files at Google Docs and Dropbox from far apart geographic locations.

BUSINESSES

The digital environment enhances business processes and activities across the entire organization. Employees from a variety of disciplines work together in cross-functional teams worldwide using computer networks to share and apply knowledge for increased efficiency and profitability. Financial experts communicate shareholder information and file required

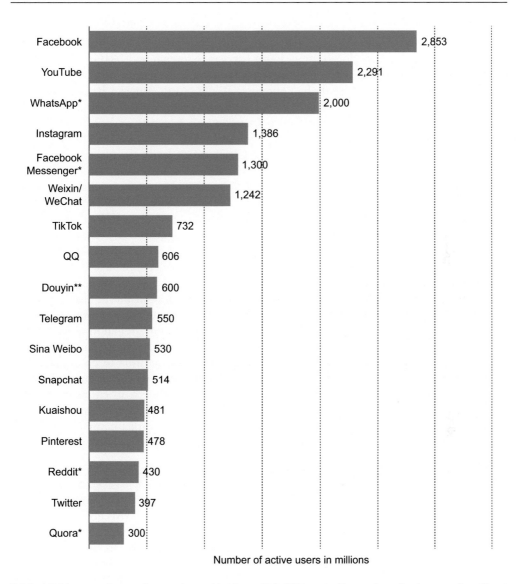

Exhibit 1.2 Most popular social networks worldwide as of July 2021, ranked by number of active users (in millions)
Source: Statista

government statements online. Human resources personnel use the internet for electronic recruiting and training. According to Statista, 57 percent of recruiters have not hired a candidate because of what they found about that candidate on social media. Production and operations managers adjust manufacturing based on the internet's ability to give immediate sales feedback—resulting in just-in-time inventory and building products to order.

Strategists at top corporate levels leverage computer networks to apply a firm's knowledge in building and maintaining a competitive edge. Digital tools allow executives easy access to data from their devices and show results of the firm's strategies at the click of a mouse or the tap of a mobile screen.

SOCIETIES

Digital information enhances economies through more efficient markets, more jobs, information access, communication globalization, lower barriers to foreign trade and investment, and more. But the internet's impact is not evenly distributed across the globe. Internet penetration rates around the globe differ greatly by continent. While North America has a penetration rate of 95 percent, it only makes up 6.7 percent of all users online, which is dwarfed by Asia, making up 53.4 percent of all internet users (according to internetworldstats.com). Stories abound about indigenous peoples in remote locations gaining health, legal, and other advice or selling native products using the internet (see Chapter 4). Clearly, the internet is having a huge, worldwide impact on various societies.

A networked world creates effects that some see as undesirable. Societies change as global communities form based on interests, and worldwide information access slowly decreases cultural and language differences. Some say that the existence of a truly global village will have the effect of removing cultural differences, which is seen as negative. As well, many in the United States are concerned by the high degree of technology outsourcing. This inevitable result of a global economy, greased by the internet, means there will continue to be big changes in many countries.

Easy computer networking on mobile devices from any location means that work and home boundaries are blurring. Although this option makes working more convenient, it may encourage more workaholism and less time with friends and family. Yet another issue is the digital divide—the idea that internet adoption occurs when folks have enough money to buy a computer, the literacy to read what is on webpages, and the education to be motivated to do it. Internet critics are justifiably concerned that class divisions will grow, preventing the upward mobility of people on lower socioeconomic levels and even in entire developing countries. Finally, the problems of **spam** (unsolicited e-mail), online fraud, and computer viruses slow down the positive impact of the internet and digital marketing practices. These kinds of problems are the unavoidable results of all new and evolving technologies.

Digital Marketing's Past: Web 1.0

The internet is over 50 years old. Started in 1969 as the ARPANET, it was commissioned by the US Department of Defense's Advanced Research Projects Agency (ARPA) as a network for academic and military use. The first online community, the **USENET**, began 10 years later. Over 800 million messages from that early community are now archived in Google Groups. The first Web pages and internet browsers appeared in 1993, and that was the internet's tipping point. This was Web 1.0: organizations created content on Web pages and in e-mail, and users consumed the content. The first form of online marketing appeared as a banner ad from AT&T on the website HotWired.com in 1994 (LaFrance, 2017). This ad ushered in a new era of digital marketing with companies, media, and users flocking to the Web as it grew more quickly than any other medium previously (Exhibit 1.3).

This first generation of digital business was like a gold rush. Start-ups and well-established businesses alike created a Web presence and experimented plenty. Many companies quickly attracted huge sales and market shares, but only a handful brought anything to the bottom line. In early 2000, many firms experienced 12-month sales growth between 100 percent and 500 percent with negative profits. Between early 2000 and 2002, however, more than 500 internet firms shut down in the United States alone, owing to the so-called dot-com bust. After the bust dust had settled, almost 60 percent of the public dot-com companies making it through hard times were profitable by the fourth quarter of 2003.

1969 ARAPNET commissioned by US Department of Defense for academic and military use.

1975 First mailing list created to use the new computer network.

1979 USENET established to host discussions. First post in 1981. Later managed by Google Groups (800 million archived messages).

1984 Number of connected computer hosts reaches 1,000.

1987 Number of connected computer hosts reaches 10,000. First e-mail connection with China.

1988 First virus, affects 10% of the 60,000 hosts.

1993 Early Web sites appear, and businesses and media take notice.

1994 First banner ads, "Jerry and David's Guide to the World Wide," appear on hotwired.com (later named Yahoo!).

1995 eBay opens its doors and disrupts the classified advertising business.

2000 Napster.com shows the world that peer-to-peer networking can work. Businesses show that digital commerce doesn't always work (the dot-com crash).

2002 Running your own blog is now considered hip.

2003 The Recording Industry Association of America (RIAA) sues 261 people for illegal music downloading.

2004 16% of the world's population uses the internet. Businesses figure out how to be profitable with digital business models.

2012 34.3% of the world's population is online. Internet usage in industrialized nations reaches maturity. Social media use moves the balance of power from organizations to internet users.

2017 51.7% of the world's population is online. Internet usage in developing nations grows increasingly popular. Corporate social media use becomes an accepted business practice among companies and consumers.

Exhibit 1.3 Internet Timeline for Interesting and Amusing Facts

Source: Some of this information is from Hobbes' Internet Timeline (available at www.zakon.org). Internet adoption rates from www.worldinternetstats.com

Brick-and-mortar retailers, such as the bookseller Barnes & Noble and Wall Street investment firms, may have felt relief as their online competitors were failing but quickly noted that internet technologies had fundamentally changed the structure of their industry and several others. In what *Business Week* called the "first wave of internet disruption," firms such as Amazon, Expedia, E★TRADE, and the former CDNow (purchased by Amazon) transformed the way books, travel, investments, and music were sold ("E-Biz Strikes Again!", 2004). Disrupted industries in the first wave generally offered tangible products that were easily compared online and purchased for the lowest price.

Having gone through the boom and the bust in developed nations (the internet is still booming in many emerging economies), businesses then entered what Gartner, Inc., called the *slope of enlightenment* (Exhibit 1.4). It was a time when marketers returned to their traditional roots, relying on well-grounded strategy and sound marketing practices but using information technology in ways that increased the company's profit—no more throwing money at ideas that don't return a desired amount on investment. During the dot-com shakeout from 2000 to 2002, industries experienced much consolidation (the Gartner "Peak of Inflated Expectation" and subsequent "Trough of Disillusionment" in Exhibit 1.4). Some firms, such as Levi Strauss, stopped selling online both because it was not efficient and because it created *channel conflict* between manufacturer Sears Roebuck and Company and other long-time retail customers. Other firms merged, with the stronger firms typically acquiring smaller ones.

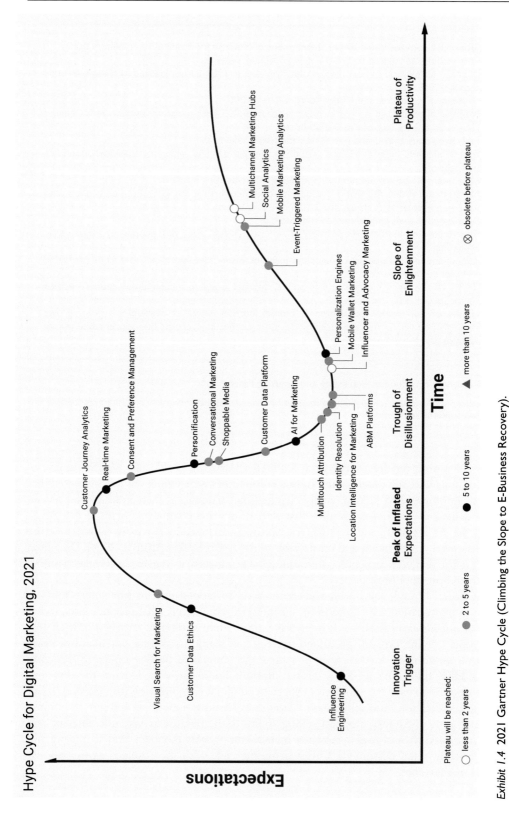

Exhibit 1.4 2021 Gartner Hype Cycle (Climbing the Slope to E-Business Recovery).

Source: Gartner, Inc. Hype Cycle for E-Commerce, 2010, Gene Alvarez, Aug. 3, 2010. Note: Gartner material speaks as of the date of publication and is subject to change without notice

The E Drops from eMarketing

Gartner predicted that the *e* would drop, making electronic business just part of the way things are done (refer to Exhibit 1.4). This means that e-business is just business, and eMarketing is just marketing. This is now mostly true, as evidenced by the majority of marketing managers and executives who say that online marketing is an integral part of the company's marketing effort. However, e-business and eMarketing will always have their unique models, concepts, and practices with special considerations for integrating them into marketing communications (and that is why we have not dropped the "E" from the name of this book, although the term "digital marketing" is used synonymously throughout the text).

Markets and traditional marketing practices continue to change, sometimes in fundamental ways, due to information technology. For instance, the concept of online search is intrinsic to digital marketing, continues to evolve, and has important implications that marketers must understand. However, most marketing processes stand the test of time—technology has just given them a new twist. Marketing research is greatly enhanced with online data collection, but the process of identifying research problems, collecting data, and using the results to make marketing decisions will never change. In short, marketers must stay well-grounded in the discipline and simultaneously be current on new information technologies and changing digital marketing concepts to remain competitive. This is necessary because the moment marketers feel comfortable about the *e* dropping, new technologies will challenge traditional practices. For example, the digital marketing landscape is now changing rapidly due to consumer-generated content, mobile internet access, social media, and many disruptive technologies.

An example of a company that has already gone through the entire Gartner cycle is Charles Schwab, which allowed e.Schwab.com (now schwab.com) to cannibalize the larger brick-and-mortar securities firm in 1998. Dubbed "eat your own DNA" by former CEO Jack Welch of General Electric, Schwab astutely pitted the online and offline business models against each other and allowed the most profitable methods to win. The Schwab model resulted in lower prices, incorporation of successful digital marketing strategies, and faster-growing accounts and assets. For this brokerage firm, digital business is just business.

Marketing Implications of Internet Technologies

Early marketers who grasped what internet technologies could do were better poised to integrate information technology into marketing practice. Compare the properties in Exhibit 1.5 to those of the telephone. The telephone is a mediating technology, has global reach, and has network externality. In contrast, the internet has properties that create opportunities beyond those possible with the telephone, television, postal mail, or other communication media. It is these differences that excited early marketers and had them wondering how to best capitalize on them.

These internet properties not only allow for more effective and efficient marketing strategy and tactical implementation but also actually changed the way marketing is conducted. For example, the fundamental idea of digitizing data (bits, not atoms) has transformed media and software and music delivery methods, as well as created a new transaction channel. This is why traditional newspaper circulation is declining in comparison with the digital online versions. Also, the internet as an information equalizer has shifted the balance of power from marketer to consumer.

Marketers must understand internet technology to harness its power. They do not have to personally develop the technologies, but they need to know enough to select appropriate suppliers and direct technology professionals.

Property	Marketing Implications
Bits, not Atoms	Information, products, and communication in digital form can be stored, sent, and received nearly instantaneously. Text, audio, video, graphics, and photos can all be digitized, but digital products cannot be touched, tasted, or smelled.
Mediating Technology	Peer-to-peer relationships, such as auctions, social networks, and business partnerships, can be formed regardless of geographic location. Technology allows timely communication and data sharing, as with businesses in a supply chain.
Global Reach	New markets are opened allowing for worldwide partnerships, employee collaboration, and salesperson telecommuting.
Network Externality	Businesses can reach more of their markets with automated communication, and consumers can disseminate brand opinions worldwide in an instant.
Time Moderator	Consumers hold higher expectations about communication with companies and faster work processes within companies.
Information Equalizer	Companies employ mass customization of communication, and consumers have more access to product information and pricing.
Scalable Capacity	Companies pay for only as much data storage or server space as needed for profitable operations and can store huge amounts of data.
Open Standard	Companies can access each other's databases for smooth supply chain and customer relationship management, which connects large and small firms.
Market Deconstruction	Many distribution channel functions are performed by nontraditional firms (e.g., Edmunds.com and online travel agents), and new industries emerged (e.g., ISPs).
Task Automation	Self-service online lowers costs and makes automated transactions, payment, and fulfillment possible.

Exhibit 1.5 Internet Properties and Marketing Implications

Source: Properties adapted from Allan Afuah and Christopher Tucci, *Internet Business Models and Strategies* (New York: McGraw-Hill/Irwin, 2001)

The internet has a number of unique properties when it comes to business applications:

- *Lower costs.* Reach the right customers at a much lower cost than with traditional marketing methods.
- *Trackable, measurable results.* Obtain detailed data about customer responses to marketing campaigns.
- *Global reach.* Access new markets across the globe.
- *Personalization.* Connecting a database to a website allows for individually targeted offers. The more they buy, the better the data and more effective the marketing.
- *One-to-one marketing.* Gain instant access to individual customers on computers and mobile phones.
- *More interesting campaigns.* Use of creative multimedia content to engage customers through two-way interactivity.
- *Better conversion rates (increased purchases).* Online customers are only a few clicks from a purchase, whereas when offline they must make a phone call or visit a store.
- *Twenty-four-hour marketing.* Allows 24/7 access to the firm's products and services, even when the office is closed.

Digital Marketing Today: Web 2.0

The unique properties and strengths of internet technologies provided a springboard from the first to the second generation (Web 2.0), as described by NetLingo:

The components of Web 2.0 sites (and the popularity of blogs and social networking) exist because of the ability to offer mini-homepages, a gig of storage, your own e-mail, a music player and photo, video and bookmark sharing . . . all of which were initially "first-generation" technologies.

(www.netlingo.com)

Technology only opens the window of opportunity. Marketers and their markets create new products that capitalize on Web 2.0 technologies. Whereas Web 1.0 connected users to computer networks for receiving content, Web 2.0 technologies also connect people with each other for producing and sharing content. These webpages allow for social networking and are primarily authored by internet users (also called user-generated media [UGM] or consumer-generated media [CGM]). Social media sites are increasing in number and attracting users more quickly than are traditional media sites. And with any new technology, this creates opportunities and challenges for marketers, some of which are outlined next.

Power Shift from Sellers to Buyers

As noted previously, the connected customer is now the CEO online. "Marketers of all sorts are now being urged to give up the steering wheel to a new breed of consumers who want more control over the ways products are peddled to them," according to Stuart Elliott, a *New York Times* columnist (Elliott, 2009). Both individual and business buyers are more demanding than ever because they are just one click away from a plethora of global competitors, all vying for their business. As well, the internet's social media provide a communication platform where individual product comments can spread like wildfire in a short time and quickly either enhance or damage a brand image. Consumer and business customer word of mouth has long been a powerful market force, but now individuals are not limited to their friends, colleagues, and families. The internet allows a disgruntled customer to tell a few thousand friends with one click of the "share" button: this electronic word of mouth ("eWOM") is something marketers have never seen before. One growing challenge related to eWOM is the vast amount of information available and how consumers navigate and make sense of it.

This phenomenon is only one part of a trend that has been growing for years because of the internet—the power balance has finally shifted from companies to individuals, as shown in Exhibit 1.6. How did this happen? It started with consumer control of both the television

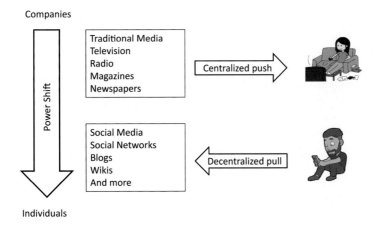

Exhibit 1.6 Power Shift from Companies to Individuals

Source: Based on Dion Hinchcliffe's ideas (web2.socialcomputingmagazine.com)

remote control and the computer mouse. This meant that marketers could no longer hold an individual captive for 30 seconds in front of a TV screen or even for 10 seconds in front of a computer screen. With **cloud** and **streaming services and mobile devices**, consumers can easily navigate and capture countless hours of programming for later viewing—fast-forwarding through or completely eliminating commercials.

Let's Get Technical—TV: Content Over Platform

It is Saturday night at 7:50 P.M. Your friends want you to go with them to the 8:30 showing of the latest movie, and you know that your favorite actor is the lead. However, you also do not want to miss the season finale of your favorite reality show, which airs at 8:00 P.M. You could watch it on demand on the network's app. But the thought of missing the live broadcast truly annoys you because you know that your phone is going to be blowing up with texts and Twitter feeds during the episode, which will spoil the plot for you . . .

There was a time when content was tied to its delivery platform. Radio broadcasts were listened to on radios; TV broadcasts were watched on TVs; records were played on a record player. One of the extraordinary developments of the internet era is the divorcing of content from its platform. Once content is digitized, it can be transmitted and played back on a variety of devices. This causes a degree of worry for cable and satellite TV companies that made their fortunes by developing and selling access to costly platforms. When platforms become a commodity, then value shifts back to content. There are four themes that we will see repeated in some of these Let's Get Technical pieces:

1. Superior content beats out a superior delivery platform.
2. Over time, the inferior delivery platform will catch up in quality.
3. Younger users drive these trends in two ways.
   a. Younger users tend to be more price sensitive.
   b. Younger users value constant connectivity.

A short walk back through history will illustrate these points. There was a time when almost every home in the United States had a dedicated phone line. With the advent of cell phones, younger consumers did not see the need to own and pay for both a land line and a cell phone. They chose to go exclusively with the cell phone for two reasons. First, the cell phone was always with them. Second, the early generation cell phones had texting, which was not available on land lines. With the advent of the iPhone in 2007, the content difference grew even more pronounced with the addition of apps. In the beginning the quality of cell reception was not as good as land lines, but it didn't matter. People were willing to put up with reduced quality to enjoy the enriched content (texting and apps) and to stay universally connected. Over time, cell phone quality has improved so that now 5G exceeds landline voice quality and do a good job with video as well.

Why do platforms catch up in quality? Because at the end of the day only two things matter—bandwidth and signal quality. Bandwidth is the amount of information transmitted per unit time. Signal quality refers to how much of the information is transmitted cleanly. Over the last 10 years we have seen bandwidth and signal quality increase tremendously both over wired and wireless connections. Necessity is the mother of invention.

Cable and satellite TV are beginning to go the way of the land line. Cord cutters now receive streaming content over the internet. They represent 24 percent of US households, and their numbers are growing (Stoll, 2021). Already much of the same content that is available over cable and satellite has come to internet TV. The cord cutters pay a reduced rate, but to protect their broadcast channels, the networks often make the cord cutters watch on tape delay.

Many internet streaming providers like Netflix, Disney+, and Amazon are *producing their own proprietary content*! This type of content really started taking off in the 2020s, and if the content continues to be engaging, the users will follow.

Internet TV—Watch Anything, Anytime, Anywhere, on Any Device

TV over the internet is the future. The internet may provide viewers with the opportunity to sidestep traditional cable and satellite services.

Hulu, Roku, Amazon, Netflix, YouTube, and Apple TV are just a few of the internet services available. All of these services require some sort of device that receives and decodes the internet signal. The box also verifies access rights for premium services. The data pathway is typically internet to your cable modem, cable modem to your router, router via WiFi to the decoding device, decoding device to the screen.

Sensing these trends, most TV manufacturers now create internet-ready smart TVs that have one or more of the decoding devices programmed into the TV itself. Just plug in the TV, give it the password to your wireless router, and the service is ready to go.

Will smart TVs eliminate the need for decoding devices? Maybe. Most of the streaming services would be just as happy not to provide the box. They make their money off of selling content or ads.

Apple TV is an exception that proves the rule. Apple has apps that run on Apple TV. So the *apps comprise much of their content*, and of course you can only run the apps if you buy the box from Apple. This creates two revenue streams for Apple: selling the Apple TV and their commission on each paid app that users buy.

Pay services such as Netflix omit commercials and allow fast-forward, pause, and rewind of content. Netflix even allows you to download content for later connectionless viewing on your iPhone. Major broadcast networks (ABC, CBS, NBC) offer online services that run commercials throughout the content and do not allow skipping and fast-forward and are also starting to offer their own subscription-based apps. Every viewing is another opportunity to sell ads.

The great advantage of internet TV for consumers is the ability to watch anything, anytime, anywhere, on any device. Unlike using a DVR, the consumer does not have to remember to program the show in advance. Just find it online and watch it on the platform of choice to match your device—whether that be a phone, tablet, laptop, or even a regular old TV.

Other trends affecting consumer attention are as follows (and many more throughout this book):

- *Consumers trust each other more than companies.* According to Crowdriff, consumers trust user reviews 12 times more than they trust marketing communications from the organization. For example, the Tripadvisor.com site allows travelers to review hotels worldwide, and other travelers rely upon it to pick hotels for upcoming trips—they trust it more than the corporate sales monologue they see at the hotel websites.
- *Market and media fragmentation.* The mass market has been slowly disintegrating since about 1992, as evidenced by the decline in prime-time television ratings, growth of cable television, and increasing number of special-interest magazines. The internet put finality to this trend by extending it to its ultimate—a market size of one customer—and prompted marketers to create products, mobile apps, webpages, and communication to small target groups.
- *Connections are critical.* Social networking is the name of the game today. Job recruiters scour social networks for job candidates, and business deals are made among LinkedIn members who have never met in person. Taylor Swift has over 88 million followers on Twitter, and this has helped to build her music empire. It is about whom you know online and what they say about you.
- *Everyone is a content producer.* Consumer-generated content also includes multimedia material. With smartphones, consumers always have the ability to take photos and videos and instantly upload to TikTok, Instagram, and other sites. Wearable recording devices enable action footage while skiing or during other activities. This opens the door to images of products that customers enjoy or ones that do not meet expectations and can be shown malfunctioning in YouTube videos.
- *Information transparency.* Because consumers create online product reviews and share other information, marketers must be authentic with brand and company information, or they will be exposed in social media. The same holds true for consumers, who present much personal information in social network profiles and wall posts.
- *Social commerce.* This is an evolution of digital commerce, using social media and consumer interactions to facilitate online sales. Customers chat about products online while they are shopping and post products they like on social media sites like Pinterest.

Voice of the customer is "a systematic approach for incorporating the needs of customers into the design of customer experiences," according to Bruce Temkin (2007) at Forrester Research. Forrester outlines five components: relationship tracking, interaction monitoring, continuous listening, project infusion (including customer insights in strategies and tactics), and periodic immersion (by employees with customer interactions). Companies are buzzing about this new technique for capturing a 360° view of customer preferences and behavior in every online and offline channel.

Many years of exposure to marketing strategies have made consumers more demanding and more sophisticated, and marketers will continue to become better at delivering customer value.

Customer Engagement

What do marketers do when this new breed of consumer finds their Web properties? Marketers are in a "new age of engagement, participation, and co-creation," according to Nielsen Media ("Super Buzz or Super Blues?", 2008). **Engagement** occurs when internet users connect or collaborate with brands, companies, or each other. This involves connecting with a user both

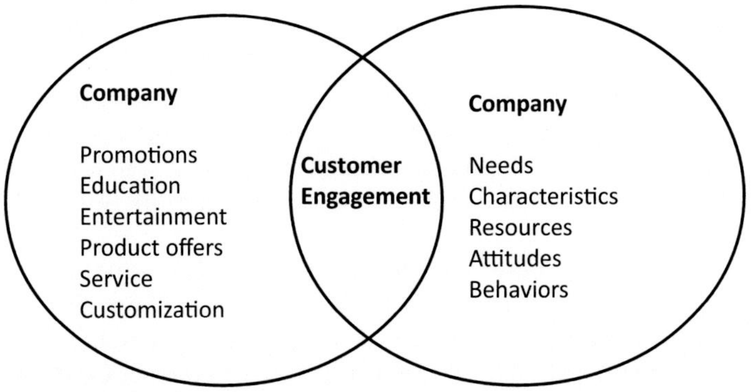

Exhibit 1.7 Customer Engagement Connects Company Content with Consumer Characteristics

emotionally and intellectually. Online engagement is analogous to offline experience marketing, such as the famous Build-A-Bear retailers or Disney theme parks. Online marketers engage users by enticing them to participate in their content or media (as seen in Exhibit 1.7).

One way to engage online users is through **crowdsourcing.** This is the practice of outsourcing ads, product development, and other tasks to a people outside the organization. For example, Doritos held an annual contest where users create 30 second television commercials. Site visitors vote on the finalists, and the winner's ad is shown during the Super Bowl game. Marketers capitalize on consumer desires for control by soliciting input on product development. Software developers ask users to test beta versions of websites or next-version software and suggest improvements. Customer engagement via crowdsourcing also involves consumer uploading videos or photos, posting comments on a blog, becoming a fan of the brand Facebook page, and so forth. Inventors also ask consumers to help fund new products through sites such as kickstarter.com. When buyers are engaged with a company's content, they become more attentive and often feel more favorable toward the brand.

Content Marketing

In addition to crowdsourcing, marketers use their own content to engage users online. **Content marketing** is a strategy involving creating and publishing content on websites and in social media. All online content can be considered content marketing, and it ranges from websites, social network pages, and blog posts to videos, white papers, and digital books. For example, when a business buyer receives an e-mail offering a free white paper about a hot topic, this engages them to click on the link and download the paper. In the process, the marketer receives the user's e-mail address and can follow up with a sales e-mail or call. Although the consumer is CEO, content is the king online. What is new about this is that marketers are beginning to see themselves as publishers, creating engaging content and enticing users to visit and consume the information or entertainment.

Inbound Marketing

Customers no longer appreciate marketing messages that interrupt them from what they are doing. Today, marketers must ask for permission to deliver communication if they want it to be attended and generally give customers what they want when they want it.

This change in customer behavior gave rise to the concept of **inbound marketing**—getting found online, as opposed to interrupting customers with outbound marketing to get them to pay attention to the ads, website, products, and so forth. Outbound tactics include traditional and online media advertising, telephone calling prospects, trade shows, and e-mail blasts. The components of inbound marketing are content (e.g., blogs, videos, digital books, white paper pdf files), social networks (e.g., Twitter, Facebook, blogs), and search engine optimization techniques to help get the social media or website come up on the first page of results for a keyword search.

Inbound marketing works. For instance, the majority of marketers indicate that blog content creation is their top inbound marketing priority, according to HubSpot (2017). One challenge for marketers involves developing new metrics to monitor the success of inbound marketing's social media tactics. The internet allows for tracking every mouse click and mobile screen tap, and marketers now have well-established measures for online tactics (as outlined in Chapter 2 and throughout the book). However, the standard measurement of number of site visitors or click-throughs from an ad does not measure site engagement well. Nielsen Media and others are now measuring the length of time spent on a site, number of comments posted, time spent watching a video, and other metrics to determine site engagement. Other performance metrics used by marketers include the amount of conversation about a topic for a specific time period, the number and growth of fans, friends, or followers and "likes" on a social network page, rate of pass-along for videos and other content, number of downloads or uploads of content, number of ratings, reviews, subscriptions, or social bookmarks, amount of interaction with a webpage, and many more.

New Technologies

Marketers constantly watch technology advances that spawn new marketing tactics. In this section, we discuss a sampling of important recent changes that affect internet technologies.

Wireless Networking and Mobile Computing

For cellular service, 5G is a fifth-generation high-speed wireless technology that replaces 4G (fourth generation). Although not yet widespread, 5G is likely to take over the billions of 4G subscribers worldwide. Mobile phones, tablets, and laptop computer technologies support a wide range of bandwidths for receiving and sending e-mail and large amounts of data, and for Web browsing in many different countries.

Using wireless mobile devices, customers check social media at Starbucks in Shanghai, receive flight information in the smallest of airports, and catch the latest sports scores while at the Gare du Nord train station in France (Exhibit 1.8). Consider the following:

- Many major airlines offer internet connections on airplanes.
- Verizon and other mobile carriers offer wireless hotspots, allowing users to access the internet anytime, anywhere.
- Coffee drinkers listening to music in Starbucks can instantly identify the artist, track, and album by asking Siri to listen to the song and then download it to their iPhones via iTunes.
- There are 362 million public WiFi spots worldwide (Vailshery, 2021a).

The rapid growth of wireless access points, when coupled with the large number of individuals worldwide owning mobile phones and the huge numbers owning smartphones, tablets,

Exhibit 1.8 WiFi at the Gare du Nord Train Station in France
Source: Courtesy of Reinier Evers (www.trendwatching.com)

or notebook computers, indicates a continuing growth in wireless networking. As this trend plays out, customers will demand information, entertainment, and communication whenever and however they desire and in small file sizes for fast downloading. We discuss many mobile strategies in this book, such as the Square device that allows businesses to swipe credit cards from their iPhones.

Cutting the Cord

In 2002, the number of mobile subscriptions began to surpass landline telephones (Meeker, 2012). Consumers are increasingly cutting the cord on their landline phones and moving to purely mobile phone use. They are also cutting the cable to their televisions. IPods and digital music downloads have changed the music industry, with physical CDs being produced and consumed less and less. These examples are indications of the huge disruption that continues to evolve the entertainment industries.

Appliance Convergence

Digital media are simply data that can be sent to viewers a variety of ways, as seen in Exhibit 1.1. Television programs, radio shows, news, movies, books, and photos are sent by their creators in electronic form via satellite, telephone wires, or cable and then viewed by the audience on receiving appliances such as televisions, computers, radios, smartphones, and others. Contrary to popular terminology usage, the receiving appliance is separate from the media type. In other words, watching a television set doesn't mean one must be viewing television programming—many watch YouTube videos on their televisions via WiFi connections in their homes. Computers can receive digital radio and television transmissions, and television sets can receive the Web and satellite radio content.

The idea of separating the medium from the appliance is both mind-boggling and exciting because of the business opportunities. It opens the door to new types of receiving appliances that are also "smart," allowing for saving, editing, and sending transmissions. For instance, smart refrigerators allow consumers to view television programs, movies, family photos, and webpages on a touch screen located right on the refrigerator door. Consumers can also read e-mail and messages entered by members of the household, listen to downloaded music, and track food inventory in the refrigerator.

The smart refrigerator is a good example of receiving-appliance convergence—many digital appliances in one. This convergence trend is far from over—many opportunities still exist for new technology and appliance development.

What does this mean for marketers? Marketers now realize that the medium and the appliance are no longer the defining way to reach customers (i.e., the term *television commercial* will soon lose its meaning). Instead, marketers will create multimedia communication for distribution to audience members anytime, anywhere, to any device—on demand by the user. In this light, social media and traditional media become simply media.

Exciting New Technology-Based Strategies

Demanding consumers jump on anything that saves them time. One new idea that works is one-click delivery. Take Uber Technologies Inc. as an example. The company offers an iPhone and Android app that allows consumers to simply tap once, and a taxi or luxury car and driver will appear to pick them up (uber.com). This is currently available in most US cities. Uber has even expanded this service to food delivery with its product Uber Eats, which gained tremendous popularity during the COVID-19 global pandemic, when consumers quarantined in their homes and were unable to pick up their own products from grocery stores and takeout meals from restaurants.

Voice navigation is another development, initiated by the iPhone's Siri. Acting on a user's voice commend, Siri can send an e-mail or text message, make a phone call, add a calendar item, check the weather or answer many questions using the Web. Siri decides which app or website will best answer the user's question and presents this to the user. The implications for marketers are huge. For example, if the user asks Siri for the best Thai restaurant, Siri might check Yelp for the answer, as opposed to a Google search (thus ignoring marketers' search engine optimization efforts).

Moreover, augmented reality (AR) and virtual reality (VR) give marketers unique opportunities to integrate the digital and real worlds. Some say such technologies can even keep physical retail stores fresh by allowing consumers to take virtual tours in brick-and-mortar shops or try on accessories virtually and compare looks.

Other Opportunities and Challenges in Web 2.0

Let's examine some of the other key elements of today's Web 2.0 landscape.

- *Internet adoption matures.* Today, the internet has matured in industrialized nations. High adoption rates have leveled, and heavy Web and e-mail use are commonplace.
- *Growth of online retail sales.* The National Retail Federation estimated holiday sales hit over $656 billion in 2016, which encompasses $117 billion in "non-store sales," including

e-commerce activity. This growth is expected to continue as more lucrative options become available online.

- *Search engines are now reputation engines.* Relevance is one of Google's search algorithm variables. The more high-traffic, similar-topic webpages that point to a site, the higher it appears on search engine results pages for specific keywords—meaning it is more relevant to the user. Popularity, as measured by incoming links, improves brand exposure, awareness, image, site traffic, and ultimately sales. Search marketing is now a key part of online marketer budgets.

- *Image recognition takes root.* **Image recognition** is technology that sees the content within an image. TinEye is an image recognition search engine that will find images online based on their content, not on text-based keywords or metatags describing the image. This service has indexed over 2 billion images and can help users locate copies of pictures of themselves or any other object (www.tineye.com).

- *Improved online and offline strategy integration.* This integration is especially evident in **multichannel marketing**—offering customers more than one way to buy something, such as a website, retail store, and catalog. Retailers manage customers via databases accessible by all employees.

- *Intellectual capital rules.* Imagination, creativity, and entrepreneurship are more important resources than financial capital. This was true of the first-generation internet and continues to this day. The difference today is that marketers now know how to use solid marketing and business principles to monetize creative ideas.

- *Decline of print media.* In early 2012, the Encyclopedia Britannica announced that it will no longer produce a printed version (the first edition was published in 1768). Printed newspapers are also declining in number due to subscriber and advertiser declines. Wikipedia's start in 2001 paved the way for growth in digital encyclopedia content with online access. This applies to other areas as well, such as Twitter, YouTube, and e-mail for breaking news and digital book readers for longer texts (such as Amazon's Kindle).

- *Online fundraising increases.* Kickstarter.com allows inventors to raise funds from users for innovative new products (crowdfunding).

- *Location-based services.* Many companies use the smartphone's GPS (global positioning system) features to provide local search (e.g., Google local search). Others also allow user check-in so friends can see where they are (e.g., Facebook).

- *The long tail.* Made famous by Chris Anderson's book, this term refers to the economy of abundance and explains how cheap computing and storage make it possible to increase revenue by selling small quantities of many products online. A typical Barnes & Noble brick-and-mortar store might have approximately 100,000 books, whereas an online retailer such as Amazon.com has millions of books. Amazon can sell a large variety of hard-to-find books in smaller quantities, and the sale of products not available in offline bookstores makes up 57 percent of Amazon's total sales. Furthermore, Amazon can deliver a given book in a matter of just a couple of days. This idea has turned economic models upside down.

- *Everything is "FSTR."* Everything is faster in the Web 2.0 environment. Users are overloaded with entertainment and information opportunities, and marketers need to be fast to gain their attention.

Many of these changes made traditional marketing more efficient and effective in reaching and selling to markets. However, some truly changed traditional marketing in fundamental and critical ways. The opportunities are stimulating, and marketers must be ever vigilant to capitalize on the internet's new frontiers.

The Future: Web 3.0

Plenty of other thrilling new opportunities lie ahead, but companies move with caution, watching the results of every goal, strategy, and tactic for signs of effectiveness. In the following sections, we describe several important trends that will further solidify in the future.

Semantic Web

Conceptualizing information and entertainment as data that are separate from the receiving appliance is one way that marketers can give customers exactly what they want when and where they want it. Web 3.0 will be able to handle more complex tasks than ever before. For example, you could ask your semantic Web electronic agent to book a flight to see a client on Monday in San Francisco, California, and then a lunch at a good Mexican restaurant. The agent would book a flight via the airline databases early in the morning with an aisle seat because it has stored your preferences. The agent would further charge your credit card and bill the flight to the client's account in your software program. It would then organize restaurant options for you to choose from and make a reservation once you decide. Then the agent would remind you that you will miss a dentist appointment at home on Monday and ask if you'd like it cancelled in the dentist's database. The evolution from Web 1.0—content creator makes a Web page and the content consumer views it—to Web 2.0—every user is both content creator and consumer and they share with one another—to Web 3.0—individual data presented and shared as desired—is an exciting transition. One thing keeping this from being a reality is that computer software cannot interpret data meaning based on the context, as in this example. Enter the semantic Web.

Sir Tim Berners-Lee, the Web's co-inventor, has been working with many others since 2001 on the technology to organize the Web's data for greater user convenience. His idea, the **semantic Web**, is an extension of the current Web, in which information is given well-defined meaning through HTML-like tags. The current Web carries text documents, photos, graphics, and audio and video files embedded in webpages that search engines struggle to catalog for users to find. The semantic Web will make it easier by providing a standard definition protocol so that users can easily find information based on its type, such as a person's name (e.g., <person> in the HTML code), the next available appointment for a particular doctor (found by searching the doctor's database), details on an upcoming concert, the hours of the library, the menu at the local restaurant, and so forth (for more information, see Berners-Lee, Hendler, and Lassila, 2001 and www.w3.org).

The value of the semantic Web is truly information on demand. Using an analogy, think for a minute about the development of time-telling devices. All clocks before 1929 required user effort to find the time. The sundial took a lot of user effort, to go look at the time and reposition the instrument as the sun's position changed. Later, mechanical, wind-up clocks displayed time only if the user wound the watch or clock pendulum to keep it running (Exhibit 1.9). In 1929, the quartz crystal changed things dramatically. From that point, the piece of data called *time* was pushed to users on demand with no effort on their part, a fundamental change from user finding or pulling the time to automated delivery of the time data. Afterward, time appeared in lots of devices, controlling lawn sprinklers, microwave ovens, manufacturing processes, and so forth. Individuals have come to depend upon that piece of data arriving reliably when and where they want it.

Now, think of the text, images, video, and audio available via the internet. Users must go find what they want, and it is not easy: they must spend effort searching, just as with early clocks, especially if they seek to find the highest quality information. We believe that the

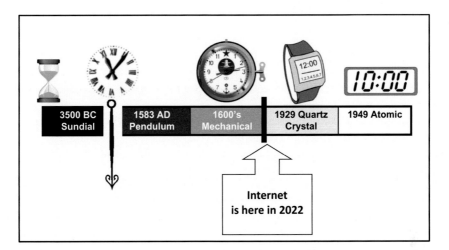

Exhibit 1.9 Internet—Time Analogy: Awaiting the Next Technological Breakthrough

internet is awaiting the next big technological leap, similar to the quartz crystal. Imagine the information on the Web arriving just as reliably as time, on demand. Some data is available this way now, such as flight delays, but consumers must sign up to receive these. Other data arrive automatically, such as text messages, e-mail, and Facebook comments or friend requests. However, these data all arrive from the source with no distinction between what the user wants or does not want to receive. With the semantic Web, consumers will define tasks for their personal digital agents, which will search for pieces of data and return them as movies to the television set, appointments to the smartphone calendar, contact information to the address book, and more. The semantic Web holds the promise of being this next huge advance: worldwide access to data on demand without effort. Get ready for the internet's "quartz crystal" and the next wave of disruption.

Stepping Stones to Web 3.0

Many predict that Web 3.0 will continue to integrate high-speed and large-bandwidth networks with distributed computing backed by powerful servers. Such a seamless integration will also feature applications support by artificial intelligence and an ever-connected internet of things (IoT). The following are predictions by industry experts, some of which are already accessible to consumers:

- Wearable computing will deliver data into goggles, wristbands, and other devices. University of Washington researchers have already produced a contact lens containing electrical circuits that can receive the internet via a WiFi connection (the internet in your eye) (see dailyuw.com).
- Additive manufacturing, or 3D printing, will become more accessible and useful to consumers. This is a process of using a digital design in a printing machine that builds up a 3D object, layer by layer (using liquid, powder, or sheets of plastic and other material).
- Distance online education will become more pervasive and perhaps eventually make the traditional university obsolete. The COVID-19 pandemic required higher education institutions to dramatically increase their online education offerings in 2020 and 2021, which will likely have lasting impacts for the future of higher education.
- "Big data" refers to the sea of information available about consumers, organizations, and all internet users. Some predict that these data will provide more transparency online and

create better productivity and marketing strategies. Marketers currently struggle to shape this sea into usable customer insights.

- Some people believe that digital currencies and wallets will become the ubiquitous standard, with technologies like Apple Pay becoming increasingly available and consumers' adoption growing, too.
- Relatedly, consumers will use smartphones to pay for everything in physical retail stores: No more cash or credit cards.
- Cloud computing will continue to grow, such that most data will be stored in the "cloud" for accessibility to any internet connected device.
- Forms of artificial intelligence and machine learning will become more prevalent, automating levels of consumer decision making and actions.
- Augmented reality is a combination of computer and real-world data, such as digital information superimposed on reality. The digital information can be graphics, text, sound, or video. For example, a person might be in the stands watching a football game and see a red line across the field to indicate where the ball needs to go for a first down. Augmented reality can also be viewed on a mobile device or computer. Marketers use augmented reality to display what is inside a package or to integrate traditional print and digital advertising. Advances like Apple's ARKit make this more possible for companies to develop for.

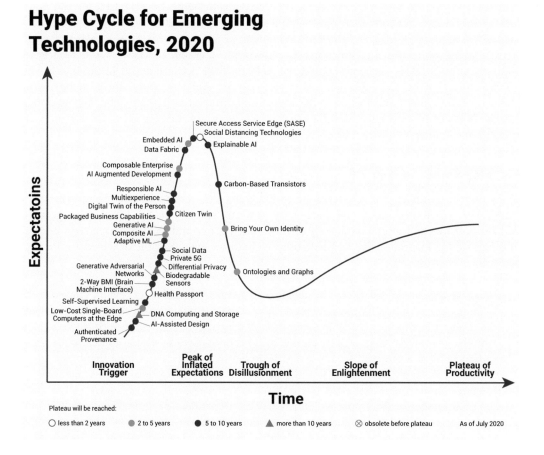

Exhibit 1.10 2017 Hype Cycle for Emerging Technologies

Source: Gartner, Inc. Available at www.gartner.com. Note: Gartner material speaks as of the date of publication and is subject to change without notice

The Gartner Group creates a new "hype cycle" each year. See Exhibit 1.10 for Gartner's 2020 hype cycle, which presents Gartner's view of new technologies and when they will become mainstream (from less than two years to over ten years). The important themes in this hype cycle are artificial intelligence, transparently immersive experiences, and digital platforms. These themes affect marketing strategies as follows:

- *Artificial intelligence everywhere.* Artificial intelligence will give marketers radical computational power and amounts of data, empowering our society to solve problems like never before.
- *Transparently immersive experiences.* Technology will become more adaptable and fluid, and thus more consumer-centric.
- *Digital platforms.* Digital platforms such as Bitcoin could revolutionize entire industries, moving them away from silos and toward interconnected ecosystems.

Read On

This book follows the structure of traditional marketing processes but discusses effective and efficient digital marketing concepts and practices. Technology is an important aspect of the digital marketing environment, and because it is critical for marketers to understand it, we integrate "Let's Get Technical" boxes throughout the text to help marketers understand some of the basics. *eMarketing* is organized into four parts.

Part I: "Digital Marketing in Context" (Chapters 1–3) introduces strategic digital marketing and the digital marketing plan. The discussions include digital business models, performance metrics for measuring digital marketing success, and the steps involved in a digital marketing plan.

Part II: "Digital Marketing Environment" (Chapters 4 and 5) explains the legal and global environments that are critical to the success of any digital marketing effort. We place special emphasis on the next frontier: emerging and important markets such as China.

Part III: "Digital Marketing Strategy" (Chapters 6–8) deals with digital strategy formulation, including the marketing knowledge base and customer behavior data needed for designing what we call tier 1 strategies: segmentation, targeting, differentiation, and positioning.

Part IV: "Digital Marketing Management" (Chapters 9–15) covers tier 2 strategies: the marketing mix and customer relationship management best practices, focusing on social media.

Chapter Summary

Digital business is the continuous optimization of a firm's business activities through digital technology. Digital commerce is the subset of digital business focused on transactions. Digital marketing is the marketing activity, set of institutions, and processes for creating, communicating, delivering, and exchanging offerings that have value for customers, clients, partners, and society at large. It is the application of information technology to traditional marketing practices.

The dynamic digital marketing environment offers opportunities to develop new products, strategies and tactics, new markets, new media, and new channels. Individual buyers have more power today because of technology, input devices, and mobile accessibility allowing the ability to compare products and pricing online, as well as the ability to upload content that affects brand images. Web 2.0 social media communities form online to discuss products, connect, and more, and this activity is out of marketers' control. Today's marketers use inbound marketing to get found online and attempt to engage customers with content; however, it is a challenge to measure the success of these strategies. Internet adoption and retail sales in most industrialized nations have reached maturity levels. The internet deeply affects the citizens of many countries.

The internet consists of computers with data, users who send and receive the data files on a myriad of receiving appliances, and a technology infrastructure to move, create, and view or listen to the content. An intranet is a network that runs internally in a corporation using internet standards. An extranet is an intranet to which proprietary networks are joined for the purpose of sharing information. The Web is the part of the internet that supports a graphical user interface for hypertext navigation with a browser. The internet's properties allow for more effective and efficient marketing strategy and tactical implementation and are changing marketing in Web 2.0 by realizing that customers trust each other more than companies, increasing market and media fragmentations, inbound marketing, and customer engagement, shifting power from sellers to buyers; empowering search engines as reputation engines; social commerce; and improving online and offline strategy integration (especially multichannel marketing). Content is still king online, but connections are critical in this climate of high broadband connectivity and intellectual capital rules. In the Web 2.0 environment companies try to engage customers through content marketing, crowdsourcing, and inbound marketing. Finally, new technologies such as wireless networking, cutting the cord, appliance convergence, and many other exciting inventions open the door to new marketing strategies and tactics.

The internet has evolved from Web 1.0 (content creator makes a Web page and the content consumer views it) to Web 2.0 (all users are both content creators and consumers, and they share with one another) and the future Web 3.0 (individual data presented and shared as desired).

Web 3.0 will be a time of continued receiving-appliance convergence, merging of traditional and social media, increased wireless networking, wearable internet devices, big data, cloud computing, and the semantic Web, and this will change the marketing landscape. It is essential for marketers to realize that television programs, radio shows, news, movies, many books, and photos are simply digital data sent by their creators in electronic form via satellite, telephone wires, or cable and then viewed by the audience on receiving appliances such as televisions, computers, radios, cell phones, smartphones and others. This understanding opens the door for many new product opportunities that provide value to the demanding customers of the future. Web 3.0 will be defined by better technology and Web applications and automatic receipt of individual data to any connected device.

Exercises

Review Questions

1. Define digital business and digital marketing.
2. What are metrics, and why are they important?
3. How does technology change traditional marketing?
4. What are some of the marketing implications of internet technologies?
5. Describe the important internet properties that affect marketing.
6. What fundamental changes has the internet brought to marketing?
7. What is the difference between inbound and outbound marketing?
8. Contrast the key elements of Web 2.0 and Web 3.0.

Discussion Questions

1. **The Piano Guys Story.** Explain how The Piano Guys capitalized on Web 2.0 properties and trends.

2. **The Piano Guys Story.** In the future, when Web 3.0 is a reality, what additional tactics will businesses campaigns use (also refer to Exhibit 1.10 for ideas)?
3. What are the implications of the differences in various country internet adoptions?
4. As a consumer, what difference does it make if digital business is "just business?" Explain your answer.
5. Some economists suggest that the increase in digital commerce within the business-to-business (B2B) market will lead to greater competition and more goods and services becoming commodities, meaning they will compete solely on price. How do you think this competition is likely to affect buyers within the B2B market? How would it affect sellers?
6. How has a power shift from companies to consumers occurred in the marketplace?
7. What concerns about consumer privacy are raised by the increased use of wireless computing and handheld devices outside the home or workplace?
8. As a consumer, how will your life change when the semantic Web becomes a reality?
9. How do social media and consumer-generated content change the way marketers operate? Explain.

Web Activities

1. See if you can find the portion of your university's website that is for students and employees only (intranet). What information is contained on those pages? Should outsiders be excluded from accessing the pages? Why or why not?
2. Visit the McDonald's website. List each stakeholder it reaches and tell what basic content is targeted to each stakeholder.
3. Visit Facebook.com and find a company profile. How many likes does it have? Why would Facebook users want to "like" a company?

Chapter 2

Strategic Digital Marketing and Performance Metrics

The main goal of this chapter is to help you understand strategic planning and the way companies seek to achieve their objectives through strategies and tactics involving digital business and digital marketing. You will become familiar with common digital business models implemented at different organizational levels and with the application of performance metrics to monitor progress toward objective accomplishment.

After reading this chapter, you will be able to:

- Explain the importance of strategic planning, strategy, digital business strategy, and digital marketing strategy.
- Identify the main digital business models at the activity, business process, and enterprise levels.
- Discuss the use of performance metrics and the Balanced Scorecard to measure digital business and digital marketing performance.
- Enumerate key performance metrics for social media communication.

THE AMAZON STORY

After opening its virtual doors in 1995, Amazon.com was one of the first to prove that the online retailing business model can be profitable, reporting its first-ever net profit in the fourth quarter of 2001 ($3.1 billion in net sales). Now a Fortune 500 company, Amazon.com announced $386 billion in 2020 net revenue (an increase from $280.5 billion in 2019)—an impressive growth rate. Amazon's strong customer service strategy (focusing on consumers, companies, digital commerce sellers, and content creators) has paid off big time.

Amazon, a dot-com survivor, is quite adept at leveraging its competencies into many different digital business models. It started as the world's biggest bookstore but soon branched out into the "everything" store. First is its core business—online retailing. Amazon sells merchandise and content purchased from manufacturers and resellers to consumer markets. Sales of paper and electronic books, Kindle manufacturing, music, and DVDs account for the largest proportion of Amazon's sales, but nonmedia sales now comprise the majority of all sales (toys, tools, health and beauty aids, prescription drugs, home furnishing, electronics, apparel, and more). A truly global organization, Amazon now sees 27 percent of its revenue occurring outside of North America.

Second are Amazon's digital commerce partnerships with many retailers. These partnerships bring revenue through differing commitments, but they typically involve Amazon earning fixed fees, sales commissions, or per-unit activity fees by offering third-party merchandise on Amazon.com. Customers can purchase items in dozens of product categories and complete the transaction in one checkout process. Amazon also offers to undertake marketing, customer

DOI: 10.4324/9781003247319-3

service, and product fulfillment services (inventory storage and delivery) on behalf of its part-ners. This partnership business model can be more profitable than the pure retailing model because Amazon earns a fee by leveraging its automated services, digital commerce experience, and huge customer base.

Amazon has evolved from online retailer, to digital commerce partner, and now to developer service provider. It sells many different Web services and space for computing, storing, and retrieving data from anywhere on the Web through Amazon Web Services (AWS), a suite of software-as-a-service tools aimed at business users around the globe. Amazon offers over 200 different Web services in 25 regions worldwide.

Amazon is also a content provider, offering authors and publishing companies an online platform for selling digital content for the Kindle and the Fire platform. Amazon also created the first affiliate program (called Amazon Associates), giving hundreds of thousands of website owners up to 10 percent commission for referring customers who purchase at Amazon. These partners integrate merchandise seamlessly into their websites via Amazon's Associate program. It is like having lots of salespeople all over the world, and in fact, Amazon classifies this com-mission as a marketing expense in its annual reports.

Strategic Planning

Amazon, like every other marketer, uses strategic planning for a profitable and sustainable business future. **Strategic planning** is the "process of developing and maintaining a strategic fit between the organization's goals and capabilities and its changing market opportunities" (Kotler and Armstrong, 2010). Part of this process is to identify the company's goals, such as the following:

- *Growth.* How much can the company reasonably expect to grow in terms of revenues, and how fast? The answer to these questions involves a thorough understanding of the competition, product life cycles, and market factors.
- *Competitive position.* How should the company position itself against other firms in the indus-try? Viable positions are industry leader (Google), price leader (Walmart), quality leader (Mercedes), niche company (eMarketer), strong customer service (Apple), and so forth.
- *Geographic scope.* Where should the company serve its customers on the continuum of local to multinational? Is the company prepared to ship tangible products purchased online to foreign countries?
- *Other objectives.* Companies often set objectives for the number of industries they will enter, the range of products they will offer, the types of channels they will use, ways to reduce costs, and so on.

For example, Facebook switched strategic direction in 2007, choosing to open its network to third-party developers—expanding customer benefits in the process. Other companies, such as Coca-Cola, Starbucks, and most recently Ocean Spray, have shifted to leverage user-generated content via social media taking advantage of consumer engagement strategically. These companies and many others today find value in gathering opinions and feedback from their customers for immediate consideration—like Salesforce's Trailblazer Community (see trailblazer.salesforce.com/ideaSearch).

Environment, Strategy, and Performance

The digital marketing plan is normally a part of an organization's overall marketing plan, flow-ing from its overall goals and strategies. For better understanding, we discuss the digital marketing plan in isolation in this book (Chapter 3). It starts with the business environment, where legal, ethical, technological, competitive, market-related, and other environmental factors external to the company create both opportunities and threats. Organizations perform SWOT (strengths, weaknesses, opportunities, threats) analyses to discover what strengths and weaknesses they have to deploy against threats and opportunities, leading to digital business and digital marketing strategies. Organizations select digital business models, and then marketers formulate strategy and create marketing plans that will help the firm accomplish its overall goals. The final step is to determine the success of the strategies and plans by measuring results. **Performance metrics** are specific measures designed to evaluate the effectiveness and efficiency of the digital business and digital marketing operations.

This chapter and Chapter 3 describe digital business and digital marketing strategies, the digital marketing plan, and performance metrics. Chapters 4 and 5 explore environmental factors particularly important for digital marketing and leading to the SWOT analysis.

Strategy

The term *strategy* has been used to describe everything from "the course we chart, the journey we imagine and, at the same time, the course we steer, and the trip we actually make" (Nickols, 2000, p. 6). Although the term is used in many different contexts to mean many different things, most strategists agree that **strategy** is the means to achieve a goal. It is concerned with how the company will achieve its *objectives*, not what its goals are. Interestingly, strategy has its roots in military action. For example, the country's objective is to win the war, its strategy is to deploy troops to a particular country, and its tactics are to land a particular battalion in a specific location at a specified day and time. This process translates well to business strategy because the company sets its growth and other objectives, then decides which strategies it will use to accomplish them. The tactics are detailed plans to implement the strategies. For example, Salesforce's objective might have been to improve its product mix using a strategy of seeking product ideas from consumers and then creating the IdeaExchange Website as a tactic to achieve the objective.

It is important to note that objectives, strategies, and tactics can exist at many different levels in a company. Thus far, we've been discussing high-level corporate strategic planning. Functional areas within a company also develop goals, strategies, and tactics to support corporate-level objectives. If a company wants to grow by 10 percent in the coming year, the marketing function may set supporting goals to engage customers in social media and increase market share. Similarly, finance, human resources, and other functional areas set goals to help achieve the company's overall objectives.

From Strategy to Electronic Strategy

How does traditional strategy differ from digital business strategy? **Digital business strategy** is the deployment of enterprise resources to capitalize on technologies for reaching specified objectives that ultimately improve performance and create sustainable competitive advantage. Thus, when corporate-level (also called *enterprise-level*) business strategies include information technology components (social media, digital data, databases, etc.), they become digital business strategies. As an example, Tchibo, the German retailer, has two key strategies for reaching its growth goals: first is the corporate-level business strategy of building new retail stores in selected European cities, and second is the digital business strategy of selling products on its website. Using strategic planning, Tchibo elected to use a digital business strategy only after careful analysis of its internal capabilities and the needs of its customers, retail competitors, and other environmental issues.

In a parallel fashion, marketing strategy becomes digital marketing strategy when marketers use digital technology to implement the strategy. **Digital marketing strategy** is the design of marketing strategy that capitalizes on the organization's electronic or information technology capabilities to reach specified objectives. In essence, digital marketing strategy is where technology strategy and marketing strategy wed.

For example, Grupo Posados, with over 150 hotel properties in South America, maintains a sophisticated, large customer database. It can send customized e-mails by customer segments, such as customers who are high value or recent visitors or who booked through a travel agent. By targeting special offers to relevant customers, it has increased hotel bookings and profits. This relevant targeting keeps customers happy and supports Grupo Posados's customer relationship management digital marketing strategy—ultimately supporting the corporate growth strategy.

Most strategic plans explain the rationale for the chosen objectives and strategies. They are especially important for a single digital business project trying to win its share of corporate resources and top-management support. Consider the following types of rationale managers must consider:

- *Financial justification*, such as break-even analyses, cost-benefit analysis, and return on investment (ROI), often lead the argument to gain funds for tactical implementation.
- *Operational justification* is also important: does the company have the staff capability to engage customers in social media?
- *Organizational justification* involves the corporate culture and its fit with the new strategy.
- *Strategic justification* involves the strategy fit with the organization's overall mission, goals, and strategies.
- Finally, *technical justification* is hugely important for digital business. For example, does the company have the technical expertise needed to implement hardware, software, and/or cloud-based solutions to executive strategic plans?

From Business Models to Digital Business Models

One more piece of this puzzle needs to be explained before we get into the really interesting content of digital business and digital marketing strategies. The term *business model* is often mentioned in print and by executives. Based on current use of the term, we suggest that a **business model** is a method by which the organization sustains itself in the long term and includes its value proposition for partners and customers as well as its revenue streams.

A business model does not exist in a vacuum. It relates to strategy in that a company will select one or more business models as strategies to accomplish enterprise goals. For instance, if the firm's goal is to position itself as a high-tech, innovative company, it might decide to use the latest online platforms to connect and communicate with its suppliers and customers, as does technology company Microsoft.

Presented with many opportunities, how does a company select the best business models? The authors of *Internet Business Models and Strategies* suggest the following time-tested components as critical to appraising the fit of a business model for the company and its environment (Afuah and Tucci, 2001):

- *Customer value*. Does the model create value through its product offerings that is differentiated in some way from that of its competitors?
- *Scope*. Which markets does the company serve, and are they growing? Are these markets currently served by the company, or will they be higher-risk new markets?

- *Price*. Are the company's products priced to appeal to markets and achieve company share and profit objectives?
- *Revenue sources*. Where is the money coming from? Is it plentiful enough to sustain growth and profit objectives over time? Many dot-com failures, for example, overlook this element.
- *Connected activities*. What activities will the company need to perform to create the value described in the model? Does the company have these capabilities? For example, if 24/7 customer service is part of the value, the company must be prepared to deliver it.
- *Implementation*. The company must have the ability to actually make it happen, which involves the firm's systems, people, culture, and so on.
- *Capabilities*. Does the company have the resources (financial, core competencies, etc.) to make the selected models work?
- *Sustainability*. The digital business model is particularly appropriate if it can create a competitive advantage over time. Will it be difficult to imitate, and will the environment be attractive for maintaining the model over time?

Digital Business Models

Traditional business models such as retailing, selling advertising, and auctions have been around ever since the first business set up shop. What makes a business model a digital business model is the use of information technology. Thus, a **digital business model** is a method by which the organization sustains itself in the long-term using information technology, which includes its value proposition for partners and customers as well as its **revenue streams**. For example, the internet allows education, music, video and software firms to deliver their products over the internet, thus creating a new distribution model that cuts costs and increases value. Digital business models successfully take advantage of the internet properties described in Chapter 1 (i.e., global reach, time moderator, etc.).

Digital business models can capitalize on digital data collection and distribution techniques without using the internet. For example, when retailers scan products and customer data or reward cards at the checkout, these data can become a rich source of knowledge for inventory management and promotional offers—digital marketing without the internet. Similarly, when these data are available through the company's proprietary computer network (intranet), the firm is applying digital marketing without the public internet. For simplicity, we use the term *digital business models* to include both internet and offline digital models throughout the rest of our discussion.

Value and Revenue

As part of its digital business model, an organization describes the ways in which it creates value for customers and partners. This description is in line with the **marketing concept**, which suggests that the social and economic justification for an organization's existence is the satisfaction of customer wants and needs while meeting organizational objectives. And at no time is this truer than right now. Customers discuss brands on social media, and if companies do not satisfy customer needs, the world will hear about it in a second. This often hinders the company's goal achievement.

Business customers and partners might include supply chain members such as suppliers, wholesalers, and retailers or firms with which the company joins forces to create new brands (such as the Microsoft and NBC alliance to create MSNBC). Organizations deliver stakeholder value through digital business models by using digital products and processes.

Whether online or offline, the value proposition involves knowing what is important to the customer or partner and delivering it better than other organizations. **Value** encompasses the customer's perceptions of the product's benefits, specifically its attributes, brand name, and support services. Subtracted from benefits are the costs involved in acquiring the product, such as monetary, time, and psychic costs. Like customers, partners evaluate value by determining whether the partnership provides more benefits than costs. This concept is shown as follows:

Value = Benefits − Costs

Information technology usually, but not always, increases benefits and lowers costs to stakeholders. Conversely, it can decrease value when websites are complex, information is hard to locate, and technical difficulties interrupt data access or shopping transactions.

As shown in Exhibit 2.1, digital business strategies help organizations to decrease internal costs, often improving the value proposition for customers and partners. Importantly, as businesses seek to improve their value proposition, they must keep in mind what their brand stands for. For example, when Amazon purchased Whole Foods in 2017, the company must have recognized synergies between the two brands' customers and the digital marketing communications strategies used to reach them. Digital business strategy alignment can also increase the enterprise revenue stream, an important part of the digital business model.

Digital Marketing Increases Benefits

- Online mass customization (different products and messages to different stakeholders)
- Personalization (giving stakeholders relevant information)
- 24/7 convenience
- Self-service ordering and tracking
- One-stop shopping
- Learning, engaging, and communication with customers on social networking sites

Digital Marketing Decreases Costs

- Low-cost distribution of communication messages (e.g., e-mail)
- Low-cost distribution channel for digital products
- Lowers costs for transaction processing
- Lowers costs for knowledge acquisition (e.g., research and customer feedback)
- Creates efficiencies in supply chain (through communication and inventory optimization)
- Decreases the cost of customer service

Digital Marketing Increases Revenues

- Online transaction revenues such as product, information, advertising, and subscription fees; or commission/fee on a transaction or referral
- Adds value to products/services and increases prices (e.g., online FAQ and customer support)
- Increases customer base by reaching out to new markets
- Builds customer relationships and thus increases current customer spending (share of wallet)

Exhibit 2.1 Digital Marketing Contributes to the Digital Business Model

Menu of Strategic Digital Business Models

A key element in setting strategic objectives is to take stock of the company's current situation and decide the level of commitment to digital business in general and digital marketing in particular. The possible levels of commitment fall along a continuum that is appropriately represented as a pyramid because fewer businesses occupy the top position (Exhibit 2.2). As a general rule, the higher the company travels up the pyramid, the greater its level of commitment to digital business, the more its strategies are integrated with information technology, and the greater the impact on the organization. Also, the more strategic moves are at the top, while the more tactical activities are at lower levels; as a result, higher levels carry more risk and have higher positive impact than lower levels for most companies.

Bear in mind that one company's activity may be another's enterprise-level strategy. For example, digital commerce may be a small activity for a ski shop with 1 percent of its business from the online channel, but it is an enterprise-level activity for FedEx, the package delivery service.

Each level of the pyramid in Exhibit 2.2 indicates numerous opportunities for the company to provide stakeholder value and generate revenue streams using information technology. Because no single, comprehensive, ideal taxonomy of digital business models is available, we categorize the most commonly used models based on the company's level of commitment. This scheme is not perfect either, because the level of commitment for each model varies by company, as previously mentioned. Also, the activity-level items generally add value by saving costs but may not generate a direct revenue stream—although evidence shows that blogs and Twitter activity can result in sales and build customer loyalty. Nonetheless, we present it as a good menu of strategic opportunities, arranged by level of commitment to digital business, focusing primarily on models that involve digital marketing. We'll briefly describe many models here and expand upon them in later chapters.

Although we are discussing individual digital business models, many companies combine two or more digital business models. For example, Yahoo! is both an online retailer and a content publisher. It also uses many processes and activities listed in Exhibit 2.3, such as e-mail and customer relationship management.

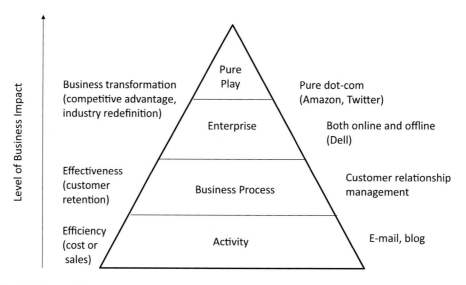

Exhibit 2.2 Level of Commitment to Digital Business

Source: Adapted from www.mohansawhney.com.

Activity Level	Business Process Level	Enterprise Level
1. Order processing	1. Customer relationship management (CRM) and social CRM	1. Digital commerce, social commerce, direct selling, content sponsorship
2. Online purchasing	2. Knowledge management (KM)	2. Portal
3. E-mail	3. Supply chain management (SCM)	3. Social networking
4. Content publishing	4. Community building online	4. Broker models (online exchange, auction)
5. Business intelligence (BI)	5. Database marketing	5. Agent models (manufacturer/ selling agents, shopping agent, reverse auction)
6. Online advertising and public relations (PR)	6. Enterprise resource planning (ERP)	
7. Online sales promotion	7. Mass customization	
8. Dynamic pricing strategies online	8. Crowdsourcing	
9. Social media	9. Freemium	
10. Search marketing		

Exhibit 2.3 Digital Business Model Classification

Activity-Level Digital Business Models

The lowest level of the pyramid affects individual business activities that can save the firm money if automated using information technology or the internet. In this low-risk area, the firm realizes cost reductions through digital business efficiencies (e.g., order processing, **competitive intelligence**, or surveys online). The following is a brief description of activity-level models:

1. *Online purchasing.* Companies can use the Web to place orders with suppliers, thus automating the activity. Normally this activity is not a marketing function, but when retailers such as Wal-Mart created automated order processing throughout the supply chain, it had a huge impact on marketing, made even more challenging by the increased demand and lack of supply of many goods during the COVID-19 pandemic. While this is called digital commerce from the seller's perspective, here we only consider the business customer's online purchase activity.
2. *Order processing.* This model occurs when online retailers automate internet transactions created by customers.
3. *E-mail.* When organizations send e-mail communications to stakeholders, they save printing and mailing costs.
4. *Content publishing.* In this model, companies create valuable content or services on their websites, draw lots of traffic, and sell advertising or generate sales leads. In another type of content publishing, the firm posts information about its offerings on a website, thus saving printing costs. See the "Let's Get Technical" box for car audio in the next section.
5. *Business intelligence (BI).* This activity refers to the low-cost online gathering of secondary and primary information about competitors, markets, customers, and more.

6. *Online advertising and public relations (PR).* As an activity, the company buys advertising on someone else's e-mail or website. When the company sells advertising, it is engaging in content sponsorship, a higher-level process. Online PR includes a company's own website, as well as online press releases and more.

7. *Online sales promotions.* Companies use the internet to send samples of digital products (e.g., music or software) or to run sweepstakes, among other tactics. Group promotions include coupons that provide deep discounts on products if a required number of people purchased it (such as Groupon.com).

8. *Pricing strategies.* With dynamic pricing, a company presents different prices to various groups of customers, even at the individual level. Online negotiation through auctions is one type of dynamic pricing initiated by the buyer instead of the seller. Technology allows this activity to be automated.

9. *Social media communication.* Companies use Facebook pages, Twitter accounts, Instagram Stories, TikTok videos, blogs, and more to engage and build relationships with customers and prospects.

10. *Search marketing.* It is all about getting found online, and the search engines are one key tool for inbound marketing. Organizations optimize websites and incoming links and place content all over social media so they can appear high in a search engine results page for relevant keywords.

Let's Get Technical—CarPlay versus Satellite Radio

You're buying a new car. It comes with Apple CarPlay, Android Auto, and satellite radio. The satellite radio is free for the first 6 months. Do you renew after that or just move to CarPlay?

Since 1929, cars have had a broadcast radio installed. These began with AM, then FM, and now satellite radio. AM receives signals over a longer range but has less fidelity. FM receives signals over a shorter range but has higher fidelity. Satellite radio has virtually unlimited range together with even higher digital fidelity. In addition, the satellite signal allows for many more channels than either AM or FM.

Since 1965 cars have also had an on-demand playback device installed. The first of these was 8-track tapes, followed by cassettes, then CDs, and finally MP3 players. More recently, cars have conceded that customers already have their music player built into their phones and so they only need to provide an interface to connect the phone to the car's speakers.

CarPlay and Android Auto are both technologies that allow you to connect your phone either wired or wirelessly to the car's stereo. When connected, a driver-safe version of the phone's display appears on the car's dashboard. The functions available include music, navigation, voice calls, and messages from the phone.

In this piece we will focus on the music. Most phone carriers offer virtually unlimited data. This means that you can stream music to your phone from a cloud service like Apple Music or Spotify wherever you have a cell signal. With the advent of LTE networks and, most recently, 5G technology, that cell signal has become very fast. High speed means more bits per second to carry a high-quality music signal.

So is there still a reason to pay for satellite radio? It depends. As of today, satellite radio still has more complete coverage, especially in rural areas. You turn the radio on, it works. That's no small advantage when a safety priority is to keep a driver's focus on the road.

Over 80 percent of cars sold in the United States support Apple CarPlay, and 23 percent of consumers consider it a "must have" feature. There are still some challenges in using CarPlay, but that might not matter. Recall our three themes from earlier:

1. Superior content beats out a superior delivery platform.
2. Over time, the inferior delivery platform will catch up in quality.
3. Younger users drive these trends in two ways:
   a. Younger users tend to be more price sensitive.
   b. Younger users value constant connectivity.

Let's start with content. Even with hundreds of channels, satellite radio still cannot compete with the virtually limitless music content on a phone. The phone may have the music stored locally or may be streaming it over the cell network from a cloud service like Apple Music or Spotify.

There are two aspects to music quality. The first is the quality of the user interface—how easy is it to find and play the music that you want while driving. The second is the quality of the music itself. The fidelity of music played on a smartphone is already outstanding. So the only real issue is the user interface. And unfortunately, this is a case of too many cooks in the kitchen.

Most cars include their own wireless technology to interface with your phone. And here is where the problems begin. If your phone is simultaneously connected to CarPlay and the car manufacturer's system, then one of them has to win in a conflict. Typically, it will be the car manufacturer's system, which may not be what the user wants.

In addition, the systems sometimes operate in unpredictable ways. For example, you may be on the phone when your friend, who has borrowed your car, drives up. The car senses the phone and immediately transfers the call away from you and inside the car.

There is no doubt that all these interface issues will be resolved in the near future. At that point the intelligent and on demand features of the phone will tip the scales away from satellite radio.

Because smartphones *are* computers with intelligent assistants, they enable voice commands. For example, "Hey Siri, play music by Colbie Caillat." Note that this request makes use of intelligence to interpret the request and on-demand delivery to find and play the content. Because satellite radio is a broadcast rather than an on-demand medium, it cannot offer the same functionality.

Young, price-sensitive users will not want to pay an additional monthly fee for satellite radio. Furthermore, they want to stay connected even while driving. The iPhone now uses GPS to sense when you are driving and shuts down texting to improve driver safety and comply with laws. That means that the only way to text and drive safely is by using the voice commands of CarPlay. And if CarPlay is already connected, then those users would naturally be inclined to use it for music as well. Finally, for those who are already iPhone users, the seamlessness of the Apple ecosystem across multiple apps and devices is likely to be a big draw.

Still skeptical? On the most recent economy car bought by one of the authors, the ubiquitous CD player had been relegated to the glove compartment. This is hardly a convenient location for what used to be the marquee technology. Meanwhile, the CarPlay interface was prominently featured in the center console and touted as a major selling point by the dealer. Yes, the car also has satellite radio and a free 6-month trial. But after that . . .

Business Process—Level Digital Business Models

The next level of the pyramid changes business processes to increase the company's effectiveness.

Customer relationship management (CRM) involves retaining and growing business and individual customers through strategies that ensure their satisfaction with the company and its products. CRM seeks to keep customers for the long term and to increase the number and frequency of their transactions with the company. In the context of digital business, CRM uses digital processes and integrates customer information collected at every customer "touch point." Customers interact with organizations in person at retail stores, via phone, or over the internet, including chatbots powered by artificial intelligence. The results of interactions at all these touch points are integrated to build a complete picture of customer characteristics, behavior, and preferences—all stored in electronic databases. Social CRM (SCRM) adds a new dimension when companies interact with customers as they chat about products in social media.

Knowledge management (KM) is a combination of a company's database contents, the technology used to create the system, and the transformation of data into useful information and knowledge. KM systems create a storehouse of reports, customer account information, product sales, and other valuable information managers can use to make decisions.

Supply chain management (SCM) involves coordination of the suppliers and distribution channel to deliver products more effectively and efficiently to customers. For example, when a customer orders from certain websites, FedEx's computers receive the instruction to pick up product from a warehouse and deliver it quickly to the customer. Similarly, when consumers buy a product at the grocery store, the barcode scanner at the checkout tells the store's computer to reduce the inventory count by one and then automatically orders more cases of the product from warehouses or suppliers if inventory in the back room is low.

With **community building**, companies use social media to engage with groups of special interest users. In this model, firms invite users to interact and post comments on their platforms with the purpose of building buzz online and attracting potential customers. Firms often communicate and contribute content among community and social networking sites that their customers frequent. Through community building, marketers can create social bonds that enhance customer relationships while building their images as experts in specific knowledge areas.

Database marketing involves collecting, analyzing, and disseminating electronic information about customers, prospects, and products to increase profits. It is one of the oldest and most important strategies for digital marketers. Database marketing systems can be a part of the company's overall knowledge management system.

Enterprise resource planning (ERP) refers to a back-office system for order entry, purchasing, invoicing, and inventory control. ERP systems allow organizations to optimize business processes while lowering costs. Many ERP systems predate the Web. ERP is not a marketing function, but it is so important that it must be included in this list.

Mass customization refers to the internet's unique ability to customize marketing mixes electronically and automatically to the individual level. Companies use this practice when they collect information from customers and prospects and use it to customize products and communication on an individual basis for a large number of people.

Crowdsourcing is the practice of outsourcing ads, product development, and other tasks to a people outside the organization. Starbucks did this when setting up its ideas.starbucks.com page so the public could make product suggestions on its website.

Freemium is a combination of "free" and "premium," where companies offer a basic product for free and then provide upgraded versions for a fee. For example, customers can use some basic software for free but need to upgrade and pay for more functionality. This can be contrasted to a sales promotion sampling technique or a pricing strategy.

Location-based marketing delivers local and relevant content to a user's mobile device using GPS technology. The content can include promotional offers designed to motivate the user to visit a retail store, restaurant, bar, or other business.

Enterprise-Level Digital Business Models

At the enterprise level of the pyramid, the company automates many business processes in a unified system—demonstrating a significant commitment to digital business. Firms relying heavily on these models (such as Dell, Google, and Facebook) believe that their future will depend on digital business activities.

Digital commerce refers to online transactions: selling goods and services on the internet, either in one transaction or over time with an ongoing subscription price (e.g., *Wall Street Journal Online*). Following traditional marketing terminology, online retailers are firms that buy products and resell them online. However, any company that sells online, whether it produces its own products or purchases products for resale, is commonly known as an online retailer. One type of online retailer sells physical products and uses traditional transportation methods to deliver them. The other type sells digital products such as information, software, and music and delivers them via the internet (and usually ground transportation, too). Many online retailers maintain brick-and-mortar stores as well. **Virtual worlds** often create revenue through subscriptions—these are sites where users can take the form of avatars and socialize in an online space of their own making, with the most popular associated with gaming. However, others such as Second Life focus on interpersonal interaction and relationships to form communities, exchange ideas, share experiences, and even sell goods and services.

Social commerce is one type of digital commerce that uses social media and consumer interactions to facilitate online sales. Tactics include "buy now" widgets on social media pages and software agents that put buyers and sellers together on social sites, such as online travel site Tripadvisor.com.

Direct distribution refers to a type of digital commerce in which manufacturers sell directly to consumers, eliminating intermediaries such as retailers (the Dell model—although Dell also sells in brick-and-mortar retailers). **Content sponsorship** online is a form of digital commerce in which companies sell advertising on their owned content Web pages, YouTube videos, or other online media. It is called content sponsorship because this model sprang from the media, which depends on advertising sales to pay for editorial content. Today, many sites use consumer-generated content to build their sites, for example, Yahoo!'s Flickr—the digital photo hosting site.

A **portal** is a point of entry to the internet that combines diverse content from many sources, such as the MSN and Yahoo! websites. They are portals because they provide many services in addition to search capabilities. They are destinations for news, games, maps, shopping, mail, and so forth, in addition to being jump-off points for content provided by others. AOL uses its portal to communicate with members, help them find other websites, offer entertaining content, and conduct digital commerce—driving tens of billions of dollars in sales per year to partner merchants. Some portals focus on vertical industries, such as government portals, Edmunds.com for automobiles, and TheKnot.com for couples planning a wedding. Although portals have lost much traffic with the rise of social media platforms, they still net massive amounts of traffic, especially since most Web browsers direct users to a default portal.

Social networking sites are those that bring users together to share interests and personal or professional profiles. They use the community-building model previously described, but social network site owners are creating and hosting communities with the purpose of connecting like-minded individuals for friendship or business—such as LinkedIn for professionals and Facebook for businesses, nonprofits, or simply friends and family. Social networking site owners monetize the model by selling advertising, charging recruiters for searching profiles, and by partnering with third-party developers for adding valuable applications to benefit users.

Online brokers are intermediaries who assist in the purchase negotiations without actually representing either buyers or sellers. The revenue stream in these models is commission- or fee-based. Examples of companies using the brokerage model are E★TRADE (**online exchange**), Guru.com (exchange for freelancers looking to connect with project managers), and eBay (**online auction**). Brokers usually create a market space for exchanges to occur, taking a piece of the action. A **business-to-business (B2B) exchange** is a special place because it allows buyers and sellers in a specific industry to quickly get connected. Online auctions occur in both B2B and **business-to-consumer (B2C)** markets, with the online broker providing the website and technology in exchange for a commission on all sales.

Unlike brokers, **online agents** tend to represent either the buyer or the seller and earn a commission for their work. **Selling agents** help a seller move product (such as real estate agents). Many selling agents work in the B2B market. In the B2C market, affiliate programs, discussed earlier, are also examples of the selling agent model.

Manufacturer's agents represent more than one seller. In traditional marketing, they often represent manufacturing companies that sell complementary products to avoid conflicts of interest. However, in the virtual world, they generally create websites to help an entire industry sell products. For example, Expedia.com, the online travel agent, is a manufacturer's agent in the travel industry (as well as a social network and recommendation site).

Purchasing agents represent buyers. In traditional marketing, they often forge long-term relationships with one or more firms; on the internet, however, they represent any number of buyers, often anonymously. For example, **shopping agents** help individual consumers find specific products and the best prices online (e.g., www.bizrate.com with its tagline, "Search, Compare, Conquer"). Another model, the **reverse auction**, allows individual buyers to enter the price they will pay for particular items at the purchasing agent's website, and sellers can choose to agree or not (e.g., Priceline.com). Purchasing agents often help buyers form cooperatives online for the purpose of buying in larger quantities to reduce prices (such as Groupon.com).

Pure Play

The final level of the pyramid is comprised of internet pure plays. **Pure plays** are businesses that began on the internet, even if they subsequently added a brick-and-mortar presence. We did not include pure plays in Exhibit 2.3 because they start right at the top of the pyramid with a very distinct business model rather than progressing upward, as do traditional brick-and-mortar companies. For example, E★TRADE is a pure play, beginning with only online trading.

Pure plays face significant challenges: they must compete as new brands and take customers away from established brick-and-mortar or online businesses. The successful ones have been able to do so by industry redefinition (i.e., changing the rules of the game) (Modahl, 2000). One way to change the rules is to invent a new digital business model, as Yahoo!, Google, Twitter, Flickr, and eBay did. Opendoor.com is attempting to shake up the process of buying and selling homes with an online-only model. The key to pure play success is offering greater customer value. For example, Buy.com increases customer value by using a content sponsorship model combined with direct sales. The ad inventory sold on the site helps to subsidize prices for the consumer.

Performance Metrics Inform Strategy

The only way to know whether a company has reached its objectives is to measure its results. **Performance metrics,** also called key performance indicators (KPI), are specific measures designed to evaluate the effectiveness and efficiency of an organization's operations, both online and offline. For example, if the company strategy calls for 30 percent of its sales to come from the online channel, it needs to continually measure revenue from various channels to determine whether it is achieving the goal. Note that this means monitoring sales from brick and mortar stores, too, and integrating online/offline metrics for the entire business success. The managers also monitor all the tactics used to drive sales to the online channel to see which ones are working well. Armed with this information, the company can make tactical corrections to make sure it accomplishes the goal.

For instance, meal-kit delivery company HelloFresh is excellent at converting website visitors to buyers and constantly watches this metric, making tactical refinements to improve performance. The company also integrates its online data with offline data to target potential customers in pursuit of a full picture of strategy and tactic effectiveness. Such tactics lead to great success for HelloFresh, whose revenue doubled from 2019 to 2020 during the global lockdowns resulting from the COVID-19 pandemic.

Because strategy is the means to the end (the way of accomplishing objectives), performance metrics should be defined along with the strategy formulation so that the entire organization will know what results constitute successful performance. Albert Einstein famously noted: "Not everything that can be counted counts, and not everything that counts can be counted." Marketers are drowning in metrics, and many go for the easy metrics, such as number of clicks. It is critical for them to be effective and efficient in metric selection and measurement so that the results of their efforts will help improve marketing communications toward meeting the company goals.

When a company designates the performance metrics it will use to measure strategy effectiveness, it does four important things:

1. It translates its vision, strategy, or digital business model into components with measurable outcomes. Some digital marketing goals needing metrics include attracting visitors to the website for selling more advertising or converting them to sales and building visitor loyalty to the site.
2. The performance metrics must be easy to understand and use. They should be accessible to employees using them for decision making. It is difficult to choose from among all the available data, so organizations often settle on KPI to monitor progress toward important goals.
3. Metrics must be actionable. Companies use benchmarking and last year's metrics to decide where they are, after which they can set metric goals for the future (such as increase the amount of time visitors spend on the site from 5 minutes to 10 minutes per session).
4. Finally, when employee evaluations are tied to the metrics, people will be motivated to make decisions that lead to the desired outcomes. Even though the metrics are usually set by top management, successful companies collect employee input throughout the process so that the measurements are relevant and the organization gains consensus on their importance—thus, the adage, "What you measure is what you get."

Web analytics is the digital marketing term for the study of user behavior on Web pages. Companies collect data as users click through pages and take actions, such as registration or purchase. Companies use these data to optimize their online investments. These metrics help firms manage Web content, improve user targeting and personalization, and increase user engagement (and much more). Commonly collected metrics include which tactics generated the site traffic (e.g., click-throughs from online advertising or search engine optimization), which pages are viewed most often, how many comments were posted on a blog, how many fans there are on a company Facebook page, and how many interactions there are with pieces of content. Of course, a key metric involves conversions to sales or other desired behaviors, such as signing up for an e-mail newsletter. Finally, organizations want to know which of their new tactics are working well—things such as a new one-day shipping price or special promotion on the site to increase sales. These data for Web analytics are collected in several ways:

- **Website server logs** record the user's IP (internet protocol) address, which browser the visitor is using, his or her location before arriving at the company site, the time of the day, and every user click through the site. The IP address helps companies understand where users live (e.g., .jp for Japan).
- **Cookie files** are small data files written to a user's hard drive when visiting a site. They are necessary for using shopping carts and other site operations. The cookie file data are retrieved and used to understand how many visitors are returning. Amazon.com uses cookie file data to display the user name on its home page instantaneously.
- **Page tags** are one pixel on a page that is invisible to users (a pixel is one dot of light on a computer screen). Page tags activate a special script when users are on the page, providing information such as when items are removed from a shopping cart. Tags can also be activated based on cookie files on the visitor's hard drive from a previous visit—creating data about the return visit and what the user did.
- **Geolocation** uses many different technologies to locate an internet-enabled device (and its owner) at its physical world address: for example, WiFi, GPS (global positioning satellite coordinates), or simply IP addresses. Marketers can use this for market segmentation when they observe consumer behavior from various countries or other more precise locations.

Web analytics software helps companies analyze all these data on server logs to uncover usage patterns. They can do this through free services like Google Analytics or through purchased software, with thousands of different performance metrics evaluated within a sea of data.

In this chapter you'll learn the basics and see examples, and throughout this book you'll find many more very specific metrics for each type of tactic. Next time you purchase something online, think about how you found the site and navigated through it to the product you bought. Know that the company is tracking your every move and click in order to both optimize its tactics and be more relevant to your needs.

The Balanced Scorecard

Several well-known performance metrics systems include these data in dashboards individualized to an organization's needs. The Balanced Scorecard is a good framework for understanding digital marketing metrics; thus, we present it as an organization scheme for many important performance metrics.

For years, organizations valued financial performance or market share as the most important success measure. The large companies fostered competition among their brand groups or retail outlets and measured success by the bottom line (profits). Many still do so. During the mid- to late-1990s, the dot-com firms ignored financial measures and focused on growth, much to their dismay. These approaches are narrowly focused and place more weight on short-term results rather than on addressing the company's long-term sustainability through customer retention strategies and more.

These weaknesses paved the way for enterprise performance management systems which measure many aspects of a company's achievements. The **Balanced Scorecard**, developed by two Harvard Business School professors in 1990, is one such system with a huge adoption rate (over 7,500 professionals worldwide, according to estimates as reported at www.balancedscorecard.org). The scorecard approach links strategy to measurement by asking companies to consider their vision, critical success factors for accomplishing it, and subsequent performance metrics in four areas: customer, internal, learning and growth, and financial. In the following sections, we describe the typical goals and digital business metrics in each perspective. We start with the basic definitions and then adapt the system for digital marketers. However, it is important to remember that each company defines the specific measures for each box—the system is very flexible.

Four Perspectives

The customer perspective uses measures of the value delivered to customers. These metrics tend to fall into four general areas: time, quality, performance and service, and cost. They also include measures such as time from order to delivery, customer satisfaction levels with product performance, amount of sales from new products, and industry-specific metrics such as equipment uptime percentage or number of service calls.

The internal perspective evaluates a company's success at meeting customer expectations through its internal processes. The items with greatest impact in this area include cycle time (how long it takes to make the product), manufacturing quality, and employee skills and productivity. Information systems are a critical component of the internal perspective for digital business companies.

The learning and growth perspective is one of the Balanced Scorecard's unique contributions. Here, companies place value on continuous improvement to existing products and services as well as on innovation in new products. These activities take employees away from their daily work of selling products, asking them to pay attention to factors critical to the company's long-term sustainability, which is especially important for digital business organizations. Measures in this area include a number of new products and the percentage of sales attributable to each, penetration of new markets, and the improvement of processes such as CRM or SCM initiatives.

If the projected outcomes result from the previous perspectives and performance metrics, the financial perspective will be on target, too. Financial measures include income and expense metrics as well as return on investment, sales, and market share growth. Companies must be careful to relate measurements from the first three perspectives to the financial area whenever possible.

Each company will select metrics for the four perspectives based on its objectives, business model, strategies, industry, and so forth. The point is to understand what the company wants to accomplish and devise performance metrics to monitor the progress and see that the goals are reached.

A US regional airline developed a Balanced Scorecard to build and sustain its unique position as a high-frequency, short-haul carrier (see www.balancedscorecard.org for examples). Consider the performance metrics goals it associated with each goal:

- *Customer perspective*. On-time flights, more customers, and lower prices. Metrics included being the first in the industry according to FAA on-time arrival ratings, customer satisfaction rankings of 98 percent, and a healthy percent change in number of customers.
- *Internal perspective*. Improve turnaround time as measured by on-ground time of less than 25 minutes and 93 percent accurate departure time.
- *Learning and growth perspective*. Align ground crews better with company goals, measured by percentage of ground crew trained and percentage of ground crew who are stockholders. The airline wanted 70 percent of one-year employees, 90 percent of four-year employees, and all of six-year employees to own the company's stock.
- *Financial perspective*. Profitability increase of 25 percent per year, lower costs, and increased revenue (based on market value, seat revenue, and plane lease cost).

Applying the Balanced Scorecard to Digital Business and Digital Marketing

We'll say it again: digital marketers are swimming in data. They have huge databases full of customer information, website logs that automatically record every click of every page visitor and how long the user stays, customer service records, sales data from many different channels, number of comments from a blog post, and so forth. One service company manager reported: "Since I've got all these things to measure, I'm paralyzed by all the opportunities." In spite of these difficulties, measurement is vital to success.

Metrics for the Customer Perspective

The most important of these metrics measure customer loyalty/retention and lifetime value. However, many other metrics can help a company optimize customer value, for example, customer perceptions of product value, appropriateness of selected targets, and customer browsing and buying patterns. The company must also measure value created for partners and other supply chain members because many can easily partner elsewhere if they are not satisfied. Customer engagement online is an important metric involving the number of comments, photos, videos, or other user-generated content posted to a site, among other things. As an example, Exhibit 2.4 displays several possible measures for some customer goals of a company employing digital business models.

Metrics for the Internal Perspective

The internal perspective is critical to a successful digital business. Many goals in this perspective affect human resources, information technology, and other areas that directly and indirectly affect marketing. Of particular note is that the entire supply chain is considered *internal* in this analysis. Obviously, the manufacturing company cannot control the employees of its online retailers. At the same time, neither business customers nor consumers differentiate among organizations in a supply chain—they just want quality products on demand. Thus, recent work on the Balanced Scorecard includes measures for the entire supply chain. See Exhibit 2.5 for example goals and measures in the internal perspective.

Metrics for the Learning and Growth Perspective

The learning and growth perspective typically falls under the human resources umbrella. Two exceptions include product innovation and continuous improvement of marketing processes,

Customer Perspective

Example Goals	*Possible Measures*
Build awareness of new website service	Survey target awareness of service Number of visitors to the site
Engage customers on a site	Number of comments on the site
Increase number of software downloads or subscriptions	Form completions or Web analytics goals
High customer satisfaction on the website	Survey of target at website Number of visits and activity at site
Increase the amount or frequency of online sales from current customers	Mine database for change in frequency of purchases over time
Build customer relationships	Number or purchases per customer Customer retention percentages
Appropriate target markets	Data mining to find purchase patterns by targeting criteria
Buy-to-delivery time faster than competition	Number of days from order to delivery Competition delivery
Increased visits from sweepstakes offers	Number who enter
Build communities on the site	Number of registrations Amount of content uploaded
Value for Business Partners	
Increase number of affiliates in program	Number of affiliates over time
Cross-sell to partner sites	Number of visitors to partner site from our site

Exhibit 2.4 Customer Perspective Scorecard for Digital Business Company

both of which are important for digital business firms due to rapid changes in technology. Exhibit 2.6 includes a few sample goals and measures affecting digital marketers.

Metrics for the Financial Perspective

Marketing strategies clearly drive revenues both online and offline. They can affect profits as well, but other operational factors enter the equation when figuring company expenses. Nevertheless, marketers who manage brands have responsibility for their profits. When marketers propose new products or online services, they must forecast the potential sales over time, estimate the expenses to deliver that level of sales, and project the amount of time needed to break even (create enough revenues to cover expenses and start-up investments). In most cases, the product or internal project with the fastest break-even period or best potential for meeting the company's return on investment hurdle will get funded.

Two of the most frequently used metrics are profits and return on investment (or return on marketing investment). This section will outline basic ideas without considering taxes and other details. Net profits are revenues minus expenses. Revenues are the actual amount of dollars customers give the company in exchange for products. Expenses include many things, most commonly the variable costs for producing the product, the selling costs (advertising, free product giveaways, and other customer acquisition costs [CAC]), delivery, customer support, and other administrative costs.

Internal Perspective

Example Goals	*Possible Measures*
Improve the quality of online service	Target market survey Number of customers who use the service Number of complaints on social media
Quality of online technical help	Amount of time to answer customer e-mail Number of contacts to solve a problem Number of problems covered by website FAQ Customer follow-up survey
High product quality for online service	Product test statistics on specific performance measures
Web server size adequate and operational 24/7	Number of actual simultaneous page requests/maximum possible Percentage of uptime for the server Number of mirrored or backup sites
Optimized number of customer service reps responding to online help	Number of inquiries to customer service rep ratio Number of chat sessions with site visitors
Superior website content management	Number of updates per day Website log traffic pattern statistics
Optimized inventory levels	Average number of items in warehouse Inventory turnover Supplier speed to deliver product
Supply Chain Value to Company	
High supplier satisfaction	Supplier profits from our firm's orders
Partner value	Number of visitors from our partner site to ours and number who purchase Partner contribution to product design

Exhibit 2.5 Internal Perspective Scorecard for Digital Business Company

Learning and Growth Perspective

Example Goals	*Possible Measures*
Online service innovation	Number of new services and products to market in year Number of new service features not offered by competitive offerings Percent of sales from new services
Continuous improvement in CRM system	Number of customer complaints and fixes Number/type of improvements over time
High internet lead-to-sales conversion	Number of customer complaints and fixes Number/type of improvements over time
Increased value in knowledge management system	Revenue per sales employee from internet leads Number of conversions from online leads Number of accesses by employees Number of knowledge contributions by employees
Successful penetration of new markets	Percentage of firm's sales in each new market

Exhibit 2.6 Learning and Growth Scorecard for Digital Business Company

---

Financial Perspective

Example Goals	Possible Measures
Increase market share for online products	Market share percentage (firm's sales as percentage of industry sales)
Double-digit sales growth	Dollar volume sales from one time period to next
Target 10% ROI within one year for each product	ROI
Lower customer acquisition costs (CAC) in online channel	CAC (costs for advertising/number of customers)
Increase conversion rates at website	Number of orders/number of visitors to site
Increase individual customer profit	Average order value Profit contribution over time less CAC
Achieve at least a 10% net profit in first year of new product	New profit as a percentage of sales

Exhibit 2.7 Financial Perspective Scorecard for Digital Business Company

Return on investment (ROI) is calculated by dividing net profit by total assets (fixed plus current). Marketers often evaluate ROI for specific digital business projects by dividing the project's profits by its investment dollars, such as the research, development, and the testing funds needed to introduce the new service. As an example, a company might invest $100,000 in software to analyze Web traffic patterns, use the results, change the website for better usability, and realize an additional $75,000 in digital commerce revenues: a 75 percent ROI. In addition to sales and profits, marketing ROI, along with customer acquisition, customer retention, and brand value are important financial and marketing performance metrics by marketing executives in 2017 (The CMO Survey, 2017).

The financial perspective scorecard relies heavily on sales, profit, and return figures. Exhibit 2.7 presents some common financial perspective performance metrics used by digital marketers.

Social Media Performance Metrics

Social media metrics are different from most standard website metrics because users interact with brands' social media accounts in many different ways. For example, when an internet user views an online video, he or she might spend four minutes viewing it, but another might stop it immediately. And if the user uploads, comments on, or shares a brand's video, how can this interaction be counted? For example, Starbucks wanted to engage customers and learn ways to better meet their needs at physical stores through its Ideas microsite. Starbucks can count the number of suggestions, measure the sentiment (as positive/negative), and identify the number of product changes to see if its engagement and learning goals were achieved. This is quite different from the metrics Starbucks might use on its main website (such as impressions and conversions to purchase). We will discuss social media strategy, tactics, and specific measurement items more thoroughly in Chapters 12, 13 and 14; however, this section presents a general framework and some popular metrics for measuring the success of communication efforts through social media.

As with all performance measurement, it is important to select metrics that can easily be measured on a continuous basis and apply them directly to the organization's social media objectives. Exhibit 2.8 displays five general measurement areas, from awareness through

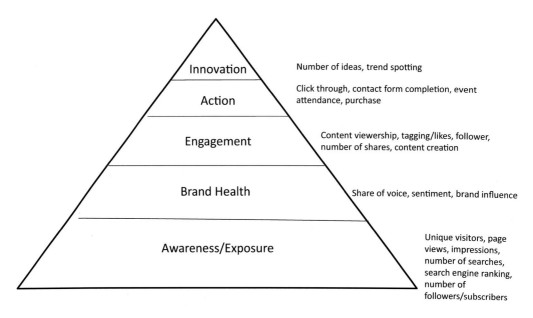

Exhibit 2.8 Social Media Measurement Areas

innovation, along with sample metrics used in each area. The pyramid shape represents the fact that the number of people decreases at higher levels: for example, (1) the most people will become aware of a viral video, (2) fewer will like or dislike and post positive or negative comments about it (brand health), (3) fewer still engage more deeply with the brand by sharing or using social bookmarking to tag the video (engagement), then (4) even fewer visit the video sponsor's site to read about the products and purchase one (action), and (5) the smallest number are loyal customers who post collaborative type comments that the company can use to improve the product (innovation).

We next describe some exemplary metrics at each pyramid level. Note that companies also use many of these metrics to monitor their competition.

Awareness/Exposure Metrics

The most accurate way to measure an increase in brand awareness is to conduct survey research using a representative sample from the company's target market. However, this is very expensive and difficult to accomplish due to declining response rates on surveys, so organizations use many other proxy metrics to gain some measure of progress toward this goal. These metrics assume that if users land on an organization's Facebook page or other social media content, they will become aware of the product features discussed in an ad or on the pages:

• *Unique visitors* measure the number of visitors—without repetition—who access a site, application, video, or other social media content within a specific period of time. Unique visitors is measured by user registration, cookie files, or by a third-party measurement service such as Nielsen or comScore. Search engines also visit these sites, so companies must filter out visits from automated "bots." Video views on YouTube are visible for all to see under the video itself.

- *Page views* refer to single pages that are viewed on a social media site. One unique visitor can view many different blog entries on one blog site. Obviously, the more pages users view, the longer they are on the site and the more opportunity they have to learn about the brand.
- *Impressions* refer to the number of times an ad loads on a user's screen. Marketers use this popular metric for all Web properties.
- *Number of searches* measures the number of times users search for the brand, company, or associated keywords selected by the organization while typing the keywords in on a search engine.
- *Search engine ranking* evaluates where the organization's social media content appears in the search engine results pages for desired keywords. For instance, if a user types in the name of the company, brands, or executives, ideally the links will appear in the first ten results/ on the first page of results.
- *Number of followers, registrations, or subscribers* to the blog, social network page, video channel, or other content. These are also used to measure earned media engagement.

Brand Health Metrics

In this category, companies want to measure the influence their brand and communications have on consumers. Brand health refers to the amount of conversation and what proportion of the sentiment is positive or negative—and more. Measures in this area include the following:

- *Share of voice (SOV)* is the proportion of online conversations about one brand versus its competitors. In the offline world, SOV measures the weight of advertising space in traditional media, but in social media, it usually is only measured by conversation. For example, Brandwatch found the SOV for different luxury fashion brands for a two-month period by analyzing over 630,000 tweets: Calvin Klein (20.4%), Chanel (16.3%), Burberry (11%), Dior (11%), Versace (10%), and other brands making up the remainder (Smith, 2015).
- *Sentiment* refers to the proportion of online conversation about a brand that is positive, negative, or neutral. Sentiment is generally measured using natural language processing (NLP) powered by artificial intelligence to uncover whether words and combinations of words mean something that is positive or negative.
- *Brand influence* can include a number of other metrics such as number of inbound links to a social media property, number of tweets that are retweeted on Twitter, number of comments on posts, and number of times content is shared or linked (Jones, 2011).

Engagement Metrics

There are many ways to engage social media users, as discussed in later chapters. Engagement metrics are endless, and the ones companies select depend on the specific content, promotion, or other communication tactics. The following are some of the most common measures relating to the depth of engagement:

- *Content viewership* refers to the number who consume content, such as by reading a blog (page views), watching videos or listening to podcasts, and downloading white papers.
- *Tagging, bookmarking,* "likes," or **"favorites"** of content demonstrate interest in and favorability toward the content.

- *Membership/follower* metrics count the number of RSS subscribers, members in a community, such as a LinkedIn or Facebook group, or number of followers on Twitter.
- *Number of shares* measures how many times viral content is shared with others.
- *Content creation* counts the number who upload ads for a contest, such as the Frito Lay Super Bowl promotion, entries for which were primarily collected via social media. Companies can also measure the number who rate or review products and write comments on blogs or videos, or also the retweeting and other content-related items measured in previous categories.

Action Metrics

Although engagement metrics demonstrate actions taken by users, this category steps it up to a higher level of action (closer to purchase):

- *Click through* to an advertiser's site. This is measured by the proportion of all people who are exposed to a communication message and those who click to visit the site.
- *Contact form completion* or *registration*, allowing the company to add the person to their database of names, e-mail addresses, and more.
- *Event attendance* online or offline, based on a social media promotion for a Webinar or other event.
- *Purchase* is the ultimate goal for company marketers. Companies measure conversion rates (proportion of all site visitors who purchase), number of purchases, average order value, and many other metrics that evaluate communication effectiveness toward this goal. Note that many other factors lead to purchase, such as product quality, price, and availability; however, social media communication (especially discount promotions) can play an important role in motivating purchase.

Innovation Metrics

In this category, companies want to know if their social media communications are driving customers to comment and review in ways that help the company improve its products and services. Many of these metrics are also included in other categories, but we single innovation out because it is a very high level of brand engagement and builds customer loyalty. A few measures include:

- *Number of ideas* shared in a company's social media site (such as IdeaExchange from Salesforce).
- *Trend spotting* helps companies know what is hot in their target markets. Google Trends displays "hot" search keywords and allows users to search trends. Trendsmap displays real time Twitter trends worldwide, and many blogs and other sites provide word cloud displays of the most popular words in posts.

Measurement Tools

Many companies offer excellent tools for measuring the metrics previously referenced, allowing marketers to build sophisticated analytic dashboards that continuously monitor and report on key performance measures. These tools help companies monitor progress toward objectives and tactical effectiveness while identifying negative conversations about their products as they occur, which is just as important.

Perhaps the simplest free tool is Google Alerts. Anyone can use this tool by entering a topic for monitoring along with sources (video, blogs, news or discussions), and Google will send e-mails based on the selected criteria at the requested frequency (as it happens, daily, weekly). Companies monitor their names, brand names, executive names, and taglines or slogans in advertising campaigns. Google also provides free website or blog analytics to measure the awareness metrics, such as page views and action level click-throughs (Google Analytics). In addition, many social media platforms (i.e., Facebook, Twitter, etc.) also provide free access to measures for monitoring user activities and engagement. Beyond that are complex dashboards, such as those provided for a fee by Alterian, Meltwater, Salesforce, Keyhole, and many more. To view many dashboard samples, simply type "social media dashboard" into a Google image search.

Although performance metrics affect the entire organization, this book focuses on digital marketing metrics. Many of the measures mentioned earlier will be described in more detail in later chapters.

In Chapter 3, we move to the digital marketing plan and discuss how this plan flows from corporate digital business strategies and how the marketing mix and CRM enter the picture. The digital marketing plan is a management guide and road map that paves the way to achieving performance goals.

Chapter Summary

A business or digital business needs strategic planning to develop and maintain the proper fit between the organization's objectives, skills, and resources and its ever-changing market opportunities. Key goals for growth, competitive position, geographic scope, and other areas must be determined.

Strategy is defined as the means to achieve a goal. Digital business strategy is the deployment of enterprise resources to capitalize on technologies for reaching specified objectives that ultimately improve performance and create sustainable competitive advantage. Digital marketing strategy is the design of marketing strategy that capitalizes on the organization's electronic or information technology capabilities to reach specified objectives.

A digital business model is a method by which the organization sustains itself in the long-term using information technology, including its value proposition for partners and customers as well as its revenue streams. Companies deliver value by providing more benefits in relation to costs, as perceived by customers and partners. Digital marketing improves the value proposition by increasing benefits, decreasing costs, and increasing revenues.

Companies can become involved in digital business at the activity level, business process level, enterprise level, or through a pure play. Commitment and risk are lower at the activity level and rise with each level. The main digital business models at the activity level include online purchasing, order processing, e-mail, content publishing, business intelligence, online advertising, online sales promotion, dynamic pricing strategies, and social media communication. The main digital business models at the business process level are customer relationship management, knowledge management, supply chain management, community building online, database marketing, enterprise resource planning, and mass customization. The main digital business models at the enterprise level are digital commerce, portal, social networking, online broker (online exchange and online auction), and online agent (manufacturer's agent, shopping agent, and reverse auction).

Performance metrics are specific measures designed to evaluate the effectiveness and efficiency of an organization's operations. Web analytics helps to analyze user behavior on a website by using server logs, cookie files, and page tags.

The Balanced Scorecard links strategy to measurement by asking companies to consider their vision, critical success factors for accomplishing it, and subsequent performance metrics in four areas: customer, internal, learning and growth, and financial. The customer perspective uses measures of the value delivered to customers. The internal perspective evaluates a company's success at meeting customer expectations through its internal processes. The learning and growth perspective looks at continuous improvement to existing products and services as well as innovation in new products. The financial perspective looks at income and expense metrics as well as return on investment, sales, and market share growth. Each company selects metrics for the four perspectives based on its objectives, business model, strategies, industry, and so forth. In this way, the company can measure progress toward achieving its objectives.

Organizations using social media require many different types of performance metrics because they want to measure levels of user engagement and how that influences brand awareness and product purchase. This chapter discusses exemplary metrics in five areas: awareness/exposure, brand health, engagement, action and innovation. The chapter concludes with mention of various free and paid services that help marketers track performance metrics.

Exercises

Review Questions

1. What is strategic planning, and why do companies prepare a SWOT analysis during the strategic planning process?
2. How does digital business strategy relate to strategy on the corporate level?
3. Define digital marketing strategy and explain how it is used.
4. Give examples of digital business models.
5. What is the formula for determining value?
6. What are the four levels of commitment to digital business? Give some examples of each.
7. What is customer relationship management (CRM), and why do companies create strategies in this area?
8. How is digital commerce defined?
9. What is an internet pure play, and what are some examples?
10. What are four ways of collecting Web analytics?
11. What is the Balanced Scorecard, and how do companies use it in digital business?
12. List six important social media awareness/exposure metrics.
13. List three important social media brand health metrics.
14. List four important social media engagement metrics.
15. List four important social media action metrics.
16. List two important social media innovation metrics.

Discussion Questions

1. **Amazon Story:** identify the business models Amazon used and at which level of digital business commitment each falls (Exhibit 2.3).
2. **Amazon Story:** What performance metrics might Amazon use to measure progress toward its growth and customer service objectives?
3. Why is it important for a digital business model to create value in a way that is differentiated from the way competitors' models create value?
4. Based on the opening vignette and your examination of the Amazon.com site (or your experience as a customer), what strategic objectives do you think are appropriate for

this digital business? What performance metrics would you use to measure progress toward achieving these objectives—and why?

5. The Balanced Scorecard helps digital businesses examine results from four perspectives. Would you recommend that digital businesses also look at results from a societal perspective? Explain your response.

6. Should digital businesses strive to build community with noncustomers as well as customers? Why or why not?

7. Do you agree or disagree that the page-view metric is nearly useless in the Web 2.0 environment?

8. If you wrote a blog about your experiences at the university you attend in order to help high school students understand what college was like, which metrics would you use to measure the blog's success, and why?

Web Activities

1. Visit www.dell.com. Write down what you think the company's goals are for its website. Then make a list recommending relevant performance metrics from each of the four perspectives.

2. Visit www.BizRate.com. Do a search for this book (*eMarketing*). What is the lowest price available for the book? The highest? Compare these prices with those found at the brick-and-mortar stores like Barnes & Noble. Check out the used bookstore site www.abebooks.com. Explain in terms of value why customers might buy the book at a higher price.

3. Search Google images for "social media dashboards." Look at the dashboards and follow their links to the companies that created them. Which one do you think best for a large consumer goods company, such as Coca-Cola? Why do you recommend the one you do?

Chapter 3

The Digital Marketing Plan

The primary goal of this chapter is to explain the importance of creating a digital marketing plan and present the seven steps in the digital marketing planning process. You will see how marketers incorporate information technology in plans for effectively and efficiently achieving digital business objectives such as increasing revenues and slashing costs.

After reading this chapter, you will be able to:

- Discuss the nature and importance of a digital marketing plan and outline its seven steps.
- Show the form of a digital marketing objective and explain the use of an objective-strategy matrix.
- Describe the tasks that marketers complete in tiers 1 and 2 as they create digital marketing strategies.
- List some key revenues and costs identified during the budgeting step of the digital marketing planning process.

THE TWITTER STORY

How did a brand-new internet concept go from an idea in a brainstorming meeting in 2006 to a social media platform with 206 million daily active users (Twitter Q2 2021; Shareholder Letter, 2021) a decade later? Twitter is a social networking and microblogging service using instant messaging, a Web interface, or SMS (short message service, commonly called "texting"). Jack Dorsey recalls the naming of his brainchild:

> We wanted to capture that feeling: the physical sensation that you're buzzing your friend's pocket. It's like buzzing all over the world. So we did a bunch of name-storming, and we came up with the word "twitch," because the phone kind of vibrates when it moves. But "twitch" is not a good product name because it doesn't bring up the right imagery (interestingly, Twitch has become a very popular live streaming social media platform for gamers, highlighting the importance of a brand selecting an appealing name). So we looked in the dictionary for words around it, and we came across the word "twitter," and it was just perfect. The definition was "a short burst of inconsequential information," and "chirps from birds." And that's exactly what the product was.
>
> (Sarno, 2009)

Twitter traffic took off after a South by Southwest (SXSW) festival in 2007, where attendees were sending text messages that displayed on large televisions at the conference. The number of tweets grew from 2 million in all of 2007 to more than 500 billion per day today (Smith,

DOI: 10.4324/9781003247319-4

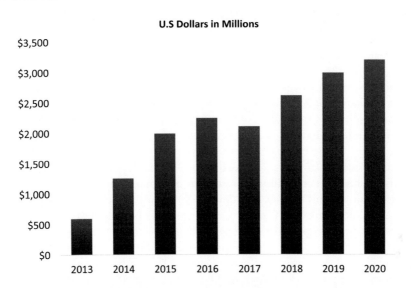

U.S Dollars in Millions

Exhibit 3.1 Twitter Annual Advertising Revenue from 2013 to 2020

2020). In November 2013, Twitter went public through an IPO valued at over $24 billion (Pepitone, 2013). Twitter continues to add features, such as enabling users to stream live video to engage with users.

Twitter began its business with venture capital. This begged the questions: What is the business model, and where is the revenue stream? However, with an increasing number of tweets and users, Twitter found a way to monetize this traffic by selling advertising (Exhibit 3.1). Following the Google AdWords model, Twitter began selling ad products (e.g., promoted Tweets, promoted trends, and promoted accounts) by targeting users based on their Twitter searches.

Twitter is an example of an internet start-up turned major social media player that continues to mature. The platform has also been used for education in China, the United Kingdom, Austria, and the United States for reporting in emergency situations, for gathering opinions in surveys, for business fundraising and public relations, and for news announcements. Many companies also use Twitter for customer service.

Overview of the Digital Marketing Planning Process

How can information technologies assist marketers in building revenues and market share or lowering costs? How can firms identify a sustainable competitive advantage with the internet when the landscape is constantly changing and filled with international competitors? The answer lies in determining how to apply digital data and information technologies both effectively and efficiently. The best firms have clear visions that they translate, through the marketing process, from digital business objectives and strategies into digital marketing goals and well-executed strategies and tactics for achieving those goals. This marketing process entails three steps: marketing plan creation, plan implementation, and plan evaluation/corrective action (using performance metrics, as discussed in Chapter 2). This chapter examines the first of these steps: the digital marketing plan.

Creating a Digital Marketing Plan

The marketing plan is a blueprint for digital strategy formulation and implementation. It is a guiding, dynamic document that links the firm's digital business strategy (digital business models) with technology-driven marketing strategies and lays out details for plan implementation through marketing management. It should be integrated with the firm's overall marketing plan. The marketing plan guides delivery of the desired results, measured by performance metrics, according to the specifications of the digital business model embedded in the firm's digital business strategy. Exhibit 3.2 shows where the digital marketing plan fits in the process.

The digital marketing plan serves as a road map to guide the firm in the direction it wishes to take. It also helps marketers allocate resources and make adjustments as needed. Many companies short-circuit this process and develop strategies ad hoc. Some are successful like Twitter, but many more fail. The Gartner Group correctly predicted that up to 75 percent of all digital business projects prior to 2002 would fail due to fundamental flaws in planning (Gartner, Inc. 2010). Nonetheless, some of the best firms discover successful digital commerce tactics accidentally and then use those experiences to build a bottom-up plan. Such was the case with Schwab.com, the online stock trading firm, which allowed its online channel successes to change the entire brick-and-mortar firm. Whether the result of top-down or bottom-up planning, firms must plan for long-term sustainability.

This chapter is structured around a seven-step traditional marketing plan. It presents a generic plan that includes a menu of tasks from which marketers can select activities relevant to their firm, industry, brands, and internal processes. It assumes that a higher-level corporate plan is already in place, outlining the firm's mission, goals, digital business strategies, and selected enterprise-level digital business models. If such a plan has not already been formulated, marketers must go through the **environmental scan** and SWOT (strengths, weaknesses, opportunities, and threats) analyses prior to creating the plan. Two common types of digital marketing plans are the napkin plan and the venture capital plan, discussed next.

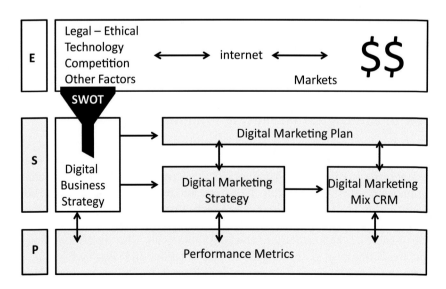

Exhibit 3.2 Focusing on the Digital Marketing Plan

The Napkin Plan

In what one marketer calls the *napkin plan*, many entrepreneurs simply jot their ideas on a napkin over lunch or cocktails and then run off to find financing. See the 2006 social network blueprint sketch created by Twitter's founder Jack Dorsey on Wikipedia (search for "Twitter"). It is simply a white legal-pad sketch that inspired this great company. Dorsey went on to create Square in a similar fashion—the card reader that allows smart phone users to swipe credit cards for product purchases. The big-company version of this process is the just-do-it, activity-based, bottom-up plan. As an example, Kevin Rose had an idea about how to set up a website to host the most-liked stories of the day, which resulted in Digg.com. In another example, a marketing university student who works for a local ski shop approached the owner, asking for $500 for software and $50 a month for Web hosting to start an experimental digital commerce site. He placed a few pictures of skis on the site and included information about how to call the store to order. The site brought in several orders per week, quickly paying off the invest-ment. These ad hoc plans sometimes work and are sometimes even necessary, given a stodgy corporate culture, but they are unique occurrences and not recommended when substantial resources are involved. Sound planning and thoughtful implementation are needed for both raising capital and long-term success in business and digital business—a principle that became increasingly evident during the dot-com shakeout.

The Venture Capital Plan

Small to mid-sized firms and entrepreneurs with start-up ideas often begin with a *napkin plan* and do not initially go through the entire traditional marketing planning process. One reason is that one or two leaders generally plan the whole venture, intuitively understanding the marketing environment and how their hot new idea is positioned for success. Such was the case for Jerry Yang and Dave Filo when in 1994 they started *Jerry's Guide to the World Wide Web*—later named Yahoo! However, as the company grew and needed capital, Jerry and Dave had to put together a comprehensive digital marketing plan. Without an emphasis on strategic planning, Yahoo! would not have been an internet survivor.

Where does an entrepreneur go for capital? Some of it is debt financed through bank loans, though most of it is equity financed. Start-up companies tap private funds (friends and family), angel investors, and venture capitalists (VCs). Angel investors provide funds with fewer requirements than those of venture capitalists. In general, friends and family are the smallest sources of capital; angel investors invest hundreds of thousands of dollars; and venture capitalists invest millions of dollars. Some banks, corporations, and consulting firms have established venture capital branches to finance internet start-ups. Some VCs even finance companies operated out of college dorm rooms. Crowdfunding has grown as a popular method to raising capital to fund a business. The Coolest Cooler was a project released on Kickstarter.com that raised over $13 million to create a cooler on wheels with a built-in speaker system.

There are tremendous amounts of venture capital available for innovative businesses that utilize the internet. This financing can range from a few thousand dollars to billions of dollars in funding depending on the idea. The conventional wisdom is that money is scarce, but talent is really the scarce resource. Investors tend to be savvy. They are looking for a well-composed business plan and, more importantly, a good team to implement it. After all, it was Steve Jobs and his carefully-formed team that drove Apple to be the success it is today.

This kind of thinking relieves some of the planning pressure on entrepreneurs but does not eliminate the need for planning to maximize organizational resources. The plan prepared by entrepreneurs for VCs should be about 8–10 pages long and contain enough data and logic to prove that (1) the digital business idea is solid and (2) the entrepreneur has some idea of how to run the business. In addition to product benefits and costs, it should include information about the competition, the target market and its potential, and the cost to acquire and retain customers.

Venture capitalists typically look for an exit plan—a way to get their money and profits out of the venture within a few years. The golden exit plan is to go public and issue stock in an initial public offering (IPO). As soon as the stock price rises sufficiently, the VC cashes out and moves on to another investment. VCs don't even pretend that all their investments will be successful. But even if 1 out of 20 is a big success, the risk is well worth the reward. The employees of these start-ups typically work for very low wages—deferring their compensation in stock options. Of particular interest to investors are projects that tap new markets with high margins. First came a boom in B2C investments, and then B2B investments, and now social media investments. As soon as observers feel that the markets are becoming saturated, another opportunity arises. Now it is mobile marketing that is taking off.

A Seven-Step Digital Marketing Plan

The seven key planning elements are (1) situation analysis, (2) strategic planning, (3) plan objectives, (4) digital marketing strategies, (5) implementation plan, (6) budget, and (7) plan for evaluating success (Exhibit 3.3). We cannot overemphasize the need to include feedback mechanisms to assess the plan's success and to use in making course corrections along the way. In fact, some marketers recommend contingency plans that if reached will invoke strategy refinement.

1. Situation Analysis	Review the firm's: • Environmental and SWOT analyses • Existing marketing plan and any other information that can be obtained about the company and its brands • Digital business objectives, strategies, and performance metrics
2. Digital marketing Strategic Planning	• Determine the fit between the organization and its strategic planning market opportunities. Perform marketing opportunity analysis (MOA), demand and supply analysis, and segment analysis. • **Tier 1 Strategies:** Segmentation, Targeting, Differentiation, Positioning
3. Objectives	• Identify general goals from digital business strategy • Identify revenue streams suggested by digital business models
4. Digital marketing Strategy	• **Tier 2 Strategies:** Design the offer, value, distribution, communication, and relationship management strategies to create a competitive edge • Modify objectives as needed.
5. Implementation Plan	Design: • Digital marketing mix tactics: product/service offering, pricing/valuation, distribution/supply chain, integrated communication mix • Relationship management tactics • Organizational structures for implementing the plan
6. Budget	• Forecast revenues • Evaluate costs to reach goals
7. Evaluation Plan	• Identify appropriate performance metrics

Exhibit 3.3 Digital Marketing Plan Process

A good way to think about the marketing plan is through the analogy of preparing for a football game. While reviewing game films, a situation analysis reveals each team's strengths and weaknesses (e.g., the home team has a good passing game, the visitors have an excellent run defense). A likely objective would then be to win the game by throwing the ball. Strategies are developed to meet this objective (e.g., use play action to draw in the coverage; throw deep). Next, tactics implement the strategies (e.g., use a play action pass on first down; run on second down to keep them honest; pass on third down). Finally, Monday morning quarterbacking provides the postgame evaluation.

Step 1—Situation Analysis

As with creating a business or marketing plan, the best place to start is to conduct a situation analysis. The marketing environment is ever changing, providing plenty of opportunities to develop new products, new markets, and new media to communicate with customers, plus new channels to reach business partners. At the same time, the environment poses competitive, economic, and other threats. Three key **environmental factors** that affect digital marketing and are part of any situation analysis are market-related, legal, and technological factors. They are covered in depth in Chapters 4, 5, and 7, as well as in the "Let's Get Technical" boxes throughout the text.

The **SWOT** analysis flows from a situation analysis that examines the company's internal strengths and weaknesses with respect to the environment and the competition and looks at external opportunities and threats. Opportunities may help to define a target market or identify new product opportunities, while threats are areas of exposure. For example, when Amazon.com launched as an online bookstore in the mid-1990s, it had no significant competition. Its biggest threat was a full-scale push by a large bookstore chain to claim the online market. The company's greatest weakness was that it had no experience selling books or even processing credit card transactions. What's more, it had no experience boxing books for shipment and originally packed them on the floor until a visiting carpenter suggested building packing tables (Spector, 2000). The company's greatest strength was a smart and talented team that stayed focused and learned what it didn't know. Fortunately for Amazon, the big stores were caught napping. The delay by the bookstore chains gave Amazon the opportunity to establish its online brand at a time when many firms didn't fully understand the power of the internet. Barnes & Noble (www.bn.com) did not fight back until Amazon was on the eve of a stock offering. By then it was too late. Further proving Amazon's strategy skills, CEO Jeff Bezos began experimenting with brick-and-mortar stores in 2015. However, the threats are not over for Amazon or any company. Amazon's 2020 annual report lists numerous potential risk factors such as increasing competition, resource constraints, expansion risks, performance fluctuations, data security issues, and foreign currency exchange rate fluctuations ("Amazon.com Annual Report", 2020).

Bear in mind that a company's strengths and weaknesses in the online world may be somewhat different from its strengths and weaknesses in the brick-and-mortar world. For example, Amazon is worried about data security and intellectual property. Barnes & Noble has strengths in the brick-and-mortar world, but this did not necessarily translate into strengths in the online world. Barnes & Noble can easily find itself in the unfortunate position of channel conflict—having to explain to channel partners why customers can purchase for less online than in the store.

Step 2—Strategic Planning

After reviewing the situation analysis and currently used marketing plans, marketers engage in strategic planning. As you recall from Chapter 2, the strategic planning process involves determining the fit between the organization's objectives, skills, and resources and its changing market opportunities. For clarification throughout the book, we present these tasks as *tier 1 strategies*, including segmentation, targeting, differentiation, and positioning. During this phase, marketers uncover opportunities that help formulate the digital marketing objectives.

Marketers conduct a **market opportunity analysis (MOA)**, including both demand and supply analyses, for *segmenting* and *targeting*. The demand analysis portion includes market segmentation analyses to describe and evaluate the potential profitability, sustainability, accessibility, and size of various potential segments. Segment analysis in the B2C market uses descriptors such as demographic characteristics, geographic location, selected psychographic characteristics (such as attitude toward technology and mobile communication device ownership), and past behavior toward the product (such as purchasing patterns online and offline). B2B descriptors include firm location, size, industry, type of need, technological savvy, and more. These descriptors help firms identify potentially attractive markets. Firms must also understand segment trends—are they growing or declining in absolute size and product use?

Companies use traditional segmentation analyses when they enter new markets through the online channel; however, if the firm plans to serve current markets online, it will delve more deeply into these customers' needs. Which of the firm's customers will want to use the internet? How do the needs of customers using the organization's website differ from those of other customers? For example, most internet users expect e-mails to be answered within 48 hours but will be satisfied if a postal letter is answered within weeks. In addition, firms often discover new markets as these customers find their way to social media sites such as Facebook or Pinterest. Marketers can use Web analytics to discover how best to serve these new markets.

The purpose of a supply analysis is to assist in forecasting segment profitability as well as to find competitive advantages to exploit in the online market. Only by carefully analyzing competitive strengths and weaknesses can a firm find its own performance advantages. Therefore, companies should review the competition, their digital marketing initiatives, and their strengths and weaknesses prior to developing digital marketing initiatives. They must also try to identify future industry changes—which new firms might appear online, and which will drop away? For example, who could have envisioned Facebook's successful growth in 2005 to 2008 when MySpace was the hugely popular social network at the time? In addition, they must try to prepare for the unexpected such as when the COVID-19 pandemic really started to hit companies in 2020, many of whom were unprepared for conducting most of their business online.

With a thorough MOA, the company can select its target market and understand its characteristics, behavior, and desires in the firm's product category. Furthermore, firms will want to understand the value proposition for each market. For example, marketers at Jay's Ice Cream might decide to target several Hispanic markets. In doing so, the company first assesses its strengths as having a strong customer service department and websites. Its weaknesses, however, include having a low-tech corporate culture and a seasonal nature to its business. A pending security law means that Jay's could face costly software upgrades, as the company's main competitor, Ruby's Soft Serve, begins to aggressively use Facebook for marketing purposes. Jay's recognizes that Hispanic markets are growing and untapped in the industry and that they could save on postage costs if they engage in Facebook marketing.

Another tier 1 step in digital marketing strategic planning is identifying brand *differentiation* variables and *positioning* strategies. Based on an understanding of both the competition and the target(s), marketers must decide how to differentiate their products from competitors' products in a way that provides benefits perceived as important by the target. In the case of Facebook, management opted to add third-party applications to differentiate the site from its competitor, MySpace. Flowing from this differentiation is the positioning statement: the desired image for the brand relative to the competition. If the positioning strategy was already decided upon in the traditional marketing plan, digital marketers must decide whether it will be effective online as well. If planning for a new brand or market, digital marketers must decide on branding strategies of differentiation and positioning at this point in the process.

Step 3—Objectives

In general, an objective in a digital marketing plan includes the following aspects:

- Task (what is to be accomplished).
- Measurable quantity (how much).
- Time frame (by when).

Assume that Chevrolet wants to increase the number of visitors to the "Build & Price" page on its website from 215,000 to 216,000 in one year. This type of objective is easy to evaluate and is a critical part of the digital marketing plan. The plan will often include the rationale for setting each objective—why each is desirable and achievable given the situation analysis findings, digital marketing, and digital business strategy.

Even though digital commerce transactions are a revenue producing and an exciting dimension of a digital business presence, other objectives are also worthwhile, especially when the firm is using technology only to create internal efficiencies, such as to target market communication to build long-term customer relationships. In fact, most digital marketing plans aim to accomplish multiple objectives, such as the following:

- Increase market share.
- Increase the number of comments left on a blog.
- Increase the positive sentiment of comments.
- Increase sales revenue (measured in dollars or units).
- Reduce costs (such as distribution or promotion costs).
- Achieve branding goals (such as increasing brand awareness).
- Increase database size.
- Achieve customer relationship management (CRM) goals (such as increasing customer satisfaction, frequency of purchases, or customer retention rates).
- Improve supply chain management (such as by enhancing member coordination, adding partners, or optimizing inventory levels).

An important part of the planning process is to define potential revenue streams, using a viable business model from Chapter 2. The organizational digital business plan might contain a SWOT analysis like the Jay's Ice Cream example, leading to the firm adopting a digital business model of digital commerce. Digital marketers take over from here, setting a measurable objective of generating $500,000 from digital commerce sales within the first year.

Step 4—Digital Marketing Strategies

Next, marketers use the 4 Ps to craft strategies to achieve plan objectives regarding the offer: (product), value (pricing), distribution/supply chain (place), and communication (promotion). Further, marketers design CRM and partner relationship management (PRM) strategies. For clarification, we call these *tier 2 strategies* throughout the book. In practice, tiers 1 and tier 2 strategies are interrelated (Exhibit 3.4). For example, marketers select the best target market and identify a competitive product position, which dictates the ideal type of advertising,

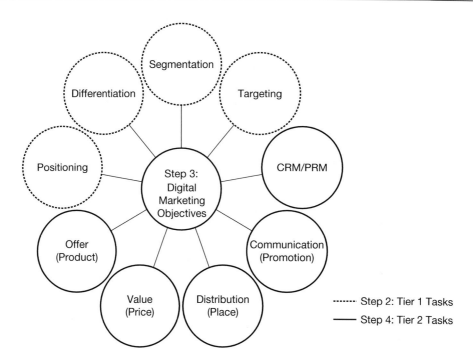

Exhibit 3.4 Steps 2, 3, and 4 of the Digital Marketing Plan

pricing, and so forth. Steps 2, 3, and 4 are an iterative process because it is difficult to know what the brand position should be without understanding the offer that comprises the brand promise (i.e., the benefits the firm promises to customers). Tier 2 strategies discussed in detail in subsequent chapters.

The Offer: Product Strategies

The organization can sell merchandise, content, services, or advertising on its website. It can adopt one of the digital business models discussed in Chapter 2, such as *online auctions*, to generate a revenue stream. The firm can create new brands for the online market or simply sell selected current or enhanced products in that channel. Such analyses will reveal many opportunities. If the firm offers current brands online, it will need to solve many different problems, such as the way colors appear differently on a computer screen than in print. The most astute firms take advantage of information technology capabilities to alter their online offerings. For example, the Porsche AR–Imagine app uses augmented reality to allows users to customize a Porsche vehicle, examine it from numerous angles, and even take it for a test drive.

The Value: Pricing Strategies

A company must decide how online product prices will compare with offline equivalents. To make these decisions, firms consider the differing costs of sorting and delivering products to individuals through the online channel as well as competitive and market concerns. Two particularly important online pricing trends are the following:

- *Dynamic pricing.* This strategy applies different price levels for different customers or situations. For example, a first-time buyer or someone who hasn't purchased for many months may receive discounted prices to motivate purchase, or prices may drop during low-demand periods. The internet allows firms to price items automatically while users view pages.
- *Online bidding.* This approach presents a way to optimize inventory management. For instance, hotels allow guests to bid for hotel rooms on slow days, instructing its reservation agents to accept various minimum bid levels depending on occupancy rates for any given day. Priceline.com, eBay.com, and many B2B exchanges operate exclusively using this strategy.

Distribution Strategies

Many organizations use the internet to distribute products or create efficiencies among supply chain members in the distribution channel. Consider the following examples:

- *Direct marketing.* Many firms sell directly to customers, bypassing intermediaries in the traditional channel for some sales. In B2B markets, many firms realize tremendous cost reductions by using the internet to facilitate sales.
- *Agent digital business models.* Firms such as eBay and E★TRADE bring buyers and sellers together and earn a fee for the transaction.

Marketing Communication Strategies

The internet spawned a multitude of new marketing communication strategies both to draw customers to a website and to interact with brick-and-mortar customers. Firms use webpages, social media, and e-mail to communicate with their target markets and business partners. Companies build brand images, create awareness of new products, and position products using online content. Database marketing is key to maintaining records about the needs, preferences, and behavior of individual customers so companies can send relevant and personalized information and persuasive communication at strategic times.

Relationship Management Strategies

Many digital marketing communication strategies also help build relationships with a firm's partners, supply chain members, or customers. However, many firms up the ante by using CRM or PRM software to integrate customer communication and purchase behavior into a comprehensive database. They then use CRM software to retain customers and increase average order values and lifetime value. Social CRM is a recent development that uses social media conversation to engage and build relationships with prospects and customers. Other firms build extranets—two or more proprietary networks linked for better communication and more efficient transactions among partner companies.

One informative way to present the company's goals and accompanying digital marketing strategies is through an objective–strategy matrix, an example of which is shown in Exhibit 3.5. This graphical device helps marketers better understand their implementation requirements. Each cell contains a *yes* or *no* depending on how the marketer will link particular goals and strategies.

Online Goals	Online Advertising	Online Videos	E-Mail	Online Sales	Social Networking
Increases customer engagement	Yes	Yes	Yes	No	Yes
Increase customer database	Yes	No	No	Yes	Yes
Improve customer service	No	No	Yes	Yes	Yes
Build brand name awareness	Yes	Yes	Yes	No	Yes
Increase online sales	Yes	Yes	Yes	Yes	Yes
Reposition brand	Yes	Yes	Yes	No	Yes
Increase Facebook "likes"	Yes	No	Yes	Yes	Yes
Generate sales leads	Yes	Yes	Yes	Yes	Yes

Exhibit 3.5 Digital Marketing Objective–Strategy Mix

Step 5—Implementation Plan

Now comes the fun: deciding how to accomplish the objectives through creative and effective tactics. For example, at Halloween, GoPro posted an Instagram video of people skydiving while dressed as witches and riding broomsticks in an effort to connect with its audience and take advantage of the Halloween season in a creative way. Marketers select the marketing mix (4 Ps), relationship management tactics, and other tactics to achieve the plan objectives and then devise detailed plans for implementation (the action plans). They also check to be sure the right marketing organization is in place for implementation (i.e., staff, department structure, application service providers, and other outside firms). The right combination of tactics will help the organization meet its objectives effectively and efficiently.

Unfortunately, many companies try to start the digital marketing plan process at step 5. For example, instead of first conducting a situation analysis, engaging in strategic planning, and considering plan objectives and strategy, they begin by creating photos and captions for social media content and posting it to "see how it goes." While this may seem to move things along quickly, it also fails to capture the importance of making strategic decisions at the bigger picture level before diving into the more granular tactics. Indeed, it is easy to engage in content creation, but without strategy, companies could be damaging the brand's reputation and wasting resources, both financially and in terms of employees' time and effort. Digital marketers pay special attention to information-gathering tactics because information technologies are especially adept at automating these processes. Website forms, cookies, feedback e-mail, social media comments and likes and online surveys are just some of the tactics that firms use to collect information about customers, prospects, and other stakeholders. Other important tactics include the following:

- Website log analysis software helps firms review user behavior at the site and make changes to better meet the needs of users.
- Business intelligence uses the internet for secondary research, assisting firms in understanding competitors and other market forces.

Step 6—Budget

A key part of any strategic plan is to identify the expected returns from an investment (ROI). These returns can then be matched against costs to develop a cost/benefit analysis, for ROI calculation, or for calculating internal rate of return (IRR), which management uses to determine whether the effort is worthwhile. Marketers today are especially concerned with adequate return on marketing investment (ROMI). During plan implementation, marketers will closely monitor actual revenues and costs to see that results are on track for accomplishing the objectives. The internet is terrific for monitoring results because technology records a visitor's every click. The following sections describe some of the revenues and costs associated with digital marketing initiatives.

Revenue Forecast

The firm uses an established sales forecasting method for estimating the site revenues in the short, intermediate, and long terms. The firm's historical data, industry reports, and competitive actions are all inputs to this process. An important part of forecasting is to estimate the level of website traffic over time, because this number affects the amount of revenue a firm can expect to generate from its site. Revenue streams that produce internet profits come mainly from website sales, advertising sales, subscription fees, affiliate referrals, sales at partner sites, commissions, and other fees. Companies usually summarize this analysis in a spreadsheet showing expected revenues over time and accompanying rationale.

Intangible Benefits

The intangible benefits of digital marketing strategies are much more difficult to establish, as are intangible benefits in the brick-and-mortar world. How much brand equity is created, for example, through an American Airlines program in which customers receive periodic e-mail messages about their frequent-flyer account balances? What is the value of increased brand awareness from a website? Putting a financial figure on such benefits is challenging but essential for digital marketers.

Cost Savings

Money saved through internet efficiencies is considered soft revenue for a firm. For example, if the distribution channel linking a producer with its customers contains a wholesaler, distributor, and retailer, each intermediary will take a profit. A typical markup scheme is:

	Markup	Cost
Original Cost to Manufacturer	0%	$50.00
Markup to Wholesaler	10%	$55.00
Markup to Retailer	100%	$110.00
Markup to Consumer	50%	$165.00

For example, if a producer manufactures a product for $50 and sells it to a wholesaler for $55, the consumer ultimately pays $165. If the producer cuts out the intermediaries (disintermediation) and sells its product online directly to the consumer, it can price the product at $85 and increase revenue by $30. Whether this approach translates into profits depends on the cost of getting the product to the consumer. Other examples include the $5,000 a marketer might save in printing and postage for a direct-mail piece costing $1.00 per piece to 5,000 consumers, or the $270 million Cisco saved in one year on handling costs for its online computer system sales.

Digital Marketing Costs

Digital marketing entails many costs, including costs for employees, hardware, software, programming, and more. In addition, some traditional marketing costs may creep into the digital marketing budget—for example, the cost of offline advertising to draw traffic to the website (e.g., GoDaddy.com's Super Bowl ads). For simplicity, this section will discuss technology-related cost items only. See the "Let's Get Technical" box for the steps required to build a website. Consider that the cost of a website typically ranges from $5,000 to $50 million. Following are just a few of the costs site developers incur:

- *Technology costs.* This includes software, hardware, internet access or hosting services, educational materials and training, and other site operation and maintenance costs.
- *Site design.* Websites need graphic designers to create appealing page layouts, graphics, and photos.
- *Salaries.* All personnel who work on website development and maintenance are included in the budget.
- *Other site development expenses.* Expenses not included in the technology or salary categories will fall here, such as registering multiple domain names and hiring consultants to write content or perform other development and design activities.
- *Marketing communication.* All advertising, public relations, and promotions activities, both online and offline, that directly relate to drawing site traffic and enticing visitors to return and purchase are included here. Other costs include search engine optimization (SEO), online directory costs, e-mail list rental, prizes for contests, and more.
- *Social media communication.* Staff costs can really escalate when companies engage customers on Facebook, Twitter, or other social media pages. Organizations should also allocate resources to monitoring their brand and other company mentions in social media through services such as Keyhole.com so they can catch and respond to negative posts.
- *Miscellaneous.* Other typical project costs might fall here—expenses such as travel, telephone, stationery printing to add a new URL, and more.

Let's Get Technical—Building a Web Site

You have been added to the team charged with redesigning your company's website. You have heard that colleagues in graphic design and information systems will also be on the team. You are not quite sure who is responsible for what function or even what all the issues are. You would like to appear articulate and informed in the meetings.

How are professional websites actually built? The process is similar in some ways to building a home. In home building, an architect works with clients to determine their needs, draws up a design to meet those requirements, and then hands that design over to a developer who builds the home. The sequence moves from requirements to design to development. Similarly, the marketing department draws up a creative brief that specifies in detail the requirements for the site and specific design elements (e.g., fonts and colors that will go into the site). The next step is to create a mockup of the homepage and a few interior pages in a design tool such as Adobe Photoshop. Mastery of Photoshop and of design theory in general requires training and practice. In a large shop, the marketing department would look to the visual communication or graphic design team to produce the design. The design is run past the client and adjustments are made. Once the design is finalized, the development team takes over. The development team takes the design and makes it functional. The development team has five major goals for the site. The site should be:

1. *Easy to update.* Content changes should be easy to implement. Ideally, an input screen should allow an authorized user to type or paste content directly into the site without technical assistance. Any continuous updates such as stock feeds or weather updates should be programmed to take place automatically, without human intervention.

2. *Optimized for quick download.* Each page on the site should load on the user's computer within seconds. Research shows that users have little patience for slow sites. Optimizing involves compressing the graphic elements on the page as GIF, JPG, or PNG files. GIF files are used for line art that has areas of flat color (e.g., a corporate logo) and support having one color transparent so that white backgrounds disappear. JPG is used for continuous tone images such as photographs. PNG files do the best of both. HTML 5 allows for animation and movies. Text does not require compression because it loads quickly.

3. *Easy to find.* The site should be easy for search engines to index and find. Among other things, this accessibility involves the careful placement of keyword terms in locations that the search engines will rate highly.

4. *Interactive.* Simple interactivity is generated by including hyperlinks to link the pages together. However, more complex interactivity can require some sophisticated programming. Examples of complex interactivity include the following:

   - A search box on the site.
   - Validation of user input (e.g., checking to see that the e-mail address contains an "@" symbol or that a credit card number is valid).
   - Processing of transactions such as shopping carts and checkout.
   - User log-ins.
   - Connection to backend databases, which could be public databases such as sports scores, news feeds, stock tickers, and weather updates. They could also be private databases containing sensitive company or personal account information.

     Interactivity is accomplished using development tools such as Macromedia Dreamweaver or Microsoft Visual Web Developer. These tools develop computer code in HTML, JavaScript, Java, and a variety of other computer languages. Mastery of these tools requires a considerable degree of training and practice.

5. *Secure.* In this age of hackers and viruses, the site needs to be protected against malicious attack. Oftentimes, organizations attempt to quantify the dollar value of their exposure to attack to determine whether to even continue with development.

Want to try it yourself? There are some great online site development tools that are free. Two of the more impressive tools are Wix and Google Sites. Both create a polished-looking site. Wix has more options, but Google Sites is a bit easier to use. If you have a Gmail e-mail account, then you are already authorized to use Google Sites (find it at sites.google.com). Google Sites integrates well with other Google products such as YouTube, Google Docs, and Google Gadgets. Google's seamless integration makes it a fairly easy exercise to create an interactive site—something that only a few years ago would have required lots of coding expertise.

Step 7—Evaluation Plan

Once the digital marketing plan is implemented, its success depends on continuous evaluation. This type of evaluation means digital marketers must have tracking systems in place before the electronic doors open. What should be measured? The answer depends on the plan objectives. Review the Balanced Scorecard for digital business and social media metrics (in Chapter 2) to see how various metrics relate to specific plan goals.

In general, today's marketers are quite ROI driven. As a result, digital marketers must show how their intangible goals, such as brand building or CRM, will lead to higher revenue down the road. Also, they must present accurate and timely metrics to justify their initial and ongoing digital marketing expenditures throughout the period covered by the plan. For example, the huge German chemical company BASF must provide an ROI measure for its global search engine advertising. It is very difficult to follow lead activity because website leads are sent to salespeople worldwide who take many months to close the deals.

Chapter Summary

The digital marketing plan is a guiding dynamic document for digital marketing strategy formulation and implementation. The purpose is to help the firm achieve its desired results as measured by performance metrics according to the specifications of the digital business model and digital business strategy.

Creating a digital marketing plan requires seven steps. The first is to conduct a situation analysis by reviewing environmental and SWOT analyses, existing marketing plans and company/ brand information, and digital business objectives, strategies, and performance metrics. In the second step, digital marketers perform strategic planning, which includes a marketing opportunity analysis to develop segmentation, targeting, differentiation, and positioning strategies (tier 1 strategies). In the third step, digital marketers formulate objectives, usually setting multiple objectives; they may use an objective–strategy matrix to guide implementation. In the fourth step, digital marketers design digital marketing strategies for the 4 Ps and relationship management (tier 2 strategies).

In the fifth step, digital marketers develop an implementation plan with a suitable 4 Ps marketing mix, select appropriate relationship management tactics, design information-gathering tactics, and select other tactics to achieve their objectives. They must also devise detailed implementation plans during this step in the process. In the sixth step, digital marketers prepare a revenue forecast to estimate the expected returns from the plan's investment and detail the digital marketing costs to come up with a calculation that management can use to determine whether the effort is worthwhile. In the final and seventh step of the plan, digital marketers use tracking systems to measure results and evaluate the plan's success on a continuous basis.

Exercises

Review Questions

1. What are the seven steps in a digital marketing plan?
2. What is the purpose of the marketing opportunity analysis and the segment analysis?
3. What four elements in tier 1 and five elements in tier 2 are devised for digital marketing strategy?
4. What are common digital marketing objectives?
5. What is the purpose of a digital marketing objective–strategy matrix?

6. How do managers use budgeting within the digital marketing planning process?
7. Why do digital marketing plans need an evaluation component?

Discussion Questions

1. What details about Ruby's Soft Serve's Facebook marketing strategies might Jay's Ice Cream want to know as it is conducting its SWOT analysis?
2. **Twitter Story:** Referring to the business models in Chapter 2, what other models would you recommend to Twitter for generating profit, in addition to selling advertising?
3. What kinds of questions should a firm ask in developing a digital marketing plan to serve customers in current markets through an online channel?
4. Why is it important for digital marketers to specify not only the task but also the measurable quantity and time frame for accomplishing an objective?
5. Why would the management of American Airlines expect its digital marketers to estimate the financial impact of intangible benefits such as building brand equity through e-mail messages to frequent flyers?
6. How should Facebook calculate the ROI for adding a third-party app?

Web Activities

1. Consider a local business with which you are familiar and draft a digital marketing plan for it.
2. Visit WordPress.com, a company that offers website building services. What steps does it recommend? What does it charge to develop a website?
3. In some ways, university websites are a marketer's nightmare. Universities tend to be decentralized in their management, with colleges and even departments having a great deal of autonomy, which they assume extends to what they post on their websites. However, marketers want a consistent brand image projected over all of the university's webpages. Go to the websites for your university, college, and department and describe how well you think these site fulfill the marketing objectives of the university. Is there a consistent brand image? What improvements could be made?

Part II

Digital Marketing Environment

Chapter 4

Global Digital Marketing 3.0

The primary objective of this chapter is to help you gain an understanding of the main country-by-country differences in internet access and usage as a foundation for segmenting and targeting specific markets. You will learn about some of the barriers to internet adoption and digital commerce in emerging economies and see how these barriers are being addressed. You will learn how consumer behavior and attitudes, payment methods, technological issues, and both economic and technological disparities within nations can influence digital marketing in less developed countries.

After reading this chapter, you will be able to:

- Discuss overall trends in internet access, usage, and purchasing around the world.
- Define emerging economies and explain the vital role of information technology in economic development.
- Outline how digital marketers apply market similarity and analyze online purchase and payment behaviors in planning market entry opportunities.
- Describe how digital marketing strategy is influenced by computer and telephone access, credit card availability, attitudes toward internet use, slow connection speeds, website design, and electricity problems.
- Review the special challenges of digital marketing on the wireless internet in the context of emerging economies.
- Discuss the controversy related to the digital divide.
- Explain how digital marketing is being used with very low income or base of the pyramid consumers.

IDOL GOES GLOBAL

The singers Carrie Underwood, Clay Aiken, Kelly Clarkson, and Jennifer Hudson, are well known in America. These are all individuals connected with the American TV program *American Idol*. But what about Prashant Tamang, Jessica Mauboy, or Žanamari Lalić? These are also well-known names, but to TV viewers, internet surfers, and text messaging devotees in India, Australia, and Croatia, respectively. All these individuals are winners of local versions of the *American Idol* franchise in countries outside the United States or, as it is known in Germany, *Deutschland sucht den Superstar*. These adaptations of *American Idol* play to a worldwide audience of approximately 3.2 billion people even while audience share in the United States declines.

Georgians can follow the rise (or fall) of that season's music contestants by searching You-Tube keyword Geostari. Although the Georgian alphabet is distinctive, the blue logo with its curvy neon letters that greets each viewer on the homepage brands the Web page as connected

DOI: 10.4324/9781003247319-6

with *American Idol*. Ethiopians living anywhere in the world can stay current by either logging onto Jump TV to see rebroadcasts of *Ethiopian Idol* or by becoming an Ethiopian Idol fan on Facebook. *Ethiopian Idol* also has Feleke Hailu, a straightforward, sometimes rude, judge in the mold of Simon Cowell, an *American Idol* judge known for his candidly critical comments. Feleke alternates between his catch phrase "alta fakedem," or "you didn't make it" in Amharic, and blunt judgments like "You sing like a donkey."

SMS (text messaging) is very popular in India where Indian viewers not only vote for singers but can also apply to be a contestant on *Indian Idol* through SMS by typing the keyword "IDOL" into their handset when they call Sony Entertainment TV Asia, the cable system that carries *Indian Idol*. Avid *Idol* fans in India also have energetic debates on the all-India entertainment portal (www.india-forums.com), where contestants are thoroughly critiqued. Tensions can run high in the Middle East, where the Arabic-language version is called *Arab Idol*. As a semi-final show drew near, for example, an ice cream shop in Amman, Jordan, offered free ice cream to anyone who voted for the Jordanian contestant, Diana Karzon. In Syria, a mobile phone company hung posters in the streets urging people to vote for the Syrian singer Rowaida Attiyeh as a way of tangibly showing country pride. When a popular Lebanese singer was eliminated in the semifinals, Lebanese audience members threw chairs and anything else they could find. In that mayhem, the two remaining singers fainted. In the end, free ice cream might have made the difference: Diana Karzon won.

The *American Idol* franchise—and shows that have spawned from it such as *The Voice* and *Dancing with the Stars*—is big business worldwide. *American Idol* was one of the first to ask fans to vote for contestants via SMS text, which has become a worldwide phenomenon for many reality television programs. It is still one of the most discussed TV series on social media, along with other popular reality programs such as *The Bachelor, America's Got Talent*, and *Dancing with the Stars* (Nielsen, 2019). The convergence of TV, internet, mobile phones, and short message services, when added to the unpredictability of what will happen on each show, keeps global and national audiences tuning in each week. As one cynic said, probably the only place in the world that *Idol* does not have a franchise is Antarctica—at least not yet.

Overview of Global Digital Marketing Issues

Geoffrey Ramsey, eMarketer statistician, envisioned the striking evolution of the Web as consumers in the twenty-first century have come to know it. In 2000, Ramsey saw that ultimately the internet would have significant amounts of local content, that languages other than English would dominate the Web, and that because of the Internet's extensive reach, a truly global marketplace would develop ("New eGlobal Report", 2000). ICANN, the official body that assigns internet domain names, has recognized the internet's changing language and usage patterns. Beginning in 2010, digital marketers could create Web addresses that use characters other than the 26 letters of the Roman alphabet. Until then, Web users whose native language was written with non-Roman characters (e.g., Russian, Hindi, Japanese, Greek, Hebrew, and Arabic) had to use keyboards that could type both Roman and local characters. KIA Motors' Web address in Egypt, for example, is www.kia.com.eg. The final two letters, .eg, are part the top-level domain address and stand for Egypt (مصر). With the ICANN change, KIA's Egyptian Web address could soon end in مصر. Digital marketers living in Saudi Arabia (السعودية [AlSaudiah]) and the United Arab Emirates (امارات [Emarat]) have the same opportunities. As Paul Hoffman, the US-based programmer who created these standards, noted, these new domain names are not for the Web's current 1-billion plus users but for the next several billion users who are now not on the Web (Rhoads, 2007).

How can marketers capitalize on these changing dynamics when planning global digital marketing strategies? Foremost, global digital marketers must understand that a country's digital readiness profile significantly influences marketing strategy and tactics. It is important to differentiate between the industrialized nations of North America and Europe that hold the majority of internet users and the emerging economies of India, China, Russia, and Brazil that provide great promise in the future. We briefly introduce the global market context in this chapter but focus primarily on emerging economies. Digital marketing strategies and internet usage in industrialized nations are generally similar to those in the United States (and will be discussed extensively in the rest of the text), while those in emerging markets are not. This chapter is about two paradoxes: (1) that although convergence may make global markets superficially look the same, there are still meaningful differences that digital marketers must understand and account for when working in emerging economies and (2) that in some instances, emerging markets (which have traditionally been thought of less advanced than fully industrialized markets) may be more advanced than Western, fully developed markets and thus require a different mix of digital marketing strategies.

Global Markets

Globalization has changed the way marketers conduct business. Marketplaces that have been difficult to access either because of their physical distance from company headquarters or because of a consumer buying profile that did not match the firm's core customer are increasingly being targeted. Significant advances in telecommunications and computer technologies are driving this change, thus creating a whole world of opportunity for digital marketers. An organization such as Haier illustrates this point. Haier is a Chinese company with one overriding ambition: It wants to have a world-class global brand that is acknowledged as equal to (and Haier's CEO would say "better than") the best global brands from Japan, the United States, Germany, and South Korea. Indeed, some readers may already know the Haier brand name: Walmart and other big box retailers sell Haier's popular mini-fridge, which has developed a cult following among college students living in campus dorms.

Haier continues to take major steps toward achieving its goal of being a best-in-class global brand. Domestically, Haier is China's leading manufacturer of refrigerators, washing machines, and air conditioners. Globally, Haier has offices or production facilities in more than 160 countries (including a $15-million headquarters in Manhattan). Haier's internet presence supports its global ambition. For instance, check out their English-language homepage (www. haier.com) highlighting Haier's Web presence in a number of countries, including China, Pakistan, Korea, Russia, Australia, the United Arab Emirates, Vietnam, Indonesia, and Poland.

On haierappliances.com, Haier presents the face of a contemporary online retailer. Consumers can shop and register for products, subscribe to a Haier newsletter, follow Haier on social media, access warranty information, locate after-sales support, inquire about becoming a Haier distributor, and find tips and hints for maintaining Haier products. Haier is poised to become a fierce global competitor in the twenty-first century, and the continued development of its Web presence will help it achieve that goal.

Digital marketing is flourishing all around the world. However, global digital marketers must be alert to the significant differences that influence digital marketing strategy wherever they occur. Savvy global digital marketers recognize that successful digital marketing is dependent on a solid understanding of country context. For example, mobile marketing campaigns are much more common—and successful—in Africa than they are in other parts of the world. In countries like Kenya and India, effective mobile campaigns can be text-based rather than graphics-based, as they are in fully developed economies like the United States and Western

Europe. Social media campaigns differ significantly by country as well. For instance, WeChat was the most popular social media site in China in 2020 (Digital, 2021: China). While the globe is a world of opportunity for digital marketing, successful digital marketers know that what works in one's home market may not work as well in other markets.

Exhibit 4.1 shows that worldwide internet usage increased more than 1,300 percent between 2000 and 2022 ("Internet Usage and Population Statistics", 2022) and the total number of internet users was over 5 billion. Yet absolute numbers and rates of growth vary considerably by continent. Africa saw the greatest growth in internet use, with an increase of 227.5 percent. Asia has the most internet users, with slightly more than 1.9 billion users. Asia is home to China and India, both of which have populations greater than 1 billion and are experiencing significant economic growth. Yet when internet penetration rates (internet use divided by population) are determined, a different global picture emerges. North America has the highest internet penetration rate, with 88.1 percent of individuals having internet access. Europe is a close follower with 80.2 percent of its population using the internet. In Africa, the world's second most populous continent, internet penetration of just over 31.2 percent, even with its huge 227.5 percent increase between 2011 and 2017.

The internet has continued to grow as countries continue to develop and provide potential users with the means of access. As of January 2021, there are estimates of over 4.7 billion internet users around the world. This means nearly 60 percent of the world's population (7.9 billion) uses the internet. While this is a massive number of total users, penetration rates based on region provide a different context to the story. For instance, North America hosts slightly under 5 percent of the world's total population but makes up over 8 percent of internet users, with 88 percent of the population accessing the internet in some way. Over 55 percent of the world's population lives in Asia, and people living here make up 49.7 percent of internet users. However, only 46.7 percent of people who live here use the internet, highlighting where growth in users may be coming from in the future.

Most digital markers prefer to evaluate individual countries for online-strategy profitability. Internet use varies greatly from country to country. Country population, while always an important consideration for marketers, might not always directly correlate with internet penetration levels. The world average for Internet penetration is 60 percent with a high of 97 percent in Northern Europe and a low of 0 percent in North Korea (Internet Usage Worldwide, 2021).

World Regions	2022 Population (millions)	Percent of Population	2022 Internet Users (millions)	Internet Usage as Percent of Population	Percent of User Growth 2000–2022	2022 Percent of Internet User Population
North America	372.5	4.7	347.9	93.4	222	6.7
Europe	841.3	10.6	743.6	88.4	608	14.1
Asia	4,350.8	54.8	2,790.1	64.1	2,341	53.1
Latin America/Caribbean	663.5	8.4	533.1	80.4	2,851	10.1
Africa	1,394.5	17.6	601.3	43.1	13,220	11.4
Middle East	268.3	3.4	205.0	76.4	6,141	4.0
Oceania/Australia	43.6	.5	30.5	70.1	301	0.6
Worldwide Total	7,934.7	100.0	5,251.7	66.2	1,355	100

Exhibit 4.1 Worldwide Internet Usage and Population Statistics 2022

Source: Internet World Stats at www.internetworldstats.com/stats.htm

Bhutan, a small country in the Himalayan Mountains, is a good example of how emerging markets can leapfrog fully developed economies and present new digital marketing opportunities in the process. Bhutan was literally excluded from the internet revolution until 1999. The Bhutanese can now send e-mail, surf the Web, play online games, and establish online businesses just like citizens in other countries. With an internet penetration rate of 48.1 percent, internet access in Bhutan is still limited to major cities (Internet Penetration Rate in Bhutan, 2021). Yet the modern-day Bhutanese entrepreneur or farmer does not have to go to an internet café or have a computer in his or her home or work space for internet access. Mobile phones are the preferred way to access the internet in Bhutan. The Bank of Bhutan even has an active mobile banking division (www.bob.bt) for mobile, connected Bhutanese. While digital marketing is a demanding activity, we believe the greatest challenges for the global digital marketer lie in countries with emerging economies—countries such as Russia, India, Nepal, Egypt, and China—which present different and sometimes difficult digital marketing decisions.

Emerging Economies

Countries vary in their level of economic development. Some countries, such as the United States, Canada, Japan, Australia, Great Britain, and Germany, have high levels of economic development with economists classify these countries as *developed*. Developed countries include all of Western Europe, North America, Japan, Australia, and New Zealand (Case and Fair, 2001). Countries such as these are highly industrialized, use technology to increase their production efficiency, and, as a result, have a high gross domestic product (GDP) per capita. A high GDP means that citizens have enough discretionary income to buy items that will make their lives easier, richer, and fuller. Developed countries are, therefore, ideally suited for the broad range of digital marketing activities discussed throughout the text.

It is difficult to find a single label to describe the rest of the world's economies. Rapid economic growth has brought some countries, such as South Korea and Chile, much closer to developed economies. One term often used for countries with rapidly developing economies is emerging. The single most important characteristic of emerging economies is that they all have a rapidly developing middle class. A growing middle class in any country creates substantial demand for a broad range of products and services. Countries with large populations thus have the greatest potential for developing a vibrant middle class—all things being equal. Four countries, Brazil, Russia, India, and China, represent the largest growth markets in the world. Collectively, these four countries are called **BRIC countries** or BEMs, big emerging markets. BRIC countries have more than 40 percent of the world's population and have received significant attention from many multinational corporations and entrepreneurs. For example, IKEA, the Swedish furniture retailer, has a strong Web presence in Russia (www.ikea.com/ru/ru/), China (www.ikea.com/cn/zh; www.ikea.com/hk/zh/), and India (http://ikea.in/).

The BRIC classification is useful, yet the dynamic market potential of other countries in the world has led some individuals to describe the next group of emerging market economies as **CIVETS** (Colombia, Indonesia, Vietnam, Egypt, Turkey, and South Africa). Digital marketers will see opportunity in a country such as Colombia, where over half of the population (58%) is internet connected. A similar relationship exists for Vietnam, where more than two-thirds of the population has internet access (How the Vietnamese Use the Internet, 2018). Digital marketers also see long term opportunity in CIVETS because of the large number of youths in each country (Arno, 2012). Globally, youth are digitally connected in ways that their parents never were and present ready-made segments for marketers.

Importance of Information Technology

Every country can improve its level of economic development through increased efficiencies in the production, distribution, and sale of goods and services. For countries with emerging economies, technology plays an especially important role. Although technology can, in general, boost a nation's overall production capacity and efficiency, it is through the application of information technology that countries with emerging economies can really open up new, exciting, global markets. Today, the internet, along with its supporting information technologies, can jump-start many national economies. India is a prime example of such efforts.

Bangalore, a city well known in India mainly for its wonderful gardens and mild temperatures, is now famous as the center of India's explosive growth in software and IT services. The epicenter of all this activity is a sprawling 330-acre industrial park called Electronic City. In Electronic City, one will find the corporate headquarters of Wipro and Infosys, two global giants that are leaders in this Indian information revolution. In addition, Electronic City is home to both well-known American companies (like Hewlett-Packard) and European companies (Siemens) that are outsourcing call center operations, medical transcription, and even income tax processing to India.

The internet allows businesses in emerging economies to instantaneously tap a global marketplace. While this is true for all companies that use the internet to communicate and deliver products through the Web, businesses that are completely Web-based at their founding are given a distinctive name. They are called **born global firms**. Born global firms understand that the Web, along with e-mail and digital communications, enables them to tap global markets immediately. Born global firms illustrate that successful marketing on the internet can leapfrog a company from nowhere to somewhere overnight.

Digital marketers from countries with emerging economies still have many challenges. Not only must they confront all the marketing issues and decisions described throughout this text, but they must also address some unique challenges related to the conditions of operating within a still developing nation. Some of the internet marketing differences between developed and still developing countries are fewer computer users, limited credit card use, lack of secure online payment methods, and unexpected power failures. We will now look at these challenges in more detail.

Country and Market Opportunity Analysis

As noted in Chapter 3, a digital marketing plan guides the marketer through the process of identifying and analyzing potential markets. Market similarity is very powerful, and the savvy digital marketer will understand and use it to her or his advantage. According to the concept of market similarity, marketers often choose foreign markets that have characteristics similar to their home market for initial market entry (Jeanette and Hennessy, 2002). Thus, a US-based company would first target countries such as Canada, the United Kingdom, and Australia before targeting France, Japan, or Germany. The well-known technology giant Amazon used a market similarity strategy to begin its international expansion. After developing its domestic presence in the United States, Amazon first entered Canada, then the United Kingdom. It then targeted France, Germany, and Japan. Three markets (the United States, Canada, and the United Kingdom) share a common language (English), but there are other market similarities across each foreign market: All these countries have high literacy rates, high internet usage rates, and clearly defined market segments willing to shop for books (and other products) online; in each country credit cards are widely used for purchases; each country has secure, trusted online payment mechanisms; and each country has efficient package delivery services.

While these may not seem like anything out of the ordinary for many of today's consumers, these are key features of smoothly implementing digital business practices. For Amazon, market similarity not only reduces (but doesn't eliminate) the risk of entry into foreign markets but also helps explain why it targeted these countries in the first place. Similarly, the increasingly well-known Brazilian cosmetic company Natura began its international market expansion by first targeting Spanish-speaking countries within South America (Argentina, Chile, and Peru) before entering Mexico (McKern, Yamamoto, Bouissou, and Hoyt, 2010). Common language and geographic proximity, supported by a Web presence that is adapted to each country, helped Natura become a global cosmetic brand whose more than 2,000 products are now available in more than 3,800 pharmacies worldwide.

Companies like Amazon continue to expand leveraging innovative strategies to enter new markets. In 2017, Amazon acquired the popular digital commerce company Souq to enter the Middle Eastern market (TechCrunch). This was in part to gain an instantaneous foothold by purchasing one of the leaders in the region along with its 45 million visitors per month. Such a strategy allows Amazon to take on the operations of an already successful online business instead of having to build up an organic following in Middle Eastern markets on its own.

Pankaj Ghemawat developed a framework called **CAGE** that helps explain the balancing act that digital marketers must engage in when they evaluate the similarities and differences between markets. Each letter stands for an important consideration that every global marketer, including digital marketers, must understand as they evaluate global markets: C stands for culture, A for administration, G for geography, and E for economics. Ghemawat suggests that the more similar two countries are in terms of CAGE, the more attractive they are for target market development (Ghemawat, 2007). The implication for digital marketers is simple: target similar markets before targeting dissimilar ones.

Diaspora Communities

Globalization helps explain the increased migration of individuals from one country to another. When a large number of people leave their home country and live together in a common neighborhood or city abroad, they become part of a diaspora community. Diaspora communities often want to maintain a relationship with their homeland. Digital businesses in countries with emerging markets use market similarity to target their own diaspora communities living abroad. For example, Tortas Peru (www.sorpresassperu.com) specifically targets members of the Peruvian diaspora community who would like to surprise friends and family living in Peru with homemade, traditional Peruvian cakes. All of the cakes are made in Peru for delivery to a Peruvian home market. Peruvian homemakers who need a second income to help support their families do all the baking.

Market similarity can also be seen in the phenomenon called **market convergence**, in which markets that were once very different become more similar over time. The Czech Republic is an excellent example of how consumers have matured into accepting online marketing and appear to have online shopping preferences and attitudes mirroring those of consumers in developed countries. By 2007, however, 97 percent of Czech consumers who used the internet said they were aware of online shopping. Sixty-two percent said that they either "loved" or "liked" the online shopping experience. When asked what motivated their online shopping, respondents said that it saved them money (65%) and time (24%) (Gemius, 2009). Today, the digital commerce market is expected to grow by more than 10 percent annually until 2023, with segments such as groceries, hobbies, cosmetics, and toys leading the way (2020 E-Commerce Payment Trends Report, 2020).

The Czech Republic has several online mega online retailers, such as www.heureka.cz, www.vltava.cz (a site where users can buy music, books, videos, and software), www.alza.cz (where one can shop for consumer electronics in English and German, as well as Czech), and finally www.aukro.cz, the Czech version of eBay. Market convergence is also evident in websites that enable Czech consumers to buy sports equipment like "jumping stilts" online (www.apo-vystoupeni.cz) to feel the adrenaline rush of bungee jumping (www.bungee.cz), and to experience a similar rush from listening to music from independent metal and deadhead rock bands (www.czechcore.cz).

One area where emerging digital markets differ significantly from developed digital markets involves online purchasing. We turn to this topic next.

Digital Commerce Payment and Trust Issues

Digital commerce in emerging markets is often hampered by the limited use of credit cards and the lack of trust in safely conducting online transactions. In contrast to the prevalent ownership of credit cards in high income countries, credit card ownership in low-income countries is quite different. In Egypt, Senegal and Pakistan, for example, a small percent of the adult population in each country owns a credit card (Togan-Egrican, English, and Klapper, 2012). While entrepreneurs and corporations use the Web to communicate with customers in each of those countries, the limited use of credit cards makes online purchasing more difficult until alternatives are available.

Marketers must also analyze relevant buyer behavior within a market. In addition to knowing how many credit cards are in circulation and what alternative payment platforms can be used in the country, digital marketers working in emerging economies should understand consumer attitudes toward online purchasing. A KPMG International study found that 13 percent of consumers avoid online transactions because they do not trust the online security ("The Truth About . . .", 2017).

Online security is essential for any digital commerce transaction. Some Brazilian websites have a unique security feature. Any individual that wants to make online purchases in Brazil must supply his or her CPF number. CPF stands for "Cadastro de Pessoas Fisicas" and is a unique number given to each individual who wishes to participate in the formal economy. A CPF is needed to open a bank account, to make major purchases (such as a TV set), buy real estate, apply for a job, and shop online. Without a CPF, Brazilian consumers can only buy major purchases from the informal gray and black markets. See the "Let's Get Technical" box for more details concerning online security.

Let's Get Technical—Transaction Security

You've been asked to launch a website in Brazil. Upon investigating you find that the Brazilians tend to be wary of internet credit card transactions. That wariness is understandable because in the past Brazilians were liable for all transactions made with a stolen credit card number. Because your company prefers to take credit transactions, you are worried. You need to educate consumers that credit transactions on your site are secure. But how? You are not sure that you understand much about it yourself.

Is concern over transaction security a legitimate concern? Are users afraid of the unknown, or are their fears the result of media hype? The answer to all three questions is "yes." Ironically, transactions are probably much more secure on the internet than in the brick-and-mortar world. To understand why requires exploring the technology behind transaction security.

Credit Card Number Theft

A credit card number could potentially be stolen in three different places on the internet. It could be stolen from a user's home or business computer; it could be stolen in transit from the user's computer to the merchant's website; or it could be stolen once it reaches the merchant's site. How likely is each of these scenarios?

1. *Stolen from the user's computer:* Unlikely unless users store credit card numbers on their computers.
2. *Stolen in transit:* Almost impossible. In fact this situation is unlikely to arise as long as vendors use a secure internet connection (https). Encryption algorithms (described later) make this possibility remote.
3. *Stolen at the merchant's site:* Probably the most legitimate user concern given the following possibilities:

   - The merchant may be fraudulent.
   - The merchant may be honest but have a dishonest employee.
   - The merchant may be honest but fails to adequately protect its database of credit card numbers from hackers. This is the scenario that regularly makes the news. For example, in August 2021, T-Mobile was hacked and information on 50 million customers was stolen (T-Mobile Hacker Who Stole Data, 2021). Interestingly, the response of hacked companies is surprisingly consistent. They offer users free credit monitoring for a year, and after that the user has to pay an annual fee in perpetuity in order to be protected.

One way digital marketers are addressing transaction security is through the use of encryption algorithms.

Encryption Algorithms

Encryption algorithms cannot stop dishonest merchants or employees; but they are designed to protect transaction information in transit. Try to read the following encrypted phrase:

JCRRA JQNKFCAU

You may have guessed that the key to decrypt this message is 2. All letters have been shifted two characters to the right in the alphabet.

A-B-C-D-E-F-G-H-I-J-K-L-M-N-O-P-Q-R-S-T-U-V-W-X-Y-Z

To decrypt we shift back two letters to the left.

J becomes **H**
C becomes **A**
R becomes **P**
R becomes **P**
A becomes **Y**

With continued decryption, the message "HAPPY HOLIDAYS" is revealed. Encryption on the internet works in a similar fashion except that the key is a big number that is almost impossible to guess, and the encryption scheme is a good deal more sophisticated than shifting along the alphabet. In fact, the industry standard RSA encryption scheme (named after the inventors Rivest, Shamir, and Adleman) has never been broken outside of university laboratories, and then only with weeks of effort by high-speed computers. This level of sophistication means a user's information is quite secure in transit.

When two computers on the internet communicate in secure mode, the messages are encrypted in both directions. The user's browser encrypts the credit card number and then sends it to the merchant; the merchant in turn encrypts confidential information sent back to the user. Each side uses a key to decrypt the other's message.

But how does the user get the merchant's key? If the merchant sends the key unencrypted, it could be stolen in transit. As amazing as it may seem, it is not a problem. In fact, merchants willingly give out what is known as a public key. However, the encryption algorithms are so clever that while the public key can encrypt the message, the same key cannot decrypt it. Only a complementary private key, which the merchant does not distribute, can decrypt the message—a process involving complex polynomial calculations and extremely large prime numbers.

Encryption protects the transaction while it is in transit between the user's computer and the retailer. Sometimes, however, the retailer does not adequately protect the records stored on its computer. In one security breach years ago, the online storefronts of ESPN SportsZone and NBA.com were "broken into." The hacker stole the credit card numbers and e-mail addresses of hundreds of customers. As proof, he then sent each person an e-mail message containing his or her card number.

How does this sort of theft happen? Most Web servers are secure if properly installed and maintained following best practices. But in the rush to get things done, information system professionals sometimes get sloppy: passwords are set to easily guessed names, passwords are loosely shared, or some accounts are enabled without passwords. Hackers usually begin by obtaining access to an account with limited access to protected computer resources. Using that account, they compromise an account with a bit more access. They continue to work their way up from account to account until they have sufficient access to compromise the system.

The exposure to hackers creates an incredible headache for the end user. You might want to use the same password on every site you visit. But if just one of the sites does not secure your password, then a hacker can obtain your e-mail address and password.

One solution is to use different passwords on different sites. But then how do you remember them all? Gatekeeper programs such as OnePass or LastPass store all of your passwords for every site that you visit. Even browsers such as Google Chrome and Safari will offer to remember passwords for you. Then you only need to remember the password for the gatekeeper.

But what if the gatekeeper password is compromised? Companies have become so worried about this potential breach of security that they highly recommend that users enable two-step verification on their accounts. Two-step verification is based on something you know—your username and password—and something you have—your phone. When you sign on, the company will text a code to your smartphone that you then enter as the second step of verification. That way someone who knows your username and password still cannot access your account since they don't also have your phone. If you have not set up two-step verification already, you really should for every site that accepts it. Usually once the device (phone or computer) has been verified, you don't need to two-step verify again.

Facebook and other sites protect their users by letting them know anytime their accounts are accessed from an unusual location—like a country halfway around the world. Facebook security is becoming increasingly important since a number of sites now offer to let you sign in using your Facebook credentials. With an increasing number of Facebook users growing concerned about their privacy on the site in its "post-trust era" (Pelletier, Horky, and Fox, 2021), this issue is likely to continue to be of interest.

Merchants can protect themselves from hackers by trying to break into their own systems or hiring professionals to do so. Professionals are able to recognize flaws in the security system of the merchant's computer and suggest remedies to make it more secure. Computer programs such as NESSUS, SARA, and SAINT are available for merchants to use to attack their own sites. And, of course, corresponding intrusion detection systems, such as Snort, Bro, Prelude, and OSSEC, can notify the merchant of an actual attack by recognizing the digital signatures of these attack programs. These software systems experience short-but-sweet product life cycles: first, a new attack program comes along, then a detection program is upgraded to counteract it, then a new attack program is designed, and the cycle continues with increasing sophistication.

One innovative solution to the credit card and online payment dilemma is eBanka (www. ebanka.com), which was founded in the Czech Republic. Established in 1998, eBanka is the oldest purely internet bank in Central and Eastern Europe. The bank issues credit cards (Eurocard, Visa, and MasterCard) and handles secure and efficient online money transfer accounts for online purchases. A customer simply opens an eBanka account, deposits money, uses that money to make online purchases, and deposits more money when the account balance is low. It is a version of digital cash. Because of eBanka's success, in July 2006, Raiffeisen International (RI), an Austrian bank, bought eBanka for €30 million. Polish online shoppers stated that the second most frequently used payment method was through bank transfer, a la eBanka (or an electronic postal money transfer to the online business's bank account). The most preferred payment method for Polish online shoppers? Cash on delivery (Polasik and Fiszeder, 2010).

Infrastructure Considerations

A country's physical infrastructure also influences online marketing strategy. Unless the firm's product is completely digital, online retailers of tangible products still need to solve the logistics problems of physically moving the product from one location (a warehouse) to another (a retail outlet, the consumer's home, or some other collection point). Road conditions in emerging market countries vary greatly, including the roads in major cities. India is well-known for congested city streets, with cars, auto rickshaws, carts drawn by water buffalos, and cows all vying for space on many roads. Transaction costs increase as the length of transportation time increases.

Countries with emerging economies are also prone to electricity blackouts. Nepal is a good example. One of the poorest countries in the world, with a gross national income per year of $1,155 per capita, Nepal is rich in many natural resources, including water (World Bank Open Data, 2020). Through the efforts of the United Nations and other international aid organizations, Nepal has built a series of hydroelectric dams throughout the country to address electricity access issues throughout the country. Most people living in Nepal's major cities of Kathmandu, Pokhara, and Nepalgunj have electricity. However, Pakistan averages 75 blackouts per month, Bangladesh has 64, and Lebanon 50 (Power Outages in Firms, 2020). When lack of electricity forces a digital business offline, the business is effectively closed. Running a digital business in countries with electricity shortages can be challenging, to say the least.

Technological Tipping Points

Solving credit card payment and trust issues are only two of several marketing challenges in emerging economies. Equally important for global digital marketers is the need to understand the seismic changes occurring in how consumers access online content. "Tipping point" is a phrase popularized by Malcolm Gladwell in a book with that title (Gladwell, 2000). A **tipping point** is that moment when an emerging trend or phenomenon becomes so big that it becomes irreversible. As the metaphor suggests, a tipping point changes the balance of things forever; there is no going back. Computer and mobile phone technology, along with the rapid development of broadband, are changing the way markets access and understand information, products, and services.

Legacy Technologies: Computers and Telephones

Clearly, customers need a mechanism for connecting to the internet. Historically, in every country, this has been through desktop computers and an internet service provider (ISP). For digital businesses operating in developed, high-income countries, connecting to the internet is generally not a problem. For consumers in emerging economies, however, owning a computer has been a significant barrier to access. For example, in a global survey done by the Pew Charitable Trust in 2015, the country with one of the lowest ownership rates was Uganda, with only 3 percent individual ownership ("Internet Seen as . . .", 2015). In Latin America, Chile had the highest computer ownership rate, with 72 percent, while Venezuela had 61 percent. Africa had some of the lowest computer ownership rates, such as 26 percent in South Africa and only 10 percent in Nigeria.

In Peru, 90 percent of households have internet access. However, most of that access is through mobile internet. The slower speeds of mobile connectivity do not seem to be a barrier to adoption (Chevalier, 2021a). Mobile internet represents a dramatic shift in usage trends from the telecenters (see Exhibit 4.2) or "cabinas publicas" of the early 2000s.

China is a highly stratified society. While luxury goods marketers such as Gucci, Louis Vuitton, and Prada find a growing market for their brands, the majority of Chinese consumers are in much lower income categories. Cyber cafes in China provide significant access to the internet, with hundreds of thousands of cafes operating in the country, and the trend is only expected to grow with the rise of augmented reality and virtual reality. All internet cafes

Exhibit 4.2 Peruvian Telecenter

provide access through desktop computers. Exhibit 4.3 shows a typical internet café in rural Guatemala, with older model desktops for customer use.

As wireless technology increases in its availability, landline telephones will become increasingly less useful and ultimately obsolete. When consumers depended on landline connections to the internet, many consumers were excluded from the market. The truly explosive growth of mobile technology has created a tipping point in many developing countries, and it is this phenomenon that we discuss next.

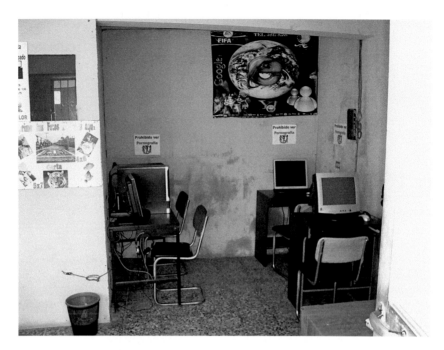

Exhibit 4.3 Guatemalan Internet Café

Wireless Internet Access: Mobile Phones

The explosive growth and diffusion of cellular telephones throughout the world has dramatically changed online marketing. Indeed, it is the most significant tipping point in computer information technology—ever. In 2007, John Tysoe, cofounder of the British mobile phone company The Mobile World, made this statement, "[The cellular industry] took over 20 years to connect the first billion subscribers, but only 40 months to connect the second billion. The three billion milestone will be passed in July 2007" (Ridley, 2007). Tysoe was on target. Forrester Research expects global smartphone subscribers to reach 5 billion by 2024. Indeed, mobile phone—and now internet-connected smartphone—use is huge.

Nowhere is this great sea change more evident than in Africa, the most underserved—and underdeveloped—continent in the world by traditional measures of connectivity (number of landline phones and number of internet users). But while less than 1 percent of the African population has fixed broadband connectivity, over 33 percent have mobile data through their phones. Contrast this with Europe, where 33 percent have broadband connectivity and 99 percent have mobile data (Ericson Mobility Visualizer, 2021). Just having a cell phone, however, does not eliminate the challenges of wireless digital marketing. Digital marketers must still determine how to modify existing website content for the smaller screens on cell phone displays; how to develop new content that consumers will want; how to price services; and how to develop easy, secure payment methods. Digital marketers must also understand that consumer behavior with the mobile internet differs from consumer behavior with stationary desktop computers or even laptop computers.

Sixty-five percent of the world's population, or 5 billion people, send text messages. So even in countries with relatively low broadband internet, marketers can still use text messaging (44 Mind-blowing SMS, 2021). Zalora (www.zalora.com), an online retailer in the Philippines, used SMS messaging when it wanted to increase both brand awareness and online sales in the Philippines. Since SMS is a high volume, quick response strategy, Zalora was able to not only find lower income men and senior Pinoy consumers (Pinoy is the colloquial term for Filipinos) but was also able to further develop a marketing relationship with them through the responses to multiple SMS messages. Similarly, Pantene shampoo used SMS messaging as a strategy to increase its short-term sales with women living in Jakarta. Pantene sent women an SMS message offering them a discount on shampoo. When interested women replied, they not only received a personalized message telling them the benefits of Pantene but were also sent a discount voucher redeemable at Carrefour, a well-known hypermarket. Pantene sales increased 31 percent in two days.

Wise digital marketers, however, must look not only look at the magnitude of these numbers but also at the consumer behavior that stands behind them. For example, Chinese consumers are much more likely to use messaging apps such as WeChat than default messaging platforms that come installed on smartphones such as Apple's iMessage.

Finally, a short note on the impact of mobile phone connectivity. Cambodia is a country that does not receive much attention outside of Southeast Asia. But in 1993, Cambodia became the first country in the world to have more mobile telephone subscribers than fixed-line telephone subscribers. Why? Price is part of the answer. Even in 1993, cell phones and the accompanying technology for mobile networks were less expensive than fixed-line telephones. But country history also provides a clue. Cambodia's recent political history includes a long and violent civil war (the movie *The Killing Fields* is about this war). During this conflict, the Khmer Rouge, one of the warring political parties, planted 4 million to 6 million land mines throughout the country (U.S. State Department, 1998). Digging up the ground to lay telephone cable is simply too risky in Cambodia. As a result, mobile phones and mobile phone networks found and satisfied a large unmet need in Cambodia. Digital marketers are served well when they place technology within a country's historical context.

Smartphones

Globally, smartphone use is on the rise. In fact, a recent study noted that smartphone adoption rates were the fastest of any technology innovation—ever. This study found that smartphones are being purchased and used ten times faster than the computer revolution of the 1980s, two times faster than the internet boom of the 1990s, and three times faster than social media adoption ("iOS and Android Adoption Explodes Internationally", 2012). China is the leading market for smartphones in 2020, followed by emerging Asia/Pacific and North America ("Global Smartphone Sales", 2021). Given the wide use of smartphones in the United Kingdom and United Arab Emirates, PizzaExpress, a London-based pizza restaurant, leveraged a successful domestic digital marketing campaign when it entered the United Arab Emirates. Downloads of a PizzaExpress app in the United Arab Emirates allowed not only fast and simple pizza ordering but also easy identification of UK expatriates working in the United Arab Emirates. Identification of UK citizens living outside the country is another example of diaspora marketing. PizzaExpress also encourages easy interactions with consumers through its relatable posts that invite people to order in-person and online and then share their dining experiences using #PizzaExpress.

Broadband

Broadband, or high-speed internet access, illustrates another significant tipping point. There are nearly 1.8 billion broadband lines worldwide in 2020, with the largest percentage growth predicted to come from emerging markets. Only 15 percent of households worldwide have a fixed (wired) broadband connection, with a high of 33 percent in Europe and a low of less than 1 percent in Africa (Johnson, 2021a). The laws of supply and demand generally apply to broadband pricing, and it is not surprising that global prices continue to decline as more individuals and firms subscribe to broadband. The United States ranks 15th in terms of average download cost per megabit, at $1.50/mg. Average monthly cost for a broadband subscription in the United States is $80. Consumers in other countries pay less for broadband on a per month basis, with China averaging $60 and the United Kingdom averaging $55 (Weinschenk, 2017). The rapid development of broadband networks in developed and developing countries is creating new opportunities for digital marketers.

However, hope is on the horizon, literally, in the form of satellite broadband and high-speed mobile. The recently launched SpaceX constellation of satellites aims to provide broadband access to underserved areas worldwide. This will create broadband access where there was none before and broadband competition where providers previously had a monopoly. The key to the SpaceX constellation is that the satellites are in low earth orbit, which means that there are few signal delays. On the mobile side, LTE and 5G networks provide wireless broadband connectivity. The penetration rates for mobile broadband are much better with a worldwide rate of 75 percent and a high of nearly 100 percent in Europe and a low of 33 percent in Africa. So the future may indeed be wireless.

The Digital Divide

Computer and information technologies are changing how consumers access and use information, yet from a marketing perspective there are still significant differences between countries and consumers in those countries. This division between those who have access to information and those do not is termed the **digital divide**. Even in fast-developing China, there is a digital divide. In urban areas, internet penetration rate is around 80 percent, while in rural China, internet penetration is 56 percent ("The 47th Statistical Report on China's Internet Development", 2021). However, this gap is rapidly narrowing due to massive government investment in internet infrastructure for underserved areas. CNNIC (2010, 2012), the Chinese government agency that reports internet statistics, reported that this gap was caused by a combination of high internet costs relative to rural income, less knowledge of the internet itself, and inadequate infrastructure ("The 47th Statistical Report on China's Internet Development", 2021). Although we have described the explosive growth of mobile phones in emerging market economies, there is a gender divide that is especially pronounced in least developed countries (LDCs), where 15 percent of women access the internet, compared to 86 percent of women in developed countries ("Bridging the Gender Divide", 2021). The digital divide raises challenging questions for global policy makers, international businesses, and local entrepreneurs. What responsibilities, if any, do these different groups have for narrowing the gap between those that have and those that do not have access to technology? Should a digital business in Calcutta, India, be competitive with a digital business in Cali, Colombia? Numerous initiatives around the world are working to bring internet technology and digital commerce capabilities to LDCs. One such effort is the "One Laptop per Child" campaign spearheaded by Nicholas Negroponte. Negroponte's goal was to design a portable laptop that would cost around $100 for children living in LDCs. Some innovations in Negroponte's laptop were using Linux as the laptop's operating system, having a sunlight-readable screen so that children can use it outdoors, and building in a hand crank to generate power. The laptop does not need electricity to work. Exhibit 4.4 shows a picture of the laptop, production of which began in November, 2007. Further information can be found at Laptop.org.

Exhibit 4.4 One Laptop Per Child (www.laptop.org)

Building Inclusive Digital Markets

Peter Drucker, perhaps the greatest management theorist of the twentieth century, said that business has only two core activities: marketing and innovation. Drucker's strategic insight is nowhere better illustrated than by the innovation that is occurring in the poorest of global markets—at the base of the world's economic pyramid. That phrase, **base of the pyramid**, has been used to describe the 4 billion people who live on less than $2 per day. The United Nations, the World Bank, the World Economic Forum, the Asian Development Bank, and the Inter-American Development Bank, among others, are working to reduce the income inequality that exists in many least developed and emerging market countries. Microfinance and microlending, both of which are clearly targeted at helping poor individuals develop economically sustainable businesses, are also part of this revolution. As noted previously, the explosive growth of mobile phones throughout the developing world is enabling digital marketers to reach base of the pyramid consumer segments in interesting and creative ways.

Mobile banking is the one of the most successful digital marketing efforts in countries that are the least economically developed. Low-income individuals around the world lack security for their money. Many of the worlds "unbanked" (the shorthand phrase used to describe this market) live either in rural areas or in tightly packed slums. Slum life can be very violent and is often filled with material and financial theft. Banks generally do not operate in such environments. Poor individuals living in rural, remote areas face a different problem: there are simply not enough people living in any one village to make it profitable for a bank to have offices there. Mobile banking is the innovative, market-based solution that solves these problems.

Safaricom, the African subsidiary of the UK-based cell phone giant Vodafone, is a good example of m-banking. In 2007, Safaricom developed a new product called M-PESA (www.

safaricom.co.ke). *Pesa* is the Swahili word for *money*. An agent, usually a dealer of a cell phone service authorized by both the bank and Safaricom, registers users and installs an application onto customers' phones. This application allows other users with the same application to send money to each other. Once installed, customers can pay bills, send money, and store money—all through their mobile phone. This means that a migrant worker who lives in a remote rural area but has traveled to Nairobi to find work can easily send money back home. Taxi drivers also find benefit in mobile banking, since they now have less cash on hand for would-be bandits.

The success of M-PESA in Kenya has been impressive. Seventy-two percent of Kenyans are M-PESA m-banking customers—not too bad for a country that had about 38 million inhabitants and 13 million cell phone users in 2007 (Kelsey, 2020). Success has also brought competition. MTN, Africa's largest cell phone carrier, headquartered in South Africa, and Zain, a Kuwait-based, pan-African cell phone carrier, are also aggressively marketing mobile banking services throughout Africa (Economist, 2009). Banks and cell phone carriers profit from the resulting transaction fees.

Least developed countries (LDCs) have low annual per capita incomes, and one of their dominant characteristics is that many or most inhabitants work in agriculture, sometimes subsistence agriculture. These farmers are often stereotyped as having no discretionary income. This is incorrect, and digital marketers are leading the way in breaking that myth. Digital marketers know that creating value for target markets is essential for market success. In countries that are heavily agricultural, mobile applications for farmers are making them more productive. For example, Farmer's Friends in Uganda is a Web application that allows rural farmers to ask questions ("How can I get rid of tomato blight?" or "My chicken's eyes are bulging. What should I do?"), to receive answers to their questions through SMS, and to find out what the daily commodity prices are for their crops so that they can sell them at fair market prices. Digital marketers have developed similar mobile apps for farmers in India: M-KRISHI® ("krishi" means "agriculture" or "farming" in Hindi). Often, farmers need specific information about weather as well as about pesticide and fertilizer use. M-KRISHI® allows rural Indian farmers to send questions about the any of these items through a simple text, voice or picture interface (see Exhibit 4.5). Farmers receive prompt responses and, most importantly, information tailored to *their* specific plots of land. Productivity and crop yields have increased.

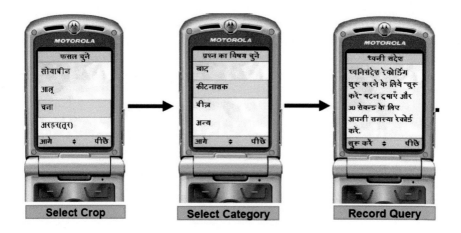

Exhibit 4.5 Screenshot of M-KRISHI® for Rural Indian Farmers

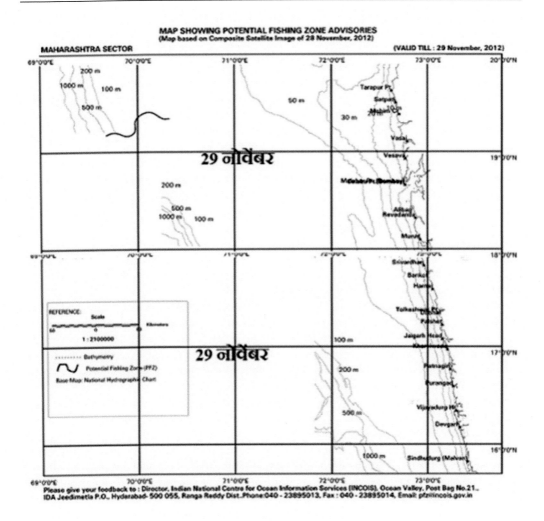

MAP SHOWING POTENTIAL FISHING ZONE ADVISORIES
(Map based on Composite Satellite Image of 28 November, 2012)

Exhibit 4.6 Demonstration of M-KRISHI® for Fishermen

Rural Indian farmers pay 200 rupees (about $4.20) for a three-month subscription. The success of M-KRISHI® for farmers has recently led to the expansion of the service for fishermen (see Exhibit 4.6). Digital marketers know that consumers will pay for services that create value.

Digital marketers targeting rural consumers in India face another challenge. Many of these consumers live in media dark parts of the country. *Media dark* refers to those rural Indian communities that have no access to radio and TV. A combination of factors may make a village media dark. A village, for example, may not have electricity; no one living in the village may actually own a TV or radio; or no one in the village can afford the monthly subscription fee for a satellite connection. Hindustan Unilever, the Indian subsidiary of Unilever, developed an innovative way to reach media dark rural Indian consumers through its iShakti program. IShakti consists of electronic kiosks set up in rural villages through which local residents can obtain free health, hygiene, employment, agricultural, and legal information. Content is delivered through voice and streaming video, since many rural consumers, especially women, are illiterate. IShakti complements Hindustan Unilever's main Shakti project in which rural women are trained as Shakti ammas to sell Unilever products in their village. ("Amma" means "mother" in Hindi and is often used as a general term of respect for elder women in India). IShakti positions Hindustan Unilever as a socially responsible partner within the village, while it simultaneously co-brands Unilever products.

Digital marketers targeting low-income consumers in urban areas can use a wider array of electronic strategies, since urban life incorporates all consumers within a rich media landscape. Casas Bahia, the largest retailer in Brazil, selling electronics, appliances, and furniture, illustrates the creative use of Web strategies with base of the pyramid consumers. Casas Bahia's core consumers are street vendors, maids, cooks, and construction workers—individuals who earn minimum wage and who often work several jobs. These individuals tend to live in the densely populated Brazilian slums called *favelas*. In 2008, Casas Bahia, in fact, opened a retail store right in heart of Paraisópolis, one of São Paulo's largest slums.

Extending credit to very low-income consumers is at the center of Casas Bahia's success. In contrast to banks and other lending organizations that would never extend credit to low wage consumers and seasonal workers, or if they did would charge very high interest rates, Casas Bahia has developed a unique in-store financing process. Consumers apply for purchase financing at an individual store. The store approves credit based on proof of address and not being blacklisted by a Brazilian credit rating agency.

Casas Bahia (www.casasbahia.com.br) was clever in its digital marketing strategy. On the one hand, for the small percent of consumers who can pay with a credit card, the website functions as a standard online digital retailer. On the other hand, the site's primary purpose is to drive traffic into the store. Once inside the store, Casas Bahia staff have the possibility of upselling customers and, of course, including them in the store's branded consumer credit program—where the higher profit margins are to be made.

Another example of clever digital marketing from Brazil involves the most popular soap opera ever to air on Brazilian TV: *Avenida Brasil* (*Brazil Avenue*). Like all soap operas, the plot is complex, yet the main story line is about the romance between a single mother living in a *favela* and a soldier sent into the *favela* to keep the peace because one of the main characters is seeking revenge for the death of her father in that same *favela*. The final episode brought all of Brazil to a halt—literally, with even the president of Brazil viewing. The final episode alone had over 500 advertising deals, and Proctor & Gamble aired 10 commercials for brands such as Pampers (www.pampers.com.br/), Oral-B (www.oralb.com/brazil/), and Wella Koleston (www.koleston.com/pt-br/), all of which have localized Brazilian websites. Other global brands advertising on the final episode also included Volkswagen (www.vw.com.br), Kia (www.kiamotors.com.br/), Trident chewing gum (www.tridentbrasil.com.br), and Mastercard (www.mastercard.com/br) (Chao, 2012). Additionally, one of the characters, Monalisa, operated a beauty shop in the soap opera and now has her own line of branded beauty products in the home market, which are available on cosmetics website embelleze.com (www.embelleze.com), keyword search "monalisa."

Social Networking

Perhaps nowhere is the convergence of new technology (the increased use of mobile and smartphones) and access to information (mobile broadband) more evident than in the increased importance of social media in the digital marketing integrated communications toolkit. As of 2021, 4.2 billion social media users were reported worldwide. This is over half of the world's population, and users average over two hours per day on social media. Filipinos spend the most time on social media, averaging over four hours per day, while Japanese spend just under an hour (We Are Social, 2021).

Facebook is the social network giant; there are Facebook users in about every country in the world. Yet Facebook penetration varies by country and, in fact, may not be the dominant social networking site in certain countries. VKontakte (vk.com) dominates social networking in Russia. Hence, when the Clearasil brand of skin care and acne medication products wanted to increase its market share with Russian teens, it created a brand page on Vkontakte that allowed users to post photos and exchange information on the site (vk.com). When integrated with Clearasil apps (one of which would allow users to remove blemishes and pimples from their photos), Clearasil experienced a 30 percent sales increase within one year. Of course, if Clearasil was to launch a similar marketing program today, they would certainly add the social network site Odnoklassniki (www.odnoklassniki.ru), which is a popular social network site in Russia.

Global digital marketers understand that Russia is not unique in having strong, very popular local social networking sites. In 119 countries, Facebook is a market leader. Instagram is more popular in countries such as Botswana, Namibia, and Indonesia, and some African countries prefer LinkedIn. Twitter dominates Japan, while QZone leads in China ("World Map . . .", 2017).

Although the number of Facebook users varies widely by country, forward thinking digital marketers are integrating Facebook into their overall marketing strategy. Debenhams, a large mid-market retailer from the United Kingdom, is but one example. Debenhams now targets consumers living in Armenia through its Armenian Facebook page. Debenhams is a very popular Facebook page in Armenia, along with LightStyle clothing and Ashtakrak Kat, a local dairy. Debenhams was an early adopter of branded Facebook pages targeting consumers in emerging market countries. Marketing to Nigerian shoppers has been especially successful. The flagship store in London has multilingual Facebook ads that include Hausa, one of the local languages in Nigeria. Through Debenhams' Facebook page in Armenian, Debenhams is now reaching shoppers in the Trans-Caucasus region with hoped-for similar results.

Finally, Sproxil is a company that integrates many of this chapter's ideas. Sproxil is a born global firm that was founded in 2008 by Ashifi Gogo, a Ghanaian entrepreneur with a strong telecommunications background. Sproxil markets a mobile phone app specifically designed to combat the $200 billion trade in counterfeit drugs. Gogo had witnessed firsthand the consequences of taking counterfeit medications. Ghana had low internet access through desk and laptop computers but had high mobile phone and mobile internet penetration rates. Consumer ease of use, driven by a mobile product authentication (MPA) app that uses simple text messaging to tell a consumer whether the drug she or he has purchased is fake or not, has helped grow the company significantly. Sproxil's business model is to sell the printed labels with authentication numbers and SMS directions directly to pharmaceutical companies and distributors who, in turn, place them on their products to assure authenticity. For consumers, the authentication process is not only simple but also duplicates the process of recharging (i.e., adding money) to a SIM card. Sproxil first tested its mobile app in Nigeria and has since expanded into Ghana, India, and East Africa. Sproxil's parent company, Devex, uses social media such as Facebook, Twitter, Instagram, LinkedIn, and YouTube to reach consumers. Sproxil is a born global firm that uses mobile phones and social media in emerging market countries not only to generate profit but also to make the world a better, more humane place to live.

Chapter Summary

Within a worldwide business-to-consumer (B2C) market of billions of consumers, some countries have higher penetration rates of internet access, usage, and shopping. Among the many factors affecting internet penetration are income, infrastructure, computer ownership, telecommunication availability and pricing, social and cultural traditions, business attitudes, and wireless Web access. Digital marketers must carefully research each country's current market conditions and environmental factors before selecting specific targets for entry.

Internet usage is growing so rapidly outside the United States that users from other countries will increasingly dominate the internet. This growth is creating opportunities and challenges for digital marketers to target or operate in countries that are less developed than the most highly industrialized nations. Emerging economies are those with low levels of GDP per capita that are experiencing rapid growth. Not only can technology generally boost a nation's overall production capacity and efficiency, but also information technology can help countries with emerging economies open up promising global markets.

In the course of analyzing country and market opportunities, digital marketers in emerging economies that target markets in developed countries must understand market similarity. Digital marketers in emerging economies that market within their own countries or those in developed economies that want to target groups in an emerging economy must understand market differences. In general, digital marketers that target emerging economies must deal with a variety of challenges, including limited credit card use, lack of secure online payment methods, consumer attitudes toward online purchasing and payment, limited computer and telephone access, slow connection speeds that affect webpage download rates, and unexpected power failures. Enterprising digital marketers have reacted to these challenges with innovative solutions.

Many countries, including those with emerging economies, have more mobile telephone subscribers than fixed-line telephone subscribers. As a result, digital marketers must consider how to modify Web site content for small cell phone displays; how to handle text entry using tiny keypads; how to develop appropriate content for wireless Web users; how to price services; and how to develop appropriate payment methods. Digital marketers also must understand how consumers behave with the mobile internet.

Consumers living at the base of the world's economic pyramid are increasing being targeted by digital marketers. Perceptions of low-income consumers as not being able to use technology, as not wanting quality products and services, and as not being able to afford such products are shown to be inaccurate. Low-income consumers provide significant market opportunity for digital marketers when products and services fulfill meaningful consumer needs. The extensive use of mobile phones by base of the pyramid consumers is providing a new platform for digital marketers to reach this new market.

Exercises

Review Questions

1. What is an emerging economy?
2. How can countries with emerging economies make use of information technology?
3. What is the concept of market similarity, and how does it apply to companies that target foreign markets?
4. Why is credit card payment a conundrum in emerging economies?
5. How do computer and telephone ownership affect digital marketing in emerging economies?
6. Why must website designers consider connection speeds in emerging economies?
7. What are some of the electricity problems faced by digital marketers in emerging economies?
8. How is wireless internet access likely to influence digital marketing around the world?
9. What is the digital divide, and what does it mean for digital marketers?

Discussion Questions

1. *American Idol* **Story.** What differences do you see between the US version of *American Idol* and those in other countries? Use material from this chapter to explain the reason for those differences.
2. *American Idol* **Story.** Do you think that this brand needs to be consistent worldwide to maintain a desired brand image? Explain.
3. Do you agree with the observation that the global internet will drive styles, tastes, and products to converge and create a more homogenous global marketplace? Why or why not?
4. Knowing that many consumers in emerging economies are wary of buying online, what would you do, as a digital marketer, to encourage them to change their attitudes and behavior?
5. What are the advantages and disadvantages of digital marketers creating fast-loading, low-graphics versions of their websites to accommodate slower connection speeds in emerging economies?
6. What responsibility do you think digital marketers should assume for helping to close the digital divide? Do you think consumers and governments should assume some responsibility as well? Explain your answers.
7. What is the advantage of a mobile currency such as M-PESA? How can digital marketers leverage this type of technology?
8. How serious is the online threat from Chinese companies? Are Chinese companies more likely to succeed globally in some product or service categories than others? Explain your answer.

Web Activities

1. Visit Internet Usage Statistics at www.internetworldstats.com. According to this site, what percentage of the world is currently online? How has that changed since this book was written? Divided by region, which areas of the world show the highest percentage for online usage? In comparison to the United States, what are the usage patterns of those in Europe and Asia? What trends in internet adoption and usage do you think will occur as the internet continues to mature?
2. Visit the UPS Website at www.ups.com. If you wanted to deliver a package to Paris, France, what steps would you have to take to complete the transaction? How has UPS made the process easier? What languages other than English are available to UPS customers? What difficulties might you run into when delivering to an address that doesn't use English characters? How does UPS address these issues?
3. More Web sites are providing pages in languages other than English. Visit Google.com and select language tools. What types of services does Google provide for specific languages and countries? Try translating an entire Web page into a different language and view the results. What languages are compatible with these feature sets? What efforts is Google making to translate sites from languages that are currently unavailable?

Acknowledgment

This chapter was contributed by Al Rosenbloom, Associate Professor of Marketing at Dominican University in Illinois (arosenbloom@dom.edu). In 2001, Rosenbloom was a Fulbright Scholar and taught internet marketing to MBA students in Nepal. This chapter is based on his experiences in a number of emerging economies, with particular emphasis on Far Eastern nations, including Nepal, India, and China. Research for this chapter was conducted by Juan David Gomez.

Chapter 5

Ethical and Legal Issues

The main goal of this chapter is to help you explore the ethical and legal issues that digital businesses face in marketing online. You will learn about the current and emerging issues that have caused concern among a variety of stakeholders, including digital businesses and consumers.

After reading this chapter, you will be able to:

- Compare and contrast ethics and law.
- Discuss the implications of ethical codes and self-regulation.
- Identify some of the main privacy concerns within traditional and digital contexts.
- Explain some of the important patent, copyright, trademark, and data ownership issues related to the internet.
- Highlight key ethical and legal concerns related to online expression.

SOFTWARE INFRINGEMENT

Have you ever broken the law while sitting at your computer? Most people would probably say no—not recalling the times they installed computer software that they did not purchase (sometimes called software **piracy**). Infringement of copyright in software occurs when people download copyrighted software from the internet without a license, loan copyrighted software to others, or install copyrighted software on more computers than is allowed under their software licenses. Counterfeiting occurs when copyrighted software is duplicated and distributed to others without the consent of the copyright owner. Both infringement and counterfeiting violate US copyright laws and are illegal.

So what is the big deal? Suppose you spent months writing a best-selling novel and then learned that thousands of people were copying it instead of buying it. That copying would cut into your income and reduce your enthusiasm for writing more novels. Infringement of software copyrights creates a similar situation. The firms creating software use the income from their software sales to pay for innovative upgrades and new products, which they cannot do or do as much if they lose income. Also, software makers must raise the price paid by legitimate buyers to replace income lost to infringement.

This cause-and-effect relationship between protection and innovation plays out around the globe. The United States, Japan, and most of the countries in Europe are examples of countries producing and protecting trillions of dollars' worth of new software every year. In stark contrast, Asian-Pacific countries with very weak software copyright enforcement—like China, India, and Vietnam—cost software owners billions of dollars in lost revenue. The United States has the lowest rate of software infringement in the world but still lost $9.5 billion in

DOI: 10.4324/9781003247319-7

commercial revenue due to piracy in 2018, according to The Software Alliance (BSA). Globally, approximately 37 percent of the software sold is an infringing version. Cutting this number by even a third would create millions of jobs and generate hundreds of billions in new economic growth around the world.

What can companies do? Microsoft, one of the main victims of software infringement, uses several methods: it proposes intellectual property legislation, files civil lawsuits, and creates non-infringement technologies such as digital rights management (DRM) security programs embedded in its software. Critics have argued that security measures like DRM do little to stop sophisticated international counterfeiters while making legal use of the software more difficult for the average user. Microsoft has tried numerous such measures, including the implementation of a system that sniffs out users' hard drives while they were online, but privacy advocates objected. In the end, Microsoft and many companies like it believe that education is the best weapon. Many people who use infringing software do not know they are stealing, and it is not against the law or against cultural norms in many countries. For example, executives in some countries believe that if they buy one copy of the software, they can use it as they please, as with other products. Infringement and counterfeiting remain huge problems for the software industry—problems that are unlikely to be solved for a long time.

Overview of Ethics and Legal Issues

Scholars often treat ethical and legal issues as separate, even unrelated, subjects. In reality, ethics and law are integrally related. As we will see, **ethics** frequently concerns the values and practices of professionals and others who have expert knowledge of a specific field. Ethics is also a general endeavor that considers the concerns and values of society as a whole.

Law is similar to ethics in the sense that it, too, is an expression of values, but while ethics may be directed toward individual or group endeavors, laws are normally created for broader purposes, with the goal of addressing national or sometimes international populations. In the Anglo-American tradition, law is made by legislatures such as Congress or Parliament, enforced by executives or agencies, and interpreted by the courts. In all these instances, it is a public endeavor, which is reflected in the fact that law is often the result of political and social compromise. Additionally, law attempts to be consistent in both time and place, so that citizens will be familiar with their rights and obligations.

Because law results from combinations of interests, beliefs, and goals, the processes that lead up to the making of laws are often slow and complex. Unfair laws, a common by-product of one-sided lobbying efforts, overly generous political contributions, and other special influences, have been the focus of criticism and call for reform. The problem has become so unwieldy that it prompted one of the world's premier copyright scholars, Lawrence Lessig, to consider a bid for Congress, running primarily on the platform of reducing political corruption.

Even in a perfect world of no political corruption, new laws cannot anticipate every nuance of how people and companies will push the proverbial legal envelope months or years down the road. New laws regulating the internet are at a particular disadvantage. Given the speed with which the internet landscape changes and the slowness with which laws are enacted, some laws are nearly obsolete by the time they are passed. Similarly troubling, even when Congress passes "good" laws, many questions remain concerning the meaning of the law itself or about how the law is to be enforced. Thus, aggrieved parties file lawsuits demanding courts interpret these laws and determine their impact on particular conflicts. Administrative agencies such as the **Federal Trade Commission (FTC)** also promulgate rules and opinions governing online activity, although many of these may be guidelines as opposed to laws. Given the complexity of the task, efforts to tame online transactions can be slow, particularly within the new and often unfamiliar context of digital communication. For example, social media influencers long promoted brands without disclosing that they were being paid to do so, until the FTC stepped in with a disclosures guide for influencers to help social media users understand their relationships with brands (FTC, 2019).

Ethics make important contributions to legal developments, influencing lobbyists, legislators, and eventually judges. The filtering that takes place as an ethical tenet moves from idea, to law, to **enforcement** interferes with what would ideally be a seamless legal enforcement of an ethical precept. As a result of this imperfect system, laws do not correlate directly with ethics. Ethics can be a casualty of the debates and compromises that end up dictating the metes and bounds of a resulting law. Problems like legislators' weak grasp of complex information technology issues, biased lobbying efforts, and the large time lag between online innovations and laws that govern them mandate that the law itself be merely the beginning and not the end of the ethical inquiry.

Laws lag far behind online innovations. Ethical debates surrounding these innovations, however, happen in real time, which is why consumer monitoring is top of mind for many companies today. It is critical that lawmakers understand innovations clearly before trying to mold the laws governing them. Digital marketers play a crucial role in assisting legislators. Legislators seeking insight into the complex ethics of a particular online issue look to experts and real-world entities for guidance. Impressions from the trenches are lawmakers' most unvarnished source of information concerning the ongoing ethical debate.

Ethics and Ethical Codes

The study of ethics has been in existence for more than 2,500 years. The central focus of this study is the analysis and description of such basic concepts as right and wrong and how we judge the difference. An important dimension of this investigation concerns the types of conduct that make up ethical behavior. These tasks necessarily involve the examination of rights, responsibilities, and obligations. Ethical inquiry is not limited to purely theoretical boundaries. Rather, questions are studied at all levels of human interaction and often appear as political, legal, and commercial issues. Consequently, the scope of ethics is virtually as wide as its subject matter. Similarly, many types of ethical positions compete against each other for acceptance.

A particularly important aspect of ethical inquiry involves the study of professional activities. Traditionally, groups of individuals possessing special skills or knowledge have established codes and systems of fair practice. A classic example is the Hippocratic Oath of physicians. Ethical standards work both externally and internally. They help to communicate consistency and trustworthiness to the community at large while also assisting in maintaining stability and integrity within the profession. In these ways, ethics are both pragmatic tools and essential elements of professional identity.

Documents such as the American Marketing Association's (AMA) *Statement of Ethics* reflects the recognition of a commitment to the exercise of honesty, responsibility, transparency, respect, citizenship and fairness within all professional transactions (see http://ama.org/codes-of-conduct/ for the full code). In addition to articulating overall values, professional codes provide members with guidelines that are specific to their pursuits. They are often products of the combined experiences of practitioners, scholars, and the public that are passed along to the entire membership and eventually published. Historically, codes have been interpreted or revised to respond to changed circumstances and new issues. In the past, these processes have been relatively gradual, with modifications often coming in conservative degrees. Today, this situation has changed.

Modern technology presents a radical challenge to marketing ethics as well as to those of other professions. The extent of this demand is perhaps best reflected in the revolutionary features of the computer itself. When compared with other major technical advances such as the printing press, telephone, or automobile, digital media is arguably unique in its capacity for speed, ubiquity, and versatility. Computers serve as data collectors, compilers, and disseminators. They represent the fastest-growing form of communication and, through the internet and similar systems, forge global links of unprecedented proportion.

These factors create vacuums in ethical policy. Although they do not directly challenge such general ideals as fairness or honesty, digital processes and potentialities are so new that ethics, like many other social endeavors, is only beginning to adapt itself to the computer revolution. Currently, many critical issues confront those who work within electronic environments, including the ownership of intangible data, often termed *intellectual property*; the role of privacy in a virtual world without walls, locks, or doors; the extent to which freedom of expression should be allowed; the uses of data, including methods of collection; and the special status of children who use digital networks.

Easy solutions are seldom achieved within ethics or law, and in the electronic context, progress is complicated by a lack of comparative historical situations. Likewise, the ability to analogize computers to objects or institutions with which society has had greater experience is often questionable. Is the computer network more like a broadcast station, a printing press, or a public library? Our current lack of experience in these matters makes it difficult to say for certain. Finally, the fact that electronic spaces are global in nature accentuates the earlier observation that ethical positions are by no means agreed upon. What is accepted in Europe may be rejected in Asia or America.

The seemingly limitless opportunities afforded by computers also suggest the need for the constant assessment of their implications. Each participant in electronic marketing is given not only the responsibility to adhere to professional codes but also, in a very real sense, the unique opportunity to contribute to these standards in a meaningful way.

The Problem of Self-Regulation

Although law and ethics are frequently directed toward the same goals and often provide mutual assistance in the examination of complex problems, one emerging area of conflict involves the role of formal law in the regulation of online conduct. Throughout their tenures, the administrations governing the United States throughout the internet years have expressed the position that the development of the internet should be largely left to the free operation of the market. Within such a system, rather than mandate behavior through legislation, **ethical codes** developed by trade associations, commercial standards groups, and various professional organizations dictate appropriate behavior of participants.

Supporters of the self-regulation model point to the private sector's ability to rapidly identify and resolve problems specific to its areas of competence, particularly when compared to the seemingly confusing, contradictory, and lengthy processes of the law. According to this view, problems encountered within technological environments are particularly amenable to the expertise possessed by market actors. Once consensus is reached, uniformity is achieved through members' compliance with ethical codes, as well as by ongoing education of providers and consumers. Although the law cannot normally force anyone to adhere to these codes, many believe that improved consumer confidence resulting in enhanced economic opportunities will ensure voluntary compliance.

The most stunning example of self-regulation took place in the wake of the US Capitol riot of January 2021. Following the riot, social media giants Twitter and Facebook banned

President Trump from their platforms, effectively cutting off his voice and his ability to incite another riot. Arguably there is no way that such swift action could have taken place through legal channels. On the other hand, opponents of the ban argue that private companies should not have more power than the president of the United States.

Critics of self-regulation argue that its incentives are insufficiently compelling. They note that perpetrators of fraud and deception frequently benefit from schemes of short duration and are rarely interested in the long-term gains offered by adherence to ethical codes. On a broader level, it has been suggested that commercial self-interest and pressures to maximize profits compromise the private sector's ability to police itself and that, absent the type of sanctions only the law can provide, true deterrence cannot be achieved.

Although the resolution of this debate is far from over, recent policy-making activities indicate that governments are asserting themselves more frequently in internet regulation and control. Issues of online privacy, data protection, and particularly internet crime and fraud prevention already have been addressed by many countries.

The Australian Competition and Consumer Commission (ACCC), the Office of Fair Trading in the United Kingdom, and the consumer protection agencies in several other countries, including the United States, have already implemented various programs aimed at decreasing the spread of online deception.

The International Consumer Protection and Enforcement Network (ICPEN), an organization uniting consumer protection authorities from more than 65 countries, conducts annual internet sweeps to detect online traders that defraud consumers. In 2001, the ICPEN created the "econsumer," a network website that gathers digital commerce consumer complaints and shares this information with the participating law enforcement agencies. Today, the organization runs a series of educational campaigns during Fraud Prevention Month seeking to educate consumers and businesses about online protection.

The Interactive Advertising Bureau (IAB) in the United States comprises hundreds of leading companies who develop and execute digital marketing campaigns reaching consumers all over the world. The association also sets standards and promotes ethical guidelines among members while advocating for the industry. Independently operated, there are more than 45 IABs globally located in North America, South America, Africa, Asia, Asia Pacific, and Europe.

The FTC in the United States likewise considers detection and suppression of domestic and international fraud to be a priority. It regularly holds different seminars and trainings sessions for internet users as well as posts many useful tips and recommendations on https://consumer. ftc.gov/identity-theft-and-online-security/online-privacy-and-security, the website developed specifically for the purpose of online fraud prevention.

The number of new governmental agencies, private and non-for-profit companies, and associations fighting online fraud keeps growing worldwide. With a wave of new devices and users connected to the internet, organizations assist in developing safeguards for consumers who are not always aware of the apparent risks.

The "Get Safe Online" campaign in the UK provides helpful information and practical guidance to internet users and prevent internet fraud.[1] The project, also broadly supported by major businesses, has proven to be very successful. The National Cyber Security Division (NCSD), a division within the Department of Homeland Security (DHS) created the "Stop. Think. Connect"[2] campaign aimed at improving internet security awareness and educating the public about common methods to detect cyber threats.

Even though heightened governmental involvement appears to be an increasing response to many online issues, it is significant to note that lawmakers in the United States and elsewhere have entered into a close dialog with private entrepreneurs, public interest groups, and commercial associations. Such arguably unprecedented instances of cooperation and sharing of resources suggest that future regulations will take the form of "networked responsibility" among many participants.

Privacy

The concept of **privacy** encompasses both ethical and legal aspects. It is also relatively new to both disciplines. Perhaps more than any other legal or ethical issue, privacy is a product of the twentieth century. Although many cultures follow established customs of social boundaries, detailed consideration of this subject did not come about until 1890, when Samuel Warren and future Supreme Court justice Louis Brandeis published an article that urged the recognition of a right to privacy within American law. This protection was defined as the "right to be left alone."[3] Significantly, many of the justifications for this new idea were reactions to the phenomena of a maturing industrial and technological age, including the mass distribution of newspapers, the development of listening devices, and the widespread use of photography. In essence, privacy's young tradition has always been about information and the means of its delivery.

Although it has been the subject of constant debate since the Warren and Brandeis article, privacy has proven to be an elusive concept, both ethically and legally. One reason for legal confusion is the lack of any specific privacy provision within the Constitution. This situation was recognized in the US Supreme Court's 1965 decision of *Griswold v. Connecticut*,[4] which held that privacy in the use of contraceptives could be inferred from a number of enumerated Constitutional rights, including those of association, freedom from illegal searches and seizures, self-incrimination, and the quartering of soldiers. Through the Fourth Amendment to the US Constitution, the privacy of the home has been established against governmental agencies, which are required to obtain warrants before entering upon and searching a dwelling. This provision is, however, applicable only to officials or those acting on their behalf and not against private individuals.

In addition to Constitutional developments, privacy has been addressed in the common law. **Common law** refers to decisions, presumptions, and practices traditionally embraced by Anglo-American courts. The common law has established a series of privacy violations that, both individually and together, form the basis of invasion of privacy lawsuits. They are arranged into four categories: unreasonable intrusion into the **seclusion** of another, unreasonable publicity of another's private life, the appropriation of another's name or likeness, and the publication of another's personal information in a false light. These elements are codified in many state statutes and appear in the influential legal treatise *Restatement of Torts*.[5]

Despite these developments, much disagreement remains as to what privacy entails. Identified central attributes fall into three general areas. The first is the Warren and Brandeis concept of a right to be left alone, often referred to as the *seclusion theory*. Privacy within this perspective is the ability to remain isolated from society. This model encourages laws and ethical standards that are oriented toward maintaining personal distance and punishing those who cross the limits set by individuals. A second intermediate theory, known as **access control**, does not presume isolation as a norm but places its emphasis upon laws and standards that enable persons to reasonably regulate the information that they are giving up. Expressions of this model can be found in laws and standards that empower individuals to protect personal material from unauthorized release.

Both seclusion and access control models provide measures of protection, but their focus is concerned more with how information is released and less with what actually constitutes private data. A third theory, known as the *autonomy model*, attempts to provide such a definition. It does so by identifying private matters as those necessary for a person to make life decisions. This model entails freedom from the coercive use of personal information as well as the ability to be alone when reflection is necessary.

In addition to presenting difficulties in definition and scope, privacy exists as one value among many. Within society, privacy interests routinely compete against concerns of personal and public safety, economics, and even the social and psychological need for association with others—a process that can require the divulging of sensitive information. The ways in which these interests are coordinated involve complex balances that can result in difficult choices. Often people are willing to give up personal information for benefits they perceive to be worthwhile—credit cards, frequent flyer mileage, and security precautions in airports are but a few examples. In such cases, ethics and law attempt to provide guidelines helpful in critically examining definitions, priorities, and implications.

Privacy Within Digital Contexts

Information plays a pivotal role in the concept of privacy, as well as that of marketing and electronic commerce. It is, therefore, not surprising that conflicts about how data should be collected and used have developed.

A starting point for this discussion is the privacy policy of any corporate brand website or social networking site. Such policies often promise to uphold the privacy of users, which can be difficult to apply to the internet's many information-gathering mechanisms and parties with whom information can be shared.

The most common means by which this type of data is obtained is through the use of cookies. Cookies are packets of data created within a user's hard drive in response to instructions received from a webpage. Once stored, cookies can be retransmitted from a user's computer to a pertinent website. Cookies serve many purposes. For example, they may handle online information, creating features like shopping baskets to hold purchases. They may recall stored sales information to remind users of items already ordered or to suggest new products. Significantly, cookies may collect other data, such as full name, e-mail and postal addresses, phone numbers, a computer's geographic location, and the time logged online.

Although cookies may be configured within a browser to run only with explicit permission, they are normally automatically executed without any user action. Cookie packets may be combined with other digital information and may be transferred between servers or sold on the open market. User tracking occurs when cookies are appended and examined in the course of a user's online travels. The result is an ability to pinpoint an individual's online behavior. With the integration of offline data, such tracking takes on a more encompassing, and more troubling, dimension.

They presume most users wish to receive the benefits of targeted advertising. This position reflects the view that privacy is only one of many values to be balanced. It generally supports an opt-out policy which presumes that data collection will take place but still allows users to withdraw consent by a variety of methods, including sending e-mail to collectors requesting removal from their databases.

Pro-privacy critics of opt-out presumptions point to the fact that most users have no significant knowledge of how computers operate or process data. They question whether the average person will take the steps necessary to withhold data and suggest that many opt-out routines are confusing and thus are unlikely to be successfully accomplished. Commercial proponents of opt-out solutions emphasize consumer surveys that reveal a preference for targeted advertising and argue that the data necessary to provide this service should be collected unless otherwise denied. Industry has not developed a widely accepted solution to the challenge, although opt-in is considered a best practice. Some companies have developed routines that do not allow the sharing of their visitors' information with other websites.

Apple Computer has made privacy a hallmark of their brand and part of their marketing campaign. In December 2015, Apple refused to help the FBI unlock the iPhone of a San Bernadino terrorist, arguing that giving law enforcement a back door to the iPhone created a potential for exploitation by criminals as well. In fact, the iPhone was designed so that even Apple could not unlock it. In April 2021, Apple announced App Tracking Transparency to deal with marketing privacy. Apps are required to ask iPhone users if they wish to be tracked. The preliminary results are that only 3 percent of users choose to be tracked. Predictably, many companies, especially Google and Facebook, lobbied vigorously against the feature, since it prevents them from precisely targeting ads to individuals. The position taken by Google and Facebook is that they are doing consumers a service by giving them targeted ads rather than ads for products for which they have no interest. The position makes sense even if it is a little self-serving.

More recently, websites like Facebook have come under fire for using the personal information of their users. Facebook has been accused of using users' personal information in advertisements and sharing this information with third parties.

While Facebook provides methods for limiting the disclosure of personal information, critics argue these methods are intentionally complex and often misunderstood by users. While some users have deleted their Facebook accounts in response to the distribution of their personal information, deleting a Facebook account can be as difficult as trying to prevent disclosure of personal information in the first place. Users have even called for the creation of an "open source" alternative to Facebook, which gives users the ability to control all aspects of how their personal information is displayed and shared.

While wholesale exploitation of personally identifiable information has decreased since the turn of the century, technology has increased the ways in which such information is collected. Accordingly, while the impact may not be as noticeable to consumers, the usage is more widespread. Adding to the problem is the confusion over what websites do with the information they collect. Nearly every major website collects some type of personally identifiable information. Many, however, do not specify exactly how the information will be used. For several years, industry has recognized that privacy is a significant consumer concern. This realization has prompted a greater use of privacy policies, including a more extensive use of opt-in routines.[6] It remains to be seen, however, whether these outward expressions will translate into greater protection of private information or merely serve as a cover for greater, more widespread exploitation of personally identifiable information.

In addition to issues of data collection, the problem of access to data is of fundamental significance within the context of online privacy. In this area, the status of sensitive information is not only a matter of hardware security but also one of administrative policy. The majority of privacy-related debates focus on traditional methods of data processing and the recently developed but already well-established use of cookies. Beyond these technologies, cutting-edge applications promise to gain popularity and to raise additional issues.

Java is a Web-friendly programming language that allows the downloading and running of programs or applets on individual computers. These applications are increasingly used to provide such enhancements as dynamic animation, Web-based simulations, and other useful additions to plain hypertext. Java may also be used to design programs known as **hostile applets**, which can be used to surreptitiously access and transmit data on hard drives, including e-mail addresses, credit card records, and other account information.

Intelligent agents are a growing topic of interest within Web marketing and computer science research. The products of developments in artificial intelligence agents are programs that, once released by a user, can function autonomously online to make electronic decisions. Some potential tasks include the searching of sites or the buying of products that conform to an individual's tastes or interests. Critics of agents worry that the preferences they hold may be chosen or controlled by entities other than their "owner." Such a situation would limit the individual's ability to make autonomous decisions and could create an incentive to distribute personal information contained in the agent applications.

Cookies, Java applets, and intelligent agents are ubiquitous applications; that is, they are able to function in the course of nearly any online session without a user's knowledge or control. The ease of their operation explains why some sites would not want to inform users that data is being collected. This objectionable attitude places technological ease above ethical principles. Similarly, because much of the information is not of an explicitly confidential character, it may be tempting to disregard privacy implications. This argument ignores the fact that even apparently innocuous data may, when combined, result in very specific information.

In addition to application-based collection, sites may gather information through online forms and e-mail, often in exchange for browsing privileges or other benefits with or without the full disclosure of the terms of use. Regardless of how it is elicited, the use of information as a form of currency has raised ethical questions, particularly when most average users (as well as information experts) are understandably uncertain of the ultimate value of the data. Although such valuation may indeed be challenging, consumer education about all uses of revealed data has been suggested as a solution to help users make informed judgments in this area. Information may also be gathered through explicitly fraudulent methods—an approach that has unambiguous ethical and legal implications.

A particularly active area of study involves the collection of material from children. In response to research, reports of abuses, and lobbying from parents and other advocates, Congress passed the **Children's Online Privacy Protection Act (COPPA)**[7] in 2000, which requires that websites and other online media that knowingly collect information from children under 13 years of age (1) provide notice to parents; (2) obtain verifiable parental consent prior to the collection, use, or disclosure of most information; (3) allow parents to view and correct this information; (4) enable parents to prevent further use or collection of data; (5) limit personal information collection for a child's participation in games, prize offers, or related activities; and (6) establish procedures that protect the "confidentiality, security, and integrity of the personal information collected." In addition, the FTC, as required by Congress, enacted specific rules to govern and enforce the act.[8] One major change brought about by the act is the increasing presence of data collection policies on sites used by children and the provision of an active means, such as a click button, for parents to confirm their awareness of these practices. The challenge is that in today's environment, where parents share information about their children on social media (a practice known as "sharenting"), often at the request of brands (Fox and Hoy, 2019), COPPA may not be enough to uphold children's online privacy and safety.

While federal laws relating to internet privacy remain in debate, many explicit offenses can be addressed by conventional criminal statutes. Sanctions for misuse of consumer data are present in the **Fair Credit Reporting Act**[9] and the **Electronic Communication Privacy Act (ECPA)**.[10] Additionally, organizations such as TrustArc have developed comprehensive guidelines and even software for Web privacy. One troubling development within this area is a decision of a federal trial court to dismiss a class action suit that alleged breaches of privacy policies by an airline. The dismissal was based, in part, upon the court's finding that even though an allegedly violated privacy policy was posted at the airline's site, the plaintiffs did not claim to have read its contents and therefore had few actual privacy expectations. Critics of this decision claim that requiring such a showing would impose an enormous burden upon those attempting to enforce Web privacy policies, essentially making those policies worthless.

The problem of privacy within e-mail remains an unsettled aspect of online interaction. Under US law, users who operate e-mail accounts on private services (those that are not advertising supported) are generally assured of their legal privacy through service agreements with their internet service provider (ISP). In addition, the ECPA addresses the privacy of ISP clients, with certain exceptions that include situations in which e-mail is inadvertently discovered through system maintenance. The opposite condition applies to employees who use their organizations' computers or networks to communicate. Here, the current law generally extends no expectation of privacy to workers, particularly those employed by nongovernmental entities. Many companies emphasize this status in memoranda of policies, but even when such notices are absent, the employee's wisest course of action is to assume that all material that passes through workplace facilities is monitored. Ethical questions remain as to whether strict surveillance policies adequately reflect reasonable expectations or values of personal autonomy and integrity. Compare this to laws that prohibit unlimited monitoring of employer-owned phone systems or dressing rooms.

Most recently, the **California Consumer Privacy Act of 2018 (CCPA)** addresses new privacy rights for California residents. According to the State of California Department of Justice, it offers increased consumer protection in the form of the right to:

- know about how a business collects, uses, and shares personal information;
- delete personal information collected;
- opt-out of the sale of personal information; and
- not be discriminated against for exercising CCPA rights.

While the CCPA is a step in the right direction for consumer privacy protection, it is still critical that consumers are educated about the importance of protecting their data so as to make the best possible decisions about their online safety and security as they arise.

International Privacy Issues

On an international level, privacy issues have also received close attention. The most comprehensive privacy legislation so far has been developed by the European Union (EU). In 2018, the General Data Protection Regulation (GDPR) was passed by the EU and applies to any organization that targets or collects data related to people in the EU. The new regulation sets forth stricter rules for personal data processing and greater responsibility for those personal data operators that violate legislative requirements. According to GDPR.eu, it focuses on data protection principles such as lawfulness, fairness, transparency, data minimization, accuracy, storage limitation, and accountability.

While most Asian countries have no overarching privacy laws, there is growing attention being paid to the issues of personal data protection. For instance, in Thailand, the Personal Data Protection Act (PDPA) became law in 2019 and is largely based on European policies. The PDPA recognizes that individuals have the right to control how their personal data is collected, stored, processed and disseminated. Because of the global pandemic, companies have until 2022 to comply. Although there is much debate over which privacy policies most evenly balance corporate and individual interests, the following norms identified by the FTC

Exhibit 5.1 FTC Online Privacy Policy

Source: www.ftc.gov/

represent a consensus regarding the minimum requirements in the ethical use of consumer information (Exhibit 5.1):

1. *Notice:* Users should be aware of a site's information policy *before* data is collected.
2. *Consent:* Users should be allowed to choose participation or exclusion from the collection.
3. *Access:* Users should have the ability to access their data and correct them if erroneous.
4. *Security:* Policies to ensure the integrity of data and the prevention of misuse should be in place.
5. *Enforcement:* Users should have effective means to hold data collectors to their policies.

The FTC has been actively involved in development of additional recommendations for the internet community that would help to improve personal data protection. It has established an extensive framework for companies involved in the collection and processing of personal data.[11]

The framework expresses concerns about the methods used by large internet service providers to process personal data of online users. It also encourages personal data operators to promote consumer privacy; introduce reasonable safety measures for personal data protection, retention, and disposal; limit collection of personal data only to such information that is specifically necessary for their business purposes; and to ensure accuracy of personal data and implement procedural protections (e.g., internal policies and regulations) in order to enforce the data protection principles. It also indicates that companies should develop clear and transparent privacy guidelines for consumers and provide them with an adequate mechanism to access, modify, and control their personal data and its collection. The FTC report demonstrates a current global trend that even though the government allows self-regulation in data collection, it is gradually increasing its control over it.

Digital Property

A primary function of law is to define ownership, but this is constantly being challenged by the mercurial nature of digital technology. Traditionally, the law protected intangible or intellectual property through three basic mechanisms—patent, trademark, and copyright laws. It is important to note that none of these areas of law protect ideas. Rather, they protect inventions, expression, and brands.

Patent law is centered upon inventions and the ability to reproduce or manufacture an inventor's product. **Copyright** addresses the realm of creative expression—specifically, the right to publish, duplicate, or alter expressions of ideas. **Trademark** is concerned with brands—source identifiers that consumers use to identify and distinguish products and services in the marketplace. It is important to note that these categories have been flexible, and often the boundaries between them have been modified by legislation and the courts. In addition, international treaties can redefine both distinctions and protections.

Computer-based communication poses particularly difficult problems for intellectual property. These communications may incorporate elements of patent, copyright, and trademark or any combination thereof. A single communication may contain (a) a novel way of communicating covered by a patent; (b) text and pictures protected by copyright; and (c) proprietary branding covered by trademark law.

Patents

The application of patent law to computing is a continually developing field. Under conventional American law, patents are granted by the US government for inventive processes or steps.[12] Grounded in English legal foundations and the heritage of conventional invention, the law is tailored toward industrial or mechanical concerns. In 1998, the case of *State Street Bank & Trust Co. v. Signature Financial Group, Inc.* held that a computer program could be patented. This ruling has since been expanded to include other methods of doing business. Since *State Street*, online businesses have been making use of this type of patent protection. A primary motivation for this may lie in the fact that, unlike copyrights, patents prevent competitors from doing the same thing a different way. However, like copyright, American patent powers derive from constitutional concerns. Thus, public access to patented material is assured after the term of the patent has expired and the patent itself is always on file with the government.

The inclusion of software under patent law is largely based upon the assertion that programs describe inventive processes. A contrary opinion holds that software at its root consists of algorithms—formulas that are generic in nature and therefore cannot be owned by anyone. A similar criticism states that programs are merely schemes or plans that machines actually execute. The details of both sides' arguments are complex and promise to be the subject of much future debate, litigation, and, perhaps, congressional action. An area of current internet focus centers on the use of *business patents* that describe such activities as marketing approaches and methods for conducting commerce. Patent protection has been claimed for reverse online auctions, secure credit card processing, and incentive-based methods for reading website advertising. When the Patent Office first started granting patents on business methods, the review process was less than vigorous. Many overly broad patents were issued in a short period of time. Opportunistic companies bought large numbers of these patents and began filing infringement lawsuits around the country. These patent trolls are still around, reaping millions of dollars in royalties every year for doing nothing but threatening to sue on somewhat suspect patents.

An example of the attempted enforcement of a software patent is found in the claim that secure digital time-stamping is a unique and protected process. Critics fear that if this assertion is upheld, the majority of online encryption routines will be affected. Similarly, in *Amazon.com v. Barnesandnoble.com*, the plaintiff (Amazon.com) relied upon a patent to allege that it alone had the ability to use *1-Click* ordering routines—a now-common practice within the internet.[13] The matter was settled in 2002 without final judicial resolution, and the details of the settlement have not been disclosed.

The US Patent Office recently decided to increase the rigor with which it reviews applications for software-related protection. Likewise, both courts and Congress are being called upon to carefully examine whether historical data supports the inclusion of software and business practices within a patent's ambit. Advocates of inclusion argue that the granting of patents in these areas will encourage productivity and innovation. Critics argue the opposite, stating that both the encryption matter as well as the unanswered issues of the *Amazon* case point to the potentially stifling and monopolistic effects of patent law's strong protections.

Copyright

At this comparatively early stage of online legal development, copyright appears to be established as the primary means of protecting most expression on the internet, including text and other data. In the conventional world, copyright has protected expressions of ideas in such formats as books, recordings, and film. Under American law, copyright law is derived from the Constitution as a protection established for the benefit of the public. Chief among these protections are the doctrines of fair use and of first sale.[14,15,16] Fair use consists of the ability to copy—without cost—reasonable portions of protected material for purposes of such public activities as education, news reporting, and editorial comment. The doctrine of first sale limits the ability of a copyright holder to obtain profit from the sale of his or her work after the initial time at which the material is sold. Purchasers are subsequently given the ability to transfer or otherwise dispose of their copy. The first sale doctrine is viewed as benefiting such institutions as public libraries and can also increase access to intellectual material through discounts such as those offered by used bookstores. The issue is unsettled when it comes to digital property such as music downloads.

The **No Electronic Theft (NET) Act**[17] became law in 1997, conferring copyright protection for computer content and imposing sanctions when infringement is committed for commercial or private financial gain or by the reproduction or distribution, either commercial or noncommercial, of one or more copies of copyrighted works having $1,000 or more in retail value. Punishment under this provision may include criminal prosecution. While proponents believe that the NET Act will encourage innovation by protecting material placed on the internet, critics believe that the definition of *infringement* has been made problematically broad by shifting its traditional meaning, which is normally associated with permanent or semipermanent reproduction (known as fixing), to now include electronic distribution without reproduction. It is argued that such acts could include the mere perusal of digital material through a Web browser and thus make criminal activities of what has been previously protected by the First Amendment. Additional criticism has been directed to the use of criminal sanctions, particularly at a time when there is great debate about the economic value of electronic material.

A related law is the **Digital Millennium Copyright (DMCA) Act**.[18] The DMCA is a complex piece of legislation that contains several provisions. It grants ISPs protection from acts of user infringement as long as certain procedures are followed, including the prompt reporting and disabling of infringing material. Supporters of this legislation claim that the DMCA will free ISPs from liability for its users' illegal actions and thus encourage industry growth. Critics believe that the reporting and disabling requirements may cause innocent behavior to be presumed infringing and wrongfully censored.

The DMCA also criminalizes the circumvention of software protections and the development or distribution of circumvention products.[19] As with the NET Act, DMCA supporters believe that this law will increase commercial willingness to place material on the internet by deterring online infringement. Although some exceptions exist for educational and scientific activities, critics maintain that the DMCA goes well beyond this goal by banning the development of innocent and useful applications that may have minor circumvention capabilities, giving copyright holders a veto over any development that they perceive as a challenge to their profits.[20]

The DMCA was enacted in part to comply with the World Intellectual Property Organization's (WIPO) Copyright Treaty and the WIPO Performances and Phonograms Treaty.[21] These documents set forth international standards for copyrighted material and were recently ratified by the United States. Treaty proponents argue that, in a global networked environment, international consensus regarding ownership, protection, and transfer of digital property is essential. As with the DMCA, critics argue that the specific laws required by the treaties unfairly favor copyright owners.

There have been serious efforts made by Congress to pass legislative acts aimed at establishing stricter guidelines for internet companies operating websites involved in copyright infringement. The **Stop Online Piracy ACT (SOPA)**[22] and the **PROTECT IP (Preventing Real Online Threats to Economic Creativity and Theft of Intellectual Property, or PIPA) Act**[23] have called for enhanced enforcement against individuals and companies engaged in copyright infringement. The introduction of these bills caused a great storm of protests among the internet community and its supporters. Google, Mozilla, Facebook, Twitter, Yahoo, and many other internet companies opposed these acts, warning consumers against the fatal consequences of the proposed legislation to the open internet. Due to the enormous pressure caused by numerous boycotts and picketing, the bills were rejected. But the issues of online copyright infringement remain very important, and an open dialog between the internet service providers and those lobbying for stricter regulation is needed.[24] While privacy tends to be a bipartisan issue, consumers are wise to carefully investigate the positions of all parties and look past the talking points.

Trademarks

Trademark law is the area of intellectual property that governs source identifiers for goods or services. At its heart, trademark law is a consumer protection law. Under the federal **Lanham Act**,[25] trademarks may be registered with the government. Registered or not, however, they may still be protected under the act. To pursue an infringement case, claimants must prove that the trademark is *protectable*. Generally, the more distinctive (unique) the mark, the greater the strength of this claim. The act also prohibits **dilution**—the unauthorized use of famous trademarks in association with goods or services that is likely to lead to a lessening of the uniqueness of the trademark.

There are two types of dilution: **blurring** and **tarnishment**. Blurring results from activities that reduce the "distinctiveness" (uniqueness or brand recognition) of the famous mark. Tarnishment occurs when the famous mark is cast in an unflattering light.

Trademark law has recently been applied to the internet-naming system. Domain names (aka domains) are unique configurations of letters or numbers that are used to route data. The most familiar examples of domains are addresses of websites, for example, www.google.com. In addition to designating websites, domain names are also used in e-mail addresses. As the primary means to reach commercial destinations, the significance of these identifiers is obvious.

Although the creative application of language provides for many distinctive names, it is inevitable that some similarity will occur. For example, "General Signpost" can plausibly be thought to resemble "General Sign," but traditionally, trademark law has been able to allow such similarities because trademark protection is typically limited to a particular class or classes of goods or services. When enough dissimilarity of goods or services exists, overlap in the similarity of brands is permitted.

Another type of trademark violation is known as **cybersquatting**. This activity involves the registration of domain names that resemble or duplicate the names of existing corporations or other entities. The initial registrants are typically unrelated to the institution at issue. The domain name is then offered for sale at a price far greater than that originally paid. Under the **Anticybersquatting Consumer Protection Act (ACPA)**,[26][27][28] a person is liable if, in bad faith, he or she registers, traffics, or sells a domain bearing a name that is identical or confusingly similar to a protected trademark or which would dilute the worth of the trademark. The act makes it easier to place notoriously elusive cybersquatters under the control of the court system and allows for swift possession by a successful complainant of the disputed domain name. Heralded by trademark holders, the act has received criticism similar to that lodged against the DCMA, specifically, that the swiftness of the transfer of contested domain names may unfairly deprive a defendant of a proper hearing and due process.

Let's Get Technical—Digital Products as a Paid-for Service

There was a time when music, movies, and software were primarily distributed on CDs and DVDs. In the old model, when you bought a disk, you licensed the music or software with the right to play or install it. The primary distribution method now is over the internet. Internet distribution supports a different pricing model—one that relies more on subscription services.

A by-product of this shift is that producers can offer low-end products for free (or ad supported) with the ability to upgrade to a fully featured or ad-free offering. One reason for the free offerings was to stem the tide of music and software piracy. In the not-so-distant past, there was a feud between music fans and the music industry over the illegal distribution of music. Users, especially younger users, would regularly download thousands of illegal songs from websites, robbing the industry of revenue. There were even high-profile cases of the music industry going after college students for piracy. The industry fought back by encoding the music so that it could not be copied. But fans wanted to copy their music to play it on different platforms. Furious fans smashed and burned CDs in public displays of outrage. This adversarial dynamic was not good for business.

Now users can get free music online as long as they are willing to listen to ads. Spotify is a great example—80 million Spotify users listen to ad supported music; another 60 million have upgraded to an ad-free account. Either way, the music industry gets its revenue and the fans are happy. Some internet users even access music through YouTube, where artists often upload music videos as part of their social networking efforts.

But if this works for music, then why not software? Software is a little trickier. You are not going to be happy if Microsoft Word stops for 30 seconds to show an ad in the middle of writing your term paper. An alternative solution is for Microsoft to offer a limited functionality version of Word for free, with the ability to upgrade to a fully functional version (Office 365). Younger users will normally be happy with the free version; business will need the functionality (e.g., mail merge) of the paid version. And the paid version is now a subscription rather than a one-time cost.

Similarly, in the smartphone space, there are often free and paid versions of the same product. The free version usually has more limited functionality or is ad supported. The paid version has full functionality and is ad free. Power users and businesses have the need and can afford the paid version. Meanwhile, the company is building goodwill and developing future paying customers with the free version.

So the real issue for software vendors is how to stop piracy of the paid version. They do this by tying each version to a unique user with an authentication key. Upon installing the software, the computer user is allowed to either run the software for a certain number of days or open it a certain number of times. Once the user activates the software online, the limitations are removed. The activation stops software piracy because it allows the software associated with the product key to be activated only once, and thus it can be installed on a limited number of computers—usually from two to five.

Apple, always an innovator, was one of the first to acknowledge that some forms of copying are reasonable. Buy an app on your iPhone or iPad, and you can install it on multiple devices that you own as long as all the devices are tied to your Apple ID. This works especially well for families that have multiple devices and do not wish to buy separate apps for all the devices. Buy a movie on iTunes and you can watch it streamed from the cloud or download it to your iPad or computer. All of the permissions are keyed to your Apple ID.

A big advantage to users of a subscription service is automatic updates. There is no financial incentive to stay with an old version of the software if free updates are available to you as a subscriber. Many vendors even allow users to choose automatic updates. This is also an advantage for vendors. Users are likely to be happier and promote the product by word of mouth if they are using the most advanced version of the product.

There are other advantages to vendors as well. Customers continue to pay each year in perpetuity. The incentive to steal software and music is removed by the free services. Finally, vendors know who their customers are and can market other products and services to them.

Trade Secrets

The field of trade secrecy has taken on new proportions with the advent of online technology. A trade secret is an economically valuable business secret that is not generally known or readily ascertainable. The federal **Economic Espionage Act** of 1996[29] was enacted in part to address digital advances and now makes it a criminal offense to divulge trade secrets, which are broadly defined to include such areas as commercial, scientific, and technical endeavors. Trade secrets can include but are not restricted to formulas, market data, algorithms, programs, codes, and models. They may be stored online or in tangible formats. Significantly, computer-based disclosures such as e-mails, downloads, Web publications, and similar means are within the scope of the act.

Employees with access to trade secrets may be prohibited from engaging in similar businesses for a period of time—so long as the time and geographic scope of the restriction are reasonable given the nature of employment. In one notable case, a court determined that an employee's particular skills in Web marketing were sufficiently protected under a noncompetition agreement with a former employer to prevent him from working for a competitor within a one-year period following his departure from a company.[30]

Another important act in trade secrets law is the **Uniform Trade Secrets (UTSA) Act**, which was introduced by the Uniform Law Commission in 1979 and amended in 1985. Forty-eight states have adopted it.[31] The main purposes of the UTSA is to unify the existing trade secrets legislation across all 50 states and, consequently, to provide certainty to US businesses that their confidential information will be protected uniformly throughout the country.

Data Ownership

It is not an overstatement to say that the online world runs on data. Not surprisingly, access and ownership questions relating to data and databases abound in current legal and ethical debate. As the electronic market becomes more competitive, attempts to obtain the advantages provided by control of information are becoming more numerous.

Until recently, data relating to such technical issues as website usage were easy to access and were often shared among site owners, marketing professionals, advertisers, and consumers. Currently, a new technology is being introduced that would make information collected from banner advertisements invisible to site owners and their clients. These *click data* have been important in determining such factors as site content and marketing strategy. Such protective technologies raise new issues concerning the ownership of information that is both a necessary element of online interaction and of extreme value in itself. A particularly significant question is whether the *fencing in* of data will achieve the same status as the more formal application of copyright, patent, trademark, or licensing laws. This process will challenge the model of cooperation that has been a characteristic of online dynamics and, arguably, a primary reason for the success of the interactive digital medium.

Another complex issue involving online data is an activity known as **spidering**. This process involves the use of software applications called *robots* to enter targeted websites and obtain data for the use of their owner. A final area of consideration is that of the special protection of data relating to facts. As previously noted, US copyright law protects *expressions* of ideas but not the ideas themselves. This distinction is owing to the public policy emphasis of protecting the raw material of free expression and national learning. For similar reasons, copyright cannot be used to protect facts. Because electronic databases often contain arrangements of facts, a movement is growing within the law to protect specially compiled or *sui generis* data.

The **Agreement on Trade Related Aspects of Intellectual Property Rights (TRIPs)** of 1995 is part of the World Trade Organization's (WTO) program of international treaties. Provisions within this agreement set forth *sui generis* protection. The EU's Database Directive[32] also includes protection for compiled facts. Currently, the US Congress has not adopted a *sui generis* law.

Arguments favoring *sui generis* protection revolve around the belief that this type of protection will afford an incentive for database vendors to create more of their products by assuring them of potential return on their investments and that their product will not be copied or diluted. In the long run, society will benefit from the increase of databases, which would in turn help decrease the price of information.

Critics of these laws argue that no economic proof indicates that such incentives would produce an increase in databases or that, with an increase, prices would necessarily come down.

Instead, they state that worries about copying and dilution can be addressed through encryption and similar methodologies. In the balance, they claim that *sui generis* protection could erect legal barriers that stifle innovation and lead to a monopolization of the basis for all education and learning. Another troubling fact is that many current proposals allow a virtually infinite term under which data could be kept out of the public domain. Under US law, settling these issues will involve a close examination of the reasons underlying the constitutional aversion to the ownership of facts, and it will raise ethical questions about whether facts are merely commodities or are so valuable that exclusive control can never be granted to one individual.

Online Expression

The mass distribution of unsolicited e-mail or spam has been the subject of much complaint within the online world. The practice has been criticized on many levels. Internet service providers point to the burdens that spamming places upon network resources. Spam is, by definition, unrequested, and users complain of the unwanted intrusion into their affairs. Privacy-related worries are not restricted to transmission alone. Much spam is derived from mailing lists that are collected from e-mail addresses posted to such locations as Web bulletin boards or **newsgroups** without any intention to participate in mass mailings. Similarly, many users are disturbed to find that information given to individuals or entities for one purpose may be collected and sold for mass distribution. The frustration with spam is further compounded by the fact that often these messages are sent without valid return addresses or other contact information, making spam nearly impossible to stop.

Although spam has been the subject of much justified criticism, its regulation must be approached with some caution. First, the topic implicates freedom of expression, which is a right protected under the First Amendment in the United States. Disagreement remains between those who believe that participation in mass e-mails should be restricted to those who voluntarily agree to receive mailings and those who advocate an opt-out-only approach. An opt-in e-mail approach is considered the best approach for today's digital marketing practice.

Within the law, spam has become a major issue. In the case of *Cyber Promotions, Inc. v. America Online, Inc.*,[33] the court held that a spam producer had no First Amendment right to send its product to AOL subscribers and that consequently the ISP could block its messaging activity. Similarly, a court ruled that spamming activity violated the federal Computer Fraud and Abuse Act.[34] Additionally, Congress passed and President George W. Bush signed the **Controlling the Assault of Non-Solicited Pornography and Marketing Act** of 2003, better known as the CAN-SPAM Act.[35] The act creates a comprehensive national framework for the use of marketing-directed e-mail. The act permits federal and state authorities as well as ISPs to initiate both civil and criminal actions against advertising deemed to be conducted through spamming activities. Currently, the FTC is taking steps to help consumers limit the amount of spam they receive, including communications containing deceptive information, misleading statements, and false representations of an e-mail's content as displayed on the subject line. E-mail recipients must be provided with clear instructions on how to terminate further contact, and the use of autonomous data collection applications (such as spidering) is prohibited. To many critics, a significant deficiency of the legislation is the absence of a private right to pursue actions against spammers. In the interim, e-mail providers such as Gmail provide easy-to-use spam filters. In this way, they are effectively crowd-sourcing the identification of spam.

The issue of expression directed to children remains a highly visible issue within online law and ethics. In 1996, the federal Telecommunications Act of 1934 was amended to include the

Computer Decency Act (CDA), which in relevant part made it a criminal act to send an "obscene or indecent" communication to a recipient who was known to the sender to be under 18 years of age. An additional provision made it an offense to use an interactive computer service to present material that "depicts or describes, in terms patently offensive, as measured by contemporary community standards, sexual or excretory organs" in a context available to minors. In 1997, in the case of *Reno v. American Civil Liberties Union*,[36] the US Supreme Court found that these provisions were unconstitutionally vague, prohibiting, among other things, the exchange of information about such subjects as AIDS and reproductive decision making. It further noted that the provisions would hinder or *chill* adult speech through the placement of undue burdens. Today, this continues to be a challenge due to "sexting" and other communication trends among young people that are facilitated by the constantly connected nature of social media.

Although the broad regulatory attempts of the CDA failed, a number of efforts are underway to provide more narrowly defined regulations for children's content. In December 2000, Congress passed the Children's Internet Protection Act (CIPA). The legislation links federal funding to libraries with the use of filtering software in public internet terminals. In May 2002, after hearing extensive evidence, a federal judicial panel invalidated the act, stating that blocking software cannot adequately guarantee that only material harmful to minors would be screened. The decision was appealed to the US Supreme Court, and on June 23, 2003, a plurality opinion reversed the lower court, holding that public funding can be made contingent upon the use of filters. Significantly, this declaration was effectively limited because, in the course of the proceedings, the government stated that libraries would retain the ability to remove filtering software if simply requested to do so by a patron. This concession was cited by two individual concurrences and likely played a determinative role in the outcome.[37]

Other current online expression-related issues are focused on social media platforms specifically designed for children such as Facebook's Messenger Kids and the hotly contested Instagram for Kids, which critics feel only contribute to mental health issues among youth such as low self-esteem and depression. These examples strongly suggest that the boundaries of expression will continue to be challenged by the internet. Although specific outcomes remain open to question, it appears that expression will be protected when the courts and the legislatures realize the purpose and importance of electronic communication. Education of all parties involved may prove to be the best security for the continued flourishing of online speech.

Emerging Issues

Along with the more conventional problems of online dynamics, additional challenges are particularly unique to the internet at its current stage of development. The responses to these challenges will require the same levels of imagination and creativity demonstrated in the internet's creation.

Fraud

The use of deception and false claims to obtain profit is, of course, not unique to the internet. However, the nature of online dynamics introduces several factors that affect prevention efforts. The first general factor relates to the technical nature of networked communication. The average person is not in a position to understand exactly how information is displayed, transferred, or stored, and this lack of knowledge provides opportunities for novel deceptions. Included within this category is the use of e-mail or websites to impersonate individuals or corporations. This activity, known as **spoofing**, is often used to extract sensitive information

SCAMS AND SAFETY

Protecting Your Kids | On The Internet | Common Scams And Crimes | Sex Offender Registry Websites

On the Internet

Learn tips for protecting your computer, the risk of peer-to-peer systems, the latest e-scams and warnings, Internet fraud schemes, and more.

New E-Scams & Warnings

To report potential e-scams, please go the Internet Crime Complaint Center and file a report. Note: The FBI does not send mass e-mails to private citizens about cyber scams, so if you received an e-mail that claims to be from the FBI Director or other top official, it is most likely a scam.

If you receive unsolicited e-mail offers or spam, you can forward the messages to the Federal Trade Commission at spam@uce.gov.

Exhibit 5.2 The FBI Warns against Cyber Scams

Source: www.fbi.gov/

by leading a user to believe that a request is coming from a reputable source, such as an ISP or a credit card company. Other common swindles involve the use of programs that secretly dial long-distance locations for which the unknowing user pays the fees or false log-in pages that record account information.

A second factor involves the psychology of digital environments. The media is full of stories concerning technological advances and opportunities for profit. Unfortunately, many people are unable to differentiate genuinely worthwhile endeavors from those presented by mere opportunists. Messages originating from the online world are likely to be viewed by some as having an air of authority, solely due to their association with the digital revolution. Many investment opportunities make use of this rhetoric, often promoting breakthrough technologies and applications.

The problem of consumer **fraud** is being addressed on several dimensions. Federal agencies such as the FTC and the FBI have increased their efforts to track and prosecute fraudulent conduct (Exhibit 5.2). Likewise, many state agencies have begun to prosecute criminal activity within their borders. The range of sanctions available includes stipulated lifetime bans in the conduct of internet commerce, civil judgments, forfeiture of property, and referrals for criminal prosecution. In 2009, the FTC issued new guidelines prohibiting online reviews that do not disclose the relationship between the reviewer and the owner of the product reviewed, with the Consumer Review Fairness Act being enacted in 2016. Similar initiatives have been undertaken by authorities of other countries.

The basis of fraud is usually incomplete or false information. Thus, a consumer's ability to evaluate online material is essential. Promotion and adherence to codes of ethics such as those promulgated by the AMA are one means of inspiring consumer confidence. Codes may include requirements that members refrain from doing business with questionable clients or third parties. Many online and real-world businesses, particularly those within the finance and credit industry, require that their licensees follow strict legal and ethical protocols and may withdraw affiliation in cases of violation.

Although the establishment and enforcement of laws are necessary responses to the problem of fraud, the internet's global reach continues to frustrate even the most comprehensive of enforcement plans. On the other hand, a weakness of purely private regulation is the potential for conflicts of interest or less than rigorous enforcement of rules. Recent revelations of unpunished violations by members of eTrust,[38] the internet's largest nongovernmental privacy watchdog, have caused many to wonder whether industry-based enforcement is truly possible.

Even though law must frequently play a reactive role, the conditions of the online environment create unique opportunities for marketing professionals to educate potential victims of fraud. Professional associations have particular abilities to establish sites that outline and explain minimum standards and consumer protections. They may also serve as clearinghouses, reporting unethical or illegal conduct. Even within the information-rich environment of the internet, online knowledge continues to be a need without limits.

Chapter Summary

Ethics is concerned with the values and practices of professionals and experts as well as the concerns and values of society. Law is also an expression of values but created for the broader goal of addressing national or even global populations. Groups of individuals with special skills or knowledge have established ethical codes over the years. Differing views exist of the role of law and self-regulation in ethical online behavior.

The notion of privacy emerged during the twentieth century as a key ethical and legal concern. Key aspects include seclusion, access control, and autonomy. Online privacy issues in the United States and other countries relate to how data should be collected and used. US firms can participate in a safe harbor plan to protect data from EU internet users. The FTC set forth five basic norms for ethical use of consumer information, including provisions for user notice, consent, access, security, and enforcement.

Intangible or intellectual property is protected through three basic legal mechanisms: patent law (covering inventions), copyright (covering the expression of ideas), and trademark (covering brands). A company can license its intellectual property while restricting unauthorized duplication or distribution. Companies are concerned about legal protection for trade secrets and about the ownership of information such as Web site content, usage data, and facts. Online expression issues include concerns about spam, criticisms of products or industries, and expression directed to children. Three emerging legal and ethical issues are online governance, jurisdiction, and fraud.

Changes within the ethical and legal framework of networked communication are occurring with swiftness equal to the technical, economic, and social transformations this medium has brought about. As critical participants within the online world, marketing professionals will not only be required to remain well informed of regulations and accepted practices but also be increasingly called upon to contribute to the global dialog on electronic spaces.

Exercises

Review Questions

1. Define ethics and law and show how they are different and similar.
2. What are some of the threats to internet user privacy?

3. According to the FTC, what are the minimum requirements for ethical use of consumer information?
4. Evaluate the current trend and direction in copyright law.
5. How does copyright differ from patent and trademark law?
6. Which types of trademark dilution exist, and how do they differ from each other?
7. What are the NET Act and the DMCA?
8. What is the doctrine of first sale? How should it be applied online?
9. What is the doctrine of fair use, and how should it be applied online?
10. What are the EU safe harbor provisions, and why are they important for US companies doing business in Europe?

Discussion Questions

1. **Copyright Infringement.** Do you think education is the answer for stopping copyright infringements in other countries? Why or why not? If yes, what type of education might work?
2. **Copyright Infringement.** If you were a famous recording artist, what would you do to protect your income from pirating (illegal sharing and downloading of your music) in the United States?
3. Is it better to regulate industry via laws or let industry self-regulate? Support your claim.
4. Which is more ethically problematic: attacking a former employer via online discussion or making the same attack by e-mailing current employees?
5. Deep linking takes place regularly over the internet. Anytime a webpage links to another site and bypasses the homepage of that site, deep linking occurs. Should this practice be allowed? Explain your position.
6. The CEO of Amazon.com publicly questioned the advisability of granting patents for business processes such as his company's 1-Click ordering process. Do such patents put a chilling effect on the expansion of digital commerce? Justify your position.
7. What court should have jurisdiction over the internet? Why?

Web Activities

1. Visit https://marketingplatform.google.com/. Do you find any of its services ethically objectionable? Why or why not?
2. Visit the FTC site at www.ftc.gov. What cases is it currently reviewing that relate to the internet? Describe several and give your opinion about how the agency should rule.
3. The World Wide Web is a borderless medium that spans the globe. Check out the Internet Law and Policy Forum at www.ilpf.org. What attempts have been made to regulate the internet both domestically and overseas? What recourse do users have if they are wronged in activities such as gambling and if the servers are physically located outside the United States? What about spam outside the United States?
4. Visit www.walmart.com and www.amazon.com and review their privacy policies. Are they easy to locate? What sorts of things do they cover? Which one has a better policy in your opinion?

Acknowledgment

An earlier version of this chapter was updated and augmented by Lara Pearson, Esq., and Inna S. Wood, Esq. Lara is Vice President & the Sustainability Steward at Exemplar Law and the Chief Pontificator at BrandGeek.net, a branding law blog where IP law and corporate social responsibility collide. Inna's expertise is primarily focused on corporate and business law. She holds an LL.M. degree from the University of California, Berkeley, School of Law, and a degree in jurisprudence from the Moscow State Law Academy. Inna is admitted to practice law in the State of California as well as the Russian Federation.

Notes

1 American Marketing Association, *Statement of Ethics* (Chicago, IL, American Marketing Association, 2021).
2 https://www.cisa.gov/cisa-cybersecurity-awareness-program; www.getsafeonline.org.
3 S. Warren and L. Brandeis, *The Right to Privacy*, 4 Harvard Law Review 193 (1890).
4 381 U.S. 479 (1965).
5 410 U.S. 113 (1973); *Restatement (Second) of Torts* § 652 (1977).
6 Relevant cases include *Lane v. Facebook, Inc.*, No. 08–03845 (N.D. Cal., filed Aug. 12, 2008) and *In re Google Buzz User Privacy Litigation*, No. 10–00672 (N.D. Cal., filed February 17, 2010). Also, see Elec. *Privacy Info. Ctr. v. F.T.C.*, 844 F. Supp. 2d 98, 100–101 (D.D.C. 2012). For more information on recent privacy cases please go to: business.ftc.gov/legal-resources/8/35. Another resource is W. Adkinson, J. Eisenach, and T. Lenard, *Privacy Online: A Report on the Information Practices and Policies of Commercial Web Sites*, (The Progress & Freedom Foundation, 2002). Available at www.pff.org.
7 Children's Online Privacy Protection Act of 1998, 15 U.S.C. 6501 et seq.
8 Federal Trade Commission, *Children's Online Privacy Protection Rule*, Final Rule, 16 CFR 312 (1999). Available at www.ftc.gov/privacy/privacyinitiatives/COPPARule_2005SlidingScale.pdf.
9 Fair Credit Reporting Act, 15 USC 1681 (1992).
10 Electronic Communications Protection Act (ECPA) 18 USC §2510–21, 2701–11 (1994).
11 ftc.gov/os/2012/03/120326privacyreport.pdf.
12 35 U.S.C. §101, et seq.
13 *Amazon.com v. Barnesandnoble.com* (W.D. Wash., filed October 21, 1999).
14 *Bilski v. Kappos*, 130 S. Ct. 3218 (2010).
15 *Bilski v. Kappos*, 130 S. Ct. 3227–3229 (2010)
16 17 U.S.C. §§107 and 109 (1998).
17 17 U.S.C. §506(a) (as amended 1997).
18 17 U.S.C. §512 et seq. (1998).
19 17 U.S.C. §1201et seq. (1998).
20 Electronic Frontier Foundation, *Unintended Consequences: Three Years Under the DMCA*, May 3, 2002.
21 *WIPO Copyright Treaty*, adopted by the Diplomatic Conference on December 20, 1996, WIPO Doc. CRNR/DC/94 (1996), and *WIPO Performances and Phonograms Treaty*, adopted by the Diplomatic Conference on December 20, 1996, WIPO Doc. CRNR/DC/95 (1996).
22 *Stop Online Piracy Act*, H.R.3261, 112th Cong. (2011).
23 *Preventing Real Online Threats to Economic Creativity and Theft of Intellectual Property Act*, 112th Cong., S. 968 (2011).
24 www.sopastrike.com/. See Macon Phillips, *Obama Administration Responds to We the People Petitions on SOPA and Online Piracy* (The White House Blog, 2012). Available at www.whitehouse.gov/blog/2012/01/14/obama-administration-responds-we-people-petitions-sopa-and-online-piracy.
25 15 U.S.C. §1051 et seq.
26 15 U.S.C. §1125 et seq.
27 15 U.S.C. §1125(c).
28 15 U.S.C. §1125.
29 *Playboy Enterprises, Inc. v. Calvin Designer Label*, 985 F. Supp. 1220 (N.D. Cal. 1997); *Playboy Enterprises, Inc. v. Welles*, 279 F.3d 796 (9th Cir. 2002); *Estée Lauder Inc. v. The Fragrance Counter and Excite, Inc.* (S.D.N.Y. complaint filed March 5, 1999); *Ticketmaster Corp. v. Microsoft Corp.*, No. 97–3055 DDP (D. Cal. filed April 28, 1997); *Washington Post v. TotalNEWS, Inc.*, 97 Civ. 1190 (PKL) (S.D.N.Y., filed February 28, 1997); *Kelly v. Arriba Soft Corp.*, 336 F.3d 818 (9th Cir. 2003); *Perfect 10, Inc. v. Amazon.com, Inc.*, 508 F.3d 1059–1062 (9th Cir. 2007); *M. A. Mortenson Co. v. Timberline Software*, 998 P. 2d 305 (Wash. 2000); *Groff v. America Online*, 1998 WL 307001 (R.I. Super. Ct., May 27, 1998); 18 USC §1831 et seq.

30 *New England Circuit Sales v. Randall,* No. 96–10840-EFH (D.Mass., June 4, 1996).

31 See the list of states at www.ndasforfree.com/UTSA.html.

32 *eBay, Inc. v. Bidder's Edge, Inc.,* 100 F.Supp. 2d 1058 (N.D. Cal. 2000); *Directive 96/9/EC of the European Parliament and of the Council of March 11, 1996 on the legal protection of databases.*

33 *Cyber Promotions, Inc. v. America Online, Inc.,* 948 F.Supp. 436 (E.D. Pa. 1996).

34 *America Online v. Christian Brothers,* No. 98 Civ. 8959 (DAB) (HBP) (S.D. N.Y., December 14, 1999).

35 15 U.S.C. §7701, et seq.

36 *Intel Corp. v. Hamidi,* 1 Cal Rptr. 3d 32 (Cal. 2003); 267623 *Ontario Inc. v. Nexx Online,* No. C20546/99 (Ontario Super. Ct., June 14, 1999); 47 U.S.C. §230(c)(1) [Communications Decency Act of 1996]; *Zeran v. America Online,* 129 F.3d 327 (4th Cir. Va. 1997), cert. denied, 524 U.S. 937 (1998); 117 S.Ct. 2329 (1997).

37 *United States et al. v. American Library Association, Inc., et al.,* 539 US 194 (2003).

38 *Zippo Manufacturing Company v. Zippo Dot Com, Inc.,* 952 F. Supp. 1119 (W.D.Pa., January 16, 1997); *Digital Control Inc. v. Boretronics, Inc.,* 161 F. Supp. 2d 1183 (W.D. Wash. 2001); *ALS Scan, Inc. v. Robert Wilkins,* 142 F. Supp. 2d 793 (D.Md. 2001); *Net2Phone, Inc. v. Superior Court,* 109 Cal. App. 4th 583 (Cal. Ct. App. 2003); vmag.vcilp.org/; www.arbiter.wipo.int/center/index.html; www.etrust.org.

Part III

Digital Marketing Strategy

Chapter 6

Digital Marketing Research

The objective of this chapter is to develop your understanding of why and how digital marketers conduct online marketing research and how they turn data into marketing knowledge that provides insight for marketing activities. You will learn about the three categories of internet data sources, consider the ethics of online research, look at key database analysis techniques, and explore the use of knowledge management metrics.

After reading this chapter, you will be able to:

- Identify the three main sources of data that digital marketers use to address research problems.
- Discuss how and why digital marketers need to check the quality of research data gathered online.
- Explain why the internet is used as a contact method for primary research and describe the main internet-based approaches to primary research.
- Describe several ways to monitor the Web for gathering desired information.
- Contrast client-side data collection, server-side data collection, and real-space approaches to data collection.
- Explain the concepts of big data and cloud computing.
- Highlight four important methods of analysis that digital marketers can apply to information in the data warehouse.

THE PURINA STORY

The Nestlé Purina PetCare company knows that Purina websites and online advertising increase offline buying. How? Through a carefully conducted study that integrated online and offline behavioral data.

Switzerland-based Nestlé S.A. operates full lines of dog- and cat-care brands such as Friskies, Alpo, Purina Dog Chow, and Fancy Feast. The firm manages branded websites that serve the following markets: consumers, veterinarians/veterinary schools, nutritionists/food scientists, and breeders/other enthusiasts. Nestlé started its inquiry with the following three research questions:

1. Are our buyers using our branded websites?
2. Should we invest beyond these branded websites in online advertising?
3. If so, where do we place that advertising?

Combining comScore Media Metrix's representative panel of 1.5 million internet consumers and the Knowledge Networks, Inc.'s frequent-grocery-shopper panel of 20 million

DOI: 10.4324/9781003247319-9

households revealed 50,000 consumers belonging to both panels. Researchers created three experimental groups (cells) from survey panel members, with two of the cells receiving Purina O.N.E. banner advertising as they naturally surfed the internet: a control cell (no ads), a low-exposure test cell (1 to 5 exposures), and a high-exposure test cell (6 to 20 exposures). Banner ads were randomly sent as exposure-cell subjects viewed webpages anywhere on the internet. Next, the firm surveyed all cell members to assess the brand awareness of Purina, purchase intent, and advertising awareness. Finally, the researchers compared survey results with offline buying, as measured in the Knowledge Networks panel.

Nestlé's marketers were very interested in the study's findings. First, banner click-through was low (0.06% on average). Second, when study participants were asked, "When thinking of dog food, what brand first comes to mind?" 31 percent of both exposure-cell subjects mentioned Purina. In contrast, only 22 percent of the no-exposure subjects mentioned the brand; this result clearly showed an advertising effect. Further, 7 percent more of the subjects in the high-exposure group mentioned the brand compared with those in the low-exposure group. Next, researchers reviewed the internet panel's website-viewing habits of those who purchased Purina products and determined that home/health and living sites receive the most visits from these customers. This information helped the firm decide where to place banner ads. Among the sites frequented by Purina's market, petsmart.com and about.com enjoyed heavy usage and were thought to be great ad buys.

Data Drive Strategy

US marketers account for nearly two-thirds of the global market share for the marketing research industry. This's a lot of data! Information overload is a reality for most consumers and marketers alike. It is an especially difficult problem for marketing decision makers as they gather survey results, Web analytics, mobile app usage information, call center data, product sales information, secondary data about competitors, social media conversations, and much more. The problem is compounded by automated data gathering at websites, brick-and-mortar points of purchase, and all other customer touch points. For example, Susan is following a brand on Twitter and sees the following tweet from the brand while scrolling through her feed: "Click here and get $10 off your next purchase." When she clicks on the link, she will be prompted to enter her e-mail address and other information prior to receiving the coupon. At this point, her Twitter response and data go into a database. If she purchases on the company's website, this information is also recorded, and thus the database grows with her address and other information. If she calls to ask a question about the product, then that becomes part of her record in a database. Geo-enabled applications also enable the collection of behavioral data within retail environments. This cycle continues as the company gathers more information about Susan and her behaviors. Multiply this by the number of all the other customers, and there is a lot of actionable data, ready to help marketers achieve their objectives of building or retaining a relationship and increasing customer value.

What to do with all the data? Purina marketers sorted through lots of consumer data to build a road map for their internet advertising strategy and must continue to do so to maintain currency. As you read this chapter, keep one important thing in mind: data without insight or application to inform marketing strategy are worthless.

Exhibit 6.1 displays an overview of this process. Data are collected from a myriad of sources, filtered into databases, and turned into marketing knowledge that is then used to create marketing strategy. This chapter discusses internet data sources, describes important database analysis techniques, and, most importantly, examines the purposes and payoffs for all this work.

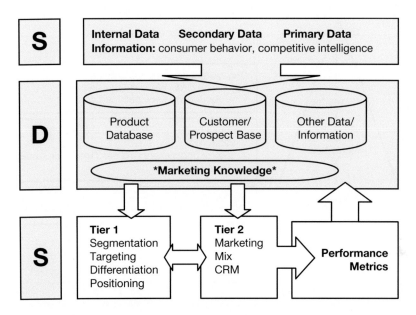

Exhibit 6.1 From Sources to Databases to Strategy (SDS Model)

Most of these techniques are well grounded in marketing practice; however, new technology brings new applications that are both helpful and confusing for market researchers. Web analytics and performance metrics permeate each of these processes—these were discussed in Chapter 2 and are described in subsequent chapters as they relate to specific marketing tactics.

Marketing insight occurs somewhere between information and knowledge. Knowledge is more than a collection of information but something that resides in the marketer, not the database. It can be compared to the difference between teaching and learning. A professor might spout information in a lecture or from a textbook, but it is not usable unless the student ponders over it, relates it to other pieces of information, and adds insights that result in acquired and useful knowledge. People, not the internet or computers, create knowledge; computers are simply learning enablers.

Big Data

Big data refers to data sets that are so big they are difficult to manage with currently available software. For example, how can a marketer turn 500,000 tweets a day into actionable brand tactics? Furthermore, what can a marketer do if this data is not structured and organized in a meaningful way?

Data growth rates are astounding and expected to increase by more than 180 percent by 2025, reaching 180 zettabytes, necessitating an increasing amount of storage hardware space, which is only growing at a rate of 19 percent a year (Holst, 2021a). This presents a problem for information technology managers, and digital marketers must determine how to glean insights from this enormous amount of bytes.

IBM maintains that businesses must manage four aspects of big data: volume (the quantity), velocity (handling time sensitive data quickly), variety (ranging from social media conversation to customer click patterns and census data), and veracity (is the information reliable and

Exhibit 6.2 From Data to Decision at Nestlé Purina PetCare Company
Source: "Does Online Marketing . . .", 2002

trustworthy?) ("What is Big Data?", 2012). Although marketers recognize the value of data, they cite three pain points as problematic:

- Getting data fast enough to act can be a challenge, especially given marketers' increasing desire for meaningful insights.
- Generating significant business and consumer insights is a major challenge.
- Difficulty with making use of data to generate a unified customer view (Ugboma, 2017).
- Moreover, increasing concerns about consumer privacy are adding to marketers' challenges to effectively target consumers. Amazon certainly takes advantage of big data. It tracks page views and purchase history of individual customers and uses that information in real time to offer buying suggestions—see the Let's Get Technical box about data mining in this chapter.

The Purina research vignette is a good example of how a firm sorts through hundreds of millions of pieces of data from about 21.5 million consumers, collects even more data, and makes decisions (Exhibit 6.2). Organizations must go through this process with all the data they collect, or their data will simply be an overwhelming bunch of facts and numbers.

Let's Get Technical—Data Mining

The Target department store chain used data mining to predict which customers were pregnant. Through extensive analysis of past customer purchases over a long period of time, Target researchers found that pregnant women made a series of specific changes in their shopping habits—for example switching to unscented products and buying lots of cotton balls. Not only could the researchers predict pregnancy, but they could even predict due dates within a narrow time frame. Understanding that pregnancy is one of the few times in life that a company can garner a loyal customer, Target would then send ads for baby products to the expectant mother. So as not to spook her, Target would include ads on the same page for unrelated items—such as lawnmowers. Nonetheless, one father of a high school girl took offense and asked a confused store manager why his daughter was receiving ads for baby products. A short while later the father called back to apologize. Indeed, sometimes the predictive nature of data mining can cross the line of invasion of privacy.

Data mining is the search for information hidden in large databases. It is much like scientific inquiry except that the subject of study is human-made data rather than nature. The larger the database, the more the need for specialized data mining tools to spot patterns and relationships in the data. The tools themselves are quite sophisticated, and data miners tend to have advanced degrees—with special emphasis on statistical training.

A common form of data mining familiar to online shoppers is cross-sell data. Based on past sales patterns, marketers can predict which products sell well together. They then present this information to the shopper with a friendly note saying something like, "customers who bought the iXT widget also bought . . . ." The same idea is behind streaming music sites that learn your preferences. They look for pattern matches with other customers that listen to your same music and then suggest other songs that they listen to. The larger the database of customers, the more accurate the predictions are likely to be.

Here is how cross-sell data mining works. Imagine that Joe buys the iXT widget and the alpha widget. As it turns out, 200 other customers buy both widgets together. For each customer, the database examines what items they bought in combination. Then it counts the frequency with which each combination appears. Finally, it sorts the counts from largest to smallest and presents future customers with the most likely cross-sell.

Amazon has taken cross-sell analysis one step further by tying page **views** to purchases. For example, look at a camera on Amazon and you are likely to see the message, "What Other Items Do Customers Buy After **Viewing** This Item?" (emphasis added). Maybe you are on the fence between two camera models. Amazon will tell you what others on the fence ultimately purchased! They do this by counting page views of every customer and correlating those views with purchase behavior. So as you click around Amazon's website you are creating a massive amount of data that is automatically mined.

Note that the cross-sell data is the process of fishing for relationships. We are looking at the strength of correlation between *every* combination of variables in the database, which is sometimes called *factor analysis*. However, factor analysis does not show the direction of dependence—which variable causes which. Nor does factor analysis incorporate subtle hypothesis variations to find just the right fit with the data.

But data mining can be more directed—a form of hypothesis testing. The investigator forms a hypothesis (e.g., advertising dollars are best spent on existing customers) and then uses a statistical technique such as regression to test the hypothesis. This process is the foundation of most academic research. However, it is somewhat slow and requires inventive hypothesis formation. Typically, tools to carry out this analysis include SPSS and SAS.

More sophisticated still is a data mining technique called evolutionary programming. A computer program adopts the role of scientific investigator. The program forms and tests hypotheses. When it finds a hypothesis that looks promising, it varies it slightly, forming a series of daughter hypotheses. Each of these hypotheses is tested in turn, looking for the best match with the data. After churning away for a while, the program reports back to the user on which hypotheses show interesting relationships in the data.

Tasks solved by data mining include predicting, classifying, detecting relationships, and market basket analysis (the cross-sell data). The packages themselves are becoming more user friendly, which is good news for marketers. Companies such as Megaputer may one day make sophisticated data mining commonplace.

Marketing Knowledge Management

Knowledge management is the process of managing the creation, use, and dissemination of knowledge. Thus, data, information, and knowledge can be shared with internal marketing decision makers, partners, distribution channel members, and sometimes customers. When other stakeholders can access selected knowledge, the firm becomes a learning organization and is better able to reach desired ROI and other performance goals.

Marketing knowledge is the digitized "group mind" or "collective memory" of the marketing personnel and sometimes of consultants, partners, and former employees as well. Oftentimes the knowledge management technology allows marketing staff or even an artificial intelligence-powered chatbot to chat in real time for problem solving, which is why the system also includes contact information. For example, a Context Integration, Inc., consultant working on a digital commerce problem at the client's offices can enter a "911" help call into the webpage and immediately chat with other internal experts to solve the problem. A complete marketing knowledge database includes all the data about customers, prospects, and competitors, the analyses and outputs based on the data, and access to marketing experts, all available 24/7 through a number of digital receiving appliances. Consider the following examples:

- An international technology firm uses Salesforce.com to manage the sales pipeline. When someone downloads a white paper from the website, registers online, or sends an e-mail inquiry, it goes into the Salesforce.com software for all salespeople and managers to view—and pick up contact information for e-mail or phone follow-up. The CEO gets a text message for each new lead.
- An insurance firm with 200 independent agents allows them access to claim data from more than 1 million customers. This access allows the agents to avoid high-risk customers as well as to compare claim data with their own database of customers.
- Johnson & Johnson, the pharmaceutical company, learned through survey research that contact lens wearers communicate with frequent text messages, so it created a game for mobile phones featuring its ACUVUE brand of contact lenses.

The Electronic Marketing Information System

A **marketing information system (MIS)** is the process by which marketers manage knowledge. The MIS is a system of assessing information needs, gathering information, analyzing it, and disseminating it to marketing decision makers. The process begins when marketing managers have a problem that requires data to solve. The next step is to gather the data from internal sources and from secondary sources or by conducting primary marketing research. The process is complete when these managers receive the needed information in a timely manner and usable form. For example, Web advertisers need audience statistics prior to deciding where to purchase online display ad space (the problem). They want to know how many people in their target market view various Web or social media sites to evaluate the value of Web ads versus TV and other media ads (information need). One way to get this information is through secondary sources such as comScore or Nielsen. Such companies rate websites and monitor traffic statistics by researching the internet usage habits of large panels of consumers. Web advertisers use the data to make effective and efficient media buys.

In the past, marketers needing answers asked information technology or information systems personnel what software they had on the shelf. Today, however, digital marketing actually drives technology change. Digital marketing changed the MIS landscape in several ways. First, many firms store electronic marketing data in databases and data warehouses. These data warehouses enable marketers to obtain valuable, appropriate, and tailored information anytime—day or night. Second, marketers can receive database information in webpages and e-mail on a number of devices in addition to desktop computers and laptops: smartphones, basic cell phones, and even home appliances connected through the internet of things. Third, customers also have access to portions of the database. For example, when consumers visit Amazon.com, they can query the product database for book titles and also receive information about their account status and past book purchases. Business customers, channel members, and partners often have access to customer sales data to facilitate product planning. Customer inquiries are usually automated, with personalized webpages created instantaneously from customer databases. These databases are also updated through user interactions, helping keep them up to date. Finally, most firms recognize that data and information are useless unless turned into knowledge to increase profits. Therefore, cutting-edge firms make one employee's project reports, proposals, and data analyses available to other stakeholders in the MIS network. In sum, all the data, the output from their use, and stakeholders' contact information that are gathered via an MIS make up a firm's marketing knowledge.

The internet and other technologies greatly facilitate marketing data collection. Internal records give marketing planners excellent insights about sales and inventory movement. Secondary data help marketers understand competitors, consumers, the economic environment, political and legal factors, technological forces, and other factors in the macroenvironment affecting an organization. Marketing planners use the internet, product barcode scanners, and other technologies to collect primary data about consumers. Through online e-mail and Web surveys, online experiments, focus groups, app usage, and observation of internet user discussions, marketers learn about both current and prospective customers.

Source 1: Internal Records

Internal records such as sales data are one important source of marketing knowledge. Accounting, finance, and production personnel collect and analyze data that provide valuable information for marketing planning. The marketing department itself collects and maintains much relevant information about customer characteristics and activities. For example, logistics personnel use the internet to track product shipment through distribution channels—information that can help marketers improve the order-to-delivery and payment cycles.

Sales Data

Sales data come from accounting systems and the company **website log**, retrieved via the Web analytics discussed in Chapter 2. When a customer makes a purchase online, the transaction is recorded in a database for access. Marketing managers review and analyze these data to determine conversion rates (proportion of visitors who purchase online) and to see if online ads and other communication are driving sales. Marketers can also access analytics about online shopping cart behavior, such as when products are removed from the purchasing process or if a particular event triggers a user to buy an additional item.

Sales information systems, such as Salesforce.com or other customer relationship management systems (CRMs), allow representatives to input results of communications to both prospective and current customers into the MIS. Many sales reps use their laptop or smartphone to access the product and customer databases both for input and review of customer records while on the road. For example, one office products firm has salespeople from different divisions calling on the same large customer. When the customer has a complaint, the sales rep must enter it into the database, and other reps review the customer record prior to making a visit to the same customer. This firm has a rule: if four reps record the same complaint, a warning is issued, and they must immediately visit the customer as a team and solve the problem. Sales reps are also instrumental in entering competitive and industry information gained in the field. For cutting-edge firms, marketers enter proposals, reports, and papers written on various topics into the knowledge database to ensure sales teams on the ground have access to the best practices that resolve customer issues.

Customer Characteristics and Behavior

Perhaps the most important internal marketing data involve individual customer activity. Exhibit 6.3 gives a hypothetical scenario for a computer company that collects data from its customers online and by telephone and uses the information to improve products. At a minimum, database entries include an electronic list of prospective and existing customers, along with their addresses, phone numbers, e-mail addresses, and purchase behavior. Firms have used this technique for many years, but new storage and retrieval technologies and the availability of large amounts of electronic information recently escalated its growth. For example, visitors to Expedia are asked to register before using its services. This firm has a large database that includes e-mail addresses, customer characteristics, and Web viewing and purchase behavior. Each customer file in a database might also include a record of calls made to customer service reps, product service records, specific problems or questions related to various products, and other data such as coupon and other promotional offer redemption. A complete customer record will include data from every customer touch point (contact with the company),

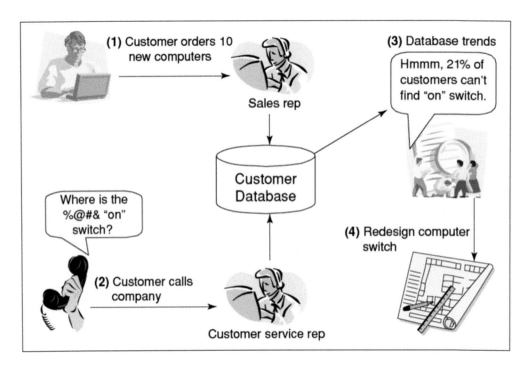

Exhibit 6.3 Digital Marketers Learn from Customers

Source: Adaptation of ideas from Brian Caulfield (2001)

including internet orders and e-mail interaction, and product purchases and coupon redemption at the retail store. Data on in-store behavior are gathered through scanning universal product codes (UPCs), or barcodes, on products. Firms use the data in customer databases to improve sales rep effectiveness, refine the product mix, identify optimum pricing for individual products, assess promotion effectiveness, and signal distribution opportunities. For example, have you ever wondered why your local retailer asks for a ZIP code when you make a purchase? The retailer adds this information to the marketing database and uses it to decide whether a new store location might be profitable.

Many organizations with websites track user movement through the pages and use these data to improve site effectiveness. They also track how users found the site (via Google or another search engine or from a link on another site). By knowing how users find the site, how much time they spend on each page, how long they are at the site, and what path they take through the site, Web developers can reorganize pages and content frequently and in a timely manner. In addition, companies can identify the website users visited immediately before and after the firm's site. This information provides competitive insights, especially if a user is reviewing certain products. These data are all generated automatically in the website logs and can be part of a firm's marketing databases. FedEx is especially adroit at gathering customer information automatically using electronic networks. Through its website, customers can dispatch a courier for package pickup, locate drop-off points, track shipments, obtain shipping rates, prepare shipping documents, and request a signature proof of delivery in many different languages. All this information can be analyzed by FedEx's marketers for planning purposes. FedEx maintains an extranet for frequent shippers, providing them with individualized rate books and other special services. In addition, FedEx maintains an intranet hub that serves over 20,000 visitors a month for human resources management and workplace and marketplace integration—a thorough system of internal data input for effective marketing knowledge management.

That said, integrating internal and external data is a difficult task because the data are quite different in type, timing, and quantity. Unifying data often requires digital marketers to establish processes and procedures while integrating systems that were not designed to work together. Despite these challenges, data integration can potentially minimize errors, improve data quality, reduce resource needs through collaboration, and lead to actionable strategy (Foote, 2019).

Source 2: Secondary Data

When faced with a need for specific information not available in company or partner databases, the digital marketer first looks for secondary data, which can be collected more quickly and less expensively than primary data—especially on the internet, where up-to-date information from more than 200 countries is available 24/7, from home or work, delivered in a matter of seconds. Syndicated research is available via the internet with a credit card sign-up and password entry.

Recent innovations in this space have caused website developers to revisit how users might register to keep the process smooth. Single sign-on (SSO) services allow users to log on to a website using identification from another services, such as a Google or Facebook account. This innovation enables greater collection of data across multiple platforms and websites, allowing marketers to increase their collection of relevant data related to a consumer.

On the other hand, secondary data may not meet the digital marketer's information needs, because they were usually gathered for a different purpose than the one at hand. Another

View by Topic

| 2020 Census Data | Data Tools | Data Science & Visualization | Population & Housing Characteristics | Business & Economy | Geography |

Exhibit 6.4 The Biggest Database of All: The US Census Bureau

Source: www.census.gov

common problem is the quality of secondary data. Marketers have no control over data collection procedures, so they should always evaluate the quality of secondary data. Samples used to generate statistics may also be incomplete even if they appear authoritative. Finally, secondary data are often out of date. The US Census Bureau provides numerous population statistics; its heavy data collection periods occur only every 10 years, and most results will not appear on the website until a year or two later. A marketer using data from www.census.gov must read the fine print to see when and where the data were collected (Exhibit 6.4).

Marketers continually scan the company's macroenvironment for threats and opportunities. This procedure is commonly called **business intelligence**. What type of information do marketing managers need? An environmental scan seeks market information about the following:

- Demographic trends.
- Competitors.
- Technological forces.
- Natural resources.
- Social and cultural trends.
- World and local economies.
- Legal and political environments.

For example, an organization wanting to understand the characteristics and behavior of the millennial demographic group can visit the US Census Bureau site, read appropriate articles in online magazines and newspapers, and monitor general research websites such as Clickz or sites that target this group. The following sections present examples of public and private sources of data about the firm's macroenvironment. We then move to secondary sources for understanding consumer behavior.

Publicly Generated Data

Most US agencies provide online information in their respective areas. The US Patent Office homepage can explain how to apply for a patent and research pending trademarks. Many global organizations, such as the International Monetary Fund (www.imf.org), are also good sources of data for environmental scans involving countries other than the United States. Generally speaking, however, US agencies collect and disseminate a great deal more data than do governments in other countries. For example, the *CIA World Factbook* is an excellent source of information on internet adoption and telecommunications in every country. In the not-for-profit category, most universities provide extensive information through their libraries, and many faculty post their research results online. Finally, industry- or profession-specific information is available at the sites of professional associations such as the American Marketing Association and is disseminated in many forms, from white papers to podcasts.

Google offers several tools for marketers to leverage regarding search interest on particular topics around the world. While the numbers provided are not exact, one can begin to identify trends of what consumers are searching for. One of these tools is Google Trends, which allows a user to input various search terms and compare their popularity based on geographic area and other factors.

Wikipedia, a social media database with over 53 million entries, is edited by some 325,000 contributors that make more than 27 million edits monthly (see www.wikipedia.org). Many other wikis exist to provide specialized information, such as Wikihow.com, with articles and videos about how to do just about anything from building a workbench to cleaning beeswax. Most of this public information is free and available to all internet users. A sampling of important public sites is displayed in Exhibit 6.5.

Website	Information
US Patent Office www.uspto.gov	Provides trademark and patent data for businesses.
World Trade Organization www.wto.org	World trade data.
International Monetary Fund www.imf.org	Provides information on many monetary issues and projects.
Mohanbir Sawhney and Dave Chaffey www.mohansawhney.com www.davechaffey.com	Academicians who generously publish many digital marketing articles on their websites.
Securities and Exchange Commission www.sec.gov	EDGAR database provides financial data on US public corporations.
Small Business Administration www.sba.gov	Features information and links for small business owners.
Federal Trade Commission www.ftc.gov	Shows regulations and decisions related to consumer protection and antitrust laws.
US Census www.census.gov	Provides statistics and trends about the US population.

Exhibit 6.5 Sample of Public Online Data Sources in the United States

Privately Generated Data

Company websites provide a great overview of the firm's mission, products, partners, and current events. Individuals often maintain sites with useful information about companies as well. Politicians and other public figures create sites containing commentary about political issues. An important source of current information and commentary comes from leading bloggers in various industries, such as well-known marketing author Seth Godin's blog (seths.blog).

Another good resource is large research firms, such as comScore and Forrester Research, which put sample statistics and press releases on their sites as a way to entice users to purchase full research reports. Nielsen posts the top websites and advertisers in a survey period. Several large research firms now also offer e-mail newsletters that are sent automatically to subscriber desktops. For digital business information, free newsletters from the Interactive Advertising Bureau (www.iab.net) and eMarketer (www.eMarketer.com) are especially helpful. Although often incomplete, these tidbits of information are generally useful in an environmental scan and help marketers decide whether to purchase the full report.

Commercial online databases contain publicly available information that can be accessed via the internet. Thousands of databases are available online covering news, industry data, encyclopedias, airline routes and fares, Yellow Page directories, e-mail addresses, and much more. Marketers increasingly access syndicated data via the internet from well-respected firms such as the Nielsen Media television ratings and the Simmons annual survey of over 25,000 consumers listings of media advertising rates and specifications. Students and faculty often access articles from a number of respected media via the university library databases from home—using the internet.

Note that many of these databases are not available on webpages but are simply electronic versions of articles and other information ordinarily found in the library. Some databases are free, but others charge a fee for access.

See Exhibit 6.6 for a sample of privately generated data sites.

Website	Information
Nielsen Corporation www.nielsen.com	Global data and analytics company specializing in audience measurement and consumer research services.
Gartner www.gartner.com	Specializes in digital business and usually presents highlights of its latest findings on the website.
IRI Worldwide www.iriworldwide.com	Data analytics and market research company focused on consumer package goods, retail, and health care intelligence and analysis
Commerce Business Daily www.cbd-net.com	Lists of government requests for proposals online.
Experian www.experian.com	Consumer data used by marketers for a variety of industries involving audience and message measurement as well as campaign strategy.
Dun & Bradstreet www.dnb.com	Global provider of business data and analytics.
Lexis-Nexis www.lexis-nexis.com	Articles from business, consumer, and marketing publications.
Statista www.statista.com	International market and consumer data company.

Exhibit 6.6 Sampling of Privately Generated Data Sources in the United States

Competitive Intelligence Example

Competitive intelligence (CI) involves analyzing the industries in which a firm operates as input to the firm's strategic positioning and to understand competitor vulnerabilities. It is a legal activity conducted by many companies. It can be very difficult because companies know others are watching and put out information that can lead competitors astray. Specialists at Fuld + Company suggest the following intelligence cycle (www.fuld.com):

1. Planning and direction.
2. Published information collection.
3. Primary source (human intelligence) collection.
4. Analysis and production.
5. Report and inform.

The Fuld + Company website includes a thorough review of software to aid in CI activities as well as seminars on the topic. Astutely, they note that companies should not invest in technical CI software tools unless they have the right processes in place, or it is a waste of money—just like everything else internet-related!

A few sources of CI include competitor press releases, new products, alliances and co-brands, trade show activity, and social media conversations. The internet simplified CI. Companies can observe competitive marketing strategies right on competitors' websites and can sometimes catch announcements of new products or price changes prior to media reports about them.

Marketers should be sure to check the websites linked to competitors' pages. One technology-enabled CI activity involves analyzing a firm's website log to see which webpage users visited immediately prior to and after visiting the company's site. If, for example, Honda marketing managers noticed that a user visited the Toyota Matrix Web page prior to checking out Honda models, they would gain a consumer perspective on competitive shopping behavior. In a later section, we discuss online monitoring techniques in more detail.

Third-party industry-specific sites can also provide timely information about competitive activities. An airline will monitor online travel agents to watch competitive pricing and route changes (e.g., Expedia and Travelocity) and social media sites such as Tripadvisor.com (where travelers post hotel reviews). Company profiles for public firms are available in the Securities and Exchange Commission's (SEC) online EDGAR database as well as at many investment firm sites (e.g., E★TRADE).

Another valuable source of CI comes from user conversation on social media, as will be discussed in the primary data collection section later—Facebook has over 2.8 billion registered users, and they each have something to say about brands they like and dislike. Companies can often find consumer conversation about competitive product strengths and weaknesses via keyword searches, but much more sophisticated monitoring is now available with social media dashboards. For example, social media listening tools such as Keyhole and Sprout Social allow marketers to track social media user-generated conversations about one's own brand as well as those about other companies.

Information Quality

Secondary and primary data are subject to many limitations; thus, marketers should use all information with caution and with a full understanding of how the data were collected. It is advisable to be as objective as possible when reviewing data prior to using it for making marketing decisions—especially before using information on webpages. Why? Because anyone can easily publish on the Web without being reviewed by a publisher or being screened for accuracy or appropriateness and because so many different methods are used to generate research data. Special care is needed when dealing with secondary data from international sources because of cultural and data collection differences.

Digital marketers should not be seduced by good design: the best-designed sites may not be the most accurate or credible, and vice versa. For example, the Securities and Exchange Commission publishes reports filed by public companies in simple text, spending little taxpayer money to make them pretty. The following steps can be taken to evaluate the quality of secondary data collected online:

- *Discover the website's author.* A site published by a government agency or well-known corporation has more credibility than one by an unknown author. Sometimes discerning the difference is quite tricky: For example, the same musical group usually has a number of sites—some official and some published by individual fans. A search in Google for *Taylor Swift* yielded more than 3,520,000 results in 2017. Which of these sites are authorized by the singer?
- *Try to determine whether the site author is an authority on the website topic.* For example, an economist from Harvard University or Merrill Lynch might have more credible information about interest rates than a politician. Furthermore, the university's website may be more objective than the financial firm's site.
- *Check to see when the site was last updated.* Many websites change every day, but some have not been maintained for years. Obviously, the more current the information is, the more useful it will be for decision making. Check the hyperlinks. Although many sites contain occasional broken links, a site with many inoperative links is a site that has not been updated recently.
- *Determine how comprehensive the site is.* Does it cover only one aspect of a topic, or does it consider the broader context?
- *Try to validate the research data by finding similar information at other sources on the internet or in hard copy at the library.* If the same statistics are not available elsewhere, look for other ways to validate the data. For example, one validation of the number of people using the internet might be to check the number of people with computers (the latter should be larger). In general, it is also a good idea to compare sites that cover the same topic.
- *Check the site content for accuracy.* If a site has lots of errors or if the numbers don't add properly, it is a sign that the data cannot be trusted.
- Consider the site security certificate. Many websites are moving to the https:// protocol for security, so it may be worth checking to ensure the URL of the website you are on is preceded by https://.

Don't stop looking when the first good screen full of hyperlinks appears. Remember that this site is only one of many potential sites to research, and the list of related hyperlinks is provided as a service—so these sites are not necessarily the best sources for the topic.

What about Wikipedia—is it accurate? Students like to use this site in their research, and many professors believe it is not accurate because all content is created and edited by citizen journalists—anonymous internet users who contribute their perspectives by posting content to online blogs, forums, and websites, usually without editorial review. *Nature*, an international science and medicine journal, conducted a study that compared articles from both *Wikipedia* and *Encyclopedia Britannica* for accuracy. *Nature* received 42 peer reviews from a preselected field of science experts and found that Britannica had 2.92 mistakes per article and Wikipedia had 3.86. However, Wikipedia articles were on average 2.6 times longer than the Britannica articles, indicating a lower error per word ratio in Wikipedia (Terdiman, 2005). Wikipedia is fairly accurate partially because there are so many citizen journalists editing the articles and they keep each other from making too many errors. As with all Web pages, however, it is always better to check Wikipedia's original sources and validate the information by looking for similar work by other authors.

Source 3: Primary Data

When secondary data are not available to assist in planning, marketing managers may decide to collect their own information. Primary data are information gathered for the first time to solve a particular problem. Gathering primary data is usually more expensive and time consuming than it is to gather secondary data; on the other hand, the data are current and more relevant to the marketer's specific problem. In addition, primary data have the benefit of being proprietary and thus unavailable to competitors.

This section describes traditional approaches to primary data collection enhanced by the internet: experiments, focus groups, observation, content analysis, and survey research. **In-depth interviews (IDI)** are another important form of primary data collection, but they are better done offline because the questions tend to be less structured and more open-ended (of course, the researcher could use a Skype phone call online for this). A subsequent section discusses several other nontraditional primary data collection techniques only made possible by internet technologies. Whether collected on the internet or offline, all electronic data gathered at any customer touch point (e.g., e-mail, telephone, website, grocery store purchase, social media site, and store kiosk) end up in a marketing database and become part of the marketing knowledge to be used for effective planning.

As a review, we present the steps for conducting primary research and then discuss each approach along with its particular uses, strengths, and weaknesses.

Primary Research Steps

A primary data collection project includes five steps (Exhibit 6.7).

1. *Research problem.* As with secondary data, specificity is vital. Exhibit 6.8 shows some typical internet marketing research problems that electronic data can help solve.
2. *Research plan.*

    - *Research approach.* On the basis of the information needed, researchers choose from among experiments, focus groups, observation techniques, and survey research, or Web conversation monitoring, real-time techniques, and real-space techniques.
    - *Sample design.* At this stage, researchers select the sample source and the number of desired respondents.

A primary data collection project includes five steps

Exhibit 6.7 Primary Research Steps

Online Retailers	Web and Social Media Sites
Improve online merchandising	Pages viewed most often
Forecast product demand	Increase customer engagement
Test new products	Increase number of comments posted to a blog
Test various price points	Path users take through the site
Test co-branding and partnership effectiveness	Site visit overall satisfaction efficient?
Measure affiliate program effectiveness	Social media conversation sentiment
Customers and Prospects	**Marketing Communication**
Identify new market segments	Test social network application
Measure loyalty among registered users	Test new promotions
Profile current customers	Optimize site usability and revenue
Test site-customization techniques	Measure display ad click-through

Exhibit 6.8 Typical Research Problems for Digital Marketers

- *Contact method.* Ways to contact the sample include traditional methods such as the telephone, mail, and in person, as well as the internet and other technology-enabled approaches.
- *Instrument design.* If a survey is planned, researchers develop a questionnaire. For other methods, researchers develop a protocol to guide the data collection.
3. *Data collection.* Researchers gather the information according to plan.
4. *Data analysis.* Researchers analyze the results in light of the original problem. For quantitative research, this step includes using statistical software packages for traditional survey data analysis or data mining and other approaches to find patterns and test hypotheses in databases.
5. *Distribution of findings/addition to the database.* Research data might be placed in the marketing knowledge database and be presented in written or oral form to marketing managers.

Internet-Based Research Approaches

The internet is fertile ground for primary data collection. One reason is declining cooperation from consumers when using traditional research approaches. Telephone survey response rates are less than 10 percent (Kennedy and Hartig, 2019), and 33 percent didn't even answer the mailed 2020 US Census. It is difficult to obtain a representative sample of respondents when survey research response rates are so low. Do Not call registries also curtail the abilities of sample generation using smartphones as many home phone numbers are phased out. Although it is also difficult to obtain a representative sample online, with a large number of consumers online, conducting research using this inexpensive and quick method makes sense. Here are four examples of successful online research:

- *Creative test.* Leo Burnett, the advertising agency, built a panel of 50 elementary schools for the purpose of testing advertising directed to the "kid" market. Burnett put some advertising posters online and sent e-mails directing students to the webpages displaying the posters. After viewing the posters, students completed a survey to select the best one. In this test, more than 800 kids helped decide the best creative approach for the poster.

- *Customer satisfaction.* British Airways posted a questionnaire on its website to gather opinions of company services among Executive Club members. More than 9,000 people completed the questionnaire within nine months.
- *Product development.* The University of Nevada, Reno, posted a questionnaire on the marketing program website, inviting practitioners and academics to give opinions about what should be included in digital commerce programs at the university level; 140 respondents helped to shape new courses.
- *Reputation management.* A large manufacturing company made a small mistake and shortly afterward found negative comments in 90 percent of the first page and 80 percent of the second page of Google search results for the company. These included bloggers talking about the incident and YouTube visitors posting negative comments under the company's videos. Primary research data collection takes on a new meaning when companies, brands, and executives must monitor for internet conversation.

Marketers combine online and offline data effectively and efficiently, as in the Purina example and as done by some brick-and-mortar retailers that also conduct digital commerce. This task involves merging data from older legacy systems, incoming call centers, retailer barcode scanners, government statistics, and many other places that are difficult to integrate. In one example, comScore Media Metrix installed PC meters on the computers of several thousand Information Resources, Inc. (IRI) Shoppers Hotline panel members. Web data include exposure to ads, sites visited, and purchasing frequency and patterns. These data are combined with offline panel data: actual packaged goods purchased at brick-and-mortar grocery stores, as well as volume purchased, timing of purchases, promotional effectiveness, and brand loyalty.

Social networking sites have also launched tools that are useful for marketers, even if they don't allow the depth of questioning traditional methods do. One can post a poll-like question on Twitter and receive instantaneous feedback from Twitter users who see it in a company feed. Furthermore, engaging on social media opens the door for further engagement for more traditional methods of primary data collection.

In addition, primary data are collected online using experiments, focus groups, observations, in-depth interviews, and survey research, as discussed in the following sections.

ONLINE EXPERIMENTS

Experimental research attempts to test cause-and-effect relationships, as in the Purina example. Offline, a researcher will select subjects, randomly put them into two or more groups, and then expose each group to different stimuli. The researcher then measures responses to the stimuli, usually in the form of a questionnaire, to determine whether differences exist among the groups. If the experiment has been carefully controlled (i.e., only the experimental stimuli have been varied), group differences can be attributed to the stimuli (cause and effect). Of course, these effects must be tested in other situations and with other subjects to determine their degree of generalizability.

Online, marketers tend to use experiments to test alternative webpages, display ads, and promotional offers online. This is commonly called "A/B" testing: one group sees a particular ad or webpage and another group sees a different version (A page or offer and B page). Marketers use this quite successfully for improving response rates and sales online. For example, a company might send e-mail notification of two different pricing offers, each to one-half of its customer database. If a hyperlink to two different webpages at the sponsoring firm's site is included in the e-mail, it will be quickly apparent which offer "pulls better." In another example, when a consumer searches for a particular product on Google, the company might randomly link to one landing webpage for half the group and another page for the other half and see which results in better sales.

A/B testing with biometric technology can be a useful method for understanding which version(s) of an advertisement are most effective in capturing consumer attention. For example, when Rovio, creator of popular online games such as Angry Birds, was seeking to increase the effectiveness of their advertisements, they partnered with SPARK Neuro to test new advertising formats that would increase consumer attention to their ads. IMotions Biometric Research technology was used to track eye movements and measure brain activity to analyze how consumers looked at and reacted to ads while playing online games. As a result of this testing, SPARK Neuro helped Rovio develop ads that were more effective in calling the attention of online game players and making the ads more memorable after game play was finished (iMotions, 2021). By assessing even tiny movements of the eye and changes in brain activity, biometric technology can go a long way in conducting effective marketing research.

ONLINE FOCUS GROUPS

Focus group research is a qualitative methodology that attempts to collect in-depth information from a small number of participants. Focus groups are often used to help marketers understand important feelings and behaviors prior to designing survey research.

This contact method provides some advantages over traditional focus groups, where all participants are in one room. First, the internet can bring together people who do not live in the same geographic area, such as a focus group with consumers from five different countries discussing online shopping experiences. Second, because participants type their answers at the same time, they are not influenced as much by what others say (known as *groupthink*). Finally, by using the Web, researchers can show participants animated ads, demonstrate software, or use other multimedia stimuli to prompt group discussion.

Conversely, focus groups can accommodate 8 to 12 participants at a time. The reason behind the small group size is the difficulty in managing simultaneous overlapping conversation online. Some researchers avoid this problem by using online bulletin boards and keeping focus groups going on for weeks. Also, nonverbal communication is lost online—in offline groups, facial expressions can be revealing in a way that typed smiley faces do not match, although personal computers and smartphones with webcams make it easy to record video footage during a focus group, which can be post-processed to automatically analyze facial expressions. Another disadvantage of online groups is the authenticity problem. Without seeing people in person, it is difficult to be sure they are who they say they are. For example, it is quite common for children to pose as adults online. This dilemma can be solved by verifying **respondent authenticity** and requiring password entry to the group. Technical problems can also stall an online group.

In a crowdsourcing example, TechSmith, the company that created the Snagit software for taking high-quality screenshots, used crowdsourcing for research during the beta testing stage of software development. Over a 10-month beta test period, over 400,000 people joined the TechSmith community to discuss and comment on the software (Barker, 2012). TechSmith estimated that they saved $300,000 to $500,000 by conducting research this way. We think it is safe to say that the internet has expanded the definition of focus group to include an increasingly large number of participants over a specified time period that is longer than the few hours for face-to-face groups.

ONLINE OBSERVATION

Observation research monitors people's behavior by watching them in relevant situations. For example, retailers videotape shoppers to see the pattern they choose in moving through the store and to monitor other shopping behaviors. Some researchers believe that actions speak louder than words, making customer observation stronger than surveys that record people's statements from memory about what they believe and do. Of course, as a qualitative approach, observations of a small number of people cannot be used to describe how all people might act.

An interesting and important form of observational research, available only on the internet, involves monitoring consumer conversation in social networks, bulletin boards, and other social media. Such information is extremely important for a company and its competitors. Other ways to monitor customer chat are to provide space on the firm's website or to subscribe to e-mail lists on product-related topics.

Citizen journalists post multimedia all over social media, and companies must now observe to see which of the 500 million tweets generated per day concern their brands, company, or executives. This has become a huge problem because a quick Google search is no longer enough to catch a potentially damaging rumor or competitive announcement as it breaks. For example, an MSN.com reporter posted a story "Is Home Depot Shafting Shoppers?" and within one day he received 10,000 e-mails and 4,000 posts on MSN.com that told tales of poor customer service at Home Depot. The company needed automated tracking to catch something like this in time to make a response and control the crisis. This rapid spread of citizen journalist content is part of the reason that companies are losing control of their brand images. Sometimes they pay public relations firms or online reputation management firms to help (such as ReputationDefender.com). However, companies can easily set up an automated monitoring system on their own, using e-mail, RSS feeds, or special software. Google Alerts offers e-mail alerts for any keywords of the user's choice—such as a person's name, a brand name, or a competitor's brand name, and so forth. Users can set up an alert e-mail for the entire Web, blogs, news, videos, or groups and have them sent automatically as they happen, daily, or weekly.

RSS (Really Simple Syndication) feeds are an **XML (extensible markup language)** format designed for sharing headlines and other Web content. When individuals subscribe to a blog or other social media site via RSS, the content goes to reader desktops as it is published. Customers can read the RSS feeds by downloading a free reader. This is the way that most companies follow influential bloggers in their industry and watch for posts about their company and brands so they can add comments or react when crises hit.

Where should companies look online for such conversation? Consider these 12 channels for online reputation monitoring (Beal and Strauss, 2008):

- Your own content channels—any blogs, comment sections on the company site, or other websites owned by the company that allow user posting.
- Social media and blogs alerts and RSS feeds.
- Google's network of video, news, groups, and more.
- Industry news via e-mail newsletters or competitive site monitoring.
- Stakeholder conversations that occur at any other website not monitored in other ways.
- Social communities in the company's industry, such as Tripadvisor.com for the travel industry.
- Social bookmarking sites such as delicious.com, which allows users to tag websites for sharing with others.
- Multimedia content such as video at YouTube and photos at Flickr.

- Forums and message boards such as Reddit.com, and any website in the company's industry that hosts them.
- Customer reviews at sites such as Amazon.com reviews or epinions.com—this is important for companies selling products online.
- Brand profiles at social networks such as LinkedIn.com and Facebook.com.
- Web analytics will help companies monitor the traffic coming to their own sites, the keywords they used at Google to find them, and the sites they visited previously to landing at the company site.

We categorize this nearly real-time monitoring as observational research, but it can also be considered content analysis when social media conversation is analyzed at a later date.

Content Analysis

Content analysis is the examination of text or images in order to evaluate the communication content. Market researchers have used this technique for evaluating press releases or other text and for examining advertising models or their settings (e.g., what roles do men play in advertisements?). Researchers have used content analysis for a long time to understand the communication context, antecedents, trends, persuasive techniques, and much more. This research method can be quantitative or qualitative in nature and fits somewhere between secondary and primary research depending on the project goals, but usually researchers will count words or concepts and report quantitative results.

The river of social media conversation online has opened a floodgate of opportunities for market researchers. They can learn many things about internet users through content analysis, such as:

- Consumer characteristics (e.g., Facebook profiles).
- Customer preferences (e.g., company and competitor site traffic and Twitter streams).
- Brand images (e.g., product review and rating sites and Google group discussions).

Solve Media's Brand Tags provides content that helps thousands of marketers understand their brand images, in what it calls "the world's first brand sentiment network." Displays a word cloud based on a free association qualitative research technique from over 3,000 consumer participants: "describe this brand with any word(s) . . . Purina." This is a great way for companies to understand the current image and sentiment of their brands, using qualitative research collected for free by another company.

Online Survey Research

Survey research is primarily conducted online. Digital marketers conduct surveys online in several ways:

- *Intercept sampling* is used when website users are browsing or shopping on a website and get a pop-up window asking them to participate in a survey. This is a form of self-selection that marketers sometimes call "river" sampling. This is parallel to offline intercept surveys when interviewers stop potential respondents in a public place asking them to answer survey questions. BizRate is a good example of a firm that has built its business using intercept survey research. BizRate presents Web questionnaires to a random sample of shoppers at client sites for the purpose of helping the sites improve marketing efforts.

- *Direct targeting* occurs when organizations send invitations to individuals via e-mail with a link to a survey form on the Web. Organizations either draw a probability sample of e-mail addresses or contact specific people from their databases. They can also purchase a list of e-mail addresses of a specific demographic, geographic, or professional group from a vendor (and addresses based on many other segmentation variables).
- *Panels* are opt-in communities with a large number of people who have agreed to respond to surveys, usually for some incentive (discussed in a subsequent section).
- *Bulletin board/forum groups* are sometimes asked to complete surveys or respond to new products, such as in the Snagit example previously mentioned—although that was mostly based on pure discussion versus a structured questionnaire.

WEB SURVEYS

Many companies post questionnaires on their web-pages. Respondents type answers into automated response mechanisms in the form of radio buttons (users click to indicate the response), drop-down menus, or blank areas for open-ended questions. One such Web survey was conducted to determine what beverages students consumed as the basis of a positioning assignment. Exhibit 6.9 displays question types from the Web survey. Sometimes the purpose of these questionnaires is to gather opinions from a site's visitors (e.g., website registration);

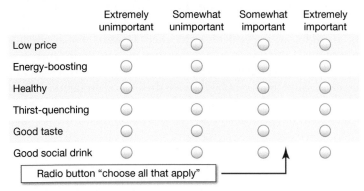

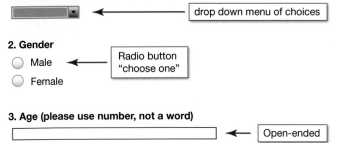

Exhibit 6.9 Web Survey Question Types

sometimes it is a more formal survey research. For example, New Balance asks random website visitors to rate the importance and performance of various site features: customer service, navigation ease, product selection and prices, site security, and shopping. Through this process it learned that customers are willing to pay for shipping, which is why the firm added that element to the pricing structure.

As previously mentioned, researchers often create a Web survey and then send e-mail and use other forms of publicity to direct respondents to the website. The best response rates come from members of e-mail lists, such as customers and prospects, because they usually have a special interest in the topic. Advertising on social media (or using poll widgets) or via banner ads and links from other websites will also drive amount of traffic to a Web survey. In general, response rates to online surveys are as good as or better than surveys using traditional approaches, sometimes reaching as high as 70 percent for opt-in panels (Keeter, 2019).

Online survey research has many advantages and disadvantages over traditional contact methods. Some are discussed in the next paragraphs; Exhibit 6.10 contains a more extensive list.

Online survey research is fast and inexpensive, especially when compared with traditional survey methodologies, perhaps its most important advantage. Questionnaires are delivered nearly instantaneously worldwide over the internet without paying for postage or an interviewer. Web surveys are created as HTML files and do not need lengthy printing, collating, and mailing time. Those who complete the questionnaires generally do so in the first three days, making the entire process very quick. It is also easy to send multiple reminders if using e-mail invitations.

Some researchers believe that Web surveys reduce errors. For example, contingency questions are those that the computer automatically presents depending upon responses to previous questions. If a respondent answers "c" to question 9, the software can immediately skip three questions and present question 12. This technique reduces the complexity and time involved for respondents. In addition, respondents enter their answers, which eliminates data entry errors found in traditional methods when converting answers from paper questionnaires. In addition, some researchers have discovered that respondents will answer questions more honestly and openly on a computer or mobile device than when an interviewer is present—and will answer sensitive questions about private matters over the internet. The reason may be that the device is perceived as impersonal and no one is watching what the respondent types.

Advantages	Disadvantages
Fast and inexpensive	Sample selection/generalizability
Diverse, large group of internet users worldwide to small specialized niche	Measurement validity/self-selection bias
Reduced researcher data entry errors because of respondent data entry	Respondent authenticity uncertain
Honest responses to sensitive questions	Frivolous or dishonest responses
Anyone-can-answer, invitation-only, or password protected	Duplicate submissions
Easy tabulation of electronic data	Declining response rates
Less interviewer bias	Perception that research solicitation is spam

Exhibit 6.10 Advantages and Disadvantages of Online Survey Research

Sample representativeness and measurement validity are the biggest disadvantages of online surveys over their offline counterparts; however, some researchers think the idea of sample representativeness is no longer possible for any type of market research. Marketers cannot draw a scientific **probability sample** because no list of internet users currently exists—unless the sample is only from a firm's customer list, they all use the internet, and the firm has all the e-mail addresses. In contrast, researchers employing in-person or mail contact methods have population lists and can draw probability samples. Although no public lists of all telephone numbers exists, random-digit-dialing technology solved the probability problem for this contact method—at least until great numbers of the population cut the cables on their land lines and only have mobile phones. Without the ability to draw a random sample, researchers cannot generalize results to the entire population being studied. Therefore, researchers can send e-mail questionnaires to samples of respondents or put a Web survey online, but they must be careful when interpreting the results. What does it mean when 15,000 online survey participants click off the products they've shopped for online? How does the result relate to all Web users? This problem is one of generalizability. Some firms, such as BizRate.com, compensate for **sampling** problems by offering the questionnaire to every *n*th visitor at a website. This technique works well if the firm wants information from a good sample of site visitors.

Online research entails several measurement issues. First, because of many different browsers, computer/tablet/mobile screen sizes, and resolution settings, researchers worry that colors will look different and measurement scales will not display properly online.

Another concern with Web questionnaires is respondent authenticity. This problem affects any self-administered survey methodology, but it seems particularly acute on the internet. Many Web users pose as the opposite sex on the internet, and children often pose as adults online. This situation is not easy to correct and obviously biases survey results. Many researchers are attempting to screen out illegitimate or flippant respondents. One way is to watch for frivolous results such as responses that form a pattern (e.g., each response is increased by one: 1, 2, 3, 4, and so on).

Another problem concerns duplicate responses to surveys. However, it is easy to remove duplicate responses from a database by just checking for identical responses submitted near the same time.

Finally, when researchers use e-mail to solicit responses to Web-based questionnaires, it may be perceived as spam unless the sample consists of a firm's customers.

Note that survey forms are not nearly as easy to create as most other types of Web pages. Also, in order to make the form interactive, developers must place a special program on the Web server that "tells" the server what to do with the respondent information. A few enterprising firms created software to assist in this process, such as the Web-based surveymonkey. com. Google Forms software allows researchers to create a free Web form survey nearly as simply as other webpage authoring tools or word processing software. Researchers then put the webpage on their site, and all the interactive work is done on the Google server. Survey responses can be downloaded by the researcher as tables or data appropriate for analysis in spreadsheet or statistical software.

Online Panels

Most researchers are using online panels to combat sampling and response problems. Also called **opt-in** communities, **online panels** include a group of people who have agreed to be the subject of marketing research. Usually they are paid, and they often receive free products as well. Panel participants complete extensive questionnaires after being accepted so that researchers have information about their characteristics and behavior. This way, when panel members are asked to test a product, are given questionnaires to complete, or are sent coupons and other promotions, researchers can correlate results with already collected demographic data. In turn, the research firms can use shorter questionnaires, thus increasing response rates (i.e., no need for demographic questions). An advantage to large panels such as those in the Purina opening story is that smaller groups of members can be targeted based on behavior or demographics. Firms with large online panels include America Consumer Opinion, Nielsen, NPD Group, and Harris Interactive.

In one interesting use of panel testing, global multibillion-dollar sports apparel brand Under Armour partnered with Qualtrics (i.e., an international research and customer experience company) to support product development. Using the Qualtrics platform, Under Armour was able to efficiently scale to over 10,000 panel members for product testing and data capture distributed across product design and marketing teams. The digitally based platform shortened feedback time and increased product tests leading to the development of Under Armour's award-winning HOVR running shoe (see www.qualtrics.com/case-studies for more successful examples) On the downside, panel access is often more expensive for client firms than traditional methods of sample generation. Also, because research firms sometimes recruit panel members in nonscientific ways, the generalizability of survey results from panels is questionable. Large numbers of respondents and high response rates minimize this problem, however. One other problem with panels is that they are paid for their participation and sometimes cheat to get the participation money in three different ways:

1. Cheat by answering "yes" to questions they think will keep them from getting terminated mid-survey because of not using particular products or other screening criteria (they don't want to be terminated because they don't get paid).
2. Inattentive behavior so they can get through it quickly—for example, just clicking random answers without reading carefully, or "straight lining" (clicking all of one number for several questions in a row). Researchers check this by setting traps, such as oppositely worded questions that respondents must closely read to avoid giving inconsistent responses.
3. Closely related to inattention is speeding. Researchers detect this by timing how long it takes respondents to answer a survey, and if they took 5 minutes on a 15-minute questionnaire, their responses are not counted.

Ethics of Online Research

Many companies conducting marketing research on the Web have considered its "gift culture" and decided to give something to respondents as appreciation for participating. With traditional research, respondents are sometimes offered a nominal fee (e.g., $5) to complete a questionnaire, which increases the response rate. Some researchers draw names from those who submit responses, offering them free products or cash. Others donate money to charities selected by respondents (e.g., $3 to one of three charities listed on the Web page for each questionnaire submitted). Many post the entire results in downloadable form, and most provide at least some results on the websites after the survey period is completed.

Marketers face several other ethical concerns regarding survey research on the internet.

1. Respondents are increasingly upset at getting unsolicited e-mail requesting survey participation.
2. Some researchers "harvest" e-mail addresses from internet forums and groups without permission. Perhaps this practice is analogous to gathering names from a telephone book, but some people object because consumers are not posting with the idea of being contacted by marketers.
3. Some companies conduct "surveys" for the purpose of building a database for later solicitation. Ethical marketers clearly mark the difference between marketing research and marketing promotion and do not sell under the guise of research.
4. Privacy of user data is a huge issue in this medium, because it is relatively easy and profitable to send electronic data to others via the internet.

These and other concerns prompted ESOMAR, the European Society for Opinion and Marketing Research, to include guidelines for internet research in its International Code of Marketing and Social Research Practice (www.esomar.org).

In spite of serious shortcomings, the internet is critical for conducting primary research and is an important tool for marketers. However, when using any primary or secondary data, marketers must evaluate their quality carefully and apply it accordingly.

Other Technology-Enabled Approaches

The internet is an excellent place to observe user behavior because the technology automatically records actions in a format that can be easily, quickly, and mathematically manipulated for analysis. Computer client-side and server-side automated data collection are two technology-enabled approaches deserving of special emphasis. Real-time profiling at websites is one particularly powerful server-side approach. These techniques are especially interesting and unusual because they did not exist prior to the internet and because they allow marketers to make quick and responsive changes in Web pages, promotions, and pricing.

Client-Side Data Collection

Client-side data collection refers to collecting information about consumer click behavior right at the user's PC. One approach is to use cookies when a user visits a website. Cookie files are quite helpful, and even necessary, for digital commerce and other internet activities. Some cookies help marketers present appropriate promotions and webpages to individual users using database information. Exhibit 6.11 displays an example of the sales funnel. It shows how cookie files and website logs can identify the number of visitors to a website that view desired pages and eventually purchase the product. As discussed in Chapter 2, these numbers are a result of Web analytics software.

One important client-side data collection method involves measuring user patterns by installing a PC meter on the computers of a panel of users and tracking the user clickstream. This approach is similar to the ACNielsen "people meter" used on TV sets to determine ratings for various programs.

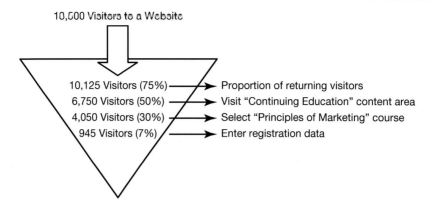

Exhibit 6.11 Website Logs Assist in Sales Funnel Analysis

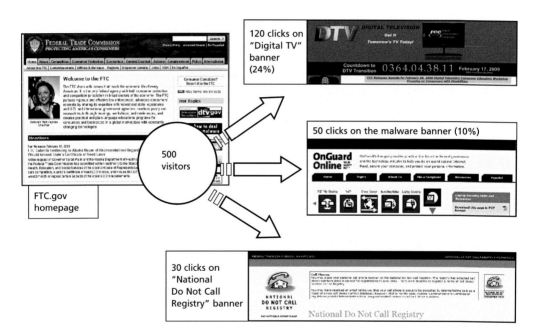

Exhibit 6.12 Following the Clickstream

Server-Side Data Collection

Web analytics uses site log software to generate reports on numbers of users who view each page, the location of the site visited prior to the firm's site, and what users buy at a site— fundamental elements in **server-side data collection**. For example, because of its online registration requirement, Expedia can track visitors' ticket purchases, browsing patterns, and how often they visit the site. It uses the information to send special offers to customers as well as to offer services such as the fare watcher. Amazon.com, through collaborative filtering software, keeps track of books ordered by customers and makes recommendations based on customer trends in its database. These observational data help firms improve online marketing strategies, sell advertising, and produce more effective websites. See Exhibit 6.12

for an example of the clickstream at FTC.gov that Web analytics software would help analyze. Armed with these data, the FTC can determine which pages are the most relevant to citizens and should remain as prominent banner links from its homepage.

Increasingly, firms use server-side data to make frequent changes in Web pages and promotional offers. **Real-time profiling** occurs when special software tracks a user's movements through a website and then compiles and reports on the data at a moment's notice. Also known as "tracking user clickstream in real time," this approach allows marketers to analyze consumer online behavior and make instantaneous adjustments to site promotional offers and Web pages. Real-time profiling is not cheap—one estimate puts the software at $150,000 to start and $10,000 a month thereafter. The ability to predict future behavior based on past behavior and thus offer customized Web pages to appropriate customers while they are visiting a website can, however, pay off handsomely.

Real-Space Approaches

Real-space primary data collection refers to technology-enabled approaches to gather information offline that is subsequently stored and used in marketing databases. The most important real-space techniques are barcode scanners and credit card terminals at brick-and-mortar retail stores, although computer entry by customer service reps while talking on the telephone with customers might also be included here.

Real-space primary data collection occurs at offline points of purchase. Offline data collection is important for digital marketing because these data, when combined with online data, paint a complete picture of consumer behavior for individual retail firms. Smart card and credit card readers, interactive point of sale (iPOS) machines, and barcode scanners are mechanisms for collecting real-space consumer data. Even though the universal product code, also known as the barcode, has been in grocery stores since 1974, its use has grown to the point where such codes are now scanned billions of times a day. Product sales data gathered by scanning the UPC at retail stores are currently used primarily for inventory management. As UPC data go from the cash register into the computer, the software reduces accounting inventory levels automatically and sends communication to suppliers for replenishment of physical goods. This immediate inventory updating is quite efficient for retailers, wholesalers, and manufacturers. It is also an example of the big data problem discussed earlier in this chapter—how to store, analyze, and take action on that much data.

Catalina Marketing uses the UPC for promotional purposes. This firm places small machines next to the cash registers of grocery stores to generate coupons based on each customer's purchase. For example, if a customer buys Smucker's jam, the machine might spit out a $0.50 coupon for Knott's Berry jam. When the consumer redeems the Knott's coupon, the barcode scanner records it. In the process, Catalina Marketing and the retailer are building huge databases of customer purchases and responses to various offers. If consumers redeem only a small proportion of the Knott's coupons, Knott's Berry Farm might choose to increase the coupon size to $0.75. Marketers always attempt to combine data collected at the brick-and-mortar retail store with that of the online version of the store. Most multichannel retailers amass a huge amount of data by combining server-side data from their website with telephone and mail orders from the catalog and UPC real-space data from the brick-and-mortar stores. This data compilation gives their customer service representatives a complete customer record from the database whenever needed.

Marketing Databases and Data Warehouses

Regardless of whether data are collected online or offline, they are moved to various marketing databases, as shown in Exhibit 6.1. Product databases hold information about product features, prices, and inventory levels; customer databases hold information about customer characteristics and behavior. Transaction processing databases are periodically copied into a data warehouse (Exhibit 6.13). Data warehouses are repositories for the entire organization's historical data (not just marketing data). They are designed specifically to support analyses necessary for decision making. Sometimes the data in a warehouse are separated into more specific subject areas (called data marts) and indexed for easy use. These concepts are important to marketers because they use data warehouse information for planning purposes.

Because websites are so complex, often including thousands of pages from or for many different corporate departments, content management is an important area. Many software vendors, including Microsoft, are attempting to solve the website maintenance problem with their software. These programs have features such as press release databases that automatically put the newest stories on a designated page and archive older stories, deleting them on a specified date.

The current trend in data storage is toward **cloud computing**: a network of online Web servers in remote locations from the company used to store and manage data (Exhibit 6.14). Authorized employees can access or upload data from any internet-connected device. The advantages to companies include no investment cost for server space, no software investment to manage the data, and access to free applications such as those offered by the US Post Office or Google Earth. Of course, the company pays to use the cloud computing service. Amazon.com and Salesforce.com are two of the most well-known cloud computing options for companies.

Individuals can also access cloud computing, such as the iCloud for storing all the data on an Apple device (photos, contacts, calendar, and so forth) and retrieving it on any Apple

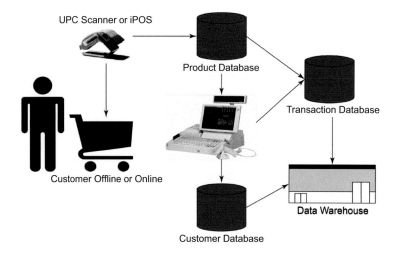

Exhibit 6.13 Real-Space Data Collection and Storage Example

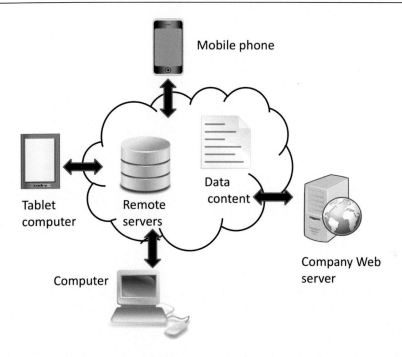

Exhibit 6.14 Cloud Computing Allows Internet Data Access Anytime, Anywhere with Any Device

phone, computer, or tablet. Dropbox.com and Microsoft Teams are other great applications for individuals who want to store data on a server and have it automatically sync to any computer. The authors used Microsoft Teams to write this book, holding virtual meetings and sharing files from thousands of miles away. When one author updates a chapter, it automatically saves to the other author's computer via Teams.

Note that cloud computing is not just for data storage. Data processing can also take place in the cloud. For example, Facebook and all its many apps live in the cloud, as do Twitter, Gmail, YouTube, and a host of other services. Many multiplayer games similarly live in the cloud.

Data Analysis and Distribution

Data collected from all customer touch points are stored in the data warehouse or cloud knowledge management system, ready for analysis and distribution to marketing decision makers. Four important types of analysis for marketing decision making include data mining, **customer profiling**, RFM analysis (recency, frequency, monetary value), and report generating.

Data mining involves the extraction of hidden predictive information in large databases through statistical analysis (see the "Let's Get Technical" box). Here, marketers don't need to approach the database with any hypotheses other than an interest in finding patterns among the data. For example, a marketer might want to know whether a product's heaviest users tend to purchase more during particular months or how many people in a social network share applications with others. Patterns uncovered by marketers help them to refine marketing mix strategies, identify new-product opportunities, and predict consumer behavior. Using data mining helped Fingerhut, the $2 billion catalog retailer, discover that customers who move their residence triple their purchasing in the 12 weeks after the move. Data mining also revealed that movers tend to buy furniture, telephones, and decorations but not jewelry or home electronics. Fingerhut used this information to create a special Mover's Catalog, selecting appropriate products from among the 15,000 items it sells. In addition, it stopped sending other specialty catalogs to movers during the 12-week window. Data mining also helped the American Automobile Association (AAA) Mid-Atlantic office to streamline its marketing communication process, decreasing the amount mailed by 96 percent, from 1.2 million to 40,000 pieces per year. This reduced costs by 92 percent without a membership-enrollment decline.

Customer profiling uses data warehouse information to help marketers understand the characteristics and behavior of specific target groups. Through this process, marketers can really understand who buys particular products and how they react to promotional offers and pricing changes. Some additional uses of customer profiling include the following:

- Selecting target groups for promotional appeals.
- Discovering the best way to engage customers in social media.
- Finding and keeping customers with a higher lifetime value to the firm.
- Understanding the important characteristics of heavy product users.
- Directing cross-selling activities to appropriate customers.
- Reducing direct-mailing costs by targeting high-response customers.

RFM analysis scans the database for three criteria. First, when did the customer last purchase (recency)? Second, how often has the customer purchased products (frequency)? Third, how much has the customer spent on product purchases (monetary value)? This process allows firms to target offers to the customers who are most responsive, saving promotional costs and increasing sales. For example, an online retailer might notice that the top customer segment generated 32 percent of the sales, with a $69 average order value (AOV), or $22 of sales per thousand exposures to a keyword ad on Google. Now the retailer can estimate the value of this type of advertising and take steps to reach the top customer segment as directly as possible.

Individual marketing personnel can perform data mining, customer profiling, and RFM analyses at any time through access to the data warehouse and distribute the results to other staff members involved in a particular decision. Report generators, on the other hand, automatically create easy-to-read, high-quality reports from data warehouse or cloud information on a regular basis. These reports may be placed in the marketing knowledge database on an intranet or extranet for all to access. Marketers can specify the particular information that should appear in these automatic reports and the time intervals for distribution, as in the earlier example of a retailer that sends online weekly sales reports to all managers. Some firms provide collaborative software that automatically integrates data from both the firm's **macroenvironment** and its **microenvironment**. For example, when a marketing manager working on a marketing plan saves the data, the system can automatically put the file on the server for other managers to access. Internal data are seamlessly integrated with the firm's website, external websites, newsgroups, and databases—all with search capabilities. Such software helps firms distribute the results of database analyses. Cloud computing vendors also have this capability.

Knowledge Management Metrics

Marketing research is not cheap. Marketers often weigh the cost of gaining additional information against the value of potential opportunities or the risk of possible errors from decisions made with incomplete information. They are also concerned about the storage cost of all those terabytes of data coming from website logs, social media conversations, online surveys, Web registrations, and other real-time and real-space approaches. The good news is that data storage costs have declined steadily over the last couple of decades, and marketers can now buy disk drives for a dollar per gigabyte or online storage for anywhere from $10 to $23 per gigabyte. Online storage has many additional benefits, such as duplicate storage and fast recovery on demand, and more. Two metrics are currently in widespread use:

- *ROI.* Companies want to know why they should save all those data. How will they be used, and will the benefits in additional revenues or lowered costs return an acceptable rate on the storage space investment? For hardware storage space (either on site or in the cloud), ROI usually means total cost savings divided by total cost of the installation (Gruener, 2001). Notably, companies use ROI to justify the value of other knowledge management systems as well.
- *Total cost of ownership (TCO).* Largely a metric used by information technology managers, TCO includes not only the cost of hardware, software, and labor for data storage but also other items such as cost savings by reducing Web server downtime and labor requirements.

For example, the American sports-themed beverage brand, Gatorade, recently sought to increase their social media marketing effectiveness by adding Facebook and Instagram in-stream video advertising. Gatorade is manufactured by PepsiCo and distributed in over 80 countries worldwide. They were looking to achieve a higher return for the Gatorade Zero product. Targeting their core audience of adults (ages of 25–54) with an interest in fitness and wellness, Gatorade conducted a split test delivering video ads through traditional news feeds (i.e., scrolling) or via in-stream placement to viewers already watching videos. The goal was to determine whether in-stream ad placement drove incremental sales and greater value on the campaign spend while optimizing the budget automatically across the best-performing ads in real time. After six weeks, in-stream advertising reached more than 47 million consumers while increasing market penetration by 1.2 percent—which is a significant return within a global multi-billion dollar industry (see Facebook for Business for more examples).

Chapter Summary

Digital marketers need data to guide decisions about creating and changing marketing mix elements. These data are collected from a myriad of sources, filtered into databases, and turned into marketing knowledge that is then used to develop marketing strategy. Knowledge management is the process of managing the creation, use, and dissemination of knowledge. A marketing information system is the process by which marketers manage knowledge, using a system of assessing information needs, gathering information and analyzing it, and then disseminating it to decision makers.

Marketers can tap three sources of marketing knowledge. (1) internal records (such as cash flow, sales force data, and customer data), (2) secondary data (publicly and privately generated, from online databases, and for competitive intelligence), and (3) primary data (gathered for the first time to solve a particular problem). Competitive intelligence (CI) involves analyzing the industries in which a firm operates as input to the firm's strategic positioning and to understand competitor vulnerabilities. Marketers must evaluate the quality of data before relying on them to solve research problems.

Primary data are collected on the internet by nearly all companies. The steps to conduct primary research are as follows: (1) define the research problem, (2) develop a research plan, (3) collect data, (4) analyze the data, and (5) distribute findings. Internet-based research may include any of the following activities conducted online: experiments, focus groups, observations, and surveys. Surveys may be conducted by e-mail invitation to a website. Advantages to online surveys are that they are fast and inexpensive, have broad reach, reduce errors, elicit honest responses, can be restricted to authorized participants, and are easy to tabulate. Disadvantages include poor generalizability of results due to poor sample selection, self-selection bias, inability to confirm the respondent's authenticity, frivolous or dishonest responses, and duplicate submissions.

Online panels are increasingly being used to combat sampling and response problems of online surveys. Although some of these panels are small, others contain millions of participants. Some ethical concerns of online research include unsolicited e-mail, harvesting e-mail addresses from newsgroups, selling under the guise of research, and lack of privacy of user data.

Companies must constantly monitor social media and other websites to identify content about their brands and personnel that are posted by citizen journalists and other stakeholders. New technologies such as e-mail alerts, RSS feeds, and special software make this an easy and automated process.

Marketers use technology to observe user behavior on the user's computer (client side) via cookies and PC meters or the server (server side) via the use of log files and real-time profiling. Real-space data collection takes place at offline points of purchase such as smart card and credit card readers, iPOS machines, and barcode scanners. The data can be used for inventory control and to target promotions.

Data warehouses are repositories for the organization's historical data. Data marts are subsections of the warehouse categorized by subject area. Data from all customer touch points are stored in the warehouse. Four types of analysis are conducted with the data: data mining, customer profiling, RFM (recency, frequency, monetary value) analysis, and report generation. Data mining extracts hidden predictive information from the warehouse via statistical analysis. Customer profiling helps marketers understand the characteristics and behavior of specific target groups. RFM analysis allows firms to target offers to customers who might be most responsive. Sophisticated report generation tools can automatically schedule and publish reports.

Exercises

Review Questions

1. What are the three main sources of data for solving marketing research problems?
2. Contrast primary with secondary data and explain the advantages and disadvantages of each.
3. Why is big data a problem for marketers?

4. What is competitive intelligence, and what are some sources of online CI data?
5. Why and how do digital marketers evaluate the quality of information on a website?
6. What are the strengths and weaknesses of the internet for primary and secondary data collection?
7. Identify the key primary research methods and the appropriate use of each one.
8. What is A/B testing and why is this important?
9. How do marketers turn marketing data into marketing knowledge?
11. What is real-space data collection? Why is it important?
12. Is data mining possible without a data warehouse? Why or why not?
13. What is cloud computing, and how does it help marketers?
14. Give an example of how data mining uncovers new knowledge.
15. Identify the steps in a primary marketing research project.

Discussion Questions

1. **Purina Story:** Review Exhibits 6.2 and 6.14. What conclusions can you make about Purina customers and brand based on these and the opening story?
2. **Purina Story:** classify each of the research methods used by Purina, using concepts from the chapter.
3. What online research method(s) would you use to test a new-product concept? Why?
4. What online research method(s) would you use to test the brand image of an existing product? Why?
5. What combination of techniques would you recommend for conducting competitive intelligence?
6. Of the ethical issues mentioned in the chapter, which are you most concerned about as a consumer? Why?
7. Can you think of a marketing research technique that could not be supported online? Explain your answer.
8. What are the current limitations for undertaking market research on the general population on the internet? How might these be overcome now and in the future?
9. Given that the cost of sending an e-mail questionnaire to 10,000 people is no higher than the cost of sending it to 10 people, why would market researchers bother devising samples if they were planning to undertake some research online?
10. What do you think a company should do if it receives a Google Alert or RSS feed showing that customers are speaking poorly about its products?
11. What are the pros and cons of cloud computing?
12. How would you monitor a brand image in the social media?

Web Activities

1. Join the American Consumer Opinion online panel and take a survey (www.acop.com). Did it screen for a particular type of respondent? What observations can you make about the client and research problem?
2. Look for the cookies file(s) on your hard drive (on a Microsoft PC, use the *find file* function and search for *cookie*). Do you see sites there that you have never visited?
3. Find information on the US Census and Nielsen TV ratings, either online or in the library. What methodology does each use? Evaluate their strengths and weaknesses based on what you've learned about research methods in this chapter.

4. Toyota has asked you to test the effectiveness of its new banner ad using four primary research techniques. Design these tests.
5. Visit allfacebook.com and report on the top pages. What statistics does this site provide, and how can it help marketers?
6. Visit Google Trends and check out two competitive brands (like Coke and Pepsi). What are the differences in brand image?

Chapter 7

Consumer Behavior Online

Time is the only commodity worth anything anymore. Consumers will pay you to save them time. The internet saves people time.

— Scott Reamer, S.G. Cowen

Consumers are empowered in a way that's almost frightening.

— Peter Weedfald, Samsung Electronics North America

The primary objective of this chapter is to develop a general understanding of the online consumer population. You will explore the context in which online consumer behavior occurs, the characteristics and resources of online consumers, and the outcomes of the online exchange process.

After reading this chapter, you will be able to:

- Discuss general statistics about the internet population.
- Describe the internet exchange process and the technological, social/cultural, and legal context in which consumers participate in this process.
- Outline the broad individual characteristics and consumer resources that consumers bring to the online exchange.
- Highlight the four main categories of outcomes that consumers seek from online exchanges.

THE CUSTOMER'S STORY

This is the story of a typical one-hour adventure on a weekend afternoon in the life of a 25-year-old professional male, Justin. It begins when he streams news from his iPhone while having the television tuned to a soccer game and answering a text message from his smartwatch.

Partway through the newscast, the newsperson mentions @NASA_Astronauts, a Twitter account of interest to Justin. Justin opens the Twitter app on his iPhone to find the Twitter account mentioned in the newscast. He is captivated by photos of the astronauts' latest trip to the International Space Station. As he browses the account, Justin tweets to a friend who lives in a different time zone: "You gotta see these photos."

As Justin continues to peruse @NASA_Astronauts, he sees a link to their website, follows the link to see that there are careers available at NASA. He follows NASA on LinkedIn to learn more about its culture and stay up-to-date on employment opportunities. The more

DOI: 10.4324/9781003247319-10

Justin reads about NASA, the more he could see himself working for a company like this. Justin returns to Twitter and retweets several of @NASA_Astronauts' tweets, and pretty soon other messages about NASA appear. The buzz quickly spreads.

This is the new consumer. He is a multitasker, attending to many different electronic media simultaneously. He is difficult to catch online and won't stick around one website for long. His connections with friends and colleagues are enhanced by the internet, where they like to share their online conversation in a myriad of ways from e-mail, to text, to micromedia sites. They are often routed to traditional websites after connecting with others and viewing content in social media. Justin is an important consumer because if brands can't attract the young demographic, they will eventually head into the decline stage and die. How can a marketer capture dollars from this—advertising online, selling streaming music access and other products, fees for premium social media subscriptions? That is a problem marketers are trying to solve as you read this.

Consumers in the Twenty-First Century

This chapter is about the majority of US consumers who use the internet. Before we delve into understanding their behavior, it is important to think about the small percent of Americans who don't use the internet. It would not benefit a company to invest in a significant Web presence if its market were mostly in that minority percentage. The less-connected groups tend to be older, less educated, live in rural areas, and have a lower income (according to Pew Internet & the American Life Project). Pew suggests that nonusers may have no interest in going online and do not think that doing so enhances their lives, while others find it too difficult to use. Still others cite the expense of the internet or owning a computer as the reason they do not use the internet (Anderson and Perrin, 2016). Chapter 4 describes many social, cultural, technological, legal, and political issues as the main reasons that consumers do not use the internet in emerging economies. Without major shifts, some countries may not ever achieve high levels of internet adoption among individual consumers, although high cell phone adoption may change this picture eventually.

The number of non-internet users has continued to decline over the last couple of decades (Exhibit 7.1). Globally, internet use is still growing, but at a slower pace than in the past. As of January 2021, 4.6 billion people had access to the internet, representing 60 percent of the worldwide population (Johnson, 2021a). Internet usage in developed nations has reached a

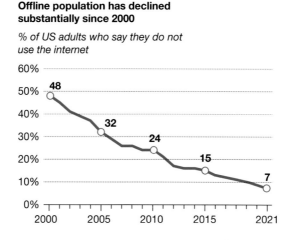

Exhibit 7.1 Offline Population has Declined Substantially Since 2000 (Pew Research Center)

critical mass, and marketers now ask practical questions such as whether a firm's target market is online, what these customers do online, what determines whether they will buy from a site, and how much of the marketing effort should be devoted to online channels. This chapter addresses typical consumer behavior among internet users in the United States in order to discover the answers to some of these questions.

Inside the Internet Exchange Process

Many stimuli, characteristics, and processes explain consumer buying behavior. Stimuli that can motivate consumers to purchase one product rather than another include marketing communication messages and cultural, political, economic, and technological factors. Individual buyer characteristics such as income level and personality also come into play, along with other psychological, social, and personal aspects. Finally, consumers move through a variety of decision processes based on situational and product attributes. Marketing knowledge about consumer behavior is quite complex, and although we make many generalizations, individual differences are also important.

To create effective marketing strategies, marketers need to understand what motivates people to buy goods and services, both in the short and long term (i.e., develop brand loyalty). **Exchange** is a basic marketing concept that refers to the act of obtaining a valued object from someone by offering something in return. When consumers purchase a product, they are exchanging money for desired goods or services. However, many other types of marketing exchanges can be made, such as when a politician asks citizens to exchange their votes for his or her services.

Exhibit 7.2 summarizes the basic internet exchange process—a graphical representation to help focus this discussion. Individuals bring their own characteristics and personal resources to the process as they seek specific outcomes from an exchange. This process occurs within a technological, social/cultural, and legal context. The exchange is often motivated by marketing stimuli—the topic of Part IV of this book.

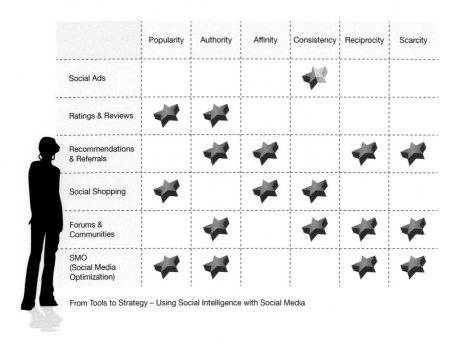

Exhibit 7.2 The Basic Internet Exchange Process

Technological Context

The internet has moved from novelty to utility in the United States and most developed nations. It is critical for digital marketers to understand the current state of ever-changing internet technology if they want to entice consumer exchanges. "Let's Get Technical" boxes within this text assist in this process, and the semantic Web and other innovations mentioned in Chapter 1 bear watching. Here we focus upon two important developments affecting online consumer behavior today—home connection speeds and the changing landscape of digital receiving devices such as cell phones.

Three-quarters of Americans connect to the internet at home with broadband (fast) internet service (Pew Research, 2021). Consumers connecting with broadband exhibit different online behavior than do those accessing from a mobile handheld device. Broadband users enjoy more multimedia games, music, and entertainment because data caps are typically higher than those of mobile devices (see the "Let's Get Technical" box).

The number of consumer internet and media devices, such as smartphones, TVs, digital devices, computers, etc., connected to the internet (i.e., internet of things—IoT) is more than 10 billion and is expected to reach 25 by 2030 (Holst, 2021b). Media streaming services have grown more popular than ever. Netflix, one of the most popular streaming services that allow customers to watch television and movie content for a monthly fee, has grown from 25 million subscribers in 2012 to more than 207 million in 2021 (available at Netflix.com). Streaming services adoption continues to grow, including the ability to watch any video content on demand while at home or on the road.

As shown in Exhibit 7.3, among online US residents, internet use has surpassed television (451 minutes per day for internet versus 229 for television), according to Statista. Time spent reading newspapers and magazines is just about 15 minutes per day, according to this study.

Average Minutes with Major Media Per Day

☐ Digital ☐ TV ■ Radio ■ Newspapers ■ Magazines

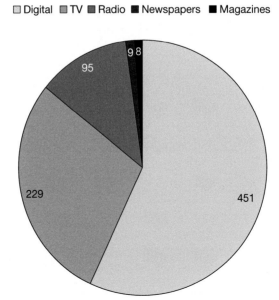

Exhibit 7.3 Americans' Daily Media Use as of 2020

The key is to learn which devices a firm's customers and prospects own and prefer to use. Companies then target customers' digital devices to deliver messages, interact, facilitate exchange, and manage relationships. Users can now access stock prices, FedEx package tracking information, airline schedule changes, weather, and more over their smartphones while in an Uber car on the way to a client meeting or the airport.

Let's Get Technical—Broadband Options

You are trying to decide whether to get a high-speed internet connection for your apartment. You know of the different options—**cable modems, DSL**, satellite, and LTE—you are not quite sure how they are different and would rather not buy more than you need. You need to know about broadband connections to the home and their options.

The information channels that form the internet's backbone have amazing carrying capacities and are constantly being upgraded by firms such as Cisco, Sprint, and AT&T. However, consumers pay for the last mile along the path to the internet, the connection to the consumer's home. Various wired and wireless alternatives are available.

The wired alternatives make use of two wires that are already connected to the user's home—the phone line and the cable TV line. These wires can do double duty to carry internet content on one channel while they perform their normal functions on the other channels.

Digital Subscriber Line

Digital subscriber line (DSL) technology refers to a family of methods for transmitting at speeds up to 8 Mbps (8 million bits per second) over a standard phone line. DSL uses the phone line already installed in consumer homes, allowing users to simultaneously make phone calls and surf the Web because the data travel outside of the audible voice band. Users must install a DSL modem; some computer manufacturers offer these modems as a preinstalled item, and some phone companies supply them. The major phone companies have deployed the infrastructure to support DSL technology, but they were a bit late to the game and have been playing catch-up with cable modems. As a result, phone companies aggressively price DSL service to attract cable subscribers.

Cable Modems

Cable modems allow transmission of internet traffic over the cable TV wire connected to the home. The speed of transmission over a cable modem ranges between 20 Mbps and 100 Mbps. The major problem cable companies may face is having too many subscribers! This problem arises because subscribers in a cable neighborhood share bandwidth. The more the subscribers who share, the less bandwidth is available to repartition. Therefore, if a neighborhood becomes saturated with subscribers, each subscriber will experience delays.

Cable companies have two big advantages—early market penetration and a much bigger information pipe. The **early adopters** opted for cable modems because they were the first technology available. This early usage also gives cable modems the advantage of diffusion via word of mouth. The cable companies solved their infrastructure issues early and can now focus on establishing value-added services such as the following:

- Video-on-demand.
- CD-quality audio.
- Online games available for download and purchase.

Each value-added service provides a barrier to entry for the phone companies. Why purchase a service with fewer features? And because providing each service requires a learning curve, phone companies will experience difficulty catching up.

Cable also has a higher maximum speed than DSL. Nonetheless, phone companies continue to question the actual versus advertised speed of cable. However, if both networks are properly supported, cable still wins the battle.

One way the phone companies are competing is through price. DSL typically undercuts cable, though there are regional variations in price. In some cases, the companies will waive the installation fee if the user signs up for an extended period of service.

Wireless Broadband Options

Three smaller competitors in the broadband game are satellite, fixed wireless, and mobile wireless. There are two types of satellite service—geostationary and constellation. Geostationary is the older technology. The satellite is placed so high in the sky that it rotates in synch with the earth. The advantage of being so high is that you need very few satellites since a single satellite can communicate with an enormous area—for example all of North America. The disadvantage of being so high is that it takes a quarter of a second for a signal to go up and back. This is a noticeable and annoying delay especially when using a real-time service such as video conferencing. SpaceX recently introduced a competing system based on a constellation of thousands of satellites flying in lower orbit. Because they are in lower orbit, the satellites cannot keep pace with the earth's rotation. Nonetheless, there are so many of them that as one passes out of range, another moves into range so you are constantly connected. Your cell phone operates in a similar way when driving. Your call gets passed from tower to tower but appears to you to be a continuous connection. The advantage of flying in lower orbit is that there is almost no latency delay in the signal. It feels real time. The other advantage of thousands of satellites is that they are sharing the load so that no one satellite becomes overwhelmed.

Fixed wireless access is best categorized by distance and bandwidth. Some systems are designed to work over a range of miles, effectively replacing wired access to the home. Other systems operate over a range of up to hundreds of feet, providing local connectivity within the home or office. In either scenario, the bandwidth of the system determines its suitability as a broadband connection. There is a good chance that a competitively priced SpaceX offering will take significant market share from fixed wireless.

Mobile wireless is available over the cell phone network. With cell phone towers already in place in many areas, Web access via cell phone would seem to be a natural outgrowth. The cell phone network is reliable and in most areas the communication is already digital. LTE networks operate up to 36 Mbps for download and 16 Mbps for upload, and 5G networks operate even faster—up to 20 Gbps. This is on par or faster than cable for most meaningful applications. With so many vendors offering unlimited data, it will be interesting to see if homeowners abandon their cable modems and transfer all data through their cell phones, in the same way that many abandoned their voice land lines when cell phones became available. Smartphone users and laptop road warriors are leading the charge to popularize LTE and 5G services. Ultimately, users want access to anything, anytime, anywhere, and from any device.

Social and Cultural Contexts

The days of marketers holding consumers captive for 30 seconds of a TV commercial are quickly coming to a close, and captivity in front of a display ad online is virtually nonexistent. Ad content is increasingly being shown in shorter formats such as five-second skippable ads at the start of a YouTube video. Furthermore, the Web is training individuals and organizations to help themselves to information, products, and practically everything they want when and where they please. Thus, the power has shifted to consumers, as mentioned in Chapter 1. For example, consumers today walk into brick-and-mortar car dealerships and open their smartphones to discuss automobile options and pricing with salespeople.

One of the most important social trends is that consumers trust each other more than they trust advertising or companies online. The increase in user-generated content in special interest communities has consumers looking to each other for advice. For example, Askapatient (www.askapatient.com) hosts thousands of posts about side effects of various medicines. Consumers visit the site to see if other people experience the side effects that they experience and what to expect for a new drug, and many find it to be more reliable than information from pharmaceutical companies. As the COVID-19 vaccination was rolled out in early 2021, it was met with consumer skepticism about its effectiveness given the newness of this type of virus. Consumers turned to Twitter and other social media sites to learn about the side effects that others were experiencing as they received the vaccine to help inform their own decisions. These examples highlight the importance consumers place on user-generated content, and the truly in-tune marketers are not only monitoring this content but engaging in the conversation.

The following general social/cultural trends also greatly affect online exchanges:

- **Sophisticated consumers** know they are in control and have choices—for example, they use the information provided by Askapatient.com to help their medical doctors make treatment decisions.
- **Information overload** overwhelms consumers. It creates an **attention economy**—the idea that information may be infinite but the demand for it is limited by human capacity. This serious problem is compounded by the internet and is one reason why consumers have little tolerance for spam (unsolicited e-mail).
- **Multitasking** speeds up normal processes and lowers attention to each task. By example, the **millennials**, a consumer segment born between 1974 and 1994 (also called Generation Y), are great multitaskers, likely to watch several television screens with sporting events at home, connect with friends via their smartphones, and monitor sports scores on the internet at the same time.

- **Home and work** boundaries are dissolving. Many US internet users have access to the internet both at home and at work, with this trend growing tremendously in an effort to stay safe during the COVID-19 pandemic. Home has become more like a center of life and home office for many; this trend will increase as more Americans work and live in different cities and rarely visit the physical office.
- **I want what I want when I want it**. Anywhere, anytime convenience is critical for busy people. They want to view online content, shop or pay bills anytime of the day or night from any geographic location, online or not, and receive deliveries when convenient for them, not for the firm or package delivery service, which explains the popularity of services such as Amazon Prime (two-day delivery) and Prime Now (two-hour delivery). Online users access the internet from mobile devices, sending e-mail, text messages, photos, and searching the Web for a variety of content. Consumers have high expectations that firms will answer e-mails and social media posts quickly and generally perform as expected—otherwise they will take to Twitter to share the news about the underperforming company.
- **Self-service** is required. Empowered customers want to log on, find information, make purchases, track package shipments, check their accounts, and make inquiries anytime, 24/7. Furthermore, they want to do these tasks on a computer via the internet and on the go. It is an interesting contradiction: consumers want to help themselves when they feel like it and be pampered by firms at other times.
- **Privacy and data security** are paramount. Customers want marketers to keep their data confidential. They also want to safeguard children from websites they find objectionable. Consumers want marketers to ask permission before sending commercial messages to their devices. However, internet of things (IoT)-connected devices such as voice-controlled speakers, which listen for consumers' voice commands to know when to be launched into action find and share information with consumers, may present more privacy and data security challenges as they continue to grow more popular among consumers.

Individual Characteristics and Resources

Beyond general social and cultural trends, individuals vary in their online behavior. Some of this variance is based on differences in characteristics, such as demographics and attitudes, and some is based on the resources consumers bring to the exchange process.

Individual differences. Internet users have several characteristics that differentiate them from nonusers, and similarly, users differ in their needs and desires. The first variable involves demographics. Age, income, education, ethnicity, and gender all affect internet use. For example, 99 percent of 18- to 29-year-olds use the internet, as compared with 75 percent of those ages 65 and older. While adoption gaps are declining, differences continue to persist across population characteristics ("Internet/Broadband Fact Sheet", 2021).

The second variable is a positive attitude toward technology. Internet users who purchase products online tend to hold the attitude that technology helps make their lives richer and easier. See the "Let's Get Technical" box for differences in broadband option selection, indicating technology differences. Third, online skill and experience play an important role in the exchange process. Consumers who have been using the internet for more than three years tend to be more adept than new users at finding information and products quickly, resulting in less frustration and less shopping cart abandonment.

Consumers may be interested in engaging in online shopping for different purposes. For example, goal-oriented behavior often includes going to a specific website with a purpose in mind or searching for the lowest price for a particular product. Experience orientation relates to having fun, bargain hunting, or just surfing to find something new. Goal-oriented individuals like the idea that they don't have to deal with salespeople or crowds in the online environment, and they appreciate the online product selection, convenience, and information availability. When consumers are engaged in experiential shopping, it makes sense that they would find this element more often in brick-and-mortar stores than online.

Marketers thoroughly explore the differences in online behavior for their target markets and then design marketing mixes accordingly. It is especially important to provide options as markets continue to fragment to increasingly smaller target groups.

Consumer resources. Chapter 2 introduced the value equation, showing that consumers perceive value as benefits minus costs. These costs constitute a consumer's resources for exchange: money, time, energy, and psychic costs.

Monetary cost. Consumers need enough discretionary income to exchange for the goods and services they want—and to afford a computer and ISP connection for internet access. What makes the internet exchange different, however, is that consumers usually can't pay cash or don't write paper checks for online transactions. Instead, consumers pay by credit card, debit card, or another form of digital currency. While many consumers in developed nations use credit cards, not everyone is able to acquire or wants a credit card. This problem is big for marketers targeting the huge teen market online and for those targeting consumers in countries with low credit card availability.

Time cost. Time poverty is a problem for today's consumers, so they want to receive appropriate benefits for the time they spend online. Companies want to ensure that users get what they desire for the time invested by making their sites well organized and easy to navigate so users can quickly find what they want.

The internet's property of time moderator, discussed in Chapter 1, helps consumers manage their scarce time. Users can shop, e-mail, or perform other activities anytime, 24/7—a big advantage for working parents who can only find the time to shop late at night after the kids are in bed.

Time resource is a critical topic because online attention from consumers is a desirable and scarce commodity. The clutter of websites now parallels that of other media—with some differences. Some researchers believe that consumers pay more focused attention to websites than to the content in any other medium. When in front of a television, consumers are easily distracted by other people or activities in the environment. The same holds true for the passivity of radio listening. Consumers seem to pay more attention to print media but may still flip pages quickly.

Flow refers to a psychological state consumers experience when they are 100 percent involved and not easily distracted when they are online (Hoffman and Novak, 1996). Whether they are in a goal-oriented or experiential shopping trip online, they are focused. Therefore, once digital marketers can capture a pair of consumer eyeballs or earlobes, they can make a big impression in a short time as long as the website is enjoyable, self-reinforcing, and engaging.

Psychic costs. Closely related to time are psychic resources. Consumers apply psychic resources when webpages are hard to figure out or when facing technological glitches. Baymard Institute (2017) estimates that $260 billion in sales for online retailers can be recovered by improving factors impacting design and flow in the checkout experience. At one time or another all users abandon carts due to technical problems and other issues—buying just gets to be too much trouble. Consumers may abandon their shopping carts because they got distracted, weren't sure of the return policy or shipping price, or couldn't remember their username or password, among other reasons.

Internet Exchange

Then comes the actual moment when exchange occurs. Browser favorites help consumers quickly jump to their favorite online retailer when looking for a product or making a purchase. In addition, e-mail messages from firms often contain hyperlinks to bring consumers directly to specific information, news reports, or advertised specials. The internet has the added feature of automation to facilitate exchange. For example, news sources often send one-sentence e-mails several times a day or week with breaking news for those who sign up for the service. Also, Amazon.com sends consumers a link to a new book by a previously purchased author. These automated e-mails facilitate the exchange process.

Exchange Outcomes

Just what benefits do consumers get by exchanging all that money and time? Organizations such as Pew Research Center, comScore Media Metrix, Nielsen, ClickZ, and others have enabled a rich understanding of what American consumers do online and how the internet has changed the way people behave. Using these generalizations, marketers look for differences in their target markets and then build online and off-line strategies to meet their needs.

People typically engage in five basic behaviors online—connect, create, enjoy, learn, and trade. Each is ripe with marketing opportunity. In the following sections, we categorize the myriad of online activities into these areas of consumer need and desire. Looking at it this way helps marketers remember that profits come from focusing on the customer.

Connect

Unlike any other medium, the internet allows consumers to interact with individuals and organizations using multimedia two-way communication. Around 4 billion consumers use e-mail worldwide ("Number of E-mail Users Worldwide from 2017 to 2025", 2021). E-mail is still the internet's "killer app" worldwide, in spite of spam. Consumers communicate online because it is an inexpensive way to keep in touch, and because it is usually text based so it can be easily accomplished over a wireless handheld device. In addition, consumers make new connections with the people and business partners they meet online that sometimes carry over to the physical world.

Consumers also spend time instant messaging (IM), making phone calls using the internet (Skype) and video calling (FaceTime), using online dating applications, and more. Consumers exchange time and energy to build relationships with friends and family and even to work out problems with companies.

Create

The need to connect was one springboard for the Web's social networking sites, where users can create profiles, upload pictures and other content, and connect with friends and colleagues. Content creation is the highest form of user engagement because users are participating by adding to the Web's offerings, as discussed in Chapter 1. Facebook is the most popular site, nearing 3 billion monthly active users worldwide. For professionals, LinkedIn sets the standard, with over 740 million members in 2021 (Osman, 2021). LinkedIn members include executives from all Fortune 500 companies.

User-content creation for uploading has grown so quickly and is so vast that we created a separate category of exchange outcome for this edition of *eMarketing*. The biggest activity involves digital sharing at sites such as Facebook, which reports that nearly 56 percent of average daily content shared are photos (Newberry, 2021). Users also create or post comments to blogs and create videos for YouTube and for a myriad of online contests for user-created television commercials (e.g., the Doritos Super Bowl Contest). It is no wonder that users create all these videos for uploading—nearly half of all internet users enjoy watching videos on social media sites. You'll find social media strategies to capitalize on this trend in later chapters.

Enjoy

Many consumers use the internet to enjoy entertainment (Exhibit 7.4). Two-thirds browse for fun, sometimes on experiential shopping trips, as previously mentioned. One of internet's big promises, however, is audio and visual entertainment. American adults ages 18–64 watch hundreds of minutes of online video per week, and this will continue to rise in coming years due to the increasing popularity of streaming services. As this occurs, online entertainment content will grow considerably and become just one of the choices for consumers deciding how to spend time online.

One way for marketers to keep their fingers on the pulse of internet users is to monitor search terms entered at Google, Bing, and other search engines. Popular search items tend to change every month with breaking news events, and a glance at the most-entered searches in 2020 validates this, with the top five being (1) Election results, (2) Coronavirus, (3) Kobe Bryant, (4) Coronavirus update, and (5) Coronavirus symptoms according to Google.

Learn

Consumers access information to learn things online such as news, driving directions, travel information, jobs, weather, sports scores, and radio broadcasts over the internet. Digital marketers have known for some time that consumers only have a limited amount of time to exchange for media consumption and that the internet takes away from off-line media time, as consumers are increasingly turning to the internet to access the news.

How do internet users find information for learning? Many are loyal to particular media sites, often prompted by breaking news e-mails and push notifications. Queries range from the vanity search ("How many times does my name come up on Google?") to the soul searching ("Who is God?") and ridiculous ("what is what") to the heartbreaking ("My mom has breast cancer—what should I do?").

Outcome	Percent
Online videos	90.6
Gaming	86.9
Make purchases online	76.8
Listen to streaming services	73.2
Seek news	55.6
Access social media	53.6
Watch video blogs	51.4
Listen to online radio	47.1
Listen to podcasts	44.1

Exhibit 7.4 Percent of Global Internet Users Enjoying Types of Content Each Month

Trade

Most consumers shop, buy, or conduct other transaction-oriented activities online (85 percent worldwide) (Tighe, 2021). Due to its popularity, several firms offer special software to assist bidders in finding value at eBay, one of the most popular and longest running online auction websites. It is important to note that many internet users seek information online prior to buying products. Sometimes they use this information to purchase online, and sometimes they purchase at a local brick-and-mortar store—many consumers purchase offline based on information they get online.

Chapter Summary

The internet has grown more quickly than any other medium in history. In 2021, 93 percent of US consumers had access to the internet. Yet the remaining 7 percent are not online due to various issues, as well as the idea that many activities cannot be replaced by the internet.

The basic marketing concept of exchange refers to the act of obtaining a desired object from someone by offering something in return. Individual consumers bring their own characteristics and personal resources to the process as they seek specific outcomes from an exchange. All of this interaction occurs within a technological, social/cultural, and legal context. Among the US social/cultural trends affecting online exchanges are consumers' paramount trust in each other, information overload, multitasking, I want what I want when I want it, home and work boundary blur, self-service, and concerns about privacy and data security.

Internet users tend to have a more positive attitude toward technology and be more adept and experienced with computer usage. Gender affects attitudes toward use of internet technology, and age and ethnicity can also affect internet usage. Online shoppers tend to be more goal oriented and be either convenience or price oriented.

The main costs that consumers exchange for benefits are money, time, and psychic costs. The internet exchange can be facilitated by browser bookmarks, e-mail messages with hyperlinks, automated e-mails from websites seeking to attract visitors, and social media updates. The main consumer activities online can be categorized by these general outcomes: connect, create, enjoy, learn, and trade. Each outcome represents a marketing opportunity for savvy digital marketers.

Exercises

Review Questions

1. What is an exchange?
2. What are some of the trends affecting online exchanges in the United States?
3. What individual characteristics influence online behavior?
4. What are the costs that constitute a consumer's resources for exchange?
5. How can digital marketers facilitate internet exchange?
6. In what ways do consumers create content for the Web?

Discussion Questions

1. Can an attention economy exist in countries where internet penetration is low? Explain your answer.
2. What might digital marketers do to accommodate consumers who are experiential shoppers?

3. Do you consider the concept of flow an explanation for what some observers call internet addiction? Explain your answer.
4. How might digital marketers capitalize on consumer interest in relationships as an outcome of internet activity?
5. What are the reasons for the growth in social networking online?
6. Why do you think that consumers trust each other more than they trust companies? What can marketers do about this?

Web Activities

1. Customers face many barriers when purchasing online. It has been estimated that as many as 88 percent of all online shopping carts are abandoned. Working in groups, try to develop ways that online retailers can help more site visitors be converted to buyers.
2. Check out your local newspaper classified ads online, then examine Facebook Marketplace for your local area. Why do you think that Facebook Marketplace have taken share from newspaper classifieds? What advice do you have for newspapers to regain customers?

Chapter 8

Segmentation, Targeting, Differentiation, and Positioning Strategies

The main goal of this chapter is to help you examine the various bases for market segmentation and the classifications and characteristics of several important digital marketing segments. It also provides examples of product differentiation and positioning strategies for digital marketing.

After reading this chapter, you will be able to:

- Outline the characteristics of three major markets for digital business.
- Explain why and how digital marketers use market segmentation to reach online customers.
- List the most commonly used market segmentation bases and variables.
- Outline several types of internet usage segments and their characteristics.
- Describe two important coverage strategies digital marketers can use to target online customers.
- Define differentiation and positioning and give examples of online companies using them.

THE 1-800-FLOWERS STORY

Jim McCann is a guy who keeps up with technology. He started with 14 retail flower shops in New York City in 1976 and is now a multichannel retailer who understands his target customers. Ten years later, he acquired the incoming toll-free number 1-800-Flowers so that customers could order flowers over the telephone from any location for New York delivery. In 1995, McCann was quick to jump onto digital commerce with an early website to extend the brand (1-800-flowers.com) and offer 24/7 worldwide delivery. By this point, the company had expanded to plants, gourmet food, gift baskets, and other gift-related merchandise.

The website worked well, and the company generated much data about prospects and customers who registered and purchased online. How to sort it all out and use it for increasing profits? McCann used data mining software from SAS to identify customer segments for better targeting. The software sifted through website clickstreams and purchasing patterns of the firm's millions of customers and generated some interesting findings.

Thus, 1-800-Flowers can respond to the segment of one person who only purchases every year on Valentine's Day or the larger segment of people who want several birthday reminders a year so they don't forget to honor their friends and family. All of this individual attention is possible at McCann's place. As a result, 1-800-Flowers.com has appeared on the Internet Retailer's "Best of the Web Top 50 Retail Sites" and been a *Forbes* magazine "Best of the Web" site (according to 1-800-Flowers.com site information).

1-800-Flowers also has an active Facebook page with over 1.3 million likes in 2021. This page engages users with its frequent posts of very creative floral bouquets and other ideas for upcoming holidays. Its Twitter account has over 45,000 followers, and its Instagram account is growing, with more than 37,000 followers.

DOI: 10.4324/9781003247319-11

Currently, 1-800-flowers.com uses SAS business analytics to compete by managing customer relationships and building customer value. This process resulted in millions of dollars of additional revenue, partially due to increased customer satisfaction—customer problems dropped by 40 percent after implementation (according to www.sas.com success stories). As well, the company discovered and developed Mother's Day flower offers targeting the female segment because they are the biggest buyers of flowers for their mothers and mothers-in-law. The company can analyze multichannel sales data in real time and adjust its website offers based on retail demands in various geographic zip code (geographic) segments.

A focus on customer service by using business analytics and narrow customer segment targeting is working well for 1-800-Flowers. Revenues have grown more than 100 percent since 2012, with a gross profit of 41 percent on sales of over $2 billion annually, including 6.5 million new customers in 2021 (see 1800flowers.com/investors for more information). Founder McCann attributes this to the company's leadership with its 15 brands, from 1-800-Flowers, to Shari's Berries, to BloomNet, and success in the rapidly growing social and mobile channels.

Segmentation and Targeting Overview

Clearly, 1-800-Flowers understands the needs and behaviors of its various target markets. A company must have in-depth market knowledge to devise a savvy segmentation and targeting strategy, especially in today's multichannel commerce environment. As explained in Chapter 3, digital marketing strategic planning occurs in two highly interrelated tiers. The first involves segmentation, targeting, differentiation, and positioning topics covered in this chapter. Second-tier strategies involving the 4 Ps and customer relationship management (CRM) are discussed in Chapters 9 through 15.

Marketers make informed decisions about segmentation and targeting based on internal, secondary, and primary data sources (see Exhibit 8.1). **Marketing segmentation** is the process of aggregating individuals or businesses along similar characteristics that pertain to the use, consumption, or benefits of a product or service. The result of market segmentation is

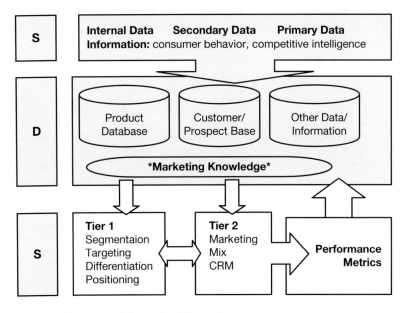

Exhibit 8.1 Sources and Databases Inform Tier 1 Strategies

groups of customers called market segments. We use the word *groups* loosely here. A market segment can actually be any size—an important point because the technology of digital marketing allows companies to easily tailor market mixes for targeting individuals. It is also important to note that segments are worth targeting separately only when they have bigger differences between them than within them. For example, if consumers behave differently online at work than at home, marketers can capitalize on these differences by targeting each as a separate segment—otherwise why bother separating these users into two targets with different marketing mix offerings?

Market targeting is the process of selecting the market segments that are most attractive to the company. Some criteria companies use to select segments for targeting include accessibility, profitability, and growth potential.

Three Markets

Sergio Zyman, formerly chief marketing officer of Coca-Cola, has been quoted as saying, "Marketing is supposed to sell stuff." One way information technology helps sell stuff is by facilitating relationships before, during, and after the transaction with prospects, customers, partners, and supply chain members. Yet all the latest technology can't help marketers sell stuff if they don't identify appropriate markets. Exhibit 8.2 highlights three important markets that both sell to and buy from each other: businesses, consumers, and governments. Although this book focuses on the **business-to-consumer (B2C)** market, with some coverage of **business-to-business (B2B)** activities, all three markets are important. Note that after B2C and B2B markets, the **business-to-government (B2G)** and **consumer-to-consumer (C2C)** markets are where most digital business activity occurs.

Business Market

The business market involves the marketing of products to businesses, governments, and institutions for use in the business operation, as components in the business products, or for resale. Online B2B marketing is huge because a higher proportion of companies are connected to the internet than consumers, especially in developing countries. Much of the B2B online activity is transparent to consumers because it involves proprietary networks that allow information and database sharing (e.g., extranets). Consider FedEx, the package

	To Business	To Consumer	To Government
Initiated by Business	Business-to-business (B2B) The Idea Factory www.ideafactory.com	Business-to-consumer (B2C) Classmates.com www.classmates.com	Business-to-government (B2G) W. Australian Gov. www.ssc.wa.gov.au
Initiated by Consumer	Consumer-to-business (C2B) Better Business Bureau www.bbb.org	Consumer-to-consumer (C2C) eBay www.ebay.com	Consumer-to-government (C2G) GovWorks www.govworks.gov
Initiated by Government	Government-to-business (G2B) Small Business www.sba.gov	Government-to-consumer (G2C) California state www.state.ca.us	Government-to-government (G2G) USA.gov www.usa.gov

Exhibit 8.2 Three Basic Markets

Source: Updated in 2012 from Wood, Marian. (2001). *Prentice Hall's Guide to E-Commerce and E-Business.* Upper Saddle River, NJ: Prentice Hall

delivery company. This company maintains huge databases of business customers' shipping behavior and account information. Its customers can schedule a package pickup using the website, track the package using a laptop or smartphone, and pay the shipping bill online. Sometimes the shipping order is automatically triggered when a consumer buys something online from a FedEx client; then FedEx sends an e-mail notification of its delivery progress to the retailer.

Information technology created tremendous efficiencies in the B2B market, yet businesses that sell online face increasing competition due to globalization and lower market entry barriers brought about by the internet. As well, many companies are changing their entire supply chain structures, which often results in conflict between different marketing channels. This conflict is especially problematic when manufacturers sell directly to consumers online, thus taking business from retail partners. On the other hand, many companies experience greater interdependence in their value chain due to electronic collaboration practices. Many challenges and opportunities exist for companies in the B2B market.

Finally, companies in unlikely industries find it relatively easy to use the internet to forge partnerships that supply value to customers. Consider, for example, the joint venture that created MSNBC (Microsoft and the NBC television network). In this environment, companies compete not only for customers but also for partners and sometimes even form partnerships with rivals. As an example, the major airlines came together to form an airline reservations hub—thus undercutting online travel agents (e.g., Star Alliance with United Airlines and 26 others). As another example, the major US auto manufacturers have a shared procurement hub to link to their suppliers.

Government Market

The US government is the world's largest buyer. Add to this the purchasing power of US states, counties, cities, and other municipal agencies, which makes for huge markets. The governments of other countries are also major purchasers. The state government of Western Australia, for instance, buys $14 billion in goods and services annually and authorizes more than 40,000 work contracts.

Businesses wishing to sell to governments face challenges unique to this market. Government agencies have many rules for suppliers to follow regarding qualifications, paperwork, and so on. Additionally, companies often must compete to be on the government list of approved suppliers and then compete yet again for specific work contracts through a bidding process. Government agencies are generally very particular about timely delivery of quality products at reasonable prices.

The good news is that small and large businesses usually have an equal chance of selling to governments, and government websites announce their buying needs in advance of the bidding process. The US government maintains a searchable website with thousands of opportunities (see SAM.gov—Exhibit 8.3). Internet technology has helped businesses to be more effective when selling to government markets because they can upload proposals at the site and handle much of the bidding process online.

Consumer Market

The consumer market involves marketing goods and services to the end consumer. This chapter describes many consumer market segments, and most of this text is dedicated to digital marketing in the consumer market.

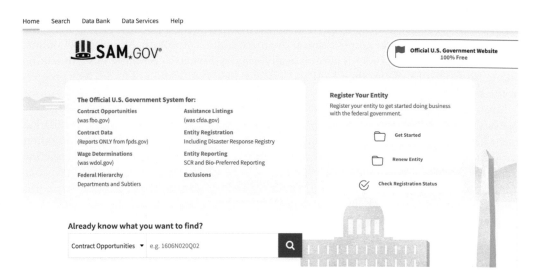

Exhibit 8.3 US Government Federal Business Opportunities
Source: www.fbo.gov

Market Segmentation Bases and Variables

Marketers can base their segmentation of consumer markets on demographics, geographic location, psychographics, behavior, and many combinations of these. Within each base, many **segmentation variables** come into play (see Exhibit 8.4). For example, McDonald's demographic segmentation uses the variables of age and family life cycle to target adults, children, senior citizens, and families. One way to understand segmentation bases is as a few general organizing categories and segmentation variables as numerous subcategories.

Companies often combine bases and focus on categories such as **geodemographics** (geography and demographics). For example, the Claritas PRIZM system, owned by The Nielsen Company, contains over 68 geodemographic segments (with segment names such as Blue Blood Estates and Young Digerati). Similarly, marketers can build segments using any combination of variables that make sense for their industry. The important thing to remember is that marketers create segments based on variables that can be used to identify, enumerate, and reach the right people at the right time.

After using any of these four bases alone or in combination, marketers profile segment members using many other variables. For example, after a website such as CafeMom.com uses demographic segmentation, targeting women, it can create a list of mothers who register at the site, and then use Web analytics and other online research to develop profiles that describe these mothers (such as how old their children are and what activities the family enjoys). These profiles might indicate that 30 percent of mothers like to search for places to take their children for a family excursion. CafeMom can then determine which other Web and social media sites reach this target market (for advertising) and what content and products to display on its own site and in e-mail communication to this market. It is much more difficult to figure out how to reach these women when they are offline and want to find places to take their children. Thus, marketers use profile variables to refine the marketing mix, including website content and advertising. Sites such as 1–800-Flowers also do this type of segmentation analysis, as discussed in the chapter opening story.

Bases	Geographies	Demographics	Psychographics	Behavior
	City	Age	Activities	Benefits sought
Identifying/	County	Income	Interests	Usage level
Profiling Variables	State	Gender	Opinions	Online
Examples	Region	Education	Personality	engagement
	Country	Ethnicity	Values	User status

Exhibit 8.4 Segmentation Bases and Examples of Related Variables

The next sections describe geographic, demographic, psychographic, and behavior segments used in digital marketing.

Geographic Segments

Most companies target specific cities, regions, states, or countries with their product offerings. Even the largest global companies usually develop multi-segment strategies based on geographics.

Product distribution strategy is a driving force behind geographic segmentation. A consumer goods online retailer such as Rakuten.com will want to reach only customers in countries where it distributes products. Similarly, companies offering services online will only sell to geographic areas where they can provide this service and follow-up customer assistance in the appropriate language. Before an organization decides to use the internet channel, it must examine the proportion of internet users in its selected geographic targets.

Important Geographic Segments for Digital Marketing

According to internetworldstats.com (2017), China boasts the largest number of internet users in the world, with more than 980 million people connecting to the web. India has the second highest number of users, with 755.8 million and a 54.2 percent penetration rate. The United States is the third largest geographic segment, with 312.3 million users and a high penetration rate (95.6%). Appendix A (toward the end of the book) lists all countries in the world with available statistics on internet usage, and this would be a good starting point for geographic segmentation. Marketers using geographic variables for segmentation also evaluate online markets by region, city, urban area, and so forth. For instance, the entire North American and Scandinavian regions contain attractive markets, and most urban areas, such as Mexico City, Mexico, are more wired than are rural areas. Many factors indicate market viability for digital commerce and other digital business activities in countries outside of the United States, as explained in Chapter 4.

Global Facebook and Search Engine adoption

While China is the big bang in internet adoption, the market is cut off from players in this space like Facebook. It is important to realize that Google and Facebook are international, but other countries have their own similar search engines and social networks that gain many more local adopters. For example, China's Sina Weibo is similar to Twitter and has over 530 million active users. In the search engine market, Google pales in China, with less than 3 percent share of market compared to industry giant Baidu (with over 76% market share) (StatCounter,

2021). Obviously, a global digital marketer must study geographic markets carefully before planning internet strategies and tactics.

Languages on Web Pages

English has not been the language of most webpages and online bulletin boards for many years, yet it has seen a slight increase recently. The top internet languages are English (25.9%), Chinese (19.4%), Spanish (7.9%), Arabic (5.2%) and Portuguese (3.7%), according to internetworldstats.com data (2020) (Exhibit 8.5). These findings obviously have huge implications for marketers desiring to reach global markets via the internet; until more online text appears in local languages, users in those countries will not be able to participate in digital commerce or other online activities. Unfortunately, Web developers in many Asian and Middle Eastern countries face technical challenges because local languages require double-byte character sets (versus single byte for European languages) and, therefore, need more database and transaction customization along with complicated search algorithms.

Another factor is that many countries recognize more than one national language, such as Canada, with both English- and French-speaking citizens. Consider the US Small Business Administration (SBA) (Exhibit 8.6). This government agency serves citizens speaking both Spanish and English, and, like many companies and nonprofits, the agency has created website content in different languages.

Local Marketing

Finally, local marketing efforts work well online, thanks to locally tailored searches and company review sites such as Yelp and TripAdvisor. Social media platforms also offer methods of displaying locally curated content to users. Small companies, such as the local physician or car repair shop, can be listed in these searches even if they don't have websites. Google offers amazing applications for smartphones, allowing owners to get from where they are and to any local business.

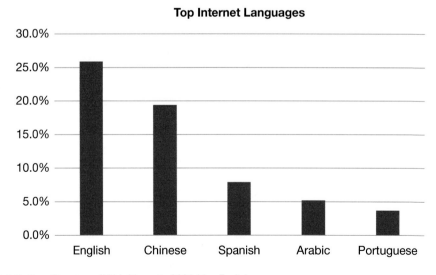

Top Internet Languages

Exhibit 8.5 One-Quarter of Web Users in 2021 Use English

Source: Data from www.internetworldstats.com

Exhibit 8.6 US Small Business Administration Site in Spanish and English

Source: www.sba.gov

Demographic Segments

In the internet's early years, the typical user was a young male, college educated, with a high income—except for gender, the description of a typical innovator. This picture is generally repeated in countries with low levels of internet adoption and in most social media adoption rates at this point. In developed nations, users look more like the mainstream population, with a slight skew toward younger people with higher incomes and more education.

To reach these segments, marketers identify attractive demographic niches. The following sections describe two market segments that have recently caught the attention of digital marketers: millennials and kids. Obviously, these are important because they represent the internet's future.

Millennials

In the United States, 72 million people born between 1981 and 1996 are coming of age in the twenty-first century. Pew Internet and American Life calls millennials "confident, connected, and open to change." They are the hyper-connected generation. They can handle multitasking and information overload better than older internet users because they grew up with the internet. They are the folks who can easily operate any receiving appliance and see information, communication, and entertainment as just one data stream available on multiple devices. They often use pop-up ad blockers online and use streaming services to watch television programming on demand. They are heavy social networking users, always have their smartphones nearby, and are always communicating via text messages.

Millennials are an important market segment because they are the first generation to control information quickly, use many technology gadgets at once, and totally ignore marketers. Many millennials watch television and use the internet at the same time, sometimes voting online while watching *American Idol* or other reality television programs. They use numerous social media platforms (e.g., Facebook, Twitter, YouTube, Instagram, Snapchat, etc.), e-mail, smartphones, connected gaming systems, tablets, and augmented worlds.

If marketers can get their attention and entertain them, they will listen and spread the news through online word-of-mouth (viral marketing) and social networks. However, marketers must attend to the millennial's thirst for instant gratification by responding to tweets instantly and generally mimicking millennial behavior—an especially difficult task for those marketers over 40 years of age. This group is a real challenge and is important to digital marketers as the proving ground for the future—if brands can't capture the younger markets, they eventually become obsolete.

Gen Z

Consumers born in the mid-1990s and beyond are known as Gen Z (Parker and Igielnik, 2020). This segment of the population globally accounts for 40 percent of the population and are known as "digital natives" due to their immersion in the digital world. According to The Center for Generational Kinetics, Gen Zers can't go more than four hours without internet access, have "only online" friends, and believes the internet brings us closer together. Consumers in this segment are also far more willing to share information with brands that they trust and contribute to social causes ("Generation Influence: Gen Z Study Reveals a New Digital Paradigm", 2020). With a purchasing power of over $140 billion, this segment will continue to build wealth as they come of age (Davis, 2020).

Kids

The number of kids under the age of 17 online is increasing and have become the most influential household audience in the world, according to SuperAwesome, a technology company that focuses on children. They love to consume videos online, often on their smartphones, and tend to check YouTube as an initial source of inspiration for their purchases. The proliferation of mobile devices causes worry for parents on how their children access the internet.

Many parents worry about the security and privacy of their kids online, but they can't stop marketers from targeting this huge potential new market. Instead, many parents censor Web content for children (see the "Let's Get Technical" box on content filtering). Kids are responsive to marketing messages; however, digital marketers must be careful not to irritate parents, who might perceive promotional messages as manipulation. Nonetheless, this is a hugely important demographic segment, following in the footsteps of millennials and definitely worth watching.

Let's Get Technical—Content Filtering

> Somehow, you were sucked into babysitting your 7-year-old cousin. He asks you if he can go online while you are making his dinner—macaroni and cheese with hot dog chunks, of course. However, you think to yourself, "How am I going to monitor him while I am downstairs cooking?" You know that you, or his parents, would never want him to experience inappropriate material online. As you pause to mull over this dilemma, your cousin says, "Don't worry! My mom and dad made the computer safe for me."

One growing segment of Web users is children under the age of 18. Children often have their own personal e-mail accounts and online nicknames. Many families are concerned that their children will be exposed to unwanted material online, such as pornography or violence, which can be considered objectionable. Even children not seeking such material may be exposed when conducting innocent searches. For example, a simple search for "girls' sites" using one of the top search engines resulted in numerous objectionable links to sex sites, such as a link titled "Naked Girls Sites Teenager Drunk and Naked."

Many solutions are available to serve the needs of user segments that do not want exposure to this type of material. One group of solutions aims to curb exposure to offensive material through education or legislation. Another group of solutions aims to limit exposure by use of technology. Education- and legislation-based solutions include the following:

- Educate children not to pursue offensive online material.
- Ban offensive material through legislative means.
- Require or encourage providers of offensive material to put age warnings on their sites (i.e., "if you are under 18, do not enter here").
- Require or encourage providers of offensive material to run an age verification system. Such systems require users to purchase a password using a credit card or require a valid credit card number to verify age. The presumption is that minors do not have access to credit cards.
- Require or encourage providers of offensive material to rate their material using industry-standard ratings similar to those used by the television or film industries.
- Require companies that collect information from children ages 13 and under to comply with the Children's Online Privacy Protection Act (COPPA).

Technology-based solutions include the following:

- Ask the internet service provider (ISP) to filter the content coming to the user.
- Filter the content right on the user's own computer using specialized software.
- Use search engines that filter the results based on user preferences.

All solutions mentioned have pros and cons, and they have been the subject of lively debates. This section focuses only on solutions that are technology based.

The internet comprises many different types of computers, and when users access web-pages, they are metaphorically hopping from computer to computer until the destination is reached. At any one of these hops, the content can be scanned and filtered for appropri-ateness. In the corporate world, employees are typically barred from objectionable sites by software running on a corporate computer that serves as the gatekeeper to the internet. This computer is called a **proxy server**. All communication between any corporate com-puter and the internet passes through the proxy server. It is an efficient solution and even allows employers to record attempted accesses to objectionable sites and to take disciplinary action when desired. Proxy servers have also been used to reduce employees' leisure surfing while at work. For example, some corporations have chosen to block sports-oriented sites, such as espn.com, or social networking sites such as Facebook. Of course, blocking is fairly futile when employees can get the same content on their phones.

The home Web user typically does not have access to a similar service; ISPs are reluctant to filter content because many users want to access this type of material. Some countries, such as China and Vietnam, filter content at the ISP level for everyone (adults as well as children). Incidentally, censorship is at the heart of the ethics debate on this issue.

Normally, the home user installs software on his or her computer to filter content. A number of products can perform this task, including Net Nanny and CYBERsitter. As their names indicate, these products are intended to impede children's access to the objectionable sites. Many provide password overrides so other household members can have full internet access if they wish. Filters are also customizable, allowing users to set the strength of the filter for each user.

One way the products operate is by maintaining a "can't go" or "can go" list. Under the "can't go" scenario, the products maintain a list of banned sites—tens of thousands of sites.

Each time the child attempts to access a site, the software checks the site address against the list of banned sites. If it matches, the software can take one of the following actions:

1. Allow access to the site and silently make a record of the access for the parent to see later.
2. Allow access to the site and mask out objectionable words or images.
3. Block any access to the banned site.
4. Shut down the browser completely.

Under the "can go" scenario, the child can visit only sites that are on an approved list and nothing else. These sites might include G-rated sites such as disney.com or toysrus.com. The parents can always add to this list according to requests from the children. The same series of actions would be available should a child try to access a site not on the "can go" list.

Most products provide free updates as the list of objectionable sites grows. Updates are a major concern due to the constant production of new adult sites. However, filters that block access to sites based on words in the site name (e.g., cybersextalk.com) or the words in the webpage itself (e.g., "this site contains graphic sex") provide increased protection against the new sites. Even incoming e-mail or Microsoft Word documents can be scanned. In all cases, the same list of foregoing action options is available.

The products can also monitor outgoing e-mail messages to ensure that children do not give away private information such as name, phone number, or address to a cyber pedophile. To accomplish this monitoring, the software is programmed to recognize the name, phone number, and address of household members and then scan for these keywords in any outgoing message. ISPs have also begun to offer e-mail filtering. Users are drawn to the e-mail filtering services but still reject the idea of ISPs filtering their Web content. Google's Gmail takes a multilayered approach to filtering out spam. This includes:

- Checking if the e-mail address has been blacklisted before.
- Looking for misspelled words.
- Checking for malicious links.
- Scanning attachments for viruses.
- Looking for suspicious words and phrases.
- Using a machine learning program called TensorFlow to assist with the above tasks.

Using all these features, Google is able to filter 100 million spam e-mails per day, thereby improving the security of its customers.

Apple builds parental controls right into its operating system. In addition to limiting the sites visited, the controls can also limit the overall amount of time that a child spends on the computer each day. One can even limit the time of day that a child is on the computer so late-night surfing when the parents are asleep can be eliminated. The time limits are a welcome feature for parents who tire of nagging their children to get off the machine.

Many feel that **content filtering** products do provide the level of protection that families need. Some communities also install content filtering software in public libraries. These products are an example of a unique marketing mix that is tailored to a target market based on both demographics (age) and **psychographics** (beliefs). However, none of these products is completely foolproof, because Web sites change too quickly, and determined kids are very clever.

Psychographic Segments

User psychographics include personality, values, lifestyle, activities, interests, and opinions (**AIO**). *Personality* characteristics are traits such as other-oriented versus self-oriented and habits such as procrastination. *Values* are deeply held convictions such as religious and green environment beliefs. *Lifestyles* and *activities* as psychographics refer to non-product-specific behavior such as playing sports, writing product reviews online, or eating out. For example, 85 percent of consumers in the United States claim to be online daily, with 48 percent between the ages of 18–29 report never being offline (Perrin and Atske, 2021). *Interests* and *opinions* are attitudes and beliefs people hold. As an example, some people believe that Facebook is a waste of time, and others think they could not exist without e-mail.

Interest Communities

The internet is ideal for gathering people from all corners of the globe into communities with similar interests and tasks. Social media and other online communities attract users, who then post their comments and profiles and upload content for others to see—sometimes paying a subscription price for the benefit. Communities can form around social media or other Web sites and forums, or via e-mails to the entire group membership. We've identified ten important types of online communities ripe with marketing opportunity (Exhibit 8.7).

Community Type	Description and Example	Community Type	Description and Example
1. Entertainment communities	People join to play multiplayer games.	6. Advocacy communities	Nonprofit communities form to influence public opinion.
2. Social networking communities	Users join and visit these communities to meet others, such as for dating (Match.com), getting a job (Monster.com), or finding a business connection (LinkedIn.com). Users are willing to pay a fee to join these communities, especially if they are large. Some sites exist purely for connecting to meet and make friends with like-minded people. These include Twitter.com, Facebook.com, and many others.	7. Brand communities	Firms create CRM communities around their brands on websites by allowing user posting. Examples include product reviews (Amazon.com), travel experiences (Tripadvisor.com), and tips for using your electronic gadget (engadget.com) or SAP software (Sap.com). Many companies also create branded social network pages.
3. Trading communities	These communities exist so that users can exchange goods and services. Examples include online auctions in the consumer market (eBay.com) and business market (Guru.com).	8. Consumer communities	Consumers post product reviews on epinions.com and discuss their product experiences on Google Groups. What differentiates these from CRM communities is their lack of brand sponsorship, and thus, they are basically unedited opinions.
4. Education communities	These communities form around particular education disciplines, such as Elmar for marketing educators (ama.com), educational software, or students participating in class or university discussion groups.	9. Employee communities	One example is the large network of former Microsoft employees who use e-mail and a private bulletin board to discuss Microsoft gossip and to network for professional purposes. LinkedIn.com is a good example of this.
5. Scheduled events communities	When *The Walking Dead* would air, usually an episode called *The Talking Dead* would also follow and enable much communication on social networks.	10. Special topics communities	In addition to the others on this list, some sites exist purely for user chat and bulletin board posting on a narrow topic of interest. This could also include knowledge communities like Quora.com.

Exhibit 8.7 Ten Important Types of Online Communities

Perhaps the most important type is **social networking**—the practice of expanding the number of one's business and social contacts by making connections through individuals online. It is based on the idea of *six degrees of separation* (that any two people are connected through contacts with no more than five others). LinkedIn is a great example of a professional network, with hundreds of millions of professionals using the platform in over 200 countries. Recall that people trust others like them more than many company professionals, so social networking and other communities will continue to grow in importance.

There are three ways to target online communities. First, a company can build a community at its own website through online discussion groups, a company app, and online events or through company-owned social network pages. When folks with similar interests gather at the virtual watering hole to discuss issues, the value they receive in both information, and **social bonding** keeps them returning. Second, companies can advertise on another company's community site or via blog comments and e-mails to community members. Finally, many companies actually join the communities and listen and learn from others who are talking about their industry. Several advantages and disadvantages characterize community targeting online. When an organization builds and maintains the community, it can present products and controlled messages customized to the group's interests, such as at Amazon.com. These communities are good targets for products of interest to them. For example, online gamers are always interested in hearing about the latest subscription-based game, and members of the Harley Owner's Group enjoy hearing about Harley-Davidson-branded products. Perhaps most importantly, communities are good places for companies to learn about customer problems and suggestions. Conversely, online community conversation will often gather negative product postings and offensive language. When companies sponsor a community, they must watch the content; however, if they edit it too heavily, they will discourage future postings. Besides, if a company removes negative posts, users will just post elsewhere online and discuss it all over the Web in blogs and on Facebook, so it is better to host the conversation at the company's own website. Finally, it takes a lot of time to participate in and monitor social media and other online communities.

Attitudes and Behaviors

How do attitudes and behavior differ? Attitudes are internal evaluations about people, products, and other objects. They can be either positive or negative, but the evaluation process occurs inside a person's head. Behavior refers to what a person physically does, such as talking, eating, registering at a website, posting a comment on a blog, "Liking" a Facebook page, or visiting a website to shop or purchase a product. However, marketers do not include product-related behaviors in psychographic segmentation. Product behaviors are such a vital segment descriptor that they form an entirely separate category (see the next section). Thus, when marketers discuss psychographics, they mean the general ways that consumers think and feel, but when they discuss "behavior" it is usually about product-specific behaviors.

Psychographic information helps marketers define and describe market segments so they can better meet consumer needs. It is especially important for webpage design and deciding what social media to use for connecting with prospects and customers. For example, Japanese users do not like the flippant and irreverent tone at some US sites. Japan's websites are more serious and do not include content such as political satire. Baby boomers prefer earth tone colors and positive, well-worded conversation on Web and social media sites, and the millennials prefer more hip, bright colors and authentic talk. This type of attitudinal information is increasingly available about Web users.

Most marketers believe that demographics are not helpful in predicting whether a person will purchase online or offline. Demographics help marketers find target markets for communication, but other variables are more valuable for prediction, so marketers try to find a balance between both types of variables to identify and then profile segments. One valuable psychographic scheme is the segment's attitudes toward technology to forecast whether or not users will buy online.

Attitudes Toward Technology

Forrester Research measures consumer and business attitudes using a proprietary segmentation system to better identify and predict industry change. By conducting hundreds of thousands of surveys annually worldwide, they seek to discover how consumers think about, buy, and use technology in many categories of devices and media in health care, financial services, retail, and travel industries, among others.

Broadly, they start by thinking about what empowers consumers and organizations to evolve with their use of technology, how they interpret or act upon new innovations, and their preferences around data privacy (see Exhibit 8.8). First, researchers ask questions to determine whether a person is more or less likely to use emerging technologies. Next, they seek to understand how customers adopt and integrate digital tools and experiences within their lives. Finally, they query users about their beliefs associated with personal skill and confidence using, evaluating, and navigating technologies. After many years of collecting data, Forrester is able to apply their research framework globally. Exhibit 8.8 illustrates this approach involving five common segments that identify how consumers adopt technology.

Influencers

Many online marketers target influential people who are opinion leaders online. These could be company stakeholders who are passionate about the brands and have big social network followings or others who hold some type of status that is instrumental in influencing purchase behavior. In traditional marketing, public relations personnel targeted media reporters because

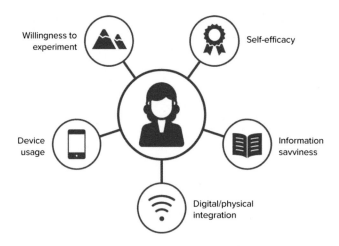

Exhibit 8.8 Empowered Customer Segmentation

Source: "Segmenting Customers by Technology Preference" (2017). Forrester Research, Inc. Reprinted with permission

of their influence when writing about the company in published media. Now the field of influencers has considerably expanded to include the following (and more):

- **Online journalists**. There are a wide range of online news platforms that consumers rely on for information. These platforms are staffed by influential journalists who maintain a following on the platform and on social media sites.
- **Industry opinion leaders**. These vary by industry but commonly include industry analysts, traditional journalists, prominent bloggers, thought leaders, and CEOs of leading firms. It is difficult to seed opinion leaders with new ideas that spread, but if an idea rides the tide of an emerging social trend, opinion leaders will be quick to create a buzz when given the right information. Example: Brian Solis, author, speaker and analyst, maintains a blog with the latest developments in social media and their effects on business, marketing, and culture (www.briansolis.com).
- **Influential social network authors**. In addition to traditional celebrities being influencers on social media, there are now celebrities who have been made by social media. These individuals hold much clout over their networks, who take their recommendations seriously. Lady Gaga was the first to gain over 20 million followers on Twitter. When she tweets about a restaurant or hotel she likes, readers pay attention. Many consumers or business customers are also opinion leaders in their social networks, and when marketers locate those customers with big networks, they want to friend and chat with them.
- **Innovators and entrepreneurs**. Elon Musk has been pivotal in launching companies like Tesla, SpaceX, and others, but one of his most interesting stories thus far has been with The Boring Company. Musk uses social media to promote purchase of a $20 hat that says "The Boring Company" to raise money for this company.

We shouldn't ignore the influential "citizen journalists." Even a relatively unknown person can post something negative about a company that will spread all over the internet in a "blogstorm." Jeff Jarvis's complaining post about Dell computer had a huge impact in 2005 in what is known as "Dell's Hell." Individuals often post videos or images of product malfunctions online. Of course, they also post positive product comments, but those don't tend to get the same high readership. Importantly, there has been great debate over whether citizen journalists take things too far, with less-than-credible information being portrayed as the truth. This can be quite problematic, given how quickly information can spread online.

It is important for marketers to determine who the influencers are in their industry. They must also decide how to entice them to write about the company/products and to monitor for product and company mentions online.

Behavior Segments

Two commonly used behavioral segmentation variables are benefits sought and product usage. Marketers using **benefit segmentation** often form groups of consumers based on the benefits they desire from the product. For example, what benefits do you seek when searching travel sites online? Most people want to check flight prices and routes at airline or travel agent sites (such as Expedia.com), some want to find hotel ratings by other travelers (people like "me"), and some look for discussions about what to do or see at specific locations. These desired benefits help travel site owners, such as Travelocity and TripAdvisor, design content that will appeal to these benefit segments. If done well, the people looking for these benefits may actually purchase as well.

Product usage is applied to segmentation in many ways. Marketers often segment by light, medium, and heavy product usage. As a hypothetical example, heavy internet users might be those who go online constantly using either a PC or a mobile device; medium users, those who go online using a PC only while at work and a smartphone at other times; and light users, those who connect only once every day or two. Companies must research to determine actual usage and decide how to split their target into appropriate user categories. For example, Amazon.com offers free shipping for users in an effort to move them from light to medium use: those who purchase at least $25 in one order. Amazon also heavily suggests shoppers join its Prime program for free two-day shipping on any of its products that are Prime-eligible. Another approach is to categorize consumers as brand loyal, loyal to the competitive product, **switchers** (who don't care which site they use), and nonusers of the product. Next, we discuss some of these variables as they apply to the internet.

Benefit Segments

Clearly, the internet offers something for everyone. If marketers can form segments based on the benefits sought by users, they can design products and services to meet those needs. This approach is often more practical than simply forming demographic segments and trying to figure out what, say, professional women in Peoria want from the Web. Marketers will use all segmentation bases to define, measure, and identify target markets, but "benefits sought" is the key driver of marketing mix strategy.

What better way to determine benefits sought than to look at what people actually do online? Marketers can evaluate online activities, such as those presented in Chapter 7. (Recall that the six basic online activities are connect, create, learn, enjoy, trade, and give.) Marketers also check which websites are the most popular. Several sites report each month on the top online properties. Listed here are the top Web domains as of 2021, according to Alexa.com. Social media platforms and Google properties are consistently among the top sites in most (but not all) countries, and sites like Baidu and Qq, which are popular in countries such as China, top the list as well. The list demonstrates that many people search, use social networks, and seek entertainment. Comparing these data with activities in Chapter 7 presents a rich picture of current and emerging benefits desired by internet users.

1. Google.com
2. YouTube.com
3. Tmall.com
4. Baidu.com
5. Qq.com
6. Sohu.com
7. Facebook.com
8. Taobao.com
9. 360.cn

Usage Segments

Marketers also segment internet users according to many technology-use characteristics such as smartphone, tablet, or PC access and where they access the internet. Following are two important internet usage segments: mobile access and online engagement level. Many others are worth exploring, such as video watchers, social network users, and online gamers. New technologies and platforms, like voice assistants, are opening up even more ways to segment users based on how they interact with such devices.

Mobile Access

Clearly, the type of internet connection and the information-receiving appliance affect usage behavior. Eighty-five percent of Americans own smartphones, according to the Pew Research Center (2021). Mobile internet use is paralleling the early days of internet adoption, with the younger, better educated and higher-income consumers using their smartphones online more than the reverse demographics. The main two reasons cell owners use the internet is because it is convenient and the cell is always with them, according to Pew.

Obviously, wireless users do a lot more than talk on their cell phones and get e-mail. They send and receive all kinds of voice, text, video, music, and graphic data—anyplace, anytime. They shop online, check the weather, stream video, read the news, interact with friends, play games, and much more. Below are some recent statistics about the leading mobile-first online activities worldwide:

- Use a chat or instant messaging service/app (86%).
- Watch a video clip or visited a video-sharing site (85%).
- Use a map or directions service/app (73%).
- Visited a news website/app/service (68%).
- Checked the weather online (61%).
- Uploaded/shared a photo (60%).
- Used an internet banking service (57%).

In 2019, Statista reports that 52 percent of Americans have a tablet. In another interesting study conducted (Anderson and Perrin, 2016), Pew provided tablets to individuals who had never accessed the internet before. What they found was these new internet users played games (33%), looked up the news (26%), took pictures and video (26%), downloaded apps (21%), and tried online shopping (11%). Pew Internet and American Life studied mobile users versus "the Stationary Media Majority," and devised five segments in each category (Exhibit 8.9). It

Mobile User Segments (39%)	Stationary Media Majority (61%)
• **Digital Collaborators** (8% of the population) are very much concerned about continual information exchange with others, as they frequently mix it up with online collaborators to create and share content or express themselves.	• **Desktop Veterans** (13%) are tech-oriented but in a "year 2004" kind of way. They consume online information and connect with others using traditional tools such as e-mail on a home highspeed connections. They are not heavy users of cell phones for much beyond a voice call.
• **Ambivalent Networkers** (7%) are extremely active in using social networking sites and accessing digital resources "on the go" yet aren't always thrilled to be contacted by others. They sometimes yearn for a break from online use and pervasive connectivity.	• **Drifting Surfers** (14%) have the tools for connectivity but are relatively infrequent users of them. They say they could give up their internet and cell phones. In spite of years of online experience, they seem to have checked out of the digital revolution.
• **Media Movers** (7%) are the accelerants of user-generated content as they use their ICT assets to send material (say, a photo or video they've taken) out onto the Web.	• **Information Encumbered** (10%) have average amounts of connectivity but suffer from information overload and have a tough time getting their gadgets to work without help from others.
• **Roving Nodes** (9%) are active managers of their social lives using basic applications-texting and e-mailing-to connect with others, pass along information, and bolster personal productivity.	• **Tech Indifferent** (10%) have limited online capability at home, and even though most have cell phones, they bristle at the intrusiveness cell phones can foster.
• **Mobile Newbies** (8%) are occasional internet users, but many in this group are recent cell phone adopters and very enthusiastic about how mobile service makes them more available to others. They would be hard pressed to give up their cell phones.	• **Off the Network** (14%) lack the tools for digital connectivity, as they have neither online access nor cell phones.

Exhibit 8.9 Mobile and Stationary User Segments

Source: ("The Mobile Difference . . .", 2009) Pew Internet & American Life Project

is very interesting to review these segments and devise product opportunities, especially when combined with the usage statistic previously mentioned.

The mobile wireless segment creates huge opportunities for companies wanting to produce wireless portals: a customized point of entry to the internet where subscribers can access websites and information in a low-bandwidth format. Big technical problems face global digital marketers, so marketers must be clever to provide both wireless and wired users with desired services. At the same time, the wireless market is unstoppable and will grow considerably, and has even penetrated household items such as refrigerators. The value of the data being generated by such products is high for digital marketers, yet consumers' increasing concerns about their privacy is at odds with the availability of this data.

Online Engagement Level

Chapter 1 introduced the concept of customer engagement online—the idea that many users actively participate by adding content for others to view. In Chapter 7, we discussed several forms of content creation, as measured by Pew: uploading photos, rating products, tagging online content, posting comments to a blog, creating a blog, and creating an avatar for a virtual world. Because this is an important new concept born from social media use, Forrester Research identifies consumer engagement segments through survey research. Exhibit 8.10 displays four common categories they use for aggregating consumers around a typology involving social engagement.

Forrester asks questions that categorize social media users according to segments such as skeptics, samplers, supporters, and savants based on their desire to engage with companies using social media. Social skeptics despise any type of social interaction online and do not want to share their thoughts or perceptions with the world. Social samplers appreciate social interactions but do not seek them out. In turn, social supporters actively engage within social media and welcome interactions with companies. Lastly, social savants demand interactions with companies through social media and openly endorse or complain about brands using social tools.

Social Skeptics

They spurn social interactions with companies. They prefer to interact with companies through established channels.

Social Samplers

They appreciate social interactions with companies. They don't shy away from branded social interactions, but they don't seek them out.

Social Supporters

They expect social interactions with companies. They consider social tools to be an everyday part of their lives.

Social Savants

They demand social interactions with companies. They consider social media a leading choice for interactions with companies across the customer lifecycle.

Exhibit 8.10 Four Types of Social Consumers.

Source: Forrester Social Marketing Playbook, Forrester Research, Inc. 2021

If a company uses Forrester's services, it will learn which of its customers are in these and other segments. If the company's customers are social skeptics, then a contest asking them to create a video commercial for the company will not be effective (unless the company attracts new customers). Conversely, if the company has nearly three-quarters of social samplers in its customer base, it knows that they will still view or read their social media content even without commenting. Marketers are continuing to figure out how deeply to engage with social media initiatives and how to communicate with customers, influencers, and prospects in these venues. Segmentation by social media engagement level provides data that helps drive digital marketing social media tactics.

Industry-Specific Usage Segments

Segmenting by usage varies widely from one industry or business type to the other. For the automotive industry, technology and digital media have ushered in new purchasing behavior, forcing car dealers to adapt and evolve. Contrary to initial beliefs, young consumers—especially millennials—don't dislike cars. They dislike the traditional car-buying process (i.e., showroom visit, paperwork, sales pitches, negotiations, etc.) and have altered how they make purchase decisions using technology. According to Google Trends, 92 percent of car buyers research, compare, and make selections online in less than three weeks. In fact, the vast majority of consumers start at third-party sites (e.g., TrueCar.com, Cars.com, etc.), with millennials twice as likely to purchase without visiting a dealership, giving rise to online car-buying services and platforms such as Shift, Vroom, and Carvana (Furchgott, 2021).

Targeting Online Customers

After reviewing many potential segments, marketers must select the best for targeting. For this selection, they review the market opportunity analysis (see Chapter 3), consider findings from the SWOT analysis, and generally look for the best fit between the market environment and the firm's expertise and resources. Sometimes, this task is as easy as discovering a new segment that visited the company's website and then experimenting with offers that might appeal to this group. Other times, it is a lengthy and thorough process. To be attractive, an online segment must be accessible through the internet, be sizable and growing (if possible), and hold great potential for profit.

Next, digital marketers must select a targeting strategy. This might include deciding which targets to serve online, which in the brick-and-mortar location, and which via catalog. The internet is especially well-suited for two targeting strategies:

- **Niche marketing** occurs when a company selects one segment and develops one or more marketing mixes to meet the needs of that segment. Amazon adopted this strategy when it targeted Web users exclusively. Cyberdialogue/findsvp (now Fulcrum) calls the internet "a niche in time," indicating its ripeness for niche marketing. This strategy has real benefits but can be risky because competitors are often drawn into lucrative markets and because markets can suddenly decline, leaving the company with all its eggs in one falling basket.
- **Micromarketing**, also known as **individualized targeting**, occurs when a company tailors all or part of the marketing mix to a small number of people. Taken to its extreme, it can be a target market of one person, which can be risky, given the small size of the micromarket, or pay off well if the micromarket is lucrative.

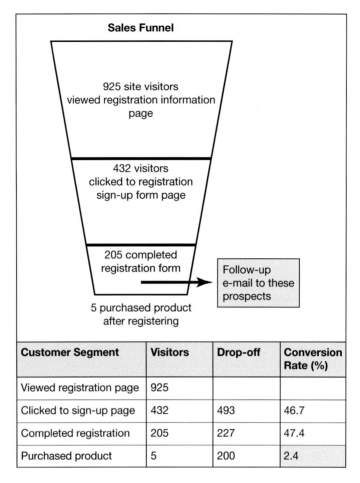

Sales Funnel

925 site visitors viewed registration information page

432 visitors clicked to registration sign-up form page

205 completed registration form

Follow-up e-mail to these prospects

5 purchased product after registering

Customer Segment	Visitors	Drop-off	Conversion Rate (%)
Viewed registration page	925		
Clicked to sign-up page	432	493	46.7
Completed registration	205	227	47.4
Purchased product	5	200	2.4

Exhibit 8.11 Targeting the Right Customers

The internet's big promise, one that is currently being realized by many companies, is individualized targeting. Exhibit 8.11 shows a sales funnel that allows marketers to follow users as they go through the website registration and purchase processes. Each step creates a user segment that can be targeted with persuasive communication based on behavior, such as e-mailing those who completed registration but did not purchase. Amazon.com builds a profile of each user who browses or buys products from their website, apps, or hardware devices. It tracks the products that its purchasers read and makes recommendations based on their past purchases. Amazon also sends e-mail notifications about products that might interest particular individuals. This approach is the marketing concept at its finest: giving individual consumers exactly what they want at the right time and right place. The internet technology makes this mass customization possible in ways that were unimaginable 20 years ago.

Differentiation Online

What do marketers do with all these extensive target market profiles? Prior to designing any marketing mix strategies, the company makes differentiation and positioning decisions based on target market needs and competitive offerings. The goal is to obtain a **differential advantage**:

1) A property of any product that is able to claim a uniqueness over other products in its category. To be a differential advantage, the uniqueness must be communicable to customers and have value for them. The differential advantage of a firm is often called its distinctive competencies, and 2) An advantage unique to an organization; an advantage extremely difficult to match by a competitor.

(Reprinted with permission from American Marketing
Association's Online Marketing Dictionary)

In short, differentiation is what a company does to the product, as opposed to positioning, which is what it does to the mind by attempting to convince the market that the product indeed has the specified differential advantage. A company can differentiate its offering along many dimensions. The following are just a few online examples:

- *Product innovation.* Pinterest was a brand-new concept online: saving images online and creating an online bulletin board, called a "pinboard." See the "Let's Get Technical" box about Apple's iPod/iPad for another product differentiation by innovation example.
- *Mass customization.* Blue Nile has very different features compared to other similar jewelry sites because visitors can customize diamond rings and other jewelry online.
- *Service differentiation.* Amazon.com excels in customer service. It is part of the company's mission, and it delivers.
- *Customer relationship management (CRM).* CRM is closely related to service differentiation and involves gaining a 360-degree view of the customer through many different touch points (see Chapter 15). Shelby Farms Park is a massive park in the city limits of Memphis, TN. One of the biggest draws to this park is a herd of buffalo that calls it home. When the park is welcoming a new buffalo to the herd, they promote a contest on their social media channels to receive entries from visitors and build park membership.
- *Personnel differentiation.* Zappos.com also excels with customer service because of its employees (see the Zappos opening story in Chapter 11).
- *Channel differentiation.* Netflix and Hulu differentiate by offering streaming television programming and movies to internet connected devices, such as televisions, tablets, computers, and smartphones. This digital channel created a competitive advantage for these companies when disrupting the conventional television distribution model.
- *Image differentiation.* Google versus Bing for search.
- *Site atmospherics.* This involves a Web or social media page that is user friendly, provides appropriate content, and has a great visual design. Companies can differentiate their sites through graphic design, typography, scaling for smartphone/small screen viewing, social media integration (e.g., log in with Facebook), and advanced technology behind the sites. For example, The Webby Awards have been in existence since 1996 to honor the leading international internet sites in many categories. See the websites and mobile apps that won a recent Webby Award (www.webbyawards.com).
- *User-Generated Content (UGC).* A company can differentiate by using effective crowd-sourcing to generate content or simply providing an active online space for users to share comments and ideas.
- *Efficient and timely order processing.* Some companies excel at this in their industries. When you order something online, sometimes it arrives in a very short time, and the company sends several confirmation e-mails to update the delivery status.

Let's Get Technical—Apple Ecosystem: iPhone, iPod, iPad, MacBook, CarPlay

You are making a cross-country trip in your late model Mini Cooper. For 200 miles you have driven through what appears to be an unbroken string of corn fields and flat earth. Though your car has a great sound system, for the last four hours you have been listening to country stations and talk radio. Suddenly you remember that your car has CarPlay. Plugging your phone into your car's speakers, you bathe the car in rock and roll. Before you know it, the hours melt away and the Rocky Mountains loom gracefully in the distance.

Apple Computer has long been the master of the simple and stylish user interface. Their products work seamlessly with one another. One way that they ensure this interoperability is by controlling both the hardware and the software that run on their devices.

Consider the opposite scenario. Microsoft does not make most of the computers that run Windows. Google does not make most of the phones that run Android. By contrast, you can only run OSX on a MacBook or iOS on an iPhone, iPod, or iPad.

In the Windows and Android worlds, all the different manufactures are supposed to design their hardware to common specifications. However, in practice there are differences. And any one of those differences can potentially cause the software to fail in unexpected ways.

Even Apple, which does manufacture all of the hardware and software, sometimes has compatibility issues. But because they control the entire ecosystem, they can quickly isolate the problem and resolve it in a software update.

Now put yourself in the shoes of a software tester. You need to try the software on every device that will potentially run the software. In the Windows and Android worlds, this involves thousands of possible configurations; in the Apple world there are only dozens.

Furthermore, Apple can make sure that their devices smoothly hand off to one another. If you are on your computer and a call comes into your phone, it automatically transfers it to the computer. If you are wearing your Apple Watch, the call comes there.

We see the importance of interoperability with CarPlay. Apple still does not manufacture a car or even a car stereo. Therefore, they have to rely on the hardware of others for CarPlay. Small wonder then that some users (including one of the authors) have experienced more problems with CarPlay than any other Apple product.

At the end of the day, most customers want their smartphones, tablets, and computers to just power on and work without problems. Right now they are far more likely to get that wish in the Apple ecosystem—which also promotes strong brand loyalty. Brand loyal customers feel a strong sense of dedication, positive feelings, and bond toward Apple, leading to heavy use and advocacy. And that is why they are willing to pay a premium for Apple products.

Online Positioning Bases

Positioning is a strategy to create a desired image for a company and its products in the minds of a chosen user segment (consumers, business or government buyers, and so forth). The first step in positioning is to determine the product category in which the brand competes. For example, when tablet computers were first introduced, it was unclear whether they were competing with laptops or smartphones. Does bottled water compete with soft drinks? This is a hard question that must be answered. Once the company decides who the direct competition is, then it determines whether the brand is differentiated in that product category and thus has a competitive advantage to form the basis for competitive positioning.

The previous discussion on differentiation provided many examples of companies who do have a competitive edge for creating their product's position. Marketers often position based on technology (the new smart speaker or the smartphone with the most apps), benefits (fastest product delivery from an online order), user category (Nick.com is one of the most popular sites for kids), or competitive position (Android phones are generally less expensive than an iPhone). Some internet marketers position as an integrator: TheKnot.com offers everything to do with weddings, from gift registry to wedding planners and other consultants.

Regardless of the selected positioning basis, the brand story must be told from the customer's viewpoint – otherwise it is self-aggrandizing and chest thumping. Digital marketers only have a short time to capture and engage their market's attention, and this is accomplished with interesting content that reaches the right consumers and business prospects, resonating and engaging them.

Chapter Summary

Online commerce occurs primarily in three markets: business-to-business (B2B), business-to-consumer (B2C), and business-to-government (B2G), although businesses also become involved in the consumer-to-consumer (C2C) market. The majority of dollars change hands in the B2B market, with many companies connected to the internet. Information technology is creating efficiencies while increasing competition. The consumer market is huge and active online. The government market consists of numerous states, cities, counties, municipal agencies, and countries buying goods and services. Businesses must pay close attention to the rules for selling to this market. Numerous trends are affecting the ability of marketers to tap new growth areas and become successful digital marketers.

Marketing segmentation is the process of aggregating individuals or businesses along similar characteristics that pertain to the use, consumption, or benefits of a product or service, which results in groups of customers called market segments. Targeting is the process of selecting market segments that are most attractive to the company and choosing an appropriate segment coverage strategy.

The four consumer market **segmentation bases** are demographics, geographic location, psychographics, and behavior with respect to the product. Each basis is further refined into segmentation variables—such as age and gender variables within demographics. Currently, digital marketers are targeting a number of demographic niches and look forward to newly important segments: millennials, Gen Z, and kids. Different strategies are used to target each segment.

User psychographics include personality, values, lifestyle, attitudes, interests, and opinions. The internet is an excellent way to gather people with similar interests and tasks into online communities for effective targeting. An important segmenting variable to predict online purchase behavior is attitude toward technology. Important behavioral segmentation variables commonly used by digital marketers are benefits sought (based on the benefits customers desire from the product), product usage (based on how customers behave on the internet) and influentials (journalists and others who influence opinions). Forrester's Social Technographics® is an important social media engagement segmentation scheme.

User segments can be divided according to home or work access, mobile access, online engagement level, and industry-specific usage segments.

Marketers use two important coverage strategies to reach the segments: (1) niche marketing and (2) micromarketing (individualized targeting). The internet holds tremendous promise, especially for effective micromarketing.

Differentiation is what a company does to the product. Positioning is what it does to the customer's mind. The proliferation of information, products, and services available on the internet means companies must find ways of differentiating their products and services in order to attract customers and build long-term relationships. Many traditional differentiation strategies can be applied to a digital marketing strategy, such as product, service, personnel, channel, and image differentiation. These require some additional and unique differentiation strategies for digital marketing, focusing on site/environment atmospherics, trust, efficiency, pricing, and customer relationship marketing and inviting user-generated content.

Traditional offline positioning strategies also apply to the internet. However, digital marketers can use internet-specific strategies such as positioning on the basis of technology, benefit, competitor, or integrator.

Exercises

Review Questions

1. What are the three main markets of digital business, and how do they differ?
2. Define the four main segmentation bases and list at least two segmentation variables for each.
3. Why are millennials and Gen Z important market segments for digital marketers?
4. Why do digital marketers need to measure attitude toward technology? What measures are available?
5. What benefits do consumers seek online?
6. How do benefit segments differ from usage segments?
7. What are the three most important online engagement segmentation levels? Describe Forrester's Social Technographics® segmentation scheme.
8. How does micromarketing differ from niche marketing?
9. Why would a digital marketer want to create or nurture a Web site for building a community?
10. How does differentiation differ from positioning?

Discussion Questions

1. **1-800-Flowers Story:** Identify the types of consumer segments used by this company to build revenue. What other segments might be profitable?
2. **1-800-Flowers Story:** What is this company's competitive advantage, and thus its differentiation and positioning bases?
3. Underdeveloped countries tend to have sharper class divisions than those that exist in the United States. It is not uncommon for 2 percent of the population to control 80 percent of the wealth. As a marketer, how would you use this knowledge to develop a segmentation strategy for targeting consumers in these countries?
4. Many parents are upset that some websites specifically target children and young teens. Outline the arguments for and against a company using this segmentation and targeting strategy. Which side do you support, and why?

5. Some company managers forbid employees from using the internet for non-work-related activities. What are the implications for digital marketers that segment their markets using the variable of home and work access?

6. Forrester Research suggests a segmentation scheme for online engagement. Interview some of your classmates to see what proportion of your class falls into each segment.

7. Looking at the list of 10 community types in Exhibit 8.7, name one Web company that capitalizes on each for marketing purposes.

8. How can a company identify influencers that might affect its product sales or branding efforts?

9. How can marketers use the data about smartphone use to build profitable target market segments?

10. Why would a digital marketer choose to use competitor positioning? Integrator positioning?

11. Which mobile or stationary market segment fits you the best? What kinds of products would succeed in this segment?

12. How might an online company react if a rival embarks on competitor positioning in an unflattering way?

13. Are customers likely to be confused by an integrator positioning that suggests a website sells anything and everything? What are the advantages and disadvantages of this positioning?

Web Activities

1. Strategic Business Insights features the Values and Lifestyles Program (VALS). Many marketers who wish to understand the psychographics of both existing and potential customers use this market segmentation program. Companies and advertisers on the Web can use this information to develop their sites. Visit www.strategicbusinessinsights.com/vals/presurvey.shtml and follow the links to the VALS questionnaire. Take the survey to determine your type and then read all about your type. What is your VALS type? Does it describe you well? Why or why not? How can marketers use information from the VALS surveys?

2. Visit CafeMom and write a profile of a typical female user based on the site content.

3. Visit Google and Facebook to look for a grocer in your area. Compare the results of these searches based on effectiveness of the results and how easy they were to use.

4. Amazon.com is a site trusted by millions of customers. Visit the site and identify what makes the site trustworthy.

5. Find one website that caters to kids, one to teens, one to millennials, and one to older adults. Evaluate the site atmospherics for each and report on differences.

Part IV

Digital Marketing Management

Chapter 9

Product

The Online Offer

The primary goal of this chapter is to help you analyze the development of consumer and business products that capitalize on the internet's properties and technology by delivering online benefits through product attributes, branding, support services, and labeling. You will become familiar with the challenges and opportunities of digital marketing enhanced product development.

After reading this chapter, you will be able to:

- Define *product* and describe how it contributes to customer value.
- Discuss how attributes, branding, support services, and labeling apply to online products.
- Outline some of the key factors in digital marketing-enhanced product development.

THE GOOGLE STORY

What performs over 5.6 billion searches a day in more than 200 countries, speaks nearly 150 languages including Xhosa, Māori, and Zulu, and is the most-visited US Web site? The answer is Google.com, the fourth highest value Global Brand of the Year in 2020 after Apple, Amazon, and Microsoft, according to Interbrand ("Best Global Brands", 2020). Google is so popular that it has changed the English language—the verb *to google* has been added by two dictionaries. Google's parent company, Alphabet, had revenues of $196.7 billion in 2020, while net income was $51.4 billion (Macrotrends, 2021). The firm continues to grow in sales, new markets, number of employees, and new products offered.

This success is particularly remarkable because Google entered the market in 1998, well after other search engines were firmly entrenched with loyal customers. How did Google do it? First, it got the technology right at a low cost. Co-founders Sergey Brin and Larry Page figured out how to pack eight times as much server power in the same amount of space as competitors by building their own system from commodity hardware parts. Second, they invented an innovative new search strategy: ranking search query page results based not only on keywords but also on popularity—as measured, in part, by the number of sites that link to each webpage. These criteria meant that users' search results were packed with relevant websites. Finally, the founders maintained a customer focus, used simple graphics, allowed no advertising on the homepage, and allowed only text ads (without graphics), so search result pages download faster and are easier to read. Since then, as internet speeds have increased, Google's search results have changed to allow for display and search advertising and to include images in its Shopping results.

Google continues to excel through rapid and continuous product innovation. It makes new products available on Google Labs, moves them to beta testing when they seem useful

DOI: 10.4324/9781003247319-13

to customers, and finally adds them to the suite of products—a process sometimes lasting a year or more. Through this process, Google learns from customers and incorporates improvements based on feedback. Google is constantly revising its search algorithm, which contains over 200 variables used to present the most relevant search results based on the user's selected keywords, the details of which are never completely publicly available so that sites cannot game the system. Exhibit 9.1 displays the idea generation and external testing process used to improve user searches. Google's product mix includes many search products (Web, Earth, Maps, Alerts, and more), advertising products (AdSense, AdWords, and Analytics), applications (e.g., Google Docs, Drive, YouTube, and mobile products), hardware (Google Home and the Pixel phone), and other enterprise products to maximize revenue from Web content, increase marketing ROI, reach new customers, enhance a website, and increase productivity. All products adhere to Google's philosophies of simplicity, customer focus, speed of service, and product excellence.

Google primarily uses a digital media model, connecting users with information and selling eyeballs to advertisers. In 2020, 80 percent of Google's revenues came from advertising (Johnson, 2021b). It generates revenues from several B2B markets. It licenses search services to companies, powering a majority of all searches worldwide; it sells enterprise services; it also sells advertising to Web advertisers, sharing risk with the advertisers by using a pay-per-click model (advertisers only pay when users click on an ad). Google's advertising revenues continue to rise at its own site and on customer sites including Google ads because it delivers narrowly targeted relevant ads based on keyword searches. Google also sells hardware to access its software services, like Google Home, while also investing in "moonshots" that enable them to take massive risks to introduce new innovations to the market.

In a firm where many employees hold a PhD, the innovation continues. This fact, plus a monomaniacal customer focus, is why the company is always right on target with new services. The profitability is likely to continue as well, because Google pays close attention to

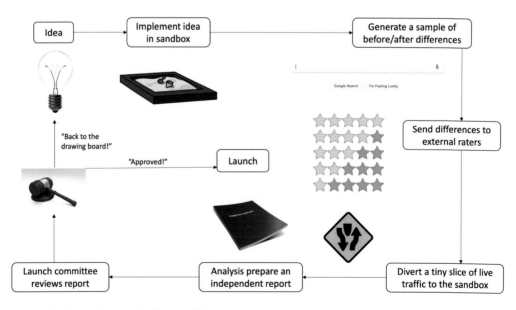

Exhibit 9.1 Google Process for Testing Changes to Its Search Algorithm

Source: Courtesy of Google (google.com)

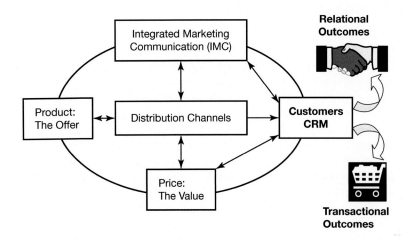

Exhibit 9.2 Marketing Mix and CRM Strategies and Tactics for Relational and Transactional Outcomes

user value, keeps costs low, and delivers eyeballs to advertisers. Google does everything extremely well.

Many Products Capitalize on Internet Properties

The success of Google demonstrates how a new and purely online product can use the internet's properties to build a successful brand. A product is a bundle of benefits that satisfies the needs of organizations or consumers and for which they are willing to exchange money or other items of value. The term *product* includes items such as tangible goods, services, ideas, places, and people (politicians, sports figures, movie and music stars, and dating services). All of these can be marketed via the internet.

Some new products such as search engines, smartphone apps, and social networks are unique digital platforms, others such as music simply use the internet as a distribution channel, and some use the internet as an electronic storefront. With the internet's unique properties, customer control, and other marketing trends, product developers face many challenges and enjoy a plethora of new opportunities while trying to create customer value using digital marketing tools. This chapter focuses on both consumer and industrial products capitalizing on internet properties and does so within the rubric of traditional product and branding strategies.

To create new products, organizations begin with research to determine what is important to customers and proceed by designing strategies to deliver more value than do competitors. In line with the sources-databases-strategy model discussed in Part III, tier 2 strategies involve the marketing mix 4 Ps and customer relationship management (CRM). Because the process of designing these strategies is closely tied to the tactics used to implement them, strategies and tactics together are presented in the chapters of Part IV. As shown in Exhibit 9.2, the marketing mix (product, price, distribution, marketing communication) and customer relationship management work together to produce relational and transactional outcomes with consumers. Assumed in the model is the parallel idea that this activity occurs in all markets—that is, marketers want the same outcomes with government and business customers (especially those in the supply chain). The present chapter begins this discussion by describing how information technology affects product strategy and implementation.

Creating Customer Value Online

Never has competition for online customer attention and dollars been fiercer. To succeed, companies must employ strategies—grounded in solid marketing principles—that result in customer value. Recall from Chapter 2 that Customer Value = Benefits − Costs. But what exactly is value? First, it is the entire product experience. It starts with a customer's first awareness of a product, continues at all customer touch points (including things such as the website and in-store experience and e-mail from a firm), and ends with the actual product usage and post-purchase customer service. It even includes the compliments a consumer gets from friends while using the latest release of the iPhone, or the fun he or she has when messaging friends on Snapchat or Facebook. Second, value is defined wholly by the mental beliefs and attitudes held by customers. Regardless of how hard the company works to develop the right value proposition, it is the customers' perceptions that count. Third, value involves customer expectations; if the actual product experience falls short of their expectations, customers will be disappointed. Fourth, value is applied at all price levels. Both a $0.05 micropayment for access to an article on NYTimes.com and a $2 million digital commerce platform from Amazon Web Services (AWS) can provide value.

The internet can increase benefits and lower costs, but it can also work in reverse. The next sections explore the value proposition online.

Product Benefits

Along with internet technology came a new set of desired benefits. In Chapters 7 and 8, we discussed many of the benefits customers seek online while connecting, creating, enjoying, learning, trading, and giving. Web users also want effective Web navigation (thank you, Google), quick download speed, clear site organization, attractive and useful site design, secure transactions, privacy, free information or services, and user-friendly Web browsing and e-mail reading. Today's connected consumers also want a place to join conversations, curate images, videos, and more, and create and upload content. Mobile users want useful and fun applications, location services, fast website downloading, and much more. Users of smart assistant hardware and software want hands-free access to information. Thousands of new products and social media sites were quickly created to fill these and many other user needs. As internet technology evolves, user needs change, and the opportunities continue to expand. Astute marketers are ready.

To capitalize on these opportunities, marketers must make five general product decisions that comprise its bundle of benefits to meet customer needs: attributes, branding, support services, labeling, and packaging. All of these can be converted from atoms to bits for online delivery—even packaging—through branding. Here we will discuss the first four in terms of the online benefits they provide to customers and their associated digital marketing strategies.

Attributes

Product attributes include overall quality and specific features. With quality, most customers know "you get what you pay for." That is, higher and consistent quality generally means higher prices, thus maintaining the value proposition. Product features include such elements as color, taste, style, size, and online speed of service, or the ability to connect and personalize. Benefits, on the other hand, are the same features from a user perspective. (That is, what will the attribute do to solve problems or meet needs and wants?) For example, Facebook hosts a lot of page profiles (attribute) that help users connect with old and new friends quickly online (benefit). Product benefits are key components in the value proposition.

The internet increases customer benefits in many remarkable ways that have revolutionized marketing practice. The most basic is the move from atoms to bits, one of the internet's key properties. This capability opened the door for media, music, software, and other digital products to be presented on the Web. Mass customization is a very important benefit. Tangible products such as laptop computers can be sold alone at rock-bottom prices online or bundled by individual buyers with many additional hardware and software items or services to provide additional benefits at a higher price. The same is true for intangible products, some offering tremendous flexibility for individual benefit bundling. For example, online research firms can offer many different business services in a variety of combinations such as white papers, podcasts, or quarterly reports; similarly, Spotify playlists combine songs from many different artists as desired by customers. It is important to realize that information products can be reconfigured and personalized easily, quickly, and cheaply, as compared to manufactured products. Consider that changing an auto design takes years, and one model may be offered in only a few versions. In contrast, changing and customizing smartphone apps is much easier and faster—consider how many update notices you receive for your apps.

Even though this type of benefit bundling occurs offline as well as online, the internet offers users the unique opportunity to customize products automatically without leaving their keyboards. For example, Blue Nile, the profitable online jewelry retailer (www.bluenile.com), allows Web users to select from among many gemstone features (e.g., stone type, clarity, and size) and pick a ring setting to match (mass customization).

User personalization is another form of customization. Through registration requests and other techniques, websites greet users by name and suggest product and promotional offerings of interest based on previous purchases. For instance, a new customer to Amazon.com receives the following pop-up: "Welcome! Enter your e-mail address for 15% off your first purchase." But a returning customer gets an item with his name on it: "Hello, Sam. We have recommendations for you." Clicking on the link reveals a list of items that Sam might be interested in examining based on his previous purchases from Amazon or those of similar buyers. Because the two are different types of customers at this point, Amazon tries to target them with information that is most relevant to their current stages of the decision-making journey.

Going one step further, Amazon allows individuals to create "wish lists," thus shifting this data storage function from the customer to the retailer: more benefits. Smart assistants address users by a name that they select, and many social media platforms show sponsored posts tailored to individual interests and behaviors. Another form of personalization occurs when sites allow registration via a visitor's Facebook or other social network membership. One big benefit is about making it convenient for the customer.

Branding

A brand includes a name (McDonald's), a symbol (golden arches), or other identifying information. When a firm registers that information with the US Patent Office, it becomes a trademark and is legally protected from imitation. According to the US government,

> A trademark is a brand name. A trademark or service mark includes any word, name, symbol, device, or any combination, used or intended to be used to identify and distinguish the goods/services of one seller or provider from those of others, and to indicate the source of the goods/services. Although federal registration of a mark is not mandatory, it has several advantages, including notice to the public of the registrant's claim of

ownership of the mark, legal presumption of ownership nationwide, and exclusive right to use the mark on or in connection with the goods/services listed in the registration. (Definition from www.uspto.gov)

It is notable that dictionary words can't be trademarked for website use—companies can own books.com or music.com but can't trademark the word *book* for a company name.

A brand is much more than its graphic and verbal representation in marketing materials, however. Many marketers have noted that a brand is also the following:

- A promise to customers.
- Beliefs in the market's mind about what the brand delivers.
- Innovation to the product that continues to improve on the brand promise.
- A symbol of trust for customers that the brand will deliver on the promise.
- The sum of all customer touch point experiences.
- A relationship between buyer and brand.

Delivering on this promise builds trust, lowers risk, and helps customers by reducing the stress of making product-switching decisions. Reducing stress is especially important online because of concern over security and privacy issues and because firms and customers are often separated by large distances. If brand names such as Amazon and Apple can generate consumer trust and add to customer-perceived benefits, they can command higher prices from consumers. See the "Let's Get Technical" box for McAfee and Symantec's Norton AntiVirus products, brands that generate a lot of trust. Of course, some brands, such as Walmart in the United States or Aldi food stores in Germany and Australia, have a brand name synonymous with low prices and fairly good quality. The value proposition is preserved in these cases with some buyers because the products provide fewer benefits for lower costs (e.g., a smaller set of features or fewer services).

Customers and prospects become aware of brands and develop beliefs and attitudes based on every brand contact, also called touch points. Some contacts are through one-way media such as advertising and packaging, and others are through two-way communication such as conversations with the firm's customer service or salespeople on the phone, at trade shows, on websites, social media comments, or in company-initiated e-mail.

Let's Get Technical—Computer Viruses and Protection

The day has finally come for your presentation to the company's largest client. You have been working on the new marketing campaign for over a year, and you were at the office until 10 P.M. every night for the past week agonizing over final changes. Wearing your best suit, you walk into work, grab a cup of coffee, and turn on your computer. You notice out of the corner of your eye that the familiar screens are not flashing while your computer starts up; there is simply a message that says, "No hard disk found." You immediately call the company's helpdesk, only to learn that someone in the human resources department opened a virus-infected e-mail attachment that has wiped out many computers across the company's network. After hanging up, you calmly plug your phone into the projector and connect to your cloud storage. Not even an annoying virus can stop you from giving this presentation today.

Computer Viruses and Spam

Computer viruses are a digital marketer's worst nightmare. They reinforce consumer perceptions that the internet and computers in general are not secure. Computer viruses are intrusive pieces of computer code that secretly attach to existing files. Viruses are often self-reproducing and have the potential to wreak havoc on data. Harmful viruses can spread throughout a computer network, overwriting data files with nonsense. On the other hand, prank-like viruses might be as small as making the computer beep on a certain day of the month when the user strikes a particular keyboard letter or opening the CD-ROM drive every so many minutes. In addition, some viruses, known as dormant viruses, can infect a computer and not cause problems until a specified date or time.

Three common types of viruses are macro viruses, worms, and Trojan horses. **Macro viruses** attach to data files and infect common desktop applications when users open the infected data file. The Microsoft Office Suite used to be susceptible to macro viruses. For example, the NightShade macro virus infected Microsoft Word 97 documents. When the user closed the infected document, the Word Assistant displayed a message with the word *NightShade* in it and password-protected the file with the same word. However, Microsoft has fought back by prompting the user to be careful before opening any document that contains a macro in case it is infected.

Worms reproduce rapidly throughout a computer's memory, destroying the stored information and eating up resources. In 2004, multiple variations of the Sasser Worm infected computers worldwide. German teenager Sven Jaschan is the alleged author, and he was arrested following the incident. Additional viruses posed as cures for the virus, causing even more chaos.

Trojan horses do not replicate and often appear as legitimate programs. The virus-like program can do damage to the computer and open doors to let hackers enter the computer to do damage. The common CodeRed worm dropped a Trojan horse that facilitated remote access to computer drives, allowing hackers to run a program on the computer.

Computer viruses can appear in data, e-mail, or software from any source. In 2000, the I Love You virus and its variants made the rounds of the world's computers and caused billions of dollars' worth of damage in a matter of days. The virus, which was transmitted via e-mail, mostly affected users of Microsoft Outlook, a common e-mail program. Old, unpatched versions of Outlook allowed small programs, called scripts, to run on the user's computer in order to automate tasks. Although this means that users can customize the program to their needs, it also means that the scripts can run almost any Windows command—including the delete command. In this case, the virus writers sent a script as a file attachment that deleted files on the user's computer. The virus also looked up addresses in the Outlook address book and sent all of the user's contacts a copy of the virus as well. The result was rapid dissemination of a destructive virus. Variants that followed were even more sophisticated and destructive. Knowing that users would be on the lookout for "I Love You" in the subject line, one variant randomly generated a new subject line on each transmittal. Also knowing that antivirus programs would be scanning messages in search of the virus script, that same variant modified the script slightly on each transmittal to escape detection. Malicious programmers often target Outlook, which is tightly integrated with Windows, and other Microsoft applications because of their popularity. However, since the release of Windows 7, Microsoft offers free antivirus protection with Windows Security Essentials.

Even though viruses most commonly affect computers, they are also beginning to infect mobile devices, such as cell phones and PDAs. A worm named Cabir infected mobile phones running the Symbian OS operating system in 2004 and spread by detecting and infecting Bluetooth-enabled devices in proximity to the infected phone.

What can digital marketers do? The best place to stop a computer virus is before it reaches the end user. All e-mail messages pass through a mail server that stores the messages on a disk drive in users' mailboxes. Software can be installed on the mail server to scan all incoming messages for known viruses and destroy them if identified as containing a virus or quarantine them if suspected. In this way, the virus never reaches the end user, and infection is avoided. Patch all programs regularly. Security updates from Microsoft and other vendors are often designed to thwart viruses. You should have your system set to auto update. Antiviral software can also be installed on each individual computer. One robust antiviral program is McAfee Anti-Virus (www. mcafee.com). Also popular is Symantec's Norton AntiVirus (www.symantec.com). The market share of these products may be threatened now that Microsoft is giving away Windows Security Essentials. Virus activity is reported to and recorded by the WildList Organization International, and information about viruses is available at its website, www.wildlist.org.

There are far fewer viruses that attack Apple computers. Much of that is due to protections built into Apple's operating system and distribution system. Much of Mac software is distributed online through the Mac App store. Before allowing the software into the store, Apple checks it for viruses. But what about software that you buy outside of the Mac App Store? The Mountain Lion operating system includes a feature called Gatekeeper. Gatekeeper checks to see if software is code signed by Apple. If not, then it won't install the software. The developer needs to register with Apple in order to get a code key. If it turns out that the developer is producing infected software, Apple will simply revoke the key.

Almost as annoying and frustrating as viruses, spam has taken over hundreds of users' inboxes. Spam occurs when unwanted messages are sent via e-mail and/or SMS to many contacts at one time. These types of cyber threats often have subject lines such as "Get rich quick!!!!" or "Cheap Prescriptions." Spam sometimes contains phishing schemes. In a phishing scheme, the perpetrator masquerades as a trusted source to trick users into giving away money or identifying information that could be used to commit fraud. According to the US Federal Bureau of Investigation (FBI), phishing attacks cost Americans millions annually. To combat phishing, a number of businesses now inform their customers that they would never request identifying information over e-mail.

Although most spam messages are harmless, viruses often mask themselves as spam. Users often increase the amount of spam they receive by signing up for services online that subsequently sell user addresses. Many ISPs and e-mail providers offer spam or junk mail filters. These filters attempt to separate the spam messages from the important messages. Software similar to antivirus software scans incoming messages and either separates or deletes them from the user's inbox. Both antivirus and antispam detection are a boon for marketers because they keep the internet clear of destructive or unwanted content, helping to focus user attention on the desired content.

Brand Equity

Brand equity is the intangible value of a brand, measured in dollars. Exhibit 9.3 displays rankings for some of the top 100 US brands in 2020. Amazon has recently experienced the greatest growth in brand value by significantly outperforming others on three brand strength factors—empathy, agility, and affinity—according to Interbrand. Note that Facebook is thirteenth on the Interbrand list but seventh on the Brand Finance list and sixth in Brand Z's evaluation. These differences arise because each company uses different criteria to evaluate brand value. It is not a perfect science because it involves an estimate of future revenues.

Amazon is not alone in growth of brand value, as Microsoft, Spotify, Netflix, and Apple are other technology firms common across all lists. How did they accomplish their equity rankings? See Exhibit 9.4 for suggestions, gleaned from many brand experts and marketers.

We add the idea that a great brand taps into the popular culture and touches consumers, as shown in Exhibit 9.5. Popular culture trends in music, entertainment, sports, and more help

Brand Value Ranking ($ Millions)

Interbrand	BrandZ	Brand Finance	Brand
1 (322.9)	2 (611.9)	1 (263.3)	Apple
2 (200.6)	1 (683.8)	2 (254.1)	Amazon
3 (166.0)	4 (410.2)	4 (140.4)	Microsoft
4 (165.4)	3 (457.9)	3 (191.2)	Google
5 (62.2)	42 (46.7)	5 (102.6)	Samsung
6 (56.8)	16 (87.6)	39 (33.1)	Coca-Cola
7 (51.5)	64 (26.9)	12 (59.4)	Toyota
8 (49.2)	67 (28.8)	13 (58.2)	Mercedes-Benz
9 (42.8)	9 (154.9)	38 (33.8)	McDonald's
10 (40.7)	33 (55.2)	22 (51.2)	Disney

Additional Digital Technology Companies, according to Interbrand

Interbrand Rank	Brand	Value in $ Millions
12	Intel	36.9
13	Facebook	35.1
14	IBM	34.8
19	Instagram	26
27	Adobe	18.2
30	YouTube	17.3
41	Netflix	12.6
46	eBay	12.2
58	Salesforce	10.7
60	PayPal	10.5

Exhibit 9.3 Highest-Value Global Brands in 2020

Sources: Interbrand Best Global Brands (2020), available at www.interbrand.com; Kantar BrandZ Most Valuable Brands (2021), available at www.kantar.com; Brand Finance Global 500 (2021), available at www.branddirectory.com

Interbrand	BrandZ
• Financial performance	• Consumer appeal
• Role in purchase decisions	• Sales performance
• Competitive strength	• Attraction
• Loyalty	• Generates "love"
• Sustainable demand	• Meets expectations
• Clarity of purpose	• Different and unique
• Authenticity	• Top of mind

Exhibit 9.4 What Makes a Great Global Brand?

Sources: Interbrand Best Global Brands (2020), available at www.interbrand.com;

Kantar BrandZ Most Valuable Brands (2021), available at www.kantar.com

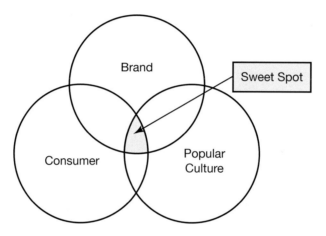

Exhibit 9.5 A Great Brand Intersects with Popular Culture and Touches Consumers

the brand touch consumers and remain current. For this reason, many firms use celebrities as spokespeople and sponsor sporting events that interest their target markets. For example, the iPad found the branding sweet spot when it gave customers the ability to flip magazine pages and enjoy many other forms of entertainment and personal connection while on the move. This strategy capitalized on consumer desires to have products and communication tailored to their individual needs and popular culture trends involving increased use of the internet for 24/7 entertainment and connection with others. Skype found the sweet spot when it brought **internet telephony** to the global masses, and LinkedIn hit the spot for business networking.

Brand Relationships and Social Media

Yahoo! has been so successful that individual customers actually created the Yahoo! yodel, subsequently used in the firm's commercials. This response is every brand marketer's dream—to build a following of cult-like customers who live, breathe, wear, and talk about their brand. Such is the case for Harley-Davidson motorcycle owners, Saab automobile owners, Apple iPhone fans, Chipotle fanatics, and others. Similarly, many Amazon users vie to become a top reviewer. How does a firm go from an unknown to this high level of acceptance? By establishing a strong affinity in the minds of consumers and elevating a brand's relationship intensity through the following (Duncan, 2002):

- *Advocacy*—customers tell others about their favorite brands, both online and offline.
- *Community*—customers in communities, such as Facebook, communicate about brands with each other.
- *Connection*—customers communicate with the company between purchase events.
- *Identity*—customers proudly display the brand name of products they use.
- *Awareness*—consumers include the brand in their list of possible purchases.

The fewest customers are at the highest level, where they have become advocates who tell everyone how great *their* brand is—YouTube and Tesla are fortunate to be in that spot today.

The explosion of social media sites have escalated this process with peer-to-peer communication about brands. Yahoo! began its Life Engine repositioning by promoting an employee contest, with 800 entries describing why Yahoo! was their life engine. This type of internal marketing helps firms communicate a consistent message at all points where customers interact with employees. (Refer to Exhibit 9.4 regarding the importance of internal commitment to the brand.)

When using the internet, a company must be sure that its online messages and employee e-mails convey a positive brand image that is consistent with messages from all other contact points. One writer coined the term *smash test* to refer to the idea that when a Coca-Cola bottle is smashed, an individual can identify the brand from any little piece of the bottle. Websites should pass the smash test as well—after removing logos and other identifying information, users ought to be able to identify the brand from any piece of the site, although this can be difficult to achieve in practice. This type of identification means that the colors, font style and size, writing tone and voice, image size and appearance, and more should communicate the desired brand image.

Although the internet can assist organizations in moving customers up the pyramid, it is particularly difficult to control brand images because internet users often receive brand messages from sources that the company has not planned and managed, such as blogs, social networks, consumer e-mail among friends, or a customer burning a faulty product in a home-made video posted on YouTube. The internet provides information—good, bad, and ugly—about brands. Marketers must monitor the Web for brand information, as discussed in previous chapters, and do their best to shape brand images using every available tool, including internet technology. See the marketing communications and media chapters for more details about managing brand reputation crises online.

More than 90 percent of US companies with 100+ employees use social media for marketing purposes. Forrester Research, Inc., summarizes three roles for social media in branding: (1) build trust through social media relationships with consumers, (2) differentiate the brand in social media to enhance the emotional connections, and (3) nurture consumers in social media to build brand loyalty. It is also important to note that the marketing leaders in this study said that in the B2C market, the Web and internet are first in importance for brand building, social media are second, search marketing third, followed by content development and e-mail marketing (and in the B2B market, social media are fourth, after Web, content, and e-mail). Yes, websites are still important for brand building.

Branding Decisions for Web Products

Companies with products for online sale face several branding decisions: whether to apply existing brand names or to create new brand names for new products; whether to lend their brand name as a co-brand with other firms; and what domain name to use for the website.

Using Existing Brand Names on the Web

An existing brand name can be used for any product extensions, and it makes sense when the brand is well known and has strong brand equity. For example, Amazon added music, streaming videos, software, electronics, food, and nearly everything else to its product mix. It is beneficial for Amazon to use its well-established online brand name for these other offerings rather than launch a new electronic storefront with another name for different product categories. Similarly, when products with offline sales introduce **online extensions**, many choose to use the same brand name (e.g., *The New York Times* became www.nytimes.com online). In fact, the dot-com crash showed that the strength of brick-and-mortar brands carried over to the internet, which is what gave many websites their staying power.

Some companies may not want to use the same brand name online and offline, for several reasons. First, if the new product or channel is risky, the firm would run the risk of jeopardizing the brand's good name by having it associated with a possible product failure. Entering the online publishing business tentatively, *Sports Illustrated* did not want to use its brand online and instead created an extension, naming it *Thrive* (www.thriveonline.com). The *Sports Illustrated* affiliation was not mentioned online. The thriveonline name was subsequently sold to Oxygen Media and today no longer exists. *Sports Illustrated* now uses its own brand online at si.com.

Also, a powerful internet success might inadvertently reposition the offline brand. Most internet products carry a high-tech, cool, and young image, which will carry over to offline branded products. For example, NBC (the television network) serves an older market than does MSNBC online. Because the network hoped to bring younger viewers from MSNBC on the internet to its television network, it made a decision to stick with the brand name—thus intending to reposition the offline brand image. In such situations, firms must ensure that online brand images will have the desired effect on the offline versions and that overextended product lines do not create fuzzy brand images. Finally, sometimes the firm wants to change the name slightly for the new market or channel, as a way of differentiating the online brand from the offline brand. For example, *Wired* magazine initially changed the name of its online version to *HotWired* to convey a high-tech image and perhaps to position the two publications differently. Perhaps due to its success, it has since reverted back to the well-known *Wired* brand name.

Creating New Brands for Internet Marketing

If an organization wants to create a new internet brand, it is critical to select a good name. Good brand names should suggest something about the product (e.g., Coupons.com and AffordableAmishFurniture.com), should differentiate the product from competitors (e.g., gURL.com), and should be suitable for legal protection. On the internet, a brand name should be short, memorable, easy to spell, and translate well into other languages. For example, Dell Computer at www.dell.com is much easier than Hammacher Schlemmer (www.hammacher.com), the gift retailer. As another example, consider the appropriateness of these search tool names: Yahoo!, Bing, DogPile, DuckDuckGo, Google, and Yelp. Which ones fit the preceding criteria?

Co-branding

This occurs when two different companies form an alliance to work together and put their brand names on the same product or service. This practice is quite common on the internet and is a good way for firms to build synergy through expertise and brand recognition, as long as their target markets are similar. If you are looking for a used car on the Carvana.com website, you can find the Carfax report with each vehicle. This cobranding example helps reassure buyers on the Carvana website by allowing them to see the history of the vehicle. Sometimes these collaborations happen in newer mediums as well. Two popular YouTube content channels around the Disney brand, Disney Dan and Defunctland, have collaborated several times on their popular channels on YouTube to reach both audiences.

Internet Domain Names

Organizations spend a lot of time and money developing powerful, unique brand names for strong brand equity. According to Internet Live Stats, in 2021, there were over 1.8 billion websites. With 201.5 million hosts for .com sites, how can a company find a unique website name (Exhibit 9.6)? Of course, it could be worse—Royal Pingdom counts 380 million abandoned site names. Using the company trademark or one of its brand names in the Web address helps consumers find the site quickly. For example, coca-cola.com adds power to Coca-Cola brands (i.e., Exhibit 9.3). Note that most of the top global brands use their brand names in the website name. Many factors must be considered when it comes to domain names.

A **URL (uniform resource locator)** is a website address. It is also called an **IP address (internet protocol)** and a **domain name**. This categorization scheme is clever; it is similar to telephone area codes in the way it helps computer users find other computers on the internet network. URLs are actually numbers, but because users can more easily remember names, a domain name server translates back and forth. Without this system a company would have to say: "Check out our site at 71.24.607.304." A domain name contains several levels, as depicted in the following:

www.support.dell.com

http://	**www.**	**support.**	**dell.**	*com*
hypertext protocol	World Wide Web sub-domain	third-level domain	second-level domain	*top-level domain*

Domain Designation	Top-Level Domain Name	Number of Hosts (millions)
.com	Commercial	203.5
.tk	Tokelau	24.2
.cn	China	23.9
.de	Germany	21.6
.net	Networks	18.5
.uk	United Kingdom	18.4
.org	Organization	14.5
.ru	Russia	9.9
.xyz	Generations X, Y, & Z	8.4
.br	Brazil	8

Exhibit 9.6 Largest Top-Level Domain Names

Source: Domain Name Stat 2020. Available at domainnamestat.com

The *http://* indicates that the browser should expect data using the hypertext protocol—meaning documents that are linked together using hyperlinks (https:// for a secure connection). The *www* is no longer necessary, and most commercial sites register their name both with and without it and then direct one to the other using an automated redirect command. Sometimes a URL is for Web-based mail, and the word *mail* will replace the "www" subdomain (e.g., http://mail.yahoo.com).

When organizations purchase a domain name, they must first decide in which top-level domain to register. Most businesses in the United States and other English-speaking countries want *.com*, because users usually type in the firm name.com as a best guess at the site's location. Other countries have top-level domains such as .jp, for Japan, .uk for the United Kingdom, and .de for Germany (*Deutschland* in German). Thus, Amazon in the United Kingdom is www.amazon.co.uk. Exhibit 9.6 displays the largest top-level domains, ranked by number of hosts. A *host* is a computer connected to the internet and may contain multiple IP addresses. For this and other technical reasons, these numbers represent the minimum number of possible IP addresses in each domain.

An interesting wrinkle on the country domains designation is that marketers outside those nations sometimes want the name. For example, many doctors registered in Moldova to obtain the .md country extension. Another interesting example comes from the Pacific Island nation of Tuvalu (.tv). DotTV agreed to pay Tuvalu $50 million in revenues for the right to sell .tv extensions—a big offer for a country with only $20 million gross national product. However, www.cbs.tv or www.nypdblue.tv did not materialize. Since the 1998 deal, the new owner of the .tv deal, VeriSign, had spent $60 million promoting the extension to yield 400,000 registrations in 2001, with only half of that remaining by the end of 2003 (Raskin, 2003). So far, most of the networks have chosen to brand through their .com websites. However, many other possible top-level domains remain as choices. The Internet Corporation for Assigned Names and Numbers (ICANN) is a nonprofit corporation that operates like a committee of experts to make decisions about protocol and names such as the latest: .xxx and .post. Incidentally, .edu and .com were introduced in 1985. In 2021, there were approximately 1,500 top-level domain names, but the top three (.com, .net, and .org) account for more than 99 percent of names (Domain Name Stat, 2021).

Recent changes in technology and ICANN policies have given rise to the ability for organizations to apply for new top-level domains. An application is required for consideration to create a new generic top-level domain, which many major brands have started to undertake. For example, Walmart has applied for the .walmart domain for their own use. Amazon already owns the .aws extension, and you can see an example of this by navigating to buildon.aws. There is even an auctioning process to determine who should gain access to such domains if there are any issues. Johnson & Johnson paid over $3 million for the .baby domain against a set of other competitors in late 2014 (icann.org, 2017).

GoDaddy, along with many other sites, provides domain registering services for a small annual fee, sometimes even including an e-mail address (www.godaddy.com). For this low price, students can leave less professional yahoo.com and other Web-based e-mail addresses behind and get a more professional address to impress recruiters (such as firstname.lastname@ lastname.com).

One problem is that with more than 97 percent of words in the dictionary already registered as domain names, the desired online name may not be available. A dictionary name is not necessarily the best option because it already has a meaning attached to it, which is generic for the product category, making it difficult to build a competitive advantage and impossible to trademark. Thus, it is more difficult to build a unique brand identity for a wine firm called wine.com than for gallo.com, a well-known brand name. Consider the brilliance of Amazon.

com when it selected a unique name and avoided the soon-to-come crowd of online booksellers using "book" in their names. The similarities in the following brand names make it very difficult to find a competitive positioning online (some now out of business, not surprisingly). See the list of select online booksellers using the word *book* in their brand names below.

1bookstreet	BooksAMillion	gobookshopping
A1Books	BookSense	Gobookshopping
abebooks	books-forsale	HalfPriceBooks
allbooks4less	BooksNow	nwbooks
AllBookstores	Bookspot	Textbooks
Alotofbooks	Bookwire	Textbooksatcost
BestBookBuys	CheapyBook	Textbooksource
BookCloseOut	Classbook	Textbookx
Bookland	CoolBooks	TheBookPeople
BookNetUSA	Ebooks	TrueBooks
BookPool	eSuccessBooks	VarsityBooks

What happens if the firm name has been registered by someone else? For example, DeltaComm, a software developer and ISP in North Carolina, was the first to register www.delta.com, preempting Delta Airlines (originally www.delta-air.com) and Delta Faucet (www.deltafaucet.com). These firms were forced to come up with alternative names. Another solution is to buy the name from the currently registered holder; that is what Delta Airlines eventually did, and today, Delta Airlines enjoys www.delta.com as its URL. In another example, Grupo Posadas, the large Mexican hotel chain owner, negotiated for 18 months to buy www.posadas.com.mx from a local family with the same last name. The company paid for the name with a free condo, many nights of free hotel stays, and *mucho dinero*. Many creative internet users register lots of popular names and offer them for sale at prices of up to millions of dollars. GoDaddy offers second-level domain name auctions, and Sedo.com allows users to buy and sell popular domain names. Insure.com went for $16 million in 2009. As you read in Chapter 5, cybersquatting—which occurs when a domain name registrant takes an already trademarked brand name—is illegal. The same is not true, however, for dictionary or personal names. A "whois" search at GoDaddy.com reveals domain name owners.

Incidentally, when registering a name, organizations would be well advised to also purchase related names for several reasons. First, this keeps them out of the hands of others. Second, users don't always know what URL to type to find a company. Posadas, the Mexican hotel firm, purchased domain names for more than 17 different spellings of its various hotels to make things easier for customers. Coca-Cola has done the same. The company owns cocacola.com, coca-cola.com, and coke.com; coca-colacompany.com, and cocacolacompany.com—which often redirect to a more concise URL—, .info, .us. .org, .me, and many more.

Bently Nevada wishes that it could own both www.bently.com and www.bentley.com due to this common misspelling of its name. Also, Compaq Computer Company paid $3 million to develop the AltaVista search engine site (www.altavista.com) only to find that www.altavista.com was already in operation as an adult site with sexual material. Fortunately, the search engine outlasted the adult site, although both Compaq and AltaVista search are no more. Picking the right domain name can make a huge difference when trying to entice users to the site and to build consistency in the firm's marketing communications.

Support Services

Customer support—during and after purchases—is a critical component in the value proposition. Customer service representatives should be knowledgeable and concerned about customer experiences. Sites that care about developing relationships with their customers, such as Amazon.com, place some of their best people in customer support. In the early days, Amazon's billionaire founder and CEO Jeff Bezos even answered some of the e-mail messages himself. Some products need extra customer support. For example, when a user purchases software such as Constant Contact to design e-mail newsletters and maintain e-mail databases, technical support becomes important. Customer service reps help customers with installation, maintenance problems, product guarantees, and service warranties, and in general work to increase customer satisfaction with the firm's products.

Online chat bots are also an important and growing part of customer service. Live chat online occurs when a user is at a site and types into a box to communicate in real time with a company customer service representative—either during the purchase process or as post-purchase customer service. Business Insider (Nguyen, 2017) reports that 45 percent of consumers state chat bots are their preferred method to resolving issues they may be having. Advances in artificial intelligence have fueled more innovative uses of bots, and now they have left the computer screen to also assist customers via voice assistant applications.

The topic of customer service online is such an important part of product design that we dedicate much of Chapter 15 to it (as part of customer relationship management).

Labeling

Product labels identify brands, sponsoring firms, and product ingredients and often provide instructions for use and promotional materials. Labels on tangible products create product recognition and influence decision behavior at the point of purchase. Labeling has digital equivalents in the online world. For online services, terms of product usage, product features, and other information comprise online labeling at websites. For example, when users download Apple Music software for organizing their music, they can first read the "label" to discover how to install and use the software.

In addition, many companies have extensive legal information about copyright use on their webpages. Microsoft, for instance, allows firms to reproduce product images without permission, but any images on its former Expedia.com site must receive special permission before being copied and used in printed materials such as this book. Like many organizations, the Federal Trade Commission has a "label" page discussing its privacy policy (see Exhibit 9.7). Online labeling can serve many of the same purposes on the Web as offline. Many brick-and-mortar businesses display the Better Business Bureau logo on their doors and websites to give the customer a sense of confidence and trust. Another validating label is the TrustArc privacy shield. If firms agree to certain terms of use regarding privacy of customer information collected at their site, they may register at TrustArc, download the TrustArc seal, and affix it to their websites as part of a label. Consumers may also check to see if they are browsing on a secure page by either a lock symbol in the URL bar or if the URL begins with "https" instead of "http."

Finally, many sites present social media logos as labels on their pages. The purpose is to allow sharing, commenting, or registering via Facebook and others. These logos add to the credibility and technology competence of the original company.

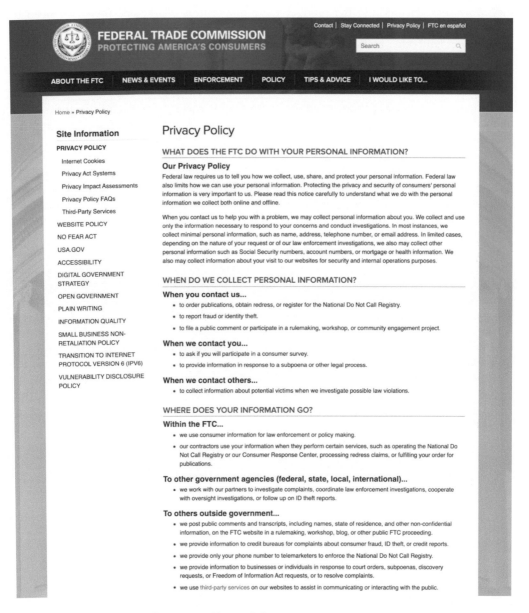

Exhibit 9.7 US Federal Trade Commission Privacy Policy

Source: www.ftc.gov

Digital Marketing Enhanced Product Development

The move from atoms to bits adds complexity to online product offers. Developers must now combine digital text, graphics, video, and audio and use new internet delivery systems (see Chapter 11 for a discussion of how to monetize digital products). They must integrate front-end customer service operations with back-end data collection and fulfillment methods to deliver products. These requirements create steep learning curves for traditional companies as they work these factors into the product value proposition. Marketers, therefore, need to consider several factors that affect product development and product mix strategies with new technologies (and other marketing mix factors in the following chapters).

Customer Codesign via Crowdsourcing

The power shift to buyers, when combined with the internet's global reach, allows for many unusual business partnerships and for both business and consumer collaboration. Partners form synergistic clusters to help design customer products that deliver value. For example, after Dell Computer contractually gave one supplier 25 percent of its volume requirement for computer monitors, the supplier assigned engineers to work with Dell's product development team (Ghosh, 1998). These engineers stood beside Dell employees when new products were introduced to help answer customer questions. Today, Dell can take advantage of online reviews and social media comments to capitalize on consumers' opinions.

Internet technology allows this type of collaboration to occur electronically among consumers across international borders as well. For example, software developers commonly seek customer input as they develop the product. You may have seen websites, mobile apps, and others listed as "Beta version." This means that the product is in a development stage, and users will try it and give feedback to the company about possible changes to improve usability. This process repeats as the company improves the product based on this feedback and releases newer beta versions for customer testing. Internet browsers, CRM software, and many others use this basic process, shown in Exhibit 9.8. When the software is good enough, the company makes the final version available to all internet users.

In another interesting example, the LEGO® Group, a toy maker, encourages consumers to upload their creations to social media and tag LEGO® for a chance to be featured on the company's social media platforms so that others can view their great designs. This is a great

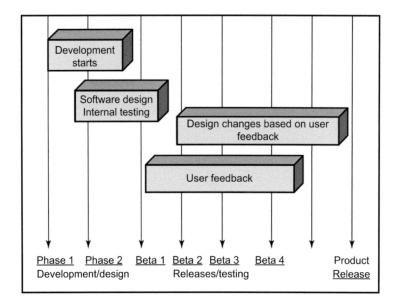

Exhibit 9.8 Customer Codesign of Software Products

way for LEGO® to engage customers and to use crowdsourcing to find new product ideas that could be used in brick-and-mortar stores.

Chris Anderson, the author of *The Long Tail*, posted draft copies of his book on his blog as he wrote and engaged readers who posted comments about the emerging theory. This dialog helped improve the final book.

Many organizations engage customers by inviting them to create advertisements and website content on their sites or social media pages. For instance, customers write product reviews and answer potential customer questions at Amazon. CNN encourages breaking news video uploads by citizen journalists. Local businesses encourage customers to express opinions and rate services via Yelp and TripAdvisor, which relies on crowdsourced reviews shared with others. Blogs are one technology that increased this co-development of Web content. Bloggers invite comments to their posts, thus increasing the content value for readers. Even popular monetized YouTube channels enable comments to provide instant feedback. Good marketers look everywhere for customer feedback to improve products, even setting up blogs for the sole purpose of gathering customer ideas and input. One great example is Salesforce Ideas, mentioned in Chapter 2.

However, sometimes this feedback comes uninvited. With the proliferation of new media platforms and smartphones, the speed and reach of the internet, and the fact that consumers trust people like them more than they trust companies, customers are quick to spread the word about product strengths and weaknesses. In this environment, savvy firms monitor customer input electronically (as discussed in Chapter 6).

Internet Properties Spawn Other Opportunities

The internet's unique properties, discussed in Chapter 1, generated unusual new products and companies. Location-based services (LBS) are one such example. Global positioning systems (GPS) in smartphones and other mobile online devices track user locations that users can send to friends via "check-ins" while at restaurants, retailers, and many other locations. This has created many marketing opportunities, discussed in later chapters.

AutoMall.com and LendingTree are two companies that aggregate services for users. LendingTree is a firm that offers online searches for the best prices for mortgages and other types of loans. These firms provide bundles of benefits difficult to achieve before the advent of the internet.

The internet is a great information equalizer, which means fierce competition, lots of product imitation, and short product life cycles. Online auctions are a perfect example. Not long after eBay came online, Amazon.com and others began offering auctions; now one restaurant in San Francisco is even auctioning meals to draw patrons during slow times. Also, Groupon and other "deal of the day" sites bring a new type of competition to the masses. Many search engines are starting to look similar. In this environment, product differentiation is key, because if consumers cannot find meaningful product differences, they will purchase based solely on price.

Devices connected to the internet offer the opportunity to "push" new features to the end-consumer product instantaneously, such as in internet-connected cars containing very powerful software. In another example, when Frank Sinatra died, BMG's five-person new-product development team created a lifetime tribute and a series of product offerings for the website in six short hours. The firm would have needed four months to produce this in a paper catalog. News sites commonly refresh stories every minute, 24/7. While all of this may sound like normal business activity to readers, it is the internet that made it possible. Organizations must respond quickly to new technology or lose. As one astute pundit said, "Eat lunch or be lunch." Despite the internet adoption flattening at maturity, innovation online is still rewarded.

New-Product Strategies for Digital Marketing

Many new products, such as YouTube and Twitter, were introduced by "one-pony" firms, built around the company's first successful product. Other organizations, such as Microsoft, added internet products to an already successful product mix (e.g., the Edge browser). This section explores product mix strategies to aid marketers in integrating offline and online offerings.

Product Mix Strategies

How can marketers integrate hot product ideas for the internet into current product mixes? Companies can choose among six categories of new-product strategies. Discontinuous innovation is the highest-risk strategy, while **me-too lower-cost products** are the least risky ones. Companies will select one or more of these strategies based on marketing objectives and other factors such as risk appetite, strength of current brand names, resource availability, and competitive entries.

Discontinuous Innovations

These are new-to-the-world products never seen before. Hula hoops and computers were discontinuous innovations when introduced. On the internet, the first webpage design software, shopping agent, and search engine fall into this category. Social networking is another discontinuous innovation—the idea that each internet user has a rich array of contacts for fun and profit when tapped. Combined with advances in new hardware, we are witnessing a shift in even more innovative internet enabled services. Many discontinuous innovations will continue to proliferate on the internet in the future.

A **disruptive innovation** is a special category of discontinuous innovation that changes the existing market in a drastic way. Sometimes called disruptive technologies, examples include digital music downloads disrupting the CD market, desktop publishing disrupting the magazine and newspaper markets, GPS devices disrupting the physical paper map market, and Facebook and Twitter disrupting the market for how people communicate and share ideas and how companies engage in promotion. This is another reason that marketers must carefully watch new technologies.

Although a discontinuous innovation strategy is quite risky, the potential rewards for success are great. Marketers planning discontinuous innovations must remember that their customers will have to learn and adopt new behaviors—things they have not done before. The company faces the risk that customers will not change unless the new behavior is easy and they perceive that the benefits are worthwhile. However, if the target group is younger, the risk is lower because technologically savvy young consumers yearn for cool new technologies.

New-Product Lines

These are introduced when companies take an existing brand name and create new products in a completely different category. For example, Microsoft created a new line when it initially introduced its Internet Explorer Web browser. Because the Netscape browser was already available at that time, Microsoft's entry was not a discontinuous innovation.

Additions to Existing Product Lines

This occurs when organizations add a new flavor, size, or other variation to a current product line. *USA Today* (www.usatoday.com) is a slightly different version of the hard-copy edition, adapted for online delivery. It is yet another product in *USA Today's* line. At the beginning of this chapter, we mentioned that Google has many different product lines (search, advertising, applications, enterprise, hardware, and more)—all leveraging the great brand name and helping to increase brand equity.

Improvements or Revisions of Existing Products

These products are introduced as "new and improved" and thus replace the old product. For example, Web-based e-mail systems improved on client-based e-mail systems such as Thunderbird or Outlook because users could check and send e-mail from any internet-connected computer. On the internet, firms are continually improving their brands to add value and remain competitive.

Repositioned Products

These are current products that are either targeted to different markets or promoted for new uses. YouTube sells subscription services for ad-free music experiences, departing from the model of only consuming ad-supported videos online.

Me-Too Lower-Cost Products

These are introduced to compete with existing brands by offering a price advantage. For example, MailChimp competes with Constant Contact by offering absolutely free e-mail marketing services for companies, and an evaluation of paid services shows $10/month for up to 500 e-mail contacts (versus $20/month for Constant Contact). The internet spawned a multitude of free products with the idea of building market share so the firm would have a customer base for marketing its other products. For example, Eudora Light, the e-mail reader software, and WS_FTP LE, the file transfer software, were two early entries with this strategy. This strategy can also be considered promotional sampling.

Although the B2C market gets most of the attention, many cutting-edge technology products and trends in the B2B markets are discussed in the "Let's Get Technical" boxes throughout this book.

A Word About ROI

Part I of this book discussed the need for performance metrics as feedback so firms can assess the success of their digital marketing strategies and tactics. This type of assessment is especially important when introducing new products, online or offline. Marketers generally forecast the expected product revenue over time, deduct marketing and other expenses, and generate a break-even point and return on investment estimate for new products prior to their launch. Usually, brand managers compete for the firm's resources by showing that their products will generate either a higher ROI or a break even in shorter time frame. By *break even* we mean that the R&D and other initial costs will be recovered at a particular date based on projected sales. In the process, they calculate a break-even date when the product is projected to start making a profit. How long is acceptable? Ten years ago, some managers were saying that internet projects had to break even within three months or they would not get funded. Of course, the exact timing varies by industry—Boeing does not expect most new aircraft to pay out for 20 years! Nonetheless, ROI and break-even point are important metrics for selling new-product ideas internally and for measuring their success in the market.

Chapter Summary

A product is a bundle of benefits that satisfies the needs of organizations or consumers and for which they are willing to exchange money or other items of value. A product can be a tangible good, a service, an idea, a person, a place, or something else. The entire product experience provides value to the customer, is defined by the customer, involves customer expectations, and applies at all price levels.

Of the five general product decisions that comprise a bundle of benefits for meeting customer needs, four (attributes, branding, support services, and labeling) apply to online products. Companies creating new products for online sale must decide whether to use existing brand names or create new brand names for new products; whether to co-brand; and what domain name to choose. Customer support—during and after purchases—is a critical component in the value proposition. Online labeling is the digital equivalent of product labeling and can serve many of the same purposes as offline labeling.

When branding products, marketers consider popular culture, the brand, and the consumer. Firms attempt to move consumers to higher levels of relationship intensity from awareness to advocacy.

When developing new online products, digital marketers can turn to customer codesign and use internet properties to spark other opportunities. They can choose among six categories of new-product strategies (discontinuous innovations, new-product lines, additions to existing product lines, improvements/revisions of existing products, product repositionings, and me-too lower-cost products) and are generally required to estimate revenues, costs, and ROI or payout for management review and approval.

Exercises

Review Questions

1. What are the arguments for and against using existing brand names on the Web?
2. List six new-product strategy categories and provide internet examples of each.
3. Why is value tied to the entire product experience?
4. What are some important criteria for naming internet domains?
5. How does labeling work on the internet?
6. What techniques can marketers employ to enhance new-product development?
7. Why do marketers need to forecast revenue, expenses, ROI, and break even for new products under consideration?

Discussion Questions

1. **Google Story:** Describe Google's strategy for creating value: attributes, branding, support services, and labeling.
2. **Google Story:** Why do you think Google's primary revenue comes from advertising? What other products do you think Google could monetize?
3. What similarities do you see in Exhibit 9.4 that makes for great brands? Do you have other ideas?
4. Under what circumstances would it make sense to take an existing brand name online? When would it not make sense?
5. Given the list of online booksellers in this chapter, what name would you pick for a new bookstore selling both new and used books online?
6. How would you use social media to build the brand of your university?

7. What discontinuous innovations have you seen since this book was written? What's next in your opinion?

8. Why do marketers often have difficulty estimating the revenues, costs, and payout or ROI of a new product under development?

Web Activities

1. Visit www.sedo.com and search keywords of interest. Do you see any names represented there that could be interpreted as cybersquatting?

2. Visit the Country-Code Top-Level Domain database at www.domainnamestat.com. Notice how websites originating in the United States do not have to append the ".us" root to the end of URLs. Which root names owned by these countries could be used for commercial purposes rather than differentiating country of origin? If you wanted to register a website ending in one of these country root names, what requirements do you have to meet? What country root names are already being offered through registrations sites like GoDaddy.com?

3. Visit godaddy.com and do a search for your own name.com. Is it available? If so, what would it cost to get it, and what services are available for that fee? If it is not available, how can you attempt to obtain it using GoDaddy's services?

4. Many companies use a new-product development process called scenario planning. For example, Microsoft executives wonder what it would be like if you could search your computer for phone numbers, e-mail addresses, and both file names and document content all at once with one search word. Think of five scenarios that would make your life easier while using the internet.

Chapter 10

Price
The Online Value

This chapter will help you examine how internet technology influences pricing strategies. You will gain an understanding of both the buyer's and the seller's perspectives of pricing online and consider whether the internet is an efficient market. You will also read about fixed pricing as well as the return to dynamic pricing, such as online auctions, and many other strategies and tactics.

After reading this chapter, you will be able to:

- Identify the main fixed and dynamic pricing strategies used for selling online.
- Discuss the buyer's view of pricing online in relation to real costs and buyer control.
- Highlight the seller's view of pricing online in relation to internal and external factors.
- Outline the arguments for and against the internet as an efficient market.
- Describe several types of online payment systems and their benefits to online retailers.

THE PRICE OF A FREE APP

How many in-app purchases does it take to generate $5.1 billion in sales a year (Clark, 2021)? Epic Games, the developer of popular game Fortnite, can answer such a question. Fortnite does not cost money to play, but Epic Games has mastered the revenue generating model, with 77 percent of players making in-game purchases (Clement, 2021). With over 350 million registered players, Fortnite is a worldwide phenomenon engaging consumers across gaming consoles, personal computers, and mobile devices (Clement, 2021). In-app purchase are not the only method of generating revenue from apps. There are several different popular pricing and revenue models in use (Golmack, 2017):

- Freemium is a combination of "free" and "premium," where companies offer a basic product for free and then provide upgraded versions for a fee—for example, Angry Birds Free. This could also include in-app purchases to engage with users spending large amounts of time using the app.
- Lite versions of apps are sold at low prices and do not include all the features of the full app versions. For example, Robinhood is a free trading and investing app that allows you to purchase more than 7,000 corporate stock offerings while also offering a "Gold Service Plan" for $5 a month. Part of Robinhood's psychic appeal is to position stock trading to have a more game-like feel.
- Subscription models offer access to content based on a monthly fee and can also remove ads, like Hulu.
- Ad-supported apps, such as Spotify, are typically free to the user but generate revenue through the serving of targeted ads.

DOI: 10.4324/9781003247319-14

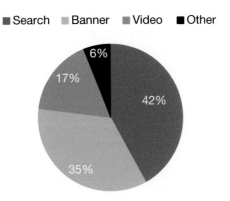

■ Search ■ Banner ■ Video ■ Other

Exhibit 10.1 Mobile Advertising Format Share

- Crowdfunding platforms, such as Kickstarter, support the development of certain types of applications, products, and projects and are an effective example of dynamic pricing, in that early investors typically receive a lower price than those that join later. Dynamic pricing will be elaborated on later in this chapter.

According to an Internet Advertising Bureau report, advertising revenue generated from mobile apps comes primarily from three formats served within applications (see Exhibit 10.1). The leading mobile app categories used by consumers each month include messaging (90.7%), social networking (88.4%), entertainment (67.2%), music (52.9%), and games (52.0%) (Hootsuite Global Digital Report, 2021).

The Internet Changes Pricing Strategies

In the narrowest sense, price is the amount of money charged for a product or service. More broadly, price is the sum of all the values (such as money, time, energy, and psychic cost) that buyers exchange for the benefits of having or using a good or service. Throughout most of history, prices were set by negotiation between buyers and sellers, and that remains the dominant model in many emerging economies. Fixed price policies—setting one price for all buyers—is a relatively modern idea that arose with the development of large-scale retailing and mass production at the end of the nineteenth century. Now, 100 years later, the internet is taking us back to an era of dynamic pricing—varying prices for individuals.

Information technologies have complicated pricing strategies and have changed the way marketers use this tool, especially in online markets. In addition, the increasing power of buyers means control over pricing in some instances—such as with online product bidding. The internet's properties, especially in the role of information equalizer, allow for price transparency—the idea that both buyers and sellers can view competitive prices for items sold online. This feature would tend to commoditize products sold online, making the internet an efficient market. But is it?

We explore the internet as an efficient market in this chapter, using the economist's view as a guide. We also discuss both the buyer's and the seller's views of price and explain why some pricing strategies are more effective online than others.

Buyer and Seller Perspectives

The meaning of *price* depends on the viewpoint of the buyer and the seller. Each party to the exchange brings different needs and objectives that help describe a *fair* price. In the end, both parties must agree, or no sale takes place.

Buyer View

Recall that buyers define value as benefits minus costs. In Chapter 9, we discussed the benefit variable, explaining that the internet creates many benefits important to consumers and business buyers alike. Here we explore the cost side of the formula: money, time, energy, and psychic costs.

The Real Costs

Today's buyer must be quite sophisticated to understand even the simple dollar cost of a product sold online. The seller's price may or may not include shipping, tax, and other seemingly hidden elements—hidden in the sense that these costs often are not revealed online until the last screen of a shopping experience. For example, Exhibit 10.2 displays the different prices for the book, *The Hunger Games* (book one in the series), as displayed by several different online booksellers. These prices are fairly clear yet complex to understand, and the burden is on the consumer to understand his or her needs and translate those into the best price. Note that tax is not included because it varies by state or country—another complexity. The lowest price bookseller, Biblio, does not have the highest rating, so is it better to pay an additional few dollars to use a more highly rated store with more reviewers and a better-known brand name? Also note how there is quite a range in shipping prices from most sellers. Finally, why is there an 80.5 percent price dispersion from the lowest to the highest price?

   This example is what is meant by the time, energy, and psychic costs that add to a buyer's monetary costs. As well, sometimes the internet is slow, information is hard to find, and other technological problems cause users to spend more time and energy, thus becoming frustrated (psychic cost). Shopping agents will find the lowest prices online, but the search adds to the time cost. For example, when buyers search for the lowest airfare at online travel agents Orbitz. com or Travelocity.com, the search time is minimal compared to the dollar savings, but users need to know that these sites do not represent all airlines (e.g., Expedia.com doesn't include Southwest Airlines). The same non-monetary savings may not be true for a book-price search—it all depends on the time it takes to search, the savings as a percentage of the item cost, and how much familiarity and experience the buyer has with the search engine (making an easier search process). The internet technologies and content are far from perfect, but as

Bookseller	Review Stars	Price	Shipping	Price with Shipping
Alibris		$1.45	$4.49	$5.94
Books-A-Million	4.8/5	$7.79	$4.99	$12.78
Barnes & Noble	4.7/5	$12.99	$4.99	$17.98
Amazon	4.7/5	$11.69	$2.99	$14.68

Exhibit 10.2 Online Search, *The Hunger Games*: book by Suzanne Collins

Source: Booksellers in column one.

broadband adoption continues to increase, technology evolves, and firms develop better online strategies, some of these costs will decline.

In contrast, buyers often enjoy many online cost savings:

- *The internet is convenient.* It is open 24/7 so that users can research, shop, consume entertainment, or otherwise use the Web's offerings anytime, anywhere, and on any stationary or mobile receiving device. Digital mail allows asynchronous communication among buyers and sellers at any location and prevents "phone tag" (both parties need not be online simultaneously to communicate). Shopping bots (automated chat and animated help programs on websites) provide synchronous help as a customer is shopping online. Powerful analytics enables automatic recommendation of complimentary products based on previous purchases.
- *The internet is fast.* Amazon Prime has normalized two-day shipping for many US users, and in some regions the company can even offer one-hour delivery services. During the COVID-19 pandemic, demand for such services surged, as consumers were unable to make in-store purchases.
- *Self-service saves time.* Customers can track shipments, pay bills, trade securities, check account balances, and handle many other activities without waiting for sales reps. In addition, technology allows users to request product information at websites and receive it immediately. Of course, all these activities take time to perform.
- *One-stop shopping saves time.* The internet opened the door for companies to increase customer convenience through one-stop shopping. AutoMall Online has partnered with a number of firms to provide automobile price comparisons, research about various models and manufacturers, financing and insurance information, and service options. This firm also offers instant online pricing from a large network of auto dealerships and gives customers a *purchase certificate* guaranteeing that the price quote will be honored at the dealership. AutoMall Online has an effective track record, proving that customers receive value.
- *Integration saves time.* Users have control over the organization and access to many popular apps, websites, and services they frequently use regardless of what device they use to view it. Adding personalized account access to many of these utilities enables the user to access relevant information as seamlessly as possible.
- *Automation saves energy.* Customers value simplicity and ease; because the internet makes some activities more complex, technology can help. For example, browsers, sites and companies that allow customer computers to keep track of passwords for user accounts (such as Dashlane) and to track previous purchases at websites save time and energy. Applications like Honey can automatically search the Web for deals and promo codes to apply toward a purchase you are making now.

Note that not everyone wants to save money in online transactions. Customer needs and their views of the value proposition vary as each individual weighs the desired and perceived benefits against all the costs. For example, some people prefer to order books from Amazon. com with overnight delivery, knowing well that Amazon prices are often higher than other online booksellers, that the book is in stock at a local bookstore, and that overnight delivery costs quite a bit more and shaves only a few days from the delivery time. Nevertheless, the Amazon brand name is trustworthy, these customers have had excellent previous experiences with Amazon, and they are familiar with the site, quickly finding what they need. And they do not have to leave their house or business to get the book they want. Thus, those benefits and time/energy-saving features overcome the higher expense.

Buyer Control

The shift in power from seller to buyer affects many digital marketing strategies, including pricing. For instance, in what is known as a reverse auction, buyers set prices for products and sellers decide whether to accept these prices. A good example is Priceline.com, where you can name the price you want to pay for hotels, flights, cars, vacations, and cruises. In the B2B market, buyers bid for excess inventory at exchanges and for products at firms such as General Electric and Caterpillar, and government buyers put out a request for proposal for materials and labor needed for a particular project. The government buyer selects the lowest price, in effect having control over the exchange.

Online sellers are more willing to negotiate than their offline counterparts in most industrialized nations, thus giving power to buyers in the exchange. Perhaps it is easier for US consumers to negotiate from behind an impersonal computer, as compared with standing face to face with the seller. Also, sellers realize that information technology can help them better manage inventories and automate frequent price changes. Buyer power online is also based on the huge quantity of information and product availability on the Web. As a result, online buyers are becoming more sophisticated—as they must be, considering the example of the *Hunger Games* book pricing options. Also, social media saves time and money when consumers can look at online reviews written by "people like them." For instance, it saves time to search for the highest rated tires at consumerreports.org or the highest recommended books in a category at Amazon. This is much faster than facing the alphabetized books on shelves at the brick-and-mortar bookseller. Social networks such as Facebook and Twitter, as well as many other sites, give consumers the power to find the best products without even consulting company sites. Also, consider the social media cooperative buying sites such as Groupon.com, where consumers can purchase an item and watch the price drop as other individuals elect to purchase the same item.

With power comes risk. Consider what happens to a substantial number of bidders in online auctions. In what has been called "the winner's curse," some people actually pay a higher price for auctioned products than they would pay an online retailer. In the B2B market, one study found that car dealers pay significantly more for used automobiles online than they do offline. In the B2C market, researchers evaluated the winning bids for new surplus computer items at Egghead.com and compared prices for the exact items sold on the retail portion of the Egghead site (Pellegrino, Amyx, and Pellegrino, 2002). They found that 20 percent of winning bidders overpaid. This holds true today. One eBay seller reported placing video games on eBay for the "buy it now" price of $10 (his cost), and they all sold for an average of $15 each plus $4 shipping ("Why do People Overpay . . .", 2011). Perhaps the entertainment benefit of an online auction keeps the value equation in balance, but just as likely, buyers do not realize they have overpaid.

Seller View

Sellers view price as the amount of money they receive from buyers, unless they are making a barter exchange. Seller costs for producing the good or service represent the pricing floor, under which no profit is made. Above that floor, marketers have the freedom to set a price that will draw buyers from competing offers. Between cost and price is profit.

The seller's perspective on pricing includes both internal and external factors. Internal factors are the firm's strengths and weaknesses from its SWOT analysis, its overall pricing objectives, its marketing mix strategy, and the costs involved in producing and marketing the product. External factors that affect online pricing in particular include the market structure, competition, and the buyer's perspective, as discussed earlier.

Internal Factors: Pricing Objectives

Marketers begin by setting overall pricing objectives from among those that are profit oriented, market oriented, or competition oriented. The most common profit-oriented objective for pricing is current profit maximization. Online research firms such as Forrester and Gartner Group are using a profit-oriented approach when they charge $1,500 to $4,500 and more to download current digital business research reports.

Companies can also select among various market-oriented objectives. Building a larger customer base may lead to lower costs and higher long-run profit. Low prices generally build market share. For example, Survey Monkey, a Web-based survey software program, offers its basic level software at a low price to build share (compared to competition) and then upsells to annual maintenance fees and programs with more functionality. Negotiation and bidding are also market-oriented approaches. For example, consumers can bid for hotel room nights on priceline.com, hotwire.com, roomauction.com, and many individual hotel websites.

The objective of competition-based pricing is to price according to what competitors charge for similar products, paying less attention to the company's own costs or to demand. The internet's pricing transparency gives firms quicker access to competitive price changes and increases the number and speed of online price changes.

Internal Factors: Marketing Mix Strategy

Successful companies use an integrated and consistent marketing mix strategy. For example, a study of more than 22,000 consumers discovered that 90 percent of consumers start researching new and used automobiles three months before purchase (Deloitte, 2018). Digital channels become significantly more important for younger buyers (i.e., Gen Y/Z) with mobile devices serving as critical information tools. However, only 11 percent report social media impacting their purchase decisions. Marketers pay careful attention to this type of research so they know how to integrate promotional channels (Web, social media, offline media), marketing communication, and pricing and coordinate these with their offline retail presences. Looking ahead, more than 50 percent indicated they were either neutral or somewhat interests in buying a vehicle online (Deloitte, 2018).

The internet is only one sales channel and must be used in concert with other marketing mix elements. Marketing managers carefully consider how to price the same product for sale in both online and offline channels. For instance, you can read unlimited *The New York Times* articles online for $25 for three months or get mail delivery of the physical paper to your home for $50 for three months (prices as of June 2021). There are also different pricing schemes for education and business market segments. No proven rules or standard practices have emerged at this point—practices vary widely by product and industry.

INTERNAL FACTORS: INFORMATION TECHNOLOGY AFFECTS COSTS

Information technology can be expensive, but once it is running smoothly it can create tremendous cost efficiencies—putting both upward and downward pressure on prices.

The Internet Puts Upward Pressure on Prices   Many companies fail with expensive customer relationship management software or other software that does not help to generate enough new revenue to cover the sites' costs due to competitive pricing constraints. Following are some of the factors that put upward pressure on internet pricing:

- *Online customer service.* In the past, customer service online provided a competitive edge for firms such as Dell Computer and Amazon. Conversely, customers now expect firms to return e-mail promptly and provide thorough help and FAQ functions online (or even on Twitter) and provide telephone and other contact information. Online customer service is no longer a competitive edge but an expensive competitive necessity.
- *Distribution.* Online retailers face hefty distribution costs for their products: each product must be shipped separately to its destination rather than by the case to brick-and-mortar retailers or centrally located warehouses. This is similar to the catalog marketer's cost structure. Retailers pass shipping costs on to their customers, thus raising prices. Not surprisingly, some customers are offended by the shipping costs if they are higher than expected and if the shipping cost is presented in the shopping cart only at the last minute. High shipping costs are one reason for shopping cart abandonment.
- *Affiliate programs.* Many websites pay a commission on referrals through affiliate programs. Affiliate sponsors reward the referring websites by paying a 7 percent to 15 percent commission on each reference that leads to a sale. This commission, like all channel intermediary costs, has the effect of inflating the price of the item or lowering company profits if referral fees are absorbed.
- *Site development and maintenance.* Website development and maintenance are not cheap. The scope of the project impacts the cost significantly. For example, Amazon may spend thousands of dollars to develop and maintain its website, whereas a local retailer can get its website up and running for just a few hundred dollars. Website developers tend to specialize within industry segments, lowering the cost and increasing the quality of the product delivered.
- *Social media maintenance.* Companies spend a lot of staff time monitoring and responding to consumer posts on Facebook, Twitter, and other social media. It is important for businesses to identify which social media are key to customer development and engagement and to focus on those (more on this in later chapters).
- *Customer acquisition costs (CAC).* The cost of acquiring new customers online is quite high; this factor caused the downfall of many dot-com firms. How many orders must a firm receive to recoup that cost, and at what price? In addition, many customers are not nearly as brand loyal online as they are offline.

The Internet Puts Downward Pressure on Prices   The internet also allows marketers to save costs, translating into lower prices and ultimately higher value for customers. When lower costs lead to higher prices, profit increases—a win for the company. The following are a few ways firms can save costs using internet technology for internal processes:

- *Order processing—self-service.* Because customers fill out their own order forms, firms save the expense of order entry personnel and paper processing. These expenses can be considerable. The average cost of producing and processing an invoice electronically is $10, compared with $100 in offline transactions. An average retail banking transaction costs $0.15 to $0.20 online versus $1.50 offline. Cisco Systems, the world's largest manufacturer of networking equipment, invites Web-based orders from customers. The paperwork reduction it reaps from its website saves hundreds of millions of dollars each year.

- *Just-in-time inventory.* Some manufacturers use electronic data interchange (EDI) to drive down costs in the digital channel by coordinating value-chain activities and allowing for just-in-time (JIT) delivery of parts and reduced inventories. Some online and offline retailers do not even hold inventory, saving considerably on financing costs. Instead, they acquire the inventory in response to customer orders or have partners drop-ship products directly to customers.

- *Overhead.* Online storefronts can lower their overhead costs because companies do not have to rent and staff expensive retail space. Amazon's physical warehouses are considerably less expensive to rent and staff than the retail space of a trendy shopping mall. Furthermore, these warehouses can be located in areas with low rents, low wages, low taxes, and quick access to shipping hubs, such as northern Nevada.

- *Customer service.* Although customer service can initially add to an organization's costs, companies save by automating some customer service functions that were formerly performed by employees. Advances in natural language processing (NLP) allow for automated chatbots to handle more complex customer requests online. Companies also save money by posting FAQs and video instructions online, as well as providing automated e-mail responses to questions. Customer service requests can average $15 to $20 in an offline call center versus $3 to $5 when customers help themselves on the internet.

- *Printing and mailing.* Online sellers do not incur mail distribution and printing costs for their product catalogs. Once the catalog is placed online, access carries little or no incremental costs. The same holds true for e-mail and social media promotions.

- *Digital product distribution costs.* Distribution costs for digital products are extremely low in the internet channel, such as when a customer downloads a purchased music file from iTunes or reads articles with Instapaper. Conversely, the internet channel has high distribution costs for tangible products because they are sent to individuals in small quantities instead of in larger lots to brick-and-mortar intermediaries.

These efficiencies usually result in lower prices for consumers online; technology enables buyers to evaluate and demand appealing prices. For example, online stock trades cost as low as $5, while broker-assisted offline trades often cost hundreds of dollars.

External Factors Affecting Online Pricing

The competition, market factors, price-demand relationship (i.e., elastic or inelastic), and customer behavior all affect a firm's pricing strategies online and offline. The buyer's viewpoint was covered earlier; online behavior affecting pricing was covered in Chapter 7. In this section, we examine two important market factors affecting pricing in the online environment: market structure and market efficiency.

MARKET STRUCTURE

The seller's leeway to set prices varies with different types of markets. Economists recognize four types of markets, each presenting a different pricing challenge:

1. *Pure competition.* This market consists of many buyers and sellers trading in a uniform commodity such as corn. Product differentiation and marketing communication play little or no role, so sellers in these markets do not spend much time on marketing strategy. Many online products could be seen as pure competition, such as music downloads; however, the retailers offering the products can differentiate based on customer service.

2. *Monopolistic competition.* This market consists of many buyers and sellers who trade over a range of prices rather than a single market price. A range of prices occurs because sellers can differentiate their offers to buyers. Online university courses are one product delivered over the internet that falls in this category.

3. *Oligopolistic competition.* This market consists of a few sellers who are highly sensitive to each other's pricing and marketing strategies. If a company drops its price by 5 percent, buyers will quickly switch over to this supplier. Online travel agents such as Expedia and Travelocity fall into this category.

4. *Pure monopoly.* This market consists of one seller whose prices are usually regulated by the government. If you are in a smaller town, your internet service provider could fall into this category.

This market structure distinction is extremely important for online sellers, because if *price transparency* eventually results in a completely efficient market for some products, sellers will have no control over online prices—the result will be pure competition as depicted in Exhibit 10.3. One example of a nearly efficient market is the stock market. Note that online stock trading firms operate in a monopolistic competition because they compete based on trade commission prices and customer service, not actual security selling prices. If other products follow suit, the internet will have a profound effect on pricing strategy. This probably will not happen, however, for reasons mentioned in the next section. Next, we examine what comprises an efficient market and discuss whether the online market is approaching efficiency.

MARKET EFFICIENCY

Economists have long theorized about consumer behavior in efficient markets. Such markets would experience perfect price competition. A market is efficient when customers have equal access to information about products, prices, and distribution. In an efficient market, one would expect to find lower prices, high price elasticity, frequent price changes, smaller price changes, and narrow price dispersion—the observed spread between the highest and lowest price for a given product. As previously mentioned, the closest example of an efficient market is the stock market. Commodity markets came close to being efficient until the government

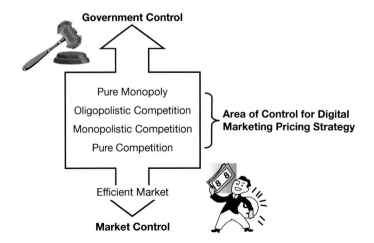

Exhibit 10.3 Efficient Markets Mean Loss of Pricing Control

intervened with controls. However, the internet is probably as close to a test ground for efficient markets as has ever existed because it exhibits so many of the appropriate characteristics. Interestingly, the behavior of consumers on the internet does not bear out all of the economists' predictions.

Is the Internet an Efficient Market?

Many people believe that the internet is an efficient market because of access to information through corporate Web sites, shopping agents, and distribution channels. For instance, a search for a flight to Bangkok at Kayak.com or Travelocity.com will display a complete array of airlines and prices. Products sold online generally exhibit lower prices, high price elasticity, frequent price changes, and smaller price changes—all symptoms of efficient markets. But do these factors actually make the internet an efficient market? The following external market factors place a downward pressure on internet prices, contributing to efficiency:

- *Shopping agents.* Shopping agents, also called comparison shopping agents, such as ShopSavvy facilitate consumer searches for low prices by displaying the results in a comparative format. While there are many websites that accomplish this function, like Bizrate. com, many popular apps give consumers flexibility to comparison shop even while in physical stores. Exhibit 10.4 displays the results for a Morphie charging case for the

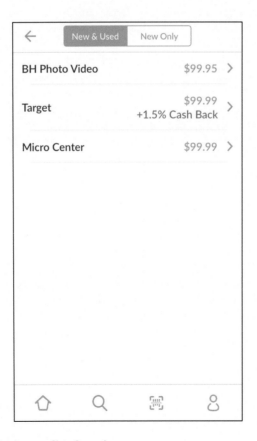

Exhibit 10.4 Example of Product on ShopSavvy App

iPhone. Shopping agents are popular, especially when they can quickly help consumers save money on a purchase.

- *Flash sales.* These are limited-time offers for site members to purchase a product at a deep discount. Gilt and Rue La were among the first to offer flash sales, such as a 20 percent discount good for only four hours. The primary way of announcing these sales is via e-mail marketing to members, and some question the viability of this business model due to the interrupt nature of the marketing communication (i.e., the e-mails create overload and are easy to ignore).
- *High price elasticity.* Price elasticity refers to the variability of purchase behavior with changes in price. As an example, leisure travel is an especially elastic market: when the airlines engage in fare wars, consumers snap up ticket inventories, creating huge demand. For many products, such as books, the online market is more elastic than the offline market, so we would expect internet users to be sensitive to price changes.
- *Reverse auctions.* Reverse auctions allow buyers to name their price and have sellers try to match that price (such as Priceline.com). This format pits sellers against one another and usually drives prices down.
- *Venture capital.* Many internet companies are financed through venture capital or angel investors. Many investors take a long-term view and are willing to sustain short-term losses to let those companies grow by establishing brand equity and grabbing market share. These companies can price lower because they do not have a profit-maximization pricing objective.
- *Competition.* The competition online is fierce and highly visible. Furthermore, some competitors are willing to set prices that return little or no short-term profits to gain brand equity and market share.
- *Frequent price changes.* The online market experiences more frequent price changes than the offline market because (1) online suppliers must jockey with competitors to attract price-sensitive consumers; (2) shopping agents give consumers excellent comparative information about prices, and vendors may frequently alter their pricing to place higher on the results; (3) sellers can easily change prices using databases to drive webpage content; (4) in a computerized environment, firms can offer volume discounts in smaller increments than in an offline environment (e.g., FedEx creates millions of different rate books based on shipping volume for posting on webpages for individual clients); and (5) experimentation is easy online, allowing firms to change prices frequently, see how demand changes, and then adjust as competition and other factors emerge.
- *Smaller price change increments.* In one study, the smallest offline price change was $0.35, whereas the smallest online price change was $0.01. Keepa.com allows users to track price changes for popular products on Amazon.com. Some of the same factors that encourage frequent price changes may play a role here as well. First, price-sensitive consumers may respond to even a small price advantage with respect to the competition. Second, shopping agents rank their results by price—even a $0.01 advantage will earn a higher ranking than the competition. Third, because it is difficult to change prices offline, retailers may wait until the need for a price change is even greater.

Is the Net an Inefficient Market?

Even though the Web exhibits many characteristics of an efficient market, it does not act like an efficient market with respect to narrow price dispersion. Prices tend to equalize in commodities markets because sellers cannot easily differentiate one bushel of peas from another. With perfect information for all, one would expect narrow price dispersion online—for example, because buyers can search many Web sellers for this book, we might expect the prices to gravitate to the same level.

Interestingly, this expectation does not hold on the internet, due to the strength of a firm's brand, the way goods are priced online as well as delivery options, time-sensitive shoppers, differentiation, switching costs, and second-generation shopping agents:

- *Branding*. In spite of the proliferation of products, brand is still a sought-after benefit. The most highly recognized and preferred branded websites get most of the traffic. Consumers will show a preference for brand when using online services such as search engines. Many consumers will pick a well-known merchant brand from the search results even if that brand does not offer the lowest price. Because of the importance of brand, the best-branded websites spend millions of dollars to attract customers. Amazon spent $22 billion on marketing expenses in 2020 according to their annual filings (Chevalier, 2021a). The brand-loyal customer base allows Amazon to charge more than bargain online retailers.
- *Differentiation*. One result of strong branding is perceived or real product differentiation, which enables marketers to price their products differently.
- *How products are priced online*. Most goods are offered at fixed prices offline in industrialized nations. By contrast, marketers use many more strategies on the Web. The same product is often available for a fixed, a dynamically updated, or an auction price on different sites at the same time—and the prices among them may vary widely. In addition, products are bundled with shipping and special services in different ways, confusing shoppers who want to compare similar products.
- *Delivery options*. The same product delivered under differing conditions (time and place) may have considerably different value to the consumer. For example, a beer served at a bar has more value than one bought at a supermarket. Similarly, a product delivered to the door may have considerably more value for some consumers than one that is bought at the store (convenience). Online grocery shopping follows this value model. Some marketers would argue that groceries delivered to the door are not the same product as the same groceries picked up at the store. By this argument, the additional benefits actually differentiate the product. Normally, the consumer has to wait longer for a product delivered to the door, but that may be changing. Amazon offers one-hour delivery of selected items in some metropolitan areas, and other firms may follow suit.
- *Time-sensitive shoppers*. Time-sensitive shoppers may not wish to invest the time and energy required to track down the best price. Also, some sites may be so complex that consumers need more time to navigate and complete the transaction.
- *Switching costs*. Customers face switching costs when they choose a different online retailer. Some customers are not willing to incur those costs and thus stick with a familiar online retailer. If an Amazon customer shops at another retailer, he or she loses access to a familiar interface, personalized book recommendations, and the 1-Click ordering that Amazon has patented. Switching costs are even higher in the B2B market. Many organizations have found that it is more effective to build relationships with a limited number of suppliers rather than offer all items out for bid. These organizations readily pay a slight premium to enjoy better service and support.
- *Second-generation shopping agents*. Second-generation shopping agents guide the consumer through the process of quantifying benefits and evaluating the value equation. If a consumer ranks certain benefits highly, that consumer may be willing to pay more to receive those benefits. BizRate allows consumers to evaluate merchants based on ratings compiled from previous customers. PriceScan and DealTime allow consumers to set filters so

that merchants delivering the desired benefits will rise in the rankings. See the "Let's Get Technical" box for more information on shopping agents.

Is the internet an efficient market? The answer is no, not now. However, it has all the features to move toward efficiency in the future. This shift would have devastating effects for digital marketers wanting control over pricing strategies; thus, marketers will watch this trend closely.

Let's Get Technical—Unwrapping Online Shopping's Secrets

Five days before the holidays . . . and you have not even started shopping for gifts. By the time you get home from work, it is after 7 P.M. and you are tired. Because you were so busy with your new job this year, you forgot everyone's birthday and only remembered to send a card a month late. If things weren't bad enough, you are strapped for cash because your old clunker of a car died last month, and you were forced to get a new one. Your sister wants a digital camera, and your mom wants a new TV for her bedroom. The convenience of online shopping is appealing, and you might just score some coupons on RetailMeNot.com. After a couple of hours of clicking and shipping, your holiday shopping is finished and you saved a bunch of dough. . . . Now it's time for some holiday cookies!

A majority of the large retailers in the United States and shoppers worldwide have all caught the bug—the online shopping bug, that is. While the Saturday trip to the mall used to be commonplace, many households are now doing a majority of their shopping online, and this only increased during the COVID-19 pandemic, when consumers had no choice. Whether it is the latest consumer electronic or a new bedspread, consumers are more than happy to shop from the comfort of their homes—wearing who knows what. Most consumers say they are lured by the convenience of online shopping. Retailers are certainly used to attracting consumers to their stores using circulars, commercials, and coupons, and similar concepts are being deployed online to get consumers to their websites.

Since the onset of online shopping, consumers' perceptions have been that better "deals" can be found online. Of course, a "deal" is based on the individual consumer's values. However, websites are cropping up to help frugal consumers find the best deals online. So instead of clipping the coupons and flipping through circulars, shoppers are giving shopping agents and coupon websites a try. It is important for digital marketers to understand the technologies employed by consumers—and for digital marketers to properly utilize them.

A *shopping agent* is a website that collects product and price information from online retail sites and displays all of the information together. For example, many websites sell digital cameras. If a consumer is looking for a certain digital camera, such as the Nikon CoolPix, he would be able to enter that information into the shopping agent's search box and receive prices from all over the Web. Many shopping agents display websites' advertised prices, but some also ask for the consumer's zip code to calculate tax and shipping costs. The final result is a list of the sites on which the item is available and the cost of the item on that site. Links are also available to go directly to the websites or the product pages. In addition to providing prices, some shopping agents review products and retailers. Consumers are invited to rate retailers and record comments about their buying experience on the site.

From a digital marketing standpoint, shopping agents are beneficial because they attract to the retailers' websites consumers who are ready to buy—what more could a digital marketer ask for? Although consumers believe that shopping agents are providing unbiased results to their queries, the truth is that most are not. Some agents list only retailers that have registered with them, and other agents list sites based on who has paid for the top spot on the results list.

Shopping agents are popular, and consumers can find hundreds of products using comparison shopping engines (CSEs). When marketing products using shopping agents, it is essential to understand how to register a product and select one that is appropriate for the digital marketing campaign.

When registering a product with a shopping agent, marketers are usually required to pay a fee and give the website a product feed. Most agents have a pay-per-click (PPC) policy. Prices range from a few cents to more than $1 for each time a consumer clicks on the link to the product. Some sites also require a deposit of $100 to $200 when registering, which would be applied to the PPC account.

A product feed contains information about the product that is being featured, such as its name, description, category, price, and availability. Agents also ask that a URL to the product be included for linking purposes. Product feeds are fairly simple to create and give marketers an opportunity to compel consumers to purchase the product from their websites. Expert digital marketers recommend that clear and concise language be used when writing product feeds, and industry abbreviations should never be used. For example, the abbreviation "DJ" may seem reasonable when marketing a Hewlett-Packard DeskJet printer, but it is better to write out the term. Agents ask that product feeds be submitted in one of a variety of ways, such as online forms or file uploading.

When choosing which shopping agent to register with, one should definitely do one's homework. Some sites are known for their ability to provide information on a wide variety of products, while others are more specialized. Also, registering with one shopping agent can have the product listed on multiple sites due to the agent's affiliation with other agents.

Shopping agents that are known for their high volume of visitors include Google Shopping, BizRate, NexTag, and ShopAtHome. Google is so far out ahead in the European market that they were sued in 2017 for $2.73 billion for monopolizing the European CSE market. The complaint was that Google featured their own shopping search engine results first.

Consumers' use of online coupons is also increasing. Coupon sites offer a variety of services for the penny-pinching consumer:

- Links to company websites that offer free coupons.
- Printable coupons for use in brick-and-mortar stores.
- Coupon codes for online retailers.
- Links to sites that will automatically give a percentage off an order.
- Information about sale and clearance-priced items at online retailers.

Some sites require consumer input to get the coupon or information listed on the site. Digital marketers can submit their coupons, promotional codes, and sales to these sites, usually via e-mail. Coupon sites include coupons.com, retailmenot.com, and coupon-cabin.com. Traditional paper coupon distributors, such as SmartSource and ValPak, are also offering online coupons. Industry experts say that the circulation of coupons and promotional codes online is high and that the best way to get noticed is to offer two deals in one, such as free shipping and $10 off an order.

Payment Options

Electronic money, also called e-money, digital cash, or digital currency, is a system that uses the internet and computers to exchange payments electronically. It can be used in offline or online transactions, using the internet to transfer money between buyer and seller accounts. In the United States, an example of offline digital money transactions occur at toll booths when autos with transponders drive through them—and drivers receive a monthly invoice. PayPal, Square, Venmo, Apple, and Google have all introduced varying degrees of services that enable currency to flow between users digitally. Apple Pay, for instance, is accepted at many point of sale devices across the United States. These services allow mobile device users to pay using integrated technology in the iPhone, like near-field communication (NFC), and even through text messages.

Online, approximately 70 percent of US consumers use online financial services, showing the huge adoption of digital money systems (as mentioned in Chapter 7) (Johnson, 2021a). Payment systems in other countries vary, and marketers must learn what technologies to offer for facilitating digital commerce. The preferred methods of payment for users in China, for instance, are much different than what is used in the United States.

For one-time payments, PayPal has become the industry standard, with over 392 million accounts worldwide (de Best, 2021). This innovative payment company allows users to pay for online purchases via credit card or bank debit. One important digital money service uses a model quite different from PayPal's—so much so that PayPal acquired the company and eventually rebranded it as PayPal Credit. Called Bill Me Later, this model allows buyers to pay for online goods and services without a credit card. They must be approved by Bill Me Later and are billed after making the purchase. This service signed up merchants such as Walmart, the Apple Store, Office Max, and Overstock.com. It is especially good for small businesses that purchase online because it costs them less than their credit card fees and interest.

Bitcoin is a form of virtual currency that has gained popularity in recent years. Unlike government-backed currencies, it operates outside of mainstream financial regulations. Scarcity of Bitcoin has increased demand, and because it is untraceable, it has become popular among hackers.

Electronic money has distinct advantages for online retailers. It is more efficient, with lower transaction fees, and draws new customers without credit risk fears. Also, these services allow online merchants to sell to internet users who do not have credit cards or who do not want to input their credit cards on a new website. Finally, offering multiple payment options can actually entice more people to buy online. Conversely, potential downsides include large economic issues involving all digital commerce, such as fewer taxes for states when transactions occur out of state, the possibilities of exchange rate fluctuations with high levels of international digital commerce, and the criminal use of the systems for money laundering and other fraudulent or illegal activities.

Electronic cash is an important pricing component for two reasons. First, when merchants use PayPal or other systems, their costs increase, and this is reflected in the product's price. Second, when online purchasing is easier for customers, this balances the higher price—recall that the costs for consumers include money, time, energy, and psychic costs.

Pricing Strategies

Price setting is full of contradictions. It has become nearly as much art as science, with lots of data needing insightful interpretation for best application. If the price is too low, profits will suffer, yet if it is too high sales may decline. And that is just the short-term view. In the long run, an initial low price that builds market share can create economies of scale to lower costs and thus increase profits. Also, how marketers apply pricing strategy is as important as *how much* they charge. PayPal's merchant pricing system demonstrates the skill that goes into pricing strategy.

Another contradiction is that information technology complicates pricing in some ways while making it simpler in other ways. Sellers easily change prices at a moment's notice or vary them according to each individual buyer's previous behavior. Next, buyer value perceptions vary between rational and emotional, and not everyone reacts the same way. For example, some high-income customers enjoy walking into the Volvo dealership with a printed webpage detailing what they want and how much it should cost, while others enjoy the emotional relationship with a favorite salesperson and return every three years for the latest model, trusting that "Joe will take care of me." Finally, firms using multichannel delivery systems must consider the varying costs of each channel and buyers' differing value perceptions about purchasing on the internet versus at the brick-and-mortar store. Pricing is a tricky business guided by data, experience, and experimentation.

In general, marketers can employ all traditional pricing strategies to the online environment. Here we focus on four types of pricing strategies particularly important to online sellers: fixed pricing, dynamic pricing, renting instead of buying, and price placement on Web pages.

Fixed Pricing

Fixed pricing (also called *menu pricing*) occurs when sellers set the price and buyers must take it or leave it. With fixed pricing, everyone pays the same price. Most US brick-and-mortar retailers use this model. Even when wholesalers and manufacturers offer quantity discounts, the price levels apply to all businesses that purchase the required amount. The basic pricing principles every marketer uses offline also apply online. Three common fixed pricing strategies used online are price leadership, promotional pricing, and freemium pricing:

- *Price leadership*. A **price leader** is the lowest-priced product entry in a particular category. Both online and offline, Walmart is a price leader, setting the pace for other retailers. With shopping agents on the Web, a price leader strategy is sweet indeed. To implement this strategy, however, marketers must keep costs to a minimum. Reducing costs can be done through internet marketing cost efficiencies previously described, but a firm must do it better than the competition. Often the largest producer becomes the price leader because of economies of scale, but on the internet an entrepreneur building mobile phone apps out of a basement constantly challenges the large producer. This strategy is productive for the internet, although competition is fierce and price leadership is often fleeting. Of course, the second-lowest-priced item will also gain sales, especially if it offers benefits perceived as better than those of the price leader.

- *Promotional pricing.* Many online retailers have turned to **promotional pricing** to encourage a first purchase, encourage repeat business, and close a sale. Most promotions carry an expiration date that helps create a sense of urgency. For example, Amazon offered free shipping with any order over $25 with such success that it became standard. It didn't arrive at that order amount, however, without trying several other price points first to find the optimum promotional offer to motivate sales. Promotional pricing on the internet can be highly targeted through e-mail messages.
- *Freemium pricing.* Many companies offer free versions of products. Skype is one of the first to successfully use a freemium pricing model. Individuals can call each other for free worldwide from computer to computer (or mobile to mobile via the Skype app). The premium part of this model is the calls from computer to a regular number—a minimal charge, but not free. Skype adds lots of other related products for a fee, such as voice mail and call forwarding. Do not confuse this with free promotional pricing, where a free product is offered for a limited time—for example, a free 30-day software download that expires and users must purchase the full software package.

Dynamic Pricing

Dynamic pricing is the strategy of offering different prices to different customers. Personalized pricing and promotions can be very effective for retailers to combat price transparency online. This was followed by improved monitoring of competitive prices. Yield management is a strategy used most often by the travel industry to optimize inventory management through frequent price changes. Airlines have long used dynamic pricing software for yield management when pricing air travel—dropping prices when traffic is light. Dynamic webpages allow travel companies to make quick and frequent changes in order to rent cars and fill seats or hotel beds.

Dynamic pricing can be initiated by the seller or the buyer (as compared with fixed pricing, which is always initiated by sellers). Two types of dynamic pricing are segmented pricing, where the company sells a good or service at two or more prices, based on segment differentiation rather than cost alone, and price negotiation, where the company negotiates prices with individual customers, who comprise segments of one. Negotiation is more often initiated by the buyer, while segmented pricing is usually set by the seller.

Segmented Pricing

Segmented pricing uses the internet properties for mass customization, automatically devising pricing based on order size and timing, demand and supply levels, and other preset decision factors. With segmented pricing online, the company uses decision rules to set pricing levels for segments of customers all the way to a segment of one person—that is, any customer that is X or does X gets Y price. For example, any person who books a flight within seven days of departure is quoted the full price (no discount), whereas advance purchasers may receive a discounted price. Segmented pricing has its roots in traditional marketing, as when theaters lower prices for consumers attending afternoon movies. Pricing according to customer behavior segments is becoming more common as firms collect an increasing amount of electronic behavioral information. See Exhibit 10.5 for an example of dynamic pricing by customer type, showing how Constantcontact.com practices segmented pricing based on the size of the customer's e-mail database. Note that Constant Contact also offers discounts for paying in advance and to the nonprofit organization customer segment.

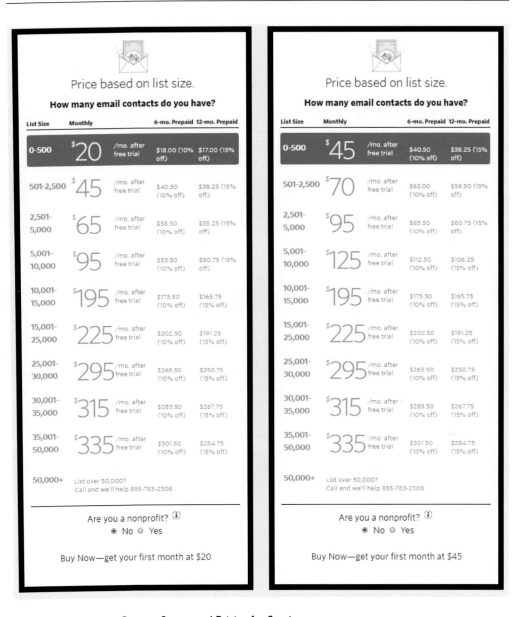

Exhibit 10.5 Constant Contact Segmented Pricing for Services

Segmented pricing at the individual level is easier online because sophisticated software and large databases permit firms to set rules and make price changes in a *nano*second—even as a buyer is clicking on a webpage. This capability has marketers quite excited—the internet's ability to customize prices, marketing communication, and products to the individual level. Using cookie files, online sellers recognize individuals and experiment with offers and prices to motivate transactions. Sometimes these individuals are particular customers, as when Amazon.com recognizes the customer and presents customized recommendations. Other times, individuals are part of a larger segment, such as those logging in from a particular geographic location or those exhibiting a behavior such as abandoning a shopping cart. Sellers define the segment and then customize prices following preset decision rules when an individual member of the segment visits the site. For example, an online retailer can lower the price by small increments on each subsequent visit to see whether the buyer will buy. Also, online firms can build loyalty programs, like frequent flyer programs, to offer special prices to individuals who return and purchase often.

Segmented pricing can be effective when the market is segmentable, the different prices reflect real differences in each segment's perceptions of the product's value, and the segments show different degrees of demand. It is also appropriate when the costs of segmentation and segmented pricing do not exceed the extra revenue obtained from the price difference. In addition, the company must be sure that its segmented pricing meets legal and regulatory guidelines. Finally, the firm must take care not to upset customers who learn they are getting prices different from their neighbors. Amazon.com created uproar when customers learned of its segmented pricing for individual customers; for some reason, airline passengers have accepted this practice, but not book buyers. Thus, digital marketers employing segmentation must use customer-accepted reasons such as giving discounts to new or loyal customers or adjusting shipping fees for purchases sent to outlying locations.

Internet users can be segmented using many variables, as discussed in Chapter 8. Two variables that are particularly important to online pricing strategies are geographic and value segmentation.

GEOGRAPHIC SEGMENT PRICING

With **geographic segment pricing**, a company sets different prices when selling a product in different geographic areas. An online seller often knows where the user resides because server logs register the user's IP address, and the top-level domain name typically indicates country of residence (e.g., a Japanese user will have a .jp designation). Geographic pricing can help a company better relate its pricing to country-by-country or regional factors such as competitive pressure, local costs, economic conditions, legal or regulatory guidelines, and distribution opportunities. For example, a Dell computer might be priced higher in the United Kingdom than the United States. This difference is because the manufacturer faces price escalation and therefore must price to reflect the higher costs of transportation, tariffs, and importer margins, among other costs involved in selling in another country. Increased transportation costs also affect product prices within a country.

Value Segment Pricing

With **value segment pricing**, the seller recognizes that not all customers provide equal value to the firm, segmenting by high, medium, and low value—and pricing accordingly. The well-known **Pareto principle** states that 80 percent of a firm's business usually comes from the top 20 percent of customers. As represented in Exhibit 10.6, a firm's five-star customers comprise a small group that contributes disproportionately to the firm's revenues and profits. These customers tend to be the most loyal and may become brand advocates to their friends and acquaintances: the frequent flyers who always go first class, the casino high rollers who return repeatedly, or the high-volume package shippers who use the FedEx website to automate all services. These customers are also brand-loyal frequent customers who provide significant value to the seller. When four- or five-star customers appear at the website, they will be recognized and receive special attention. These customers may not be price sensitive because they perceive that the brand or firm offers greater benefits (e.g., free upgrades and special treatment) and has earned their loyalty.

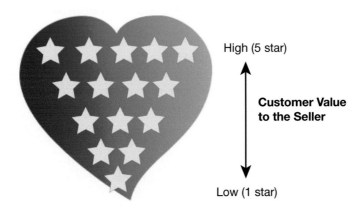

Exhibit 10.6 Customer Value Segments from Low (1 Star) to High (5 Star)

The large group of three-star customers may be price shoppers or infrequent users of the product category, not accounting for much of the seller's revenue. Two-star customers are also price sensitive and probably use the product category more than do one-star customers.

Market factors tend to drive customers to the one-star level, whereas moves such as competitive offerings and price cuts attempt to lure five- and four-star customers away. The seller's goal is to keep five-star customers brand loyal and to move all groups up to a higher level of value. Pricing strategies can help. For example, five-star customers might be allowed to bid on surplus inventory before others get a chance. Giving high-value customers the first shot at new products or promotions (e.g., Amazon's free shipping) will reinforce their loyalty. Conversely, two- and one-star customers most often seek the lowest price, so discounts are not likely to create brand loyalty—they will continue being price-shopping brand switchers. These customers might enjoy e-mail blasts with fixed prices so they can be informed of the firm's prices and competitive benefits of the brand. The seller can use this technique to build a database for moving customers up in value. Incidentally, the heart shape in this exhibit refers to the fact that companies love all their customers; however, they spend more time satisfying the high-value segment. See Chapter 15 for more about value segmentation and marketing communication techniques for building customer relationships.

Negotiated Pricing and Auctions

Sellers usually set pricing levels when using segmented pricing, and buyers usually initiate pricing when bidding for items online. Through negotiation, the price is set more than once in a back-and-forth discussion—a major difference from all other pricing strategies. Haggling over price is common in many countries; however, with a few exceptions, US consumers have shied away from such bargaining. The internet is changing this reluctance, as evidenced by the spectacular growth of online auctions. Many consumers enjoy the sport and community of an auction, while others are just looking for a good deal.

In the C2C market, trust between buyers and sellers is an issue because the transaction happens among strangers—there is no brand name to generate trust. To assist buyers, eBay uses a feedback system consisting of one, zero, or minus one points for positive, neutral, or negative comments and ratings, respectively. Points build to the star and shooting star levels and are placed near seller profiles on eBay webpages. The red shooting star is reserved for a seller with

100,000 or more points. This system works: highly rated eBay sellers are more likely to make a sale and do it at a higher price.

Yet while it seems that high levels of positive feedback mean higher prices, there are eBay scams that allow sellers to buy positive feedback.

Auctions in the B2B market are an effective way to unload surplus inventory at a price set by the market. For example, Bstock.com works with companies to help liquidate excess inventory through online auctions.

Renting Software

Companies developing software sometimes decide to rent rather than sell it to customers. Buyers want to purchase software they use on a regular basis, but if organizations want to use software for a short-term project or do not want to go to the expense of installing and maintaining it on their servers, renting makes sense. For example, Salesforce.com offers an incredibly complex and rich leading CRM software system. Its customers do not want to purchase and install the system internally and watch hidden costs emerge (estimated by Salesforce.com at 90% above the purchase price of CRM software). Salesforce rents its software instead, pricing in a range from $65 per month per user to $1,200 a year for five users (based on a minimum annual commitment). Consumers now rent the Microsoft Office suite (Office 365), whereas it used to be more of a purchase-based model. Renting software is analogous to leasing cars. When leasing, the driver does not have to pay for maintenance and many other costs that purchasers must bear.

Price Placement on Web Pages

Many physical world retailers have found that if they first offer customers a higher priced product, overall sales will be higher than if they first offer a lower priced product. For example, if similar tables sell at prices from $400 to $4,000 (with several priced in the middle), it is best to offer the $4,000 version first. The customer will often look at lower cost versions, but fewer offered the $400 table will look at much higher cost versions. Robert Cialdini discussed this "larger and then smaller request" principle in his famous book, *Influence*. This principle may also hold true online; thus, marketers might arrange online pricing pages as shown in Exhibit 10.7B

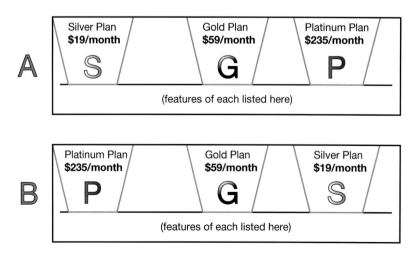

Exhibit 10.7 Price Placement on a Web page

rather than 10.7A as a way to increase the average sales price and thus overall sales (see six-teenventures.com for more commentary on this still unproven concept).

Chapter Summary

Price is the amount of money charged for a product or service. More broadly, it covers the sum of all the values (i.e., money, time, energy, and psychic cost) that buyers exchange for the benefits of having or using a good or service. Fixed price refers to one price set for all buyers. Dynamic pricing means varying prices for individual customers. Internet technology has prompted mass customization and a return to dynamic pricing—especially negotiation and pricing for segments as small as a single buyer. This capability is creating huge opportunities for marketers to optimize pricing strategies, including changing them daily or more often. However, the internet is also facilitating price transparency, the idea that both buyers and sellers can view all competitive prices for items sold online.

From the buyer's perspective, the cost of a product purchased online may be higher than that offline (due to seemingly hidden elements such as shipping costs and the time and effort needed to search out and compare prices). Yet buyers may also enjoy online cost savings due to the internet's convenience, speed, self-service capability, one-stop shopping, integration, and automation. Moreover, online buyers have more control through strategies such as reverse auctions, the availability of information and products, and negotiation opportunities.

From the seller's perspective, any price above the cost of producing the good or service has the potential to return profit. The seller's perspective on pricing covers internal factors such as pricing objectives, the marketing mix strategy, and information technology. Beyond the buyer's perspective, the market structure and the efficiency of the market are key external elements affecting online pricing.

A market is efficient when customers have equal access to information about products, prices, and distribution. Efficient markets are characterized by lower prices, high price elasticity, frequent and smaller price changes, and narrow price dispersion. The Web exhibits many characteristics of an efficient market except narrow price dispersion. Because the internet could become a more efficient market in the future, marketers who want to maintain control over pricing should differentiate their products on bases other than price, create unique product bundles of benefits, and consider the role of customer perceptions of value when determining pricing levels.

Exercises

Review Questions

1. How does fixed pricing differ from dynamic pricing?
2. What is price transparency, and why is it an important concept for digital marketers to understand?
3. List the main factors that put downward pressure on prices in the internet channel.
4. List the main factors that put upward pressure on prices in the internet channel.
5. From the buyer's perspective, how does the internet affect costs?
6. What is an efficient market? What makes the internet an efficient market, and what indicates that it is not an efficient market?
7. How do digital marketers use geographic, value segment, and negotiated pricing online?
8. Why is PayPal a good idea for merchants?
9. What are the advantages of electronic money for online retailers?

Discussion Questions

1. **Price of an iPhone App Story:** If you created a cool new app, which pricing model would you use and why? Consider all the important pricing variables in this chapter when answering.
2. **Price of an iPhone App Story:** What is the difference between a freemium model and a direct purchasing (light or full) model?
3. Near-perfect access to pricing information is a problem that airlines have faced for years. How have airlines responded to this problem? Should internet businesses adopt similar strategies?
4. Which of the online cost-saving factors do you think has the greatest effect on price? Why?
5. Which pricing strategy would you use to introduce a new internet connected appliance? Why?
6. Internet technology allows a company to price the same product differently for different customers. What do you think would be the advantages and disadvantages of Amazon offering the same book at one price to a professor and at a different price to a student?
7. As a buyer, how do you think price transparency affects your ability to develop an appropriate bidding strategy for new products auctioned by companies through eBay?
8. As a seller, how do you think price transparency affects your ability to obtain as high a price as possible for used products you auction through eBay?
9. Would you like to use your cell phone to pay for goods and services? Why or why not?

Web Activities

1. Using a website like Keepa.com, what do you notice about the price of a product you are interested in buying from Amazon.com? Did you expect the price to behave in this way?
2. Use Google Shopping to look up a specific electronic product you are interested in purchasing. Next, navigate to your local electronics store website and find the price of that item. Create a table showing how the online price from a tool like Google Shopping may differ from the price offered at a local retailer.
3. Visit PayPal.com and Braintree Payments. Review the prices and options for a new online clothing store and report on the pros and cons of each service. Which one(s) do you recommend?

Chapter 11

The Internet for Distribution

The key objective of this chapter is to help you develop an understanding of the internet as a distribution channel, identify online channel members, and analyze the functions they perform in the channel. You will learn how the internet presents opportunities to alter channel length, restructure channel intermediaries, improve the performance of channel functions, streamline channel management, and measure channel performance. Special emphasis is on digital commerce, m-commerce and social commerce.

After reading this chapter, you will be able to:

- Describe the three major functions of a distribution channel.
- Explain how the internet is affecting distribution channel length.
- Discuss trends in supply chain management and power relationships among channel players.
- Outline the major models used by online channel members.
- Distinguish among digital commerce, m-commerce, social commerce, and F-commerce.
- Highlight how companies can use distribution channel metrics.

THE ZAPPOS STORY

How did Zappos go from concept to the world's largest online shoe store worth $1.2 billion in a short 10 years? Founder Nick Swinmurn, with early investor and former CEO Tony Hsieh, built a strong brand based on customer service and produced stellar revenue growth from day one. The company started at zero in 1999 and grossed over $1 billion in 2009. In November 2009, Amazon.com bought Zappos for a hefty $1.2 billion. Even the great online retailer, Amazon.com, knows better than to change a good thing—Zappos continues with the same management team and operates as a wholly owned subsidiary with headquarters in Henderson, NV ("Running Smoothly: Online . . .", 2012).

Founder Nick was initially turned down by most venture capitalists in 1999 because they doubted that anyone would buy shoes online, without the chance to try them on first. But Nick knew that $2 billion of the then $40 billion shoe market happened via catalog, so shoes ought to sell online, too. And he showed he was right by surviving the dot-com crash and copy-cat competitors. Key success factors in this astounding digital commerce story all centered on the company culture of customer service. Zappos wants every customer to say, "That was the best customer service I've ever had," and the company even publishes a "culture book" where employees write about what this culture means to them. The customer service policies include free shipping both ways, a 365-day return policy, and a call center that is open 24/7.

DOI: 10.4324/9781003247319-15

In the first nine years Zappos offered a 110 percent price protection policy. Other success factors:

- *Great search engine marketing.* People search for shoes by brand, so Zappos didn't need to build the company name but simply optimize the site for searches for Rockport or Vans and capitalize on the strength of shoe branding. Search marketing was unheard of in 1999, so this was very forward-thinking.
- *Word of mouth.* An estimated 20 percent of new customers are referrals from current customers, who serve as brand advocates.
- *Astute competitiveness.* When the management realized that online and catalog competitors were taking an average of six days to deliver shoes to customers, Zappos surprised their repeat customers with free overnight or two-day shipping. Customers got an e-mail saying that they were upgraded to overnight shipping because they are valued.
- *Repeat customers.* This strong customer service orientation has resulted in high customer retention.

Great customer service starts with great employees. Zappos requires a two-week customer service training for every new employee, regardless of level. This includes two weeks of working in the call center and talking with customers. At the end of two weeks, employees are offered $2,000 to "quit now." The 97 percent who stay do it because they fit the customer service "wow" culture, not for the money.

All of this reminds us of the marketing adage: under promise and over deliver. Zappos continually shows that it cares about customers, and this translates to the top-line revenue. It is inspiring to know that this value, when coupled with employee happiness, translates to business success. The company has since expanded to clothing and handbags and continues to grow and delight its customers today. Tony Hsieh's death in 2020 shocked the business world because of his youth and passion for life. You can read all about Tony's formula for corporate culture and online retailing success in his book: *Delivering Happiness: A Path to Profits, Passion, and Purpose.*

Distribution Channel Overview

Marketers are concerned about distribution because it involves point of purchase decisions and whether the customer receives a product or service satisfactorily. A **distribution channel** is a group of interdependent firms that work together to transfer product and information from the supplier to the consumer. It is composed of the following participants:

- *Producers:* Manufacturers and their suppliers, or originators of the product or service.
- *Intermediaries:* Firms that match buyers and sellers and mediate the transactions among them (e.g., wholesalers and retailers).
- *Buyers:* Consumers or users of the product or service.

A customer's experience in gaining access to the product often colors his or her satisfaction with the product, brand image, and brand loyalty. This may result in online product reviews and social media conversations about the brand.

The structure of the distribution channel can either make or impede possible opportunities for marketing on the internet. If the transaction is automated, the consumer could save money. Conversely, a consumer who purchases online must perform the search function personally that is normally performed by retailers—if you have ever searched for the lowest cost flight at online travel agents, you will realize the additional time spent versus simply calling a brick-and-mortar agent. Four major elements combine to form a company's channel structure, and all affect internet marketing strategy as shown in the sections that follow:

1. Types of online channel intermediaries.
2. Length of the online channel.
3. Functions performed by members of the channel.
4. Physical and informational systems that link the channel members and provide for coordination and management of their collective effort to deliver the product or service.

Online Channel Intermediaries

A good way to understand online intermediaries is according to their business models. Many digital business models have new names, but how many of them are really new? On closer inspection, most digital business models turn out to be variations on existing marketing concepts, but technology makes them more effective or efficient. For some digital products, such as software or music, the entire distribution channel may be internet based. When a consumer buys software online, the supplier often delivers it over the internet to the buyer's computer. In most cases, however, only some of the firms in the channel are wholly or partially Web-enabled. For example, nondigital products such as flowers and wine may be purchased online but must be delivered via truck. Nonetheless, the exact location of that shipment can be tracked using a Web-based interface (the informational role of distribution). Exhibit 11.1 shows the overall classification scheme for the discussion that follows.

1.	Content sponsorship	
2.	Infomediary	
3.	Intermediaries	
	Broker:	Online exchange
		Online auction
	Agent:	Agent models representing sellers
		Selling agent (affiliate program)
		Manufacturer's agent (catalog aggregator)
		Agent models representing buyers (purchasing agent)
		Shopping agent
		Reverse auction
		Buyer cooperative
	Online retailer	Digital products
	(e-commerce, m-commerce,	Tangible products
	social commerce):	Direct distribution

Exhibit 11.1 Digital Business Models

Channel intermediaries include wholesalers, retailers, brokers, and agents.

- **Wholesalers** buy products from the manufacturer and resell them to retailers.
- Both brick-and-mortar and online **retailers** buy products from manufacturers or wholesalers and sell them to consumers.
- **Brokers** facilitate transactions between buyers and sellers without representing either party. They are market makers and typically do not take title to the goods.
- **Agents** usually represent either the buyer or seller, depending upon who hires and pays them. They facilitate transactions between buyers and sellers but do not take title to the goods. **Manufacturer's agents** represent the seller whereas **purchasing agents** represent the buyer.

Content Sponsorship

Chapter 1 discussed the many ways companies use content to increase revenues. In this chapter we discuss selling content (digital commerce) and content sponsorship: companies create websites, attract a lot of traffic, and sell advertising. Some firms use a niche strategy and draw a special interest audience (e.g., CafeMom for women), and others draw a general audience (e.g., CNN.com or YouTube.com). Web properties using the content sponsorship model include all the major portals: Google, Yahoo!, MSN, and so on. Many online magazines and newspapers also use this model; indeed, much content on the internet is ad supported. Spotify provides suggestions on music based on previous songs that users have listened to. Not only are songs curated based on preference, but ads are also delivered based on the types of songs that are being played and the listener requesting them. Spotify has become tremendously popular, with over 356 million users around the globe.

Many websites desire to sell advertising space, but it is difficult to get enough traffic to compete with the portals and news sites. See Exhibit 11.2 for some facts about advertising impressions to internet users (impressions are the number of times an ad can be viewed). Google is the king of content sponsorship, serving online ads to billions of users across the globe on laptops, desktops, tablets, and mobile phones. We include this model in the digital commerce chapter because sponsorship generates revenues in the business-to-business (B2B) market (Web companies selling ad space to other companies). In fact, digital advertising grew 22.6 percent in 2020, reaching $8.14 billion, according to eMarketer (2021a). The product, of course, is ad space on a website, and the price for it usually increases with audience size. This model has its roots in traditional media, where television, magazines, and other media sell space and airtime. In Chapter 14, we discuss the other side: companies that buy advertising space to communicate with stakeholders.

The content sponsorship model is often used in combination with other models to generate multiple revenue streams. For example, Rakuten.com, an online retailer, sells ads on its site to generate additional revenue, which in turn allows it to lower prices. Similarly, while most online newspapers offer their current edition for free, they often charge a small amount to

---

- YouTube 2.29 billion users (backlinko.com)
- Facebook 2.89 billion users (statista.com)
- Facebook ad revenue 84.2 billion USD (statista.com)
- Google ad revenue 147 billion USD (cnbc.com)

Exhibit 11.2 Facts about the Web Content Sponsorship Model

retrieve an archived article. Even Amazon.com features sponsored products first in search results, thereby generating additional revenue for Amazon.

Infomediary

An **infomediary** is an online organization that aggregates and distributes information, acting as a personal agent for users. One form of infomediary is a market research firm. Sometimes, the infomediary compensates the consumer for sharing information. For example, a comScore Media Metrix research panel member is paid; however, some intermediaries cull the information covertly and without compensation (e.g., Google uses cookies to track users as they browse online). Websites that require registration for downloading white papers and then provide the user data to authors and others also fall into this category.

Product review sites such as yelp.com are another type of infomediary. These sites accumulate ratings and written reviews on webpages that provide information to other consumers and the reviewed companies. They often receive revenue through commissions by providing click-throughs to online retailers where consumers can purchase the products.

The original idea behind the infomediary model was to give consumers more control over how they receive marketing messages. The benefit to the infomediary is that the consumer information increases the value of its ad inventory. The benefit to advertisers is that they can market to a highly targeted audience that has expressly opted into the system. Permission marketing allows advertisers to do something never before possible—advertise while the consumer is on a competitor's site!

Intermediary Models

Three main **intermediary** models are in common use on the internet: brokerage models, agent models, and online retailing.

Brokerage Models

The broker creates a market in which buyers and sellers negotiate and complete transactions. Brokers typically charge the seller and/or buyer a transaction fee, but they don't represent either party for providing exchange and negotiation services. Some brokers also charge listing fees. Brokers provide many value-added services to help attract customers and facilitate transactions. Brokerage models operate website exchanges in B2B, business-to-customer (B2C), and customer-to-customer (C2C) markets. The best example in the offline world is a stockbroker who brings buyers and sellers together at the NYSE or other exchanges. Exchanges and auctions are the most popular online brokerage models.

The primary benefits to the buyer are convenience, speed of order execution, and transaction processing. Cost savings to the buyer come in the form of lower prices, decreased search time, and savings of energy and frustration in locating the appropriate seller. The primary benefit to the seller is the creation of a pool of interested buyers. Cost savings to the seller come in the form of lowered customer acquisition costs and transaction costs.

Online Exchange

E★TRADE, TD Ameritrade, Robinhood, and a host of other online brokerages allow customers to place equity and other trades from their computers without phoning or visiting a broker. These brokerages pass along the cost savings to the buyer in the form of lower transaction fees. They also provide the benefits of executing trades quickly, providing reference resources, and allowing for program trading. Some newer services catering to day traders bypass the Web entirely and connect traders straight to the market.

Autobytel and other online brokers allow customers to receive bids from qualified dealers on vehicles available in their area without first phoning or visiting the dealer. The dealers offer a no-hassle price quoted through the service. Thus, the customer avoids the potentially unpleasant task of negotiating price with a dealer.

Alibaba.com is a marketplace for global buyers and sellers with more than 800 million registered users from across hundreds of countries (Ma, 2021). When a buyer orders something from another country, the money goes to Alibaba and is held in escrow until the goods are delivered in good shape. After the buyer completes a form as such, the money is released to the seller.

The B2B market has spawned a number of successful brokerages. Converge is the leading anonymous exchange for the global electronics market (www.converge.com), aggregating supply and demand from thousands of component, original equipment, and contract manufacturers, distributors, and resellers. The model is similar to a stock exchange. Customers contact a Converge trader on the floor of the exchange with their request (e.g., an order for 100,000 transistors). The trader locates a supplier, completes the purchase, and pockets the spread between the buying and selling price. Additional revenue comes from other fixed fees. The exchange is anonymous: suppliers ship to a Converge quality control warehouse where the goods are inspected and then forwarded to the buyer. Converge guarantees the quality of the products and has a no-questions-asked return policy. Converge online services include personal buy-and-sell portfolios, chat communication with traders, and multiple methods for issuing requests including uploading a list of items or searching for items individually.

Guru.com is an exchange for talent. Employers can find freelancers in this large global marketplace with over 250 million freelancers and 800,000 employers worldwide seeking projects. Guru employers can locate consultants in 220 professional categories, including website design, programming, graphic design, business consulting, and administrative support. When a match is made, Guru collects a fee, just as a stockbroker company would.

Online Auction

Online auctions are challenging the fixed-price model, which has been the norm for the past 100 years in most industrialized nations. Auctions are available in the B2B (bstock.com), B2C (priceline.com), and C2C (eBay.com) markets. Even though some merchants choose to host their own auctions, many more auction their surplus through auction brokers. When merchants auction items on their own websites, they become direct sellers using dynamic pricing. Third-party auctioneers are broker intermediaries.

Sellers benefit by obtaining the market price for goods and unloading surplus inventory. Buyers benefit by obtaining a good price and, in many cases, enjoying the sport of the auction. The downside is that the buyer can waste a lot of time monitoring the auction and sometimes overpay (the "winner's curse" discussed in previous chapters). Although buyers can use services to automatically proxy bid, studies show that many repeatedly visit auction sites to check on bids.

Some auction houses offer a broad range of products. Other auction houses specialize in niche markets. Industry giant eBay hosts C2C auctions in thousands of product categories. EBay has rolled out a number of innovative services to benefit the customer and facilitate the auction process, including escrow, electronic payment via PayPal company, and appraisal services.

Agent Models

Unlike brokers, agents *do* represent either the buyer or the seller, depending on who pays their fee. In some cases, they are legally obligated to represent the interests of the party that hires them. In the brick-and-mortar world, real estate agents who are hired to list a property must represent the interests of the seller.

Agent Models Representing Sellers

Selling agents, manufacturer's agents, metamediaries, and **virtual malls** are all agents that represent the seller.

Selling Agents

Selling agents represent a single organization, helping it sell its products; these agents normally work for a commission. For example, **affiliate programs** pay commissions to website owners for customer referrals. Normally the referral must result in a sale in order to qualify for the commission (Exhibit 11.3). Some affiliates demand a share of the lifetime value of the customer as opposed to just a piece of the first sale.

Amazon.com pioneered one of the first affiliate programs in 1996, calling it Amazon Associates. Every website displaying an Amazon logo graphic that links to Amazon.com is an affiliate selling agent. It has hundreds of thousands of associates—each a point of sale for Amazon products. And when an affiliate site sends a customer to Amazon.com, that affiliate will earn up to 10 percent of the transaction price.

Manufacturer's Agents

Manufacturer's agents represent more than one seller. In traditional marketing, they generally represent only firms that sell complementary products to avoid conflicts of interest, but in the virtual world they often create Web sites to help an entire industry sell its products. In digital

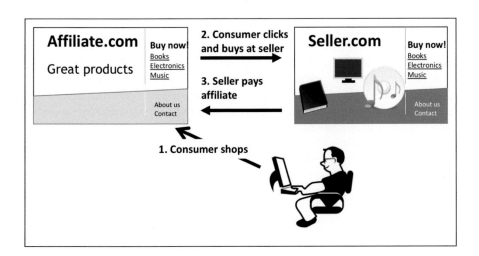

Exhibit 11.3 Affiliate Program Mechanics

marketing, manufacturer's agents are often called seller aggregators because they represent many sellers on one website.

Almost all of the travel reservations websites qualify as manufacturer's agents since their commissions are paid by the airlines and hotels they represent. Expedia, CheapOAir, Orbitz, and many other travel agent sites allow customers to make online travel reservations. In some cases, the traveler can get a better deal online, but often the greatest benefit is simply convenience.

In the B2B market, manufacturer's agents are sometimes called *catalog aggregators*. Each of the sellers these firms represent generally has a broad catalog of product offerings. Picture a purchasing manager in a small room surrounded by hundreds of catalogs, which suggests the origin of the term. The challenge for the aggregator is to gather the information from all of these catalogs into a database for presentation on the website. Normally, the catalog aggregator offers software that interfaces with the suppliers' internal database systems. The task is made easier when the suppliers use industry standard software such as Concur to manage their catalogs. Furthermore, the catalogs must be constantly maintained as product availability and prices change. While the user interface of these systems is sometimes lacking, the payoff in functionality often outweighs the inconvenience.

The more advanced manufacturer's agents support catalog customization and integration with the buyer's enterprise resource planning (ERP) systems. The customized catalogs display prenegotiated product offerings and prices. Some will even maintain spending limits for particular employees and automatically forward big-ticket orders to the appropriate officer for approval. Additional services include recommending substitutions, notifying buyers of production lead times, processing orders, and tracking orders.

With this model, the buyer gains substantial benefits, including shorter order cycles, reduced inventories, and increased control. Order processing costs are lowered through paperless transactions, automated request for proposal (RFP) and request for quote (RFQ), and integration with ERP systems.

The College Source (www.collegesource.org) is a catalog aggregator for the college market where students can search over 160,000 college catalogs at one site. There are two other intermediaries that act like agents but defy easy categorization. One represents a cluster of manufacturers, online retailers, and content providers organized around a life event or major asset purchase. They solve four major consumer problems—reducing search times, providing quality assurance about vendors, facilitating transactions for a group of related purchases, and providing relevant and unbiased content information about the purchase. These Web companies receive commissions for referrals or completed transactions. Edmunds.com is a good example in the car-buying market, providing information about new and used automobiles and advice on negotiating deals. It also refers interested customers to a car-buying service, financing information, aftermarket parts, and insurance alternatives. The Knot.com represents the bridal market, offering information about planning, fashion, beauty, grooms, bridesmaids, and moms, and so forth. It also has tools such as a gown finder, registry, checklist, and guest list.

The other intermediary hosts multiple online merchants in a model similar to a shopping mall. Hosted merchants gain exposure from traffic coming to the virtual mall. The mall gains through a variety of fees: listing fees, transaction fees, and setup fees. Amazon.com and BestBuy.com now include features that enable different sellers to leverage such trusted brands to deliver products to customers if the main company cannot fulfill an order.

Agent Models Representing Buyers

Purchasing agents represent buyers. In traditional marketing, they often forge long-term relationships with one or more firms; however, on the internet they represent any number of buyers, anonymously in many cases. Shopping agents and reverse auctions help individual buyers obtain the prices they want, while buyer cooperatives pool buyers for larger volume buys and, thus, lower prices.

As discussed in Chapter 10, when shopping agents were first developed, many feared that they would drive prices on the internet down to impossible margins. That scenario has not happened because price is not the only factor consumers consider when making a purchase. Newer, second-generation shopping agents can now measure value and not just price. TrueCar provides such services through aggregation of vehicle sales and application of that information to benefit the consumer.

Consumers who desire a quantitative performance evaluation of a merchant can shop through BizRate.com. BizRate links customers with over a million products and retailers online. BizRate Insights rates online merchants based on customer feedback. BizRate posts a report card of past consumer experiences with the merchant (generated from customer surveys) and shows the merchant's stated business policies. Sellers on Amazon.com also receive detailed ratings from customers.

A **reverse auction** occurs at a website serving as purchasing agent for individual buyers. In a reverse auction, the buyer specifies a price and sellers bid for the buyer's business. The buyer commits to buying at a specified price, and the seller either meets the price or tries to get close enough to make the sale. Priceline was the first major player in reverse auctions.

The benefit to the seller is in unloading excess inventory without unduly upsetting existing channels—a valuable benefit for sellers with perishable inventory such as airline seats or hotel rooms. The benefit for the buyer comes in the form of lower prices and the satisfaction of being able to name one's price. However, buyers have fewer choices of brand, suppliers, and product features. The reduced choice feature sufficiently differentiates the product in most cases to avoid conflict with the supplier's existing channel partners.

The **buyer cooperative** (also known as a buyer aggregator) pools many buyers together to drive down the price on selected items. The individual buyer thus receives the price benefit of volume buying. The more buyers that join the pool, the lower the price drops, usually in a step function. For example, 1 to 5 buyers pay $69 each; 6 to 10 buyers pay $58 each, and so on. The step function encourages buyers to recruit their friends to help push the price down to the next step. Buyers can make their bid contingent on the product reaching a specified price point.

MobShop, Mercata, and other promising buyer's cooperatives closed as they were not able to build profitable business models online. Some online cooperatives have had success in the education space, representing multiple buyers in the education space.

Groupon and LivingSocial are two leading buyer cooperative sites in the United States (there are many in other countries as well). They offer discounts on merchandise for a limited amount of time. Users sign up for the deal and if the minimum required number is reached, all get the discount. The advantage to sellers is that they gain a large number of new customers, often from many different locations. Another interesting example is a homeschooling cooperative buying program representing over 297,000 families (www.homeschoolbuyersco-op.org).

Online Retailing: Digital Commerce

Digital commerce is one of the most visible digital business models, with merchants establishing online storefronts and selling to both businesses and consumers (refer to the Zappos story).

What sells well online? Exhibit 11.4 displays the retail revenue in the United States by product category, with total digital commerce reaching $431 billion in 2020 and more than $4 trillion worldwide.

Category	Billions of Dollars
Computers and consumer electronics	195
Apparel and accessories	184
Furniture and home furnishings	106
Health and personal care	86
Toys and hobby	65
Auto and parts	63
Books/music/video	54
Food and beverage	54

Exhibit 11.4 What Do US Consumers Buy Online?

Source: www.census.gov

Digital goods may be delivered directly over the internet, while physical goods are shipped via a **logistics** provider such as UPS, USPS (US Postal Service), or FedEx. Companies selling physical products online can make any level of commitment from pure play to barely dabbling; however, most reasonably sized brick-and-mortar retailers offer at least some products online.

Although a pre-internet presence carries brand equity, it does not guarantee online success. Often the pure plays are free from the cultural constraints of the established businesses and can innovate more quickly in response to customer needs. Some internet pure plays established brick-and-mortar operations to enhance branding through additional exposure and an additional channel for customers to experience their products. Amazon has begun to roll out brick-and-mortar stores to test various concepts to ensure the customer receives an item as soon as possible. Some items fulfilled by Amazon can be picked up on the same day you place an order at one of these stores or lockers.

An advantage of online retailing is that companies can sell a wider and deeper assortment of products in smaller quantities than in offline stores because they are not bound by the space constraints in malls and free-standing buildings located in expensive areas. Instead, they can use warehouses on cheap land and ship from there. Named "the long tail" by Chris Anderson, editor of *Wired* magazine, this refers to the reason it is possible to increase revenue by selling small quantities of a large number of products online. Some of the friction consumers have regarding online shopping still needs to be addressed by digital commerce firms. In order to purchase online, a consumer needs a method of payment acceptable to the merchant and computer access, so this cuts out some consumers, especially in less developed countries. BigCommerce reports that nearly 30 percent of people shop online worldwide, with a 4.4 percent year-over-year increase from 2020 to 2021 (Coppola, 2021).

One of the biggest problems for online retailers is shopping cart abandonment part way through the purchasing process. The goal is to convert site visitors to purchasers, and that only happens about 1–2 percent of the time on average, according to BigCommerce.com. Exhibit 11.5 displays statistics and reasons for shopping cart abandonment. A now common tactic is to reach out to consumers via e-mail to encourage them to return to their shopping cart.

Multichannel marketing is the use of more than one sales channel, such as Web, mobile, brick and mortar, and catalog. Most large traditional retailers are multichannel marketers

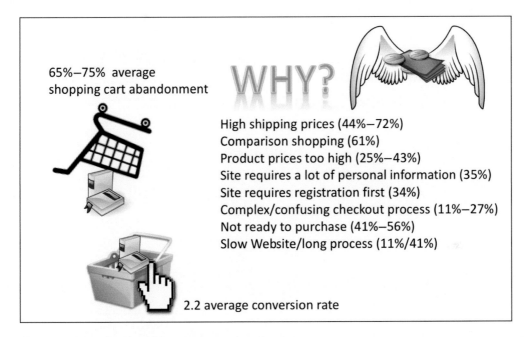

65%–75% average shopping cart abandonment

WHY?

High shipping prices (44%–72%)
Comparison shopping (61%)
Product prices too high (25%–43%)
Site requires a lot of personal information (35%)
Site requires registration first (34%)
Complex/confusing checkout process (11%–27%)
Not ready to purchase (41%–56%)
Slow Website/long process (11%/41%)

2.2 average conversion rate

Exhibit 11.5 Reasons for Shopping Cart Abandonment

because they also sell products online. Most catalog retailers also use multichannel marketing. Among catalog retailers, the majority said their return of investment (ROI) is better when both channels are used—possibly partially because they can reach different customers through each channel. Important decisions involve product selections and appropriate pricing in each channel.

Omni-channel shopping is the shopper's perspective of multichannel marketing, describing the way consumers move seamlessly through many shopping channels: Web, brick-and-mortar store, computer, mobile device, catalog, and so forth. For example, consumers (1) are in a physical store using a smartphone to research a product and do price comparisons (maybe scanning a QR code), (2) purchase online and pick up the product in a physical store, (3) research online before visiting a physical store, or (4) seek opinions about a product in social media while in a physical store. This type of customer has been known to purchase more often, spend more money, and be more loyal to specific retailers. Of course, this type of shopping may be combined with brick-and-mortar and mobile shopping channels. With this in mind, we now move to the mobile commerce experience.

M-Commerce

Mobile commerce (m-commerce) occurs when consumers make a transaction with a smartphone or other mobile device (e.g., iPhone, iPad, Android). M-commerce is a subset of digital commerce, as shown in Exhibit 11.6. An overwhelming amount of the US population has a smartphone, 85 percent, according to Pew Research Center ("Mobile Fact Sheet", 2021). Mobile user purchases include ordering products from websites (including

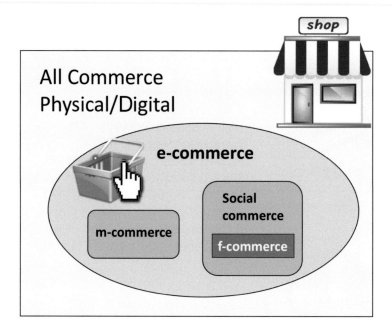

Exhibit 11.6 Relationship among Commerce, E-Commerce, M-Commerce, Social Commerce and F-Commerce

tickets, services, and more), paying for online content (such as apps or music), online banking, and more.

- M-commerce sales account for approximately 45 percent of the total US digital commerce market ("Rise of M-Commerce", 2021).
- M-commerce is a rapidly growing area of digital commerce, which involves not only the ultimate act of online purchasing but all the related digital marketing activities (most of which are discussed elsewhere in this book):
  - Mobile search (e.g., company store locators).
  - Location-based services (such as Foursquare).
  - QR code scanning (for more product information or promotions).
  - Two-dimensional barcode scanning (for building a shopping list or comparing products).
  - Image recognition (for linking to online content).
  - Voice and text message offers from businesses (e.g., airline flight delays and breaking news alerts).
  - Social networking (e.g., answering product questions via Twitter).
  - Marketing-related apps.

Near-field communication (NFC) is another tactic involving two smartphones or a smartphone and another device that communicate by touching each other or being in very close proximity. This is how Apple Pay works. NFC can also be used for checking in at hotels and conferences or downloading content.

As mobile internet continues to play a dominant role in the lives of consumers, marketers must continually adjust their tactics to respond to an ever-changing landscape. ComScore reports that 2 out of every 3 minutes spent on a digital device is a mobile one. As marketers integrate mobile tactics into digital marketing plans, they focus on customer convenience and engagement at many touch points as customers travel through the purchase funnel stages (from awareness to purchase and brand loyalty).

As an example, Exhibit 11.7 displays an iPhone with a small square plastic device that plugs into the audio jack of the phone. This allows businesses to swipe credit and debit cards for purchases on the go at trade fairs and events and e-mail the receipt to the customer. The company, Square, charges businesses a small fee and deposits the money into the user's bank account. This is quite convenient both for customers and businesses.

Social Commerce

Social commerce is a piece of digital commerce that uses social media and consumer interactions to facilitate online sales. Social media demonstrate a move from corporate to user control, yet these same social media conversations provide great opportunities for building revenue, cutting costs, and increasing customer satisfaction through social commerce.

In one social commerce example, Best Buy, the consumer electronic retailer, answers product and service questions via its Twitter account. Another example is when Blendtec, the blender company, created a number of "Will it blend?" videos that users shared with each other, and this increased blender sales.

Social shopping is one aspect of social commerce. Pinterest allows users to create digital bulletin boards ("pinboards") with everything from fashion to decorated living rooms that others can click, visit, and purchase from the sites selling featured products. When Etsy shop owners leverage Pinterest, they find there is a 20 percent increase in sales per week for many

Exhibit 11.7 Square Card Reader Facilitates M-Commerce

sellers, according to Pinterest's success stories. This is one clue about Pinterest's social commerce effectiveness.

Group buying sites such as Groupon and Living Social are also in this category. Flash sales/deep discount sites, such as Gilt, offer specials for a very short few hours that are only valid if users get friends to purchase to reach the minimum number of buyers.

Product rating, recommendation, and review sites that provide space for users to post allow for the sharing aspect critical to social commerce. Examples include Google Reviews, Trip Advisor, Amazon, and many others. Online marketplaces such as Craigslist and eBay also allow for social commerce activities. Peer-to-peer sites bring lenders and borrowers together for a transaction. This type of marketplace also occurs in the B2B market, with auction and exchange sites.

By now you are getting the picture that social commerce is initiated by customers via online spaces provided by businesses. Some of the tactics used by social commerce companies include widgets on social media sites ("buy now"), crowdsourcing that entices users to help companies develop new products, location-based commerce that offers discounts when customers share their location with friends, and many other collaboration models as seen on blogs, wikis, and other websites. Here are some examples of profitable social commerce tactics:

- Gardener's Supply Company tripled sales using Pinterest's Buyable Pins feature (see the success stories on Pinterest.com).
- Starbucks, Mountain Dew, and Dell all improved products and services through crowdsourcing on dedicated sites.

F-Commerce

F-commerce (Facebook Commerce) is a subset of social commerce where companies use Facebook to facilitate digital commerce. Because of Facebook's huge number of users and activity, many companies have attempted to sell products on the network. This involves tactics such as creating a dedicated product Facebook page, installing "want" or "own" widgets (buttons) on Facebook pages, creating dedicated Facebook apps, and making Facebook pages with searchable content. Shops on Facebook and Instagram now allow users to purchase products directly via these social media platforms. Furthermore, Facebook Marketplace offers Facebook users the opportunity to buy and sell items directly from one another.

Tangible Products

All tangible products sold online, such as books and furniture, are distributed through conventional channels. This type of distribution is relatively inefficient: rather than deliver 100 copies of a book to a brick-and-mortar store in a single shipment, the UPS truck must make deliveries to 100 individual customers. On the other hand, as ecommerce becomes the norm, the UPS truck will deliver multiple packages to each address and neighboring addresses so as to offset the distribution cost—especially in more densely populated areas. Many companies now offer free shipping when the shopping cart reaches a threshold value of, say, $50, and the consumer does not have to drive to a brick-and-mortar store. Nonetheless, local regulations sometimes impede the direct distribution of product. For example, Wine.com (the former Virtual Vineyards at www.wine.com), a wine distributor, has been forced by some state regulations to operate through local intermediaries rather than mail wine across state lines—which lengthens its distribution channel.

Digital Products/Content Sales

The internet serves as the actual distribution channel itself for digital goods and services such as news, music, software, movies, education (online classes), and so forth. This is an important part of the growing field of content marketing, as discussed in Chapter 1 and in the previous m-commerce section. Clearly, distribution costs are significantly lower for digital products compared with physical distribution. Hulu.com, iTunes, and the *Wall Street Journal Online* are all successful at selling content online. The proliferation of mobile devices such as iPads and Android tablets has increased sales of digital books, music, and many other products.

One interesting tactic involves the content subscription **paywall**: some content is hidden and only available to users who pay a fee for access. Many studies found that users expect free content prior to being asked to pay for content. Some companies include a notice on the home page that the user can read five or so articles within a month and then must pay for more. Others allow users to read part of an article and then require subscription fees for the remainder. Marketers are experimenting to see which system delivers the most revenue. For example, the *Wall Street Journal* allows nonsubscribers to read some stories in their entirety but cuts others off after a few paragraphs. Interestingly, the paper sometimes posts stories on its Facebook page that anyone can access.

Consumers purchase a large amount of online content (Exhibit 11.8). Leading the pack are music, magazines, and movies. In a global study, Nielsen asked 27,000 consumers if they would buy content online, and 85 percent said they preferred it to be free. This is definitely the internet culture, as seen in the exhibit; however, online content sales continue to grow—both because of the huge tablet use and in the B2B market, where companies purchase online research reports and database access.

Want to become a digital commerce vendor and sell your original content online? Artists sell their artwork on deviantArt and Zaarly. Crafters sell vintage and handmade items on Etsy.

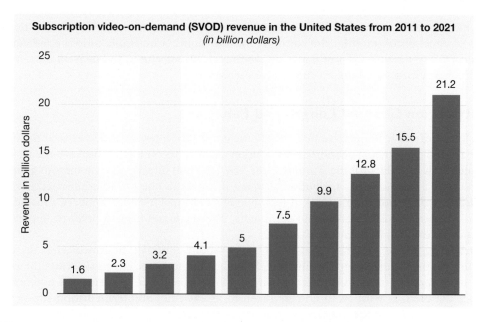

Exhibit 11.8 Subscription Video-on-Demand (SVOD) Revenue in the United States
Source: www.statistal.com

com. YouTube will pay for indie videos by splitting ad revenue with the video creator. Scribd and Amazon will let you sell your digital book online and split the proceeds. Gumroad lets you use their site for selling and link to your products on your own site. It also provides dynamic pricing so you can change the price as demand increases.

Direct Distribution

The manufacturer sells directly to the consumer or business customer in the **direct distribution** model, as does Dell, Inc. (also called direct selling). This practice is commonly used in offline selling; however, the internet made it much easier for producers to bypass intermediaries and go directly to consumers or business customers.

Direct distribution has been successful in some B2B markets—sometimes saving millions of dollars in sales-related expenses for personnel, product configuration, and order processing. Expert systems built into some online sales systems assist the customer in configuring the product with compatible components, the way Dell's system helps customers order online.

Direct distribution also has been successful in the B2C market, with sales of digital products, as previously mentioned, which require no inventory and no pick, pack, and ship logistics. Perishable products such as flowers and fresh food are also well served by direct channels. As one example, Proflowers.com delivers flowers fresh from the grower. Flowers that don't pass through an intermediary tend to be fresher, last longer, and are in many cases less expensive.

Direct distribution saves customers money by avoiding intermediaries; sometimes it leads to more rapid delivery of the product. For example, Fresh Direct calls itself a "private online farmer's market." It processes and delivers online orders of fresh produce and meat a day to its New York and Philadelphia customers. By cutting out the intermediaries and using databases to keep inventory at a minimum, Fresh Direct is able to make profits unseen by other online grocers (see www.freshdirect.com).

Benefits to the manufacturer include the ability to claim a piece of the intermediary's margin, but, of course, someone has to perform the functions of those intermediaries. The major costs of direct distribution for the customer include higher search costs to locate individual manufacturers, the time costs of transacting with each manufacturer, and delivery costs (e.g., Fresh Direct charges a minimum amount for each order).

Distribution Channel Length and Functions

The length of a distribution channel refers to the number of intermediaries between the supplier and the consumer. The shortest distribution channel has no intermediaries—the manufacturer deals directly with the consumer, the way Dell sells directly to customers in a direct distribution channel. Most distribution channels incorporate one or more intermediaries in an **indirect distribution channel**. A typical indirect channel includes suppliers, a manufacturer, wholesalers, retailers, and end consumers. Intermediaries help to perform important functions (described in the next section).

Originally, it was predicted that the internet would eliminate intermediaries, thereby creating disintermediation in distribution channels. **Disintermediation** describes the process of eliminating traditional intermediaries. Eliminating intermediaries can potentially reduce the costs, as with Fresh Direct. Taken to its extreme, disintermediation allows the supplier to transfer goods and services directly to the consumer in a direct channel. Complete disintermediation tends to be the exception because intermediaries can often handle channel functions more efficiently than producers. An intermediary that specializes in one function, such as product promotion, tends to become more proficient in that function than a nonspecialist.

Much of the initial hype surrounding the internet focused on disintermediation and the possibility that prices would plummet as the internet eliminated costly intermediaries. This line of reasoning failed to recognize some important facts. First, the US distribution system is very efficient. Second, using intermediaries allows manufacturing companies to focus on what they do best. Third, many traditional intermediaries have been replaced with internet equivalents. In many cases the online intermediaries are more efficient than their brick-and-mortar counterparts. Consider the online storefront. Online retailers do not have to rent, maintain, and staff expensive retail space in desirable shopping areas. An inexpensive warehouse provides an acceptable storage location for goods sold online. On the other hand, online stores incur the costs of setting up and maintaining their digital commerce sites. Although these charges can be significant, they do not outweigh the savings realized by eliminating the physical store.

Functions of a Distribution Channel

Many functions must be performed in moving products from producer to consumer, regardless of which intermediary performs them. For example, online retailers normally hold inventory and perform the pick, pack, and ship functions in response to a customer order. In an alternative scenario, the retailer might **outsource** the pick, pack, and ship functions to a logistics provider such as UPS. Here, the retailer forwards the order to a UPS warehouse where the product waits in storage. UPS picks, packs, and ships the product to the consumer. Distributors perform many value-added functions. The functions can be broadly characterized as transactional, logistical, and facilitating.

Transactional Functions

Transactional functions refer to making contact with buyers and using marketing communication strategies to make buyers aware of products. They also include matching products to buyer needs, negotiating price, and processing transactions.

CONTACT WITH BUYERS

The internet provides a new channel for making contact with buyers. Forrester Research calls the internet the fourth channel after personal selling, mail, and the telephone; retailers see it as the third channel after brick-and-mortar stores and catalogs. The internet channel adds value to the contact process in several ways. First, contact can be customized to the buyer's needs. For example, the Honda site (www.honda.com) allows customers to find a dealer in their area where they can buy Honda vehicles. Second, the internet provides a wide range of referral sources such as search engines, shopping agents, social networks, e-mail, webpages, and affiliate programs. Third, the internet is always open for business, 24 hours a day, seven days a week.

MARKETING COMMUNICATIONS

Marketing communication encompasses advertising and other types of product promotion (discussed in Chapters 12 through 14). This function is often shared among channel players. For example, a manufacturer may launch an ad campaign while its retailers offer coupons. Cooperative advertising is another example, with manufacturers sharing advertising costs with retailers. These communications are most effective when they represent a coordinated effort among channel players.

The internet adds value to the marketing communications function in several ways. First, functions that previously required manual labor can be automated. When American Airlines sends out a promotional message to millions of its registered users, it requires no papers to fold, no envelopes to stuff, no postage to imprint—its marketers simply click "Send" to distribute the message.

Second, communications can be closely monitored and altered minute by minute. Google's AdWords program, for instance, allows its clients to monitor the click-through rates of their online ads in real time and quickly make substitutions for poorly performing ads. Third, Web analytics software for tracking a user's behavior can be used to direct highly targeted communications to individuals. Many social networking sites offer powerful analytics solutions for business pages as well.

Finally, the internet enhances promotional coordination among intermediaries. Companies e-mail ads and other material to each other, and all firms may view current promotions on a Web site at any time. It is still all too common for brick-and-mortar headquarter firms to run promotions that retailers don't know about until consumers begin asking for the special deals—internet communication helps prevent this kind of surprise from occurring.

MATCHING PRODUCT TO BUYER'S NEEDS

The internet excels at matching products to buyer's needs. Given a general description of the buyer's requirements, shopping agents can produce a list of relevant products. Online retailers can also help consumers match products to needs. Polyvore, Pinterest, and Gap (www.gap.com) let consumers mix and match clothes to create outfits. Most automobile sites allow consumers to custom-configure vehicles. Of particular interest are **collaborative filtering** agents, which can predict consumer preferences based on past purchase behavior. Amazon uses a collaborative filtering agent to recommend products to customers. Once the system is in place, it can handle millions of users at little incremental cost. The effectiveness of the collaborative filtering agent actually increases as consumers are added to the database. Note that all of these services scale well because they are automated. By contrast, efforts to match product to buyer needs in the brick-and-mortar world can be labor intensive and are quickly overwhelmed as volume increases. Salespeople in retail outlets attempt this chore, but the internet improves on this function by being on call anytime and by matching buyers with products across retailers. Of course, this capability puts a burden on electronic retailers to compete on the basis of price or to differentiate their products in a way that is meaningful to the market.

NEGOTIATING PRICE

True price negotiation involves offers and counteroffers between buyer and seller such as might be conducted in person, over the phone, or via e-mail—a two-way dialog. Even so, shopping agents implicitly negotiate prices downward on behalf of the consumer by listing companies in order of best price first. Bidding, on the other hand, is a form of dynamic or flexible pricing in which the buyer gives suppliers an equal opportunity to bid (see Chapter 10). Many businesses currently conduct bidding online. Consumer market auctions include those held by eBay and Amazon. Businesses such as General Electric also solicit online bids from their suppliers. Online bidding effectively widens the supplier pool, thereby increasing competition and lowering prices. Many auction houses allow buyers to program an agent to represent them in bidding against other buyers or their agents.

PROCESS TRANSACTIONS

Studies show that electronic channels lower the cost to process transactions dramatically. The National Association of Purchasing Management places the cost of manually processing an average purchase order at $79—mainly due to labor costs.

Logistical Functions

Logistical functions include physical distribution activities such as transportation and inventory storage, as well as the function of aggregating product. Logistical functions are often outsourced to third-party logistics specialists. RFID tags are an important development for tracking products through the distribution channel (see the "Let's Get Technical" box). Radio frequency identification (RFID) tags are used to transmit a signal to scanners, which detect the presence of the RFID tag in products, credit cards, or even under a person or animal's skin.

Let's Get Technical—RFID Technology

Tired of waiting in long lines at the grocery store? Never again want to hear the phrase, "I'll have to send someone to check that price" when you just want to buy a carton of milk? Many customers become frustrated when making trips to supermarkets or large discount retailers. No matter when they choose to shop, the lines are often long, wasting valuable time. With the onset of RFID technology solutions, the supermarket of the future may not have lines at all. All customers might have to do is swipe their credit card and walk out the door.

Radio frequency identification (RFID) refers to tiny, embedded chips that can announce their presence to a scanner. The simplest form of RFID are tags used by retailers to detect theft at the exits. More complex forms of RFID uniquely identify the tagged product. This is similar to the unique numbers on barcodes that are read by supermarket scanners. The difference is that RFID tags do not need to be visible. That's not a small difference. The only reason you need to place your products on the belt at supermarket checkout is so that they can be run over the scanner. This requires making sure that the barcode side passes over the scanner. But if every product had an RFID tag instead, you could simply run the entire shopping cart through a scanner and have the total instantly calculated. No lines, no waiting, ever again.

The problem is cost. Even though prices have been falling, you can still expect to pay about $0.10 per tag. While that's not much to tag a $200 game controller; it is a lot to tag a bar of soap. As the popularity of RFID tags has increased, their prices have declined. The goal of EPCglobal, an industry standards group, is to have the price drop to $0.05 per tag. If the cost ever drops to $0.01 per tag, expect widespread adoption.

As the technology's name indicates, radio frequencies are used to communicate between the RFID tag and a scanner. This technology requires three components: an RFID tag, an RFID scanner, and a recording device (i.e., a computer). The RFID tag is attached to the product that is being tracked. The tag is made up of an RFID chip and a mini-antenna.

The RFID scanner, which can also be called a reader, is connected to a computer. The RFID scanner constantly sends out a low frequency electromagnetic signal (100 kHz to 5.8 GHz). The signal powers the RFID chip and antenna to transmit data back to the scanner. When the scanner receives the information, it sends this data to the computer to store and analyze. As the technology matures, increasing amounts of information can be stored in the RFID chip and transmitted to the scanner.

The distance between the RFID tag and the scanner depends on the size of the RFID chip and mini-antenna. The more sophisticated the chip and the larger the antenna, the farther the tag and scanner can be from each other.

RFID technology has many applications in the distribution and retail industries. RFIDs are already being used to track pallets of products at large distribution centers. As shipments of products enter and exit the distribution center, the movement is automatically tracked with intense accuracy.

Most credit cards now have RFID chips that guarantee that the card was present for the transaction. The card can be inserted into a chip reader. A more sophisticated and convenient variation is the tap-to-pay option, where the card simply needs to be close to the reader.

RFIDs are also being used at gas and toll stations. Specific gas companies have distributed a small plastic key chain to consumers that holds the consumer's credit card information. When the consumer purchases gas, he waves the keychain in front of a small reader at the pump. The reader receives the credit card information, authorizes the pumping of the gas, and subsequently charges the credit card. The gas companies' intent in providing this service was to increase customer loyalty because the key chains work only at their stations.

Many commuters pass through tollbooths each day on their way to and from work, and they painstakingly wait in lines at busy booths. Local and state governments, such as Pennsylvania, Virginia, and Florida have implemented RFID solutions. For little or no fee, commuters can purchase a small box that sits near the windshield of the vehicle. The number of the box and a credit card to pay tolls are registered with the transit authority. When the commuter comes to a tollbooth, he or she is allowed to enter a "Fast Pass" lane equipped with the RFID scanner. The scanner obtains the box number and bills the credit card on file. Some booths do not even require the traveler to drop their speed below 55 miles per hour. Another example of RFID in a similar application is with keyless entry systems.

Walmart uses RFID to manage the supply chain with hundreds of its suppliers. The benefits include a 16 percent reduction in out-of-stocks as well as 63 percent more effective restocking. RFID also ensures proof of delivery and eases reconciliation of purchase orders.

The goal is to eventually replace barcodes company-wide and to increase efficiency within the supply chain process.

Although the RFID solution will benefit Walmart, the large retailer also promises benefits for its suppliers. These benefits include notifications when goods arrive at stores and when they enter the sales floor, which allows suppliers to better track demand. Walmart also places RFID tags on point-of-purchase displays used as end caps and other displays for in-store promotions. These displays are often costly to produce, according to suppliers, and end up left in the back room. With the RFID tags, suppliers can track the deployment of the displays. As a result, new products reach the shelves three times faster.

With the world's largest retailer backing RFID technology, it appears poised for success. Distribution networks worldwide may need to adopt RFID standards as part of the cost of doing business.

PHYSICAL DISTRIBUTION

Most products sold online are still distributed through conventional channels. Yet digital content can be transmitted less expensively from producer to consumer over the internet: text, graphics, audio, and video content. The alternative step, physical distribution of digital product, is comparatively expensive.

AGGREGATING PRODUCT

In general, suppliers operate more efficiently when they produce a high volume of a narrow range of products. Consumers, on the other hand, prefer to purchase small quantities of a wide range of products. Channel intermediaries perform the essential function of aggregating product from multiple suppliers so that the consumer can have more choices in one location. Examples of this traditional form of **aggregation** include online category killers such as Amazon.com, with a broad product mix. In other cases, the internet follows a model of virtual aggregation, bringing together products from multiple manufacturers and organizing the display on the user's computer (e.g., Pinterest using social commerce). In the case of shopping agents, the unit of aggregation is the product page at the online store. A search for a particular product will produce a neatly arranged table with comparative product information and direct links to the vendor pages.

THIRD-PARTY LOGISTICS—OUTSOURCED LOGISTICS

A major logistics problem in the B2B market is reconciling the conflicting goals of timely delivery and minimal inventory. One solution for many companies is to place inventory with a **third-party logistics** provider such as UPS or FedEx. Taking logistics one step further, third parties can also manage the company's supply chain and provide value-added services such as product configuration and subassembly. The logistics providers will even handle the order processes, replenish stock when needed, and assign tracking numbers so customers can find their orders. Alcatel, for example, uses UPS to manage orders and distribute cellular phones in Europe.

In the B2C market a major logistics problem is product returns (reverse logistics), which can run as high as 15 percent. Customers frequently complain about the difficulty and expense of returns. Some websites offer to pay return shipping. But even with a credit for return shipping, the customer still has to weigh the package, pay shipping fees up front, and schedule pickup (or deliver to a shipping location). Many Amazon purchases allow liberal return policies to ensure the customer is satisfied.

The US Postal Service (USPS) has introduced a clever program to ease the return process. Merchants can install software on a site that allows them to authorize customers to download and print postage-paid return labels. The customer simply boxes the item, slaps on the label, and leaves it by the door for the letter carrier. UPS and FedEx offer similar services, along with a wide range of boxes that centralize the pickup process.

THE LAST MILE PROBLEM

One big problem facing online retailers and logistics managers is the added expense of delivering small quantities to individual homes and businesses. It is much less expensive to send cases of products to wholesalers and retailers and let them break the quantities into smaller units for sale. Two other problems arise: deliveries requiring multiple delivery attempts, thus increasing costs, and packages being left on doorsteps when no one is home, opening the way for possible theft. With billions of packages delivered in the United States, digital marketers are looking for ways to save costs and solve this last mile problem.

Amazon introduced Amazon Key in 2017 as a way to remotely allow select individuals into your home and see them through a camera system, like a delivery driver with a last mile service. In-garage delivery is now offered free for Amazon Prime members, wherein Amazon drivers receive temporary, one-time access to open and drop off packages in consumers' garages.

Another solution involves a retail aggregator model. Consumers can have packages shipped to participating retailers, such as local convenience stores or service stations; then consumers pick up the package from a locker or secured box of some kind. Finally, many multichannel retailers allow customers to order online for offline retail delivery. More than 150 million consumers "click-and-collect" in the United States, accounting for 9 percent of all digital commerce sales ("Click and Collect", 2021). Many retailers offer this option as a method for convenience to the shopper.

Facilitating Functions

Facilitating functions performed by channel members include market research and financing.

MARKET RESEARCH

Market research is a major function of the distribution channel. The benefits include an accurate assessment of the size and characteristics of the target audience. Information gathered by intermediaries helps manufacturers plan product development and marketing communications. Chapter 6 explored market research in detail, and Chapter 7 examined internet user behavior. This section will look at the costs and benefits of internet-based market research.

The internet affects the value of market research in five ways. First, some of the information on the internet, especially government reports, is available for free. Second, managers and employees can conduct research from their desks rather than making expensive trips to libraries and other resource sites. Third, information from the internet tends to be timelier, as when advertisers monitor banner ad click-through. Fourth, Web-based information is already in digital form, so digital marketers can easily load it into a spreadsheet or other software. Finally, because so much consumer behavior data can be captured online, digital marketers can receive detailed reports. For example, comScore (www.comscore.com) produces a site interaction report that details to what extent a site shares audience with another site—showing exclusive and duplicated audience.

Nonetheless, little market research is free. Even free government reports require a significant investment of human resources to distill the material into a useful form for making decisions. Furthermore, many firms need access to costly commercial information such as comScore reports, which sell for about $50,000 each.

FINANCING

Financing purchases is an important facilitating function in both consumer and business markets. Intermediaries want to make it easy for customers to pay in order to close the sale. Most online consumer purchases are financed through credit cards or special financing plans, similar to traditional store purchases. However, some consumers are understandably concerned about divulging credit card information online—resulting in safeguards that probably make online purchasing the most secure channel for consumers.

Online merchants have a major concern as well: how do they know that they are dealing with a valid consumer using a legitimate credit card? The major credit card companies have, therefore, formed **Secure Electronic Transaction (SET)** as a vehicle for legitimizing both the merchant and the consumer as well as protecting the consumer's credit card number. Under SET, the card number goes not to the merchant but to a third party with whom the merchant and consumer communicate to validate one another as well as the transaction. The communication occurs automatically in the background and places no technical burdens on the consumer. However, SET is so technical that most consumers do not appreciate its subtleties. Furthermore, most merchants do not want to pay for costly upgrades to a SET system.

Still, SET has been successful inside the United States, in part because of legislative protections: US consumers have a maximum $50 liability for purchases made with a stolen card. The card issuer usually waives the $50 in order to retain customers, and some issuers now advertise $0 liability for online purchases. However, that legal protection does not exist in some countries, and consumers may be liable for all charges on their card up to the time they report it stolen.

In the B2B market, brokers and agents often extend lines of credit to buyers to facilitate purchases. These lines of credit significantly speed the buying process and make the online channel more attractive.

Distribution System

The distribution channel is actually a system, when viewed by the flow of products, information, and finances along the channel—a unified system of interdependent organizations working together to build value as products proceed through the channel to the consumer. This perspective recognizes that a channel system is stronger when its participants compete in a unified way with other channel systems.

Defining the scope of the channel as a system can be done in three ways:

1. The first is to consider only distribution functions that are downstream from the manufacturer to the consumer, the traditional definition of the distribution channel.
2. The second is to consider only the supply chain upstream from the manufacturer working backward to the raw materials, the traditional definition of the supply chain.
3. The third view is to consider the supply chain, the manufacturer, and the distribution channel as an integrated system called the **value chain** (a more recent name for the value chain is *integrated logistics*). Many refer to the supply chain *as* the value chain. By this definition, the supply chain includes upstream and downstream activities as well as processes internal to the firm. See Exhibit 11.9 in which the circles represent firms in a network of suppliers, manufacturers, and intermediaries.

Redefining the supply chain to include the entire value chain is now mainstream, reflecting what a great number of practitioners mean when they talk about supply chain management. Thus, value chain, integrated logistics, and supply chain are equivalent terms.

This definition of the supply chain is used to describe the field of **supply chain management (SCM)**. SCM refers to the coordination of flows in three categories: material (e.g., physical product), information (e.g., demand forecast), and financial (e.g., credit terms). The word *flow* evokes the image of a continuous stream of products, information, and finances flowing among the channel members much as blood and nerve impulses flow through an

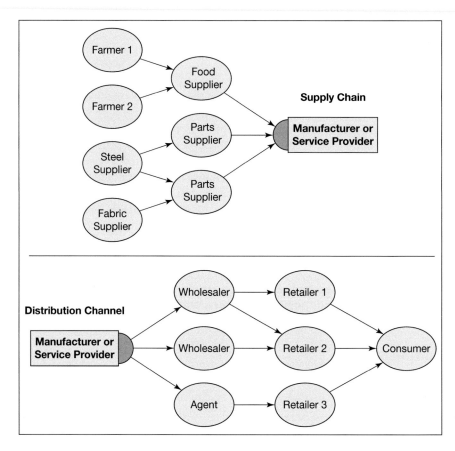

Exhibit 11.9 Supply Chain + Distribution Channel = New Definition of Supply Chain

organism. The most important flow is that of information because creation of the physical product and the financing depend on the information.

The Holy Grail in supply chain management is "scan one, make one—and deliver it fast." This process is known as **continuous replenishment**. For more complex products such as computers, the goal is to build to order and deliver quickly. Both continuous replenishment and **build to order** help to eliminate inventory. In turn, this practice reduces costs because inventory is expensive to finance; it also increases profits by avoiding unsold inventory going stale and being sold at a discount. The cost savings may be passed on to the customer in the form of lower prices, which improve the value proposition for the customer. However, creating product in response to demand almost always results in some delay in delivery. The customer's value is increased only if the increased delays are acceptable. Today's customer wants it all—lower prices, quick delivery, and custom configuration. The only way to provide these benefits is to tightly coordinate the activities of upstream suppliers, the inner workings of the firm, and the downstream distribution channel—a formidable task that would have been impossible before the information age.

A difficult problem in SCM is deciding which participant should manage a channel composed of many firms. Supply chain management allows for coordination of all supply chain functions into a seamless system, made possible by internet technologies.

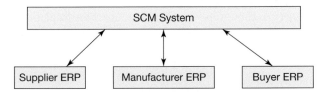

Exhibit 11.10 SCM System Interfaces with Multiple ERP Systems

Interoperability is especially important in SCM because many of the participants in modern supply chains have **enterprise resource planning (ERP)** systems to manage their in-house inventory and processes. If the individual ERP systems can seamlessly share information with the SCM system, coordination is greatly facilitated in real time. See Exhibit 11.10.

Channel Management and Power

Once a channel structure is established, its viability requires a certain measure of coordination, communication, and control to avoid conflict among its members. A powerful channel member must emerge to assume the leadership and institute these required measures. Increasingly, market competition is between entire supply chains, which is why digital marketers need to understand power relationships among channel players.

Whenever new information technology is introduced into a distribution channel, it can potentially alter the power relationships among existing channel players. Nowhere has this effect been more evident than with the internet. In many cases, buyer power significantly increased at the expense of the supplier. In other cases, the power of the supplier has come out on top. Walmart gained power over its channels when it introduced electronic systems to notify suppliers of needed product. This shift caused a major power upheaval in channels where giant manufacturers such as Procter & Gamble had previously been in control. A classic source of power for retailers and distributors has been geographic location. Retailers have built power on the place (location) utility and restricted access to manufacturers. The internet neutralizes the importance of location and offers new sources of supply for purchasing.

Just as the internet increased the power of buyers by providing access to more information and to more suppliers, it increased the power of suppliers, as well. First, the supplier that takes the early lead online will receive business from consumers and firms eager to shop in this channel. But even in cases when multiple firms are online, suppliers can gain power by establishing structural relationships with buyers. For example, Amazon establishes structural relationships with its customers using its 1-Click ordering and collaborative filtering technologies. Amazon customers switching to another site would have to reenter their billing information and, more important, they would lose access to Amazon's recommendations.

A type of business-to-business commerce known as **electronic data interchange (EDI)** is particularly effective for establishing structural relationships between businesses. Electronic data interchange is the computerized exchange of information between organizations, typically used to eliminate paperwork. A buyer logs onto the supplier's computer system and types in an order. The order is electronically conveyed to the supplier, and the buyer receives an electronic bill.

The internet puts a new face on EDI with the advent of open standards and interoperable systems. First, the internet replaces expensive proprietary networks, yielding tremendous cost savings. Second, business can use the same computer to interface with multiple suppliers. Third, networks of suppliers and buyers can more easily exchange data using a Web-based interface.

Thus, EDI is based on three key variables: the openness of the system, the transport method (internet or non-internet), and the type of technology used for implementation. Combining these variables in different ways results in many types of EDI most commonly used today, such as Application Program Interface (API) and Extensible Markup Language (XML).

The goal is to create a standards-based open system that runs over the internet so all suppliers and buyers can seamlessly integrate their systems.

Distribution Channel Metrics

Does online commerce work? To answer this question, a company must consider its effectiveness in terms of reaching target market segments efficiently and enticing them to purchase online.

B2C Market

Digital commerce has grown consistently since its inception; however, the $400 billion spent online in 2016 only represents 9 percent of all retail sales (Exhibit 11.11). The internet influences offline sales, as previously mentioned (e.g., mobile search while in a brick-and-mortar store). BigCommerce notes that 25 percent of Americans have even made a purchase from their mobile device while standing in a physical store ("BigCommerce Survey Shows . . .", 2016).

These statistics show general spending levels; however, individual retailer sales vary based on how well their online strategies work. Companies track sales from all channels (online, retail, mobile, social, and catalog) on a daily basis to determine whether they are meeting their objectives and to refine websites, cross-channel promotion, and both online and offline communication to achieve better results.

In one global study of online retailers, McKinsey and Company researchers found that two strategies are particularly effective online:

- A high-reach strategy of accumulating large numbers of customers with cost-effective conversion rates (visit the site and buy) for high-frequency purchases of low-margin products and services such as music and books (e.g., Amazon.com).
- A niche strategy with narrow focus on a particular product or service category, such as luxury items or apparel (e.g., Dell.com).

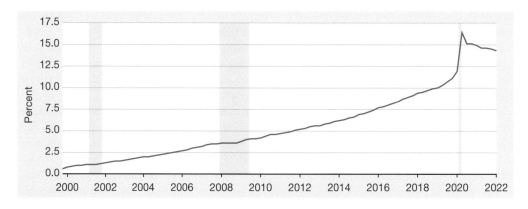

Exhibit 11.11 US Digital Commerce Retail Sales as a Percent of Total Sales

Source: fred.stlouisfed.org

For all others, the best use of online retailing is as a complement to offline channels. As you have read repeatedly, it is all about the customer, and marketers track every detail to identify winning tactics.

Chapter 2 presented many performance metrics to aid digital marketers in evaluating online retailing and supply chain management. A few of the more important include revenues (as just mentioned), ROI, customer satisfaction levels, customer acquisition costs, conversion rates, and average order values. Conversion refers to the proportion of all website visitors who actually purchase on that visit. Exhibit 11.12 shows the largest online retailers in terms of sales in 2016. What do you think the conversion rates are on websites like these?

Additional important measures relate to affiliate sites and how many customers they refer to the digital commerce site. Also, what proportion of these customers purchase at the site? Online sellers also want to know what sites their customers visit immediately prior to arriving. These measures help marketers evaluate affiliate and other partner effectiveness.

M-commerce presents another set of metric opportunities, such as click-to-call rate, secondary actions (what users do after viewing a mobile site/promotional message), click-through rate, search for store directions, text response, time spent with an app, click to social network, and many others. F-commerce also has its own metrics, discussed in later chapters. But above all, marketers want to know click-through rates, conversions to sales and average order value (including marketing/promotional costs).

B2B Market

The B2B market is big business. It is impossible to measure the amount of dollars that exchanges hands in supply chains because it happens behind company walls. Most B2B

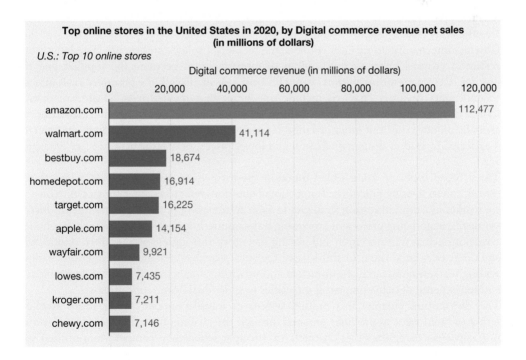

Exhibit 11.12 Top Ten Online Retailers in 2020

Source: www.statista.com

business deals still happen via the telephone, fax, and salespeople. The internet has proven to be a much more efficient way for firms to improve the quality, efficiency, and timeliness of orders from each other, spurring growth in digital procurement and process improvement. Businesses use the Web to search for suppliers, but more often they simply facilitate current relationships throughout online ordering, shipment tracking, and more.

In the B2B market, as in B2C, digital marketers should select metrics that relate to their digital marketing goals. It is critical to understand how digital commerce fits into the overall marketing strategy, what the firm expects to accomplish through it, and whether it is working. For B2B, metrics may look at time from order to delivery, order fill levels, and other activities that reflect functions performed by channel participants.

Chapter Summary

The internet increased the power of buyers and suppliers. It also changed the way electronic data interchange is used to establish structural relationships between suppliers and buyers. The major business models used by online intermediaries can be categorized as content sponsorship, direct distribution, infomediary, brokerage models (online exchange and online auction), and agent models (selling agents, manufacturer's agents, shopping agents, buyer's cooperative). Online retailing (digital commerce, social commerce, m-commerce, F-commerce) is another important model including online sales of digital or tangible products and is done by direct distribution, with intermediaries, or by using multichannel marketing (to attract the omni-channel customer).

A distribution channel is a group of interdependent firms that work together to transfer product and information from the supplier to the consumer. The transfer may be either direct or through a number of intermediaries that perform certain marketing functions in the channel between suppliers and customers. By specializing, intermediaries are able to perform functions more efficiently than a supplier could.

Channel intermediaries include wholesalers, retailers, brokers, and agents. The length of a distribution channel refers to the number of intermediaries between the supplier and the consumer. The shortest distribution channel has no intermediaries; the producer deals directly with customers. Indirect channels include one or more intermediaries. Disintermediation describes the process of eliminating traditional intermediaries. Eliminating intermediaries can potentially reduce costs, but functions must be performed by someone. Although the internet was expected to lead to disintermediation and lower prices, new intermediaries are emerging instead.

Three broad types of value-added functions performed in the channel are transactional, logistical, and facilitating functions. Transactional functions refer to making contact with buyers, using marketing communication strategies to raise awareness of products, matching product to buyer needs, negotiating price, and processing transactions. Logistical functions include physical distribution such as transportation and storing inventory and aggregating product; digital marketers often outsource these to third-party logistics providers. Facilitating functions include providing marketing research about buyers and providing financing. The last mile problem is the added expense of delivering small quantities to individual homes or businesses.

The distribution channel is a unified system of interdependent organizations working together to build value as products proceed through the channel from producer to consumer. This perspective recognizes that channels are stronger when they compete in a unified way with other channels. Supply chain management is the coordination of flow of material (e.g., physical product), information (e.g., demand forecast), and financial (e.g., credit terms). Marketers measure the success of their distribution strategies and tactics through a number of important performance metrics.

Exercises

Review Questions

1. What is a distribution channel?
2. What are the types of intermediaries in a distribution channel?
3. What are the three major functions of a distribution channel?
4. What is supply chain management (SCM), and why is it important?
5. Why are digital marketers concerned with the last mile problem?
6. What is disintermediation? Give an example.
7. What is an infomediary? Give an example.
8. What is multichannel marketing? Omni-channel marketing? Give examples.
9. How do brokers and agents differ?
10. What types of distribution channel metrics are used in the B2C market?
11. Name five reasons consumers abandon online shopping carts.
12. Compare and contrast social commerce, m-commerce, and F-commerce.

Discussion Questions

1. **The Zappos Story.** Do you think it is viable for Zappos to move to m-commerce, social commerce, and F-commerce? If yes, how could they do this? If no, why not?
2. **The Zappos Story.** This company uses a direct marketing distribution model, selling to customers directly. Review the functions channel intermediaries perform and explain what extra tasks Zappos has undertaken by eliminating intermediaries.
3. How does the value of distribution channel functions change when they become internet based?
4. Do you agree with the more inclusive definition of the supply chain to include the entire value chain? Support your position.
5. Although direct distribution often results in lower prices, what disadvantages does it have for buyers?
6. Each intermediary in the channel has to mark up a product's price to make a profit. Some retailers sell products for almost double the wholesale cost. What would a retailer have to do to add enough value to justify such a markup?
7. How would you suggest digital marketers solve the last mile problem?
8. What is the future of digital commerce, in your opinion? Will it continue to increase? Will it ever become larger in terms of sales than offline retailing? Explain your answers.
9. Which social commerce tactics are the best, from a user perspective? Explain.
10. What is your opinion of F-commerce? Do you think it is appropriate for companies to sell on Facebook? Why or why not and what tactics are appropriate, if any?
11. What digital content do you think will bring the most revenue online in five years?

Web Activities

1. Survey 20 people. Ask them to rate their online purchase experience on a scale of 1 to 10, with 10 as the best. If they have never purchased online, try to find out what stops them. Summarize the results.

2. Working in small groups, discuss online shopping experiences and what companies did to meet group members' needs, including follow-up e-mail/customer service.

3. Survey 10 people. Ask them to recall a time when they abandoned a shopping cart online while in the middle of a purchase. Query them about what the online retailer could have done to prevent that from happening. Summarize the results.

4. Visit Taggbox.com, and Chewy.com. Report on how they are using the social commerce strategy and what their business models are.

Chapter 12

Digital Marketing Communication
Owned Media

This chapter discusses how marketers use communication media and social media to connect with customers and prospects. After reading an overview of integrated marketing communication, you will learn about selecting, applying, and evaluating tools for messages in owned media, one of the three main elements of content strategy. You will also gain an understanding of the complex art and science of search engine optimization.

After reading this chapter, you will be able to:

- Define integrated marketing communication (IMC).
- Explain how marketers use the AIDA model and the hierarchy of effects model when making communication decisions.
- List the five traditional marketing communication tools and distinguish between traditional media and social media.
- Identify the differences in control and reach between owned, paid, and earned media.
- Discuss why companies use content marketing.
- Describe the most commonly used owned media and their benefits for marketing.
- Explain how and why marketers use search engine optimization.
- Highlight some of the metrics marketers can use to evaluate owned media performance.

WILL IT BLEND?

"Will it blend? That is the question." Thus opens a video starring Blendtec's CEO, Tom Dickson. Wearing a white lab coat and safety glasses, and appearing very scientific yet amused, Dickson stands next to an ordinary-looking blender on a table. The things he blends are anything but ordinary—a wood handled garden rake, a golf club, light bulbs, glow sticks, marbles, and even the sacred iPad and iPhone. The latter received 3.9 million views on YouTube in an eight-month period—and in 2021 the total was over 19 million as the company added additional videos blending bizarre products. Watching the destruction of these is like watching a train wreck—irresistible. Sending the links to friends is also irresistible. This is viral marketing at its best.

Blendtec is well known in the business market for supplying commercial blenders to Starbucks and others. The goal of the hilarious videos was to build awareness of a new high-quality blender for the consumer market. Dickson is famous for saying that before the videos, "Great products + Weak branding = Weak sales." The videos changed this equation for Blendtec. Retail sales for the $400 blender increased substantially in the first year after the video series began, and 186 videos later in 2008, sales reportedly increased by 700 percent. Not bad for an initial $100 investment in the first video. Blendtec posts videos both

DOI: 10.4324/9781003247319-16

on YouTube and on its microsite WillItBlend.com, and the latter has prompted ancillary revenue streams. Visitors could purchase "Tom Dickson is My Homeboy" T-shirts and the videos themselves.

The brainchild of Dickson, the *Will It Blend?* campaign clearly shows the product benefits in a relevant, humorous, and engaging way. This campaign shows the value of connecting with consumers versus interrupting them with unwanted advertising. It also shows the strength of consumer conversation because thousands of viewers posted responses to the iPhone-blending YouTube video, including video responses prior to YouTube disabling the comment feature. The video was marked as a favorite by over 30,000 registered YouTube visitors. It helped that Blendtec added search engine optimization and keyword advertising purchases to draw more traffic to the videos. Brilliant job, Blendtec!

Digital Marketing Communication

As the opening example of *Will It Blend?* demonstrates, internet marketing is a powerful way to build brands and start and strengthen relationships with customers. However, online marketers must be increasingly clever to design and deliver brand messages that capture and hold audience attention—because on the internet, users are in control. They can delete unwanted incoming e-mail and impatiently click away when websites do not quickly deliver desired information. Also, the internet allows consumers to widely disseminate their own views and brand experiences via e-mail and social media, shifting the balance of control over brand images from companies to consumers. In this environment, the keys to success include (1) providing relevant, interesting messages when and where target customers want them and (2) engaging internet users by enticing them to upload content, make comments, share content, or simply play with a game or other fun content.

Marketing communication (MarCom) tools that use technology to build brands, in conjunction with value-added product experiences, are important in capturing attention and winning long-term customer relationships. Advertising online still works for building brands, but there are many other innovative techniques that are often more successful—discussed here and in Chapters 13 and 14. And as a bonus, technology lowers the costs of communicating with customers and prospects.

Integrated Marketing Communication (IMC)

Integrated marketing communication (IMC) is a cross-functional process for planning, executing, and monitoring brand communications designed to profitably acquire, retain, and grow customers. IMC is cross-functional because every touch point that a customer has with a firm or its agents helps to form brand images. For example, a Home Depot retail customer might buy and use a product from the website, then e-mail or call 1-800 to complain about a problem, write about the problem on Twitter, and finally return the product to the brick-and-mortar retail store. Every contact with an employee, a website, a blog comment about the product, a YouTube video, a magazine ad, a mobile app, a catalog, the physical store facilities, and so forth helps the customer form an image of the company. In addition, the product experience, its pricing level, and its distribution channels enhance the firm's marketing communication in a variety of online and offline media to present a strong brand image. The best marketing communication can be undermined if these online and offline contact experiences do not communicate in a unified way to create and support positive brand relationships with customers.

Profitable customer relationships are key to a firm's existence. Successful firms recognize that not all customers are equally valuable—some, such as frequent flyers or buyers, are more important than others. Using technology, firms can monitor profits customer by customer and, based on this analysis, pay more attention to high-value customers both online and offline. Databases and the analysis techniques described in Chapter 6 allow firms to differentiate customers by value, send them appropriate e-mail offers and website landing pages, and track the results of company MarCom campaigns. You'll find more about online customer relationship management in Chapter 15.

IMC strategy begins with a thorough understanding of target markets, the brand, its competition, and many other internal and external factors. The Interactive Advertising Bureau suggests a four-step process good for any marketing communication campaign:

1. Set clear and measurable objectives and strategies.
2. Understand your audience motivations and behavior, especially in social media.
3. Develop a creative approach appropriate for the brand in one or more platforms (earned, paid, or owned media).
4. Define success metrics.

Many IMC experts agree that it should "(1) be more strategic than executional (i.e., more than just about 'one voice, one look'), (2) be about more than just advertising and sales promotion messages, (3) include two-way as well as one-way communication, and (4) be results driven" (Duncan and Mulhern, 2004, p. 9).

IMC Goals and Strategies

Marketers create marketing communication objectives based on overall marketing goals and the desired effects within selected target markets. For instance, Mitsubishi Motors desired to sell more automobiles, so it identified marketing communication goals of (1) driving prospects to the website, (2) increasing website registrations, and (3) increasing test drive appointments. Sales were the primary goal, and the three communications objectives helped Mitsubishi reach it.

The traditional **AIDA model** (awareness, interest, desire, and action) or the "think, feel, do" **hierarchy of effects** model is part of what guides marketers' selection of online and offline MarCom tools to meet their goals. Both the AIDA and hierarchy of effects models suggest that consumers first become aware of and learn about a new product (think), then develop a positive or negative attitude about it (feel), and ultimately move to purchasing it (do) (Ray, 1973). The thinking, or cognitive, steps are awareness and knowledge. The feeling, or attitude, steps are liking and preference.

Here are some examples of social media campaigns at each level, from awareness to behavior:

*   **Product awareness:** Popular music group The Piano Guys started out as a social media campaign for a music store. Now their videos have millions of views online and hundreds of thousands of subscribers.
*   **Interest and Desire:** October is National Pizza Month, and in 2019, Digiorno took advantage of the celebration by delivering free pizza to customers in five major US cities who tweeted #DeliveryDigiorno. According to Twitter Marketing, the hashtag

generated 8.5 million Tweet impressions and accrued a 78 percent positive sentiment rating.

- **Behavior/Purchase:** In Seoul, Korea, Dunkin' created a scent spray device that released the aroma of coffee anytime the ad appeared via the radio of the public transportation many people use to work. They followed up the radio ad with a visual ad telling them where the nearest Dunkin' store is located. More than 350,000 people experienced this ad campaign, with visitors to Dunkin' stores growing by 16 percent and increasing sales by 29 percent (Marinkovic, 2020). Mazda Motors UK ran a Facebook location "check-in" deal, offering a limited number of 20 percent discounts on the Mazda Mx-5s automobile. Sales increased 34 percent during the February 2011 campaign, selling out of 100 in stock Mx-5s model within two weeks of launching the campaign. The check-in promotion motivated 742 people to visit Mazda dealerships so that they could check in with their mobile phones and compete for the discount (see Facebook Success Stories for more information).

Consequently, brand managers must select the appropriate IMC tools, which may vary depending on the desired results. For example, digital marketers may opt to use traditional IMC tools of sales promotion, such as giving away free iPads, to create awareness and entice recipients to visit a blog; television advertising to create interest and desire; and direct selling by mailed catalog to get the desired action (purchasing). They might combine these with online tools of sales promotion (free music sampling at iTunes), keyword advertising on search engines, or direct selling via ecommerce at the online store.

If an organization wants to build its brands and inform customers, it will operate at the cognitive and attitude levels of the hierarchy of effects, perhaps using blogs, white papers (as PDF files) on websites, online advertising, e-mail campaigns, social network pages, and other promotional techniques. When Ourbeginnings.com spent more than $4 million on Super Bowl XXXIV TV ads, it was trying to build awareness of the website—and it was so eager to achieve this goal that it spent four times its annual revenue on the campaign. This strategy turned out to be a poor one, which is why now only the strongest internet firms purchase Super Bowl advertising. If a company wants to encourage online transactions (behavior), it needs persuasive communication messages that tell how to complete the transaction on the website, over the telephone, and so forth. Post-purchase behavior doesn't appear on the commonly accepted hierarchy, yet many IMC strategies seek to build customer satisfaction after the purchase. E-mail and text messaging are especially well suited for this goal.

The hierarchy of effects model is important because it helps marketers understand where consumers stand in relation to the purchase cycle so the company can select appropriate communication objectives and strategies that will move consumers closer to purchase and loyalty. Bear in mind that some traditional IMC tools are more appropriate for building awareness and brand attitudes (advertising, public relations) and others are more suited for encouraging transactional behavior (direct marketing, sales promotions, personal selling). Nevertheless, all can be used at each level.

Obviously, businesses want to be sure they find the right social media tactics to achieve their objectives and ROI requirements in this uncharted territory. The best place to start is with the company's objectives. Exhibit 12.1 displays a continuum of social media goals, from broad business strategies to specific brand tactics. We have indicated in which level of the hierarchy of effects each goal falls. Social media are especially well suited to raising brand awareness and creating a buzz, but they can also result in sales when customers read about the brand and either purchase at the website or offline. Note that many other IMC tools can achieve these goals and that an integrated strategy will be the most effective over time.

	Hierarchy Stage	Social Media Strategy
Strategic	awareness	Raise brand awareness
	attitude	Improve favorable perception of a brand/product/service
	behavior	Increase customer acquisition
	behavior	Maintain customer loyalty
	attitude	Create user advocacy Gather nonscientific/informal research Develop new insights on target market
	awareness	Create word-of-mouth and viral opportunities
	awareness	Create buzz on branded experience
	awareness	Build incremental reach
	behavior	Increase marketing ROI
	awareness	Increase consumer conversations about brand
	behavior	Drive qualified registrations (newsletter, contests, etc.)
	awareness	Support a new product launch
	behavior	Drive site traffic
Tactical	behavior	Increase sales

Exhibit 12.1 Social Media Strategies and Tactics

Source: Adapted From "IAB Social Media Buyer's Guide" (2010)

Traditional Marketing Communication Tools

Consumers tend to think that everything with a company name on it, from a Facebook contest, website, or YouTube video to an iPhone app, is "advertising." In contrast, marketers have specific definitions of the five key marketing communication tools they use (often called the "promotion mix"). These definitions help when selecting the appropriate tool(s) to create the desired effect in the target market. Following are marketing tool definitions, along with social media platform examples that the company controls (versus user-generated content):

- **Advertising:** "Any paid form of non-personal presentation and promotion of ideas, goods, or services by an identified sponsor" (Kotler and Armstrong, 2010). Social media examples: paid message placed in a YouTube video, Facebook, or LinkedIn ad, Google AdWords, promoted tweets, paid product placement in online games, and ad-sponsored content delivered to mobile phones.
- **Public relations:** "Building good relations with the company's various publics by obtaining favorable publicity, building up a good corporate image, and handling or heading off unfavorable rumors, stories, and events" (Kotler and Armstrong, 2010). Social media examples: company-created multimedia content (e.g., online videos, blogs, wikis, photos, book/product reviews, podcasts, answering questions on sites like Quora), social media press releases, viral videos and other content, social media events, participation in virtual worlds, live streaming, conversation/commenting on other people's content about brands, and social media apps for mobile phones.
- **Sales promotion:** "Short-term incentives to encourage the purchase or sale of a product or service" (Kotler and Armstrong, 2010). Social media examples: Groupon shared discounts, free sampling of digital products (e.g., music, software, research or news stories),

contests/sweepstakes, and games (e.g., advergames, where the product is featured in the game, can be a combination of advertising and sales promotion).

- **Direct marketing:**

    Direct marketing is an interactive process of addressable communication that uses one or more . . . media to effect, at any location, a measurable sale, lead, retail purchase, or charitable donation, with this activity analyzed on a database for the development of ongoing mutually beneficial relationships between marketers and customers, prospects, or donors.

    ("The Power of Direct Marketing", 2011–2012)

    Social media examples: the entire internet and social media might be considered direct marketing; however, specific examples falling only in this category include e-mail and text messaging with offers from companies, behavioral targeting (displaying ads based on user behavior online), location-based systems (such as Foursquare), and RSS feeds of content to individuals opting for it.

- **Personal selling:** "Personal interactions between a customer's and the firm's sales force for the purpose of making sales and building customer relationships" (Kotler and Armstrong, 2010). We extend this definition to the internet by noting that the 1:1 interaction can also be done online and not only in person. Social media examples: Chat bots that allow for conversation on a Web site (also called virtual agents/assistants) and sales lead generation tools.

In general, marketers have the least control over the advertising tool because they are placing messages in someone else's media platform, and the medium will have technical, legal, content, and ad-size requirements. In addition, companies must develop the advertising content and also pay for the space, whereas the other tools only require staff time or technology costs to develop the content. Also, note that marketers combine many of these tools for increased marketing effectiveness, such as when an advertisement carries a sales promotion discount offer or links to public relations content (such as a video). For example, an ad intended to build awareness of a new product will more likely compel users to purchase if the ad also carries a Web address to the product page and a limited time discount offer.

MarCom tools have been used for decades in traditional media (such as television, radio, magazines, newspapers, and outdoor spaces), but social media opportunities are really pushing marketers to redefine tactics. They still constantly use these tools; however, this way of organizing marketing communication no longer works well due to the incredible amount of digital media available that use creative technologies. Thus, marketers often discuss IMC in one of the following ways:

- **Senders and recipients.** Communication from a single marketer to a single recipient is "1 to 1," as can occur with personal selling, database marketing, and some direct marketing tactics; "**1 to many**" occurs when a single marketer sends communication to many people at once, such as with traditional television advertising, sales promotion coupons, or public relations events; and "**many to many**" occurs when consumers talk in social media to each other.
- **Media type.** Marketers speak of traditional media (television, radio, newspapers, outdoor, and so forth), new media (internet), and social media (such as social networks).
- **Owned, paid, and earned media**. This system depends on who is communicating and who owns the medium (the company owns the medium or pays for space elsewhere, or others talk about the company in social media and elsewhere). Recent trends reveal that many marketers are moving to this way of organizing, understanding, and selecting marketing communication goals and tactics. Therefore, we follow suit and organize this and the next two chapters using this system.

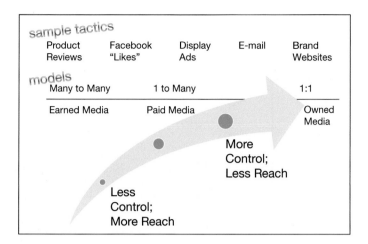

sample tactics

| Product Reviews | Facebook "Likes" | Display Ads | E-mail | Brand Websites |

models

Many to Many   1 to Many   1:1

Earned Media   Paid Media   Owned Media

More Control; Less Reach

Less Control; More Reach

Exhibit 12.2 Marketer's Control and Reach with Sample IMC Tactics and Models

One difficulty now facing marketers is how to retain control over brand images in light of social media, the amount of user control online, and the degree of trust consumers have in one another (and not in companies). The answer is that they cannot. Instead, companies can use the brand website, blogs (owned media), display ads on websites (paid media), and many social media to tell the company story; then they must monitor the internet for conversations about their brands (earned media), responding when appropriate. See Exhibit 12.2 for the varying degrees of control and audience reach marketers have over messages using various communication models and example tactics, previously discussed.

Owned, Paid, and Earned Media

The term "media" formerly meant only traditional media. Now the definition is more general: **communications media** are communication channels used to disseminate news, information, entertainment, and promotional messages. Digital media can take many different forms including text, images, GIFs, audio, or video. Examples include online video, a product review site, the online newspaper, a mobile phone app, and e-mail. Even word-of-mouth communication can be considered media (yes, your mouth or fingers on the keyboard). **Social media** are one media type with one differentiating characteristic: they blend technology and social interactions for the co-creation of content and value. That is, people use them for social interactions and conversations. In this definition, "people" collectively refers to organizations, their employees, customers, and prospects, and the general population of internet users.

For disseminating content, media can be either paid or free. By "free," we mean that marketers do not have to pay for the space to run their message, but they do often have to pay for technology, software, hardware, and an employee as well as other costs related to producing or distributing the communication piece.

Digital media can be classified into three categories, as previously mentioned (Exhibit 12.3):

- **Owned media** carry communication messages from the organization to internet users on channels that are owned and thus at least partially controlled by the company. Owned media offline include company brochures, catalogs, signs, promotional items (e.g., branded pens), and more.

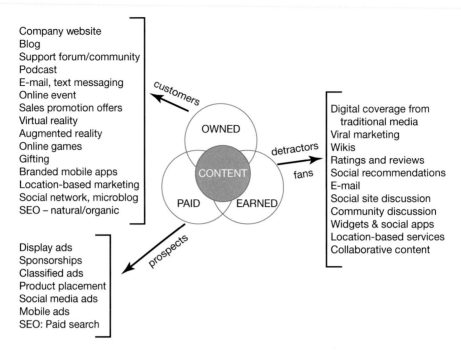

Company website
Blog
Support forum/community
Podcast
E-mail, text messaging
Online event
Sales promotion offers
Virtual reality
Augmented reality
Online games
Gifting
Branded mobile apps
Location-based marketing
Social network, microblog
SEO – natural/organic

Display ads
Sponsorships
Classified ads
Product placement
Social media ads
Mobile ads
SEO: Paid search

customers

OWNED

detractors

CONTENT

fans

PAID   EARNED

prospects

Digital coverage from
   traditional media
Viral marketing
Wikis
Ratings and reviews
Social recommendations
E-mail
Social site discussion
Community discussion
Widgets & social apps
Location-based services
Collaborative content

Exhibit 12.3 Owned, Paid, and Earned Media are All Content Driven

- **Paid media** are properties owned by others who are paid by the organization to carry its promotional messages (e.g., advertising). The company controls the content; however, the media have content and technical requirements to which the advertisers must adhere (thus, less control than owned media). Paid media offline include traditional advertising in magazines, newspapers, television, radio, outdoors, cinema, stores, and more.
- **Earned media** are when individual conversations become the channel: messages about a company that are generated by social media authors (such as bloggers), by traditional journalists on media websites, and by internet users who share opinions, experiences, insights, and perceptions on Web sites and mobile applications. This is sometimes also called user-generated media (UGM) or user-generated content (UGC). Offline, earned media includes word of mouth and stories about the company or brands in traditional media. Companies have the least amount of control over this media channel; however, they respond to customer conversation and try to guide it toward their positive brand messages.

IMC campaigns will have both owned and paid media components as their foundation in order to achieve earned media objectives—such as a YouTube video it creates (owned) and an ad on Facebook (paid). These, in turn, will help motivate earned media components, such as when consumers comment on the videos or pass the video link along on their Facebook accounts and other media (earned). If the video becomes hugely popular, bloggers and traditional journalists might discuss it (earned). Exhibit 12.4 displays this phenomenon.

You will read about owned media in this chapter, paid in Chapter 13, and earned in Chapter 14. Note that many new social and other high-tech media techniques do not fit well into traditional marketing communication tools; thus, this is a more inclusive way to organize the

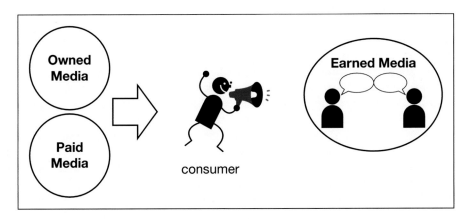

Exhibit 12.4 Owned and Paid Media Drive Earned Media

IMC field. Also, many of the traditional IMC tools are used in more than one of the three types of media.

Owned Media

In this chapter, we will discuss some of the digital marketing media channels that are fully or partially controlled by the organizations who create the lion's share of the multimedia content. For example, a company's website and e-mail are totally controlled by the company, but its Facebook page and many other tactics are conducted on "borrowed server space." This means that some company owned media take place on someone else's site, so there are more rules and requirements. Regardless, the primary goals are (1) to engage consumers with the positive brand content; (2) to entice them to pass this content along to others (earned media); and (3) to exercise CRM (customer relationship management)—all of these goals attempt to increase commerce for brand-related companies (initial and repeat purchases). Companies often inform consumers about products and sales promotion offers using some of these channels (such as discount offers, contests/sweepstakes, or free product samples) as well. Marketers use all traditional IMC tools for owned media except for advertising (paid media).

It all begins with the content produced and distributed by companies online.

Content Marketing

Content marketing is a strategy involving creating and publishing content on websites and in social media. This is an interesting trend in which companies are organizing themselves as media publishers online. Marketers have long created content offline when they create paper flyers, newsletters, brochures, catalogs, infomercials, and promotional videos ("interrupt" marketing). What is new is that marketers now use digital content as inbound marketing that attracts customers and prospects. It is about having content available to inform, entertain and engage users when they seek the company—and most internet users in both B2B and B2C markets do searches and come across this material when shopping. For example, instead of placing a banner ad that might receive as little as 0.5 percent click-through, *Will It Blend?* created video content that entertained, engaged, and enticed users to visit Blendtec's company website to learn more.

All owned media can be considered content marketing. However, now many marketers see themselves as publishers online and organize internally to include a content manager and staff with journalism or multimedia production experience. This is important and the largest expense because content needs to be fresh online. There are way too many companies with out-of-date websites, Facebook pages, and infrequent posts on blogs and Twitter.

Some companies publish small items, such as videos, press releases and blog posts. Others create lengthy white papers, infographics, and digital books. For example, we received e-mails about white papers on various digital marketing topics and clicked through to download the paper as research for writing this book. This is quite common for getting sales leads in the B2B market, thus adding prospects to the purchase funnel. See Exhibit 12.5 for a sample form used to collect contact information from prospects who want to download a free report. This tactic generates leads for the personal selling function.

As with all IMC, companies need to understand their goals and markets and decide whether their content needs to be entertaining, educational, or provide some utility, such as an interest rate or shipping price calculator. For example, RVShare provides information on RV rentals. Functioning similarly to Airbnb, the site allows users to compare rental options and book directly from RV owners.

Note that companies can monetize their owned media content in three important ways. First, they can sell digital content on their media properties, such as white papers, music, software, or online Webinars (or many other products). Second, they can accept Google's Ad Sense or other types of ads and receive payment when users click on these ads. These ads can appear on a company's own website or blog and also in multimedia content it uploads elsewhere, such as ads shown in its own YouTube videos (in this case, the company shares revenue with the site owner, YouTube). The third way is to become an affiliate of another website, such as Amazon, or subscribe to content delivered on its properties through application programming interfaces (APIs). A company receives revenue when users click on a book or other product featured on its blog or other social media property and subsequently purchase it on Amazon. The business models discussed in previous chapters outline many other ways to monetize owned media.

Next, we present some of the most used owned media.

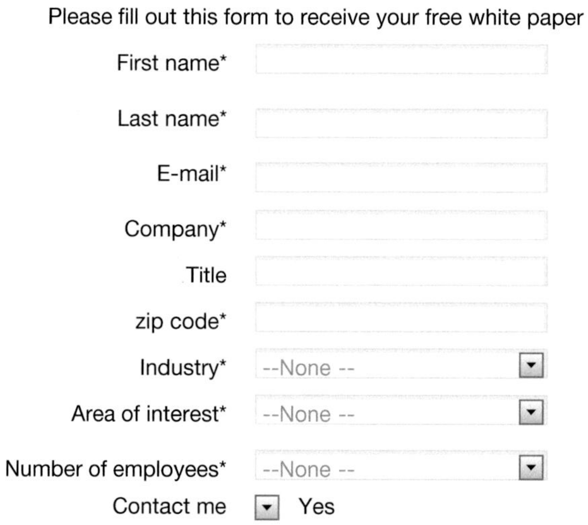

Please fill out this form to receive your free white paper

First name*

Last name*

E-mail*

Company*

Title

zip code*

Industry*   --None --

Area of interest*   --None --

Number of employees*   --None --

Contact me   Yes

Exhibit 12.5 Example Lead Generation Form

Website

Marketing public relations (MPR) includes brand-related activities and nonpaid, third-party media coverage to positively influence target markets. Thus, MPR is the marketing department's portion of PR directed to the firm's customers and prospects in order to build awareness and positive attitudes about its brands. Blendtec's *Will It Blend?* videos did a brilliant job using MPR with its owned content. MPR activities using internet technology include the website content itself, online events, and many other digital tactics discussed in this chapter.

According to one estimate, there were more than 1.8 billion websites in 2021, according to InternetLiveStats.com. Every organization, company, individual, or brand website is an MPR tool because it serves primarily as an electronic brochure, including current product and company information. In Chapter 7, you learned that most internet users purchase online and even more use the internet to gather information before shopping either online or offline. This underlines the importance of the company website and its tactics to be found via search engines. The website is far from dead, as some suggest. For example, Butterball's site (www. butterball.com), which features cooking and carving tips, can receive hundreds of thousands of visitors in one day during Thanksgiving week. Although it costs the firm money to create such a website, it is not considered advertising (paid-for space on another firm's site).

Several advantages come with using the Web for publishing product information. First, the Web is a low-cost alternative to paper brochures or press releases sent in overnight mail. Second, product information is often updated in company databases, so webpage content can be updated more easily. Finally, the Web can reach new prospects who are searching for particular products (inbound marketing). Many books and blogs discuss how to create effective websites—thus, the topic is beyond the scope of this book. The most important point is to create a site that satisfies the firm's target audiences better than the competition and to keep populating it with current content. Websites can entertain (games and media), build communities (online events, social media), provide a communication channel with the customer (customer feedback, forums, and customer service), provide information (product selection and purchase, product recommendation, retailer referrals), and assist in many other ways.

The website is a door into a company, and must provide inviting, organized, and relevant content. Exhibit 12.6 shows the Hobby Lobby home page, with a good navigation system to browse the store, see a weekly ad, or find DIY projects of interest. The departments of this retailer are organized in a clean way to help navigate through the thousands of products available for purchase in a simple way.

Microsites are websites designed for a narrow purpose, with only 3–5 pages. For example, WillitBlend.com (https://www.blendtec.com/pages/will-it-blend) is a microsite containing only the *Will It Blend?* videos. It also contains many social media hooks (such as an RSS subscription button). The company's main site is blendtec.com, and the microsite links to a store for blender purchase on the main site. However, many marketers have noticed that linking a microsite to the main company site dilutes its efforts to build a large presence on search engines (because Google sees them all as related and not separate sites warranting separate links on a search results page). Other examples of microsites include one for a specific model of automobile, individual television program, or contest site (such as "In an Absolut World").

Website Landing Pages

Landing pages are closely related to microsites because they are often stand-alone webpages. Unless headed to a particular website, most people begin their internet experience by typing keywords at Google or another search engine. Internet users also click-on ads, links in social

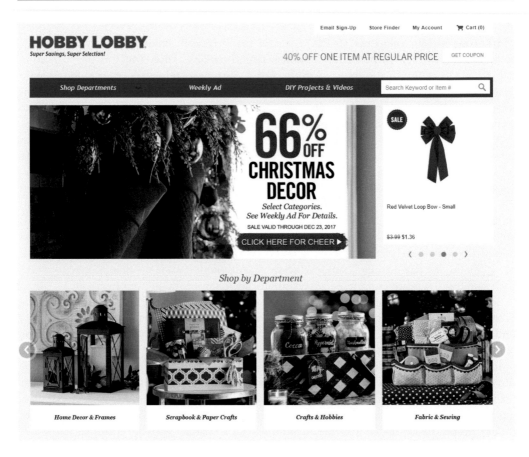

Exhibit 12.6 Hobby Lobby Home Page
Source: www.hobbylobby.com

media, e-mail links, and many other places seeded with links to company websites. A **landing page** is a unique page that appears after a user clicks on a link associated with a website. For example, if a user does a branded search for something like "Dell laptops," they will likely see the link to Dell.com/laptops, not the homepage. And below that in the Google search engine results page will be a series of other links, such as "Official Dell Coupons," "Bookmark Our Black Friday Site," "Small Office Laptop Deals," and more. Each of these links takes the user to a specific landing page appropriate to the headline. Similarly, if a user clicks on a Facebook ad for a special event, the page promoting that event will appear instead of the company home page.

The trend is for companies to create many different landing pages that match keywords, current special offers, ads, and more. These pages have attention-getting headlines that match the offer or keywords from the referring link. They also have specific images and copy on the page to match the source link and compelling words to move users to action (such as a purchase). This makes the page more relevant to the user versus linking to the generic home page.

A/B testing is when there are two versions of a webpage with similar content and images for testing which performs better. Companies conduct A/B tests on landing pages to be sure they optimize click-through rates and conversion to purchase. Some of the variations might include amount of text (heavy/light), animation versus static content, and various images (such as only the product or a person using the product). Sometime companies only change one element on the page so they will know for certain what caused the performance difference. When marketers use several different elements on the two pages, they will use multivariate testing to find statistical significance in the page differences (recall that multivariate testing is a comprehensive statistical test of more than one variable).

Companies often track landing pages at a much more detailed level, such as putting tracking links within the page to identify many other metrics. For example, they want to learn which page the customers came from prior to the landing page and where they go next (e.g., Expedia. com knows when you leave the site to check a specific airline site directly). Companies can also tell which areas of the page get more readership and how long people stay in a certain section before scrolling down. Interestingly, marketers can also gather data from mobile users, such as where they swipe or double finger to enlarge text and whether the user is viewing in portrait or landscape orientation.

CustomInk started selling custom T-shirts and hats in 2000. They are pros at landing pages, offering many different ones. They also change their home page quite often to optimize conversions, considering it a type of landing page. Exhibit 12.7 displays the CustomInk home page. Above the "fold" indicates the portion of content a user sees without scrolling down. The most important and compelling information should appear above the fold. The following is a description of various areas of CustomInk's website and how they are optimized (Exhibit 12.7):

1. Header
   - Anchor visitors with a strong logo and word-mark in the upper left; this image also doubles as a click-to-home from anywhere on the site.
   - Provide persistent links to functional site sections for returning customers and visitors such as, 'Retrieve your saved design' [this refers to the T-shirt designed by customer].
   - Prominent placement of our sales service phone number and chat service.
   - Persistent site navigation that allows users to browse quickly and efficiently.
2. Primary Messaging Area
   - Use of a rotator to communicate four core messages [rotator is an image or text that changes on each view or rotates while on the page].
   - Persistent strong Call-To-Action in a stand-out color from brand color palate.
   - Complimentary imagery/copy to communicate the offering in an impactful way.
3. Secondary Content Areas
   - Ensure that product content "peeks" above the fold as a cue that additional interesting information is only a scroll away
   - Make use of sidebar conventions to provide free shipping, pricing information and positive customer reviews for quick reference.
   - Include links to additional products and design ideas for SEO [search engine optimization] purposes.

Mobile Sites

The rapid growth of mobile internet access has marketers scrambling to create mobile versions of their websites. As of 2019, 94 percent of small businesses have mobile-friendly websites. Mobile sites are quicker to download, simpler, and focused on the key content. Adaptive design principles have helped firms build websites that automatically recognize what kind of device a user is accessing content from and scale content accordingly.

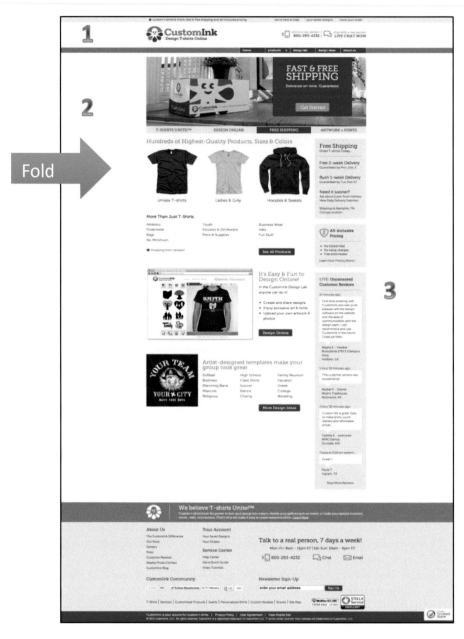

Exhibit 12.7 CustomInk Home Page Optimized for Best Results

Source: www.customink.com

Online Chat

One traditional IMC tool, personal selling, involves real-time conversation between a sales-person and customer, either face to face or with some technology mediator, such as the tele-phone or computer. Some companies provide real-time sales assistance online. Lands' End and many other companies have a live chat feature. Users can open it and ask questions about products in a real-time chat with a customer service representative. The rep can also push webpages directly to the customer so she can view the product and take the order during the chat session. With the growth in artificial intelligence (AI), automated **chat bots**, also called virtual agents, virtual assistants, and avatars, are becoming increasingly popular. These are automated figures that will answer many customer questions using a database of canned responses. The best chat bots utilize natural language processing to better serve information that is relevant to the person they are conversing with.

If you are having problems downloading a digital book at audible.com, you can chat with the customer service representative and get her technical assistance immediately. Or if you are looking for a particular clothing item on a site, you can chat and get help locating it on the site (they will send a link or display the page for you). According to Forbes, the average customer satisfaction rate for inquires handled via live chat is now more than 80 percent (Gingiss, 2019).

Blogs

Blogs (from the term *Web logs*) are websites where entries are listed in reverse chronological order and readers can comment on any entry. There are more than 600 million blogs in 2021, including those hosted on WordPress, Tumblr, and company websites. When blogs first emerged in 1999, it appeared that they contained irrelevant scribbling about miscellaneous personal topics and would probably not work their way into marketing strategy. How did this change? Marketers began paying attention to blogs because many people writing them had valuable things to say. For instance, Robert Scoble in the Microsoft marketing department wrote about his views on Microsoft's role in the industry—and competitors surely read his musings. Blogs are considered social media because of all the commenting done by blog readers (earned media).

Sometimes blogs are authored by many employees. For example, Engadget, a technology blog, offers many daily posts about new technologies, most by different authors. This blog is always listed in the top three of all blogs on Technorati because of its high readership and activity (with each post generating lots of comments) and high confidence ratings by users. It is helpful to have multiple blog authors to keep the posts frequent, as long as they all follow the goals and style of the blog. The Huffington Post is another extremely popular multi-author blog.

There are numerous types of blogs. In fact, many CEOs blog to put a personal face on their companies. When JetBlue had its huge weather-related crisis in February 2007, resulting in customers being stranded on the tarmac for hours and approximately 1,000 canceled flights in a five-day period, its then-CEO David Neeleman posted blog apologies and introduced the new company Bill of Rights. Walmart's newsroom (https://corporate.walmart.com/newsroom/) even featured CEO Doug McMillon's explanation why the legal name would change from Wal-Mart Stores to Walmart. Many consultants and thought leaders create blogs to disseminate their views and gain clients, promote books, and more. These outlets serve as a great way for experts and novices to showcase their knowledge and thoughts on a subject they have passion about.

Marketers also use blogs to draw users to their websites. For example, Dr. Pepper/Seven-Up once introduced a new flavored milk product with a blog written by a cow: Raging Cow Blog. Ghostwritten by six teenagers under the supervision of marketing staff, it sounded like a cow discussing her adventures as she traveled across country. It read like a travelogue written with a Generation Y attitude based on the product positioning: "a milk-based drink 'gone wild' because there are outrageous, intriguing and delicious flavor combinations." Within three weeks of the launch, 20,800 users logged on each day to read the crazy cow ramblings such as:

> Ho hee, we did it! Fate was on our side that night—the moon was in its final quarter (I hear a number of you asking, 'How would a cow know diddly about the phases of the moon?' Good question, but ever since that whole jumping over the moon incident, we cows and yonder moon have been TIGHT . . .).
>
> (Arnold, 2004)

This type of strategy can backfire, however. When Jim and Laura took their RV across country and camped in Walmart parking lots, they wrote a blog about it (any RV or trailer owner can spend the night for free at any Walmart). The blog gained many readers, but then a few questioned why all the reports of interactions with Walmart employees were so glowing—where were the criticisms? Finally, Laura was exposed as a freelance writer hired with Walmart funds to do the blog. This hurt Walmart's reputation. Online, transparency, authenticity, and consistency rule the day because if other bloggers discover corporate dishonesty, the entire blogosphere will be buzzing about it. Laura and Jim ended up returning the money they were paid and making a public apology.

The *Wall Street Journal* helps bloggers by sending an e-mail each day offering a link to a free online article (versus the normal subscription rate). It encourages bloggers to write their reactions to the article and link the blog to the *WSJ* website (earned media). The newspaper reports that the number of visits from blog sites is often as high as those from search engines.

There are many things to consider when companies want to start blogging, such as which platform to use, who will do the writing, how often will they post, and what the purpose of the blog is. For more details on starting a blog, we recommend *The Corporate Blogging Book* by Debbie Weil (Exhibit 12.8).

Exhibit 12.8 Consultant Debbie Weil's Blog About Corporate Blogging

Source: www.debbieweil.com

Finally, companies can become involved in blogs without starting their own. It is important to find influential bloggers in one's industry, follow their posts using RSS feeds, and add occasional comments. This keeps companies engaged in important conversations and projects them as experts in the industry. It is equally important because when they follow blogs through some automated monitoring system, as discussed in Chapter 6, they will discover a potentially reputation-damaging discussion when it breaks and can become involved in the discussion by telling their side of the story.

Support Forums/Communities

Companies create spaces for consumers, prospects, and business customers to discuss topics of interest, provide new product ideas, or seek company support with technical or product issues (among other goals). The discussion itself is earned media (Chapter 14), so here we just present a few principles for building a successful online community on a company website or other online property. It is not as simple as making a Facebook page and hoping folks will drop by—after all, marketers are competing with billions of other pages, groups, or events for viewer attention. As with most digital business strategies, research and planning precede success. Larry Weber (2007) suggests a seven-step program that works to this day:

1. *Observe.* Visit social media hangouts for users on the topics of interest in the industry of the company that wants to start a social media community.
2. *Recruit.* Find internet users who want to talk about the industry and recruit them for joining the new social media property.
3. *Evaluate platforms.* Decide whether the format should be a blog, pure online community, or social network.
4. *Engage.* Plan ways to get the community members to talk and upload content.
5. *Measure.* Identify metrics that will measure the success of the effort—for example, number of comments posted or number of members.
6. *Promote.* Plan ways to advertise or build a buzz in the social media and with search engines so the new community will attract users.
7. *Improve.* Use the metrics to continuously improve the community.

Note that many of these steps follow good CRM principles (see Chapter 15). For example, community members are more loyal because of the social bond they form with the company or the salesperson. Also, be authentic, honest, and transparent in all your posts; otherwise, you'll be found out, and it will create lots of negative conversation on social media.

Podcasts

A **podcast** is a digital media file available for download online to computers, music players, tablets, or smartphones. Podcasts began with purely audio files for the iPod and other MP3 players, but now users can download video podcasts ("vidcasts" or "videocasts") for use on many types of receiving appliances. The line between video podcasts and other online videos is quite fuzzy. Forty-eight million podcast episodes have been created (Winn, 2021), and an increase in hosting and authoring tools have provided consumers with a wide range of voices to hear from on a regular basis. Both Apple and Google have methods to subscribe to normal recordings, with Google's YouTube allowing subscriptions and Apple creating a podcast application for iOS devices.

E-Mail

Direct marketing includes such techniques as telemarketing, outgoing e-mail, and postal mail—of which catalog marketing is a big part. Due to the internet, paper-based direct marketing is declining rapidly. Targeted online ads and other forms of advertising and sales promotions that solicit a direct response are also considered direct marketing. For simplicity, and because e-mail is still so important, we focus our discussion of direct marketing communication on this application and its shorter offspring, **text messaging**—also called **short message services (SMS)**. In Chapter 15 we discuss the customer relationship-building implications of e-mail.

With billions of e-mail accounts worldwide and trillions of e-mails flying over the internet globally, it is still one of the internet's killer applications (royal.pingdom.com). E-mail remains the most important communication technique for building customer relationships, as evidenced by the 87 percent of marketers investing in e-mail campaigns (according to the Content Marketing Institute). What's more, e-mail is one of the most often-used marketing tactics in the B2B market and generally provides a good return on investment.

E-mail has not been replaced by RSS feeds, blogs, or social networking, in spite of the many people predicting its demise. Instead, marketers integrate e-mail with social media, as noted in Chapter 14. E-mail is still used to build a buzz about products. However, response rates for e-mail remain low in comparison to other IMC tactics, as shown in Exhibit 12.9. While direct mail response rates are higher, this tactic has declined over the past 20 years and maintains higher costs because of printing and postal charges.

E-mail has several advantages over postal direct mail. First, it requires no postage or printing charges. Second, e-mail offers an immediate and convenient avenue for direct response to Web and social media sites using hyperlinks. Third, and perhaps most important, e-mail can be

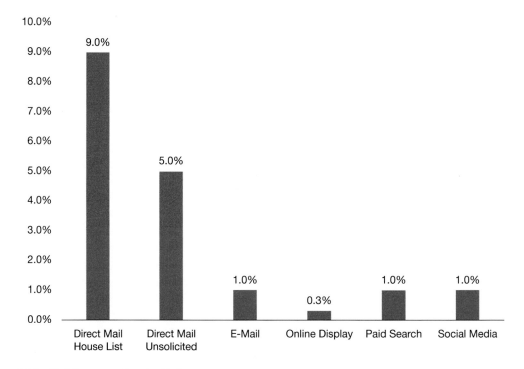

Exhibit 12.9 Response Rate by Media

Source: ANA/DMA 2018 Response Rate Report (2018)

automatically individualized to meet the needs of specific users—beyond just using a name in the e-mail. Similarly, marketers use e-mail for behavioral targeting. For example, an Expedia customer receives an e-mail about a particular travel destination after he or she searched flights on the website. Finally, e-mail is quicker than postal mail.

Conversely, e-mail must be delivered, opened, and acted upon in order to work. E-mail's disadvantages include the difficulty of making it though an ISP's **spam filters** (in 2004 AOL became famous for blocking nearly 80 percent of incoming e-mail). E-mail software, such as Microsoft Outlook, also uses spam filtering at the user's computer. According to several sources, 71 to 95 percent of e-mail worldwide is spam. Various estimates suggest that anywhere from 17 to 60 percent of legitimate e-mail is caught in spam filters. Inbox features like Focused inbox from Gmail and Clutter by Microsoft even begin to select what messages might be of importance to the reader if they make it through a spam filter. Consumers are much more upset about spam than they are about unsolicited postal mail and might not open anything looking like spam.

Then there is the difficulty in finding and maintaining appropriate e-mail lists. Lists can be built in any of three ways: (1) generated through website registrations, subscription registrations, or purchase records (the most responsive list members); (2) rented from a list broker; or (3) harvested from some newsgroup postings or online e-mail directories—though this practice is questionable for reasons to be mentioned shortly. Even though more than 4 billion consumers send or read e-mails worldwide (Chapter 7), at this time it is difficult to match a list of these e-mail addresses with individual customers and prospects in a firm's database unless the e-mail address owner supplies it, such as when ordering products online or signing up for e-mail announcements. And as soon as a good list exists, individuals often change their e-mail addresses—a problem because no forwarding system for abandoned e-mail addresses exists like the ones for telephone and postal addresses.

Digital marketers must remember that e-mail is not simply postal mail minus the paper and postage. E-mail offers the chance for real dialog with individual customers, as well as a way to develop broad and deep customer relationships instead of merely using it to acquire customers. Companies can use outgoing e-mail to make announcements, to send promotional offers, or to communicate anything important and relevant to stakeholders. When Amazon tested free shipping on orders over $49 in 2001 and over $25 in 2003, CEO Jeff Bezos sent a message to Amazon's customers informing them of the new offering. Microsoft e-mails registered users when new software patches are available for download. Some retail stores, like Home Depot, allow you to select e-mail as a method to receive a receipt for in-store purchases. Many firms send out periodic e-mail newsletters, an excellent tool for communicating with clients; small wonder that most US online customers enjoy receiving them. E-mail newsletters are a growth area because they provide many benefits:

- Regularly and legitimately promote the company name to clients.
- Personalize the communication with tailored content.
- Position the company as an expert in a subject.
- Point recipients back to the company website or social media properties.
- Make it easy for clients to pass along the information to others.
- Occasionally pay for themselves by carrying small advertisements.
- Engage consumers who might become future customers.

Permission Marketing: Opt-In, Opt-Out

When renting e-mail address lists from list brokers, marketers should search for lists that are guaranteed to be 100 percent opt-in. The opt-in qualification means that users have voluntarily given permission to receive commercial e-mail about topics of interest to them. Other types of lists are compiled from outside sources, such as public information—these recipients will not be as responsive to offers, so marketers are best advised to ignore an offer like this: "millions of e-mail addresses for $99." Brokers rent lists rather than sell them because they prefer to charge a fee for each mailing rather than give away the list for continuous use. The average cost to rent opt-in e-mail lists of consumers is $250 to $350 CPM (cost per thousand), according to Yahoo! Answers. Compare this rate to a typical B2C postal mail list rental at $100 CPM.

Web users have many opportunities to opt in to mailing lists at websites, often by simply checking a box and entering an e-mail address. Research shows that lists with opt-in members get much higher response than do lists without. Marketing messages to opt-in lists can generate response rates of up to 90 percent, because these are interested users. Opt-in lists may be successful in large part because users often receive coupons, cash, or products for responding.

When opting out, users have to uncheck the box on a webpage to prevent being put on the e-mail list. Some marketers question this practice because users do not always read a Web page thoroughly enough to evaluate the meaning of checked boxes and therefore may be surprised and upset at receiving e-mail later. Some US legislators have proposed laws banning opt-out e-mail.

Opt-in techniques are part of a marketing strategy called **permission marketing**—an opt-in form of marketing in which advertisers present marketing communication messages to consumers who agree to receive them. Permission marketing is about turning strangers into customers. How to make this conversion? Ask people what they are interested in, ask permission to send them information, and then do it in an entertaining, educational, or interesting manner (Godin, 1999).

Rules for Successful E-Mail Marketing

Knowing how to use e-mail that gets through spam filters, is opened by recipients, and is acted upon is as much science as art. Obviously, tactics vary by industry, but the following are some general guidelines:

- Use opt-in to build your lists, because your reputation for being customer oriented is more important than having a large list.
- Check your e-mail reputation to see if it will make it through ISP filters. Check e-mail blacklists and use a service such as Return Path's Sender Score Reputation Manager, which screens for 60 reputation variables.
- Use an e-mail address that is professional. Senders from Yahoo!, Hotmail, and even Gmail are more likely to be blocked than company or education e-mail addresses. For example, the best e-mail address is Firstname.Lastname@companyname.com or Firstname.Lastname@university.edu.
- Make it easy for users to unsubscribe via text link. This builds trust.
- Use microsegmentation, sending offers to smaller lists of relevant customers and personalizing them.
- A small improvement in creative layout and multimedia use in e-mail can make a big difference in terms of response rates. Test HTML e-mail approaches to see which pulls best for various offers.
- Give recipients plenty of opportunities to engage with the e-mail and act on the offer. High performing e-mails offer up to 11 links per message, according to Campaign Monitor.
- Use metrics to track the open rates, response rates, and return of investment (ROI). For instance, one author sent an e-mail to 178 recipients on an opt-in list using the Constant

Contact e-mail service. There were seven bounces for bad e-mail addresses (3.9%), one opt-out, 92 opens (53.8%), and 19 clicks on various links in the mail (20.7%). We can look to see exactly which recipients were in each category and who clicked on each link. Also, consider the cost of non-responses, which may contribute to lower brand equity if your mail is perceived as spam (and narrow the list afterward).

As previously mentioned, many organizations study effective e-mail marketing. They provide lots of advice about what works, considering everything from how to build the best opt-in list, to the creative look and subject lines, and to the unsubscribe webpage and how it might be used to build relationships. The previous list was just a sampling—much more information is available online for e-mail marketers.

Spam

Now for the dirty side of e-mail marketing. Internet users do not like unsolicited e-mail because it shifts the burden of selectivity from sender to recipient. Users developed the term *spam* as a pejorative reference to this type of e-mail. It was made illegal in the United States with the CAN-SPAM Act; however, thus far the act appears to have little ability to stop spam (see Chapter 5). Marketers must be careful, because viral marketing can work in reverse as well. Recipients of e-mail perceived as spam can vent their opposition to thousands of users in blogs, social networks, and friends on e-mail lists, thereby quickly generating negative publicity for the organization. To avoid this outcome, many companies post anti-spam policies on their websites (see Nike.com for a good example).

Spammers routinely harvest e-mail addresses from newsgroup/community postings and then spam all the newsgroup members. Spam lists can also be generated from public directories such as those provided by many universities to look up student e-mail addresses. Spammers often hide their return e-mail addresses so that the recipients cannot reply. Other unscrupulous tactics include spamming through a legitimate organization's e-mail server so that the message appears to come from an employee of that organization.

Incidentally, spam is a problem in the B2B market as well as the B2C market. Editorial staffs from the media complain about getting spam from public relations personnel at firms. Some measures have been put in place to limit spam. Many moderated groups filter spam and hide members' e-mail addresses in posts, and most e-mail programs offer users the option to filter spam as well. Also, a number of suits filed by ISPs seek to recover costs from spammers for the strain on their systems from the tremendous number of spam messages. Remember that all unsolicited e-mail is considered spam; still, as with direct mail, when the e-mail is appropriate and useful to the recipient, it is often welcomed, unsolicited or not.

It is increasingly common for opt-in lists to remind users that they are not being spammed. Usually, a disclaimer appears right at the beginning of the message, "You are receiving this message because you requested to be notified about . . ." The message also advises users how they can easily unsubscribe from the list. This notification is important because many users do not realize that they opted in—especially if they did so far in the past or in an unrelated context.

Privacy

Databases drive e-mail marketing. Such a database requires collecting personal information, both online and offline, and using it to send commercial e-mail, customized webpages, display ads, and more. Astute marketers have found that consumers will readily give personal information to firms that use it to provide value and that do not share it with others unless given permission. For example, Amazon.com has implicit permission to collect customers' purchase information in the database and serve it collectively to others looking for book recommendations. Users don't mind this service because they receive valuable information, and their privacy is guarded on an individual level. Amazon also has permission to send customers e-mail notification about books that might interest each individual. When Amazon announced that it would share customer databases with partners, it faced a huge media backlash. This reaction proves, once again, that firms desiring to build customer relationships must guard the privacy of customer data. Note that internet privacy protection is much stricter in Europe. Most European countries have much stricter regulations that protect any use of personal data by internet companies, including e-mail addresses. For example, Germany has strict laws about posting photos of others on social media websites without their permission.

The use of spyware for gathering information from personal computers is also a huge privacy issue (see the "Let's Get Technical" box on spyware). User privacy was discussed more thoroughly in Chapter 5.

Let's Get Technical—Spyware

A goofy-looking purple gorilla keeps popping up on your screen, and you do not know where it came from. Its prevalence and persistence are getting on your nerves. However, it is potentially performing much more damage behind the scenes. The purple gorilla is part of a spyware program known as Bonzi Buddy, which can broadcast your personal information onto the internet. But just how do you get rid of the pesky guy?

As far too many internet users have experienced, spyware is everywhere on the net. Any type of program that is downloaded to your computer that collects information about you can be considered spyware. Spyware can be downloaded and installed on your computer without you ever knowing, and it can also transmit the information it collects about you to a third party without being detected. For example, common spyware programs send a list of the MP3s on your computer or a list of the websites you recently visited. They can also send the contents of your address book or password and banking information.

Spyware programs that collect information about your surfing habits to feed you with focused advertisements are often considered adware. Spyware programs that perform malicious activity, such as retrieving your bank account number, are called malware. The information that is collected is stored in large databases. Adware is extremely common online (such as Google's network), and a website owner can distribute it to visitors in order to track their viewing habits and preferences. Although website owners and developers can use this information to make sites more in tune with customer preferences, they are more interested in this information because of its ability to sell advertising space.

Website owners can obtain the adware software from media networks. The purpose of media network companies is to track and record the behavior of online consumers. The information is stored in large databases and is used to target consumers. When you visit a site that is associated with the media network, the adware is downloaded and starts monitoring your internet usage. As it records your usage, it can determine certain demographic information about you. For example, if you visit babystyle.com, it might infer that you are a new parent or grandparent. Media networks lease the advertising space on websites and, in turn, sell it to advertisers. The media network then uses your profile to provide targeted advertisements the next time you visit a site in its association, such as a banner ad sold to a diaper company. When advertisers purchase ads from the media network, they are guaranteed a certain number of impressions, or the number of times their ad is displayed on a user's page.

In order for spyware to infect a computer, the computer user must visit a website that has the spyware program embedded in the programming code for the website. Spyware can also be triggered accidentally by the user when installing a regular program that is infested with spyware.

The origin of spyware is actually cookies, which are small files downloaded to and stored on the user's computer. Cookies were used by Web developers to collect usability information and were generally harmless. For example, sites that recognize who you are when you visit them most likely stored a cookie on your computer and read it upon your return to the site. The user could use his or her browser's settings to accept or reject cookies.

Today's spyware can be extremely dangerous because the information collected can end up anywhere. Spyware can also do any of the following:

- Flood your computer with pop-up advertisements.
- Send spam to your e-mail inbox.
- Slow down your internet connection speed.
- Slow down your computer's performance.
- Crash your computer.

Thousands of different spyware programs exist online. Names of software to watch out for include: CoolWebSearch (CWS), Gator (GAIN), 180search Assistant, ISTbar/AUpdate, Transponder (vx2), Internet Optimizer, BlazeFind, and Hot as Hell.

Web browsers such as Google Chrome protect against spyware by warning users when they click on a link that may lead to danger. Chrome then offers the option to return to safety—you should take that option!

Software that specifically finds and removes spyware should be installed on all computers that are connected to the internet. Some antivirus software companies have developed product line extensions to handle spyware. Popular and reliable anti-spyware programs include SUPERAntiSpyware, SpywareBlaster, and Spybot. Microsoft offers a free anti-spyware program, Windows Defender, built into its Windows 10 operating system. Similarly, Apple offers XProtect built into its OSX operating system. The advantage of the built-in products is that they are less likely to slow down your system. If you keep these products fresh by regularly installing Windows 10 or OSX updates, then you'll protect your system even more. Both operating systems allow you to automatically update—which is the best way to go. Do you need additional protection? It depends on how savvy you are. If you are really careful, then maybe not.

The same remarks apply to your mobile device. You should install updates as soon as they become available. The best way to do this is to turn on automatic updating. This convenient feature will normally update at night while you are sleeping so that you do not lose productivity. Keep in mind that Google (Android) and Apple (iOS) are as annoyed by viruses as you are since they tarnish their brand image. They will push out new updates to their systems as soon as they discover threats.

Messaging

Short message services (SMS) are up to 160 characters of text sent by one user to another over the internet, usually with a cell phone or smartphone. Twitter messages are similar; however, they are 280 characters in length and sent via mobile phone to the Twitter.com site instead of exchanged between phones. In the United States, SMS is usually commonly known as **text messaging** and is used by a majority of mobile phone users. It is different from **instant messaging (IM)**—short messages sent among users who are online at the same time. IM and SMS are also referred to in some circles as messaging, especially with the "always on" status of mobile devices. Apple's iMessage works in different ways than regular IM or SMS, which enables it to act as a platform to send SMS messages to Android users but more sophisticated attachments to other Apple users. Messaging is used both by consumers and employees (who have a quick question needing attention). Most commercial use of messaging applications today involves the ads delivered to user screens as they send messages to one another.

Messaging applications differ from e-mail because users can receive the messages instantly and inexpensively on mobile phones. SMS uses a store-and-send technology that holds messages for only a few days. Accessing SMS is easy because users do not have to open e-mail or other software to send or receive. Instead, they simply type the message on the phone keyboard. In Japan, consumers are reportedly so adept at this that they have created what is called the "thumb culture" (because they rapidly type out messages using their thumbs), and now this culture has spread worldwide. General messaging applications, on the other hand, host a wider variety of features and functions. Apple's iMessage has its own specific app store to download applications, stickers, and more. You can even send money through iMessage to other users.

How can marketers capitalize on messaging use? Most experts agree that marketers can build relationships by sending permission-based information to customers when and where they want to receive it. To be successful, the messages should be short, personalized, interactive, and relevant. Some customers might want to receive an SMS warning about pending natural disasters from their insurance firm, an SMS notification of an upcoming flight delay, or notification of an overnight shipment. Travelers receive a text message warning when their cell phone is connecting to an expensive network abroad. Shoppers at local retail stores may opt-in to receive coupons sent to their phone.

In one interesting example, Heineken, the global beer brand, used an SMS sales promotion to capitalize on the British pub tradition of quiz nights. Typically, a quiz night consists of a loyal pub customer shouting out a series of questions that other customers answer on paper score sheets. Winners receive free pints or meals. Using a combination of online and offline promotion, Heineken placed point-of-purchase signs in pubs inviting customers to call a phone number from cell phones or other mobile devices and type in the word *play* as a text message (SMS). In response, the customer received a series of three multiple-choice questions to answer. Correctly answering all the questions scored a food or beverage prize to be redeemed by giving a special verifiable number to the bartender—and 20 percent of all players won. "Feedback was that it was a great promotion . . . consumers found it fun and sellers found it to be a hook," said Iain Newell, marketing controller at Interbrew, which owns the Heineken brand.

Online Events

Online events are designed to generate user brand interest, draw traffic to a site or generate revenue with paid admission. Perhaps the most memorable early commercial online event occurred in 1999 when Victoria's Secret held a Web-based live fashion show. The company announced it in advertisements in *The New York Times*, Super Bowl football game, and other traditional media. The event drew 1.2 million visitors, an 82 percent increase in Web traffic, and the firm's Web servers went down because they could not handle all the traffic.

Companies and organizations can hold seminars (usually called "Webinars"), workshops, and discussions online. Holding online events in which clients get to "talk to" senior or prestigious people may be seen as one more valuable reason for being a client of a particular organization. It also saves considerable time and cost compared to holding or attending a physical seminar. Also, when businesspeople attend online webinars, they register, creating leads for personal selling.

Live streaming is a popular method to include viewers all around the globe as part of the event. Most of the major social media platforms offer the capability to host and be a part of such events.

Meetup.com users form special interest groups by location and then arrange offline meetings. Local residents can post to a calendar in Meetup.com that is searchable by local area. Facebook and Evite.com allow individuals to create events, such as a party, and invite a list of people via e-mail. The invitees can respond with a "yes," "no," or "maybe" and post a comment.

Sales Promotion Offers

Online sales promotion tactics can build brands, build databases, and support increased online or offline sales, but like offline promotions, most do not help to build customer relationships in the long term. Online sales promotion works, especially to entice consumers to change their behavior in the short term (e.g., visit a website, register online, purchase in the next week). Marketers report three to five times higher response rates with online promotions than with direct postal mail. Whereas most offline sales promotion tactics are directed to businesses in the distribution channel, online tactics are directed primarily at consumers—with the exception of Webinars, as previously mentioned. As with offline consumer sales promotions, many are used in combination with advertising. Sales promotions are popular display ad content. Sales promotion activities include coupons, discounts, rebates, product sampling, contests, sweepstakes, and premiums (free or low-cost gifts). Of these promotion types, only coupons, sampling, discounts, and contests/sweepstakes are widely used on the internet.

Coupons and Promo Codes

Online coupons had great promise in the internet's early days but did not gain widespread acceptance until the economy declined in the United States. According to one estimate, 31 billion digital coupons were redeemed in 2019 (Saleh, 2021). Incidentally, those who like digital coupons prefer getting them via e-mail. Promo codes are a popular method to entice users to sign up for e-mails from an organization. It is not uncommon for Expedia to send out promo codes via e-mail to users to book their next trip.

Sampling

Some sites allow users to sample digital products prior to purchase. Many software companies provide free download of fully functional demo versions of their software. The demo normally expires in 30 to 60 days, after which time users can choose to purchase the software or remove it from their system. Online music stores allow customers to sample short clips of music before downloading the song or ordering the album. Market research firms often offer survey results as a sampling to entice businesses to purchase reports. For example, comScore Media Metrix posts the results of its monthly survey of top websites for prospects to see and use and thus perhaps discover a need to purchase more in-depth data.

Contests and Sweepstakes

Many sites hold contests and sweepstakes to draw traffic and keep users returning. Contests require skill (e.g., trivia answer or photo upload), whereas sweepstakes involve only a pure chance drawing for the winners. Just as in the brick-and-mortar world, these sales promotion activities create excitement about brands and entice customers to visit a retailer. They persuade users to move from page to page on a website, thus increasing the length of time on a site (called site "stickiness"). If sweepstake offers are changed regularly, users will return to the site to check out the latest chance to win.

Virtual Worlds, Virtual Reality, and Augmented Reality

These are sites where users take the form of avatars and socialize in an online space of their own making. Companies create a presence in metaverses, such as Second Life, or create their own virtual world to support commerce, such as Webkinz—where children enter a key code from a stuffed Webkinz animal they purchased at a brick-and-mortar retailer, then create a life online for their animal while connecting with others doing the same (see webkinz.com). In Second Life, companies can create a virtual storefront, multimedia event or talk/lecture, or contest, and can also create blogs. Finally, some companies use their avatars as promotional vehicles, engaging other avatars in conversation about the brand and offering sales promotions, such as coupons. For example, the Nesquik Bunny avatar hops around Second Life, attending various events. Companies can also build virtual reality simulations and augmented reality applications much easier now that technology has started to proliferate to consumers. Apple even offers a specific developer kit to help businesses get started with augmented reality.

Online Games

Games can be played on special consoles (like Xbox and PlayStation), mobile devices, laptops, smart TVs, and virtually any other device. The mobile gaming landscape has exploded in popularity. **Advergames** combine online advertising and gaming, featuring a company's product. They are used to draw site traffic and build brands in both business-to-business (B2B) and business-to-customer (B2C) markets and are growing in popularity online. For instance, consumers can test drive a Toyota online or play any number of exciting games at the Nickelodeon website. Advergames are unabashedly commercial by nature, but if they are fun and exciting, players will enjoy them and tell their friends. The advergame is an important tactic that acknowledges the consumer's increasing power by engaging users with entertaining product-related content.

Online Gifting

JibJab allows users to create videos and eCards using images of friends or family. Consumers upload a headshot from their computers and drag it into the hilarious and charming videos, then send the link to the person in the headshot or post it on a social network. These can quickly become viral, and more people visit the site to pay $18 a year to make more eCards and videos (see jibjab.com). Online gifting doesn't even have to be personal, as it is simple to e-mail a gift card code to a receiver from many online retailers.

Branded Mobile Apps

Many companies create branded mobile applications that support social interactions and user contributions because mobile users spend 92 percent of their time using apps ("Digital 2021: Global Overview Report", 2021). Part of this growth is based on the growth of easy-to-use frameworks to build applications with little skill. Platforms like Bubble allow for the creation of basic applications without major development costs, although such applications are not very advanced.

QR Codes and Mobile Tags

QR codes are barcodes that appear as many black modules in a small square white background (see Exhibit 12.10). These barcodes were first developed for the automobile industry in 1994 to track inventory; however, they are now an extension of offline paid media that engages internet users. Consumers who have the mobile tag reader application can scan a QR code appearing in a print or outdoor advertisement by taking a picture or scanning with their phones. QR codes now appear nearly everywhere, from business cards to restaurant menus. They were particularly popular during the COVID-19 pandemic since they allowed customers to bring up their own copy of the menu untouched by anyone else.

Location-Based Marketing

Location-based marketing is growing rapidly due to the use of GPS tags in mobile applications on user devices. A few marketers have experimented with location-based marketing, including promotional offers that are pushed to mobile devices and customized based on the user's physical location. GPS data can also provide relevant information related to search queries typed into search engines and also powers voice assistants to give recommendations to businesses that are nearby. The Sam's Club Scan & Go app is offered by Sam's Club to allow users to scan items they put into their cart, pay, and leave the store without going to a checkout line. An employee scans a code for the receipt as you leave the store. Location services allow the application to ensure you are in the correct store and have the most up to date information.

Social Networks

Social networks are nodes of individuals or organizations that are connected based on common values, ideas, friendships, and so forth. They are based on the idea of six degrees of

Exhibit 12.10 QR Code to Digital Marketing Textbook

separation—that each individual is connected to every other individual in the network by up to six other people. If you join LinkedIn, a business network, you might be only six contacts away from the CEO of a Fortune 100 company. All it takes is introductions from the individuals between you and him. Social networks come in both business and personal varieties, but the lines are blurring as businesses build a presence where customers and prospects hang out.

Because today's customer researches brands online and learns about products from other customers in social media, businesses want to join in and influence the conversations—or start them when launching a new product. Social networks are one good place to do that, as long as marketers realize that they are not purely for selling but instead for communicating with and learning from users. Ninety percent of companies with over 100 employees participate in social media, according to an eMarketer.com estimate. Facebook is the giant, with over 2.8 billion users in 2021 (according to Statista). YouTube is next with more than 2 billion users who watch over 1 billion hours of video each day, with 70 percent occurring on mobile devices (see Digital, 2021 Global Overview Report).

There are many books and articles written about how companies build a successful social network presence. We've already discussed several ideas in previous chapters, and Chapter 14 discusses the earned media aspect: "likes," comments and sharing by fans and followers. Suffice it to say here that top performing company Facebook pages are those that build fan numbers by engaging users in compelling ways:

- Update the page often so there is a reason for fans to return frequently, but keep it consistent to the brand image.
- Include compelling activities (such as games, polls. and contests).
- Add attention-getting content to the timeline (e.g., videos, commercials, event announcements, status updates. and consumer-uploaded content.
- Use clear calls to action (such as "like us" or "visit our website").
- Post frequently to maintain the conversation with fans. It is about being social and fun to make the brand likable.
- Listen carefully to the comments that can help the brand improve.
- Use Facebook Audience Insights, a free service that allows companies to monitor page and app activity. Use this to keep improving the content so it is more engaging.

It is not only about inbound marketing. Ads and other paid promotions can also drive people to the social network pages (discussed in Chapter 13).

It is informative to learn from the companies that are the most successful at gathering Facebook fans and "likes." The Facebook page with the most fans in 2021 is the Facebook App page, with more than 209 million fans.

Some social networks are also called microblogs. These are blogs that hold micro content—very small posts, such as a hyperlink, image, or sentence comment. Tumblr.com offers free micro content blogs: "To make a simple analogy: If blogs are journals, tumblelogs are scrapbooks," according to Tumblr. Users can form groups or follow each other's frequently updated posts. Twitter is an even smaller mini blog, formed around the question: "What are you doing right now?" Members send text messages of up to 280 characters that post to their Twitter account. Friends follow each other's tweets either on computers or via various apps connected to Twitter.

How do businesses use Twitter? @Moonpie answers serious customer questions about the snack but also displays quite the lively side. Wendy's tweets about new products and helps direct customer service questions. Their answer to one user ended up being the most retweeted tweet of all time after Wendy's suggested 18 million retweets would garner @carterjwm free chicken nuggets for a year (they gave him a year's supply after 3.5 million retweets). Many executives use Twitter to talk about what is happening in the company and gain feedback and ideas from followers. Companies can tweet about their business and product offerings, announce sales promotions, and entice Twitter followers (as well as their own followers) to visit the virtual or brick and mortar store. For example, Virgin American gave away free flights to users with large numbers of followers to entice talk about the company's new Toronto, Canada, route.

It is extremely important to send interesting and informational posts on a microblog and not use a "hard sell" as the major topic of the tweet. People on Twitter want to know "What are you doing?" and "What can you tell me?" NOT "What are you selling?" A smart marketer will conceal the promotional message in the post or comment, such as when someone with a lot of followers gets paid to tweet where she is going to eat. A smart marketer will present himself as a subject area expert who happens to work at a particular company in the field. Twitter is cost effective for replacing other customer touch points, such as direct mail, trade shows, and paper newsletters.

Coordinating Internet and Traditional Media IMC Plans

A primary goal of marketers has always been to become monomaniacally customer driven and build long-term relationships that bring revenue to the company. Some owned and paid media do not allow for social interactions, such as some traditional websites or online ads. Traditional marketing communication media only allow one-way communication, yet these are still important for building brand awareness (e.g., an ad in the Super Bowl that reaches 60 percent of the population), creating desire and interest, and moving prospects and customers to purchase (e.g., a coupon or calendar event listing in the Sunday print newspaper). Yet marketing is moving more to the concept of inbound marketing, as mentioned in Chapter 1, because it entices customers and earns their attention.

Today, marketers face a mashup of owned, paid and earned media that can carry the promotional tools of advertising, sales promotion, direct marketing, public relations, and personal selling. The guiding force for selecting appropriate tools and media is the communication objectives in desired target markets. For example, if a company's goal is to sell its new software package to accountants, it could do any of the following: (1) use PR by describing the software on its own website and with a social media press release, (2) use Twitter to talk about software needs in the industry and offer codes for free sample downloads (sales promotion), (3) include recommendations from current customers on a LinkedIn page, (4) upload a video demonstration with software tutorials, or (5) advertise in a traditional print accounting industry magazine and on the industry's website (including testimonials from the LinkedIn pages). All this could direct prospects to a website where they can download a free sample and purchase it after a 30-day trial. This would be much more effective than giving away free iPads on Facebook because that tactic does not align with the campaign goals or target market.

There are many other tactical ways to integrate marketing communications media, and they primarily involve providing links to all the Web and social media sites in all promotional media and integrating positive conversation into various appropriate media.

The main thing to remember is that the traditional and some internet media carry corporate monologues, while social media contain dialogs with target markets: both play a role, but the dialog is becoming much more important and is truer to the well-accepted company goal of customer-driven marketing.

Search Engine Optimization

Search engine optimization (SEO) is the process of maximizing the number of visitors to a Web or social media site by ensuring that either (1) the site name and links appear high on a search engine results page for appropriate keywords or (2) ads on search engine sites get a high click-through. This reflects two types of SEO: natural search (also called organic search) and paid search. The latter is a form of paid media, discussed in Chapter 13. Here we focus on natural search as relates to owned media. **Search marketing** is an umbrella term that refers to the act of marketing via search engines, whether through improving rank in listings, purchasing paid listings, or a combination of these and other search engine-related activities.

Search marketing is a complex art and science that combines the intricacies of human behavior, linguistic preferences, marketing techniques, analytics, website usability, and technology to drive qualified visitors to a website and convert them into customers.

Search engines are **reputation aggregators**—websites that rank other websites, products, retailers, or other content according to some rating system. An aggregator gathers sites by category, value, and popularity and displays them in some organized fashion. These sites rely heavily on user input for their rankings.

The giant is Google, with 87.8 percent market share, compared to Bing at just 5.6 percent, and Yahoo! at 2.7 percent. Google ranks search engine results page (SERP) links partially based on popularity—the number of quality sites linking to each site. Many authors call Google a "reputation engine" instead of a search engine because of the way it determines these rankings. Users visit Google because the search engine results pages are so relevant and not just an unordered list of pages with just the keyword in them, with little regard to popularity. Heavy focus on meeting the needs of site visitors is what propelled Google to number one search engine.

Other reputation aggregators include social media niche sites with search capability, such as YouTube for video and TripAdvisor for hotel ratings. We discuss these in the vertical search section that follows.

Organic Search

Organic search is a search marketing strategy involving optimizing a website so it will appear naturally as close to the first search engine results page as possible. Organic search is critical because with over 5 billion search queries on Google each day, most searchers will click on a link in the first page of search engine results pages (SERP), and few scroll on to subsequent pages.

There are many ways for a site to inch its way to page one, but first it is important to understand that every reputation aggregator uses somewhat different criteria for ranking content. Google uses an ever-changing algorithm with over 200 variables, one of the most important of which is popularity, as measured partially by relevant incoming links to a site (thus its nickname as a reputation engine). Companies wanting to optimize their site for Google will seek as many relevant and high-quality incoming links as possible.

Another important tactic involves **keywords**—the words users type into the search query box to find what they seek. When websites are optimized in both their (1) content and (2) HTML meta tags that hold keywords, it will make it easy for search engines to know how to categorize the site and to provide a relevant match when users actually type in those keywords. Meta tags are not seen by visitors unless they choose to view the page source code. For example, these are the actual keywords used by eBay.com: "ebay, electronics, cars, clothing, apparel, collectibles, sporting goods, digital cameras, antiques, tickets, jewelry, online shopping, auction, online auction." When someone types in one or more of those words at Google, the search engine will consider the match as one of the 200 variables. Google finds the keywords both in the Web site text and headlines, and in the HTML tags.

To discover the best keywords, companies (1) use Web logs to see what words their visitors type into search engines before arriving at their sites, (2) use Web tools, such as Google's AdSense keyword auctions, to discover the keywords used in their industry so they can find unique words for their site (e.g., *vintage jewelry* instead of *jewelry*), and (3) by polling customers and prospects to see what words they actually use when looking for firms in the industry. Organizations also carefully craft the text on their pages to reflect this content, including even purposefully using different spellings of keywords that searchers might use (e.g., *email* and *e-mail*). Oftentimes, experimentation is the best way to see which words actually produce the highest click-throughs to a website.

Exhibit 12.11 shows a search for "email marketing" at Google. On the left side, at the bottom, MailChimp is the number one organic result for these keywords—quite a feat in a crowded field of vendors. Note that MailChimp is also the number one paid result.

Exhibit 12.11 Search for Email Marketing

Source: www.google.com

SEO is a topic that fills many books, so we will discuss only a few principles here that relate to social media and positive earned media. Visit the Google Webmaster pages for more information.

1. **Spread fresh content all over the Web**. The more sites and social media pages a company or brand maintains, the more links will appear on search engine results pages. This is important because when negative content appears in the social media, it will briefly appear within the search results, but a lot of solid, current Web content, such as images, podcasts, videos, press releases, and articles, will quickly drive the negative content to later pages in the search results. For example, when people search for "Will It Blend," the branded microsite appears first on the results page. This is followed by YouTube videos, the Blendtec company YouTube channel, a Wikipedia entry, the company's Facebook page, and then two social media columns about the company's blenders and fascinating campaign—one a humorous and positive parody of the viral videos ("will the blender blend itself?").

2. **Relevance and popularity**. Google judges relevance by incoming links to a webpage and the popularity of the site based on clicks from a SERP or number of "likes" or comments on a Facebook page. For example, if it is a musician's site and lots of credible similar sites link to it (such as a radio station blog), Google assumes it is highly relevant and popular, moving it closer to the top of the SERP. Companies seek these inbound links—for example, one blogger we interviewed for a previous book asked to be linked from our university pages because ".edu" domains have more Google credibility than do dot com sites. Social media marketers put a lot of cross-links to various sites, such as linking from the microsite to the Facebook page and cross-linking to pages within the site. For example, when searching for "blender," the Blendtec website appears in the top ten links because of the millions of people clicking, linking, and watching the viral videos on YouTube and its microsite. Google also defines "relevance" as individual-specific using social graphs (friend connections), so if you search for "the best restaurant" in your town the top result might well be one that your Facebook friends rated highly on Yelp.com, whereas someone else's SERP will reflect what their friends commented upon in other social media sites.

3. **Optimize content.** A search engine's automated robots search websites to see which words are the most important, partially by looking at topic headings, page titles (words that appear on the browser tabs), URL names, meta tags, and other things in large font. This means that marketers must understand their audiences' desired benefits and search habits so they can select keywords to populate the sites used by target markets for searching. For example, the Student Loan Down blog about student loans and Wells Fargo bank financing uses 29 keywords in its meta tag, but only three of them rank in Google's first SERP—these are the one used in the name of the blog as well (see blog.wellsfargo.com). This site needs to revise its keywords to focus on a smaller number to be used throughout the content.

4. **Use a vanity URL**. These are usually associated with a brand name to make it easier for a customer to remember (e.g., www.facebook.com/YourBrandName). The vanity URL is typically mentioned in advertising.

5. **Image search**. Increasingly, images are searchable online by the graphics, not the text descriptions. Google allows users to search for words in the image and by size, format (e.g., jpg), color, and more. Google also provides "reverse image" search, whereby users can upload an image and the engine will locate it anywhere it is posted online

(catch your friends posting your picture online). Image search will continue to grow in capability and use.

6. **Integrate social media and search strategy**. Google now considers social media activity in its organic search rankings. For example, a tweet that gets 1,000 retweets will boost a page higher in the rankings than one that gets 10 retweets. Bing considers the number of "likes" in its rankings.

7. **SEO tactics constantly change**. Google is famous for adjusting its search algorithm (several hundred times a year) both to improve results and so that sleazy site owners cannot spam the system (such as putting keywords in white text all over a white background so search engines are able to read them but users do not). For example, Google introduced "Panda" and "Penguin" in 2011 and 2012 to refine the search algorithm so that site quality and social media conversation ranked higher and pages with much advertising, especially above the fold, ranked lower. Google also announced a penalty for over-optimizing pages for search, trying to level the playing field. This means that marketers must constantly watch developments and change tactics accordingly. We recommend visiting searchengineland.com, searchenginewatch.com, and seomoz.org for the latest developments and capabilities.

Let's Get Technical—Bruening Glass Works

—John Sammons and his company, Sixth City Marketing, used SEO and WordPress to transform Bruening Glass Works into an international repair shop.

I've worked with many clients over the course of my career in internet marketing, and the story of Bruening Glass Works is my favorite one to share. Bruening Glass Works is a company that specializes in crystal and glass repair. Some of the things they repair include:

- Glass in antiques.
- Glassware.
- Lamps.
- Candlesticks.
- Prisms.

SEO and WordPress transformed Bruening Glass Works from a small business that primarily serviced Cleveland, Ohio, into an international glass repair shop. In a down economy, the company experienced incredible growth due to our recommended strategies and tactics. Because of the internet, people all across the world now know of and ship their broken pieces to Bruening Glass.

Initial Situation

We started working with Marc Konys of Bruening Glass Works in the fall of 2008. At that time, both the economy and inquiries for new business had declined. Marc approached us seeking a solution to simply be able to maintain his website on his own.

However, after having a discussion about his business, we knew that there was much more we could offer.

At the time, Bruening Glass had a very simple five-page website containing information about the business along with a page that showed before and after repair shots. The website averaged about 200–300 visits per month, and typically the company performed 6–8 repairs per year outside of Cleveland. Marc had primarily targeted people within a 15-mile radius of his shop. His primary means of advertising was through the yellow pages or trade publications.

What We Did

To help Marc increase inquiries, we did three things:

1. Search engine optimization.
2. Redesigned the website in WordPress.
3. Implemented Google Analytics.

Search Engine Optimization

Search engine optimization is essentially a smart way of writing content for your website. It is also commonly referred to as "content marketing." Search engine optimization is the process of trying to rank high on key search engines (e.g., Google, Bing) for search terms that are relevant to a business. They are often terms unconnected to your business or brand. For example, the terms we targeted for Marc's campaign included "crystal repair" and "Waterford crystal repair."

The first step in the process was to do some critical research on the business. We started by asking a few key questions:

1. Who is your target audience?
2. Where are they located?
3. What are the goals of the campaign?
4. What terms do you feel they are searching for? (Keyword brainstorming.)

One of the keys to the campaign was determining that the business had the ability to serve a global audience. We recommended that Marc emphasize his ability to repair pieces that could be shipped to him, since this could expand his potential customer base. Marc was excited to "think bigger and broader" about what he could do.

Once this was established, we took the answers to question 4 and began implementing search engine optimization.

The first phase of this process is conducting keyword research via the Google Keyword Planner. To do it properly, you'll essentially brainstorm both broad phrases (terms like "crystal repair") and more specific keyword phrases (otherwise known as "long-tail" keyword phrases).

You'll then input those phrases into the Google Keyword Planner. The Planner will show you how often keyword phrases are searched in a month. Here's an example of some of the phrases we identified for Marc:

Keyword	Avg. Monthly Searches
glass figurine repair	1,900
broken glass repair	880
glassware repair	590
repair chipped glass	590
chandelier repair	390
crystal repair	390
chandelier restoration	260
crystal glass reapair	260
antique glass repair	170
sick glass	170

Once we established this list, we then directed our attention to the website architecture or site map.

The key decisions we made with the website architecture included:

1. Creating new pages of content that would target both "crystal repair" and "Waterford crystal repair." Dedicating an individual page to a topic or service helps the search engines identify the content and rank it.
2. Knowing that many people were searching for extremely specific repairs, we recommended that Marc write about every repair project in an individual blog post. He would supply before and after pictures in the post and write a small description about each repair.

By blogging about each project and either tagging it or categorizing it as a specific type of repair, it made it easier for search engines and customers searching for very specific repairs to find Marc's site. Brueningglass.com now has over 300 individual repairs categorized as blog posts.

Here are some highlights of what we did as a result of this new strategy:

- Redesigned the site using WordPress, giving Marc the ability to update his website moving forward.
- Crafted a design strategy with the aim of keeping the site simple but also utilizing a strong "call to action" on every page.
- Implemented Google Analytics and goal tracking in order to see what online marketing channels drove leads.
- Created a YouTube video to demonstrate Marc's capabilities and personality.

Results

2,000% increase in traffic (283 in October of 2008 vs 6,145 in January of 2021). 12–20 leads from the internet per day outside of the Cleveland area.

90% of internet leads turn into business.

Ranks #6 globally for "crystal repair" (number 1 targeted term).

Ranks #3 globally "Waterford crystal repair" (number 2 targeted term).

Crystal repair is now the main focus of the business.

Receives business and inquiries from all over the globe.

Now internationally known and recommended for crystal repair.

The YouTube video has been viewed over 23,000 times and is often the reason why customers contact Marc, and it helps put a face to the company.

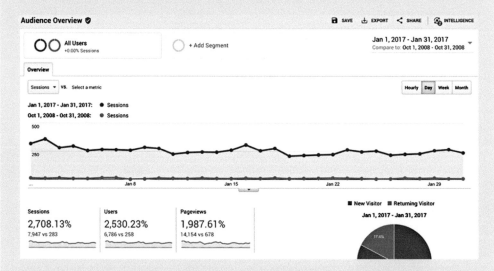

The results of the campaign have been incredible. Marc's traffic and business has increased at least 33 percent every year as he posts about new and exciting repair projects.

Note that although password protected sites such as Facebook and Twitter are crawled by search engines for public display in the SERP, users generally have to log on to these sites in order to follow the link. If a company wants its content to appear on Google and be easily viewed, it will create a public page that is available to people who are not required to be logged on to the site. Moreover, Facebook provides its own powerful search engine for users who are logged in. Companies work to be sure their content is listed by these specialty companies, who usually allow submissions if the search robots have not yet found the sites.

As with any social strategy, companies working on an SEO program first work to understand the Web behaviors and sites used by their target market and influencers in terms of publishing and sharing content. They then set SEO goals and monitor the results.

Vertical Search

Vertical search is a site-specific search on very specialized topics, such as travel, online retailers, or books. As compared with general search engines, such as Google and Bing, vertical sites are destinations for fewer users seeking very specific content. For example, in 2020 Tripadvisor.com had 884 million reviews and opinions about various hotels worldwide. Someone seeking a hotel in New York City or Bangkok can search the TripAdvisor site and get a listing of hotels ranked by popularity, with hundreds of reviews and several traveler photos per hotel. Thus, hotels want to be listed on this vertical search site. This social media site capitalizes on the fact that people trust others like themselves more than they trust the company websites.

Other vertical search site examples include ZoomInfo and LinkedIn (people search), Guru.com (vendor search in B2B market), Autobytel (automobile search), CareerBuilder (jobs), YouTube (video), and iTunes (music). The B2B Infomat fashion engine provides access to over 350,000 fashion designers, showrooms, retailers, manufacturers, and more, and DPRWorld helps dentists find everything from whitening agents to anesthesia.

Companies need to learn whether there are vertical sites for their industries and then to see if they are also indexed by the general search engines. Marmite, the English food spread, has a Facebook page with over 905,000 people liking the page—its Facebook link appears third in a Google search for "Marmite."

Vertical search is a growing area because it helps users find what they are looking for quickly—20 percent of online users search at vertical sites, according to iProspect. A consumer seeking a local pizza restaurant might do better at a Yelp vertical search or mobile application than at a general search engine, where the local entries will be buried among thousands of similar businesses nationwide (although Google now lists local results on some SERPs).

The pricing models on some vertical search sites include directory submission fee, cost per click, and cost per action, as well as the traditional cost per thousand (CPM) impressions. When the directory content is user-generated, such as with Tripadvisor.com, advertisers can pay for display ads on the site or can enter comments in response to reviews for free.

In the next section, you will learn about how companies measure owned media.

Owned Media Performance Metrics

With so many owned media choices that take a lot of participation effort, how can a marketer know which are worth the investment? The most important answer is it depends on the market and communication objectives. Referring back to Exhibit 12.1, if sales is the goal, then the number and dollars of sales are the key metrics, along with the costs, such as cost per click and ROI. If brand awareness is the goal, marketers will need a survey to determine if awareness improved (although site visits is one indicator).

For company-owned websites and blogs, marketers use Web analytics, such as number of unique visitors, time on each page, conversion to sales, and so forth (discussed in Chapter 2). Google Analytics is a free service that provides many metrics to determine the efficacy of these types of pages. For example, companies can learn how many daily visitors there are to each page, where users visited immediately prior to landing on their site, and the country from which they are accessing the site (based on IP addresses). Other metrics for owned media follow:

- Podcasts: number of downloads and length of time listening.
- Online events: number in attendance, number of questions asked (if it is a Webinar).
- Online games: number playing, length of time in the game, purchase of virtual properties, clicks on game links.
- Branded mobile apps: number of downloads and updates and number of actions that are built into the app (such as "checking in" with a location-based app or earned media "shares").
- QR codes: number of scans and actions taken at the site destination.
- Web landing pages: exit rate (view and leave the page), click-through rate and conversion rate.

Social media metrics are different from standard website metrics because users interact with branded media in many different ways. Initially, companies want to know how many fans and followers they have, number of visits and return visits, and cost per fan (especially the staff time cost). As well, there are engagement metrics, such as when an internet user views an online video, he or she might spend four minutes viewing it, but another might stop it immediately. And if the user uploads, comments on, likes or shares a branded video, this brand interaction is counted (see Chapters 2 and 14 for more detail on engagement metrics).

Next, we move to metrics for measuring sales promotion and direct marketing effectiveness.

Sales Promotion Metrics

Marketers want to know how their sales promotions contribute to the overall communication goals. For example, if the firm desires increased website traffic, how much came from the online contest? What was the conversion rate to sales at the site? As with all metrics, the selected measures depend on campaign goals. Software and music suppliers will want to measure the number of users who sampled their free online samples (e.g., 30-day trial for software or listening to a music sample) and how many subsequently purchased the product. In order to measure such performance, a baseline has to be recorded before any campaign is started.

Direct Marketing Metrics

Response rate and ROI are the most appropriate metrics for any direct marketing campaign. Additionally, many firms use direct tactics to build databases and measure success in terms of customer information growth. E-mail marketers collect metrics on every mouse click, desiring to know which offers pull best (A/B testing), which message content brings the greatest response, when is the best time to send e-mail for maximum response (by the way, it is Monday between 6 A.M. and 10 A.M. Eastern time), and so forth.

E-mail receives a widely varied and generally low click-through to the sponsor's website; however, as we have already said, the right list and offer can yield very high click-throughs. Interestingly, e-mail provides the highest ROI of any direct media, at approximately $42 on average (Sirohi, 2021).

SMS marketers also study responses other than simple click-through. In a study of more than 200 SMS campaigns, the response performance was outstanding (www.enpocket.com):

- 94 percent of messages were read by recipients.
- 23 percent showed or forwarded messages to a friend.
- 15 percent to 27 percent of recipients responded to SMS campaigns.
- Cost per response was $1.92, returning a better ROI than direct postal mail.

Chapter Summary

Integrated marketing communication (IMC) is a cross-functional process for planning, executing, and monitoring brand communications with the goal of profitably acquiring, retaining, and growing customers. When making decisions about marketing communication tools, companies consider the results they would like to achieve in moving consumers through the steps of awareness, interest, desire, and action (AIDA model) or the steps of "think, feel, do" in the hierarchy of effects model. Companies develop social media strategies and plan specific tactics to increase consumer awareness, influence attitude, and encourage behavior.

The five traditional marketing communication tools are advertising, public relations, sales promotion, direct marketing, and personal selling. In planning IMC campaigns, companies can now move beyond traditional tools and "1 to 1" (one marketer, one recipient) and "1 to many" (one marketer, multiple recipients) into "many to many" (many consumers using social media to communicate with each other). Owned media carry marketing communication messages on channels that are owned and therefore partially or entirely controlled by the marketer. Paid media are properties owned by others paid to carry marketer-controlled promotional messages (such as advertising). Organizations have the most reach and the least control over earned media, with "many to many" conversations generated by others (such as internet users' opinions).

Communication media are communication channels used to disseminate news, information, entertainment, and promotional messages. In contrast, social media blend technology and social interactions for co-creation of content and value. Content marketing involves creating and publishing content offline and online on websites and in social media. As a result, digital content functions as inbound marketing to attract customers and prospects, with appropriate content available when and where users seek information.

Among the most commonly used owned media are company websites (to provide information, entertain, build communities, and serve as a communication channel with customers); blogs (to disseminate views, attract site visitors, engage in conversations, and support expert standing); support forums and communities (for customers and prospects to discuss topics of interest, provide product ideas, or seek assistance); podcasts (to support brand-building); e-mail (for building relationships and encouraging direct response); text messaging (for instant communication and relationship-building); online events (to generate interest, build traffic, or generate revenue); sales promotion (such as coupons); online games (to engage users with product-related content); online gifting (for revenue); branded mobile apps (to support social interactions); QR codes (to provide more information); location-based marketing (to reach users who are at or near a marketing location); and social networks (connecting individuals for business or personal reasons). Given the many choices of owned, paid, and earned media, organizations have to make decisions based on their communication objectives in desired target markets.

Search engine optimization (SEO) is the process of maximizing the number of visitors to a website or social media site by landing the site name and link high on search engine results (natural or organic search) or attracting clicks on ads that appear on search engine sites (paid search). Natural search strategies depend on tactics such as site quality, achieving many relevant and high-quality incoming links or on selecting appropriate keywords. Vertical search refers to a site-specific search on specialized topics like travel or books. Marketers can use a variety of metrics to measure owned media performance, depending on the market and the objectives. For podcasts, the firm can measure number of downloads and length of time listening; for online events, the number of visitors in attendance; for QR codes, the number of scans and actions taken. Some metrics used to evaluate sales promotion performance include the conversion rate to sales at the website and the number of online samples distributed. Some metrics for evaluating direct marketing include response rate, ROI, best time for response, and cost per response.

Exercises

Review Questions

1. What is integrated marketing communication (IMC), and why is it important?
2. Why do marketers keep the AIDA or hierarchy of effects model in mind when planning social media strategy?

3. What are the five traditional marketing communication tools, and what are some social media platform examples of each?
4. How do the reach and control of marketing communications in owned, paid, and earned media differ?
5. What is marketing public relations (MPR), and how can an organization use its website as owned media for this purpose?
6. Why would a company use e-mail or text messaging instead of postal direct mail for marketing?
7. How are advergames used in marketing?
8. What are the marketing benefits of initiating, participating in, and influencing conversations on social networks?
9. How does organic search differ from paid search and vertical search?
10. Why is search engine optimization an important consideration for the company's owned media strategy?

Discussion Questions

1. **Will It Blend? Story.** What other owned media do you think this company could use to build its brand online? Explain your rationale.
2. **Will It Blend? Story.** How do the videos create earned media? Are there any other things the company could do to engage users to create more earned media?
3. "Great products + Weak branding = Weak sales." The CEO of Blendtec said this before his *Will It Blend?* videos became an internet sensation. How does the hierarchy of effects model explain the CEO's comment and the sales results that followed this marketing success?
4. Why would a company prefer the control of owned media over the extended reach of the "many to many" model?
5. What are the possible marketing consequences of not having an effective search engine optimization strategy?
6. As a consumer, how are you likely to react when you see that a company representative tweets a comment about a specific topic after other consumers have opened the conversation? What guidelines would you recommend that marketers follow for joining such conversations?
7. Have you scanned any QR codes? Do you think marketers should include QR codes in their IMC plans? Why or why not?
8. Which could be more important to an airline selling seats on its flights: a general search engine or a vertical search site? Explain your answer.

Web Activities

1. Locate the microsite for a specific brand, marketing campaign, or new product. Based on your experience finding this site and looking at its landing page, what changes would you like to see included in A/B testing, and why? List at least three specific items to be tested and explain your rationale for each test.
2. Use your favorite search engine to locate a blog written by a company CEO. How often does the CEO blog, and what topics are represented in recent posts? What marketing objectives do you think this blog is intended to achieve? List two other webpages that are linked to this blog (or that should be linked to this blog) and explain why these links make sense. If you could ask this CEO a question to be answered on the blog, what would it be?

3. Conduct a search for a nationally advertised consumer product using only its brand name and analyze the first page of search results. Who sponsors the website at the very top of the results page? How many owned paid search links do you see? How relevant are the top six search results? Which keywords do you think this brand should use to optimize its site for natural search?

4. Visit the home page of a major retailer such as Macy's (www.macys.com) or Target (www.target.com). Does this retailer offer consumers the opportunity to sign up for promotional messages delivered via e-mail or text messages (or both)? What does the retailer do to entice visitors to sign up? How is it using permission marketing? Also, follow any links to see this retailer's presence in social media and participation in online conversation. What else do you think this retailer should do to accomplish its marketing communication objectives through social media?

Chapter 13

Digital Marketing Communication
Paid Media

This chapter explores paid media, the second of the three elements of content marketing used to communicate with customers and prospects. In addition to learning about the latest trends and specific uses of paid media, you will examine some of the pricing models that apply when marketers select these tools. Finally, you will see how advertisers use metrics to evaluate paid media effectiveness and efficiency.

After reading this chapter, you will be able to:

- Outline the characteristics, benefits, and limitations of paid media.
- List the most important paid media techniques and discuss how and when advertisers use each.
- Explain the three unique aspects of social networks that attract advertisers to paid social media.
- Describe some of the advertising tactics offered by the most popular social media sites and other digital properties.
- Discuss the various ways in which marketers can reach target audiences through mobile advertising and paid search.
- Highlight how paid media can move B2B prospects through the marketing purchase funnel.
- Identify some key metrics used by advertisers to determine the effectiveness and efficiency of paid media.

LENOVO WINS BIG WITH PAID MEDIA

Lenovo is a Chinese company selling computers and other electronic items. It is headquartered in Hong Kong but maintains operational headquarters in the United States. In 1995, it acquired IBM's personal computer business and today continues to top PC market share worldwide, often competing with HP for the number one spot (Gartner, Inc., 2021). Lenovo sells to both businesses and individual consumers.

This multinational company advertises both in traditional media and online. Lenovo has long used Google display advertising for remarketing (a tactic that involves communicating with users who previously visited a website). The Google display network contains a variety of websites, from news to blogs, and advertisers can place video, text, image, or interactive ads on specific sites anywhere in the network. Remarketing allowed Lenovo to tag visitors at its own website and show them specific ads while on another site in the Google display network.

Lenovo tagged site visitors displaying three different behaviors: general visitors, those who abandoned shopping carts, and those who purchased on the site. It could then present tailored

DOI: 10.4324/9781003247319-17

ads elsewhere based on this user behavior on Lenovo. For example, general visitors got ads featuring discounts on laptops, those who abandoned shopping carts saw ads with 5 to 10 percent discounts on the exact laptop or product they viewed, and purchasers received ads offering laptop accessories, such as laptop bags.

Visitors to Levono's website from Google Display ads result in increased total site orders and decreased advertising expenses due to this specific targeting. Lenovo continues to use this remarketing strategy and many metrics to tweak tags and ads for maximum effectiveness and efficiency.

Paid Media

Lenovo used paid media to entice its target market to visit the Lenovo owned media website. As you learned in Chapter 12, paid media are properties that are paid by an organization to carry its promotional messages, as when Lenovo paid Google to present narrowly targeted ads on its Display Network. The terms paid media and advertising are often used interchangeably, as you will note in this chapter. However, there are a few paid media tactics that don't quite fit the definition of advertising, such as paid product placement in virtual worlds or online games and sponsored tweets or influencers.

The line between physical (also called traditional or offline) and digital platforms (often called nontraditional or online) for paid marketing communication messages is blurring more every day. Now that US television programming is completely digital, and as more offerings from Hulu, YouTube TV, Disney+, and Apple TV+ exist, the meaning of the terms *offline* and *online* will continue to lose their distinction—the same fate awaits the terms *traditional media* (newspapers, magazines, TV, radio, outdoors) and *nontraditional media* (everything else, including digital media). Already, newspaper ads and articles are often accessible in either location.

Note also that the medium is not the appliance: TV programming can carry content and ads that are seen on television, mobile phone, and the computer; radio audio transmission can come into many devices; and so forth. Many of the media shown in Exhibit 12.3 can be delivered on a TV set, tablet computer, or elsewhere. In this environment, the most effective tactics will be those that integrate IMC tools to reach their target markets effectively and efficiently (lowest cost)—regardless of the communication channel. This is especially important and different because of the high level of multitasking among consumers, as mentioned in previous chapters. To do this, marketers must know the capabilities, strengths, and weaknesses of each medium.

Paid media can engage target markets, moving them to owned media and resulting in social media conversation (earned media). Great content will not stay trapped in owned media but will spread (such as the *Will It Blend?* videos and white papers). Paid media often also carries sales promotions, such as the discounts offered by Lenovo in its display ads. This cycle of owned, paid, and earned media can also result in increased digital commerce sales.

Internet paid media parallels traditional media advertising, in which companies create content, draw an audience to their website or mobile app, and then sell space to outside advertisers (such as with television advertising). Sometimes it is confusing online, such as when a company includes something that looks like a banner ad promoting its own products on its website. The key is exchange—if a firm pays money or barters with goods for space in which to put the marketing message it creates, the content is considered paid media. In Chapter 11, we discussed how firms create revenue streams from selling advertising space, but this chapter discusses the flipside: buying advertising space from someone else to reach a firm's markets. These specific definitions are meaningless to consumers (who view all branded messages as advertising), but they are important to marketers because various MarCom tools help to accomplish specific goals.

In this chapter, we begin with the trends in paid media and then move to various types. We conclude with pricing models and metrics for monitoring paid media effectiveness.

Trust in Paid Media

Do you trust ads? Globally, consumers trust earned media the most, followed by owned media, and then paid media. The most trusted digital media include branded websites, opt-in e-mails, editorial content from reputable sites, and recommendations from like-minded people and social network contacts. Exhibit 13.1 displays the results of several studies that put most paid media at the bottom of the trust scale. According to Nielsen, mobile ads are the least trusted (only 43% trust mobile display ads, and 36% trust text ads). Conversely, several studies have noted that ad recall is greater in social media, and the movement of consumers to social media means that ad dollars are flowing to social media properties. Thus, marketers want to create authentic ads that drive traffic to their great owned content.

Even though most consumers love to hate advertising, they usually recognize that someone has to pay for free content in the media. Nonetheless, in addition to the much-disliked web-page pop-up ads, there are some online formats that frustrate users. Online marketers are wise to avoid banner ads below headers, ads that look like content (e.g., some sponsorships), dancing ads (across the webpage), auto-expanding half-page ads, banners next to logos, bill-boards in the top right corner, Google text links interrupting content, ads with hidden close buttons, interstitials (taking over the entire screen), and other page takeovers; in short—most interrupt advertising. Web designers have also begun to creatively force the user into scrolling down past an ad to continue reading content. Nonetheless, paid media are still very effective for building awareness and moving users to owned media; online advertising is growing, as discussed next.

Global Trust in Media

PAID. OWNED. EARNED.

PAID.	OWNED.	EARNED.
48% video ads[1]	70% Branded Web sites[1]	65% Person like yourself[2]
47% search ads[1]	56% E-mails (opt-in)[1]	62% Contacts recommending product[3]
46% social network ads[1]	61% Brand sponsorships[1]	
42% banner ads[1]		
43% mobile ads[1]		
36% text ads[1]		

Exhibit 13.1 Proportion of Consumers Expressing Trust in Media

Sources: 1. Nielsen Trust in Advertising Survey 2015 (blog.nielsen.com), 2. Edelman Global Trust Barometer, (www.trust.edelman.com)

Internet Advertising Trends

Internet advertising in the United States began with the first series of banner ads on Hotwired. com on October 27, 1994. One of these ads, sponsored by AT&T, simply invited users to "click here," with no graphics or animation. The ad ran for 12 weeks, cost $30,000, and received an amazing 30 percent click-through. Compare this ratio to the far less than 1 percent click-through rates on banner ads today. That means fewer than 10 people in 1,000 click on an ad. Google's own benchmarking tools suggest that the click-through rate for rich media is approximately .01 percent (Smith, 2018).

US online advertising reached $1 billion in 1998, grew quickly to $8.2 billion in 2000, dropped a bit in 2001–2002 due to the economic recession, and continued to grow to $31 billion in 2011, with a small drop-off due in 2009 to the economic crisis. Global online ad spend reached 84.8 billion in 2011 (O'Leary, 2012). Ad spending is expected to grow by an average of more than 16 percent annually through 2024 (eMarketer, 2021a). Most advertisers realize that the internet is an important medium for reaching their target markets, with US online advertising revenue increasing by more than $80 billion from 2015 to 2020, according to the Interactive Advertising Bureau (Exhibit 13.2). Retailers hold the biggest share of ad spend in the United States, as shown in Exhibit 13.3.

Advertising spend on the internet continues to grow and has overtaken television and other traditional media on the global stage. This power gap is only expected to widen even more with the saturation of mobile devices and new ways to serve advertisements via digital devices.

Paid Media Formats

Anything goes with paid media online: text—from a sentence to pages of story—graphics, sound, video, hyperlinks, or an animated car driving through a page. A paid search ad, prompted by keywords, is the most important technique. Keyword search is the paid part of a larger strategy called search marketing, as discussed in Chapter 12. Mobile advertising is also growing significantly and impacting digital advertising globally. Many of these ads also have interactive capability, allowing action between consumers and producers. This occurs when the advertiser provides a link, game, or direct purchase shopping cart within the ad, and the consumer can click on the ad to activate a drop-down menu or other interactive feature.

Display ads are another large spending category, with billions of advertising dollars going toward this medium. It is interesting to note how ad formats have changed over the years, reflecting the intense competition for audience attention in an environment where consumers are in charge. Next, we discuss several interesting or commonly used advertising formats. Then, due to their importance, we present mobile, social, and search engine paid media in separate sections.

Display Ads

The banner ad is a type of display ad, reflecting the traditional ad nomenclature—traditional print ads are called display ads. Online **display ads** are embedded in webpages, allowing users to click through to the advertiser's site, and can include text, graphics, and animation. These ads usually contain more graphics and white space than text and include traditional banners and many additional sizes. In 2020, display ad revenues totaled 31.5 percent of all online ad revenue, according to the Internet Advertising Bureau (IAB).

The IAB has proposed standard dimensions for display ads. It is important to have standard-ized formats so that website owners renting ad space and advertisers purchasing it can easily

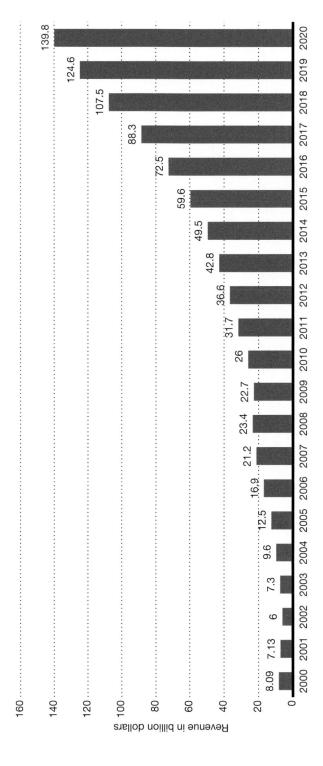

Exhibit 13.2 US Online Advertising Revenue, 2000–2020

Source: PricewaterhouseCoopers LLP/IAB Internet Advertising Revenue Reports

Share of ad spend (%)

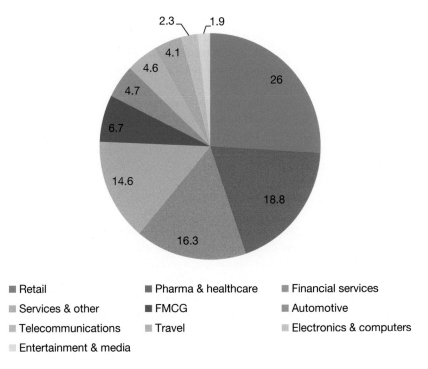

Exhibit 13.3 US Digital Advertising Spending, by Industry
Source: Statista Digital Market Outlook; July 2021

agree on the space and creative requirements. It helps companies to create a standard ad for use on many sites versus having to make many different versions, and it helps the media to design pages that allow for insertion of standard ad sizes. The IAB claims that 80 percent of online marketers follow these guidelines.

IAB discusses the concept of having LEAN advertising experiences for those viewing the ad. LEAN stands for "Light (i.e., small file size), Encrypted (i.e., https://), AdChoices supported (i.e., consumer chooses ads based on relevance), and Non-invasive (i.e., compliance with Better Ads Standards)," according to IAB. The goals of such principles enable consumers to have more control over their advertising experiences and help ensure that ads are not disrupting them. The move to LEAN principles also begins to enable the proliferation of best practices across new viewing experiences as more devices are released that could serve display ads. Visiting IAB.com allows creatives to see a wide variety of guidelines to create the best experience possible for users.

One wonders why so many advertisers still use display ads for direct response when the click-through rates are so low. The answer is that (1) display ads help build brand awareness when viewed by site visitors and (2) carefully targeted display ads can generate high click-through rates, such as experienced by Lenovo.

Although the IAB categorizes most ads as ones dictated by the LEAN principles, two additional types of display ads are a bit different from the previously discussed types: rich media ads and contextual ads.

Rich Media Ads

All ads in this category are highly interactive, at least offering click-through to the advertiser's website, where the transaction or any other objective is achieved. Some rich media display ads enhance the interactivity by sensing the position of the mouse on the webpage and animating faster as the user approaches. Other ads have built-in games or videos. Still others have drop-down menus, check boxes, and search boxes to engage and empower the user. All of the following formats can be rich media:

- **In-banner video ad:** Similar to a banner ad, except that instead of a static or animated image, actual moving video clips are displayed without the viewer having to open a video window. These can be delivered as automatic streaming or be user-activated.
- **Expandable/retractable ad:** These become larger, sometime filling an entire webpage. They can be automated or user-activated.
- **Pop-up:** A new window that opens in front of the current one, displaying an advertisement or entire webpage.
- **Pop-under:** Similar to a pop-up except that the window is loaded or sent behind the current window so that users do not see it until they close one or more active windows.
- **Floating ad:** An ad that moves across the user's screen or floats above the content. These can be animations such as the Energizer bunny hopping across the page.
- **Interstitial ad:** Also called "between-the-page," this represents a full-page ad that appears before the requested page content or as the user clicks between pages. Occasionally this type of ad can appear over a webpage as well.
- **Wallpaper ad:** An ad that changes the background of the page being viewed.
- **Trick banner:** A banner ad that looks like a dialog box with buttons. It simulates an error message or an alert.
- **Map ad:** Text or graphics linked from and appearing in or over a location on an electronic map such as on Google Maps.

One downside of video, animated, and highly **interactive display ads** is that they require more bandwidth. Keeping banner file sizes small reduces the time that they take to load, which can be problematic for mobile devices. Another downside is that the aggressive types can irritate users, similar to all interrupt advertising (such as pop-ups). Display ads that have scaling issues on mobile devices can create infinitely frustrating experiences for the user. Alternatively, they can definitely engage users if appropriate to the market.

Contextual Advertising

Ad servers maintain an inventory of display ads from clients and serve them into websites as appropriate users are viewing particular pages. **Contextual advertising** occurs when an ad system scans a webpage for content and serves an appropriate ad, such as an ad for tickets to a concert on a music site. Google's AdSense gives sites special JavaScript code to put into their HTML site code so that relevant ads can be sent into the page. Microsoft Bing Ads and many others offer this service and pay site owners when the ad appears on their sites.

Behavioral advertising is another form of contextual advertising but follows user behavior instead of webpage text. Used by Lenovo in the Google Display Network, one behavioral advertising approach is called **remarketing**—a tactic that involves communicating with users who previously visited a website. This occurs when advertising networks track user click behavior, usually through cookie files placed on their hard drive, then presents ads to the user based on their previous behavior. For example, when you search for a particular music album, an ad for that album might appear on Amazon.com on a subsequent visit. This is accomplished via ad networks that maintain a large number of website clients. The largest ad networks are search engines, such as the Google AdWords program, where the website owner gets paid when users click on the targeted ads.

Facebook also offers very specific ad targeting based on profile information (more on this later). Contextual advertising is good microsegmentation for marketers and good for users who receive relevant ads at the precise moment they want information. Contextual advertising tends to yield higher click-through rates because the ads are relevant to the user's needs.

E-Mail Advertising

Sometimes, the least expensive type of online advertising is **e-mail advertising**—paid content embedded in another firm's e-mail. Advertisers purchase space in the e-mail sponsored by others, often an e-mail newsletter. For example, Practical Ecommerce sells text-based ads for $990 or $540 in their *EcommerceNotes* opt-in newsletter, which reaches up to 35,000 subscribers each time it is sent out (www.getresponse.com). Note that HTML and multimedia e-mail messages sent from a firm directly to internet users are owned content, not paid media.

Text Link Ads

These are ads that are simply a hyperlink placed in specific text in a blog post or other owned media content—including content downloaded by mobile phone users. In a hypothetical example, a flower shop might buy a specified number of links for the word "rose" on many blogger sites, and these would have a hyperlink to the flower shop's website. The goal of these ads is to raise a site's rankings in the search engines. For example, a furniture store bought three keywords in a large number of related websites, and in over a one-year period, the store moved from a rank of 97 to 4 in a Google Search Engine results page for those three keywords.

Sponsored Content

Sponsorships integrate editorial content and paid media based on either underwritten (someone else's content) or advertiser-created content. Most traditional media clearly separate content from advertising; women's magazines are an exception. Food advertisers usually barter for recipes that include their products in these magazines, and fashion advertisers get mentions of their clothing in articles. This practice pleases advertisers because it gives them additional exposure and creates the impression that the publication endorses their products. The IAB has observed the following types of online sponsorships: content creation, mobile/Web applications, branded interaction, contests/sweepstakes, games, podcasts, polls/surveys, and trivia.

For example, a food company might pay for space on a cooking blog or wiki to insert recipes using its products as ingredients (e.g., Hershey's Brownie Recipe). The website Mental Floss frequently includes sponsored content in the form of a list or quiz. This looks like content from the site but is actually paid-for space. Companies also can pay bloggers directly to endorse products by writing positive reviews. A problem with sponsored content, however, is that bloggers often do not disclose that they are being paid (or receiving gifts) for their endorsements, even though the recent US Federal Trade Commission guidelines require this disclosure. If they do not tell and are found out, they can be exposed with a huge amount of negative discussion online (and possible federal action). Nonetheless, many marketers have paid for sponsored blog posts.

PayPerPost runs a marketplace where advertisers can find bloggers, online photographers, and podcasters who are willing to endorse advertisers' products (payperpost.com). It claims to create 220 million impressions of sponsored content a month in social media. A company begins by registering with PayPerPost and describing the type of endorsement it wants and how much it is willing to pay. A hotel, for example, might post a request for people willing to write a 50-word blog entry about their property or upload a video of themselves enjoying the hotel facilities. Bloggers create the blog post and then inform PayPerPost, which checks to see that the content matches what the advertiser asked for, and PayPerPost arranges payment. Note that the PayPerPost bloggers *are* required to disclose that they are being paid for their posting.

Some people worry about the ethics of sponsorships when consumers cannot easily identify the content author(s). Perhaps this problem is not significant, because many users view the entire internet as one giant advertisement. However, when advertising is passed off as locally generated content, it can potentially lower user trust in the website and hurt brand image. To address this important issue, the IAB established a panel to set standards for sponsor disclosure in this type of advertising.

Note that Facebook, Twitter, Instagram, and many other social media sites also have sponsored content. You will read about this in the social media section later in this chapter.

Classified Ads

Classified ads are placed both by individual consumers and companies. These usually use text but may also include photos. The ads are grouped according to classification (e.g., cars, rentals) and tend to be an inexpensive format. Classified ads can be found on dedicated sites (e.g., craigslist.org and superpages.com), as well as online newspapers, exchanges, and Web portals. In many cases, posting regular-size classified ads is free, but placing them in a larger size, in color, or with some other noticeable features is done for a fee. Craigslist postings are free for most citizens, but it covers operating costs by charging a fee for job listings and apartments for rent in large cities. Many daily newspapers have suffered big financial losses due to the classified ad business moving to the free Craigslist.

Product placement

Online gaming creates huge special interest communities. There are many types of online games with social interaction, from two-player chess to massively multiplayer online role-playing games (MMORPG)—sporting thousands of players moving about as avatars at the same time. Some games have storylines or plots, with players accomplishing goals and developing in skill and power, and others are completely nonstructured, with players designing the action. World of Warcraft is one of the most popular MMORPG, with millions of monthly subscribers worldwide. Advertisers are keenly interested in online games because they reach a broad spectrum of demographics, and the players actually like to see product placement in the games. This is because it makes the games seem more real. This is similar to movie product placement offline. For example, the online games Fortnite and Minecraft often include environmental advertisements. Some e-sport games include billboards or signs on walls behind the players.

Television programming also includes product placement. For example, a sitcom like *Ted Lasso* might have branded food items from popular fast-food chains. *American Idol* is famous for including a Coca-Cola in each of the judge's hands. Now that these programs are seen online via Hulu, Netflix, and more, this can also be considered paid online media product placement. In the social media world, product mentions in tweets, blogs, and elsewhere are the new age of product placement, as discussed later in this chapter.

Emerging Formats

On the internet, anything goes and novelty gains attention. This is fertile ground for the creative advertiser who constantly devises new ways to reach target markets with online advertising. Voice assistants are one newer frontier with advertising thinking of innovative ways to create interactive audio experiences. Devices that make any TV a smart one, like Roku, also create new opportunities for online advertising. Virtual and augmented reality are also growing segments of interest for advertisers. Internet users are attracted to novel things online, so new formats are usually attention getting and help to build brand awareness and motivate purchase.

Social Media Advertising

Social media sites sell space to advertisers who wish to reach the site's audience. In this section, we will discuss paid media on the most important of these sites. According to Smart Insights, 52 percent of businesses say that social media positively influences sales and revenue in their company (Mangles, 2017). In fact, social commerce sales are expected to grow approximately 11 percent each year through 2025 (Freer, 2021), and social media ad spending is expected to grow from 36.25 billion in 2019 to 51.51 billion in 2021 (Social Media Advertising, 2020). Advertisers also seek to meet four main objectives for this branded content paid by advertisers in social media: build brand awareness, engage existing customers, increase size of community (friends, followers, fans), and drive traffic to an online destination. Advertisers also used social media to introduce new products, build databases, and gain feedback from users.

Thus, paid social media are for building awareness, creating positive brand attitudes, collecting valuable information about customers, and motivating actions such as joining a community, clicking through to a site, and purchase. To drive sales, they require a compelling reason to click. For example, the fast-food chain Chick-fil-A ran a successful Facebook free-sample sales promotion engagement ad campaign; clicking on the ad revealed a form to receive a mail-in coupon.

Advertising spending on social media is predicted to grow at a rapid pace. Part of this growth is for display ad space on blogs and other social media. However, display ads do not take advantage of the unique properties of social networks, such as Facebook—namely, high user interactivity and free sharing of individual profiles and photos. Social networks have three unique aspects:

- *Personal profile.* Social networks contain personal profiles data, including the member's name, image and other pictures, demographic information (e.g., age, gender, and location of residence), interests, career/student status, and membership groups. These data are freely shared and usable by marketers for customizing advertising.
- *Social data graph.* Companies can make a map or list of all the connections between individuals to discover the network size for like-minded people.
- *Interpersonal interaction data.* Marketers can capture information about the amount and timing of interactions among network friends.

In contrast, behavioral targeting, discussed previously, sends appropriate display ads, webpages, or e-mail based on the user's click behavior when viewing websites. Many companies have created advertising platforms that capitalize on social media's unique features. Social media ads use these data for specific targeting and user engagement.

Advertising is the major current revenue source for social media companies. Advertisers are willing to pay a great deal for placing ads and running promotions in social networks because of the large number of visitors in the networks and the amount of time they spend there. They find it effective.

Paid Media on Facebook

Advertisers can reach over 2.5 billion active members by advertising on the Facebook social network, with over 60 percent of users logging in on any given day, according to Facebook. com. However, most advertisers prefer more narrow targeting to reach their well-defined markets, and this can easily be done via member profile information. When placing the ad, the marketer selects the desired target profile. For this ad the criteria were Facebook users with the following in their profiles:

- Live in the United States.
- Live within 50 miles of Reno, NV.
- Are age 18 and older.
- Like meditation, tai chi, reiki, power now, sound healing, metaphysics, meditating, buddhism, deepak chopra, spirituality or yoga.

This narrow targeting resulted in 4,980 Facebook users, all of whom were presented the ad on their newsfeeds and would be more likely to be interested in attending the Reno concert than if these ad criteria were not applied. The cost for the ad was based on the number clicking on it, at a rate of $0.88 per click.

This narrow targeting is important for global advertisers because Facebook is available in more than 70 different languages on the site, and over 75 percent of active users live outside of the United States. In late 2020, the company even introduced a multilingual machine translation that can translate between any two of 100 languages, which may increase the accuracy of ads even further. Facebook ads can include interactive features, links to other brand content, and are very easy to create. Advertisers simply upload an image and type the text right into the Facebook template. Facebook offers excellent metrics to see how many people were presented the ad and whether or not they took an action, like clicking on a link. Furthermore, advertisers can set a maximum daily budget.

Social Ads

A social ad has three criteria: profile data, interaction data, and social graph (friend connections). Thus, data to create these ads comes automatically from the user's profile data, social data (friends/connections), and interaction data (data about the user's interaction with friends). For example, if a Facebook user went to a particular movie and liked it, a social ad would be populated with this information. The ad is then presented to the Facebook friends that she selected to view it and thus share her excitement about this new movie (or product). A social ad also can include interactive features such as polling, votes, sharing, and other types of engagement with the ad. In general, when companies incorporate social networks into ads, Facebook advertising is quite effective.

In 2018, Facebook introduced ads via Facebook Stories, which create a full-screen, immersive experience. Because Stories content disappears within 24 hours, Facebook touts Stories as an opportunity to share "everyday moments" photos and videos, as opposed to content that will forever be a part of a company's Facebook profile (Facebook for Business, n.d.). Stories ads are becoming increasingly popular among consumers, with Facebook finding that ads in Stories alongside ads in newsfeeds can drive increased efficiency (Hutchinson, 2019).

Twitter's "Promoted Tweets," "Trends," and "Accounts"

Twitter is a strong competitor for advertisers' dollars. According to Learmonth (2011), Twitter launched its first ad product—*promoted tweets*—in 2010 and netted $45 million in ad dollars. That was due in part to the enthusiasm among brands like Virgin America, Coke, Ford, and Verizon to give the untried format a whirl. Twitter's cost-per-click on advertising content is approximately $0.58, with the click-through rate at approximately 0.86 percent. **Promoted tweets** are ads that appear as content at the top of a Twitter search page or a user's timeline. They can be targeted to Twitter users by geographic location and by whose Twitter streams they follow. Users can interact with promoted Tweets just as they can with organic Tweets. **Promoted trends** are ads placed on hot topics in Twitter that are presented near a user's timeline. **Promoted account ads** are featured in search results and in the "Who to Follow" section. These ads help users find others with similar interests. Advertisers can also pay for short videos to play near the trending section.

Using these paid media vehicles, advertisers can target Twitter users by 350 very narrow interests, such as movies that are musicals. Companies can also target @username to reach users with similar interests as the original account holder, not simply their followers.

Another interesting trend is that famous Twitter account holders often get paid to send tweets. For example, Kevin Hart has made nearly $14 million from 46 promoted tweets, while Demi Lovato has made approximately $10 million from 23 promoted tweets (Sullivan, 2021). These celebrities tweet when they visit a retailer, like Best Buy or a restaurant, and the innocuous tweets do not seem like the paid media that they are.

LinkedIn Advertising

LinkedIn is great for advertising to narrowly targeted business professionals. Advertisers can use LinkedIn Ads product to target by job title, industry, seniority, group membership, geographic location, and more. Advertisers have the choice of paying for the number of impressions or clicks (see more in the pricing model discussion later). LinkedIn can be a very effective form of online media, especially for B2B businesses.

Snapchat

Snapchat allows advertisers to create Snap Ads, Filters, and Geofilters to target different segments of their market. Snap Ads are videos that can be up to 10 seconds long and utilize many of the features that Snapchat users enjoy, as well as call-to-action buttons. Filters allow users to put an overlay on their camera and share with their friends. Geofilters allow for a quick, on-demand, and simple overlay to be added to user images and videos. This specifically targets geographic areas when a Snapchat user is taking a photo or sharing a video in a certain place.

Instagram

Advertisers can pay to promote sponsored posts in a user feed in Instagram, taking advantage of this mobile-only platform. Such posts can include a picture or a video with a button to click for further action. For example, Reese Witherspoon's clothing company (@draperjames) uses such ads to help drive traffic to purchase products at their store. Facebook Ads Manager now allows users to create ads that can appear in Facebook, Instagram, and Messenger and can make suggestions as to where the ad should appear based on ad content and which consumers the ad is targeting.

TikTok

TikTok is a short-form mobile video platform allowing users to feature music, incorporate filters, add hashtags, and engage with others through recordings and live streams. Users navigate the platform by scrolling up and down through a feed of videos with TikTok's artificial intelligence (AI) delivering content based on user likes, interactions, and/or searches. A variety of user-generated content has gone viral from the platform, including memes, lip-synced songs, music trends, and comedy videos.

TikTok, known in China as Douyin, is popular among influencers and is beginning to incorporate sponsored content as well as ecommerce partnerships enabling companies to reach consumers directly.

Paid Media in Online Videos

Organizations can place ads before, during, or after videos on a number of different sites, including YouTube and Vimeo. The types of ads include the following:

- In-stream videos are ad units that show before or during the video playback, such as pre-roll, mid-roll, and video takeovers (ad takes over the entire video screen for a short time). These are usually 15 to 30 seconds in length.
- Interactive banners and buttons run over or within the video content during play.
- Branded player skins allow companies to surround the video with their branded images. Note that text, banners, and rich media ads can also surround the video.
- In-text video ads are displayed when the viewer rolls the mouse over relevant words shown during the video play.
- Various sizes include banners, marquees, expandable ads, and full-screen takeovers.

Nearly all of these allow for interactivity. Viewers can click through to an advertiser's website or Facebook or Twitter page. Also, special buttons allow click-through to get store or dealer locations, see related videos, and receive special promotions or simply to share the video (automatically offered on YouTube but not at all video sites). As well, video ads must be prepared to play automatically for the three screens: television, computer, and smartphone.

Video ad spending is also continually growing. IAB reports the amount spent for video advertising in 2019 was $54.7 billion. Note that advertisers only pay if viewers watch at least 30 seconds or to the end of the ad. That is, when viewers click to skip the ad after a few seconds, advertisers do not have to pay for the placement.

Mobile Advertising

Mobile advertising is experiencing major growth as more people around the globe gain access to the internet through smartphones. The average time spent on mobile devices (not counting talking on the phone) for someone in the United States is 263 minutes per day (eMarketer, 2021b).

Following are the mobile advertising formats available to marketers:

- *Paid search.* Advertisers can buy keywords that appear as sponsored links on mobile search engine results pages. Because of limited screen sizes, these ads must be short and relevant in order to attract click-throughs.
- *Display ads.* Users pull content from mobile websites, and banners, flash, or other types of ad formats come along for the ride. In Virgin Mobile's "Sugar Mama" campaign, it offered cell phone owners free minutes in exchange for viewing mobile ads. For example, viewing a 45-second ad while on the Web got them one free minute of cell talk time, and receiving text message ads or completing online questionnaires got them more free minutes. According to Ultramercial, the company running the campaign, Virgin Mobile gave away over 10 million free minutes by mid-campaign.
- *Full screen takeovers.* Some mobile ads can take over the entire screen—either when the user is using an app or a Web browser.
- *Messaging.* Short message services (SMS) have broader reach than many other formats because even the lowest-end phone can receive text messages, but not all can receive larger display ads or videos. Text ads are also included with other types of content. Advances in messaging applications and the launch of applications specifically for messaging, like iMessage's own app store, means that advertisers are gaining new footholds to broaden their reach.
- *Location-based ads.* These are often text based, relying on GPS (discussed more thoroughly in Chapters 12 and 14).
- *Video.* Video ads are growing inside of applications and through use of a mobile Web browser. Companies like Vlipsy (https://vlipsy.com) also enable users to share short clips of videos with their friends, and some of these are from companies looking to expand their reach.
- *Voice.* Voice ads are increasing in popularity due to the growth of devices like Amazon's Alexa, as well as the use of streaming music through apps like Spotify.
- *Apps.* The iPhone and iPad put mobile apps on the map. Advertisers can use apps as a sampling for products (freemium model), or they can send ads with an application to offset the user's free purchase price. Tapjoy offers an ad marketplace, offering consumers virtual rewards or extra content within an app in exchange for completing some action (registering, subscribing, taking a survey and so forth). Advertisers pay Tapjoy for this service.

Following rapid mobile use growth, the Interactive Advertising Bureau and Mobile Marketing Association (MMA) is quickly trying to define advertising formats and pricing models. It is difficult for advertisers because mobile phones have many different screen sizes and resolutions. This again points to a movement of more generalizable principles about the ad experience across any device.

Which platform to choose? It all depends on the marketing goals for the campaign, the target market demographics and behavior, and other things marketers consider for any advertising format choice.

Mobile advertising continues to grow as users spend more time on their devices. However, there are still lingering issues that impact the industry. Ads that take up much of an already small screen size can cause a negative experience for app users. Furthermore, if users are expecting information on demand, a 30 second video ad to watch a 15 second clip is not desirable. Many mobile users also have data caps related to their monthly service, and paying for ads is not appealing. Mobile operating system creators are also inserting features that may help users limit their exposure to ads. Newer versions of Apple's iOS include a feature to limit targeted ad tracking, meaning that you will still receive ads, but they will not be as relevant. Combined with ad-blocking apps attempting to limit what consumers see, advertisers must be aware that tools exist to limit maximum ad effectiveness. In spite of these issues, content-sponsored advertising on mobile devices is likely to increase in the future.

Paid Search

Paid search occurs when an advertiser pays a search engine a fee for directory submission, inclusion in a search engine index, or to display their ad when users enter particular keywords. Paid search has been the paid media giant since 2006, capturing massive amounts of advertising dollars on desktop, laptop, and mobile devices. Internet users click on paid search ads (also called "sponsored links") 25 percent of the time, according to HubSpot. The most important tactic in paid search marketing is related to keywords.

Keyword advertising at search engine sites prompts sponsored text or display ads to appear on the SERP (search engine results pages). For example, advertisers can bid on the word *automobile*, and when users search using that word, the advertiser's banner or text message will appear on the resulting page. Google.com orders the ads by price paid in a keyword bidding process, the landing page URL, and the click-through rate. Thus, the most relevant ad tops the list of sponsored links on the page. Most advertisers use word groupings that describe the business rather than relying on a single word. They also use "negative" keywords to remove words that don't apply, such as a dinner only restaurant using "restaurant" and then "lunch" and "breakfast" as a negative word because it is only open for dinner. There are many other criteria, such as industry categories, and as with natural search, paid search is always changing.

Google also sends contextual ads for display on other Web sites in its AdSense program, as previously mentioned (site owners get paid whenever a user clicks on the ad at their site or in a video and so forth). See the Let's Get Technical box to understand how search engines work.

Let's Get Technical—Search Engines

You have just been hired as a junior executive in the marketing department. You would like to make a good impression. Your manager hands you a study showing that most visitors to your company's website find the site using a search engine. She asks you to improve your site's ranking on the search engines. You have no idea where to begin, and you are worried about looking bad. Fortunately, you have heard about services that help improve search engine rankings. If only you could remember what they are called and how they work . . .

The Web contains billions of pages. Realistically, it would be impossible for the search engines to search the entire Web every time someone types in a search term. The task would take days to complete. Therefore, search engines actually do the searching up to a month in advance and store the results in a huge database. They send automatic programs called **spiders** out on the Web to go from site to site, page by page, and word by word, as shown in Exhibit 13.4. These spiders build up a massive index or database of all the words found, where they are found, how many times they appear on each page, and so on.

When users type in a search term, they are actually querying this database. Because it is an indexed database, the query returns the results almost instantly. The results are generally returned in order of relevance with the most relevant site appearing first. But how does the search engine define relevance?

It is the search engine's job to figure out which sites are most likely to be relevant to the search term. Here the spider aids it. The spider does more than just count words. It also looks for the location of those words on the page and the **frequency** with which they appear. For example, if the word is in the title of a page, it is given a higher relevance value than a word appearing in the body text. A word appearing multiple times also earns a higher ranking.

So why not combine these ideas and repeat the keyword multiple times at the top of the page to fool the spider? The spiders are also trained to avoid sites that attempt to trick them by repeating words many times in a row. One technique is to ignore repeats that are not separated by at least, say, seven other words. This guards against someone loading a page with, for example, "Mazda, Mazda, and Mazda." Google will even punish sites that attempt to work the system by plummeting their search engine ranking.

Search engines also take two other off-page considerations into account—how many sites link to a particular site and how many times users have clicked through to a site. Both links and click-throughs are indicators of a site's popularity.

So again, why not just make a bunch of dummy sites that link to your site? Why not sign onto the search engine thousands of times and click through to your site to improve your ranking? The search engines are trained to spot both behaviors and compensate accordingly. The actual techniques used are becoming trade secrets because producing a search engine that returns truly useful results is actually a point of product differentiation and therefore provides a competitive advantage. Nonetheless, one Web site, Search Engine Watch (www. searchenginewatch.com), reveals many of the secrets for each of the search engines.

E-marketers would like their sites to appear high in the search engine rankings—preferably on the first page—above the fold—meaning that they show without scrolling. One way to gain this placement is to purchase paid listings, usually triggered by keywords in the search term. Another way is to hire a company that studies the search engines to determine their algorithms for ranking pages. The analysis provides information that can be used to redesign pages so they will rise in the rankings. This is called search engine optimization (SEO).

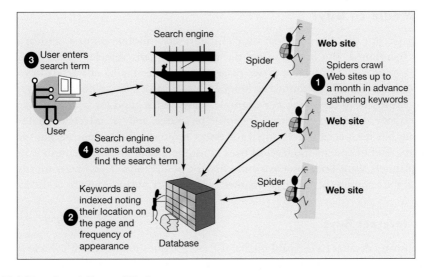

Exhibit 13.4 How Search Engines Work

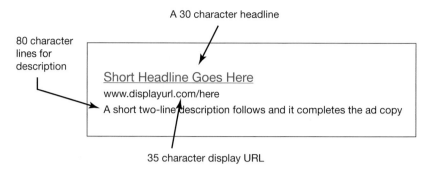

Exhibit 13.5 Google AdWords Copy Design

Paid search is commonly called pay per click (PPC) because advertisers pay whenever users click on the ads. Google charges between a few cents and hundreds of dollars per click; however, depending on the popularity of keywords, the monthly bill can range from $100 to millions of dollars. Click-through rates can vary from 0 percent to 50 percent, so picking the best keywords is key if advertisers don't want to be surprised with a huge bill. For example, American Meadows used the names of particular flowers as keywords rather than "gardening" because it got too many clicks for people looking for gardening tools and other things it didn't carry. Google and other search engines greatly increased revenues for advertisers and their own pockets by selling keyword ads because the user is more open to messages that relate to the context of their online activity.

As an example, Jerome's Furniture, a furniture store in Southern California, used the Google AdWords program and increased its sales by 93 percent due to the ads driving customers to physical stores over the course of a year. Google AdWords is a very complex service to use because it involves appropriate selections for keywords, ad group (several ads in one subject area), language, geographic area, run dates, and formulating an ad headline and text that will capture user clicks—plus, of course, deciding on the click-through rate for bidding purposes. Exhibit 13.5 displays the guidelines for the actual AdWords ad design.

Which Media to Buy?

Advertisers pay for space on Web and social media sites, mobile phones, and in e-mail, as previously mentioned. But how do they decide which media vehicles to purchase? Beyond the target, product, and campaign goals, marketers consider media characteristics, effectiveness, and efficiency. Each medium has unique characteristics for achieving goals—much of which has already been discussed. For example, television is good for building awareness and branding because it reaches the masses for some programs, and the internet can be used well for branding but is especially well suited for direct response, such as registering, purchasing, and so forth. And of course, the level of trust consumers have in each medium is important.

Media planners want both effective and efficient media buys. *Effectiveness* means reaching and gaining the attention of the target market, and *efficiency* means doing so at the lowest cost.

Effective Internet Buys

Once a company decides to use paid media, it faces the question of which vehicle (individual paid medium) to use. As noted earlier, media planners look for the media with audiences that closely match the brand's target markets. Marketers use many innovative digital strategies to reach narrowly targeted markets, including social media and e-mail ads sent using proprietary databases.

Advertisers trying to reach the largest number of users through keyword targeting will buy space at search engines. Online advertising is greatly effective at reaching niche markets due to the major amount of content existing for these segments. This reason explains the huge growth in vertical search marketing and keyword advertising.

Weather.com used search marketing effectively to drive traffic to its lifestyle content pages (weather considerations for golf, skiing, weddings, allergies, and so forth). Its goals were to increase page views by 45 percent a year, maintain leadership in the weather category (with 30% of all weather category search clicks coming to Weather.com), and to drive lifestyle page visits because they have the highest revenue value. To do this, they planned a keyword advertising campaign. Weather.com marketers tested two key phrases for its wedding pages—for people planning outdoor weddings away from home. The phrase "wedding planner" brought 1.5 visits to Weather.com per unique visitor, 3.6 webpages per visit, and 5.2 pages per unique visitor. The term "outdoor wedding" did better, with 1.8 visits per unique visitor, 6.6 pages per visit, and 12.0 pages per unique visitor. Thus, they settled on "outdoor wedding" for their keyword ad buy. "Our analytics data drives 95 percent of our decisions. We want to make sure what we changed worked and have data to back up our decisions," said Weather.com Marketing Director Derek Van Nostran.

Paid media can be quite effective at moving B2B prospects through the marketing purchase funnel. Before being acquired and shut down by LinkedIn, Bizo conceived a purchase funnel for the business market, as shown in Exhibit 13.6. First, prospects become aware of the product, then they need to learn what its benefits are as compared to competition (education). Next, prospects evaluate options and then often ask for a proposal from the seller. Hopefully, this results in purchase, and the prospect emerges from the funnel as a customer. It should be noted that not every prospect goes through all these steps in order. Also, other than the proposal stage, this is very similar to the consumer market funnel.

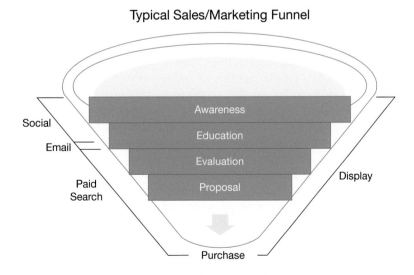

Exhibit 13.6 How Paid Media Move Prospects Through the Purchase Funnel

Source: LinkedIn Business. www.business.linkedin.com

According to Bizo, "display advertising gives marketers the opportunity to touch prospects at every stage of the funnel." As seen in Exhibit 13.6, Bizo recommends using social display ads for awareness and education and e-mail ads and paid search for the evaluation, proposal, and purchase stages. Their reasoning follows from B2B market studies:

- Top of the funnel. Bizo cites studies showing increases in awareness, aided brand recall, and website visits after users were exposed to display advertising.
- Mid-funnel. Bizo cites a ZDNet study showing a large increase in engagement and download of Web content after seeing display ads.
- Bottom of the funnel. When combined with paid search tactics, display ads prompted increases in conversions to sales, increases in event registrations, and click-through rates.

This is remarkable, when compared with the low display and search ad response rates referenced in Chapter 12. It appears that the combination is more powerful, especially in the B2B market. This is a good lesson, because marketers need to find the right blend of paid media to move prospects to owned media and generate positive earned media.

Efficient Internet Buys

If the audience for certain media vehicles matches the firm's target (*effective* buy), advertisers examine particular metrics to determine the most efficient buy. To measure efficiency *before* buying advertising space, media buyers use three important metrics: CPM (cost per thousand impressions) and two performance-based models: CPA (cost per action) and CPC (cost per click). Exhibit 13.7 displays performance-based models trends from 2004 to 2020.

CPM is calculated by taking the ad's cost, dividing it by the audience size, and then multiplying by 1,000 [(Cost ÷ Audience) × 1,000]. Internet audience size is counted using **impressions**: the number of times an ad was served to unique site visitors, regardless of whether they looked at it. For example, a full banner ad at MediaPost.com, an advertising and media internet portal, received 2.4 million impressions and cost $168,000 a month for a CPM of $70. This pricing model is often used for sponsorships, gaming and video ads. CPM is used because it allows for efficiency comparisons among various media and *vehicles* within the media (e.g., a particular video or website). Magazines are usually the most expensive medium to reach 1,000 readers; radio is often the least expensive.

Cost per action (CPA) includes social actions, such as the number of chocolate gifts sent to friends, number of posts to a profile, number of comments to a blog, number of users who play a game or view a video trailer, number of site registrations, or number of fans as a result of an advertisement. It is also commonly used in affiliate programs. For example, when a blogger recommends a book and a user clicks on the image to land on Amazon.com, the blogger will be paid if the user buys the book (not simply for clicking).

Cost per click (CPC) is a performance-based payment, often called pay per click (PPC). This includes schemes such as payment for each click on the ad, payment for each conversion (sale), or payment for each sales lead or new registered user.

Google AdWords, Facebook and many other sites use a bidding process for paid ads. Sometimes called **real time bidding (RTB)**, the advertiser only buys the number of impressions they want at a predefined price. For example, the Facebook ad in Exhibit 13.5 was bid at a maximum of $1.20 per click with a $50 total budget for the two-week campaign, and based on other competing bids, the final CPC price was $0.88. An ad using the RTB pricing model appears higher or lower in a list of ads depending on the price level of other bids (and other factors). This type of pricing is beneficial to advertisers but risky for Web sites, which must

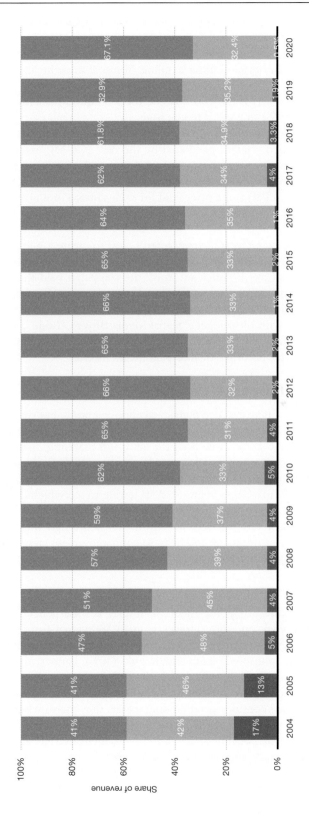

Exhibit 13.7 Distribution of US Online Advertising Revenue, 2004–2020

Source: PricewaterhouseCoopers LLP/IAB Internet Advertising Revenue Reports

depend partially on the power of the client's ad and product to yield click-throughs for revenues. Nonetheless, RTB represents an increasing number of ad buys in addition to search advertising.

There are many other pricing models online. Some of these include the following:

- Cost per install (CPI) is the cost charged for a unique installation of a widget or other application included in a social media page.
- Cost per engagement (CPE) is the cost of each user-defined engagement, such as submission of branded content generated by the user (CGM), entries to a contest, votes/polls, reviews or comments, ratings, engagement with interactive ads, replies to, clicks or favorites, a Promoted Tweet, or other social actions (clicking on "Like" button).
- Cost per visitor (CPV) is the price paid for each visitor coming from an ad to the advertiser's site.

In one interesting example, JCPenney hired Gigya to create a widget that allowed its teen market to add hats, mustaches, and other fun things to photos of their friends using a social network application. Called "Stuck on You," the campaign paid the social media property using a CPI model and realized 2.9 million installations by users. Furthermore, there were over 43 clicks for every widget install (engagement), and an average of 22 friends were reached each time a user engaged with the widget ("Social Media Buyer's Guide", 2010).

The paid media pricing models are also used during and after an IMC campaign to measure its effectiveness. At this point we turn to paid media metrics.

Paid Media Performance Metrics

There are hundreds of performance metrics to choose among, but the best ones will be those that closely match the campaign's objectives. If it is purchasing, measure the number of sales, dollar amounts, and ROI that came from the ad. If it is branding, measures could include the percent increase in positive conversations or blog comments about the brand, number of video views, increase in number of fans or friends, number of widget shares, and so forth. As mentioned in Chapter 12, marketers often use A/B testing to see which landing page pulled best. They also use this type of testing to test various display ads or other paid media tactics. Regardless, most marketers still rely heavily on click-through metrics as a starting point because it is an easy measure to get and helps to compare various tactics—for example, did the e-mail or display ad generate higher click-through?

Effectiveness Evidence

When viewed as a direct-response medium, display ads are generally ineffective: only 0.2 percent of all users click on them. However, many individual firms have received stunning click-through results with carefully targeted offers to prospects. Other tactics motivating action in one study include sponsored search engine links (40%), banner ads (28%), and pop-up ads (19%). This means that the 0.2 percent click-through for banners may not fully appreciate the effectiveness of this format in terms of brand awareness and subsequent search activity.

When display ads are considered as branding media, they increase brand awareness and message association, and they build brand favorability and purchase intent. In many studies, online ads that were bigger or contained rich multimedia delivered an even greater impact. For example, skyscrapers and large rectangles are more effective than standard size banners in increasing brand awareness and purchase intent, and video is the best. One thing hasn't changed in years—bigger and more novel ads are noticed more frequently.

Increasing evidence indicates that online and offline advertising work well together, for example, the large number of people who research online and shop offline, and the sometimes huge website visitations experienced by internet companies after advertising in the Super Bowl television event.

The best online paid media tactic depends on the target, competition, company, offer, and how novel, engaging, relevant, and creative the tactic is. Paid search and e-mail are validated in many other studies as being effective tactics, but don't forget that it all depends—a creative and scientific e-marketer can make the lowly banner ad a stellar tactic if used adroitly.

Chapter Summary

Many media are paid to carry an organization's promotional messages such as online advertising, product placement, and sponsored tweets. Paid media are generally used to build awareness, move users to owned media, and ultimately engage them in earned media. The most important paid media technique is paid search advertising, followed by display banner ads, classified ads, mobile ads, and social media. Paid display ads include rich media ads such as in-banner video ads, expandable/retractable ads, pop-up and pop-under windows, floating ads, interstitial ads, wallpaper ads, trick banner ads, and map ads, as well as contextual advertising and behavioral advertising. In addition, digital marketers may use e-mail ads, sponsored content, product placement, or text link ads as part of their paid media.

Advertisers use paid social media to build brand awareness, create positive brand attitudes, gather information about customers, and motivate user actions such as joining a community, clicking through to a site, or making a purchase. They can take advantage of three unique aspects of social networks: profile data (knowing the personal profile of members), social graph (mapping connections between members), and interaction data (capturing data about members' personal interactions). In particular, the narrow targeting available through paid Facebook, Twitter, Instagram, and LinkedIn ads enables organizations to reach well-defined markets. Advertising is also available in virtual reality applications and before, during, or after online videos on YouTube and other sites.

Because of the high penetration and heavy consumer usage of mobile devices, marketers see great promise in mobile advertising. Paid search occurs when an advertiser pays a search engine to display its ad when users type in specific keywords. When selecting media vehicles, companies look not just at the target, product, and campaign goals but also at media characteristics, effectiveness (reaching the target audience), and efficiency (reaching the right audience at the lowest cost). Paid media can move prospects through the marketing purchase tunnel from awareness and education to evaluation, proposal, and purchase. Three important efficiency metrics for paid media are cost per thousand impressions (CPM), cost per action (CPA), and cost per click (CPC). To evaluate paid media performance, advertisers use metrics that relate to the campaign's objectives, recognizing that techniques such as display ads can also have a powerful impact on brand awareness, association, favorability, and purchase intent.

Exercises

Review Questions

1. How has usage of internet advertising changed over the years? In light of this trend, how is spending on internet advertising expected to change in the future?
2. What is an online display ad, and what are some of the standard formats?

3. What are some types of rich media ads, and what are their general advantages and disadvantages?
4. Why does contextual advertising tend to produce higher click-through rates?
5. How does sponsored content help advertisers reach their audiences?
6. What three unique aspects of social network accounts, in large part, account for the expected rise in spending in social media advertising?
7. What are some of the options advertisers have when they use Facebook, Twitter, and LinkedIn as paid media?
8. What issues are likely to affect the future of mobile advertising?
9. Is keyword advertising different for laptops and mobile devices?
10. Why must advertisers be concerned about both the effectiveness and efficiency of media buys?
11. Which types of paid media tend to be most effective at each stage of the B2B purchase funnel?
12. How and why would an advertiser measure efficiency according to CPM, CPA, and CPC?

Discussion Questions

1. **The Lenovo Story.** Do you think customers might be upset if they found out Lenovo was using remarketing and keeping track of their behavior online? Why or why not?
2. **The Lenovo Story.** Identify at least five other types of paid media that might work for Lenovo, including Facebook. Explain why each might be a good idea for this company.
3. Why do you think consumers have less trust in paid media than they do in earned media or owned media?
4. Knowing that companies are always experimenting with new sizes and formats of online display ads to attract user attention and break through clutter, why would the Interactive Advertising Bureau continue to propose standard dimensions for display ads?
5. What ethical issues seem to be raised by the use of online sponsored content and product placement? How would you recommend that a marketer improve transparency when it uses such paid media?

Web Activities

1. Conduct a Google search to locate three recent news articles about "Lenovo internet advertising." Which, if any, of the paid media described in this chapter has Lenovo used during the past year, and which does it appear to be planning to use in the future? Is the company continuing its remarketing strategy, as described in the chapter-opening example? Prepare a brief written or oral report summarizing what you've learned, and include your recommendations for metrics Lenovo should use to evaluate paid media performance.
2. Select a large retailer or a particular product and conduct an internet search for one example each of its paid media, owned media, and earned media. What do you think are the marketer's objectives for each? What differences and similarities do you notice among these media? Which do you personally find the most engaging, and why?
3. Visit the Google page that describes its Google Ads Display Network. What types of formats can advertisers display through this network? What kinds of targeting tools can advertisers use to get their messages to the right audience? How does Google explain the pricing model for ads on this network?

4. Go to the Interactive Advertising Bureau's home page (www.iab.net). Browse some of its links to guidelines and best practices. Choose two of the ideas mentioned in these guidelines and best practices and explain why they're important for advertisers, based on the concepts and principles discussed in this chapter.
5. Visit business.facebook.com and read about how Facebook advertising works. If you were considering whether to participate as an advertiser, what additional questions would you ask of a Facebook representative?

Chapter 14

Digital Marketing Communication
Earned Media

This chapter examines why and how companies plan, implement, and evaluate digital marketing communication initiatives for earned media, the third element of the online content strategy. You will learn about the techniques that marketers use to engage users, encourage collaborative content creation, manage the firm's reputation online, and monitor earned media activities.

After reading this chapter, you will be able to:

- Describe the five levels of user engagement and explain what each means for earned media.
- Explain the role of trust in earned media and the implications for consumer behavior.
- List some key techniques for engaging users and discuss the importance of each.
- Outline the marketing benefits of engaging consumers in collaborative content creation.
- Highlight seven ways in which companies can attract users and move them up the engagement ladder.
- Discuss how a company can build, maintain, monitor, and repair its reputation online.
- Identify specific metrics used to monitor, measure, and refine earned media activities.

DELL STARTS LISTENING

Dell Computer has always been America's darling with its high-quality equipment, direct distribution model, and great customer service. Yet in June 2005, Dell was brought to its knees by a single blogger—Jeff Jarvis of BuzzMachine.com:

> I just got a new Dell laptop and paid a fortune for the four-year, in-home service. . . . The machine is a lemon and the service is a lie . . . DELL SUCKS. DELL LIES. Put that in your Google and smoke it, Dell.

This post brought a hailstorm of similar customer service complaints that lasted for nearly two years, and this issue has come to be known as "Dell's Hell." What happened?

Wanting to pare costs, Dell followed a current trend and outsourced its technical customer service to a firm in India in the early 2000s. Things looked great as costs dropped, and market share increased to 28.8 percent the following year (2004), according to the global market intelligence firm IDC. However, complaints about the customer service also increased: Better Business Bureau complaints rose 23 percent, and Dell's customer satisfaction declined 6.3 percent, according to a University of Michigan survey. A 2005 Google search for "dell customer service problems" returned nearly 3 million links. Clearly, the outsourcing strategy was not having the desired effect.

DOI: 10.4324/9781003247319-18

Like many companies, Dell decided to sit tight for a year and wait for the online complaint storm to pass. When it didn't stop, Dell appointed a digital media manager to "deal" with the internet chatter. Lionel Menchaca initiated several Dell blogs in multiple languages as mechanisms for handling customer complaints and ideas and to have conversations with stakeholders about the problems and Dell's actions to fix them. IdeaStorm.com (now delltechnologies.com) is a notable blog and social medium where users post ideas and vote on them, with the best percolating to the top. Dell responds to the ideas, makes changes in the company, and reports on the progress. In the first three months, the blog gathered 5,000 ideas, over 20,000 comments, and more than 350,000 idea endorsements resulting in significant changes to the company over time (see Beal and Strauss, 2008, for more on "Dell's Hell").

Earned Media

Dell was an early company to learn the hard way that companies must listen to individual customers online or pay a dear price. Listening was only a start—Dell found that a company can benefit by truly engaging stakeholders in conversation and using what it learned to improve the company. Dell's experience was a wake-up call to marketers in the early days of social media: finally, marketers were being forced to act on the concept that they must deliver on their brand promises or be exposed in a big way online.

Well-executed owned and paid media can drive prospects and customers through the steps from awareness to product purchase, repurchase, and into long-term customer loyalty. However, earned media have a multiplier effect, intensifying and spreading the communication messages far and wide online. Marketing communication is shifting from purely impression based (e.g., ads) to recommendation based (e.g., social media posting). When marketers offer compelling reasons for people to share online content, "like" on Facebook, write comments, pin on Pinterest or retweet on Twitter, it has the effect of increasing marketing spend effectiveness.

Earned media is like offline word-of-mouth on steroids: a social megaphone. When someone posts a positive comment about a product on Facebook, it serves as a recommendation to friends. Recall from Chapter 12 that earned media occur when "individual conversations become the channel" on blogs, product review sites, news sites, snaps, videos, many other places, and in comments on owned media pages everywhere they are allowed.

Earned media can be initiated by the company through branded content distribution, such as entertaining YouTube videos about the product, Snapchat Stories and filters, press releases (public relations), or other activities intended to engage users, such as placing social hooks on company brand and microsites (e.g., Facebook register, subscribe or "like," e-mail subscriptions, text opt-ins). Companies also put "follow us" links to these social sites in e-mail messages sent to customer or prospect databases or direct them to mobile applications that allow further engagement. Earned media can have a direct cost associated with it, such as when the company sponsors a contest or creates content that spreads, but it has no financial cost when it is user conversation. By definition, earned media are created by others, and companies have little to no control over this user-generated content (UGC). This communication can get ugly very quickly—and often does. Professional and citizen journalists share their own opinions and experiences all over the social media via computers and mobile phones, sometimes while company marketing personnel are sleeping. This is a fast-paced social media world, and marketers are having a hard time keeping up.

Before discussing the types of earned media, it is important to understand the possible levels of internet user engagement.

User Engagement Levels

Engagement occurs among and between the company and internet users who are actively discussing the brand. This is compared to traditional media, which only allows passive exposure, such as when a consumer is watching television. Occasionally, however, traditional media will prompt engagement when the consumer writes an e-mail to the magazine editor or sends a text to a friend about a television program. Traditional media can also prompt communication to companies about their brands when designed for this purpose, such as awarding a prize to the first 100 people who comment on a company Facebook page or *The Voice* voting by text message. However, it is not as easy for consumers to engage when they receive the information in traditional media and must move to the computer or smartphone to respond. Company-owned websites can also engage customers by offering content downloading and uploading, webpage personalization, live chat functionality, and one-to-one contact opportunities.

There are many levels of user engagement online. It is important for a company to review its marketing communication objectives and understand what proportion of its customers and prospects operate at each hierarchy of effects level (from awareness through behavior), so that it can use social media for positive discussion online and collaboration with customers. Exhibit 14.1 displays an iteration of two common models of engagement, displaying five levels from least to most engaged: consume, connect, collect, create, and collaborate.

1. The least engaged internet users **consume** online content only. They read blogs, view videos and photos, listen to podcasts, and read the reviews and opinions expressed by others occupying higher levels of engagement on websites and forums.
2. At the next level, users **connect** with others by creating a profile on a social network, such as "friending" on Facebook or joining TripAdvisor or other sites that require registration to read content. These consumers do not actively post anything, however. Connecting is a low-risk level of engagement that allows people to participate in small

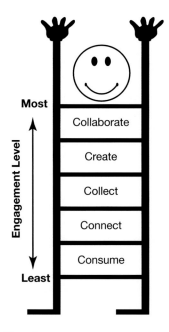

Exhibit 14.1 Five Levels of Internet User Engagement

steps. Another way to connect is through a social gathering happening either on or offline and that is facilitated by a site allowing groups to coordinate these meetings. For example, St. Supéry winery used meetup.com to create a global celebration of a wine—they called it #CabernetDay (the "#" is a hashtag). As a result, many posts were also created on social media.

3. Consumers who **collect** information go through a process of filtering content and tagging what they find valuable in social media sites. This could include Pinterest for storing and sharing ideas and Facebook for photo tagging or "liking" someone else's content. Collectors might also subscribe to RSS feeds on blog sites so that they can actively read content of interest. Finally, collectors show their preferences by voting in polls online. For example, parents can upload their children's photos to www.gerber.com/photosearch to be eligible to win the annual Gerber Baby Contest. Participants in the contest encourages other internet users to vote via the website, and Gerber uses its social media pages to promote participation as well.

4. Moving up the engagement ladder, **creators** actually write or upload original multimedia content to websites, such as videos to YouTube, photos to Facebook, or music and podcasts to iTunes. This involves creating content—which is a higher level than simply voting on someone else's content. These consumers write product reviews/ratings, create their own blogs/webpages, and comment on other people's blogs, contribute to wiki sites (e.g., eHow, Wikipedia), and generally add much more to the social media content.

5. Finally, the most engaged customers **collaborate** with the company when they work with others in discussion to find ways to improve products. For example, ProductHunt.com allows start-up companies to gather feedback from user reviews and interact with consumers who have questions about their products. Another example is delltechnologies.com, where users post questions and product problems and others view and vote the posts as important concerns or not (as mentioned in the opening story). Dell then responds on the status of each idea. Finally, hashtags (#) were created by Twitter users as a way to mark keywords and topics in tweets. This type of collaboration has now expanded to other social media websites and helps companies and bloggers improve products.

Datareportal indicates that the global social network penetration rate is 53.6 percent as of 2021; however, many of these social media users do not create content. In the next sections, you will see how companies engage customers to create earned media product discussion and multimedia content uploading.

Engaging Individuals to Produce Earned Media

When a couple becomes engaged to be married, they are expressing their trust, commitment, and caring for each other—this is also true when a brand seeks this kind of love from its markets and wants them to talk about the products. **Engagement** occurs when internet users consume, connect, or collaborate with brands, companies, or each other.

Trust is a key component of word-of-mouth communication resulting from customer engagement. In fact, 79 percent of consumers claim to trust other consumers online as much as personal friends or family, with more than 90 percent acknowledging that both positive and negative reviews influence their opinions (Statista, 2021). "A person like yourself" is someone who shares similar interests or friends—either in person or in a social network—and is often viewed as more credible than a company itself. For example, when planning trips or on the road, travelers visit the largest travel site, TripAdvisor.com, to check out the millions of reviews and opinions of hotels and sites in nearly 50 countries, which are written by other travelers as they are planning trips. Thus, when people post opinions about products, over half of the readers are likely to believe what they say, and this will influence their purchase decisions.

The popular American fast food chain Wendy's scored a tremendous win by responding to a simple question from a fan on Twitter. What started out as a tweet asking how many retweets to win free chicken nuggets for a year has become the most retweeted post of all time at over 3.6 million and almost 1 million favorites. Not only has Wendy's benefitted from the immense exposure from user Carter Wilkerson's feat, but many charitable causes have also gained another look from the innovative user's efforts. While Carter has not reached 18 million tweets yet (Wendy's initial goal), he did receive his free nuggets.

We now turn to a discussion of the "who, what, how, and where" to engage customers in conversation about a company and its brands.

Who Should a Company Engage?

It is not effective, efficient, or likely possible to get the entire internet universe talking about an organization and its products. As discussed in Chapter 12, the company will identify its target markets and objectives before developing an IMC campaign. In addition to consumers and prospects, many companies target influential bloggers and social network members, depending on their topical expertise.

Social Media Influencers

Companies identify social media influencers by observing and participating in conversations in social media locations where people discuss their industries. This will help them see who is active and has the most Facebook fans or friends, Twitter and Instagram followers, YouTube subscribers, or simply the most comments on posts. For example, the Digital Marketing group in LinkedIn had over two million members in 2021, and by clicking on the "recommended" tab, members can see posts with high engagement. These members often have the most followers in LinkedIn and contribute the most to the conversation. For a digital marketing professional, this is an ideal source for building buzz with influential colleagues. Although number of followers continues to be an important metric, engagement is just as important.

Traditional Journalists

The term "earned media" was coined prior to the internet. It referred to journalists writing or reporting on stories about companies and brands in traditional media, such as newspapers, television, and magazines. These same journalists now generate earned media in their online versions via digital channels.

Whereas printed US daily newspapers have decreased in readers from 56 million in 1995 to fewer than 25 million in 2021 (Watson, 2021), the top five general news websites today (Yahoo! News, Google News, Huffington Post, CNN) attract more than 500 million visitors (Watson, 2021). As such, and because users find news themselves via online searches, companies usually include a press room with releases about brands on their websites and also send them electronically via e-mail or the Web to media firms for publishing. This brand publicity is the result of most company marketing public relations (MPR) strategies.

The traditional press release is a typed document that includes the "what, when, where, who, and why" of something newsworthy the company sends to journalists for possible inclusion in print or online media (e.g., a new product announcement). Many companies include these text-heavy press releases as links on their websites, or worse, as PDF files for download (worse because journalists can't pick up smaller pieces of the text very easily). This is changing. Now bloggers and other social media journalists want to gain quick bits of information and expert quotes on topics they are writing about. Because they want to include images, video, and text information for articles, news releases are beginning to become social media friendly. Exhibit 14.2 is a model social media press release created by Shift Communications to be used on company websites. It includes the important facts and is largely interactive, providing links to company-created multimedia and white papers (note that the social media logos are on the press release as links but deleted in the exhibit due to intellectual property concerns). It is especially social media friendly because it allows journalists to pick up short bits of information and easily pass them along with an RSS button or Delicious bookmark link or paste it into a Wikipedia article, and more. For example, a blogger or *New York Times* reporter can easily find a quote from the company to include in an article without sifting through long documents. This means that company news can move around the internet quickly as these small information bits are shared: more earned media. The large PR firm Edelman uses this type of press release. The social media press release is the brainchild of Todd Defren, who also created a social media newsroom template for company websites, similar to what is being used by Google and others (see www. shiftcomm.com**).**

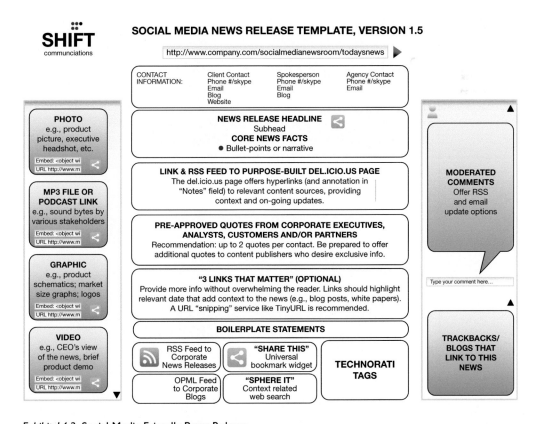

Exhibit 14.2 Social Media Friendly Press Release

Source: Shift Communications (www.shiftcomm.com)

Techniques for Engaging Users

Most social media, websites, and mobile apps provide space and tools for earned media content. You have read about many of them in this book, such as sites that allow multimedia content upload (YouTube, Flickr) and comments using hashtags, reviews, recommendations, and more. In the following sections, we focus on just a few important or new techniques not yet fully described in other chapters.

Viral Marketing

When individuals forward e-mail to friends or share Facebook newsfeed posts or YouTube videos, they are using what we like to call *word of mouse*. **Viral marketing** is the online equivalent of word of mouth and is sometimes referred to as word of mouse, which occurs when individuals forward content to each other through e-mail or social media sharing. This is analogous to the spread of physical or computer viruses. It is the opposite of the sales funnel, which narrows as prospects drop off to fewer customers, as shown in Exhibit 14.3. The viral funnel increases brand exposure as content circulates.

Viral marketing can be delivered by offline word-of-mouth or online when users forward content to others. A viral video is any video that is passed digitally from person to person, regardless of its content. This is done via a "share" link on YouTube or simply by sending an e-mail link of the video. Viral marketing was first used by the founder of Hotmail, a free e-mail

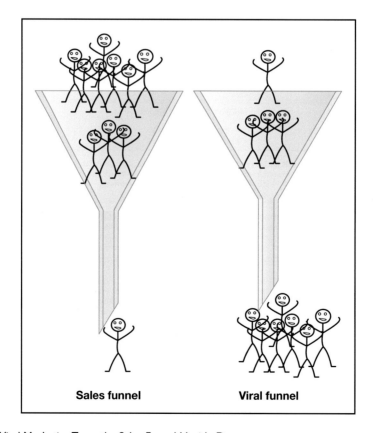

Sales funnel   **Viral funnel**

Exhibit 14.3 Viral Marketing Turns the Sales Funnel Upside Down

service that grew from zero to 12 million subscribers in its 18 initial months and to more than 50 million subscribers in about four years. Each e-mail sent via Hotmail carried an invitation for free Hotmail service. (See the Let's Get Technical Box for information about instant messaging.)

As with all engagement strategies, successful viral marketing programs involve appealing content that has a high chance of spreading. In fact, in October 2017, more than half of Facebook's users used the platform to read, watch, or share news (Newton, 2017), although recent research finds that political content, especially that which opposes one's political viewpoints, is particularly likely to cause Facebook users to tune out (Pelletier, Horky, and Fox, 2021).

Viral marketing has long been a favorite strategy of online marketers pushing youth-oriented products. For example, marketers might distribute a small game program or a video embedded within a sponsor's e-mail that is easy to forward. By releasing a few thousand copies of the game to some consumers, vendors hope to reach hundreds of thousands of others. Also known as *advocacy marketing*, viral marketing, if properly used, can be effective, efficient, and relatively inexpensive.

Viral marketing can be very successful with entertaining videos (especially on YouTube) that are spread via e-mail and by microbloggers (e.g., Twitter). The following are some successful viral campaigns:

- The Huggies #WeGotYouBaby (PRNewswire, 2021) campaign launched during the 2021 Super Bowl. Leading up to the game, Huggies encouraged parents who were expecting a child near the date of the Super Bowl to submit photos of their baby when he or she was born. The brand received many entries and could only feature five on the commercial, so they featured others on their Instagram page and website. They also gave away 25,000 newborn starter kits as a sweepstakes, according to PR Newswire.
- To celebrate Cinco de Mayo, Taco Bell released a Snapchat filter that made users' heads look like tacos. The lens was a huge success, with more than 224 million views in one day (Johnson, 2016).

Every company wants to create content that goes viral, but few accomplish this feat. The content has to be entertaining or mysterious, match popular culture, and gain user attention. In a sea of online content and information overload, sometimes even the best content does not go viral.

One downside of a viral strategy is that several e-mail hoaxes have been spread this way. Viral marketing has also been criticized by consumers because of a concern over unsolicited e-mails, which many see as an invasion of privacy.

Let's Get Technical—Text Messaging vs. Instant Messaging

Your company has two offices: one in the United States and one in India. As the director of marketing and public relations, it is your responsibility to facilitate communication between the product development team in India and the marketing and sales teams in the United States. Due to budget limitations, you need a low-cost, reliable solution, and the phone company has been unwilling to negotiate beyond its corporate packages. The teams are currently communicating via e-mail, but they are disappointed with the lag time—it often takes 45 minutes to get a simple questioned answered. An old technology—instant messaging—is now being reapplied in the business world, and it is changing the way businesspeople communicate worldwide.

Instant messaging (IM) has taken internet users by storm. Even though e-mail was the most rapidly adopted form of communication to date, instant messaging beats the speed of e-mail and maintains many of its other handy features.

Once the user is logged on, he or she views a list of contacts, which is often referred to as a buddy list or contact list. The list indicates each contact's status: online, offline, away, or idle. The list updates dynamically as friends and associates enter and exit the online world.

Sometimes instant messaging usernames are exchanged instead of e-mail addresses, especially among students of all ages. Students are known for displaying their entire days' schedules in an away message, thereby apprising friends of their whereabouts. Double-clicking a name on the buddy list initiates a conversation in most clients. A separate window opens, in which one types a message: "hi, how are you?" Only the two users can see the message and subsequent text.

The value of a communications platform is directly related to the number of users that are on it. University faculty in the United States are constantly amazed at how infrequently students check their e-mail. This is a real problem if time-sensitive content is delivered via e-mail. However, those same students constantly check their instant messaging accounts on social media. Now the tide is turning the other way. Faculty meeting on Teams or Zoom often message using the chat feature during meetings. Many faculty also instant message with their students. The broader point is that you need to meet your audience in the space that they inhabit—even if it may be a bit uncomfortable at first. In addition to instant messages, most clients offer a variety of features:

- *Chat rooms*. Multiple users can all engage in one conversation.
- *Hyperlinks*. Users can send each other active links to Web sites.
- *Files*. Users instant messaging each other can send files (e.g., Microsoft Word documents) to one another.
- *Talk*. With a microphone and speakers attached to the PC, users can talk to each other over the internet.
- *Videoconference*. With a Web camera connected to the PC, users can engage in videoconferencing.
- *Streaming information*. Up-to-date news, stock quotes, and other information can be displayed in the client application.

ICQ ("I Seek You") is considered to be the first instant messaging client. In November 1996, four Israeli entrepreneurs founded Mirabilis, Ltd., the company that developed ICQ. The thought behind the instant messaging concept was to create interpersonal communication online. The four noticed that the world was quickly adopting surfing and browsing online and wanted to create a simple solution for people to find and talk to each other. Just six months after its release, ICQ had 850,000 registered users and was considered the "World's Largest Internet Online Communication Network." By May 2002, ICQ had been downloaded more than 200 million times from CNET.com, and ICQ claimed to have 150 million registered users in 2004. ICQ believes that its success is due to viral marketing, for the software was never formally marketed. Emanuel Rosen, expert author on word-of-mouth marketing, discusses the ICQ phenomenon in his book titled *The Anatomy of Buzz*. According to Rosen, the "marketing" occurs when the ICQ client asks users if it can scan the user's e-mail address book to send friends and family an invitation to join the ICQ community.

Shortly after ICQ took off, other Web providers developed instant messaging clients. They worked hard to make sure those clients would not talk to each other so that users would be forced to stay in their networks. Keeping users in network helps monetize the service by selling ads that will reach a larger audience. Today the dominant instant messaging clients include Facebook Messenger, WhatsApp, WeChat, eBudddy, QQ, Windows Live Messenger, Skype, iMessage, SnapChat, Instagram, and GroupMe. These last four, iMessage, SnapChat, Instagram, and GroupMe are particularly popular with the North American college age crowd. These students routinely check all four accounts on a daily basis.

Instant messaging is a Web service. By contrast, text messaging is a service offered by the phone company. Therefore, you can receive a text wherever you have cell service, but you can only receive instant messaging if you have cellular data turned on or are connected to WiFi. Text messages are rather bland by comparison, since they don't include multimedia. However, that limitation also makes text messaging the lowest common denominator and guarantees its near universal adoption. Everyone can send and receive text messages. Many phone companies include unlimited texting in their cellular plans.

IMessage is an interesting example since it bridges instant messaging and text messaging. If your iPhone detects that the recipient of your message has iMessage, then they get the full multimedia message (blue thought bubbles). If it detects that they can only receive text, then that's all they get (green thought bubbles). Non-iPhone users also get a little reminder about the great content that they can't see—for example, "Message sent with balloons." So iMessage can send text messages to users of any platform but can only send rich multimedia messages to other iPhone users. So if you want to create an Animoji, you'll have to buy an iPhone.

Viral Blogging

Viral blogging is when bloggers conduct viral marketing activities. Viral blogging can be very effective with the use of tools such as Twitter. Many retailers entice WOM marketing by bloggers. For example, Paramount wanted to build awareness and box office sales for a sneak preview of the modestly budgeted "Super 8" science fiction film. Paramount sent a single Tweet and purchased advertising on Twitter via two Promoted Trends—one fairly early and the other a day before the premier. The sneak preview generated $1 million in box office sales, and the opening weekend for the film surpassed Paramount's goals by 52 percent (see more success stories at business.twitter.com).

Stormhoek Vineyards has also initiated successful viral marketing using social media (stormhoek.com). The company first offered a free bottle of wine to bloggers. Within six months, about 100 of these bloggers posted voluntary comments about the winery on their own blogs. Most had positive comments, which were read by their readers and by other bloggers. The Stormhoek example raises an interesting question: can bloggers be bought? The criticism is that bloggers are not required to disclose that they are being paid (or receive gifts) for their endorsements. Companies can pay bloggers directly to endorse products or do so via an intermediary such as PayPerPost.

Multimedia Sharing

Users upload many types of media for others to view, rate, and comment on, or build channels of other people's media. Following are the main types of sites used for this purpose, along with examples:

- *Photos and art*. Flickr (with 10 billion photos), Photobucket, deviantArt.
- *Video*. YouTube (serving over 4.9 billion videos a day), Vimeo, and traditional news sites.
- *Live casting*. This enables live audio or video streaming directly from a mobile phone, tablet internet device, PC, or Mac to a website for viewing by others. Examples: Twitch, Skype, LiveCast, FaceTime.
- *Music*. Here we are referring to sites that allow users to share and comment on music play-lists or original music, not copyright-protected music files. Examples: Spotify, Pandora.
- *Presentations*. These are uploaded, usually from PowerPoint, MS Word, or PDF documents, and then freely shared and commented upon. Examples: SlideShare, Scribd.
- *Augmented and virtual reality*. Growing capabilities in this space from companies like Apple with its ARKit are offering another way to share immersive experiences in a virtual world.

Amazon, Barnes & Noble, and other online booksellers allow anyone to self-publish content by uploading a digital e-book and selling it for download by iPad, PC, Kindle, and other digital book readers. For example, 26-year-old Amanda Hocking could not find a publisher for her young-adult paranormal novels, so she began selling them at online book-stores for $0.99 to $2.99 per digital download and sold more than 450,000 copies of the nine titles (Memmott, 2011)! Hocking earned between 30 and 70 percent of the sales price. This self-publishing capitalizes on consumer behavior trends and cuts out the book publish-ing middlemen by allowing online booksellers to offer products directly to consumers. Many other social media sites also benefit by allowing users to upload their own content. For instance, Facebook asks for users to update their safety in emergency situations, so as to let other users know which people and areas are safe. Apple Music and Amazon allow musicians to upload digital music files for sale on their sites. Musicians cannot upload music directly but must go through a distributor such as CD Baby (the largest Indie online music store), who helps them obtain a barcode and ascertains that the intellectual property belongs to said musician. Obviously, YouTube, SoundCloud, and many other multimedia sites contain only user-created content. Their business models entice users to upload content, draw many eyeballs, and sell advertising.

Wikis

Wikis are websites that allow users to post, edit, and organize multimedia content. This is closely related to crowdsourcing and user-generated content. Examples include Wikipedia (encyclopedia), Wikihow (how-to-do site), and Wikispaces (education). For example, eHow has over 2 million articles and videos created by consumers and professionals covering 30 categories and every topic from house and garden tips to business ideas. All content is created by site users and screened by site editors for quality and value (see ehow.com)

Wikis are important because a consultant can edit definitions and add material to a site like Wikipedia or Wikihow and become known as an expert. When added to other tactics like reviewing products and books or answering Yahoo! questions in his field of expertise, the consultant is building a thought leadership niche: type in his or her name and it comes up in lots of different places showing his or her expert area. Some companies, people, and brands are important enough to be allowed their own Wikipedia entries, and marketers take advantage of this.

Ratings and Reviews

Prior to a purchase, consumers like to collect information, such as what brand to buy, from which vendor, and at what price. Online customers do this via shopping aids (e.g., comparison shopping agents), looking at product review sites such as Yelp, and conducting research at company sites and other sources. Ratings and reviews in social networks facilitate commerce, both on and offline. Shoppers also resort to friends, fans, followers, and other experienced customers. With peer-to-peer engagement through social media and high consumer trust in acquaintances, retailers recognize that their customers' voices can be an extremely strong marketing tool for building sales and improving products. Therefore, retailers want to hear what customers say. A variety of tools are available to engage shoppers online:

- **Customer ratings and reviews.** This is feedback from real customers, integrated either into an e-commerce product page, a social network page, a customer's review site, or in customer news feeds (e.g., Amazon.com, Apple Music). Yelp and Google local pages are two other important review sites. Customer ratings can be summarized by votes or polls.
- **Expert ratings and reviews**. The view from the independent voice of authority, whether professional, or prosumer—professional consumer—can be integrated into a digital commerce product page, a social network page, a product review site, an online magazine, and/or in news feeds (e.g., Metacritic and CNET Reviews).
- **Business reviews**. These sites hold reviews for everything from local restaurants and retailers to national brands and professionals (e.g., Yelp, RateMDs).
- **Community questions and answers**. These sites are especially valuable to professionals who want to build a thought leadership niche, demonstrating their knowledge when answering questions in their specialty area. Examples include Yahoo! Answers and Wiki-Answers (a Wiki and a community Q&A site).
- **Sponsored reviews.** These are paid-for reviews written by either customer bloggers or by experts on social media platforms (e.g., Sponsored Reviews, PayPerPost). Expert and sponsored reviews are often generated in video format.
- **Consumer conversations**. People communicate via e-mail, blog, live chat, discussion groups, and tweets, in both original posts and in subsequent comments. Monitoring conversations yields rich data for market research, product improvements (collaboration), and customer service.
- **Customer testimonials**. Customer stories and case studies are often published to a social media site that allows comments and discussion (e.g., Bazaarvoice site reviews).

Ratings and reviews have been a cornerstone of digital commerce since 1995 (e.g., at Amazon.com) and are a proven solution for boosting traffic volume, conversions (from surfing a site to buying), and increasing average order value. Reviews may result in word-of-mouse marketing through social influence, promoting purchase decisions with credible information. Bazaarvoice measured the impact of ratings and reviews as boosting website conversion rates by up to 25 percent. Interestingly, negative reviews appear not to have a detrimental effect on sales; we do not live in a five-star world, and apparently shoppers find positive ratings more believable when they also see negative ratings.

Social Recommendations and Referrals

Whereas ratings and reviews usually are visible to all, social recommendations and referrals are personal endorsements designed to realize value for customers and advocates. The in-store analogy for this strategy is when consumers ask a fellow shopper for advice. Often, social recommendations take the form of online versions of traditional customer-get-customer and referral-rewards programs (e.g., Sky's "Introduce a Friend"), but can also use syndication tools via Twitter and Facebook to share recommendations with friends, fans, and followers. These are closely related to ratings and reviews and are sometimes integrated with them.

Traditional online product review companies such as Amazon.com, Bazaarvoice, and Power Reviews have advised many consumers. Up-and-coming social shopping start-ups such as ShopSocially now encourage *conversations* about purchases. The product recommendations come from people consumers know and are thus more trustworthy than reviews by strangers (recall the trust statistics previously mentioned). It will be interesting to see if this kind of model for product recommendations will eventually replace traditional general website recommendations and what products, services, and price ranges customers will use with traditional methods.

Sometimes social shopping portals that bundle ratings and reviews with recommendations also provide shopping tools: a prime example is provided in the Kaboodle shopping community. Common recommendation methods follow:

- **Social bookmarking**. These sites allow users to share their favorite websites and comments on them online. Pinterest provides a free Web browser plug-in so that users can simply click on a button to bookmark a website. Pinterest asks users to place the bookmark on boards, which are used to categorize the bookmark. Social bookmarking is powerful because users can click through to other users who have bookmarked the same articles to see what else they are reading on the same topic. It is a great resource for individual or collaborative research and one we have used to indicate assigned class reading lists. It is even better for marketers wanting to create a buzz about a white paper, blog post, or other online article, and that is why a Pinterest bookmark icon appears near such articles.

- **Referral programs.** These involve financial rewards for customers and partners who refer new customers (e.g., Groupon, Gilt). These programs give social media sites the opportunity to make money when a user clicks from the site to the retailer and purchases a product. For example, the Amazon.com Associate Program provides bloggers and others with banner ads or book or album images for their sites; the site owner gains revenue by sending its audience to purchase at Amazon.com. You can find examples of this on blogs where the authors have a sidebar of "books I like" or simply recommend books on a topic of discussion, complete with a link to Amazon.com.

- **Social recommendations**. Personal shopping recommendations are based on profile similarities to other customers (e.g., Apple Genius Recommendations, Amazon Recommendations).

- **Social News** These are sites where users submit links to online news stories and readers vote or comment on which are the best ones, for example, Digg.

- **Other innovative methods**. Companies such Shopify, which is a Canadian multinational digital commerce platform, are incorporating automated personal recommendations apps (e.g., Wiser, Also Bought, Product Recommendation Quiz) based on algorithms, customer purchasing histories, and profiles. Amazon's collaborative filtering software presents product recommendations by displaying additional titles purchased by consumers who also purchased the same book or product. Another recent trend is for real consumers to make recommendations instead of algorithms (e.g., yumme, Bingie, RaterFox, HBO's Recommended by Humans).

E-Mail

E-mail is widely used among businesses and consumers and is increasingly becoming integrated with social media. For example, Facebook and other social sites require valid e-mail addresses when users sign up. The task for marketers is to integrate e-mail and social media, and many studies show that the majority of marketers plan to do this. For example, Yahoo!, Gmail, and Hotmail allow integration with Facebook contacts. When users open their e-mail inbox, they might only see e-mail from Facebook friends. Facebook will integrate friends with e-mail contacts and much more. This means that companies need to be on user contact lists, or their e-mail messages might not be viewed.

In one study, nearly 60 percent of marketers said they planned to use "follow us" links in e-mail messages so that recipients could click and be transported to the company's Facebook, Twitter, or other social media page (GetResponse survey, as cited in eMarketer.com). Other e-mail tactics: 64 percent said they planned to include "sign-up" forms for Facebook-type pages, 53 percent said they would place links to e-mail messages on social media pages, and 47 percent said they would include options to share the e-mail with others.

KFC, the fast-food chicken restaurant, wanted to build awareness and create a buzz for its new Double Down sandwich (two fried chicken patties surrounding bacon and cheese). KFC sent an e-mail announcement to 3 million registered males between ages 18 and 30 at the KFC.com website, according to Rich Maynard, PR Manager (as cited in Marketing News). Immediately, social media started carrying commentary about the plusses and minuses of this product. KFC started getting calls from journalists about the buzz before the product was even on the shelf. Much of the talk centered around the unhealthy aspects of the sandwich. Social media monitoring revealed an increase in both brand awareness and negative news about the sandwich. Had KFC also engaged in the social media talk and announced the sandwich on its Facebook page, this would have been an integrated effort. Sometimes companies do the reverse: undertake social media campaigns instead of e-mail campaigns because they find their e-mail blasts caught in spam filters, unseen by customers and prospects. In fact, social media has overtaken e-mail as the most popular consumer activity, especially for the younger markets.

Groupon used a fascinating and humorous engagement technique to entice customers to continue receiving their e-mail messages about special offers. When customers click the link in an e-mail to unsubscribe, they are transported to a Web page that said "We're still sorry to see you go! How sorry? Well, we want to introduce you to Derrick—he's the guy who thought you'd enjoy receiving Groupon mails." Then the user can press a button to "Punish Derrick." The video shows a co-worker walking in, speaking to Derrick, then throwing a glass of water in his face! After that, the user can choose to resubscribe. This likely keeps some people on the mailing list or at least gives them a very positive feeling about the brand.

Social Media Site Discussions

Social media is full of comments from users, and many relate to products, companies, and brands. As well, users share images and videos, pin images on Pinterest, and upload product images from Instagram and to Flickr. Another form of earned media occurs when users submit a link to an online news story, and it appears on digg.com. On this site, additional readers can

"Digg" the story, and the more who do so, the higher on the page the story appears (this is similar to a Facebook "like").

Blog conversations occur with lengthy lists of comments, especially in the B2B market, where professionals share information on various topics. For example, Brian Solis writes about social media, technology, and business and has a huge following, often gathering many comments to his posts. He creates informative infographics and writes on cutting edge, provocative, and interesting topics. According to digital marketing expert Neil Patel (2021), industry blogs receive the most comments, and spending time commenting on those blogs can increase others' interest in your blog content as well. To engage users on business blogs, it is also important to write timely, interesting, and current content, and to include buttons so users can easily "like" on Facebook, Tweet, recommend on Google+, and share on LinkedIn. According to Sprout Social (2021), social media users who follow a company or brand have certain expectations: most commonly seek to learn about new products or services, stay updated on company news, and learn about promotions and discounts.

In one interesting blog post, Paul Dunay wrote an analysis about "Why Brands Fail to Convert Facebook Fans into Paying Customers" (Exhibit 14.4). His motivation was Hubspot's finding that although 93 percent of internet adult users are on Facebook, only 1 percent of a brand's Facebook fans ever visit the company website. His advice covers many of the things discussed in this chapter, beginning with the importance of engaging customers immediately. On Dunay's blog, he entices engagement by offering subscription options (e-mail, RSS, and podcast updates) and connection options (e-mail, Friend on Facebook, Follow on Twitter, and Network on LinkedIn). Readers can also listen to his blog in iTunes podcasts (see www.pauldunay.com). This is a good example of many ways to engage blog readers.

10 Reasons Brands Fail to Convert Facebook Fans into Paying Customers

1. Failure to Get Past the First Step (try to engage visitors immediately)
2. Poor Text and Visuals (must be relevant to brand and visitors)
3. Stagnant Page Content (use consistent fresh content)
4. Inconsistent or Sloppy Branding (Facebook page and Web site with consistent brand elements)
5. Confused Calls-to-Action (make clear offers on Facebook)
6. Too Many Clicks (create only a few clicks to target content)
7. Mystery Visitors (compile Facebook user profiles)
8. Preconceived Notions (use Facebook specific campaigns)
9. Ineffective Plugin Use (integrate "like" buttons, recommendation and comment boxes well)
10. Sticking to Stand-alone Metrics (integrate Facebook with other shopping stats)

Exhibit 14.4 How to Convert Facebook Fans into Paying Customers

Source: www.pauldunay.com

Community Discussion/Forums

Online forums, also called bulletin boards, are areas where users can post e-mail messages on selected topics for other users to read (as discussed in Chapter 12). A large public newsgroup forum is Reddit, which has 430 million monthly active users worldwide (Oberlo, 2021). The average user spends over ten minutes per visit checking out subreddits, or communities on specific topics.

Social Apps

Marketers use social applications to engage social media users. Such applications can include brand information in contests or games, be sponsorships or calls for action, or be user generated. If a company knows, for instance, that a Facebook member lives in Los Angeles, is 28-years old, and surfs, a surf shop can send a surf-related widget that allows for sharing with friends—who likely also surf. For example, see the movie app created by the author to simulate a social network widget. Note that the Facebook member's name and profile photo are automatically put into the widget, which can then be passed to friends in the network. Godiva Chocolate wanted to engage with younger prospects and build the brand image of quality and excellence. It created an "I love chocolate" widget, and Facebook friends sent over 1 million virtual chocolate gifts to each other within two weeks—some were Godiva branded and some were generic. Godiva's Facebook fan page grew to 15,000 members as a result.

Apps are not only for smartphones and tablets—they appear on websites and social media as well. Facebook features hundreds of thousands of third-party software applications on its site. One popular application area is travel. For example, one specific application is "Where I've Been," which is a map that highlights places where users have visited or hope to visit. Visitors can plan trips, organize group travel, and find and rate free in-home accommodations. This information can be sold to travel-oriented vendors, who in turn advertise their products to Facebook members. Other important apps include the following:

- Facebook Messenger allows users to send messages to friends' mobile phones anytime from a phone, tablet, or computer. This app made history at the SXSW conference (South by Southwest) as attendees messaged friends about all the new technology and gadgets they encountered.
- Pinterest has grown astronomically since its inception. We've mentioned this several times already as a site where users can "pin" images and make collections for others to see (and click on for purchase).
- Instagram allows users to take photos, add filters, and upload to the Instagram site. This aids commerce because people often take images while in restaurants, bars, and retailers and often tag the brand and location.
- Mashups. These include many types of website combinations to engage consumers. One notable example is Google My Business, which allows business owners to list their business name and location so that mobile and computer users can find the business location on a Google Map. Lil' Piddlers Pet Grooming & Boutique in Oakland Park, Florida, realized a 30 percent increase in sales within five years of using Google's location services.

Collaborative Content Creation by Consumers

As previously discussed, the most engaged customers help the company improve products and promotions because they either care deeply about the brand or are enticed by a successful engagement technique (recall The LEGO Group's virtual design uploads, discussed in

Chapter 9). In the process, the company gains market research about the behaviors and preferences of its markets. At the simplest level, when you visit an automobile company's website and click around to change the color of the car, give it leather seats, and other options, you are helping the company learn about consumer preferences as it captures your online click stream—and this will guide its future product design. Collaborative content creation is crowdsourcing at its best.

You've read about several companies using crowdsourcing to solicit product ideas, such as Dell and Starbucks. Another important crowdsourcing trend involves user-generated advertising. Frito Lay offers internet users $1 million, a free trip to the Super Bowl and the chance to work with an ad agency for creating winning 30-second television commercials about the Doritos brand chips. The winning spot each year is aired at the game. Since its inception in 2007, consumers have submitted over 30,000 ads, according to sponsor PepsiCo. This promotion was so successful that winners typically end up in of the top three spots in *USA Today*'s Super Bowl Ad Meter. General Motors tried the same strategy, providing consumers video, audio, and images to use in constructing commercials. It worked well for GM, too; however, there was a negative backlash—approximately 20 percent of the entries had superimposed text mentioning the Chevy Tahoe's part in using up the world's oil and causing global warming. These videos were posted as ad parodies on YouTube and received lots of press. The moral: in an online environment where everyone is a journalist, expect your underbelly to be exposed. Regardless, GM felt the campaign was a huge success.

Advertisers continue to experiment with user-created ads for good reason—one study found that consumers believe companies with customer-created ads are more friendly (68%), creative (56%), and innovative (55%) than those that use only professional advertising (according to AMA and Opinion Research Corporation research). Also, recall that consumers trust each other more than they trust companies, so consumer-created advertising is an appropriate tactic.

The San Francisco County Transportation Authority (SFCTA) used a crowdsourcing campaign that combined offline and online IMC. It posted ads in the city buses (in both English and Chinese) inviting citizens to propose ways to spend the $64 billion transportation budget from 2012 through 2040. Titled "How would you invest San Francisco's transportation dollars: be the City's budget czar for a day!" it consisted of a webpage that guided users through a series of transportation spending options under three expenditure categories: maintenance and operations, programs, and capital projects (Exhibit 14.5). The site operated like an online game, with participants put into a drawing for $50 transit passes. The campaign ran for two months, and approximately 600 people participated. You'll also note a QR code in the ad for easy access to the website.

Crowdfunding involves raising money online for new product ideas or for political campaigns and nonprofits. Sites such as Kickstarter.com, which has raised $3.4 billion to fund more than 136,000 projects, assist ordinary citizens in raising money for their creative projects (see Kickstarter.com for more statistics). Similarly, cause-based marketing designed to leverage social media by engaging and empowering consumers can lead to viral movements. One of the best examples of this is the ALS Ice Bucket Challenge (2021). Amyotrophic lateral sclerosis (also commonly referred to as Lou Gehrig's Disease) is a progressive neurodegenerative disease that affects motor control (ALS Association, 2021). The ALS challenge exploded virally in 2014 when Pete Frates and Pat Quinn encouraged family and friends to participate, which involves people having a bucket of ice water poured over their heads and soliciting donations before nominating others to do the same via social media. Videos of individuals and groups from around the world, including famous entertainers, athletes, and politicians, soon emerged challenging others while accumulating millions of views across multiple platforms. The viral

Be the City's Budget Czar for a Day!

How would you invest San Francisco's transportation dollars?

Between now and 2040, $64 billion dollars will be available to support San Francisco transportation. The San Francisco County Transportation Authority wants your opinion on how best to spend it. Repaving streets, building better bike lanes, constructing rapid transit lines, or making pedestrian safety improvements are just a few of the possibilities.

To create and submit your own investment plan, visit:
www.sfcta.org/mybudget

You'll also be entered in a drawing to win one of three $50 Clipper Cards.
More ways to get involved: www.movesmartsf.com or 415.593.1670

Exhibit 14.5 The San Francisco County Transportation Authority Uses Crowdsourcing

Source: Courtesy of The San Francisco County Transportation Authority

phenomenon has been heralded as one of the most successful social fundraising campaigns of all time, having raised more than $220 million in research funding for the disease.

How do Companies Entice Engagement?

As Oscar Wilde famously noted, "The only thing worse than being talked about is not being talked about." How do companies engage their markets, gaining trust and guiding people from passive content consumption, up the ladder to sparking positive brand conversations and viral activity? This involves creating content and promotions that encourage people to interact with the brand and then tag, bookmark, or rate the content and share opinions with others via comments and recommendations on social media. Because they can reach millions of people when they share, it is like the old-fashioned word of mouth on steroids.

As with all effective promotions, three basic criteria must be met—delivering the right message to the right messengers in the right media. Accomplishing this requires a deep understanding of the audience's needs, behaviors, and motivations and constant earned media monitoring.

Social media participants want to be informed, entertained, appreciated, and not bombarded with interruptive brand messages, seen in the following engagement principles and examples.

Provide High Quality, Timely, Unique, and Relevant Information

When companies like eMarketer, A.C. Nielsen, ComScore or Forrester release statistics from their primary research, bloggers will write about it, giving their interpretations for readers to comment upon and share. For example, internet marketing consultant Andy Beal started the Marketing Pilgrim blog in 2005. He began his day in the wee hours by reading his RSS streams from over 100 sites he follows. He then would write a blog post about the latest news announced by Google or another company and give his expert analysis on what it means to internet marketers. Beal built his consulting business from the blog followers, sells advertising space on his blog, participates in many interviews with mainstream media, added a team of experts to write articles, and is constantly in the top ten media and marketing blogs, as rated by *Advertising Age* (see andybeal.com).

Create Entertaining Content

Consumers will watch and share video commercials and other company-created content that is entertaining, irreverent, interesting, or unusual. TikTok launched as a short-form video creation and sharing platform and has become a popular video service worldwide. According to Business of Apps, the platform enjoys $1.9 billion in revenue as of 2020. Despite the privacy challenges it has faced along the way, the easy to create, edit, and share nature of TikTok's content has captured consumers' attention, with 837 million monthly active users worldwide as of 2021.

Offer Competitions

Many people love to compete and win prizes. For example, Yeti, a manufacturer of drinkware and coolers, teamed up with Traeger Grills to offer a user-generated photo contest to kick off the summer season. Participants were asked to post a photo on Instagram of their barbecue setup. The photo had to have tagged @traegergrills and @YETI and included the campaign-specific hashtags, #YETIxTraegerBBQ and #Sweepstakes, in the caption. Both brands promoted the sweepstakes via their social media accounts and although the details of the official rules were available via the brands' websites, consumers could participate in the contest entirely via Instagram. Winners were announced on social media and received products from both companies. But with more than 1,000 entries via the hashtag, Yeti and Traeger benefitted from the tremendous amount of earned media that they repurposed on various social media platforms (Macready, 2022).

Appeal to Altruism

People like to share stories, videos, and other content about social causes. For example, the Harvey Relief Coalition, a nonprofit coalition in Texas, created a Google Doc for people to enter their address and any details to their request for help after the hurricane damaged parts of Texas. They also coordinated volunteers who could help provide relief. Even Snapchat's snap maps proved to be very helpful for tracking people's locations and the storm's damage.

Make an Exclusive Offer

The social psychology principle of "scarcity" often motivates people to take action immediately. Sales promotion discounts and free sample product offers with expiration dates often engage recipients. Contests are another popular social media marketing tactic. For example, LOFT, a popular women's clothing brand, asks users to follow the brand on Instagram, like a post announcing the contest, and tag a friend in the comments using #LOFTsweepstakes for a chance to win a seasonal garment of their choice. In doing so, the brand puts time pressure on users to participate in the sweepstakes while encouraging engagement with its posts.

Reward Influentials and Fans

Following the famous Pareto rule, that 80 percent of the business comes from 20 percent of the customers, most of the buzz about a brand comes from a small number of fans. Rewards of appreciation can take the form of exclusive information, first chance at breaking news, or a free gift—such as the chance to review a new product that they get to keep, an exclusive offer, or a special discount. Following the principles of customer relationship management (Chapter 15), a brand will do well to occasionally appreciate its fans. In late 2020, Chipotle, an American fast casual restaurant chain, promoted its #ChipotleRoyalty contest, which invited consumers to create a TikTok video that shows why their Chipotle order is the best of all combinations. In addition to a $10,000 cash prize, three winners would have their orders added as official menu items on Chipotle's app and website for a limited time (Moore, 2020).

Incentivize Group Behavior

Following the social psychology principle of reciprocity, customers can be motivated to participate in social media if offered an incentive up front (versus the "thank you" type reward just mentioned). For example, Target will release daily deals on Twitter with limited time offers or exclusive follower discounts. These promotions initiate a sense of urgency while rewarding consistent engagement and loyalty. The goal is to incentivize customers who follow them while providing a reason to return in the future (Johnson, 2021).

A key principle of enticing engagement is to make it easy for users. For instance, most social media and many websites provide one click buttons for "liking," tagging, bookmarking (e.g., offering a Pinterest button), subscribing via an RSS feed button (which can rapidly spread the content), and sharing content on social networks. Many sites also allow users to register with one click using their social media profiles or other individualized accounts. For example, OneClickPolitics is an international nonpartisan campaign management company established to leverage digital technologies for political policy and advocacy impact. To date, they have delivered more than 28 million messages directly to elected officials with an 84 percent campaign success rate, according to CEO Chazz Clevinger (see oneclickpolitics.com).

Thus far, we have been painting a rosy picture of customer engagement and all the good it can do for a brand or organization. As hard as marketers try to deliver a good product and respect consumer communication preferences, things can quickly go downhill with earned media, such as what happened with the General Motors UGC advertising. The moral: in an online environment where everyone is a critic, expect the brand's underbelly to be exposed. This brings us to an important topic: How can a company manage its brand messages and reputation in the Wild West environment of earned media?

Reputation Management Online

In a stroke of bad luck, an employee on Chrysler's social media team tweeted an off-color message about Detroit's traffic from Chrysler's official account, when the employee had meant to tweet it from his own account. Although the tweet was deleted, Chrysler's large Twitter audience was outraged, and the company received backlash for the offensive language used in the tweet.

Reputation is a belief in the mind of the beholder. Abraham Lincoln is attributed to have said that "Character is like a tree and reputation like a shadow. The shadow is what we think of it, and the tree is the real thing." Thus, an entity's reputation is based on what other people think of it, not what it thinks of itself. With earned media, there is plenty of opportunity for other people to shape the reputations of a company, its brands, and its employees. Brands and companies have lost a great deal of control over their images and reputations and must now monitor, engage, and participate in social media conversations or pay the consequences.

Marketers must remember that although viral videos and other branded content is a plus, it is quite often changed as it gets passed along the internet. The message will be distorted (such as a mashup of a company video posted to YouTube), and oftentimes the message will turn negative. An example is the numerous YouTube videos showing the Mentos brand mints exploding out of soda bottles.

In another example, Greenpeace UK, the activist not-for-profit organization working for a green and peaceful world, posted a video on YouTube to build awareness of a perceived problem. Nestlé, the maker of Kit Kat candy bar, was purchasing palm oil extracted from forests in Indonesia, thus ruining the Indonesian rainforests, which pushed the orangutans toward extinction. The video, entitled "Have a Break?" showed an office worker taking a break by eating a Kit Kat bar. When he bit into it, blood gushed from the chocolate bar.

The video received hundreds of thousands of views; however, the damage really escalated on Nestlé's Facebook page. Immediately after the video post, viewers began complaining about the palm oil harvesting, with comments on the company's Facebook page. Some of the protesters created a graphic imitation of the Kit Kat candy bar package, replacing the brand name with the word "Killer" in the same font or stamping the package with bloody orangutan footprints. They made this image their profile picture on Facebook so every post on the Nestlé page included this image.

Nestlé responded by saying that they would delete any comments that contained the altered image. This inappropriate response created a blogstorm and many more posts and shifted the conversation away from the core issue of deforestation and animal slaughter to Nestlé's ineptitude in social media. Nestlé debated with commenters, defending its decision to censor profile pictures, and then started deleting comments as well. It got very nasty. Eventually, the Nestlé executive running the Facebook page posted an apology and said they would stop deleting comments.

What really is amazing is the speed at which this happened:

- Day 1: Greenpeace video posted on YouTube.
- Day 2: 190 Facebook complaints and 1,000s of tweets in response.
- Day 3 (morning): Nestlé responds on Facebook with the plan to delete the "Killer" bar logo profile pictures and comments.
- Day 3 (afternoon): Nestlé apologizes on Facebook and stops deleting the posts.

Several companies analyzed the social media conversations after this incident. One found that social media conversations including both terms "Nestlé" and "Facebook" jumped by 40 percent on day three, and that 16 percent of this conversation was negative, 66 percent neutral, and 16 percent positive.

Which Reputations Matter?

Brand and company reputations are very important. The majority of a company's market value is often attributable to reputation. Many executives think it is harder to recover from reputation failure than to build and maintain a reputation, and it takes companies multiple years to fully recover from a damaged reputation.

In an interesting example, Brazilian creative agency Moma Propaganda was stripped of two awards and prohibited from entering the Cannes Lions International Festival of Creativity for a year. The agency entered two fake ads for Kia Motors Brazil—"fake" meaning that they created the ads for the competition—but the ads were neither approved by Kia nor run in any traditional or online media. Cannes discovered this when it came across the firestorm of social media conversation, which criticized the campaign for overtones of lust and pedophilia. This incident created reputation-damaging publicity for both the agency and Kia Motors Brazil until the latter said it had neither seen nor approved the ads (Wentz and Penteado, 2011).

A company CEO's reputation is linked closely to the company's reputation. For example, derogatory comments made by the founder and CEO of Papa John's Pizza led to a 13 percent drop in the company's stock, which was particularly painful given that its competitor, Domino's Pizza, experienced a tremendous increase in the same period (Considine, 2020). The reputations of other company executives can also affect the company. For example, job recruiters' reputations can make a big difference when trying to attract good employees (Shih, 2011). Successful recruiters build their reputations on LinkedIn, and this helps them to build good relationships with previous job candidates and new hires.

Recently, there has been a great deal of talk and information about using social media for personal branding. This especially applies to consultants, salespeople, and other professionals, as well as to college students who are about to enter the job market.

Build, Maintain, Monitor, Repair, Learn

The reputation management process includes four steps: build, maintain, monitor, and repair. Many of the techniques for implementing these steps are elsewhere in the book, so we just touch upon it here. There are many promotional techniques for *building* a strong reputation, but it all starts with the company's actions. As previously mentioned, most social media reputation crises happen because of something the company does or does not do. Given positive actions, the company can use owned or paid media and join the conversation in earned social media to communicate its benefits to consumers and other stakeholders. This book gives many examples of how companies do this, such as engaging social media participant customers and prospects where they hang out online and building good customer relationships (Chapter 15).

Maintaining positive reputations requires constant internet and offline media monitoring and then sometimes participating when things go awry. We say "sometimes" because companies decide whether or not to respond based on three factors: (1) how valuable is the poster to the company, (2) how much potential does the comment contain for creating reputation damage, and (3) how widely can the discussion travel in social media (Flynn, 2012)? For example, if the comment came from a high value customer or influential journalist, the company will respond immediately, sometimes by direct e-mail to the author. Conversely, if the poster is a low value customer or a competitor and does not seem like a big enough conversation to spread far, the company might ignore the comment or delay its response. Interestingly, one survey found that when it comes to handling customer service issues on Twitter, customer response time expectations are longer than average (7–7.2 hours) and companies' expectations are shorter than average (3–3.4 hours) (Fox and Cowley, 2015). Indeed, the value of using social media to maintain relationships with customers is still not fully recognized by marketers.

The Nestlé example shows the need to *monitor* social media conversation 24/7 and assign appropriate personnel to Facebook and other social media for beneficial user interactions. It is also critically important to understand and fix the underlying problem, if possible, prior to responding to bloggers and other social media detractors. Without substance, responses to a crisis can be seen as empty promises to social media participants.

When a company creates a Facebook business page, it often allows other Facebook members—potentially including disgruntled customers or sleazy competitors—to post on its wall or comment on what the company has posted. However, if the page owner turns off this feature, consumers may wonder what the company fears or is hiding. Turning off the feature also precludes great customer fan conversations that could promote the products and services better than the company could do (because people trust others like them online). Companies can delete posts, but that may only encourage the post author to scream louder about being censored, as it did with Nestlé. Most social media marketing experts advise deleting only the most offensive or vulgar posts while trying to address the rest as constructively as possible. In fact, this is how a company can learn things that will improve its products and processes.

For example, Coca-Cola has more than 106 million fans on its Facebook page worldwide. The company uses geotags so that fans see relevant posts in their own language, based on the poster's IP (internet protocol) address (for example, someone posting from .de would see only German language posts). Coke posted something it thought would appeal to fans about the Day of the Student. Unfortunately, there was a glitch in the geotagging on Facebook, and for ten minutes, US fans saw this text in Portuguese instead of English. This created a firestorm of comments from US fans, the likes of "Speak English or @#* die!" (bad word deleted). Apparently, US fans think that Coke is an American brand and should stay that way. Coca-Cola removed the Portuguese post and all the offensive comments from its wall. Sometimes it is surprising to see what will upset customers.

Repairing reputations can take many years, as previously mentioned. This involves fixing the fundamental problems causing the crisis, communicating the solutions to important stakeholders, and enticing social media participants to spread the conversation.

Most good companies *learn* from criticism in social media and act upon what they hear. Negative comments add authenticity in balancing a company's one-sided owned and paid media but when handled well can boost reputations and sales. Product reviews, complaints, and positive suggestions help companies to improve products, processes, and Web content. The best way to encourage this type of posting is by hosting a conversation on the company's own social media and Web properties so it becomes easier to identify, learn, and then respond that changes have been made (if warranted). This kind of dialog often prevents complaints from becoming viral as well. For example, My Starbucks Idea site has several hundred thousand users and accepts ideas in product, experience, and involvement categories. The microsite lists recent ideas as they are sent via Twitter, Facebook or posted on the microsite and then reports on "ideas in action." Users can click on each idea to see its status and add comments. This is a brilliant way to learn from customers without doing expensive market research, and it yields a lot more actionable data as well.

One important way to avoid unwarranted reputation crises involves building a reputation management system in company-owned social media.

Reputations Management Systems

Reputation management systems use a number of various criteria and technologies for monitoring and protecting reputations. This is a solution that helps companies initiate and monitor reputations. For example, most social media platforms have a member profile feature that allows others to see more about who is posting on the medium and also to view statistics about the member's activity. Furthermore, many social networks require a reply to an automated outgoing e-mail so they know the user actually resides at that e-mail address. EBay, and other social commerce sites have feedback systems so that buyers can rate sellers for all future buyers to see. Similarly, Slashdot uses a "karma" rating system, and others also have systems where users can rate the reviews and even the ratings of other users. These reputation management systems help build authenticity and trust in contributors to the conversation.

Facebook grew and beat MySpace partially because of its reputation management system. It engaged users and built trust through e-mail authentication, privacy settings, and building the site around relationships in the offline world (Shih, 2011). Facebook started as a site for Harvard and other Ivy League schools, adding to its credibility. Today, however, Facebook is on shaky ground in terms of its reputation, with many users demanding more transparency in terms of how their data is used, stored, and shared.

In another reputation management system example, Rosetta Stone is a maker of software for language translation. It is mostly a B2B organization. To get the most out of social media, Rosetta Stone used an innovative software tool to scan posts, add them to a database, and prioritize which should be responded to, allowing for expedient customer service using a social channel (Stambor, 2010).

Earned Media Performance Metrics

As you've read elsewhere, a company specifies which metrics will be used to measure marketing communication success, and then uses these measures as feedback to (1) see if the campaign objectives were met and (2) continually refine the strategies and tactics to enhance performance. Chapter 2 discussed many social media metrics that apply to earned media in the areas of awareness/exposure, brand health, engagement, action, and innovation. These include elements such as number of likes and shares, number of ideas uploaded, share of voice and sentiment analysis. For company-owned channels (owned media), some of these earned media metrics apply if the action was on the company's own sites or pages, such as number of comments posted to a company's blog or sentiment in a forum on a company's website. Here is a summary of additional metrics that apply to earned media:

- **General earned media metrics**. Number of users who interact with an application or ad and time spent viewing a video, playing a game, or listening to music. Social media community/fan growth.
- **Actions taken by users**. Number of downloads for a white paper, MP3 music file, or other content; number of bookmarks for a website at a social bookmarking site such as Pinterest; number of uploads for user-created video, photo, or other multimedia content to a website; number of ratings at a book or online retailer; and number of games played, coupons downloaded, polls voted, and invitations sent to event.
- **Conversations on blogs and elsewhere**. Number of comments, tweets/retweets; conversation sentiment as positive/negative; conversation reach—number of visitors viewing a conversation; number of relevant conversation comments; and dates of first and last comment post.

Earned media metrics vary widely. *Individual engagement* is determined as interaction in a way that a brand defines as meaningful, for instance, a video view or content submission. *Social engagement* is defined as interaction with brand assets, which has peer-to-peer impact—for example, conversation about contributions, size, and density, comments, ratings, reviews, and content shared. Other relevant metrics include growth of followers, subscribers, media

Exhibit 14.6 Keyhole Social Media Monitoring

Source: www.keyhole.co

attention/buzz, traffic (link-backs from newsfeed items to brand pages), and search equity from links to a brand site sent by users into a social environment.

Social media dashboard. With so many social and earned media to monitor and reputations that can be damaged in a matter of hours, how can a company keep track? We discussed Google Alerts in Chapter 6, and here we present the much more sophisticated social media dashboard. It is software that pulls in company, brand, or any keyword mentions from any social media and displays them all in one place. This makes it easy for companies to monitor conversations and also displays selected metrics. Many companies are rushing to compete in this space—see Exhibit 14.6 to learn more about Keyhole, a platform that enables marketers to listen to social media activity about brands and industries, monitor a brand's social media marketing campaigns, and even manage influencer interactions. It shows whether the trend is positive or negative, builds a word cloud of keyword mentions in conversations, and offers metrics that allow marketers to keep track of performance.

Are you dizzy yet? There are many complexities to social engagement measurement, and marketers are just beginning to find robust ways for collecting these important Web 2.0 metrics as relates to their IMC goals. We'll leave you with one final example to enliven this long list of metrics. Jeep automobiles decided to engage more deeply with its already tight brand community. The "Jeep Experience" featured a showcase on Jeep.com that aggregated social media branded profiles and conversations from its own Jeep Facebook, MySpace, YouTube, and Flickr pages (using RSS feeds). The showcase page was also fed in with Jeep company content in several areas: community (branded social media profiles and content), news, Jeep events, action sports (for Jeep sponsored events), and more ("IAB Social Media Buyer's Guide", 2010). Now for the performance metrics actually used by Jeep:

- Average time on the Jeep experience site was 14.53 minutes.
- The Jeep Facebook page had 350,000 fans.

- 17 percent of the visitors to the Jeep Experience pages compared Jeep vehicles, versus only 7 percent of visitors to the website alone (Jeep.com).
- 12 percent of Jeep Experience visitors searched vehicle inventory, versus only 9 percent on Jeep.com.
- 15 percent of Jeep Experience visitors searched to locate a dealer, versus 11 percent on Jeep.com.

These are very impressive results for a campaign that had no advertising and involved engaging visitors at purely company-owned social media sites. Without these metrics, Jeep would not have known whether or not the time investment paid off.

Chapter Summary

Earned media is the third element of content strategy, resulting from owned media and paid media efforts. Unlike traditional media, which involves passive exposure, earned media is the result of user engagement. Engagement can occur at five levels: (1) when internet users consume online content (the lowest level of engagement); (2) when users connect with others online, such as by registering for a social network; (3) when users collect information, such as by filtering and tagging content on social media sites; (4) when users create original social media content, such as posting YouTube videos; and (5) when users collaborate with a company (the highest level of engagement), such as by suggesting ideas for product improvement. Compared with company-generated communications, consumers tend to put more trust in recommendations from people they know and in user-generated online reviews and opinions. Because of this trust, earned media can have a significant influence on buying decisions.

Among the key techniques for engaging users to produce earned media are viral marketing, in which individuals forward content to each other; viral blogging, with bloggers participating in viral marketing activities; multimedia sharing, in which users upload photos, video, music playlists, live audio/video, or presentations to share with others; wikis, where users can post, edit, and organize multimedia content; product ratings and reviews, which can influence purchasing online and offline; social recommendations and referrals, such as referral programs; e-mail; social media site conversations; community forums and discussions; widgets and social apps; and location-based services.

Collaborative content creation, a form of crowdsourcing, is at the high end of the engagement ladder. The marketing benefits include learning more about the behaviors and preferences of target markets, receiving new product ideas from users, and receiving user-generated advertising ideas and materials via crowdsourcing. Crowdfunding involves raising money online for new product ideas, political campaigns, or nonprofit causes.

Techniques companies can use to attract users and move them up the engagement ladder include: (1) providing information that is high quality, timely, unique, and relevant; (2) creating content that is entertaining, irreverent, interesting, or unusual; (3) devising competitions where users can win prizes; (4) appealing to users' altruism and interest in social causes; (5) making an exclusive offer that motivates immediate action; (6) rewarding influencers and fans; and (7) offering upfront incentives.

Building a strong, positive reputation for the company, its brands, and its executives starts with what the company does (or does not do), not just what and how it promotes itself. Maintaining positive reputations requires constant monitoring of internet and offline media and then determining whether or not to respond to comments. Repairing a reputation takes years, but this is a worthwhile process because the company can open a dialog and learn from any criticism. Finally, a number of metrics apply to earned media, including:

(1) general metrics such as number of users who interact with a communication or other element and growth in community or fans; (2) actions taken by users, such as number of downloads or uploads; and (3) number and sentiment of conversations on blogs, microblogs, and elsewhere. Some companies use a social media dashboard to monitor selected metrics.

Exercises

Review Questions

1. What are the five levels of user engagement? Provide an example of each.
2. In addition to consumers and prospects, which two groups should companies seek to engage for earned media?
3. How are viral marketing and viral blogging used to generate word of mouse?
4. Explain how shoppers use or contribute content to the seven forms of online reviews and ratings.
5. Why should marketers be aware of the role of trust when planning for earned media?
6. How do social recommendations and referrals differ from ratings and reviews?
7. Why are many companies integrating e-mail and social media for marketing communication?
8. What are location-based services, and how do users and marketers benefit from them?
9. In what ways does collaborative content creation help companies?
10. Which reputations should a company monitor and seek to manage? Be specific.
11. As part of the decision about responding to a comment or complaint in online or offline media, what three questions should a company ask?
12. What is a social media dashboard, and why would a company use it?

Discussion Questions

1. **The Dell Story.** Identify several ways that Dell could engage customers in a positive way, using techniques in this chapter.
2. **The Dell Story.** What might Dell have done to manage its online reputation better? Acting as Dell's consultant, give them advice that would keep them out of this kind of trouble in the future.
3. What techniques from this chapter can you adapt to manage your personal brand and reputation? List at least six tactics you might use, and why.
4. Based on the idea that "reputation is a belief in the mind of the beholder," can a firm realistically take the initiative to manage its reputation online?
5. Do you think that marketers are losing control of brand images due to social media? Why or why not?
6. Which level of engagement best describes your online behavior? How could your favorite brand move you to a higher level using the principles in this chapter?
7. Once consumers engage in collaborative content creation on behalf of a brand, what are the implications for recommendations and referrals, reputation, and purchasing?
8. If "viral marketing turns the sales funnel upside down," as shown in Exhibit 14.3, what are the potential consequences when viral marketing spreads a negative message about a company, product, or brand?
9. Should companies put more emphasis on earned media instead of investing in paid media and owned media? Explain your answer.

Web Activities

1. Visit a business news site such as www.businessweek.com or www.forbes.com and search for an article about the reputation of a company, product, brand, or executive. What happened, and what was the effect on the company? What role did social media play in this situation? What could the company have done differently to monitor, protect, and repair its reputation online?

2. Check out your personal reputation online by searching for your name on Google. If you were a job recruiter, would you hire yourself based on what you find? Why or why not? What can you do online to improve your reputation and your chances in the job market?

3. Visit the wiki of the Interactive Advertising Bureau at **www.iab.org/wiki/index.php/ Main_Page**. What information does its wiki feature? Select one entry in the wiki and look at its source and its history. Why would a marketing manager or the employee of an advertising agency contribute to this wiki?

4. Visit **www.yelp.com** and read the reviews for a restaurant, a store, or another business in your area. How many and what kinds of reviews and ratings do you see? How might the ratings and sentiment of these reviews affect the behavior of someone making a decision about buying from that business? What is Yelp doing to get users engaged and move them up the engagement ladder?

Chapter 15

Customer Relationship Management

The main objective of this chapter is to provide you with an overview of the purpose and process of building a company's relationship capital through customer relationship management (CRM). You will learn about relationship marketing's three pillars, CRM's benefits, social CRM, and the nine building blocks needed for effective and efficient implementation of CRM.

After reading this chapter, you will be able to:

- Define customer relationship management and identify the major benefits to digital marketers.
- Outline the three pillars of relationship marketing for digital marketing.
- Describe social CRM and how it relates to traditional CRM.
- Discuss the nine major components needed for effective and efficient CRM in digital marketing.
- Highlight some of the company-side and client-side tools that digital marketers use to enhance their CRM processes.
- Differentiate CRM metrics by customer life cycle stage.

THE BEST BUY STORY

Best Buy Co., Inc., is the 14th largest US digital commerce retailer, with more than $46 billion in revenue in 2020 ("Top 100 Retailers", 2021). It is famous for its "Blue Shirt" store sales force and "Geek Squad" employees who deliver technology solutions to homes and offices. The company has millions of customers each year visiting retail locations and placing online orders. With so many customers and a multichannel strategy, how can the company maintain the type of communication and customer satisfaction to maintain that huge number of customer relationships? Best Buy initiated several social media tactics just for this purpose, as described next.

Best Buy has made efforts to better engage customers and shift the role of each employee in the organization to become technology experts to help customers enrich their lives through technology. This includes a major focus on the multichannel retail experience that customers have grown to expect, especially being able to interact with retailers online and offline.

Best Buy uses Twitter to engage customers (@BestBuy, @GeekSquad, and @BestBuySupport). It is particularly important for a consumer electronics retailer to be available for answering technology questions quickly. This can retain customers and bring more business to Best Buy. Each account responds to customer needs in a rapid fashion, and employees also sign their name at the end of each tweet to ensure a more personal touch.

DOI: 10.4324/9781003247319-19

Best Buy employees are also available to immediately answer user questions in social media platforms (including its Facebook page). Multichannel strategies assist employees and customers to swiftly resolve complicated issues. And everyone benefits in the end (check out the case studies at bestbuy.com and lithium.com).

Building Customer Relationships, 1:1

Best Buy develops long-term customer relationships one at a time (1:1), not unlike those developed by neighborhood retailers in the early 1900s—except that information technology allows the company to handle millions of these close relationships. A Best Buy customer enjoying this type of employee access and high satisfaction is brand loyal and will not easily be enticed away by competition. This customer will slowly spend an increasing amount of money on additional products and services while also referring others. According to *Harvard Business Review* authors Thomas Jones and Earl Sasser, "Increased customer loyalty is the *single most important* driver of long-term performance." *Business 2.0* calls relationship capital the most important asset a firm can have ("Relationships Rule", 2000). In an environment of customer control, where attention is a scarce commodity, an organization's ability to build and maintain relationships with customers, suppliers, and partners may be more important than a firm's land, property, and financial assets. It is this relationship capital that provides the foundation of future business.

This approach represents a major shift in marketing practice: from mass marketing to individualized marketing, and from focusing on acquiring lots of new customers to retaining and building more business from a smaller base of loyal high-value customers. Although many B2B companies have practiced customer relationship management for a long time, now organizations in the consumer services market (e.g., Amazon.com) and even marketers of consumer packaged goods, such as Best Buy, work to build long-term customer relationships, 1:1. How can other companies competing within a wide range of industries profitably build relationships with each consumer? Internet technologies can facilitate relationship marketing in many new ways, yet many companies that purchase and install relationship management technologies are losing money on them. This chapter explains the process, identifies key internet tools, and presents the case for a consumer-centric customer relationship management focus throughout the entire supply chain.

Relationship Marketing Defined

Marketers have named this customer focus *relationship marketing* (also *1:1 marketing*). As originally defined, **relationship marketing** is about establishing, maintaining, enhancing, and commercializing customer relationships through promise fulfillment (Grönroos, 1990). Usually, companies try to build profitable, mutually beneficial relationships in the long term (versus the short term), as it tends to be more efficient to service existing customers than attain new ones. Promise fulfillment means that when companies make offers in their marketing communications programs, customer expectations will be met through actual brand experiences. For example, an offer on the Stash Tea website homepage promises a free box with the purchase of three, but the order page does not confirm this offer, and the total quantity shown on the final order is only three. If four do not arrive, the customer will likely consider buying tea from a competitor such as Twinings next time. Even when the four boxes arrive, the suspense may erode some of the customer's trust in the firm. Similarly, good relationships are built when company personnel meet the promises made by salespeople and promotional messages.

Mass Marketing		Relationship Marketing
Discrete transactions		Continuing transactions
Short-term emphasis	←——————————→	Long-term emphasis
One-way communication		Two-way communication and collaboration
Acquisition focus		Retention focus
Share of market		Wallet share
Product differentiation		Customer differentiation

Exhibit 15.1 Continuum from Mass Marketing to Relationship Marketing

An organization using relationship marketing focuses on wallet share more than market share. **Wallet share** is the amount of sales a firm can generate from one customer over time and thus reflects a focus on retention and growth rather than an acquisition focus (market share). For instance, Amazon wants to sell hardware, music, household appliances, and more to each customer who buys a book. Relationship marketing differentiates individual customers based on need rather than differentiating products for target groups—such as buyers of novels by a particular author. It will be more profitable for Best Buy to identify its best customers, get to know them individually, and suggest additional products based on their needs than to spend all its efforts acquiring new customers. If Best Buy is successful, clients will eventually buy all their consumer electronics products and services from the company (greater wallet share). Best Buy saves on promotion and price discounting expenditures by spending time on customer retention versus customer acquisition. Exhibit 15.1 displays a summary of these ideas, comparing mass marketing to relationship marketing.

Few companies fall on either end of the continuum but instead use varying strategies for different products and markets. For example, Procter & Gamble must differentiate its brands of laundry detergent for sale to the masses; however, it tries to build relationships with mothers who will buy increasing numbers of P&G products over the years, from Ivory powder for washing baby clothes and Pampers diapers to Crest toothpaste for the family and Olay cosmetics for themselves.

Stakeholders

Most companies also use relationship marketing techniques to build mutually supportive bonds with stakeholders other than consumers, such as employees and supply chain companies. Organizations can establish and maintain relationships with many different stakeholder groups. The four most affected by internet technologies are the following:

1. *Employees.* It is difficult for a firm to persuade buyers when employees are not happy. Because many employees are instrumental in building relationships with customers, it is critical for them to have training and access to data and systems used for relationship management. In fact, some observers say that many relationship management programs fail due to lack of employee training and commitment.

2. *Business customers in the supply chain.* With partner relationship management (PRM), companies build and maintain relationships with other businesses for the purpose of buying and selling both upstream and downstream. First are business customers: the B2B market. Procter & Gamble works with numerous wholesale and retail intermediaries, using internet technologies and databases to facilitate these relationships. Second are a company's suppliers. General Electric uses the internet to receive bids from its suppliers, a system that not only lowers transaction costs but also enhances competition and speeds order fulfillment.

3. *Lateral partners.* Other businesses, not-for-profit organizations, or governments join with the firm for some common goal but not for transactions with each other. CargoNet Transportation Community Network, a consortium of 200,000 shippers, handled 250 million trade-related documents a year in its peak for Hong Kong shippers at the world's busiest port. The internet facilitates its partner relationship management (PRM) through document tracking and customer service for manufacturers, ocean, rail, truck, and air carriers as well as banks, insurance companies, and governments associated with CargoNet (www.eds.com).

4. *Consumers.* These individuals are the end users of products and services. Marketers must differentiate between business customers and final consumers because different tactics are usually employed in the B2C and B2B markets.

Three Pillars of Relationship Marketing

Today, relationship marketing involves much more than promise fulfillment. It means two-way communication with individual stakeholders, one at a time (1:1). How can a company understand individual customer or partner needs without asking what they are and listening to the answers? Fortunately, the internet's social media allow companies to listen much better than ever before.

Author, business strategist, and CEO of the CustomerThink Corporation, Bob Thompson, believes that relationship marketing has three pillars that support customer relationships with a company's products and services (Exhibit 15.2). The first is **customer relationship management (CRM)**—the process of targeting, acquiring, transacting, servicing, retaining,

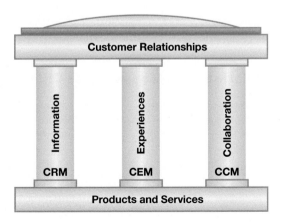

Exhibit 15.2 Three Pillars of Relationship Management

Source: Thompson, Bob (2009). "How to Use Social Media to Improve Customer Service and Cut Costs." Courtesy of Customer Think Corp

and building long-term relationships with customers that add value both to the organization and the customer. CRM is based on data, information, customer insight, and knowledge, as will be discussed in this chapter. A company needs lots of data to know how its tactics work at acquiring, retaining, and building customer relationships. The second pillar is **customer experience management (CEM)**. The difference between CRM and CEM is very slight because they both have the end goal of building loyal customers. CRM focuses more on the internal processes to maximize customer value in the long term, and CEM more on the customer expectations and touch point satisfaction/dissatisfaction (customer value). CEM can refer to one transaction experience or the sum of all transactions over the duration of the relationship. Both CRM and CEM are controlled by the marketer, who designs marketing mix strategies to build and maintain customer relationship value.

In contrast, the third and final pillar is controlled by customers but monitored and directed by companies whenever possible and grew from the social media explosion: **customer collaboration management (CCM)**, a strategy to engage customers in relationship-building conversation, often through social media. CCM is also called CRM 2.0 and social CRM.

All three pillars affect a company's brand image and revenue growth. CEM is used for nearly every product in the offline world, such as the way Disney designs the guest experience at its theme parks or a local restaurant creates an ambiance and trains servers on how to treat customers. CEM is important online as it relates to a website, company marketing communication, or customer service experience. CCM is a recent concept, and it appears that the terms social CRM or CRM 2.0 are currently gaining the most popular use for this idea. We want to make you aware of these pillars and the growing CCM area but integrate their discussion under the umbrella of the more often used CRM terminology (social CRM). This thinking follows Forrester Research's social media experts: "Social CRM augments social networking to serve as a new channel within existing end-to-end CRM processes and investments" (in a paper by R "Ray" Wang and Jeremiah Owyang with Christine Tran edited by Charlene Li).

Customer Relationship Management (CRM 1.0)

CRM is an oft-misused term that many companies use to refer to the software and other technology used to implement CRM solutions. As you'll see, CRM is much more—it is a philosophy, strategy, and process. It includes all three pillars and other tenets of relationship marketing and is grounded in customer data and conversations and facilitated by technology. Increasingly, organizations recognize that if they don't keep their customers happy, someone else will. Many have experienced one sweet tweet to increase sales and one sour tweet to hurt the business.

Social Customer Relationship Management (CRM 2.0)

Social CRM (CRM 2.0) retains all the tenets of CRM 1.0; however, it adds social media technology and customer collaborative conversations to the process (Exhibit 15.3). Social CRM means that companies must interact with customers on their terms and not based solely on the company's data, strategy, and desires. Social CRM extends CRM 1.0 but does not replace it. In CRM 1.0, customers would forward e-mails to friends or talk in business meetings about products. Social CRM added more conversation among customers due to social media and gave companies many additional media for building long-term customer relationships (and sales).

Social CRM provides many benefits to companies such as monitoring and improving reputations, learning more about customer needs, wants, and problems, improving target market selection and revenue potential, gathering data for market research on products and customer

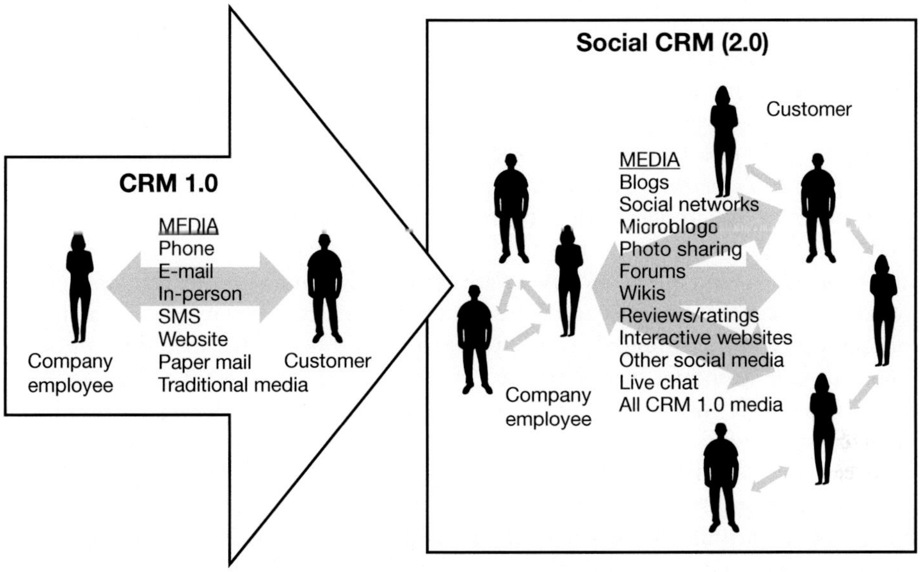

CRM 1.0

MEDIA
Phone
E-mail
In-person
SMS
Website
Paper mail
Traditional media

Company
employee

Customer

Social CRM (2.0)

Customer

MEDIA
Blogs
Social networks
Microblogs
Photo sharing
Forums
Wikis
Reviews/ratings
Interactive websites
Other social media
Live chat
All CRM 1.0 media

Company
employee

Exhibit 15.3 CRM Evolves Using Social Media

service, decreasing customer service costs, and identifying new revenue opportunities. Similarly, social CRM helps customers by getting quick problem resolution, finding unbiased product information more easily from other customers, interacting with companies easily, and improving customer satisfaction.

Qantas Airlines learned social CRM the hard way. A saxophone player protested on Facebook when he learned of a policy change: after 20 years of carrying his sax on the plane, now musical instruments had to be checked and carried in the plane's cargo area. He checked his sax and incurred $1,200 worth of damage on one flight. The sax player started a Qantas boycott on Facebook, and more than 8,700 musicians and others joined the group. Qantas discovered the group protest and subsequently changed the policy to allow smaller instruments on the plane ("Facebook Chorus Ends . . .", 2011).

Social CRM adds new technologies to CRM 1.0. Marketers need to rethink many of their current CRM strategies and tactics, as did Best Buy with its Twitter accounts and forums. Marketers are also wondering how to find the staff time to monitor conversations and manage all these 1:1 interactions with customers and prospects. Fortunately, many suppliers have stepped up to assist, as you saw in previous chapters with the social media metrics dashboards.

The explosion of social media has marketers putting "social" in front of many strategies, such as social CRM. Because social CRM simply adds new media, strategies, and tactics to traditional CRM, we organize the rest of this chapter using the basic tenets of CRM and simply add social CRM methods to current strategy and tactics.

CRM Benefits

The benefits of CRM include those previously mentioned and increased revenue from better prospect targeting, increased wallet share with current customers, and retaining customers for longer periods of time. These benefits are quantified through databases that help companies understand their customers better and use this knowledge to build loyalty and optimize lifetime value. CRM tactics can also decrease costs, resulting in greater profitability. Finally, social CRM tactics help companies work with individual customers and manage their all-important reputations in social media.

Companies often use prospect and customer data to build mathematical models that help them perform more effective customer segmentation. Effective segmentation allows them to define prospect and customer profiles that are most likely to respond favorably to particular promotional offers, or simply to identify the best segment of prospects for current or new products.

Most businesses spend more money acquiring new customers than they spend keeping current customers—but this approach is usually a mistake. Detailing our earlier statement, the cost of acquiring a new customer is typically five to seven times higher than the cost of retaining a current one, as shown in Exhibit 15.4. For example, assume that a company budgets $3,000 to acquire six customers, and the cost of acquiring each is $500. Because retaining customers costs one-fifth less (on average), that same $500 could be spent enticing five customers to stay at a cost of $100 each. If instead of spending $3,000 on gaining six customers, a firm spent $1,500 on three new customers and $1,500 on customer retention, it would be 12 customers ahead. Fortunately, most marketers now understand this, and that is why a majority see customer retention as a top priority.

One reason that retention is less costly than acquisition is reduced promotion costs, both for advertising and discounts. Additionally, higher response rates to promotional efforts yield more profits. Sales teams can be more effective when they get to know individual customers well. Another reason CRM makes sense is that loyal customers are experienced customers. They know the products well, and they know who to call in the firm when they have questions. Loyal customers cost less to service. Plus, they post positive reviews online and tell their social network friends about it.

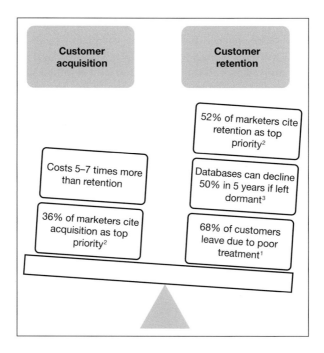

Exhibit 15.4 Maximizing Number of Customers Through Customer Retention

Having more customers leads to more sales. However, acquiring and retaining customers is only part of the equation. A firm must also attempt to increase the amount purchased by each customer. For example, Southwest Airlines and most online travel agents send e-mails to customers when the airfare to a destination of interest to them drops and to offer special hotel and car rental deals.

In addition to buying more, satisfied customers recommend websites, stores, and products to their personal and professional networks via e-mail, mobile messaging, and social media. Word-of-mouth communication among customers has been called the heart of CRM. Positive word-of-mouth can attract many new customers, but negative word-of-mouth can drive them away. One classic study reported that each dissatisfied customer tells 10 people about the unhappy experience, and for 13 percent of dissatisfied customers, each tells 20 people how bad the company and its products were (Sonnenberg, 1993). The internet outdates this offline statistic because now each dissatisfied customer can tell thousands with one keystroke on Facebook, a quick Tweet on Twitter, or through a short video on YouTube. For example, one consumer can tweet about a negative customer service experience with an airline, including nasty hashtags that can help the post gain virality. The incident may or may not have been under the control of the company, for example, if the customer's flight had to be canceled due to a snowstorm. However, the airline will still have to deal with the content, as countless firms must deal with complaints from consumers online based on their experiences.

One key CRM benefit is its cost-saving advantage. Consider that one company reported a 25 percent reduction in expenses related to solving customer services issues after using Salesforce (www.salesforce.com/customer-success-stories/activision).

CRM Building Blocks

Although companies understand CRM's benefits and are investing heavily in CRM software, many lose money on this investment. Thus, businesses are trying to determine what works and what doesn't, knowing that they have to get it right to win—especially as social media create a loss of marketing control. This section focuses on the nine important CRM components used in digital marketing, based on a Gartner Group CRM model (see Exhibit 15.5).

1. **CRM Vision:** Leadership, value proposition
2. **CRM Strategy:** Objectives, target markets

3. **Customer Experience Management (CEM):** Requirements, expectations, satisfaction, feedback, interaction
4. **Customer Collaboration Marketing (CCM):** Creating and monitoring content, listening, measuring, integrating into CRM technology

5. **Organizational Collaboration** Culture and structure. Customer understanding. People, skills, competencies, incentives, and compensation. Employee communication. Partners and suppliers

6. **CRM Processes:** Customer life cycle, knowledge management
7. **CRM Information:** Data, analysis, one view across channels
8. **CRM Technology:** Applications, architecture, infrastructure
9. **CRM Metrics:** Value, retention, satisfaction, loyalty, cost to serve

Exhibit 15.5 Nine Building Blocks for Successful CRM

Source: Adapted from Gartner Group. Available at www.gartner.com. (Note that this model was adapted in 2003, and more current information may be available at www.gartner.com)

According to Gartner, "CRM initiatives need a framework to ensure that programs are approached on a strategic, balanced and integrated basis. Such a framework will maximize benefits to the enterprise and its customers."

1. CRM Vision

Many organizations purchase expensive CRM software just because it is becoming a necessary component of successful competition. It is no wonder that so many projects fail. Some estimates note that more than twice as many companies with successful CRM strategies spent time working with employees before and while implementing CRM systems. It is the employees and not the software that make successful CRM.

Management must start with a vision that fits the company culture and makes sense for the firm's brands and value propositions. This involves both technology and employee collaboration with customers. Some say that the main reason CRM projects fail is because companies do not realize how pervasive they are and underestimate the costs. For example, when a company installs CRM software to integrate data from their website, social media, and brick-and-mortar retail operations, customer service reps need training and must be committed to the initiative. Some customer service reps bypass CRM software because it is easier to do it the old way. As well, management needs to embrace social media and put structures in place for employee interactions, as did Best Buy. To be successful, the CRM vision must start at the top and filter throughout the company to keep the firm completely customer focused.

The privacy policy also needs a vision supported by key executives. Marketers have access to lots of information about every customer and prospect, and that information is stored in databases and used for marketing communications. One key aspect of this vision is how to guard customer privacy.

Guarding Customer Privacy

Use of customer data is very important to marketers, yet the temptation to overuse it must be balanced by the need to satisfy customers and not anger them. The burden is on marketers to use customer and prospect information responsibly, both for their own business health and for the image of the profession. An increasing number of people are more concerned about their online privacy now than just one year ago ("How Concerned Are You", 2021). Actions taken by social network users to restrict personal information access include changing privacy settings to limit access (65%), deleting people from social network friend's lists (56%), blocking certain updates from some people (52%), filtering updates posted by friends (41%), deleting comments posted by others on a profile page (36%), removing names from photo tags (30%), and regretting previous postings, photos, or videos (12%) ("Americans and Privacy", 2019). Nonetheless, consumers are unaware of the extent to which real-time profiling and other techniques monitor their online behavior—and marketers must address this issue before regulators make them do it. For instance, Facebook made a huge mistake when it published customer purchasing behavior on profile pages. One Facebook user purchased an item at Overstock.com using her personal e-mail address and then saw a description of what she bought on her Facebook news feed.

CRM is based on trust. Customers must believe that the information they give companies when they purchase online, in e-mail, or in other ways will be used responsibly. It means using the information to improve the relationship by tailoring goods, services, and marketing communications to meet individual needs. It means allowing consumers to request removal of their information from databases and to opt out of e-mail lists, as well as not sharing information with other companies unless permission is granted.

Another important privacy issue concerns intrusions into people's lives. Junk mail, spam, and repeated calls requesting account upgrades by a company are all examples of interrupt-type marketing messages that can upset consumers.

What's a marketer to do? The answer is threefold: build relationships through dialog, better target profiling, and transparent data use practices. Companies must listen to customers and prospects and give them what they want. If a consumer wants to receive e-mail from American Airlines, great. If not, the firm should remove that customer from the list, perhaps checking once a year to see whether the status has changed. Why? Organizations know that retention and development of customer relationships are more profitable than one-time customer transactions and that relationship capital is one of the firm's strongest assets. Second, marketers can use consumer information to build more precise target profiles. Instead of sending a mass e-mail to everyone who visits the site, how about sending individual or small group e-mails to people who might actually need a car for the flight they just booked at the site? Individuals do not get upset with companies who send valuable and timely information to them. Finally, companies must be transparent in terms of how they collect, store, and share consumers' information. This goes beyond simply having a privacy policy that consumers must agree to, as these are often written in language that is difficult for the average person to understand. Companies should clearly communicate the content of these policies to consumers, be forthcoming when changes are made, and strive to ensure that consumers' data is as protected as possible.

Trustarc

To help websites earn the trust of their users, an independent, nonprofit privacy initiative named TrustArc was created. TrustArc provides its seal and logo to any website meeting its philosophies, as stated on the site (Exhibit 15.6). Note how well these and the following information requirements fit with good CRM practices:

- Adopting and implementing a privacy policy that factors in the goals of your individual website as well as consumer anxiety over sharing personal information online.
- Posting notice and disclosure of collection and use practices regarding personally identifiable information (data used to identify, contact, or locate a person) via a posted privacy statement.
- Giving users choice and consent over how their personal information is used and shared.
- Putting data security and quality and access measures in place to safeguard, update, and correct personally identifiable information.

In addition, sites must publish the following information on their sites to gain the TRUSTe seal (www.trustarc.com):

1. What personal information is being gathered by your site?
2. Who is collecting the information?
3. How will the information be used?
4. With whom will the information be shared?
5. What are the choices available to users regarding collection, use, and distribution of their information? (You must offer users an opportunity to opt out of internal secondary uses as well as third-party distribution for secondary uses.)

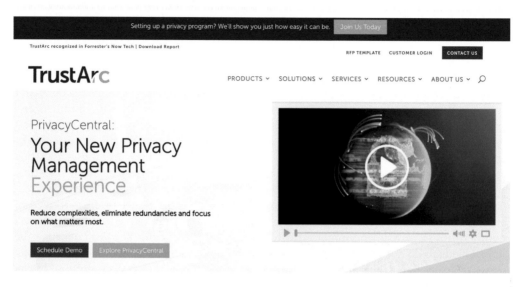

Exhibit 15.6 TRUSTe Builds User Trust

Source: www.trustarc.com

6. What are the security procedures in place to protect users' collected information from loss, misuse, or alteration? (If your site collects, uses, or distributes personally identifiable information such as credit card or social security numbers, accepted transmission protocols, including encryption, must be in place.)

7. How can users update or correct inaccuracies in their pertinent information? (Appropriate measures must be taken to ensure that personal information collected online is accurate, complete, and timely, and that easy-to-use mechanisms are in place for users to verify that inaccuracies have been corrected.)

Other organizations also provide guidelines for internet privacy. The American Marketing Association has a code of ethics for digital marketing, dealing primarily with privacy and intellectual property. See Chapter 5 for more about the legal aspects of privacy.

2. CRM Strategy

Marketers must determine their objectives and strategies for initiating CRM programs and buying technology or setting up social media accounts. These objectives may involve any stakeholders (employees, business customers, partners, or consumers) and will likely entail targeting, acquiring, retaining, and growing specified relationships. The B2B market is different from the B2C market due to its CRM focus on lead generation and follow-up for salespeople (often using the subsequently discussed sales force automation software).

Many of these CRM goals refer to customer loyalty. Most companies would be delighted if they had customers who proudly wore their brand name on clothing and tried to talk others into buying the brand on Facebook—like customers of Harley-Davidson and Apple. Chapter 9 discussed five levels of relationship intensity (awareness, identity, connection, community, and advocacy). Thus, an important CRM strategy is trying to move customers upward to advocacy.

Level	Primary Bond	Potential for Sustained Competitive Advantage	Main Element of Marketing Mix	Web Example
One	Financial	Low	Price	southwest.com
Two	Social	Medium	Personal	facebook.com
	Build 1:1 relationship		communications	
	Build community			
Three	Structural	High	Service delivery	my.yahoo.com

Exhibit 15.7 Three Levels of Relationship Marketing

Source: Adapted from Berry and Parasuraman (1991)

Another CRM goal involves building bonds with customers that transcend the product experience itself. Experts have suggested that relationship marketing is practiced on three levels (see Exhibit 15.7). The strongest relationships are formed if all three levels are used and if the product itself actually satisfies buyers. At level one, marketers build a financial bond with customers by using pricing strategies. At this lowest level of relationship, price promotions are easily imitated. Many airlines send periodic e-mail notification of price discounts to individual users. These discounts can be timed and priced to build wallet share.

At level two, marketers stimulate social interaction between customers and the company and among customers themselves. In fact, the majority of interactions with customers are non-transactional communication, thus demonstrating this strategy. Social media participation is an important way to forge level-two relationships and strengthen loyalty (as discussed in Chapters 12–14). Social CRM fits well at this level.

At level three, relationship marketing relies on creating structural solutions to customer problems. Bonds form when companies add value by making structural changes that facilitate the relationship. For example, Apple's Safari browser uses Google as its search engine (Exhibit 15.8). All of the major social networking sites and Web portals create structural bonds with their users. Services such as My Yahoo! allow consumers to customize their interface to Yahoo! so it lists local weather and movies, personal stock portfolios, and news of interest to them. Once consumers invest the time and effort to customize this interface, they will be reluctant to switch to another portal.

Social networks combine levels two and three by creating community and structural bonds. For instance, when customers create profiles on Facebook or LinkedIn, they spend time learning how to use the sites, and they invest by uploading content. Thus, customers are likely to stick with the social networking sites they use. Even TripAdvisor has this structural bond because customers have to register in order to log on and rate hotels.

3. Customer Experience Management

Amazon.com continually demonstrates its commitment to the customer experience. The great majority of its stated goals involve customer service, and fewer involve sales and profits, but of course, this customer mentality results in higher sales.

Most customers want a good experience resulting in brand loyalty as much as the companies they patronize. However, being a consumer can be difficult because of the constant bombardment by marketing communications and unlimited product choices. Consumers generally want to patronize the same website, social network, and online booksellers because doing so

Exhibit 15.8 Google Downloadable Toolbar

Source: www.google.com

is efficient. That is, consumers do not want to spend their days contemplating which brand of toothpaste to buy or how to find a good search engine. Many consumers are "loyalty prone," searching for the right product or service and then sticking with it as long as the promises are more or less fulfilled. Customers buy from Amazon.com because of good previous experiences, the convenience of having personal preferences on file, one-click ordering, and the familiar interface, regardless of price. This has extended to additional ways to engage with Amazon through voice-powered offerings like the Amazon Echo.

Customers also generally like to patronize stores, services, and websites where they are treated like individuals with important needs and where they know those needs will be met, "satisfaction guaranteed." Users believe the company cares when they get an e-mail about operating system upgrades to their smartphone, addressed to them by name, that refers to the exact product purchased. They care less when they get frequent communication pushing for general service upgrades and feel greater brand loyalty when Amazon sends an e-mail announcing a new book by an author they enjoy. Of course, companies must learn to answer e-mails sent from customers as well. Listening to hundreds of thousands of customers one at a time in e-mail or within social media can be difficult and expensive, but it satisfies customers.

Customers' preferences for communicating with each company vary by individual as well as by situation and product type. Customers might want to call and speak with a live rep about an account problem, go to a website to research product information, use e-mail to complain about a service problem, live chat with an employee, or send a tweet to Best Buy's @BestBuySupport, and so forth. Exhibit 15.9 displays these options covering many technologies, using both automated and human intervention for both synchronous (simultaneous) and asynchronous communication. This exhibit reinforces the importance of the internet in creating valued customer experiences and the idea that companies must be adept with many

	Automated	*Human*
Synchronous	Web 1:1 self-service	Telephone
	Online transactions	Online instant messaging
	Shop bots (virtual assistants)	Collaboration tools; real-time chat
Asynchronous	Automated e-mail	E-mail response
	Short message services (SMS)	Postal mail
	Web forms	Blog post comments; social media comments

Exhibit 15.9 Relationships over Multiple Communication Channels

different technologies and processes, putting the focus on customers and their preferences, not the company's capabilities.

Customer Service

Customer service permeates every stage of customer acquisition, retention, and development practices, although most service occurs post-purchase when customers have questions or complaints. Customer service is an important part of the customer experience and a critical strategic component.

Key customer experience technology tools include e-mail, online live chat, either through customer service representatives or animated shop bots, social media comments, and Web self-service through frequently asked questions, and more. For example, Mercedes-Benz combines a number of interconnected mediums to enable consumer convenience. If a consumer types a question into a form on their website, they receive an immediate phone call from a Mercedes representative. The consumer and representative can then discuss the question while viewing the same webpages. In fact, software now allows customer service reps on the telephone or a live chat with a customer to take control of the user's mouse and guide the customer around the company website. E-mail, customized Web landing pages, live chat, and package tracking using smartphones are just a few of the customer service techniques described throughout this chapter. Regardless of technique, online or offline, customer service is critical to building long-term customer relationships.

4. Customer Collaboration Management

As previously mentioned, this pillar of relationship management has been variously called social CRM, CRM 2.0, and customer collaboration management (or customer collaboration marketing). CCM recognizes the change from a transaction focus online to an interaction focus.

Interaction with customers allows companies to collect data necessary for CCM and to evaluate strategy effectiveness on a continuous basis. Peppers and Rogers (1997, p. 15) call this interaction a "learning relationship."

A **learning relationship** between a customer and an enterprise gets smarter and smarter with each individual interaction, defining in ever more detail the customer's own individual needs and tastes.

The idea here is that both the company and the customer learn from each experience and interaction. In any perfect relationship, this ongoing experience equates to increased trust, loyalty, and an increasing share of business for the company, with peace of mind for the customer. The digital technologies are uniquely positioned to deliver on this promise. When a company adopts this philosophy, it is a learning organization.

Customer collaboration management is content, people, and interaction driven, while traditional CRM is data driven. People create and upload content about brands, and companies attempt to engage users in their brand-related content. For instance, throughout this book you've seen examples of YouTube videos about brands, uploaded both by consumers (Greenpeace about Nestlé) and companies (*Will It Blend?*), all toward the end goal of company/customer collaboration.

Thus, CCM is about managing customer relationships and experiences by creating and monitoring online content. This means listening to the online chatter using technology such as Google Alerts, social media monitoring tools, and social media dashboards to assist in this difficult endeavor. It means responding to legitimate content posters with the goal of enhancing their brand experience. It involves posting content that consumers and business buyers find valuable, interesting, or entertaining—as evidenced by the success of the top blogs. This brings to mind an old saying: "We have two ears and one mouth for a reason." Listening is more important than talking when a company is selling. Altimeter summarizes CCM requirements well with its 5 M's (Wang and Owyang, 2010):

1. *Monitoring*. Provides listening capabilities to filter out noise from the social sphere, encapsulates both metrics and measurement, and extracts insights that make measurement more effective.
2. *Mapping*. Identifies social media relationships, linking social profiles to customer records for providing a holistic experience.
3. *Management*. Systems bring CRM processes to life. Without a purpose, social data is not actionable; thus, business rules and processes are needed to triage the right information to the right teams in real time.
4. *Middleware*. These are technologies that glue the social world to the enterprise. Social CRM connects to nearly every customer-facing system. Data will have to seamlessly flow between systems and advanced dashboards that provide intelligence.
5. *Measurement*. What you can't measure you can't improve; therefore, organizations must be able to benchmark what's been done.

5. Organizational Collaboration

Within a company, cross-functional teams join forces to focus on customer satisfaction to create a CRM culture (such as the numerous Blue Shirts and Geek Squad members posting in the social networks). Outside the organization, when two or more companies join forces, the results often exceed what each firm might have accomplished alone—whether it is in the distribution channel or a non-transactional-type collaboration. In fact, some marketers believe that today's marketplace consists of supply chain competition, not individual firm competition.

In the following sections, we discuss two important collaboration techniques that capitalize on internet properties: CRM–SCM integration and extranets.

CRM–SCM Integration

CRM usually refers to front-end operations, meaning that companies work to create satisfying experiences at all customer touch points: calls to customer service reps, digital commerce purchases at online stores, e-mail and Facebook contact, and so forth. This challenge is substantial because different employees and computer systems collect various information, which somehow must be integrated into appropriate customer records. In the online environment of customer control, however, even consistently good customer service is not enough. With technological advances and interoperability, online retailers can seamlessly link the back-end (e.g., inventory and payment) with the front-end CRM system and the entire supply chain management system (SCM). The entire supply chain can work together to single-mindedly focus on meeting consumer needs and make higher profits in the process. It all centers, of course, on information (Exhibit 15.10).

Imagine that a customer orders a particular shirt from a clothing retailer's website. In the past, if the shirt was out of stock, the customer might see a Web screen with that message or an e-mail notification. With an integrated CRM–SCM system, however, the system can instantly check inventory levels at the retailer and notify the customer that it is not available—usually this information appears right on the product page. The next generation of CRM–SCM integration will allow immediate inventory checking at the wholesaler or manufacturer to determine availability. Then the system could notify the customer during the ordering process and offer options: wait two weeks for delivery from the manufacturer or consider a similar shirt currently in stock, for example.

Connecting customers with supply chain businesses provides several advantages. First, all companies will share transaction data so that inventories can be kept low (thus lowering costs). If producers and wholesalers constantly receive data about consumer orders, they can produce goods in a timely manner. Second, upstream companies can use the data to design products that better meet consumer needs (see the co-designing discussion in Chapter 9). Third, if customer service reps have up-to-the-minute information about product inventories, they will be able to better help consumers immediately. Catalog companies are already fairly accomplished at this task, but the process breaks down when supplier companies are several levels upstream from the retailer.

As more companies integrate CRM and SCM activities, they will become more responsive to individual customer needs. For example, Levi's used electronic scanners to send precise measurements directly to the factory for individualized jeans, and Dell and Blue Nile (jewelry) produce and ship customized products within days. Conversely, this type of integration is quite difficult when a firm has many different channels for its brands and when each firm uses different software and hardware to manage its internal systems. Nevertheless, the systems for integration are currently available and are helping companies become market winners.

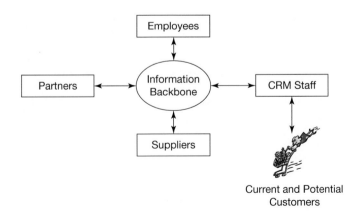

Exhibit 15.10 CRM–SCM Integration

Extranet

Extranets are two or more intranet networks that are joined for the purpose of sharing information. If two companies link their proprietary intranets, they would have an extranet. By definition, extranets are proprietary to the organizations involved. Companies participating in an extranet have formed a structural bond, the third and strongest level of relationship marketing. It is the use of extranets that allows CRM–SCM integration.

Electronic Data Systems (EDS) was a Dallas-based firm that provided, enterprise-wide, hundreds of thousands of computer desktops, managing services from procurement to network management for large clients in many countries. The word *enterprise* means that EDS focuses on all the computer desktops in an entire company, bringing them together in a network. EDS created an innovative extranet called the Renascence Channel, which links desktops of its suppliers, clients, and employees into an electronic marketplace. Forty suppliers selling more than 2,000 software products fund the private network, paying $25,000 to $100,000 each to display their products and services in a catalog-type format. Suppliers benefit because they have access to and can build relationships with lots of potential buyers. The buyers trust the suppliers because EDS selected them, and they pay lower prices because suppliers' costs are lower in this channel: one vendor reported a drop in order-processing expenses from $150 to $25 per item. Buyers benefit by having desktop access to convenient product information, click-of-a-mouse purchasing, product delivery tracking, online training, and expedited delivery. Today, EDS is part of DXC Technology to continue serving the enterprise market with innovative new solutions.

6. CRM Processes

Customer relationship management involves an understanding of the customer care life cycle, as presented in Exhibit 15.11. Companies monitor and attract customers, both online and offline, as they progress through the stages: target, acquire, transact, service, retain, and grow. This process begins with the digital marketing plan when companies select target markets. However, opportunities often arise when a new target group appears at the website—such as when Brooks Brothers noted a large number of Japanese users at the site. Thus, the cycle is circular in nature: for example, while servicing customers, a new target may emerge. This important cycle is based on one central tenet of CRM that bears repeating—it is better to

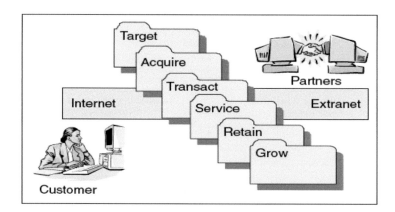

Exhibit 15.11 Customer Care Life Cycle

Source: Adapted from a speech by Tod Famous, Cisco Systems

retain and grow customers than to focus only on customer acquisition. Of course, not all customers go through this process—some do less business with the firm or leave to transact with a competitor. Sometimes companies try to reacquire these customers, as when Netflix sends e-mails to customers who have cancelled their accounts, with the line "We want you back" and an offer of free service for a certain period.

There are many CRM processes. In this section, we present a customer churn cycle that works both for retention and increasing customer value. Then we discuss two important CRM processes using internet technologies: sales force automation and marketing automation.

Hear Now or Gone Tomorrow

The Peppers & Rogers Group describes the importance of listening to customers and gathering interaction data across all marketing channels. Data help organizations predict who is likely to leave, how to keep them, and how to make changes to the marketing program to keep others from leaving. Their approach recognizes that customers you have "now" may be "gone tomorrow" unless companies focus on reducing customer defection through:

1. Obtaining transactional, behavioral, and interaction data about prospects, business customers, and end consumers through personal disclosure, automated tracking through the sales force, customer service encounters, barcode scanners at retailers, and website/social media activity.
2. Entering user information into a database that helps companies identify who is at risk for defecting. This step entails statistical modeling.
3. Segmenting customers using value analysis based on behavior, demographics, and so forth to determine which individuals might leave.
4. Identifying the root cause for possible defection by evaluating product/service flaws, competitive offers, or promotions that are not working.
5. Fixing this with a retention program that might involve promotional offers and real-time recommendations while customers are online.
6. Measuring the program effectiveness in terms of customer retention.

This model is presented because it also works within the CRM process for identifying the company's best customers. *Best* is described in many different ways, such as highest value, longest loyalty, highest frequency of purchase, and so on. CRM allows marketers to leverage their resources by investing more in the most lucrative customers. The idea is not new, but what is unique is that technology allows companies to identify high-value customers and respond with offers in real time over the internet. Value differentiation pays off when a plastics firm focused on its most profitable customers cuts its customer base from 800 to 90 while increasing revenue by 400 percent (Renner, 2000). However, not all companies have high- and low-value customers. According to the Peppers & Rogers Group, differentiation by valuation is not profitable unless a firm can say that at least half of its profits come from 20 percent or fewer of its customers (the four- and five-star customers in Chapter 10).

Some customers are clearly not profitable and thus should not get as much focus as high-value customers so that the company can allocate resources profitably. For example, casinos operate such that high rollers get anything they want and low spenders might get only a buffet discount. Casino management knows the difference because customers use player cards in slot machines that are networked and always collecting data on spending patterns. Walmart also operates in this way; due to the high volume of products they purchase and the revenue that they command, they can insist on receiving the lowest price from their suppliers.

Travel website TripAdvisor.com continually sends special reward offers to those who had contributed to their millions of hotel reviews, thus differentiating and rewarding the customers who engage by uploading content. A recent e-mail to one author offered a special digital badge for posting just one more hotel review.

Once a company identifies prospects and differentiates customers according to characteristics, behavior, needs, or value, it can consider customizing offerings to various segments or individuals—either as a retention campaign or to increase current customer value. **Customization** occurs when companies tailor their marketing mixes to meet the needs of small target segments, even to the individual level, using electronic marketing tools. Products, marketing communication messages, and dynamic pricing can all be tailored to individuals and delivered over the internet in a timely manner. These approaches were not possible before the internet except with very high-priced products such as manufacturing equipment. Through customization, companies can zero in on the precise needs of each prospect and customer and build long-term, profitable relationships.

Some writers use the term *personalize* when referring to customization. **Personalization** involves ways that marketers individualize in an impersonal computer-networked environment. For example, websites may greet users by name or automatically send an e-mail to individuals with personal account information. We use the term *customization* because it refers to much more than automated personalization.

Now, how to put this model into operationalization for retaining and building customer value?

Build a Dynamic Customer Profile

With billions of daily e-mails, millions of tweets and Facebook posts and updates, how can a marketer keep up? Lyris Technologies Inc. summarizes this current problem by suggesting that marketers gather data to profile each customer as reflected by his interactions with a brand at many touch points:

From a customer's perspective, his or her dynamic profile would look something like this:

- What I've bought.
- What I've browsed.
- What devices I use.
- When I'm online.
- Where I've visited online.
- My current status.
- What I like and dislike.
- Who my friends are."

("Field Guide to . . .", 2012)

From a marketer's perspective, the dynamic customer profile includes the data in Exhibit 15.12. Armed with this demographic, attitudinal, and behavioral information, marketers can make precise decisions to move the consumer through the CRM process from targeting and acquisition to repeat purchase. Marketers can also (1) group customers into profitable segments, (2) use the data to engage customers and deliver value, (3) integrate the data into current CRM databases, and (4) integrate data from offline sources, such as call centers and physical retail stores. All this can be accomplished in an automated fashion using databases and other technologies.

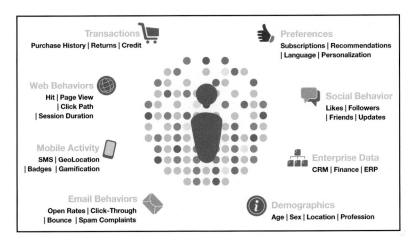

Exhibit 15.12 Building a Dynamic Customer Profile

Source: Image courtesy of Lyris, Inc., www.lyris.com

British interiors and gift store Graham & Green tested this system. The company has a large e-mail database and had been sending two product-related e-mails a week to the entire database with a 20 percent open rate. The company then sent an e-mail offering a home accessory discount to those who had visited the home accessories pages on its website and realized a 49 percent open rate and 1.1 percent conversion to purchase. Several additional tests produced similar results. This type of behavioral targeting is data driven and helps to build customer relationships and sales. Many companies, including Lyris, offer the technology solutions to make this work well.

Sales Force Automation (SFA)

"Increase your sales, not your sales force," proclaims SFA software. Used primarily in the B2B market, SFA allows salespeople to build, maintain, and access customer records; manage leads and accounts; manage their schedules; and more. In relation to digital marketing, SFA helps the sales force acquire, retain, and grow customers by accessing customer and product data from the company's data warehouses, both while in the office and on the road. Salespeople can also send the results of sales calls and activity reports to the data warehouse for access by others. Up-to-date customer and prospect records help customer service representatives and others build customer relationships. As an example, SFA leader Salesforce.com's software claims to drive sales productivity and revenues, improve customer service, facilitate partner relationship management by integrating data, improve marketing of multichannel campaigns, improve Web 2.0 content distribution, and evaluate sales operations through performance metrics.

Notably, Salesforce.com also has tools to monitor brand conversation on social media, helping companies respond quickly: customer collaboration management in a CRM tool.

Marketing Automation

Marketing automation activities aid marketers with effective targeting, efficient marketing communication, and real-time monitoring of customer and market trends. Marketing automation software usually takes data from websites and databases and turns it into reports for fine-tuning CRM efforts, such as shown in Exhibit 15.12. Software solutions include e-mail campaign management, database marketing, market segmentation, website log analysis, and more.

Marketing automation is a powerful marketing solution for CRM. SAS, business intelligence and predictive analytics software provider, offers the following marketing automation benefits with its software (www.sas.com): an integrated customer view, customer life cycle management, customer targeting, analytics, and integrated support for all business units. Companies using this software can develop multichannel communication campaigns, understand their results, and store all data in one technology solution.

7. CRM Information

As you have read up to this point, information is the lubricant of CRM. The more information a firm has, the better value it can provide to each customer and prospect in terms of more accurate, timely, and relevant offerings. Many companies entice customers to provide additional information over time by engaging them in blogs, in product reviews, or through digital commerce transactions. For example, Orbitz.com first requests a simple e-mail address from those who want information about discount offers and subsequently asks about vacation preferences so as to provide more relevant e-mailings. A customer who provides increasingly more personal information (e.g., location preferences, number of people who typically accompany one's travels) shows enough trust in the firm to invest in the relationship.

Sometimes companies gather this type of information under the guise of entertainment. For example, the Mini Cooper automobile gains valuable information about the preferences of site visitors by allowing them to configure the perfect car online, using 10 million possible option combinations (www.miniusa.com).

Companies gain much information from customers less intrusively by tracking their behavior electronically. Information technology allows companies to move beyond the traditional segment profiling (e.g., Generation X) to detailed profiles of individuals. For example, when product barcode scanner data collected at the checkout are combined with a store shopping card, the company can identify individual customer purchases over time. On the internet, software tracks a user's movement from page to page, indicating how much time was spent on each page, whether the user made a purchase, the type of computer and operating system, and more. Companies can track which sites users visited before and after theirs and use this information to guess which competitive products are under consideration and to learn about users' interests. Tracking user behavior is valuable to both users and companies, but it has its critics because of privacy considerations, as previously mentioned.

Now a customer can call the customer service representative to discuss a product purchased in the brick-and-mortar store last week, refer to an e-mail sent yesterday, and post about it on his or her Facebook account—with the data all stored in the database under one customer record. This approach is known as having a 360° customer view, or one view across channels. In her book *Customers.com*, Patricia Seybold (1998) identified eight critical success factors for building successful digital business relationships with customers. Even decades later, these factors remain a good springboard to understanding how internet technologies facilitate customer relationship management using digital marketing.

1. *Target the right customers.* Identify the best prospects and customers and learn as much about them as possible.
2. *Own the customer's total experience.* This factor refers to the customer share of mind or share of wallet previously discussed.

3. *Streamline business processes that impact the customer.* This task can be accomplished through CRM–SCM integration and monomaniacal customer focus.
4. *Provide a 360° view of the customer relationship.* Everyone in the firm who touches the customer should understand all aspects of that customer's relationship with the company. For example, customer service reps should know all customer activity over time and understand which products and services might benefit that particular customer.
5. *Let customers help themselves.* Provide websites and other electronic means for customers to find things they need quickly and conveniently, 24/7.
6. *Help customers do their jobs.* Especially in the B2B market, if a firm provides products and services to help customers perform well in their businesses, they will be loyal and pay a premium for the help. Many supply-chain management electronic processes facilitate this factor.
7. *Deliver personalized service.* Customer profiling, privacy safekeeping, and marketing mix customization all aid in delivering personalized services electronically.
8. *Foster community.* Enticing customers to join in communities and social networks of interest that relate to a firm's products is one important way to build loyalty.

8. CRM Technology

Technology greatly enhances CRM processes. Incoming toll-free numbers, interactive kiosks, voice mail, and automated phone call routing are examples of technology that assist in moving customers through the life cycle. The internet, however, is the first fully interactive and individually addressable low-cost multimedia channel—it forms the centerpiece of a firm's CRM abilities. Cookies, website logs, barcode scanners, automated Web monitoring (such as Google Alerts), social media, and other tools help to collect information about consumer behavior, conversations, and characteristics. Databases and data warehouses store and distribute these data from online and offline touch points, thus allowing employees to develop marketing mixes that better meet individual needs.

Here we discuss do-it-yourself tools that aid organizations in customizing products to groups of customers or individuals as opposed to all-in-one software packages. These include "push" strategies that reside on the company's Web and e-mail servers and "pull" strategies that are initiated by internet users. The difference is important because companies have more control over push techniques.

Company-Side Tools

Exhibit 15.13 displays important tools used to push customized information to users. Visitors are generally unaware that marketers are collecting data and using these technologies to customize offerings.

Cookies. Cookie files are the reason that customers returning to Amazon.com get a greeting by name, and that users don't have to remember passwords to every site for which they are registered. Cookie files allow ad-server companies to see the path users take from site to site and thus serve display advertising relevant to user interests. Finally, cookies keep track of shopping baskets and other tasks so that users can quit in the middle and return to the task later.

Web analytics. By utilizing Web analytics, companies can do many things, not the least of which is to customize webpages based on visitor behavior. Web analytics are tools that collect and display information about user behavior on a website (see Chapter 2). Software such as WebTrends also tells which sites the users visited immediately before arriving, what keywords they typed in at search engines to find the site, user domains, and much more.

Company-Side Tools (push)	Description
Cookies	Cookies are small files written to the user's hard drive after visiting a Website. When the user returns to the site, the company's server looks for the cookie file and uses it to personalize the site.
Web log analysis	Every time a user accesses a Web site, the visit is recorded in the Web server's log file. This file keeps track of which pages the user visits, how long the user stays, and whether the user purchases.
Data mining	Data mining involves the extraction of hidden predictive information in large databases through statistical analysis.
Behavioral targeting	Behavioral targeting occurs when software tracks a user's movements through a Web site and then sends appropriate Web content at a moment's notice.
Collaborative filtering	Collaborative filtering software gathers opinions of like-minded users and returns those opinions to the individual in real time.
Outgoing e-mail/ Distributed e-mail	Marketers use e-mail databases to build relationships by keeping in touch with useful and timely information. E-mail can be sent to individuals or sent *en masse* using a distributed e-mail list.
Social media	A firm may listen to users on blogs or social networks and build community by providing a space for user conversation on the website.
iPOS terminals	Interactive point-of-sale terminals are located on a retailer's counter and used to capture data and present targeted communication.

Exhibit 15.13 Selected Digital Marketing "Push" Customization Tools

AutoTrader.com uses Web analytics to transform 25 million rows of daily Web log data into marketing knowledge. This firm is an automotive marketplace offering more than 2 million new and used vehicles with price comparisons, performance reviews, and financing and insurance resources. More than 6 million monthly visitors view more than 200 million pages, including pages where advertisers sell cars. To make sense of it all, AutoTrader created the *Management Dashboard*, a marketing tool powered by SAS statistical data analysis software. The dashboard reports on the following:

- Visitor demographics and customer behavior online—analyzed by US region.
- Analytics about the advertisements served on the site webpages.
- Key site metrics such as number of visitors and the makes and models of cars viewed.

As an example, SAS software evaluates 30 million monthly vehicle searches, categorizing them by city, state, and zip code, as well as make, model, year, and price. The regional sales force can then quickly answer inquiries about Web traffic in different localities. The firm also uses an Oracle database, extracting e-mails, leads, and other information to generate more than 100 month-to-date reports for marketing managers. AutoTrader learns many things from these analyses. First, it knows which vehicles are in demand in various regions, which helps participating car dealers and individual sellers. Second, it can fine-tune the website based on traffic patterns. Third, and most importantly, AutoTrader can demonstrate the value of advertising on its site. Advertisers receive automatically generated reports about how many times their cars were viewed, how many visitors asked for a map to the brick-and-mortar location, and how many e-mail inquiries were received about the cars. Finally, these reports help AutoTrader bill its digital commerce partners.

Data mining. Marketers don't need *a priori* hypotheses to find value in databases but use software to find patterns of interest. For example, Nissan used CRM software to increase its sophistication with up-selling and cross-selling. Prior to using a software CRM approach, Nissan would simply attempt to sell the same model of automobile as previously owned to a repeat customer. By using data mining, Nissan identified a group of affluent, loyal customers with children ages 19 to 24 living at home who purchased the Sentra model. Nissan relied on this information to cross-sell Sentras to other customers fitting the same profile.

Behavioral targeting. This occurs when software tracks a user's movements through a website and then sends appropriate Web content at a moment's notice. Amazon uses it when it presents recently viewed products on its home page when a return customer visits. Google uses it when sending ads as users click through several different websites. This targeting uses data warehouse information to help marketers understand the characteristics and behavior of specific target groups.

American Express has used behavioral targeting for years: it sends bill inserts to groups of customers based on their previous purchasing behavior. What's new is that this type of targeting can be done online inexpensively. For example, if a customer orders a Keurig coffee maker, ads may be served to order corresponding K-cups that go along with that device. TokyoPop. com, a site targeted at Generation Y, carries behavioral targeting over to all its affiliate sites. Every time a TokyoPop registered member visits an affiliate site, it serves rule-based content, advertising, or offers. This targeting builds relationships because members are presented with relevant and timely offers, which increases their business with TokyoPop.

Sometimes consumers are greeted with personalized content upon their first visit to a website. This is generally made possible through behavioral profiling matching anonymous cookie information to serve relevant information to that user, such as information specific to a given geography the user is from.

Collaborative filtering. Individuals often seek the advice of others before making decisions. Similarly, collaborative filtering software gathers the recommendations of an entire group of people and presents the results to a like-minded individual.

BOL.com, an international media and entertainment store (owned by Germany's Direct-Group Bertelsmann), uses Net Perceptions collaborative filtering software to observe how users browse and buy music, software, games, and more at its site. The more time a user spends at the site, the more BOL.com will learn about user behavior and preferences and the better able it will be to present relevant products ("learning relationship"). BOL.com notes that it realized increased revenues from using this software and achieved a positive ROI within months.

Outgoing e-mail. As discussed in earlier chapters, outgoing e-mail from firm to customer is still the internet's "killer app." E-mail is used to communicate with individuals or lists of individuals in an effort to increase their purchases, satisfaction, and loyalty. E-mail sent to distribution lists is redistributed to the entire subscription list. Many companies maintain e-mail distribution lists for customers and other stakeholders. Automated e-mail confirming purchase or shipping activities assures customers that the company is taking care of them.

Permission marketing dictates that customers will be pleased to receive e-mail for which they have opted in. MyPoints rewards consumers with points and gift certificates, all for reading targeted e-mail ads and shopping at selected sites. MyPoints client companies pay a fee for these e-mails, part of which goes directly to customers as points. MyPoints advertises "responsible" e-mail messaging, meaning that consumers agree to receive commercial messages within their e-mails. Conversely, spam does not build relationships but instead focuses solely on customer acquisition. The internet provides the technology for marketers to easily send hundreds of thousands of e-mails, and all for less than the cost of one postage stamp. Relationship-building e-mail requires sending e-mails that are valuable to users, sending them as often as users require, and offering users the chance to be taken off the list at any time. It means talking and listening to consumers as if they were friends.

English   Español   Deutsch   Français   日本語   한국어   Polski   Türkçe

FILE A COMPLAINT   MORE STEPS TO TAKE   NEWS AND DATA   ABOUT US

Report international scams online!

econsumer.gov is a partnership of more than 40 consumer protection agencies around the world.

Your complaint helps authorities spot trends and combat fraud.

Select a complaint subject to get started

Online Shopping/Internet Services/Computer Equipment	Credit and Debt	Telemarketing and Spam
Jobs and Making Money	Impostor Scams: Family, Friend, Government, Business or Romance	Lottery, Sweepstakes, or Prize Scams
Travel and Vacations	Phones/Mobile Devices, and Phone Services	Something Else

How we use and share your data >

Exhibit 15.14 Chat Opportunities Between the US Government and Its Citizens

Sources:www.state.gov and econsumer.gov

Social media. Companies build community and learn about customers and products through blogs, social networks, and bulletin board/newsgroup e-mail postings all over the Web and at its website (for government examples, see Exhibit 15.14). Analysis of these exchanges is used in the aggregate to design marketing mixes that meet user needs. For example, if many consumers log onto a Caribbean Chat at Expedia, it might feature special tours of Caribbean islands during the next week (www.expedia.com). Expedia sends e-mail offers to users who participate in the conversation.

IPOS terminals. IPOS terminals are small customer-facing machines near the brick-and-mortar cash register used to record a buyer's signature for a credit card or digital payment transaction. They are important because they can gather survey and other data as well as present individually targeted advertising and promotions. Thousands of retailers use such devices to send receipts, enroll users in rewards programs, and collect data about purchases being made for future analysis. Such information is then used to send targeted coupons and messages to entice customers to return to the store.

Client-Side Tools

Client-side tools come into play based on a user's action at a computer or mobile device. Although the tools generally reside on a Web server, it is the customer "pull" that initiates the customized response. See Exhibit 15.15.

Agents. Software agents such as shopping agents and search engines match user input to databases and return customized information. Agent software often relies on more than one interaction. For example, a user might type "computer" on the Dell site and then be presented with either laptop or desktop options. This process continues until the search is narrowed. Similarly, when visitors to Google use a keyword search, they receive a text-based ad based on

Client-Side Tools (Pull)	Description
Agents	Agents are programs that perform functions on behalf of the user, such as search engines and shopping agents.
Web forms	Web form (or HTML form) is the technical term for a form on a webpage that has designated places for the user to type information for submission
Incoming e-mail	E-mail queries, complaints, or compliments initiated by customers or prospects comprise incoming e-mail and are fodder for customer service

Exhibit 15.15 Selected Digital Marketing "Pull" Customization Tools

the word they entered along with a customized page of website links. For example, if a user types "automobile" into the search box, an ad for Toyota might be returned, along with the list of relevant sites. Agents are the basis of all shopping comparison sites, such as BizRate.com.

Individualized web portals. The *Wall Street Journal's* online edition allows individual customers to create a personalized webpage based on keywords of interest. This capability is particularly helpful for business readers who want to monitor stories about their competitors. The *Wall Street Journal* creates a structural bond with individual customers, thereby boosting loyalty—something that was unheard of prior to the internet.

Individualized Web portals are more often used to build relationships in the B2B market than the B2C market. For example, Samsung operates a partner portal to cater specifically to business partners (https://partnerportal.samsung.com). This enables the company to specifically interact with organizations interested in joining its Samsung Team of Empowered Partners (STEP) program to access marketing materials, retrieve brochures, access training, and more.

Wireless data services. Early on in the growth of mobile devices, mobile-optimized services were created separately from many common Web applications. Now, most content is delivered to wireless devices through Web browsers interacting with reactive content, push notifications connected to the mobile device operating system, or specific apps installed on the user device. Such apps and features are customizable to the user, and users can even customize certain applications for multiple areas, like watching the weather at home and your next vacation spot. See the "Let's Get Technical" box about these "third screens."

Let's Get Technical—Mobile Trends

As you stroll through the supermarket on Sunday afternoon, you suddenly realize that you have forgotten to buy peanut butter. In what aisle do they stock the 20 different varieties of peanut butter? And how are you going to know which size is the best price? Then you remember . . . the supermarket is now offering a wireless access in the store to a searchable floor plan, weekly specials, and unit price calculator for every item. You are once again relaxed as you pull out your iPhone.

Are Your Web Sites Ready?

Many classic marketing strategies hinged on the concept of giving potential customers information about a product or service right when they are likely to need it, such as an advertising billboard stating "McDonald's, Exit 11, Turn Left" or automatic coupon dispensers attached to the shelves at the grocery store. The interesting part of these strategies is that the information was in a form that the potential customers could use: a large billboard readable from the highway and a pocket-sized coupon for use at checkout.

These days, potential customers are hungry for information on their smart devices, which include iPhones, PDAs, pocket PCs, tablet PCs, iPads, and any combination of these products. Today's customers want their smart device to be just that—smart. Just as the classic marketing strategies did, today's digital marketer must also provide information for potential customers in a form that is easy to use for the customer. In other words, websites and online services should be developed specially for smart devices using industry standards. Specially designed websites and online services should also be tested before distribution to the public. For example, frozen webpages (fixed height and width) are difficult for mobile users to view. To view the information, they must scroll both down and to the right. A better solution are responsive webpages that allow the information to be resized to the width of the device's screen.

The Third Screen

Information technology visionaries are nicknaming the screen of mobile devices the "third screen." The first was television, the second was the personal computer, and the third includes a variety of mobile devices. However, given that almost everyone has a smartphone, perhaps it should be called the first screen! The unique aspect of these screens is that users take them just about everywhere, especially the iPhone. The iPhone works off of both regular phone networks and the faster LTE and 5G networks. The iPhone is a fully functioning internet device with a very intuitive and easy-to-use interface.

Although mobile devices are convenient for users because of their size, portability, and organizer functions, they are even more convenient when they are able to access wireless networks. Popular mobile devices can access one or more of the available wireless networks: wireless phone signals, WiFi internet hotspots, and Bluetooth wireless networks. The type of network that the mobile device can access depends on the hardware it possesses.

As the ability to access wireless networks and the speed of data transfer on the networks increase, services for mobile devices are becoming more prevalent. MobiTV converts the content of such stations as MSNBC, Fox, ABC, and the Discovery Channel. The speed needed for streaming content should be at least 10 frames per second and ideally 24 or 30. MobiTV will even let you pause a show on one device and then pick up where you left off on another!

Advertisers have long used the "first screen" to reach their target market, and that trend continues on the third screen. The company feels that it should provide genuine television programming to their customers, and that includes the commercials. MobiTV sells advertisements in the same spaces where cable operators insert their ads. And due to the nature of the mobile phone, viewers have bonus interactive features, such as clicking a button to get more information on a product.

Web forms. Many corporate websites include forms, using them for a multitude of purposes from site registration, communication, and survey research to product purchase. In fact, many sites strive to build the number of registered users as a prelude to transactions. For example, the US Federal Trade Commission (FTC) allows consumers to complain about questionable business practices and advertising via its website form. Regardless of purpose, the information gathered serves to help the firm build relationships and move users through the customer life cycle.

Digital signature platforms. Platforms like DocuSign allow for secure signatures for important documents that were traditionally faxed or mailed. In addition to eSignature management, such platforms also provide businesses with the ability to build workflows to increase the efficiency of their business processes.

Incoming e-mail. Post-transaction customer service is an important part of the customer care life cycle. Normally, websites include a feedback button or form that delivers an e-mail message to the corporation. Often an automated customer service program acknowledges the message via e-mail and indicates that a representative will be responding shortly. Research shows that most companies are getting much better at responding to incoming e-mail in a timely manner. Companies should include feedback options online only if they have staff in place to respond: e-mail addresses on a website imply a promise to reply. Some companies, such as Apple, do not provide e-mail feedback from their websites and instead use automated phone routing and chat systems to assist the customer.

RSS feeds. Really simple syndication (RSS) allows users to subscribe to blogs, news, and other online information. Subscribers will receive notification as soon as there is new information posted, either in e-mail or an RSS feed reader. This technology creates a structural bond, tying user to content originator in a way that enhances the relationship.

CRM **software**. As previously mentioned, CRM, CEM, and CCM success depend on all nine building blocks, not simply technology. Nonetheless, technology and software are what grease the CRM wheel, allowing companies to gather, interpret, and use masses of customer and prospect data. There are software companies in every aspect of CRM. For example, *PCMag* presents a list of the best CRM software, including Salesforce, Zoho, HubSpot, and Freshsales. Remember that most CRM software installations fail because the firm did not take steps to fix their objectives and gain buy-in and feedback from employees at every step. The opportunities for wasting money on the wrong application are endless.

9. CRM Metrics

Digital marketers use numerous metrics to assess the internet's value in delivering CRM performance—among them are ROI, cost savings, revenues, customer satisfaction, and especially the contribution of each CRM tactic to these measures. Recall that all digital marketing performance measures assess specific tactics from different perspectives and that the metrics of choice depend on the company's goals and strategies. Here we present a few of the common metrics used to track customers' progress through the customer life cycle in Exhibit 15.16.

Armed with this and other information about what makes customers value the company's products, organizations attempt to increase conversion and retention rates, reduce defection rates, and build AOV and profits per customer over time (acquire, retain, grow). For example, the Headspace app uses Salesforce to track the effectiveness of its campaigns.

Target

- Recency, frequency, monetary analysis (RFM)—identifies high-value customers
- Share of customer spending—proportion of revenues from high-value customers as compared to low-value customers

Acquire

- New customer acquisition cost
- Number of new customers referred from partner sites
- Campaign response—click-throughs, conversions, and more from Chapters 12 and 14
- Rate of customer recovery—proportion of customers who drop away that the firm can lure back using various offers
- Number of product recommendations in social media

Transact

- Prospect conversion rate—percentage of visitors to site who buy
- Customer cross-sell rate from online to offline, and the reverse
- Services sold to partners
- Sales of a firm's products on partner websites
- Average Order Value (AOV)—dollar sales divided by the number of orders for any given period
- Referral revenue—dollars in sales from customers referred to the firm by current customers
- Sales leads from internet to closure ratio

Service

- Customer satisfaction ratings over time (see Cisco opening story)
- Time to answer incoming e-mail from customers
- Number of complaints

Retain

- Customer attrition rate—proportion who don't repurchase in a set time period
- Percentage of customer retention—proportion of customers who repeat purchase
- Sentiment of blog and other social media conversations (positive/negative discussion)

Grow

- Lifetime Value (LTV)—net present value of the revenue stream for any particular customer over a number of years
- AOV over time—increase or decrease
- Average annual sales growth for repeat customers over time
- Loyalty program effectiveness—sales increase over time
- Number of low-value customers moved to high value

Exhibit 15.16 CRM Metrics by Customer Life Cycle Stage

In addition to performance improvements, many companies use some of these methods to identify the least profitable customers and minimize interactions with them. The point is not to treat some customers poorly but to try to minimize the time invested in servicing low-profit customers.

One important CRM metric deserves discussion—**customer lifetime value (LTV)**. "Customer Lifetime Value is the expected profit that you will realize from sales to a particular

	Acquisition Year	Second Year	Third Year
Customers	100,000	60,000	42,000
Retention Rate	60%	70%	80%
Orders per Year	1.8	2.5	3
Average order size	$90	$95	$100
Total revenue	$16,200,000	$14,250,000	$12,600,000
Costs	70%	65%	65%
Cost of sales	$11,340,000	$9,262,500	$8,190,000
Acquisition Costs	$55	$20	$20
Marketing Costs	$5,500,000	$1,200,000	$840,000
Total Costs	$16,840,000	$10,462,500	$9,030,000
Gross Profit	($640,000)	$3,787,500	$3,570,000
Discount Rate	1	1.16	1.35
Net Present Value (NPV)	($640,000)	$3,265,086	$2,644,444
Cumulative NPV Profit	($640,000)	$2,625,086	$5,269,531
Customer LTV	($6)	$26	$53

Exhibit 15.17 Customer Lifetime Value Calculation

Source: Copyright 2012 by The Database Marketing Institute, Ltd. used with permission. Arthur Hughes may be reached at www.dbmarketing.com

customer in the future," according to Arthur Hughes, founder of the Database Marketing Institute. Exhibit 15.17 displays an LTV calculation over a three-year period. In the first year, the company gained 100,000 customers; however, only 60 percent were retained into year two. The table is fairly self-explanatory, except the "discount rate" refers to the interest rates into the future. Future revenue is worth less in the present year because of future interest rates. This is the net present value of future revenue. There are a few notable conclusions from this table:

- The retention rate in years two and three is higher than in year one: retained customers are more loyal than new customers.
- In this example, newly acquired customers do not become profitable until the second and third years. This is quite common because of high customer acquisition costs.
- Marketing costs decline over time, reflecting the concept that it costs more to acquire than to retain customers. In fact, it is not often profitable to acquire new customers in the first year.

Marketers use market segmentation to identify which customers have the highest lifetime value and court them accordingly. They can also calculate possible retention rates and LTV prior to undertaking marketing campaigns to analyze possible profits. This example shows why most marketers spend more effort retaining then acquiring customers.

Ten Rules for CRM Success

Many organizations lose money with their CRM efforts. This prompted industry executive Chris Selland to write a white paper about how to succeed with CRM applications for digital marketing (Selland, 2005). Following are his ten rules.

1. *Recognize the customer's role.* It is all about the customer, as evidenced by the rise in social media and the balance of control shifting from companies to customers. Customer relationship management may be a misnomer because successful companies don't "manage customers" but provide technology so that customers can manage their relationships with the company.

2. *Build a business case.* Before investing in CRM technology or processes, it is important to examine the cost versus predicted benefits. Don't forget the impact of costs such as employee training and staff. Put the metrics in place, as discussed in building block 9.

3. *Gain buy-in from end users to executives.* Many CRM installations fail because no one uses them. SFA from companies such as Salesforce.com provides tremendous benefits but only if the sales force is trained and ready.

4. *Make every contact count.* CRM means integrating data from all customer touch points, and it is likely that much of these data already exist in databases. Before starting, a company should determine how it can integrate all customer or partner data into the system.

5. *Drive sales effectiveness.* If the CRM application involves a sales force, companies should ensure that the system helps salespeople close more deals and is not simply used to manage the metrics such as sales costs and close ratios.

6. *Measure and manage the marketing return.* Marketing is bigger than sales and often responsible for generating sales leads. Good CRM solutions will monitor the marketing expenditures and their role in revenues—things such as mailing list management and how leads flow through an organization.

7. *Leverage the loyalty effect.* Customer service is one of the three CRM facets, and although most companies consider it a cost, it plays a huge part in retaining customers and building wallet share. CRM initiatives can monitor customer service efforts to see how they help increase customer loyalty and thus add to profitability.

8. *Choose the right tools and approach.* This chapter covered many types of technology solutions for CRM, from enterprise-wide tools to smaller tactics focusing on individual aspects of CRM. It is important that marketers evaluate these tools and not leave it to information technology personnel alone. As well, CRM applications can be purchased and installed on the company servers or "leased" on a contract basis, such as with the Salesforce.com solution. Which fits the problem most adequately?

9. *Build the team.* Although an effective CRM solution begins with vision from the top, it is critical to build the right team before purchasing the software and beginning the training. The team might include members from marketing, IT, sales, and finance.

10. *Seek outside help.* It is often worthwhile to hire a consultant to assist, especially if the company has little experience with CRM.

Chapter Summary

Marketers have practiced relationship marketing for some time; however, internet technologies made it possible to manage many relationships one at a time. In the move from mass marketing to relationship marketing, the emphasis has become long-term customer retention rather than many discrete transactions with new customers. The three pillars of relationship management are customer relationship management (CRM), customer experience management (CEM), and customer collaboration management (CCM)—also called CRM 2.0 and social CRM. Social CRM is an extension of CRM 1.0, involving social media to build profitable customer relationships. Social CRM adds many benefits to both companies and consumers.

Customer relationship management is used to create and maintain relationships with employees, business customers in the supply chain, lateral partners, and final consumers. CRM's benefits include cost-effective acquisition, retention, and growth of current customers as well as word-of-mouth referrals. The Gartner Group-amended model of CRM covers nine building blocks: CRM vision, CRM strategy, customer experience management, customer collaboration management, organizational collaboration, CRM processes, CRM information, CRM technology, and CRM metrics.

The CRM vision must include guarding of customer privacy and building user trust. CRM strategy starts by defining what the company wants to accomplish with CRM technology. Relationship intensity ranges from awareness (the lowest intensity) to advocacy (the highest intensity). Three relationship levels mark the bonds that digital marketers build with customers. The highest level of CRM involves creating structural bonds that raise switching costs and build loyalty. Digital marketers need to think about the experience of their valued customers, how customers prefer to interact with companies, and how they can forge ties through community building.

An important trend in CRM is integration with supply chain management (SCM). When the firm's front end, back end, and supply chain all focus on the consumer, value is delivered, satisfaction is increased, and the firm has a competitive edge. The customer care life cycle covers the stages of targeting, acquiring, transaction, servicing, retaining, and growing customers by identifying customers, differentiating customers, and customizing the marketing mix for targeted segments or individuals—customization. CRM depends on information and on technology using company-side tools (including cookies, Website logs, data mining, behavioral targeting, collaborative filtering, outgoing e-mail, social media, and iPOS terminals) and client-side tools (including agents, experiential marketing, individuals' Web portals, Web forms, digital signature platforms, incoming e-mail, and RSS feeds). Then digital marketers use a variety of software for implementation and metrics to assess the performance and value of using the internet for CRM. The chapter concludes with ten rules for successful CRM.

Exercises

Review Questions

1. Explain why relationship capital is the foundation of future business.
2. Define relationship marketing and contrast it with mass marketing.
3. Compare and contrast CRM, CEM, and CCM.
4. Define Social CRM and tell how it relates to traditional CRM.
5. What are the main benefits of CRM?
6. Why do companies use sales force automation and marketing automation?
7. What are the nine building blocks of CRM?
8. What are the five levels of relationship intensity, and why do digital marketers strive to move customers to the top level?
9. Why do digital marketers see social media as an important aspect of CRM?
10. What are the advantages to CRM–SCM integration? Give an example.
11. What are the six stages in the customer care life cycle?
12. Explain how data mining, real-time profiling, collaborative filtering, and outgoing e-mail help companies customize offerings.
13. How are company-side and client-side customization tools different? Explain your answer.
14. What are the ten rules of CRM success, according to Chris Selland?

Discussion Questions

1. Explain the difference between wallet share and share of market.
2. Describe differences among the three pillars of relationship marketing.
3. Do you agree with the idea that social CRM is simply an extension of CRM 1.0, or do you think it is different enough to spawn an entire new field? Explain.
4. If good relationship marketing means firing a company's least profitable or most costly customers, suggest how it might be accomplished without causing them to criticize the company to their friends.
5. Explain how the customer benefits from CRM–SCM integration.
6. Do you agree with the statement that the customer's goal in relationship marketing is choice reduction? Are consumers really such creatures of habit? Why or why not?
7. Which tools do you think are more powerful for building relationships—company-side tools or client-side tools? Why?
8. Compare and contrast the concept of differentiating customers with that of differentiating products.
9. As a consumer, would you be more likely to buy from a website displaying the TRUSTe logo than from a competing website without the TRUSTe affiliation? Explain your answer.

Web Activities

1. Create an account with two websites you are interested in and see if you get e-mail. Identify the ways in which those sites attempt to build relationship with you. Evaluate the sites as well as the incoming e-mail.
2. Find a company online that you think does a poor job with relationship marketing. Suggest a strategy by which it could build in phases toward a structural relationship with its customers.
3. Visit Amazon.com and list all of the ways they personalize and customize the site to retain and increase your business.

Appendix A

Internet Penetration Worldwide as of September 30, 2021

Country or Region	Size (sq. km.)	Population (06/30/2020)	Internet Users	Internet Penetration
Afghanistan	645,807	38,928,346	7,337,489	18.8%
Aland Islands	1,580	29,789	n/a	n/a
Albania	28,748	2,877,797	2,160,000	75.1%
Algeria	2,381,741	43,851,044	25,428,159	58.0%
American Samoa	197	55,191	24,000	43.5%
Andorra	464	77,265	83,887	100.0%
Angola	1,246,700	32,866,272	7,078,067	21.5%
Anguilla	96	15,003	13,665	91.1%
Antarctica	13,209,000	2,700	4,400	100.0%
Antigua & Barbuda	442	97,929	79,731	81.4%
Argentina	2,777,409	45,195,774	41,586,960	92.0%
Armenia	29,743	2,963,243	2,126,716	71.8%
Aruba	193	106,766	104,803	98.2%
Australia	7,682,557	25,499,884	21,711,706	85.1%
Austria	83,858	9,006,398	7,920,226	87.9%
Azerbaijan	86,530	10,139,177	7,991,630	78.8%
Bahamas	13,962	393,244	353,920	90.0%
Bahrain	694	1,701,575	1,615,620	94.9%
Bangladesh	142,615	168,065,920	92,061,000	54.8%
Barbados	431	287,375	234,659	81.7%
Belarus	207,600	9,449,323	7,521,628	79.6%
Belgium	30,518	11,589,623	10,857,126	93.7%
Belize	22,966	397,628	239,600	60.3%
Benin	112,622	12,123,200	3,801,758	31.4%
Bermuda	53	62,278	60,342	96.9%
Bhutan	46,650	771,608	397,499	51.5%
Bolivia	1,098,581	11,673,021	8,817,749	75.5%
Bonaire, St.Eustatius, Saba	328	26,223	20,956	79.9%
Bosnia-Herzegovina	51,129	3,280,819	2,828,846	86.2%
Botswana	581,730	2,351,627	1,116,079	47.5%
Bouvet Island	49	0	0	0.0%

(Continued)

Country or Region	Size (sq. km.)	Population (06/30/2020)	Internet Users	Internet Penetration
Brazil	8,544,418	212,559,417	150,457,635	70.8%
British Indian Ocean T.	60	0	0	0.0%
British Virgin Islands	151	30,231	25,024	82.8%
Brunei Darussalam	5,765	437,479	416,798	95.3%
Bulgaria	110,994	6,948,445	4,663,065	67.1%
Burkina Faso	267,950	20,903,273	3,704,265	17.7%
Burundi	27,834	11,890,784	1,154,568	9.7%
Cabo Verde	4,033	555,987	352,120	63.3%
Cambodia	181,035	16,718,965	8,005,551	47.9%
Cameroon	475,442	26,545,863	6,128,422	23.1%
Canada	9,976,137	37,742,154	35,477,625	94.0%
Cayman Islands	259	65,722	55,800	84.9%
Central African Rep.	622,984	4,829,767	655,466	13.6%
Chad	1,284,000	16,425,864	1,027,932	6.3%
Chile	755,482	19,116,201	17,671,546	92.4%
China	9,806,391	1,439,323,776	904,000,000	62.8%
Christmas Island	135	2,205	1,000	45.4%
Cocos (Keeling) Is.	14	596	80	13.4%
Colombia	1,141,748	50,882,891	35,936,497	70.6%
Comoros	1,862	869,901	178,500	20.5%
Congo	341,999	5,518,087	732,800	13.3%
Congo, Dem. Rep.	2,344,798	89,561,403	7,475,917	8.3%
Cook Islands	237	17,564	11,377	64.8%
Costa Rica	51,090	5,094,118	4,296,443	72.1%
Cote d'Ivoire	322,461	26,378,274	11,953,653	45.3%
Croatia	56,542	4,105,267	3,787,838	92.3%
Cuba	114,525	11,326,616	6,567,704	58.0%
Curacao	800	164,093	151,274	92.2%
Cyprus	9,251	1,207,359	1,011,831	83.8%
Czech Republic	78,866	10,708,981	9,323,428	87.1%
Denmark	43,093	5,792,202	5,534,770	96.5%
Djibouti	23,200	988,000	548,832	55.5%
Dominica	751	71,986	51,992	72.2%
Dominican Republic	48,734	10,847,910	8,227,786	75.8%
East Timor	14,604	1,318,445	410,000	31.1%
Ecuador	272,046	17,643,054	13,476,687	76.4%
Egypt	1,001,450	102,334,404	49,231,493	48.1%
El Salvador	21,041	6,486,205	3,800,000	58.6%
Equatorial Guinea	28,051	1,402,985	356,891	25.4%
Eritrea	121,100	3,546,421	293,343	8.3%
Estonia	45,226	1,326,535	1,276,521	96.2%
Ethiopia	1,127,127	114,963,588	20,507,255	17.8%
Falkland Islands	16,076	3,480	2,900	83.3%

Country or Region	Size (sq. km.)	Population (06/30/2020)	Internet Users	Internet Penetration
Faroe Islands	1,414	48,863	48,489	99.2%
Fiji	18,274	896,445	557,600	62.2%
Finland	338,145	5,540,720	5,225,678	94.0%
France	547,030	65,273,511	60,421,689	92.3%
French Guiana	83,534	298,682	120,000	40.2%
French Polynesia	3,894	280,908	209,744	74.7%
French Southern T.	7,781	120	n/a	0.0%
Gabon	267,667	2,225,734	1,307,641	58.8%
Gambia	10,689	2,416,668	442,050	18.3%
Georgia	69,700	3,989,167	2,658,311	66.6%
Germany	357,021	83,783,942	79,127,551	96.0%
Ghana	238,538	31,072,940	11,737,818	37.8%
Gibraltar	7	33,691	32,939	97.8%
Greece	131,957	10,423,054	7,815,926	70.3%
Greenland	2,175,600	56,770	52,000	91.8%
Grenada	345	112,523	69,245	61.5%
Guadeloupe	1,780	400,124	240,000	60.0%
Guam	545	168,775	134,649	79.8%
Guatemala	108,894	17,915,568	7,910,000	44.2%
Guernsey & Alderney	91	69,545	55,070	80.2%
Guinea	245,857	13,132,795	2,411,672	18.4%
Guinea-Bissau	36,123	1,968,001	250,000	12.7%
Guyana	215,083	786,552	395,007	50.2%
Haiti	27,748	11,402,528	3,650,555	32.0%
Honduras	112,088	9,904,607	4,130,000	41.7%
Hong Kong	1,085	7,496,981	6,698,252	89.3%
Hungary	92,966	9,660,351	8,588,776	89.0%
Iceland	102,928	341,243	337,194	98.8%
India	3,166,944	1,380,004,385	560,000,000	40.6%
Indonesia	1,904,443	273,523,615	175,400,000	64.1%
Iran	1,648,195	83,992,949	67,602,731	80.5%
Iraq	434,128	40,222,493	21,276,000	52.9%
Ireland	70,273	4,937,786	4,453,436	91.9%
Man, Isle of	572	85,033	56,200	66.1%
Israel	20,991	8,655,535	7,002,759	80.9%
Italy	301,323	60,461,826	54,798,299	92.5%
Jamaica	10,991	2,961,167	1,600,520	54.1%
Japan	377,812	126,476,461	118,626,672	93.5%
Jersey	116	104,318	70,000	67.1%
Jordan	89,342	10,203,134	8,700,000	85.3%
Kazakhstan	2,715,900	18,776,707	14,669,853	78.9%
Kenya	581,787	53,771,296	46,870,422	87.2%
Kiribati	832	119,449	46,500	38.9%

(Continued)

Country or Region	Size (sq. km.)	Population (06/30/2020)	Internet Users	Internet Penetration
Kosovo	10,908	1,810,366	1,693,942	93.6%
Kuwait	17,818	4,270,571	4,231,978	99.1%
Kyrgyzstan	199,900	6,524,195	2,493,400	38.2%
Laos	236,800	7,275,560	2,500,000	34.4%
Latvia	64,598	1,886,198	1,663,739	87.1%
Lebanon	10,452	6,825,445	5,546,494	81.3%
Lesotho	30,355	2,142,249	682,990	31.9%
Liberia	99,065	5,057,681	624,610	12.3%
Libya	1,777,060	6,871,292	5,100,000	74.2%
Liechtenstein	160	38,128	37,674	98.8%
Lithuania	65,300	2,722,289	2,599,678	90.8%
Luxembourg	2,586	625,978	572,242	95.9%
Macao	25	649,335	538,007	82.9%
Macedonia	25,433	2,083,374	1,652,056	79.3%
Madagascar	587,041	27,691,018	2,643,025	9.5%
Malawi	118,480	19,129,952	2,717,243	14.2%
Malaysia	329,758	32,365,999	26,353,017	81.4%
Maldives	298	540,544	370,000	68.4%
Mali	1,240,198	20,250,833	12,480,176	61.6%
Malta	316	441,543	360,056	83.1%
Marshall Islands	181	59,190	20,593	34.8%
Martinique	1,128	375,265	303,302	80.8%
Mauritania	1,035,000	4,649,658	969,519	20.9%
Mauritius	2,040	1,271,768	852,000	67.0%
Mayotte (FR)	373	272,815	107,940	39.6%
Mexico	1,967,138	128,932,753	89,000,000	69.5%
Micronesia	721	115,023	59,193	48.9%
Moldova	33,843	4,033,963	3,067,446	76.0%
Monaco	2	39,242	38,124	97.2%
Mongolia	1,564,160	3,278,290	2,000,000	61.0%
Montenegro	14,026	628,066	449,989	71.6%
Montserrat	102	4,992	3,000	60.1%
Morocco	458,730	36,910,560	23,739,581	64.3%
Mozambique	799,380	31,255,435	6,523,613	20.9%
Myanmar	676,577	54,409,800	18,000,000	33.1%
Namibia	825,112	2,540,905	1,347,418	53.0%
Nauru	21	10,824	6,418	59.3%
Nepal	147,181	29,136,808	16,190,000	55.6%
Netherlands	41,526	17,134,872	16,383,879	95.6%
Netherlands Antilles	986	337,617	n/a	n/a
New Caledonia	18,736	285,498	232,368	81.4%
New Zealand	270,534	4,822,233	4,351,987	90.2%
Nicaragua	129,454	6,624,554	3,121,000	47.1%

Country or Region	Size (sq. km.)	Population (06/30/2020)	Internet Users	Internet Penetration
Niger	1,186,408	24,206,644	2,781,266	11.5%
Nigeria	923,768	206,139,589	126,078,999	61.2%
Niue	259	1,626	1,485	91.3%
Norfolk Island	35	1,748	796	45.5%
Korea, North	122,762	25,778,816	20,000	0.1%
Northern Marianas	477	57,559	40,000	69.5%
Norway	323,759	5,421,241	5,311,892	98.0%
Oman	309,500	5,106,626	4,011,004	78.5%
Pakistan	880,254	220,892,340	71,608,065	32.4%
Palau	491	18,094	13,900	76.8%
Palestine (State of)	6,220	5,101,414	3,381,787	66.3%
Panama	77,082	4,314,767	2,899,892	67.2%
Papua New Guinea	462,840	8,947,024	1,099,945	12.3%
Paraguay	406,752	6,981,981	6,177,748	88.5%
Peru	1,285,216	32,933,835	22,000,000	66.8%
Philippines	300,000	109,581,078	79,000,000	72.1%
Pitcairn Islands	47	50	170	100.0%
Poland	312,685	37,846,611	29,757,099	78.2%
Portugal	92,391	10,196,709	8,015,519	78.2%
Puerto Rico	9,104	3,194,853	3,047,311	95.4%
Qatar	11,521	2,881,053	2,942,000	100.0%
Reunion (FR)	2,547	895,312	553,000	61.8%
Romania	238,391	19,237,691	14,387,477	73.8%
Russia	16,894,741	145,934,462	116,353,942	79.7%
Rwanda	26,338	12,952,218	5,981,638	46.2%
Sahara, Western	266,000	597,339	28,000	4.7%
Saint Barthelemy	21	7,160	7,079	98.9%
Saint Helena (UK)	410	6,077	2,300	37.8%
Saint Kitts and Nevis	267	53,199	45,476	85.5%
Saint Lucia	616	183,627	142,970	77.9%
Saint Martin	37	32,284	16,100	49.9%
St. Pierre & Miquelon	242	5,794	5,033	86.9%
St. Vincent & Grenadines	392	110,940	76,984	69.4%
Samoa	2,785	198,414	126,900	64.0%
San Marino	61	33,931	20,270	59.7%
Sao Tome & Principe	1,001	219,159	63,864	29.1%
Saudi Arabia	2,149,690	34,813,871	31,856,652	91.5%
Senegal	196,722	16,743,927	9,749,527	58.2%
Serbia	77,474	8,737,371	6,406,827	73.3%
Seychelles	455	98,347	71,300	72.5%
Sierra Leone	71,740	7,976,983	1,043,725	13.1%
Singapore	683	5,850,342	5,173,907	88.4%
Slovakia	49,034	5,459,642	4,629,641	84.9%

(Continued)

Country or Region	Size (sq. km.)	Population (06/30/2020)	Internet Users	Internet Penetration
Slovenia	20,273	2,078,938	1,663,795	79.9%
Solomon Islands	28,400	686,884	96,600	14.1%
Somalia	637,657	15,893,222	1,705,300	10.7%
South Africa	1,219,090	59,308,690	32,615,165	55.0%
S. Georgia & S. Sandwich	3,903	n/a	n/a	n/a
Korea, South	99,268	51,269,185	49,234,329	95.9%
South Sudan	619,745	11,193,725	887,722	7.9%
Spain	504,842	46,754,778	42,961,230	92.5%
Sri Lanka	65,610	21,413,249	7,169,533	33.5%
Sudan	1,886,065	43,849,260	13,124,100	29.9%
Suriname	163,820	586,632	360,000	61.4%
Svalbard & Jan Mayen	61,606	2,428	2,331	98.0%
Swaziland	17,363	1,160,164	665,245	57.3%
Sweden	449,965	10,099,265	9,653,776	96.0%
Switzerland	41,285	8,654,622	8,066,800	93.2%
Syria	185,180	17,500,658	7,609,286	43.5%
Taiwan	36,175	23,816,775	22,042,902	92.6%
Tajikistan	143,100	9,537,645	3,013,256	17.5%
Tanzania	945,087	59,734,218	23,142,960	38.7%
Thailand	513,115	69,799,978	57,000,000	81.7%
Timor-Leste	14,604	1,318,445	410,000	31.1%
Togo	58,785	8,278,724	1,011,837	12.2%
Tokelau	10	1,357	800	59.0%
Tonga	651	105,695	65,900	62.3%
Trinidad & Tobago	5,128	1,399,488	1,063,630	76.0%
Tunisia	163,610	11,818,619	7,898,534	66.8%
Turkey	773,473	84,339,067	69,107,183	81.9%
Turkmenistan	488,100	6,031,200	1,262,794	20.9%
Turks & Caicos	497	38,717	28,000	72.3%
Tuvalu	26	11,792	5,619	47.7%
Uganda	242,554	45,741,007	18,502,166	40.4%
Ukraine	603,628	43,733,762	40,912,381	93.5%
United Arab Emirates	77,700	9,890,402	9,532,016	96.4%
United Kingdom	244,140	67,886,011	63,544,106	93.6%
United States	9,629,047	331,002,651	313,322,868	89.8%
US Minor Outlying Isl.	13	300	n/a	n/a
Uruguay	175,016	3,473,730	3,059,727	88.1%
Uzbekistan	447,400	33,469,203	17,161,534	51.3%
Vanuatu	12,190	307,145	92,900	30.2%
Vatican City State	1	801	480	59.9%
Venezuela	916,445	28,435,940	23,601,504	83.0%
Vietnam	332,378	97,338,579	68,541,344	70.4%
Virgin Islands, British	151	30,231	25,024	82.8%

Country or Region	Size (sq. km.)	Population (06/30/2020)	Internet Users	Internet Penetration
Virgin Islands, US	352	104,425	67,540	64.7%
Wallis & Futuna	274	11,239	3,900	34.7%
Yemen	528,076	29,825,964	7,903,772	26.5%
Zambia	752,614	18,383,955	9,870,427	53.7%
Zimbabwe	390,784	14,862,924	8,400,000	56.5%

Sources: *Internet World Stats: Usage and Population Statistics.* Available at internetworldstats.com

References

"1–800-Flowers.com Annual Report." (2017). Available at investor.1800flowers.com.

"1–800-Flowers.com, Inc. Reports Continued Positive Trends in Revenues, EBITDA and EPS From Continuing Operations for its Fiscal 2012 Fourth Quarter and Full Year." (2012). Available at investor. 1800flowers.com.

"21% of US Pay TV Subscribers Report Cutting or Shaving the Cord." (2012). Available at www. marketingcharts.com.

"25% of the Top 100 Retailers Have No Formal Facebook Presence, Says Study." (2009). Available at www. internetretailer.com.

"44 Mind-Blowing SMS Marketing and Texting Statistics." (2021, January 4). Available at www.slicktext. com.

"45% of Americans Think Online Privacy Is More Important than National Security." (2015). Available at Trustarc.com.

"The 47th Statistical Report on China's Internet Development." (2021, February). Available at cnnic.com. com.

"2012 Shopping Outlook." (2012). Available at pricegrabber.com.

"2016 Car Buyer Journey." (2016). Available at autotrader.com.

"2020 Census." (2020). United States Census Bureau. Available at www.census.gov.

"2020 E-commerce Payments Trends Report: Czech Republic." (2020). Available at jpmorgan.com.

"2020 Mobile, Smartphone, And Tablet Forecast, Global (COVID-19 Update)." (2020, September 30). Available at www.forrester.com.

AdMob by Google. (2011). *Tablet Survey*. Available at services.google.com.

"Adult Gadget Ownership in 2006–2012." (these figures are 2010–2012 from this chart) (2012). Available at pewinternet.org.

"Advertisers Begin to Look Beyond Facebook and Twitter." (2011). *eMarketer*. Available at www.emarketer. com.

"Advertisers Will Spend $2.61 Billion on Mobile this Year." (2012). Available at www.emarketer.com.

Afuah, Allan, and Christopher Tucci. (2001). *Internet Business Models and Strategies*. New York: McGraw-Hill/ Irwin.

"Alphabet, Inc. 10-K." (2017). *GOOG*. Available at sec.gov.

"Alphabet Net Income 2006–2021." (2021). Available at www.macrotrends.com.

"ALS Association." (2021). Available at www.als.org.

"ALS Ice Bucket Challenge." (2021). Available at www.challengeals.org.

"Amazon Annual Report." (2020). Available at www.annualreports.com.

"Amazon—Statistics & Facts." Available at www.statista.com.

"Americans and Privacy: Concerned, Confused and Feeling Lack of Control Over Their Personal Information." (2019, November 15). Available at www.pewresearch.org.

"Americans Watching More TV Than Ever: Web and Mobile Video Up Too." (2009). Available at http:// blog.nielsen.com.

"ANA/DMA 2018 Response Rate Report: Performance and Cost Metrics Across Direct Media." (2018). Available at www.ana.net.

Anderson, Monica, and Andrew Perrin. (2016). *13% of Americans Don't Use the Internet. Who Are They?* Available at pewresearch.org.

"Are We Ready for Amazon Key?" (2017). Available at statista.com.

Arno, C. (2012). *CIVETS: New Global Marketing Opportunities in Emerging Economies*. Available at searchenginewatch.com.

Arnold, Catherine. (2004, March 15). "Marketers Discover Weblogs' Power to Sell—Minus the Pitch." *Marketing News*.

"Auction Results." (2017). Available at icann.org.

"Average Time Spent with Major Media Per Day in the United States." (2020, June 21). Available at statista.com.

Bailey, Jeff. (2007). *Jet Blue's C.E.O. Is 'Mortified' After Fliers Are Stranded*. Available at www.nytimes.com.

Barker, Dennis. (2012). *Outsourcing Enables 21st Century Focus Groups*. Available at bpooutcomes.com.

"Baymard Institute." (2017). Available at baymard.com.

Beal, Andy, and Judy Strauss. (2008). *Radically Transparent: Monitoring and Managing Reputations Online*. Indianapolis, IN: Wiley and Sons, Inc.

Berners-Lee, Tim, James Hendler, and Ora Lassila. (2001, May). "The Semantic Web." *Scientific American*. Available at www.scientificamerican.com.

Berry, Leonard, and A. L. Parasuraman. (1991). *Marketing Services—Competing Through Quality*. New York: Free Press.

"Best Global Brands." (2020). Available at interbrand.com.

"BigCommerce Survey Shows Americans Consider Online Shopping Essential." (2016). Available at BigCommerce.com.

"Bridging the Gender Divide." (2021, July). Available at itu.int.

Business of Apps. (2021). *TikTok Revenue and Usage Statistics*. Available at www.businessofapps.com.

Campaign Monitor. (2019). *Do Fewer Links Mean More Clicks?* Available at www.campaignmonitor.com.

Carter, Kevin. (2015). *Something Big Is Happening in Emerging Markets*. Available at digitalcommerce360.com.

Case, Karl, and Ray Fair. (2001). *Principles of Economics*. Upper Saddle River, NJ: Prentice Hall.

Caulfield, Brian. (2001). "Facing up to CRM." *Business 2.0*, pp. 149–150.

Chaffey, D. (2010). *Social Location-Based Marketing*. Available at smartinsights.com.

Chao, E. (2012). *A Soap Set in the Favelas*. Available at http://online.wsj.com.

Chevalier, Stephanie. (2021a, July 7). *Annual Global Marketing Costs of Amazon from 2010 to 2020*. Available at www.statista.com.

Chevalier, Stephanie. (2021b). *Internet Usage in Peru—Statistics & Facts*. Available at www.statista.com.

Clark, Mitchell. (2021, May 3). *Fortnite Made More Than $9 Billion in Revenue in Its First Two Years*. Available at www.theverge.com.

Clement, J. (2021, May 27). *Share of Fortnite Players Who Have Ever Spent Money on In-Game Purchases in Fortnite in the United States as of February 2020*. Available at www.statista.com.

Clement, J. (2021, September 10). *Registered Users of Fortnite Worldwide from August 2017 to May 2020*. Available at www.statista.com.

"Click and Collect, an Already Popular Option, Finds a New Gear." (2021, March 29). Available at emarketer.com.

"The CMO Survey." (2017). Available at cmosurvey.org.

CNNIC. (2010). *Statistical Survey Report on Internet Development in China*. Available at www.cnnic.net.cn.

CNNIC. (2012). *29th Statistical Survey Report on Internet Development in China*. Available at http://www1.cnnic.cn.

Cohen, David. (2012). *Facebook, ComScore Study Touts Benefits of Paid Media, Even for Larger Brands*. Available at allfacebook.com.

comScore. (2012). *2012 Mobile Future in Focus*. Available at www.comscore.com.

"comScore Introduces Mobile Metrix 2.0, Revealing that Social Media Brands Experience Heavy Engagement on Smartphones." (2012). *Press Release*. Available at www.comscore.com.

"ComScore Reports $109 Billion in Q4 2016 Total Digital U.S. Retail." (2017). Available at comScore.com.

Considine, M. (2020). *How CEO Reputation Impacts the Corporation*. Available at www.reputationmanagement.com/.

Content Marketing Institute. (2020). *B2B Content Marketing 2020*. Available at www.contentmarketinginstitute.com.

Coppola, Daniela. (2021, August 4). *Online Shopping Cart Abandonment Rate in Selected Industries in March 2020*. Available at www.statista.org.

"Customer Case Studies." (2021). Available at www.qualtrics.com/case-studies/.

Davis, Dominic-Madori. (2020, January 28). *Gen Zers Have a Spending Power of Over $140 Billion, and It's Driving the Frenzy of Retailers and Brands Trying to Win Their Dollars*. Available at www.businessinsider.com.

De Best, Raynor. (2021, August 17). *Number of PayPal's Total Active User Accounts from 1st Quarter 2010 to 2nd Quarter 2021*. Available at www.statista.com.

"Deloitte Global Automotive Consumer Study." (2018, March). Available at www2.deloitte.com.

"Digital 2021: China." (2021, February 9). Available at datareportal.com.

"Digital 2021: Global Overview Report." (2021, January 27). Available at wearesocial.com.

"Digital 2021: The Latest Insights into the 'State of Digital'." (2021, January 27). Available at wearesocial.com.

"Digital Coupons Rival Print Counterparts in Effectiveness." (2012). Available at www.emarketer.com.

"The Digital Divide." (2017). Available at census.gov.

"Disclosures 101 for Social Media Influencers." (2019, November). Available at business.ftc.gov.

"Do You Prefer Video by Companies Which Produce Cosmetic Products or from Personal Accounts and Bloggers?" (2017). Available at Statista.com.

"Does Online Marketing Really Lead to Offline Buying?" (2002). *Presentation at the Advertising Research Foundation Annual Convention*. Available at powersearch2.thearf.org.

"Domain Name Stat." (2021). *Top Level Domains*. Available at www.domainnamestat.com.

Duncan, Tom. (2002). *Using Advertising and Promotion to Build Brands*. New York: McGraw Hill-Irwin.

Duncan, Tom, and Frank Mulhern (eds.). (2004, March). "A White Paper on the Status, Scope, and Future of IMC." *The IMC Symposium*.

"E-Biz Strikes Again!" (2004, May 10). *BusinessWeek Online*. Available at www.businessweek.com.

Economist. (2009). *The Power of Mobile Money*. Available at http://people.ucsc.edu.

Elliott, Stuart. (2009, October 9). "Letting Consumers Control Marketing: Priceless." *The New York Times*. Available at www.nytimes.com.

"E-Mail + Twitter + Facebook." (2011). *Lyris*. Available at www.lyris.com.

eMarketer. (2021a). *US Digital Ad Spending 2021*. Available at www.emarketer.com/.

eMarketer. (2021b). *US Time Spent with Mobile 2021*. Available at www.emarketer.com.

"eMarketer Mobile Roundup." (2012). Available at www.emarketer.com.

"Emerging Countries Lead Broadband." (2009). Available at http://point-topic.com.

"Ericsson Mobility Visualizer." (2021, June). Available at www.ericsson.com.

"ESOMAR's Annual Global Market Research Report." (2020). Available at www.esomar.org.

"Facebook Chorus Ends Instrument Luggage Ban." (2011). *Taipei Times*. Available at www.taipeitimes.com.

Facebook for Business. (n.d.). *About Stories*. Available at www.facebook.com/business.

"Facebook Solidifies Hold on Social Sign-Ins." (2012). Available at www.emarketer.com.

"Field Guide to Customer Digital Engagement." (2012). Available at www.lyrislabs.com.

Flynn, N. (2012). *The Social Media Handbook*. Indianapolis, IN: Wiley Publishing, Inc.

Foote, Keith D. (2019, December 12). *The Fundamentals of Data Integration*. Available at www.dataversity.net.

Fox, Alexa K., and Mariea Grubbs Hoy. (2019). "Smart Devices, Smart Decisions? Implications of Parents' Sharenting for Children's Online Privacy." *Journal of Public Policy & Marketing*, vol. 38, no. 4, pp. 414–432, https://doi.org/10.1177/0743915619858290.

Fox, Alexa K., and Scott Cowley. (2015). "Customer Service on Twitter: The Effect of Company-Consumer Alignment on Service Perceptions." In Burkhalter, Janée N., and Wood, Natalie T. (Eds.), *Maximizing Commerce and Marketing Strategies Through Micro-Blogging*. Hershey, PA: IGI-Global, chapter 6, pp. 130–153.

Freer, Anne. (2021). *US Social Commerce Only Slightly Down from 2020 to 36% this Year*. Available at www.businessofapps.com/.

Furchgott, Roy. (2021, July 17). *Happy to Shun Showrooms, Millennials Storm the Car Market*. Available at www.nytimes.com.

Gartner, Inc. (2021). *Gartner Says Worldwide PC Shipments Grew 32% in First Quarter of 2021*. Available at www.gartner.com.

GDPR.eu. (n.d.). *What Is GDPR, the EU's New Data Protection Law?* Available at https://gdpr.eu/.

Gemius, Vladimir. (2009). *E-Commerce 2009: Trends and Attitudes Research into Czech Internet Users*. Available at http://gemius.pl.

"Generation Influence: Gen Z Study Reveals a New Digital Paradigm." (2020, July 7). *The Center for Generational Kinetics.* Available at www.wpengine.com.

Ghemawat, P. (2007). *Redefining Global Strategy: Crossing Borders in a World Where Differences Still Matter.* Cambridge, MA: Harvard University Press.

Ghosh, Shikhar. (1998, March–April). "Making Business Sense of the Internet." *Harvard Business Review,* pp. 126–135.

Gingiss, Dan. (2019). *Report: Customer Satisfaction with Live Chat Is on the Rise.* Available at www.forbes.com.

Gladwell, M. (2000). *Tipping Point.* New York: Little Brown.

"Global Smartphone Sales to End Users from 2018 to 2021, by Region." (2021, March 10). Available at www.statista.com.

Godin, Seth. (1999). *Permission Marketing.* New York: Simon and Schuster.

Golmack, Stacy. (2017). *Current Trends and Future Prospects of the Mobile App Market.* Available at smashingmagazine.com.

Greenberg, Karl. (2001, December 10). "Automakers Rev Up Online Efforts, But Some Dealers Are Skeptical." *BrandWeek,* p. 10.

Grönroos, Christian. (1990, January). "Relationship Approach to Marketing in Service Contexts: The Marketing and Organizational Behavior Interface." *Journal of Business Research,* vol. 20, pp. 3–11.

Gruener, Jamie. (2001). "How to Measure Storage ROI." *Network Connections,* pp. 8–10.

Hoffman, D. L., and T. P. Novak. (1996). "Marketing in Hypermedia Computer-Mediated Environments: Conceptual Foundations." *Journal of Marketing,* vol. 60, no. 3, pp. 50–68.

Holst, Arne. (2021a). *Amount of Data Created, Consumed, and Stored 2010–2025.* Available at www.statista.com.

Holst, Arne. (2021b). *Number of Internet of Things (IoT) Connected Devices Worldwide from 2019–2030.* Available at www.statista.com.

"How Concerned Are You About Your Online Privacy Compared to One Year Ago?" (2021, March 7). Available at www.statista.com.

"How the Vietnamese Use the Internet, Including Social Media." (2018, March 8). Available at blog.thepienews.com.

"How Well Do Companies Respond to Customer Complaints?" (2011). *eMarketer.* Available at emarketer.com.

Hutchinson, Andrew. (2019). *Facebook Publishes New Data on the Effectiveness of Combining News Feed and Stories for Ad Campaigns.* Available at www.socialmediatoday.com.

"IAB Internet Advertising Revenue Report," (2021). Available at www.iab.com.

"IAB Social Advertising Best Practices." (2009). Available at www.iab.net.

"IAB Social Media Buyer's Guide." (2010). Available at www.iab.net.

"Internet/Broadband Fact Sheet." (2021, April 7). Available at www.pewresearch.org.

"Internet Penetration Rate in Bhutan from 2010 to 2019." (2021, March 29). Available at www.statista.com.

"Internet Seen as Positive Influence on Education but Negative on Morality in Emerging and Developing Nations." (2015). Available at pewglobal.org.

"Internet Usage and Population Statistics." (2022). Available at www.internetworldstats.com.

"Internet Usage Worldwide." (2021). Available at www.statista.com.

"iOS and Android Adoption Explodes Internationally." (2012). Available at http://blog.flurry.com.

"iPad Use to Nearly Double This Year." (2012). Available at www.emarketer.com.

"Is the Click Still King?" (2010). *Chief Marketer Survey.* Available at www.emarketer.com.

Jeanette, Jean-Pierre, and H. David Hennessy. (2002). *Global Marketing Strategies.* Boston: Houghton Mifflin Company.

Johnson, Evelyn. (2021, July 14). *How eCommerce Stores Use Social Media Coupons to Boost Sales.* Available at http://socialnomics.net.

Johnson, Joseph. (2021a, January 27). *Most Popular Online Activities of Adult Internet Users in the United States as of November 2019.* Available at www.statista.com.

Johnson, Joseph. (2021b, February 8). *Annual Revenue of Google from 2002 to 2020.* Available at www.statista.com.

Johnson, Joseph. (2021c, April 7). *Worldwide Digital Population as of January 2021.* Available at www.statista.com.

Johnson, Lauren. (2016). *Taco Bell's Cinco de Mayo Snapchat Lens Was Viewed 224 Million Times.* Available at adweek.com.

Jones, R. (2011, August 22). "5 Ways to Measure Social Media." *ClickZ.* Available at www.clickz.com.

Keeter, Scott. (2019). *Growing and Improving Pew Research Center's American Trends Panel.* Available at www.pewresearch.org.

Kelsey, Piper. (2020, September 11). *What Kenya Can Teach Its Neighbors—and the US—About Improving the Lives of the 'Unbanked'*. Available at vox.com.

Kennedy, Courtney, and Hannah Hartig. (2019). *Response Rates in Telephone Surveys Have Resumed Their Decline*. Available at www.pewresearch.org.

Kim, G. (2010). *Social Media Buyer's Guide*. Available at www.iab.net.

Kotler, Philip, and Gary Armstrong. (2010). *Principles of Marketing*. 13th ed. Upper Saddle River, NJ: Prentice Hall.

LaFrance, Adrienne. (2017, April 21). *The First-Ever Banner Ad on the Web*. Available at www.TheAtlantic.com.

Learmonth, M. (2011). *Study: Twitter Ad Revenue Grows to $150M in 2011*. Available at adage.com.

Ma, Yihan. (2021, August 17). *Number of Annual Active Consumers Across Alibaba's Online Shopping Properties from 2nd Quarter 2016 to 2nd Quarter 2021*. Available at Statista.com.

Macready, Hannah. (2022). *12+ Creative Social Media Contest Ideas and Examples (Templates)*. Available at https://blog.hootsuite.com/social-media-contest/

Mangles, Carolanne. (2017). *How Businesses Use Social Media: 2017 Report*. Available at smartinsights.com.

Marinkovic, Pavle. (2020). *Dunkin' Donuts: A Multisensory Marketing Campaign*. Available at www.bettermarketing.pub.

"Marketers Buzz about ROI." (2010). Available at www.emarketer.com.

McKern, Bruce, Leonardo Yamamoto, Daniela Bouissou, and David Hoyt. (2010). "Natura: Exporting Brazilian Beauty." *Harvard Business Review*.

Meeker, Mary. (2012). *Internet Trends—D10 Conference*. Available at www.kpcb.com/.

Memmott, C. (2011). "Authors Catch Fire with Self-Published E-Books." *USA Today*. Available at usatoday.com.

"The Mobile Difference—Tech User Types." (2009). *Pew Internet & American Life Project*. Available at www.pewinternet.org/Infographics/The-Mobile-Difference--Tech-User-Types.aspx (accessed on September 17, 2012).

"Mobile Fact Sheet." (2021, April 7). Available at Pew Research.

Modahl, Mary. (2000). *Now or Never*. New York: HarperBusiness.

Moore, Cortney. (2020). *Chipotle's TikTok Video Contest to Give Away $10G for Best Order*. Available at www.foxbusiness.com.

Newberry, Christina. (2021, January 11). *47 Facebook Stats That Matter to Marketers in 2021*. Available at https://blog.hootsuite.com/facebook-statistics/.

"New eGlobal Report." (2000, March 28). *Business Wire*. Available at www.lexis-nexus.com.

Newton, Casey. (2017). *America Doesn't Trust Facebook*. Available at theverge.com.

Nguyen, Mai-Hanh. (2017). *The Latest Market Research, Trends & Landscape in the Growing AI Chatbot Industry*. Available at businessinsider.com.

Nickols, Fred. (2000, February 16). *Strategies: Definitions and Meaning*. Available at home.att.net.

"Number of E-mail Users Worldwide from 2017 to 2025." (2021, March 19). Available at Statista.com.

Oberlo. (2021). *10 Reddit Statistics*. Available at www.oberlo.com/.

O'Leary, Noreen. (2012). *GroupM: Global Web Ad Spend Up 16 Percent in 2011*. Available at www.adweek.com.

Osman, Maddy. (2021, July 20). *Mind-Blowing LinkedIn Statistics and Facts*. Available at www.kinsta.com/blog/linkedin-statistics/.

Parker, Kim, and Ruth Igielnik. (2020, May 14). *On the Cusp of Adulthood and Facing an Uncertain Future: What We Know About Gen Z So Far*. Available at www.pewresearch.org.

Patel, N. (2021). *8 Blog Commenting Mistakes You Need to Avoid at All Costs*. Available at www.neilpatel.com.

Pellegrino, Robert, Doug Amyx, and Kimberly Pellegrino. (2002). "A Methodology for Assessing Buyer Behavior: Price Sensitivity and Value Awareness in Internet Auctions." *Working Paper*.

Pelletier, Mark J., Alisha B. Horky, and Alexa K. Fox. (2021). "Fexit: The Effect of Political and Promotional Communication on Facebook Exiting Intentions." *Journal of Business Research*, vol. 122, pp. 321–334.

Pepitone, Julianne. (2013). *#WOW! Twitter Soars 73% in IPO*. Available at money.cnn.com.

Peppers, Don, and Martha Rogers. (1997). *Enterprise One to One*. New York: Doubleday.

Perrin, Andrew, and Atske, Sara. (2021). *About Three-in-Ten U.S. Adults Say They Are "Almost Constantly" Online*. Available at: www.pewresearchorg.

"The Piano Guys." (2017). Available at www.thepianoguys.com.

Polasik, M., and P. Fiszeder. (2010). *Factors Determining the Acceptance of Payment Methods by Online Shops in Poland*. Available at www.networkworld.com.

"The Power of Direct Marketing." (2011–2012 Edition). *Direct Marketing Association*. Available at www.the-dma.org.

"Power Outages in Firms in a Typical Month (Number)—Country Ranking." (2020). Available at www.indexmundi.com.

PRNewswire. (2021). *Huggies® Made 'Baby History' By Featuring Babies Born on Gameday in Their Latest Ad, Part of a New Global Campaign, 'We Got You, Baby'*. Available at www.prnewswire.com.

Raskin, Andy. (2003). *False Hopes on Fantasy Island*. Available at money.cnn.com.

Ray, Michael L. (1973). "Communication and the Hierarchy of Effects." In Clarke, P. (Ed.), *New Models for Mass Communication Research*. Beverly Hills, CA: Sage Publications, pp. 147–175.

Reese, S. (2011). *Quick Stat: Online Video Will Account for 6.9% of Online Ads This Year*. Available at www.emarketer.com.

"Relationships Rule." (2000, May). *Business 2.0*, pp. 303–319.

Renner, Dale. (2000). "Closer to the Customer: Customer Relationship Management and the Supply Chain." *Andersen Consulting*. Available at renner.ascet.com.

Rhoads, Christopher. (2007, October 11). "What's the Hindi Word for dot.com?" *Wall Street Journal*.

Ridley, Kirstin. (2007, June 27). "Global Mobile Phone Use to Pass Record 3 Billion." *Reuters News*. Available at www.reuters.com.

"Rise of M-Commerce: Mobile Ecommerce Shopping Stats & Trends in 2021." (2020, December 30). Available at www.businessinsider.com.

"Running Smoothly: Online Shoe Sales in the US Industry Market Research Report Now Available from IBISWorld." (2012). Available at www.prweb.com.

Saleh, Khalid. (2021). *Digital Coupon Marketing*. Available at www.invespcro.com.

Sarno, David. (2009). "Twitter Creator Jack Dorsey Illuminates the Site's Founding Document." *Los Angeles Times*. Available at http://latimesblogs.latimes.com.

"Search Engine Market Share China." (2021). Available at http://gs.statcounter.com.

Selland, Chris. (2005, September). *Customer Relationship Management: 10 Steps to Success*. Available at www.tmcnet.com.

Seybold, Patricia. (1998). *Customers.com*. New York: Random House.

Shannon, S. (2012). *Britain's Surprise Shopaholics: Nigerians*. Available at www.businessweek.com.

Shih, Clara. (2011). *The Facebook Era*. Upper Saddle River, NJ: Pearson Education, Inc.

Sirohi, Aastha. (2021). *What is the Average Email Marketing ROI?* Available at www.blogs.constantcontact.com.

"Smartphones Account for Half of All Mobile Phones, Dominate New Phone Purchases in the US." (2012). Available at blog.nielsen.com.

Smith, Brad. (2018). *What is a Good Click Through Rate (CTR) and How to Improve It*. Available at www.acquisio.com.

Smith, Kit. (2015). *Marketing: Measuring Share of Voice in the Fashion Industry*. Available at brandwatch.com.

Smith, Kit. (2020, January 2). *60 Incredible and Interesting Twitter Stats and Statistics*. Available at brandwatch.com.

"Social Media Advertising." (2020). Available at www.statista.com.

"Social Media Examiner, 2010 Social Media Marketing Industry Report." (2010). Available at www.eMarketer.com.

Solis, Brian. (2011). *Report: The Rise of the Social Advertising*. Available at www.briansolis.com.

Sonnenberg, Frank. (1993, November). "If I Had Only One Client." *Sales and Marketing Management*, vol. 56, p. 4.

Spector, Robert. (2000). *Amazon.com: Get Big Fast*. New York: HarperBusiness.

Stambor, Zak. (2010). *Why Rosetta Stone is Offering Customer Service on Facebook*. Available at digitalcommerce360.com.

"State of California Department of Justice." (2018). *California Consumer Privacy Act (CCPA)*. Available at https://oag.ca.gov/.

Statista. (2021). *Number of Monthly Active Facebook Users Worldwide as of 2nd Quarter 2021*. Available at www.statista.com.

Statista Digital Market Outlook. (2021). *Distribution of Digital Advertising Spending in the United States in 2021, by Industry*. Available at www.statista.com.

Stoll, Julia. (2021). *Cord-Cutting in the U.S.—Statistics & Facts*. Available at www.statista.com.

Sullivan, Mikaela. (2021). *Which Celebrities Have Earned the Most from Twitter Ads?* Available at www.accrediteddebtrelief.com.

"Super Buzz or Super Blues?" (2008, January 3). *Nielsen Media Company Webcast*. Available at www.netratings.com.

Temkin, Bruce. (2007). *Are You Listening to the Voice of the Customer?* Available at experiencematters.blog.

Terdiman, Daniel. (2005). "Study: Wikipedia as Accurate as Britannica." *CNET News*. Available at www.news.com.

Thompson, Bob. (2009). "How to Use Social Media to Improve Customer Service and Cut Costs." *CustomerThink Corp.* Available at www.rightnow.com.

Tighe, D. (2021, March 19). *Online Shopping Behavior in the United States—Statistics & Facts*. Available at www.statista.org.

"T-Mobile Hacker Who Stole Data on 50 Million Customers: 'Their Security Is Awful'." (2021, August 27). Available at www.wsj.com.

Togan-Egrican, A., C. English, and L. Klapper. (2012). *Credit Cards and Formal Loans Rare in Developing Countries*. Available at www.gallup.com.

"Top 10 Global Web Parent Companies, Home and Work." (2012). Available at www.nielsen.com.

"Top 100 Retailers 2021 List." (2021). *National Retail Federation*. Available at nrf.com.

"The Top 500 Sites on the Web." (2017). Available at alexa.com/topsites.

"The Truth About Online Consumers." (2017). Available at kpmg.com.

"Twitter Annual Advertising Revenue from 2013 to 2020." (2021, April 23). Available at www.statista.com.

"Twitter Marketing." (n.d.). Available at marketing.twitter.com.

"Twitter Q2 2021 Shareholder Letter." (2021). Available at https://s22.q4cdn.com/.

Ugboma, Chini. (2017). *How to Overcome the Three Big Pain Points of Data*. Available at marketingweek.com.

"The Ultimate List of Marketing Statistics." (2017). Available at www.hubspot.com.

"U.S. Online Display Advertising Market Delivers 1.1 Trillion Impressions in Q1 2011." (2011). Available at www.comscore.com.

U.S. State Department. (1998). "The Global Landmine Crisis." *Hidden Killers*. Available at www.state.gov.

Vailshery, Lionel Sujay. (2021a, January 22). *Number of Public Wi-Fi Hotspots Worldwide from 2016 to 2022*. Available at Statista.com.

Vailshery, Lionel Sujay. (2021b, January 22). *Share of Adults in the United States That Own a Tablet from 2010 to 2019*. Available at www.statista.com.

Voskresensky, Mitya. (2011). *Google Research about Smartphone Usage in 2011*. Available at www.slideshare.net and www.google.com.

Wang, R. Ray, and Jeremiah Owyang. (2010, March 5). *Social CRM: The New Rules of Relationship Management*. Available at https://silo.tips/download/social-crm-the-new-rules-of-relationship-management

Watson, Amy. *Average Weekday Print Circulation of Selected Newspapers in the United States from October 2020 to March 2021*. Available at www.statista.com.

Weber, Larry. (2007). *Marketing to the Social Web*. Hoboken, NJ: John Wiley & Sons, Inc.

Weinschenk, Carl. (2017). *Report: U.S. Median Broadband Price is $80 Monthly*. Available at telecompetitor.com.

Wentz, L., and C. Penteado. (2011). *Banned from Cannes*. Available at creativity-online.com.

"What is Big Data?" (2012). Available at http://www-01.ibm.com.

"Why Do People Overpay on eBay." (2011). Available as a consumer post in a forum on deals.woot.com.

Winn, Ron. (2021). *2021 Podcast Stats & Facts (New Research From Apr 2021)*. Available at www.podcastinsights.com.

"Women Take the Lead on Mobile Coupons." (2010). Available at www.emarketer.com.

Wood, Marian. (2001). *Prentice Hall's Guide to E-Commerce and E-Business*. Upper Saddle River, NJ: Prentice Hall.

World Bank Open Data. (2020). Available at data.worldbank.org.

"World Map of Social Networks." (2017). Available at vincos.it.

Index